The Joan Palevsky  Imprint in Classical Literature

In honor of beloved Virgil—

"O degli altri poeti onore e lume . . ."

—Dante, *Inferno*

The publisher gratefully acknowledges the generous
support of the Classical Literature Endowment Fund
of the University of California Press Foundation,
which was established by a major gift from Joan Palevsky.

Greeks, Romans, Germans

Originally published in French as *Le national-socialisme et l'Antiquité* by Presses Universitaires de France, 2008.

Greeks, Romans, Germans

How the Nazis Usurped Europe's Classical Past

Johann Chapoutot

Translated by Richard R. Nybakken

UNIVERSITY OF CALIFORNIA PRESS

University of California Press, one of the most
distinguished university presses in the United States,
enriches lives around the world by advancing scholarship
in the humanities, social sciences, and natural sciences. Its
activities are supported by the UC Press Foundation and
by philanthropic contributions from individuals and
institutions. For more information, visit www.ucpress.edu.

Originally published in French as *Le national-socialisme
et l'Antiquité* © Presses Universitaires de France, 2008.

University of California Press
Oakland, California

© 2016 by The Regents of the University of California

Library of Congress Cataloging-in-Publication Data

Names: Chapoutot, Johann, author. | Nybakken, Richard
    R., translator.
Title: Greeks, Romans, Germans : how the Nazis
    usurped Europe's classical past / Johann Chapoutot ;
    translated by Richard R. Nybakken.
Other titles: National-socialisme et l'Antiquité. English
Description: Oakland, California : University of
    California Press, [2016] | Includes bibliographical
    references and index.
Identifiers: LCCN 2016018677 (print) |
    LCCN 2016016557 (ebook) | ISBN 9780520966154 () |
    ISBN 9780520275720 (cloth : alk. paper) |
    ISBN 9780520292970 (pbk. : alk. paper)
Subjects: LCSH: Germany—History—1933–1945. |
    National socialism. | Civilization, Classical—Influence.
Classification: LCC DD256.6 (print) | LCC DD256.6.
    C4313 2016 (ebook) | DDC 943.086—dc23
LC record available at https://lccn.loc.gov/2016018677

Contents

Introduction   *1*

PART ONE. ANNEXING ANTIQUITY   *15*

1. Origin Myths: *Ex septentrione lux*   *17*
2. A Nordic Mediterranean: Greece, Rome, and the North, between German Cousins   *51*
3. *Mens sana:* Antiquity, the Humanities, and German Youth   *98*

PART TWO. IMITATING ANTIQUITY   *153*

4. From Stone to Flesh: The Body of the New Aryan Man between Aesthetics and Eugenics   *155*
5. The Racial State and Totalitarian Society: Plato as Philosopher-King, or The Third Reich as Second Sparta   *193*
6. From Empire to Reich: The Lessons of Roman Rule and Classical Colonialism   *229*

PART THREE. RELIVING ANTIQUITY   *285*

7. History as Racial Struggle: The Clash of Civilizations between East and West in Antiquity   *287*

8. *Volkstod* or *Rassenselbstmord:* How Civilizations Die   324
9. The Choreography of the End: Aestheticism, Nihilism, and the Staging of the Final Catastrophe   357
    Conclusion   393

Notes   401
Index   475

Introduction

This book was born of a surprising discovery: some preliminary research on youth movements and the idea of Europe led me to the speeches of Alfred Rosenberg, in which he claimed that the Greeks were a Northern people. As it turns out, this curious textual artifact merely repeated the canonical work of National Socialist doctrine: Hitler wrote in *Mein Kampf* that there was a "racial unity" (*Rasse-Einheit*) that linked Greeks, Romans, and Germans, and that these three peoples were united in fighting the same millenarian war.

In order to make sense of such statements, one might begin with the argument that moderns perpetually carry the weight of past centuries and their legends. And if there is indeed a specter that has haunted the powers of Europe, it is that of antiquity. Since at least the time of the Renaissance, a Romanesque monument, built on sturdy Corinthian columns, has served as a reminder of the power and glory of Rome, its sovereignty founded on arms and laws, its universalist aspirations. It is almost impossible to avoid drawing on Roman precedent in a West that cannot speak of supreme power except in Latin terms: "emperor," after all, comes from *imperator*, and "kaiser" (like "czar," among others) comes from *Caesar*. After Charlemagne, every pretender to universal domination has sought to assume the faded robes of the defunct *imperium romanum*, and German, Russian, British, French, Austrian, and Holy Roman emperors have all dreamed of *restauratio imperii*.

Greece, likewise, has never been forgotten, though less for its arms than for its words. It lives on in its abundance of spirit, the noble Greek profile, that sublime philosophy. The Munich Glyptothek was the perfect venue to marry brute force with the beauty of ancient sculpture. There was no contradiction between the philhellenic Germany of Prussia's Frederick the Great, Weimar classicism, or the Bavarian king Ludwig I and those who, with the Greece of Missolonghi, worshiped at the altar of nationalism.

Historians know all too well that, when referring to antiquity, the political use of history—appealing to the past to justify political power in the present—is a frequent phenomenon, all the more so in totalitarian regimes that seek to anchor their revolutionary political intentions in the depths of historical precedent. Stalin, for instance, commissioned Sergey Eisenstein to make *Alexander Nevsky* in order to appropriate the early Russian resistance to Germanic imperialism, and later *Ivan the Terrible* to portray a fifteenth-century Kremlin in combat against the boyars.

So in some ways this is familiar ground. Mussolini wanted to rebuild an empire when he laid out the plans for the Via dei Fori Imperiali in Rome. Italian Fascists' use of classical precedent has been the subject of many studies, in part because it was so obvious and dramatic. Still, the relationship of Mussolini's regime to the ancient world often remained little more than surface dressing and pure pomp. The possibilities afforded by the past appear to have held much greater significance, however, for National Socialism. Fascist Italy was also open to the new, as its cultural politics demonstrated; Nazi Germany, in contrast, coveted and revered the past as a sacred place of origin.

Yet the relationship between National Socialism and antiquity seems to have held little interest for historians. While we willingly concede that the Nazis developed an undeniably singular, coherent notion of *Deutschtum* (Germanness), we recoil from associating National Socialism with classical Greece and Rome.

But we can see signs of this relationship everywhere we turn: in the "neo-Grec" nudes of Arno Breker and Josef Thorak; in the neo-Doric architecture of Paul Troost; in the neo-Roman buildings of Albert Speer; in school textbooks, which presented a rather startling image of Mediterranean antiquity; and in academic studies published under the Third Reich, including such immortal titles as *The Blond Hair of the Indo-Germanic Peoples of Antiquity,* or scholarly journals full of ideologically tinged studies like "The Jew in Greco-Roman Antiquity." Indeed, the ancient world was of such interest to the Third Reich that even until the final hours of April 1945 both the *Völkischer Beobachter* and the newspaper *Das Reich* continued to publish stories on the Second Punic War and Rome's turning of the tide against a Stalinesque Hannibal.

My discovery, then, led me to a series of questions: What strange mania could have pushed the leaders of the Nazi regime, in the midst of the twentieth century, to talk—and to talk so much—about the Greeks and Romans? Or to commission neoclassical works of art and publish articles on the Rome of the Fabii? Or to subject research and education on antiquity to such ideologically driven revisionism?

We think of National Socialism as the apotheosis of racism in both words and deeds. But racism is an exclusionary practice: it is the distinction between friend and enemy based on a strict biological determinism that, taken to extremes, separates those who get to survive from those who must perish—among both the living and the dead. The biological transmission of racial traits precludes any casual dalliance outside the kinship group, any genealogical digression, and demands extreme vigilance and severe patrilineal discipline. There may be several branches of the racial tree, but the integrity and purity of its rootstock must be verified historically. The Germans thus traced their line far back into the distant past of paleontology and the primeval forest (*Urwald*), through the Teutonic Knights and the Brothers of the Sword (Fratres Militiae Christi), Frederick the Great and Bismarck, to Hindenburg and, finally, Hitler—the chosen one of the prophets and acme of the race.

The fact that, in racism, ideology partially overlaps with genealogy helps clarify the affinities that existed between Nazism and history, between the race and traces of its past, between the definition of German identity and the search for its origins. To receive official approval to marry, for example, the SS required its members to provide proof of their pure Aryan heritage dating back to 1750: some fifteen generations of racial purity. When, in 1943, two SS officers were discovered to have a common Jewish ancestor dating back to 1685, Himmler decided to extend the requirement after the war to 1650, or more than twenty generations.[1] This obsession with genealogical purity affected not only those individuals who were measured, judged, and otherwise lived in the present while being defined by their past but also the race itself: the SS and their battalions of Nazi archaeologists from the Deutsches Ahnenerbe would excavate their way through Saxe-Coburg-Gotha, Schleswig, Lorraine, Poland—but also, curiously, Mount Olympus in Greece. The German word *Ahnenerbe* means, roughly, "ancestral heritage"; did they have ancestors from Hellenic shores?

A racism as all-encompassing as that of Nazism would seem logically to exclude all traces of anything other than the most strictly defined and carefully circumscribed *Deutschtum*. What, then, made the Greeks so interesting—to say nothing of the Romans, whose speeches and statutes we will discuss later? What deep-seated need did this appeal to Greco-Roman antiquity fulfill? Was there some intrinsic deficiency, some inherent defect in the Germanic past?

German history provided a seemingly endless reservoir of models for the Nazis and their contemporaries to emulate or appropriate to bolster claims of national pride. National Socialism could draw upon examples from Prussia, the Holy Roman Empire, and the *Drang nach Osten* (Drive to the East) of the Teutonic Knights, for instance. Every era of German history offered an abundance of archetypes that glorified the ideal characteristics of the political soldier that Nazism sought to create: the Prussian army was a model of discipline, organization, and tactical prowess; "Old Fritz"—Frederick the Great—offered an enviable image of tenacity crowned by destiny; the Holy Roman Empire flattered the hegemonic ambitions of Nazi imperialism; the Teutonic epics illustrated the spirit of conquest that animated a race in search of "living space."

A triptych composed of Hermann (Arminius), Henry the Lion, and Frederick II of Prussia could by itself encompass virtually every aspect of the Nazi ethos as it was promoted in party and state propaganda. Looking elsewhere could even have been seen as a denigration of national pride; German culture could have been truly Germanic, sui generis. Indeed, the National Socialist seizure of power briefly raised the hopes of those cultural chauvinists, particularly ancient historians, who thought they might finally wipe the slate clean and toss out Latin and Greek to make way for a more truly Germanic antiquity.

Why, then, despite the numerical and conceptual wealth of Teutonic archetypes, did the Nazis resort to classical examples, sacrificing all reverence for antiquity? Were they hoping to find something more?

Teutonic exemplars demonstrated an ethos, that of the ideological warrior, a valorization of courage, tenacity, and sacrifice for the common good: the transalpine equivalent of characters from Livy or the *De viris illustribus* of Charles François Lhomond—the Camillus, Regulus, and Cincinnatus of national legends, the product of a subtle alchemy of science, folklore, and political interest, a sort of marriage between the Brothers Grimm and Ernest Lavisse.

But an *ethos* is not a *genos*, and philosophy is not genealogy. A racialized vision of antiquity offered the Nazis the opportunity to create their own mythical origins and to write their own biography of an *Urvolk* ennobled by the prestige of Augustus and Pericles.

But these Germanic origin myths alone were, to put it bluntly, simply not good enough. German history suffered from one fatal, irremediable flaw: a patent lack of cultural prestige. In the Western hierarchy of civilizations, the coarse Germans did not possess the necessary historical refinement. Hitler's goal, which he stated repeatedly, was to restore the pride of a nation humiliated by the diktat of Versailles. This sort of national therapy could not be achieved solely through rearmament and a megalomaniacal architectural politics, or saber rattling in the Saar valley, Austria, and Moravia. European history would feel the führer's wrath no less than its geography. Present time and space were not enough. The past would also have to contribute to the resurrection of a German pride gravely wounded in 1918–1919. The appropriation of the ancient past, its canonical texts, ideas, and civilizations, would assume a vital ideological significance.

In France, it was Colette Beaune[2] and Claude Nicolet[3] who introduced the study of such invented genealogies from medieval nations: While English kings invoked the pious memory of Brutus, a descendant of Aeneas, French monarchs proudly proclaimed their descent from the Hebrew king David and Francus of Troy. The nobility had their Franks, while the third estate, and later the republic, had their Gauls, in a quarrel between the two sides of France that dates back to the sixteenth century.

But it is not simply a question of fabricating ancestry. When Rosenberg and Hitler spoke of the Greeks as a "Nordic people," they did not simply claim their heritage but rather asserted a form of paternity that turned the concept of lineage on its head: what if they had all come from Germany? This appropriation of the Aryan myth, which had not previously circulated beyond a few nineteenth-century German linguists and historians—who had wistfully imagined that the Dorians of Sparta had come from the North—was legitimized and racialized by the Nazis in their desire to give credibility to the idea that Germany possessed such greatness that it had given birth to Western civilization. In this way, Rosenberg argued, imitating antiquity was neither "shameful nor incompatible with national dignity," since it was actually a legitimate reassertion of Indo-Germanic cultural patrimony.

Yet despite the presence and significance of these references to Greco-Roman antiquity under the Third Reich, the question of the relationship between National Socialism and the ancient world has attracted only cursory attention from historians, who have been interested above all in Germanic myths and the role they played in Nazi ideology.

A few historians, like Otto Gerhard Oexle[4] and Peter Schöttler,[5] have looked more closely at the fate of the historical profession (*Geschichtewissenschaft*) under the Third Reich, which they argue engaged in a "scientific legitimation" of Nazi ideology. The fate of antiquity and the historiography of the ancient world under the Third Reich seem to have held greater fascination for classicists, who have looked at its impact on the ethics and methods of their profession, than for historians of the previous century. Art historians have also been slightly more intrigued by the issue; Alexander Scobie, for instance, has written extensively on the relationship between antiquity and Nazi architecture.[6]

But there is no comprehensive survey of the Third Reich's systematic appropriation of antiquity, of the many vectors by which its messages were transmitted, or of the functions they were designed to serve. This book seeks to fill this gap and to examine what deeper meanings such references had in the broader overall economy of Nazi discourse.

Such references to antiquity were abundant and varied and emerged from a multiplicity of sources. Together they formed part of a coherent discourse of appropriation, imitation, and analogy, which drew upon rhetorical techniques of citation, allusion, and repetition. These sources and references competed for prominence in this rich, widely disseminated discourse, which was the subject of a propaganda campaign befitting the significance assigned to it.

I will show how history was rewritten in order to annex the ancient Greeks and Romans to the Nordic race. The lust for power unleashed by Nazi totalitarianism expressed itself everywhere, in the desire to master not only the present and the future but also the past, in order to establish absolute domination of the present and mastery over the future.

Hannah Arendt showed how totalitarianisms of both left and right sought to build an "entirely fictitious world."[7] This fictitious world is a fundamental premise of any totalitarian doctrine, which claims to understand the laws that will govern the world to come. In the case of Nazism, its organizing premise was that of race war, a war that the Semitic peoples fought not in the honorable spirit of open combat but in the sinister shadows of conspiracy. Such a premise is unfalsifiable, in the sense defined by Karl Popper: it cannot be invalidated, and is accepted uncritically into a narrative discourse of reality that then becomes a self-fulfilling prophecy, thus offering a reassuring coherence to the totalitarian lie. Arendt noted that the lie responded to the demands of a public predisposed to accept it, to quench its "vulgarized thirst for knowledge"[8] that betrayed the "longing ... for a completely consistent, comprehensible, and predictable world."[9] The chaos of history, all sound and fury, is conveniently tidied up by monocausal explanation. Imagined conspiracies, in particular, possess the great merit of being immune to contradiction; any inconsistencies are muted or glossed over by their simplicity and accessibility, offering a total hermeneutics of the real.

Arendt emphasized how totalitarian propaganda was marked "by its extreme contempt for facts as such" and showed how its mendacity concealed an exaggerated desire for power: the totalitarian lie "betrays its ultimate goal of world conquest, since only in a world completely under his control could the totalitarian ruler possibly realize all his lies and make true all his prophecies."[10]

Totalitarian logic, however, did not limit itself to synchronic reality; it also functioned diachronically. As the Nazis' territorial conquests multiplied, mere geography became insufficient, and history itself was subject to appropriation and rearrangement according to the tenets of their ideology.

In the specific case of National Socialism, this lie became a form of power, sinking its mythical roots into the depths of the most distant past. The construction of their fictive world was not limited to the present; the Nazis ransacked the past and exhumed the dead, excavating through their remains to find any and all proof to validate the claims of their fabricated world view. As in George Orwell's classic novel *1984*, the palimpsest of the past was conscientiously scraped clean to fit the needs of the totalitarian present. All history was contemporary.

National Socialism offered a myth. Its narration, by the state and its institutions—and especially its artistic and academic organizations—was presented as reality. Its lies were passed off as truth: Nazi discourse did not adapt to describe an external, objective reality; rather, this discourse was shaped, internally and self-referentially, to fit the preconceived notions underlying the discourse itself.

The word *lie* might sound inappropriate, like a value judgment or sign of moral disapproval, traits that were clearly not entirely absent from Arendt's work. What we see and condemn as a lie was certainly not perceived that way by actors at the time. While one can certainly find examples of classicists who were cynics or avid opportunists, the sincerity of Hitler himself—who spoke at length of the Indo-Germanic roots of the Romans in his famous table talks—or of a scholar like Fritz Schachermeyr,[11] who obsessed over the clash between East and West in antiquity well after 1945, is beyond doubt. The myth of a Nordic

Greco-Roman people engaged in mortal combat with the Jewish enemy validated ideological concerns, satisfied restless minds in search of intellectual coherence, and built to some degree upon certain elements of nineteenth-century German historiography—all factors which, to paraphrase Pierre Bourdieu, make such beliefs believable.

The question of the uses of antiquity also takes us to the heart of the regime's construction of the ideal citizen-subject: rewriting the history of the race to employ Greece and Rome as evidence of its greatness was a central part of the Nazi project to forge a new man. But how was this new man to be built? How could they liberate him from "cultural Bolshevism" (*Kulturbolschewismus*) to make him a true ideological warrior, proud of his country and his race, devoted to his führer, and ready to march off to war?

The physical sculpting of the new man was the goal of eugenics, a sort of state-sponsored selective breeding employed by the new regime to promote a new ethic and aesthetic of the body that emulated an idealized Greek figure held up to represent their glorious ancestor. Sport, the organized activities of the Kraft durch Freude—"Strength through Joy," the workers' leisure time organization—and the promotion of new regimes of physical health would develop the physique of this new man.

In addition to corporeal training, however, the new man would be subjected to psychological molding, a process entrusted to state propaganda. Nazi propaganda had many objectives, and multiple means and channels at its disposal: it could draw upon art, advertising, radio transmissions, public speeches and spectacles, easy-to-remember (and seemingly omnipresent) slogans and catchphrases—but also the schools and universities, various party organs, and the instruction these institutions provided. The ultimate aim of this propaganda was to endow the new man with a new personality and identity, to create the perfect Nazi subject, fanatically devoted to *Führer, Volk und Reich,* as the obituaries of fallen soldiers proudly proclaimed. The question of identity, of course, raised the question of origins: Where do I come from? What is my race? What is the history of this group that I belong to? The regime's ideologues thus aimed to tell the history of the race, the epic story of the Nordic people, to bestow a new past upon the new man. National Socialism engaged in this vast exercise of rewriting that is the invention of the past in order to respond to needs that derived from its own ideology, which it had itself created and imposed.

It was not just the past, and the legitimate pride that one could take from it, that was at stake here, but the future as well. Germans' new identity, built upon the Nazis' version of antiquity, was at once a story of origins and an indication of future horizons.

In one of his public speeches, Heinrich Himmler neatly connected these three temporal planes: "A people lives happily in the present and the future so long as it is aware of its past and the greatness of its ancestors."[12] This commingling of past, present, and future loses some of its triviality when one realizes that it constituted the incipit to every publication of the Ahnenerbe. Little wonder, then, the attention paid to the work of all the historians, archaeologists, and linguists employed by Himmler's Black Order to explore the origins of the race and preserve its heritage; a demonstration of their ancestral greatness would mold a firm and confident character, and thus encourage repeated deployment.

The heroic myth of the race thus not only played a role in the creation of identity but also contained a mobilizing function. An appeal to the past can also be a call to duty in the present; the conduit flows in both directions. Origins provide comfort but also bring responsibilities. The nobility of the race exists on a temporal continuum that is neither discrete nor divisible. The past engenders the present, which in turn gives birth to the future, in complete logical and ontological continuity, according to a malleable but inviolable law. Blood never lies; so long as it remains pure, it preserves its latent potential. Its past greatness is continually called forth, even if over time it suffers terrific blows and temporary setbacks. The Napoleonic Wars, the end of the Great War, and the Weimar Republic represented just such moments, when its greatness was snuffed out by circumstance, by dissolution of the blood, by malign conspiracy.

The history of the race, however, also taught never to despair; it could console or cajole in equal measure. The potential for greatness, by ontological necessity, would always rise again.

We now have a better grasp of the ideological importance of the rewriting of ancient history, presented as the first great era of a common Nordic and Indo-Germanic past. We understand how this revision did not remain marginalized in the unread pages of a few farsighted works but was instead made the subject of a large-scale publicity campaign that was communicated in a number of ways. The nudes of Breker and Thorak, official state-sponsored architecture, classroom instruction and ideological indoctrination, film, the press, many of the vast public ceremonies staged by the regime: everything was a potential medium for the dissemination of this new version of the past and the history of the race, and thus its identity, everything a means to transmit a message whose coherence and logic constituted a world unto itself (*Umwelt*), saturated by unequivocal and unilateral signifiers that characterized the totalitarian control of space. This discourse, understood in the broadest sense of the word, was inseparable from practice: the relationship with antiquity was expressed not only through words but through a variety of means and acts that were far more than mere theater staged in time and space, acts that were not just decorative or cosmetic but eminently significant. Placing Athena at the head of a parade of German art; building neo-Doric temples in Munich; planning for the construction of a giant Pantheon in the heart of Berlin; designing Roman standards for the Nazi Party and the SS: these were not anodyne acts but rather the expression of a racist seizure of classical Greek and Roman identity that was annexed in the service of the Nordic race.

We are faced with such a multiplicity of references to antiquity that they constitute a system, a symbolic universe whose signs require clarification. Faithful to the Hegelian reading of history as a succession and alteration of symbolic universes, Ernst Cassirer, in his *Essay on Man*, defined the historian as a linguist and the practice of history as the reading of a lost language, the re-creation of the symbolic code of an epoch whose speech cannot be understood without a key. Similarly, one cannot understand the curious words of Rosenberg or Hitler without delving into the work of contemporary historians of the period, the essays of the racial scientists, the sculptures of a Thorak, the designs of a Speer. It is this approach that has informed the goals and synthetic method of this book, inspired by those works of history that aimed to re-create an entire mental universe, like *Rabelais* by Lucien Febvre, *Pensée grecque* by Jean-Pierre Vernant, or the writings of the philosopher and historian Lucien Jerphagnon. I would be remiss if I did not also acknowledge my debt to Erwin Panofsky, Denis Crouzet, George Mosse, and Fritz Stern.

Viewed in proper context, it is clear that this creation of a symbolic universe from words, sculptures, columns, and films was not a spontaneous act. It was in part a legacy of the German nineteenth century, but it was also strongly encouraged by the desire of the Nazi Party, and subsequently the Nazi state, to create a historical narrative capable of shaping reality.

To collect a full measure of the richness of this symbolic system, I have analyzed a wide range of sources, which correspond to the many channels by which this discourse was transmitted and also the many themes of this study. The narration of antiquity engaged ideologues, historians, philosophers, imperial advocates and race theorists, cineastes, sculptors, architects, artisans, athletes, and many others.

I begin by analyzing the canonical texts of National Socialist ideology, the speeches and theoretical writings, journals, memoirs, and table talks by Hitler, Rosenberg, Goebbels, Göring, and Himmler—the men who, above all others, created, framed, and explained Nazi dogma.

The academy in this era made an equally significant contribution, through the many scholarly articles published in various fields, such as eugenics, anthropology, and history, in pamphlets, collective works, and the numerous journals distributed extensively throughout the period 1933–1945. In particular, the rich body of iconography issued by the official art review of the Third Reich, *Die Kunst im Dritten Reich,* with its multitude of sculptures, monuments, models, marquetry, mosaics, medals, stamps, fashions, and advertisements, reveals the wealth of artistic media influenced by antiquity.

One cannot ignore the press. I've consulted the German Newsreel Archives in Berlin concerning certain events relevant to the subject, as well as newspapers—the *Völkischer Beobachter, Das Reich,* and *Das Schwarze Korps,* the weekly paper of the SS—that contained detailed stories of those events, many quite illustrative in their references to antiquity, as in the case of the Berlin Olympic Games and the final battles of March–April 1945. The cinema, particularly Leni Riefenstahl's *Olympia* but also the overlooked comic musical *Amphitryon* by Reinhold Schünzel, was no less useful, as was the opera: Richard Wagner's work *Rienzi* appears to have made a considerable impression on the young Hitler, helping inform his idea of history. Beyond the world of art, various laws and regulations mandated the content of school curricula in Latin, Greek, and history; the memoranda outlining the preliminary debates surrounding these issues helped me understand how the Nazi discourse on antiquity was disseminated, as did the resulting school textbooks and histories of Germany, all of which helped popularize and spread their version of history.

The archives of the Reich Education Ministry, the Propaganda Ministry, and the Chancellery helped me clarify the details of certain official debates regarding antiquity: What names, for instance, were initially proposed in 1936 for the Olympiastadion in Berlin—Greek or German? What script did official party and state documents use in 1941, Gothic or Latin?

The archives in Berlin-Lichterfelde concealed an imposing number of files on the ideological training required in various party organizations.

The pamphlets of the SS, the SA, and the Hitler Youth (Hitlerjugend), designed to mold and shape the ideological warriors of the new Germany, dedicated a not insignificant amount of space in their political catechism to the official state narrative of ancient history.

How could I handle such an abundance of sources? This question confronts every historian of the modern era overwhelmed by the volume of materials at their disposal. I have simply tried to listen, read, and observe these sources in order to relay, one bit at a time, the echoes, reports, or reflections revealed by the presence and resonance of these texts, films, mosaics, statues. Were there any recurring themes and concepts? What constants or obsessions structured the rewriting of ancient history? I thus hope to draw the general outlines of this discourse of historical mythology placed in the service of ideology.

There are still some chronological distinctions in the way that certain themes are discussed. The image of Rome, for example, was strongly conditioned by the relationship between the Reich and Fascist Italy and its evolution over time—from a 1935 article that denigrated Latin through the publication in 1943 of *Rom und Karthago,* which closed ranks around the Rome-Berlin axis by claiming that Rome was an Indo-Germanic empire fighting off the Semites and Phoenicians of Carthage, portrayed as a precursor of contemporary England. One can also read the change over time in Hitler's comments on Roman history, from its appropriation as a model to emulate, in *Mein Kampf,* to its use as a warning or foreshadowing of imminent doom, as in the table talks of 1942. In Landsberg Prison, Hitler still sought inspiration from Rome to build the Third Reich; in the radically different context of the Second World War, Rome came to mean all-out resistance against Germany's racial enemies until finally, in 1945, it signified decline and fall, and death among the ruins.

In general, however, the portrait of Greco-Roman antiquity nevertheless retained a remarkable consistency. In the canon of Nazi ideology—from *Mein Kampf* to the construction of the great edifices of Nuremberg and throughout all the school textbooks and scholarly treatises published during the period—there was a coherent discourse on antiquity, which depicted the era as the first and, other than part of the Ottonian (Saxon) Middle Ages and the Hanseatic League, the only great epoch of Nordic Indo-Germanic history. Greco-Roman antiquity was reread and rewritten through a variety of media to forge a world view that offered the reader, listener, spectator, student, and subject of the new empire a vigorous and robust narrative of their past.

This fable made Greco-Roman history into a site or screen for the transfer or projection of all the dreams, obsessions, and fears of National Socialism itself. The fantasy of the perfect male body thus found expression in the harmonious, ideal form of the young Greek Adonis. The dream of totalitarian control over a society built upon legions of ideological warriors found nourishment in the myth of Sparta, the hegemonic vision of global imperial domination its archetype in Rome. The Nazi obsession with race war was justified by the Persian and Punic Wars, the paranoia regarding conspiracy by the irruption of Christianity and Judaism in Rome. The Nazis' greatest and most basic fear, that of their mortality, needed no confirmation beyond the crumbling columns and ruins of Greek and Roman temples, shadows of two great ancient civilizations that had declared they would last for all eternity, only to suddenly disappear.

I hope to illustrate the outlines of this discourse, this other ancient history, by studying the three functions it performed for a party and a state preoccupied with creating a new man, building a new empire, creating a new society: that of glorification, of imitation, and of prophetic premonition.

PART ONE

Annexing Antiquity

But three or four thousand years before our birth, we are absolutely free. . . .
 That is why it happened that one day I wrote: in the beginning was the Fable!
 Which means that any derivation and any beginning of things is of the same substances as the songs and stories which surround us in the cradle. . . .
 All antiquity, all causality, every human principle, are fabulous inventions and obey the simple laws of invention.
—Paul Valery, "On Myths and Mythology"

"In the beginning was the Fable": Paul Valéry's sober observation, somewhere halfway between amazement and disillusionment, the basis for his healthy sense of skepticism regarding all discourses on origins, might as well have been a Nazi motto. National Socialism taught the Germans that all of known civilization, with the potential exception of the most distant pre-Columbian cultures, had been the work of the Nordic peoples. It thus symbolically appropriated the very concept of civilization out of a desire to define and defend the race, an appropriation that foreshadowed later, far more tangible territorial claims. If the Indo-Germanic race had created all of the great civilizations, then its purest and most direct descendants—contemporary Germans themselves—could claim the entire world for their ancestral home. Hitler, the thwarted artist and lover of beauty and culture, would become a plunderer of museums; the Nazis, pillagers of history, would reveal themselves to be brutal conquerors of lands they claimed were still their native soil.

CHAPTER I

Origin Myths

Ex septentrione lux

For a good ending, one needs a good beginning. (It is important to begin well, because of course the main thing is to continue well—this is storytelling.) Such is the implicit but all-powerful rule that a community anxious to edify by telling its story—to itself, to others, to posterity—should follow.

—Nicole Loraux, *Born of the Earth: Myth and Politics in Athens*

History also teaches how to laugh at the solemnities of the origin. . . . The origin always precedes the Fall. It comes before the body, before the world and time; it is associated with the gods, and its story is always sung as a theogony. But historical beginnings are lowly: not in the sense of modest or discreet like the steps of a dove, but derisive and ironic, capable of undoing every infatuation.

—Michel Foucault, "Nietzsche, Genealogy, History"

Questions of identity are often linked to those of origins. The conceptual bond between the two is such that the celebration of the former frequently involves the embellishment of the latter.

The Nazis developed a coherent origin myth and provided the German people with a distinguished ancestry precisely because they wished to glorify a nation severely humiliated in 1918, first by a military defeat that was rarely acknowledged as such and subsequently by a peace at Versailles that was perceived as a diktat.

This discourse on origins was conceived and transmitted in various ways, including academic and scholarly research. History and anthropology, often perceived as auxiliary sciences, were thrust into the service of the new reigning discipline, racial science (*Rassenkunde*), producing the kind of scholarship under the Third Reich that its leaders demanded. Many scholars did not need much convincing, however, because the Nazis were merely injecting new life into a vulgate widely accepted within the German academy since the nineteenth century: that of the Nordic origins of all civilization.

AUTOCHTHONY AND GERMAN NATIONAL IDENTITY

In his essay "What Is a Nation?," the French historian Ernest Renan—a man well acquainted with neighboring Germany and its historiography—wrote: "A heroic past, great men, glory (by which I mean genuine glory), this is the social capital upon which one bases a national idea."[1] For much of the nineteenth century, Germany saw itself as "late," a *verspätete Nation*,[2] backward or behind in comparison with the other Great Powers of Europe. The contrast with France, in particular, had appeared striking to educated Germans since the turn of the century: France was a united nation, brought together first by its great monarchs, then by its newly centralized state, with its codified laws and language established by the general will of the Revolution after 1789. Powerful in its unity, France had achieved a great victory over the so-called Holy Roman Empire of the German Nation; the people represented by the last two words of that august title, meanwhile, still stinging from their defeat in 1806, remained yet to be defined.

But how should German national identity be defined? The answer was certainly not of a political nature: unlike the French, the Germans were divided among a multitude of tiny states, kingdoms, principalities, margraves, free cities, bishoprics, and baronies—more than three hundred in all when the Peace of Westphalia in 1648 had flattered their rulers' desires for power and autonomy by generously granting them territorial sovereignty (*Landeshoheit*) in exchange for maintaining the scarcely tenable fiction that was the Holy Roman Empire.

Was German identity cultural? Yes and no. Certainly, German humanists had taken pride in their strong linguistic identity since the Renaissance, when Martin Luther erected the first monument to the German tongue by translating Jerome's Bible into the vulgate in 1522. But the German language could not boast of uniformity or a regulatory authority equivalent to that of the Académie française. It remained a Babel of dialects, many of which continue to possess a baffling amount of vigor even today (at least to a French observer raised with the type of linguistic standards imposed by the Académie of Condorcet and Jules Ferry). Furthermore, after the Reformation the Germans were divided yet again, this time along religious lines, between the largely Protestant north and a happily Catholic Rhenish and Alpine south. This partition ran along a boundary given the picturesque nickname *der Weisswurstäquator,* or "the white-sausage line"—north and south being equally split by their gastronomic preferences.[3]

Faced with a dearth of political, linguistic, or religious alternatives, nineteenth-century Germans turned to anthropology. Surely they could not fail to find the elusive key to German identity by studying the race of a people that had lived on Germanic soil since the dawn of time?[4]

Evidence of this race's existence dated back at least two millennia. Since the Renaissance, German scholars could look to no less of an authority than Tacitus, who had briefly described the barbarians that the Romans had encountered and fought north of the Danube and east of the Rhine. In *De origine et situ germanorum,* the official historian of the Flavian dynasty conferred a patina of classical prestige on a people without their own written history. French subjects and citizens had much earlier chosen to appropriate the writings of Caesar, who had preserved and maintained for them the pious memory of their Gauls.[5] But the Germans could boast of their Germania: for a nation not yet fully born, such acknowledgment from the pen of a great Roman author was like a birth certificate, proof of its authenticity and worthiness of veneration, as well as of its continuity throughout history to the present day.

Germany, then, was the land populated by the Germans. But where did these early Germans themselves come from? Tacitus had set forth only a hasty genealogy of the Germanic peoples. With an evident lack of imagination, and not knowing to whom they belonged, he had simply repeated an idea borrowed from the Greeks—an idea destined for a long and healthy life. He planted the roots of their family tree firmly into the soil where the Romans had found them:

> The *Germani* themselves are indigenous, I believe, and have in no way been mixed by the arrivals and alliances of other peoples.[6]

These two Latin words, *Germanos indigenas,* would form the foundation of the myth of Germanic autochthony. In Latin, the adjective *indigena, -ae* is derived from *unde,* the relative pronoun or interrogative that designates origin, in this instance transposed into the correlative prefix *inde-*. The *indigena* is thus "one who comes from here," "here" being the place in question. The Latin term used by Tacitus thus corresponds precisely with the meaning expressed by the Greek roots of the word *autochthony*: the Germans were born of themselves (*auto-*), without the addition, assistance, or agglomeration of outside peoples, in their own native land (*-chthony*). In this regard, they saw themselves much like the Athenians, whose conviction in their own superiority over other Hellenes was based on the belief that they were born there—unlike the Spartans, for instance, who were the product of Dorian immigration.[7]

This autochthony, the spontaneous generation of a people from their own soil, a veritable parthenogenesis from a fertile land engorged with blood, was joined by a second topos: that of racial purity. After their immaculate conception, the Germanic peoples had never miscegenated with other races:

> For myself, I agree with the views of those who think that the inhabitants of Germania have not been tainted by any intermarriage with other tribes, but have existed as a distinct and pure people, resembling only themselves.[8]

Having bequeathed the Germans their ancient lineage, Tacitus also flattered them with his description of their impressive physical and moral stature. His ethnography established the anthropomorphic caricature that defined the Teutonic stereotype and has dogged the German people ever since. Their perfect physiques were endowed with equally laudable moral traits. The Teutonic ethnotype was thus admirable in both body and spirit. It is not hard to see how Tacitus earned his lasting pride of place in the development of German national identity.

ARYAN MIGRATIONS: THE TRIALS AND TRIBULATIONS OF A MYTH

In the centuries that followed its rediscovery between 1450 and 1500, Tacitus's *Germania* and the ideas it contained were a source of continual speculation about the purity, content, and universality of the German character.

In the meantime, however, the myth of German autochthony was shaken by the emergence of a competing discourse on origins that captured the imagination of Western intellectuals during the Enlightenment: the idea that the peoples of western Europe had come from India.

The origin myths adopted by the newly forming European nations all drew upon a common source: the story of Genesis, set down in scripture as an incontestable truth handed down from God. Each of these myths strove to synthesize biblical revelation with the history of antiquity and classical mythology in a single, unified fresco of all human history since Adam.

The Genesis myth began to pose a problem in the eighteenth century, however, for its roots were at once both Jewish and Christian; it thus stood in direct conflict with the antireligious, anticlerical sentiments of many enlightened minds of the time. Any truly free thinker could never admit to viewing scripture as the unsurpassed fount of all truth. He (or occasionally she) was far more eager to appeal to the sciences of history, geography, or linguistics when discussing the origins of humanity.

Furthermore, the Jewishness of the Adam story ran counter to the prevailing anti-Semitism of the era. The heritage of Christianity was firmly anchored in the Western mentality, and anti-Judaism—an ambivalent mixture of mistrust and disdain, at times shading toward outright hatred—was an almost universal sentiment, one shared even by Abbé Grégoire, who otherwise defended the cause of Jewish emancipation. The Adamic myth implied a shared kinship with the Jews, a taint of Semitic parentage that many simply could not countenance.

The eighteenth century thus witnessed a search for a suitable alternative. The cradle of humanity would no longer be found in Adam or the Palestine of the prophets but rather in India—a hypothesis supported most notably by the famously anticlerical and fundamentally anti-Semitic Voltaire. This was the idea that gave birth to the Aryan myth, later studied in such great depth by the great Russian-French historian Léon Poliakov.[9]

Interest in India was growing at the time as a result of British exploration and conquest. Travel narratives from various explorers told of the wonders of Indian culture. A general climate of Anglophilia helped these ideas spread throughout Europe's educated classes. It was also around this time that geographers began to speculate that the interior of the Indian subcontinent was unlike any other land on earth. The presence of seashells on virtually every global landmass corroborated the myth of the Great Flood, which man could not have survived except on the highest reaches of the planet—the towering peaks of the Himalayas.

The idea that humankind came from India also pleased the most fervent of Christian believers. After all, the Garden of Eden was supposedly located somewhere to the east, and the wonders of India strongly resembled that earthly paradise so desperately sought after since the

Middle Ages. What's more, the Mountains of Ararat, where Noah and his Ark came to rest, could very well have been located among the Himalayas.

The Out-of-India theory (also known as the Indian *Urheimat* theory) was also apparently reaffirmed by the new study of comparative linguistics. In 1788, a British judge posted to Bengal named William Jones decided to relieve his boredom by delivering a series of lectures in which he claimed to have found a connection between Sanskrit—the oldest language in the world—and the ancient and modern tongues of Europe: Latin, Greek, German, English, and French. Citing a number of homologous grammatical structures and lexical relations, he concluded that Sanskrit was the original mother tongue of all modern European languages, from which each contemporary vernacular had emerged.

A second conclusion followed from the first: the only way this language could have reached Europe was if the people of India had migrated west to occupy and populate Europe itself. The modern Western man was a direct descendant of these Indian invaders, who in the nineteenth century would subsequently be called Indo-Europeans: a superior tribe of white peoples, the creators of all culture, who had come down from the summits of their homeland one fine day to wander and subjugate the world and had thus created all of civilization.

Indo-European studies were created and developed as the science of ancestry. In 1808, the German writer, historian, and philosopher Friedrich Schlegel published his essay "On the Language and Wisdom of the Indians,"[10] thus becoming the first Indo-Europeanist. This was the same Schlegel who, in another of his essays, published in 1819, introduced the word *Arier* into German in order to describe these migrant conquerors who had given birth to the languages, peoples, and cultures of modern Europe. Schlegel coined the term after the Sanskrit *Arya*, for "noble," which he believed also nodded toward the root of the German word *Ehre*, or "honor."

More than the French or the British, the Germans happily adopted this origin myth and took pride in their Aryan genealogy; so much so, in fact, that in addition to the word *Aryan*, they coined the term *Indogermanisch* (Indo-Germanic),[11] to describe not just these glorious ancestors but also their contemporary descendants, who could thus claim that they had preserved traces of their forebears' timeless purity on sacred German soil. Direct linguistic affiliation only further bolstered their claims of racial kinship. In Germany, then, Indomania was transformed into Germanomania. The Indians had sown the fertile German soil and brought into the world a people who were at once German, Indo-Germanic, and Aryan.

All the enlightened minds of the time accepted this new origin myth. Hegel gave it a scholarly imprimatur and raised it to the level of metaphysics in his *Lectures on the Philosophy of World History*,[12] tracing the development of the world spirit (*Weltgeist*), which, having dawned in the East, moved to the West to find its fullest expression in the German concept of liberty. Jacob Grimm, in the preface to his 1848 *Geschichte der Deutschen Sprache* (History of the German language),[13] echoed similar ideas.

It should be noted that Germany at the dawn of the nineteenth century was in the midst of an identity crisis whose roots went much deeper than the Napoleonic invasion and occupation. In this context, the Aryan myth conferred on Germany a sense of unity and invincibility with respect to all other nations; the Germans believed theirs was the chosen land of Europe's Aryan invaders.

But if the Germans were initially content to view India as their Aryan *Urheimat,* or "ancestral home," they gradually moved this cradle of human civilization farther to the west, choosing instead to find it in modern-day Germany and Scandinavia.

The myth of the Nordic origins of all civilization would become the ideological foundation of the nationalist and racialist movements that sprouted up throughout Germany and Austria in the second half of the nineteenth century. In this view, the Nordics or Indo-Germanics were the world's sole creative people; all of Western culture had come from this prolific warrior race from the North, which had given birth to the world's great civilizations.

The propaganda literature of these various racist groups,[14] which the young Hitler read voraciously during his indolent, itinerant years in Vienna,[15] formed the bridge that introduced the nineteenth-century Aryan myth to the National Socialist movement. Hitler's reading of the Ariosophists Guido von List and Jörg von Liebenfels[16] directly inspired the composition of his ominous ideological speech "Why Are We Anti-Semites?,"[17] delivered in Munich on 13 August 1920. In his address, Hitler recounted the origins of the two primary racial types—Aryans and Jews—and made the myth of Nordic origins the central racial-genetic platform of the Nationalsozialistische Deutsche Arbeiterpartei, or NSDAP:

> In the northernmost part of the world, in those unending icy wastes, ... perpetual hardship and terrible privation worked as a means of racial selection. Here, what was weak and sickly did not survive, ... leaving a race of

giants with great strength and vigor. . . . The race we now call Aryan was in fact the creator of those great later civilizations whose history we still find traces of today. We know that Egypt was brought to its cultural heights by Aryan immigrants, as were Persia and Greece; these immigrants were blond, blue-eyed Aryans, and we know that, apart from these states, there have never been any other civilized countries on earth.[18]

THE INDO-GERMANIC ORACLE: HANS GÜNTHER AND NORDICISM

The idea that the Indo-Europeans were originally a Nordic people was vigorously promoted and staunchly defended in the German academy as well as the broader public sphere by the official racial anthropologist of the Nazi Party, Hans Friedrich Karl Günther (1891–1968), a pedantic scholar and prolific evangelizer of the Nordicist racial gospel.

Originally from Freiburg, where he studied for a doctorate in biology and anthropology, Günther was also a fervent nationalist and combatant in the trenches during the First World War before becoming one of those radicals, desperadoes, and "outlaws"[19] who fought in the Freikorps until 1921.

A *Privatdozent* (untenured professor) in Sweden and Norway during the 1920s, he nevertheless made a name for himself in Germany through a never-ending stream of publications, which helped make him the father of German racial science in the eyes of the educated public; his *Rassenkunde des Deutschen Volkes*[20] sold some 270,000 copies from its first printing in 1922 until its final edition in 1943. The success of this and other titles earned him, in party circles, the rather clever nickname of Rassengünther: "Günther the Racialist."

Although he was not formally a party member until 1932, Günther maintained close ties with the Nazis and published his books with the Munich house of Julius Friedrich Lehmann (1864–1935), who founded J. F. Lehmanns Verlag in 1890 and soon turned it into a clearinghouse for racist and Pan-Germanist literature.[21] Lehmann was a Nazi of the first hour. He joined the party in 1920 after spending time in the Freikorps, and in addition to Günther he edited Eugen Fischer, Paul Schultze-Naumburg, Richard Walther Darré, Ferdinand Ludwig Clauss, and several other well-known names in contemporary racialist circles.

Günther's racism contained a mélange of ideas from the French writers Arthur de Gobineau and Georges Vacher de Lapouge, as well as the British author Houston Stewart Chamberlain, all substantiated by the scholarship of contemporary German prehistorians. Like Gobineau, he believed that the "pure" races had forever disappeared, but he also argued that the implementation of a state policy on race—an active and vigorous "selectionism," in the formulation of Vacher de Lapouge—could protect the Nordic element in Germany and perhaps even help return the German people closer to the original Aryan type.

Günther had never managed to win a permanent position in the German academy prior to 1930. That year, however, Thuringia elected the first National Socialist majority to govern a German state, and the Nazi interior minister Wilhelm Frick immediately asked the University of Jena to create a chair in racial science specifically for him. Günther gave his first lecture on 15 November 1930, in the presence of the party's most distinguished leaders: in addition to Göring, Sauckel, Darré, and Frick, Adolf Hitler himself came to listen to the master.

The Nazis' rise to power reinforced his political connections and scholarly credentials. He was named a professor at the University of Berlin in 1935, then Freiburg in 1939, and helped inspire the writing of the Nuremberg Laws through his activities with the Reich Interior Ministry's Sachverständigenbeirat für Bevölkerungs- und Rassenpolitik (Expert committee on questions of population and racial policy), to which he was appointed in 1933. Günther accumulated a number of official accolades: in 1935, he received the Staatspreis der NSDAP für Wissenschaft (Nazi state prize for scientific research), and Hitler himself awarded him the Goethe-Medaille für Kunst und Wissenschaft (Goethe medal for art and science) as well as the Goldenes Parteiabzeichen (Golden party badge) in 1941, a rare honor for services rendered in the name of National Socialism.

Günther made his name synonymous with the Nordic theory of the origins of civilization, a theory he championed in his more general works on German and European racial science but also in two specialized monographs dedicated to Greco-Roman antiquity and the racial history of India.

That all culture came from the North was an indisputable fact, as were all signs of the Nordic race and its greatness. Günther vehemently disagreed with supporters of the Out-of-India theory—he considered the Indians "Asiatic"—and he did not back down from polemical exchanges with his opponents, unleashing a salvo of counterarguments: Whoever supported this Asiatic hypothesis, he maintained, would have to show proof of the immigration of Indo-Germanic elites sometime between the third and fourth millennia BC. Yet, he claimed, "research on prehistoric times has not come up with any evidence to support a migration of this sort."[22]

Furthermore, scholars of the prehistoric period had already abandoned the notion of a migration out of Asia, which was a fundamentally biblical idea: "It is thus not surprising that prehistoric research ... has given up the antiquated hypothesis of the Asiatic migration of the Indo-Germans, a hypothesis that originated with the Old Testament."[23] The mere mention of the Old Testament, a text at once Jewish and Christian, was enough to dismiss the concept of such a migration as an outrage against the Nordic race and a blight upon its immaculate origins: how could one believe that the pinnacle of humanity came from the East,[24] that the Germans, of all peoples, could have come from Asia? In his book, Günther called out his detractors by name, inadvertently introducing his readers to the complexity of these debates and unintentionally acknowledging that his ideas were neither as obvious nor as universally accepted as he claimed.

In his *Kleine Rassenkunde des Deutschen Volkes* (Brief racial ethnology of the German people), a cynical effort to reach a popular audience, Günther was even more assertive, offering a facile synthesis of ideas and sparing the reader the bothersome details of complex debates, subtle arguments, or sophisticated hypotheses. Its aim was more obviously pedagogical, its tone resolute and decisive: "One must look for the native lands of the Nordic race in those regions of Paleolithic Europe that had not been subsumed by glaciers."[25]

Günther continued beating the drum of Nordicism, for it was not perceived to be self-evident in universities or scholarly circles, as his colleague and accomplice Carl Schuchhardt noted in an article on the "Indo-Germanization of Greece": while "the idea of an Indo-Germanic homeland in Central Asia, as supported a century ago by comparative linguistics in a rush of juvenile impetuosity, no longer maintains any scientific validity," intellectual laziness and the weight of tradition had artificially kept it alive, such that "even educated people are surprised to hear that our German ancestors and their relations, the Celts, the Italic peoples, the Greeks ... had nothing to do with Asia but rather came from northern and central Europe, and from there expanded to the south and east, until finally reaching India."[26]

Ultimately, Günther triumphed by virtue of what might politely be described as the repetitive and categorically assertive quality of his overflowing body of work.

But to establish the validity of his own ideas, he needed to deliver a mortal blow to the heart of the Asiatic migration theory, destroying it once and for all. So Günther wrote a book on the Nordic origins of the

Indo-Germanic peoples of Asia. In *Die nordische Rasse bei den Indogermanen Asiens: Zugleich ein Beitrag zur Frage nach der Urheimat und Rassenherkunft der Indogermanen* (The Nordic race and the Indo-Germans in Asia: A contribution on the question of the homeland and racial origins of the Indo-Germanic peoples),[27] published in 1934, he sifted through the genealogy of the Iranian, Indian, Persian, and Afghan civilizations: if these peoples, who represented the elite of the East in antiquity, could be shown to have originally migrated from the North, then the old chimera *ex oriente lux,* "the light from the East," would finally be discredited. Günther eliminated any pretense of the hypothetical or conjectural from his work, and after 1933 his word was taken as gospel thanks to the apparatus of intellectual censorship developed by the Nazi party-state.

Nordicist theory was also endorsed by the three musketeers of Nazi racial medicine, Eugen Fischer, Erwin Baur, and Fritz Lenz,[28] the authors of a multivolume reference on eugenics and scientific racism. Though nominally dedicated to the modern period, the "Baur-Fischer-Lenz," as it was known, frequently used Persia, India, or the Greeks and Romans as examples of Nordic destiny.[29] In his volume on eugenics, for instance, Lenz repeatedly referred to Greek and Roman history as Indo-Germanic precedents useful to understand for their contemporary implications.[30]

In addition to biology and eugenics, anthropology and archaeology also adopted Nordicist ideas. The journal of the Ahnenerbe, the Nazis' "ancestral heritage" organization under the aegis of the SS, multiplied its efforts to prove its worth in academic circles. Its director, Walther Wüst, contributed a piece on "India and Germany,"[31] while the prolific archaeologist Franz Altheim contributed a series of articles on "Germans and Iranians,"[32] as well as more tightly focused essays on the *Elchrune* (the so-called life rune), found throughout the lands occupied by Indo-Germanic peoples, much like the figure of the stag, an important animal in bestiaries from the same regions.[33] The widespread distribution of these artistic forms and symbols, which appeared to share the same cultural significance,[34] was taken as a sign of a uniform pattern of occupation and thus of the inhabitants' shared racial origins. A common race produced a common spirit and a common culture; in this strict deterministic logic, there was a clear line of continuity between the corporal and the spiritual, biology and culture.

Blood kinship, a common racial inheritance, was thus equivalent to a shared cultural heritage. The same blood had created the same symbols, just as the Indo-Germans spoke similar languages—all derived from a common Nordic tongue—and shared a common symbolic universe, as the swastika demonstrated. These common symbols were a sign, much like their use of fire;[35] Germanic rites to mark the solstice had called for a bonfire, akin to the flame carefully tended and transported by the Greeks or the sacred flame jealously guarded by the Vestal Virgins of Rome. In essence, the racial scientist thought, worked, and acted like an anthropologist who had forgotten the meaning of culture and attributed everything to nature.

THE NORDICISM OF THE NSDAP

As the historian Cornelia Essner has shown, in her work with the anthropologist Édouard Conte, the Nordicism of Hans Günther became the official doctrine of the Nazi Party and thus the country between 1933 and 1934.[36] By vigorously promoting his Nordicist ideas, Günther also rallied the most radical troops of the *Völkisch* movement. In turn, his theories, cobbled together from the xenophobic and nationalist literature of the late nineteenth century, fueled the party's most virulent racists, who largely gravitated toward the SS. Himmler, Richard Darré, and Alfred Rosenberg all obsequiously adopted Nordicist ideas, which promised to lend racial and historical legitimacy to future policies of conquest and annexation—since, after all, the idea of an all-conquering Nordic race fit perfectly with their concept of a once and future Greater Indo-Germanic Reich. Significantly, the strongest opposition to Nordicism came from within the ranks of the SA, the left wing of the party, with its "red-brown" variant of Nazism that fit uneasily with the elitist, exclusionary idea of a Nordic aristocracy threatened by the other racial strains within the German population, which Günther, Darré, and the SS had denounced as dangerous vectors of "de-Nordification" (*Entnordung*). The elimination of the SA leadership during the Night of the Long Knives on 30 June 1934, and the subsequent political discrediting of this popular—and populist—gang of Nazi thugs, tipped the scales in favor of the SS and their racial mentor.

By this time, the concept of the Nordic origins of Indo-European civilization was no longer seen as a theory but was elevated to the level of state dogma, a dogma that Günther gave a lyrical twist in one of his most popular books. In *Rassenkunde des Deutschen Volkes* (Racial ethnology of the German people), Günther—citing Jordanes, a medieval historian famous for his work on the Goths—noted that "the writers of antiquity called the North of Europe the womb of nations [*vagina nationum*]."[37]

The ideological indoctrination given to the SS duly reflected Günther's dogma. The soldiers of the Ordnungspolizei, for instance, were taught that "the homeland of the Nordic race can be found in the western, northwestern, and central Europe of the Ice Age. The geographic center of the Nordic race encompasses the territories of modern-day Thuringia, the North and Baltic Seas, Jutland, and Scandinavia."[38] For its part, the SS weekly newspaper *Das Schwarze Korps* declared in its inaugural issue that the cradle of the Nordic peoples could be found near the North Pole.[39]

Promoted by racial scientists and anthropologists, the Nordicist vulgate was also accepted unreservedly by historians of classical antiquity, who were all too happy to promote the legitimacy of their field of study by adopting "modern" racial theories. The classics thus quietly became a branch of Nordic studies.[40]

Official Nazi policy disseminated Nordic theory as well. We have already seen how Hitler adopted Nordicism as party doctrine as early as 1920.[41] In the following decade, these ideas were tirelessly promoted by the man destined to become one of the party's chief ideologues, Alfred Rosenberg, after 1934 the *Beauftragter des Führers für die Überwachung der gesamten geistigen und weltanschaulichen Schulung und Erziehung der NSDAP* (führer's commissioner for the supervision of the intellectual and ideological education of the NSDAP).

This new incarnation of the Aryan myth made it much easier to claim Greco-Roman antiquity and the other prestigious civilizations of the ancient world as integral parts of the history of the Nordic-Germanic race. In previous versions of the myth, Greece and Rome remained on the periphery, as if they were extraneous to the core history of the race: Greeks, Romans, and Germans were merely related. Though they may have been members of the same family, they did not hesitate to fight and even to annihilate one another—as their history, particularly the Peloponnesian Wars and the sack of Rome, amply demonstrated.

But by making modern-day Germany the *Urheimat* of the Nordic-Germanic race, the Nazis' version of the Aryan myth resolved these historical contradictions by fundamentally rearranging its genealogy, making their relationship no longer one of mere kinship but rather one of direct parentage. The trunk of the family tree was now Nordic-Germanic, its various branches Greek, Roman, Indian, or Persian.

Now that the racial rootstock had been planted firmly in German soil, it was easier to see how the branches had grown and spread from their ancestral home. They had emigrated from Germany toward the more temperate climes of the south, particularly Greece, India, and the Italian peninsula, where they had given birth to the most prestigious and powerful of all world cultures and civilizations.

The paternity of Greek culture and the Roman Empire could thus be traced straight back to the Nordic-Germanic race: the Parthenon and the Acropolis, the Apollo Belvedere and the Roman Pantheon were now the expression and demonstration of Nordic racial genius.

THE ARYAN: "PROMETHEUS OF MANKIND"

That all civilization came from the North was a point repeatedly hammered home by Hitler himself. In *Mein Kampf,* the führer had outlined a cultural hierarchy of peoples in which he defined the Aryans as the world's only "creative" race, a *Kulturbegründer* locked in mortal combat with its eternal archenemy, the Jews, parasitic destroyers of Aryan civilization:

> If we were to divide mankind into three groups, the founders of culture, the bearers of culture, the destroyers of culture, only the Aryan could be considered as the representative of the first group. From him originate the foundations and walls of all human creation, and only the outward form and color are determined by the changing traits of character of the various peoples. He provides the mightiest building stones and plans for all human progress and only the execution corresponds to the nature of the varying men and races.[42]

In this same passage, Hitler also described the Aryan as a figure from Greek myth, "the Prometheus of mankind from whose bright forehead the divine spark of genius has sprung at all times."[43] Hitler thus couched his own thoughts in Greek allegory: just as Prometheus brought fire and light to all of humanity, so the Greeks—those Nordic giants—laid the foundations for all of Western civilization.

Prometheus was also a recurring theme in Nazi sculpture. Beginning in 1937, visitors to the ring of honor in the new Reich Chancellery designed by Albert Speer were welcomed by two nude warriors, sculpted by Arno Breker, which flanked both sides of the primary entrance. One nude, armed with a sword, represented the Wehrmacht; the other, holding aloft a fiery torch, represented the Nazi Party. The allusion to Prometheus was not explicitly stated in the statue's name (*Die Partei*), but the reference to classical mythology and its echo in *Mein Kampf* were obvious from the presence of the flame. Breker later revisited the legend of Prometheus for a second giant statue unveiled in 1938. The party, meanwhile, the bearer of fire and light, would lead the German people out of a period of historical darkness and into a radiant new day, dignified and strong, following the motto *Deutschland erwache!* (Germany, awake!), flown proudly on party standards.[44]

A stamp issued in 1938 by the Reich post office, the Reichspost, to commemorate the fifth anniversary of the seizure of power included a nod to both Prometheus and the Olympian ideal, with the profile of an athlete holding the torch before the Brandenburg Gate, the German equivalent of Paris's Arc de Triomphe, celebrating military power and victory. Such symbols were not reserved for just government offices under the regime; Nazi iconography decorated private spaces as well: themes of awakening and the turning of night into day were also the subject of Josef Wackerle's *Durch Nacht zum Licht* (1939) in Jena—a Promethean man with a flame lighting the way for a prostrate woman on her knees.

Prometheus's central place in the Nazi political and artistic vocabulary was perhaps due to the influence of Goethe. In his poem "Prometheus" (1776), a monument of Weimar classicism familiar to all German schoolchildren, Goethe celebrated the courage of a man who rebelled against the gods to become the master of his own destiny. Party schools were infused with this Promethean spirit, Nazi shorthand for the enlightenment and willpower of a man determined to create his own history. The National Socialist elite, for instance, were trained in select academies, the Ordensburgen, where they were taught to see themselves as Prometheus on the rock—the party's metaphor for its special role in molding the destiny of the German people. The Sonnenwendplatz (Solstice plaza) at the Ordensburg Vogelsang in North Rhine–Westphalia contained a Prometheus by the sculptor Willy Meller; the adjoining wall bore an inscription addressed to the cadets: "You are the torchbearers of the nation—you carry the light of the spirit forward into battle for Adolf Hitler."[45]

CONFUCIUS WITH BLUE EYES AND BLOND HAIR, OR NOTHING GREAT IN THE WORLD HAS EVER BEEN ACCOMPLISHED WITHOUT ARYANS

We might define a cardinal principle of the Nazi rewriting of history by parodying Hegel: "Nothing great in the world has ever been accomplished without Aryans."[46] This was, of course, a bit of circular logic; historical narration requires that such assertions be illustrated with evidence. While Germany's ancient history might occasionally leave those lovers of high culture weaned on the classical treasures of the Orient and the Mediterranean on display in Berlin's Museeninsel with a certain skepticism about their own past, their patriotic sentiments were nevertheless buoyed by the belief that, as the Indo-Germanic or Aryanist vulgate had it, all of the world's great civilizations were the expression of Nordic racial genius. If the Germanic North had fallen behind culturally over the course of millennia, the fault, as Hitler argued, could be attributed to the harsh climate—less favorable to the flowering of Nordic creativity—or to any one of a number of other historical factors that his specious reasoning could come up with.

Nordic theory allowed the Indo-Germanic race to claim all the prestige, glory, and grandeur associated with thousands of years of Mediterranean and Eastern cultural development for itself. Although this book concerns itself primarily with the Greeks and Romans—who were the focus of artistic, historical, and ideological attention at the time—it is nevertheless interesting and somewhat amusing to examine the fate reserved for ancient Egypt and, more rarely, China in the Nazi historical world view.[47]

Wherever there was a glorious ancient civilization to be found, Nordic elites came, saw, and conquered, leaving behind worlds of wealth and refinement, inimitable works of art, powerful armies and states, Great Walls and pyramids. Over time, these imaginative, all-conquering elites had been subsumed by the native masses, their racial purity corroded by qualitatively inferior but numerically superior peoples, which explained why contemporary Egyptians now had dark skin or why the Chinese had yellow skin and slanted eyes. Nevertheless, it remained impossible to comprehend the cultural richness and historical grandeur of these civilizations without the divine intervention of the Nordic creative spark. For Hitler, there was no doubt that the Egyptians had been Aryan before an untimely wave of racial miscegenation with Asiatic or Semitic elements had literally cast a shadow over their white skin. In his table talks, Hitler waxed poetic about the Egyptian body—which was comparable to that of the Greeks: "If we consider the ancient Greeks (who were Germanics), we find in them a beauty much superior to the beauty such as is widespread today.... If one plunges further into the past, one comes again with the Egyptians upon human beings of the quality of the Greeks."[48]

The Egyptians had thus initially been tall and dolichocephalic (long skulled), with blond hair and blue eyes, as had the Chinese. In a small pamphlet on comparative racial science, Richard Walther Darré noted a similar Indo-Germanic kinship between Lycurgus's Spartans and the Confucian Chinese: "The Chinese of the upper classes—the members of the elite, that is, like Confucius— ... were not far removed from the type of man of the Nordic race.... Everything points to the fact that the Chinese ruling class, at least, were blond haired and blue eyed, and thus of Aryan or Indo-Germanic descent."[49]

As if the physiological argument he put forward were not enough to satisfy the skeptical reader, Darré added further cultural evidence: the Chinese were, like all self-respecting Aryans, a patriarchal society, and placed great emphasis on music in the education of their offspring, just like the Spartans.[50] *Quod erat demonstrandum.*

HEGEL TURNED SIDEWAYS, OR THE GREAT MIGRATION FROM NORTH TO SOUTH

Contrary to the ancient Latin adage *ex oriente lux*—"the light from the East"—the Nazis proclaimed a rather different concept of the history of civilization: *ex septentrione lux*. It was from the North, the Septentrion, and not the East, that enlightenment came into being.

A believer in the original Aryan myth—the Out-of-India hypothesis—and a man well acquainted with the ancient and medieval notion of *translatio studii et imperii,* Hegel had defined the migration of the *Weltgeist* (world spirit) as a movement from East to West, a mirror image of the sun's daily journey across the skies. The world spirit, then, followed the sun, flooded man with light, and progressed from the Orient to the Occident. Invoking "the great day of the spirit"[51] in a fever of teleological self-congratulation, Hegel wrote: "World history moves from East to West, where Europe is the absolute end of history and Asia the beginning,"[52] the *terminus ad quem* being axiomatically and ontologically superior to the *terminus a quo*.

For the Nazis, rewriting the Aryan myth meant nothing less than drafting an alternative philosophy of history, one that turned Hegel sideways. Alfred Rosenberg took it upon himself to defend the North's honor, formulating a systematic counterattack against the classic Hegelian notion of the spirit in *The Myth of the Twentieth Century:* "The march of world history has radiated from the north over the entire planet, determining in vast successive waves the spiritual face of the world—influencing it even in those cases where it was to be halted,"[53] as in Persia, Egypt, Iran, and India, or even China.

Rosenberg made an even more explicit attack on Hegel and the Aryan myth in a 1935 speech at Lübeck:

> The old doctrine of light from the East, together with the idea that the peoples of Europe emigrated from Asia, that is, that the physical and spiritual

fatherland of Europe lay in Asia, today has been proved completely false. The march of history did not, as a superficial and sectarian view of history would have us believe, follow a path from East to West. Rather, the creative spirit of the millennia that concern us radiated ceaselessly from the racial might of the North, which emigrated south and southeast.[54]

Ex septentrione lux: the Aryan or Nordic man had shone his light across the world and created all high culture. All the great civilizations of history were the fruit of his labor—including, of course, the glorious and immortal achievements of Greece and Rome: "The migrations of the Nordic peoples, which once gave birth to the civilizations of India, Iran, Greece, and Rome, are well known today, and wherever we look, the emergence of cultures and states was not the product of fortunate circumstance or magical revelation but the product of a special race and its development, but also of its struggle with other races and racial types."[55]

It was from towns precisely like Lübeck, indeed from across all of northern Germany, that "these never-ending waves of Indo-Germanic people set forth to create the civilizations of antiquity."[56]

The womb of civilizations was no longer India but Germany. Once the cradle of Aryan peoples, India found itself reduced to the status of a welcome mat for an influx of Nordic immigrants, a territorial repository on the same level as Italy or Greece, the jewels of the South set in the crown of their common mother to the north.

In another speech a few months later, Rosenberg reiterated the regime's new historical orthodoxy before a group of scholars of the prehistoric era specializing in the Germanic lands: "Asia once passed for the cradle of mankind, the wellspring of all the great civilizations. Now new research has shown that the nineteenth-century notion of the spiritual relationship between the Indo-Germanic peoples was not one of influence moving from southeast to north but the reverse. Much earlier, Germanic peoples with Nordic roots migrated from central and northern Europe in countless waves, reaching as far as Central Asia, in Iran and India."[57]

Cartography visually captured the shift in this discourse on racial origins, all too clearly depicting the inversion of these two concepts of history and the replacement of one historical paradigm with another. In a 1937 pedagogical manual for the training of history instructors in secondary schools,[58] for example, two maps juxtaposed a representation of the "old concept of history"—that is, the Out-of-India hypothesis and Hegelian philosophy—to the Indo-European theory of the late nineteenth century. The first map highlighted Indo-European migrations with four arrows: from India, from the Golden Triangle of Mesopotamia, from Palestine, and from Egypt.

The second map proudly presented "the new concept of history, the result of research on prehistoric events." Endowed with the imprimatur of objective truth, it depicted the Indo-Germanic race as coming from a single Nordic home, along with its dispersal patterns and waves of expansion around the globe.

A MYTH TOO FAR: ATLANTIS AND
THE ATLANTEAN HYPOTHESIS

In the midst of all this discussion of origins, an old white whale of the Western imaginary also returned to the surface: Atlantis.

The history of that fertile and powerful island, the fatherland of an all-conquering and civilizing race of peoples, had been conjured up by Plato in two of his dialogues, *Timaeus* and *Critias*. Ever since, the existence and location of Atlantis were the subjects of ceaseless speculation, the absence of evidence leaving plenty of room for the mythopoetic imagination.[59]

In certain German racist or Aryanist circles, such as the Thule Gesellschaft (Thule society),[60] Atlantis was sometimes equated with the "Ultima Thule" identified by the Greek geographer Pytheas of Marseilles.

It was in this vein that the Aryanist Karl Georg Zschaetzsch published his 1922 book *Atlantis: Die Urheimat der Arier* (Atlantis: Homeland of the Aryans),[61] in which he defended the idea that the first Indo-Germanic migration had originated on the vanished island.

His thesis caught the attention of Alfred Rosenberg, who could not refrain from mentioning the Atlantean hypothesis in *The Myth of the Twentieth Century*, apparently driven by his penchant for the frenzied compilation of half-baked ideas, as well as his taste for any and all ravings on the mythical and occult. But he did not accept the idea of Atlantis as the Aryans' ancestral home in bold, unequivocal terms. While "it seem[ed] far from impossible" that such an island had existed and given birth to a race of "seafarers and warriors," the essential point behind the hypothesis remained that of civilization's Nordic origins: "But even if this Atlantis hypothesis should prove untenable, a prehistoric Nordic cultural center must still be assumed."[62] This lukewarm reception of the idea did not prevent Rosenberg from describing hypothetical Atlantean migrations in the pages that followed before dropping the subject, never to mention it again, either in the rest of the book or in his many public speeches.

In the end, the Atlantean hypothesis was too weak to hold up as a genealogical myth, and it should be noted that it never really caught on: setting aside the work of Zschaetzsch and a few pages of Rosenberg, the list of published German work on the subject is rather anemic. Between 1933 and 1945, only one book specifically addressed the idea, and that was by an archaeologist, Albert Herrmann, who in 1934 published *Unsere Ahnen und Atlantis: Nordische Seeherrschaft von Skandinavien bis Nordafrika* (Our ancestors and Atlantis: Nordic naval hegemony from Scandinavia to North Africa).[63] A professor at the University of Berlin, Herrmann maintained a regular correspondence with Heinrich Himmler. Fond of esoterica and mythology and little inclined to let science detract from a good story, the *Reichsführer-SS*—a great fan of the work of Jules Verne, among others—looked favorably upon such speculation regarding Atlantis.[64] For Himmler, the Platonic myth, as filtered through the eyes of some imaginative racists, was to be taken as the literal truth: the original homeland of the Nordic race could very well have been an island in the farthest reaches of the North, an enigmatic enclave that the lover of mysteries and absolutes would later ask his scholars in the Ahnenerbe to go and discover.[65] The exact site was alleged to reside in the waters somewhere between the English Channel and the Heligoland Bight, the latter the location preferred by Himmler himself.[66]

None of this speculation found its way into more serious Nordicist literature: it lacked scholarly rigor in the eyes of those for whom scientific genealogy was their profession, who largely agreed that the original Nordic homeland lay somewhere between Scandinavia and northern Germany. The Atlantean hypothesis was too flimsy, too bloated with legend and mystery, and too shot through with uncertainty to support the scholarly pretensions of a young Nordicist science. Atlantis produced only a few internal debates between Himmler and the Ahnenerbe but no publications, research, or formal expeditions; Himmler's demands for deep-sea explorations around Heligoland never came to fruition, because of the Reich's wartime defeat.[67] *Das Schwarze Korps* made little mention of Atlantis save for a review of an important work by Wilhelm Sieglin, which we will return to later.[68]

Perceived as purely speculative and barren of import, the Atlantean hypothesis never gained any traction in the pedagogy of the Third Reich: neither school curricula nor the ideological propaganda distributed to the SS mentioned it, for example, nor did any of the other tools used to disseminate teachings on the history of the race—a true testament to how marginal and frivolous it was believed to be.

OUR ANCESTORS THE ARYANS: ORIGIN MYTHS IN THE SCHOOLS

Nordicist concepts were, however, promoted vigorously by historians and educators: indeed, Nordicism became the official state history of the race under the Third Reich, as a series of three pedagogical texts from 1933, 1935, and 1938 amply demonstrate.

That this was so was due to the initiative of the Reich interior minister Wilhelm Frick, who on 9 May 1933 gave a major address on the teaching of history in the schools.[69] His remarks inspired a number of "Richtlinien für die Geschichtslehrbücher" (directives for school history textbooks) addressed to the Länder on 20 July 1933 and subsequently published in the official bulletin of the Prussian Ministry of Education.[70] This document outlined the general principles that would guide the composition of all future textbooks and the shape of history curricula. Such oversight was essential to ensure that "the importance of the race be given just consideration" and to give prehistory the attention it deserved, since it "places the starting point of our continent's historical process in our people's original central European fatherland" and constituted the "national science par excellence (Kossina), for which there can be no substitute in combating the traditional devaluation of the level of cultural development of our Germanic ancestors."[71]

The remainder of the document was dedicated to the new interpretation of various historical eras. Despite its opening manifesto, the prehistoric period was the subject of only about one-seventh of the text, while antiquity as a whole took up about one-third.

The teaching of ancient history would begin "with an account of prehistoric central Europe" that would show how "European history is the work of peoples of the Nordic race," whose "high level of culture" was not necessarily visible in "the record of stone and bronze tools" of primitive peoples but legible in "the development of that original Nordic (Indo-Germanic) tongue, which triumphed over the languages of all the other races of Europe, save for a precious few."

Texts and courses would together "trace a path to Asia Minor and North Africa, following the first Nordic migrations, which must have already taken place by the fifth millennium before our era," as evidenced by "the skulls of Nordic peoples in the most ancient tombs of

Egypt and the well-known presence of blond peoples along the coasts of North Africa." Here Frick named Georges Vacher de Lapouge and his 1899 book *L'Aryen, son rôle social* (The Aryan and his social role),[72] just as he had previously cited Gustaf Kossina.

A litany of the ancient peoples with supposedly verified Nordic ancestry followed: the "Sumerians," whose "racial provenance," while not completely "clarified," nevertheless suggested "a group of Nordic conquerors" as the sole causal factor explaining the similarities of Sumerian with the Indo-Germanic languages; then the "Indians, Medes, and Persians, as well as the Hittites," whose "fate the student must relive as though they were related by blood;" up to the Germans themselves, peoples who had "created superior civilizations in India and Persia" before "disappearing beneath the numerically superior masses of those with foreign blood."

But of course it was the Greeks and the Romans who assumed the starring roles in the new pedagogy. It was important that neither teachers nor students be left with any doubt about their racial origins, since both "the history of the Greeks" and "the history of the Nordic peoples of Italy" must have "proceeded from the lands of central Europe."

The instructor would "once again emphasize that [the Greeks] are our closest racial brethren, which explains our intimate understanding of Greek art"—an implicit and piously reverential reference to Winckelmann, Hölderlin, Burckhardt, and Nietzsche. Greece had been colonized by "Nordic Greeks, who as conquerors had formed the dominant class of the country."

The Romans, having also come from Nordic countries, would also be depicted in such a way that "their racial kinship should be deeply felt" by the student. It should not come as too much of a surprise that Hans Günther, and particularly his work on the Greeks and Romans, was made recommended reading for instructors, whose textbooks and ancient history courses would henceforth be designed by the illustrious professor.

A year and a half later, on 15 January 1935, an official decree by Bernhard Rust, the Reich minister for science and education, reaffirmed the Prussian guidelines and outlined the teacher's role: "We must portray world history as the history of racially determined peoples. In lieu of the doctrine *ex oriente lux,* there must be a firm conviction that all of Western culture, at least, has been the world of the Nordic peoples, who established their dominance over the other races of Asia Minor, in Greece, in Rome, and in the other European countries."[73]

These two decrees of 1933 and 1935 were capped off by the institution of new secondary-school curricula in 1938, which declared that the "object of the teaching of history" was "the German people" and their "fight for their existence."[74] Since the "idea of race"[75] was at the center of all instruction, the history of the Indo-Germanic race was to be the focus of all inquiry: "confidence in a great national destiny that encompasses the past and the future"[76] rested on a belief in a "consistent genetic heritage" that linked "the past directly to the present through blood inheritance."[77]

This new conception of the history of antiquity was not limited to the pious hopes and regulatory proclamations of ministerial decrees nor to the elaboration of new curricula. It was also echoed in school textbooks published after 1933, and made the subject of ongoing professional development courses for teachers and instructors in secondary schools, like that held in Vienna from 14 to 21 September 1941 by the Reich Ministry for Science and Education, attended by some fifty-two primary- and secondary-school teachers. After two opening sessions dedicated to concepts of race and space in history, further sessions were dedicated to each of the periods of "German history":[78] after "German prehistory," teachers were introduced to "the Orient and antiquity in the new history," followed by the Middle Ages, the modern era, and the contemporary period. Eastern and Greco-Roman antiquity were thus subsumed as a period unto themselves within Nordic-Germanic history—that is, into the new history of Germany. This was a message with much broader implications.

There are many examples of this mental cartography of the origins of the Nordic race, whether from the four *German History* volumes published between 1937 and 1940 (popular works designed for the general public), the textbooks used in secondary-school classrooms under the Third Reich, the ideological pamphlets distributed to the Ordnungspolizei by the Hauptamt-SS, or *Die deutsche Polizei,* the house organ for information and coordination among the various branches of law enforcement. In all of them, the Aryan family appears to blossom from its Nordic cradle: the North, a rich fount of great migratory flows, as the womb of civilizations. Arrows represent the largest migrations, usually labeled with the name of the people or civilization begotten by Nordic seed: the Greeks, the Romans, the Celts, the Persians, the Indians. If the arrows lacked a label, the map's title or legend removed any ambiguity, as in one example from an SS pamphlet: "Nordic blood created the civilizations of Greece and the Holy Roman Empire."[79] It could hardly be made any more obvious. All these textbooks, histories, pamphlets, and articles were often no more than mindless explanations of maps, mere verbal mimicry: Nordic dogma on the origins of the great civilizations of antiquity needed to be ritually repeated, almost word for word, the maps themselves all drawn to the specifications of the same master.

The National Socialist discourse on origins thus enjoyed widespread currency beyond the schools: anything can be a form of pedagogy, and the Nazis' message could be transmitted in many different ways. Such maps quickly reveal themselves to be a stylistic exercise, an obligatory feature of all discourse on the history of the race: they adorned school textbooks, of course, but also more popular works on German history and more generally any textual discourse rooting the present and future in a past defined by blood. The diverse means by which this idea was communicated demonstrate an ambitious effort to reach several segments of the public. The Nordicist rewriting of the great Indo-Germanic racial past was not just the work of a small intelligentsia, destined solely for rote repetition in the schools and reserved only for the instructor and the parroting of their pupils. It was aimed at the entire German people: homemakers and heads of families, schoolmasters and students, police and SS, and both the secular and armed wings of the regime—whose relentless work of domestic surveillance and military conquest required continuous motivation from a belief system rooted in the depths of time.

THE INVENTION OF AN INDO-GERMANIC HERITAGE

It is easy to see, then, how Nordicism and the discourse on origins that it helped establish constituted a symbolic appropriation of antiquity to the point that "the history of Europe" became, in essence, "the history of the Nordic race."[80] This equivalence, the Nazi youth magazine *Wille und Macht* argued, allowed them to claim paternity for the great achievements attributed to civilizations like those of Greece and Rome: "The superior civilizations created by the Indo-Germans in India, Persia, Greece, and Rome provide ample proof of the creativity of the Nordic spirit. The deterioration of the Nordic elite caused them to vanish. But today we still feel an essential kinship with these cultures, which come from the same origins."[81]

Germany could boast of a rich and eclectic patrimony cobbled together from all the great Indo-Germanic cultural traditions, a potpourri of the great and the sublime, a grandiose patchwork quilt of scattered elements drawn from across the centuries, whose only common thread lay in the blood of those who had produced them. A fine example of this invention of Indo-Germanic heritage is the short volume edited by Kurt Schrötter and Walther Wust in 1940 on the concept of death in various Indo-Germanic cultures, a slender handbook modeled on the *consolatio*—the elegiac oration for the soldier who departs for the front and faces the possibility of making the ultimate sacrifice. Titled *Tod und Unsterblichkeit: Aus indogermanischem Weistum* (Death and immortality: Indo-Germanic wisdom),[82] this eighty-page pamphlet gathered eleven classical Greek and Latin texts, along with eleven from the Norse *Edda*, seven from Indian traditions, and fifty-eight other excerpts from German philosophy and literature, from Meister Eckhart to Alfred Rosenberg. In this compendium of Indo-Germanic culture, the words of Nietzsche, Homer, Empedocles, Tyrtaeus, Cicero, Marcus Aurelius, Seneca, and the *Edda* rested happily alongside those of sacred Brahman texts, linked by their racial bond; the work of the Spartan poet Tyrtaeus (an author of rhythmic verse that exhorted Spartan soldiers marching off to combat) was juxtaposed to the letter of a contemporary young German soldier, whose final missive home from the field of battle, full of the elevated rhetoric of sacrifice and honor, rested side-by-side on the page with the Doric poet. Yet if the abundant historiography on the Nazi plundering of the great European art collections is to be believed,[83] it appears that there was no systematic approach or policy regarding the seizure of antique art. The primary prey of the Nazi *Kunst- und Kulturgutraub*, entrusted to specific units and ad hoc commando groups,[84] seems to have been paintings from the sixteenth through nineteenth centuries, or alternatively prehistoric and medieval archaeological artifacts that had attracted the attention of the Ahnenerbe.

This symbolic annexation of European culture was also employed to justify subsequent, more substantial territorial and military occupations—an act of foreshadowing, for all great civilizations were but branches of the Nordic tree, and the Indo-Germanic race was simply returning to its ancestral home to reclaim possession of what was already rightfully its own.[85] A secondary-school text by Johannes Mahnkopf, published in 1942 at the apex of the Nazis' military and territorial expansion, went by the provocative title *On the Prehistory of the Greater German Reich:* the roots of this Greater Reich were buried deep in the fertile soil of the distant past, just as the ideas and books of Hans Günther had conjured them up from deep in the mists of time.[86]

That the Aryans found themselves at home wherever they turned was amply reinforced by the presence of the swastika, which, from its beginnings as a mere political symbol, would become a piece of scientific evidence and a sign that the Nazis were reconquering lands where Nordic peoples had once planted their flag long, long ago.

A creation of the North, according to Rosenberg, the swastika had migrated along with the Indo-German peoples: "Since long before 3,000 B.C., Nordic folk waves carried these symbols, as can be proved, to Greece, Rome, Troy and India."[87] As a symbol of German rebirth, the hakenkreuz, or crooked cross, now evoked "*Volk* honor and . . . living space," a souvenir of "the time when, as a symbol of the Nordic wanderers and warriors, it went ahead to Italy and Greece."[88]

One short monograph published in 1934 claimed to offer a definitive history of the swastika.[89] After arguing that "the hakenkreuz originally belonged to the Indo-Germanic family that fanned out from northern Europe"—and that, as a consequence, "as descendants of these Germanic peoples, the Germans have an uncontested right to employ it"—the author delved into a detailed history of the symbol in Greek art, citing the great historian of art Alexander Conze[90] regarding the abundance of vases with the hakenkreuz recovered during the excavations of the Dipylon cemetery in Athens before noting that Schliemann had also unearthed a large number of artifacts with the swastika at Troy and Mycenae.[91] The oldest swastikas, however, had been discovered in Scandinavia; according to the author, the antecedence of these "Germanic" traces to their Greek and Mycenaean counterparts helped explain the Nordic provenance of the peoples of the classical world. This proved that the Out-of-India hypothesis was false and must therefore be categorically rejected.[92]

One of a series of party propaganda pamphlets aimed at the political commissars of the Wehrmacht—the Nationalsozialistische Führungsoffiziere (NSFO)[93]—repeated Rosenberg's claims and the book's conclusions. After detailing at length the history and significance of the swastika, the leaflet offered a genealogy of the symbol: "The oldest archaeological finds in the Saale region prove that the Indo-Germanic peoples who lived in central Germany during the Paleolithic recognized the hakenkreuz. . . . From there it spread through the cultures along the Danube before extending its horizons to include the entire Mediterranean region. It migrated into Greece. It accompanied the Aryan expeditions into India, where it was found some two thousand years before our era."[94]

The swastika was thus the sun sign of Indo-Germanic conquest, evidence of the contiguity of the territories the race had once subjugated and henceforth the banner under which they would be ruthlessly recaptured.

In September 1935, with the proclamation of the Nuremberg Laws, the black swastika on a circular white background surrounded by a field of red became the new flag of the German state. One year later, during the Olympic Games held in Berlin, the exhibition *Sport der Hellenen* (along with its catalog)[95] presented reproductions of Greek cups and vases decorated with athletes throwing a discus embossed with the swastika: Indo-German Hellenism, and the profound racial and spiritual solidarity of the German and Greek peoples, on public display.[96]

THE GODDESS EUROPE

The rewriting of ancient history led to the resurrection not of the vaguely oneiric, rose-colored antiquity of Weimar classicism but rather one remade in the image of a Greek goddess: a geographic metaphor with distinct political implications. After the attack on the Soviet Union on 22 June 1941, Nazi propaganda began promoting a vision of Europe as a Nordic continental empire, united in combat against a Bolshevik and Semitic Asia, whose solidarity and identity drew strength from its common Indo-Germanic heritage.

One SS propaganda pamphlet took the idea of their Nordic heritage even further, declaring that "the history of the Germans is the history of the West, and likewise, the history of Europe is the history of the people who form its heart. . . . German history is, from its beginnings, not just that of a single nation but that of the entire continent." This strict equivalence drew on racial identity, the vision of a Europe mobilizing for a common future goal, the construction of a new order, and the conquering of land to the east, built on a foundation of history with a sprinkling of biology thrown in. The same document drew a map, sketched in broad strokes, of Europe and its surrounding environment, situated in the broader, all-encompassing context of the history of the Nordic race: "The birth of Europe, a geographic concept that captures at once the goal and boundaries of our imperial idea, dates far back in time, to the birth of the Indo-Germanic peoples. The fate of the continent, the original homeland of the Nordic race, is closely linked to the evolution of the Indo-Germanic peoples, who came from there. The Indians and Iranians alone emigrated, wandering off into the vast lands of Asiatic space and losing their identity. The Greeks and Romans moved within Europe, while the Celts and Germans remained far longer in their original home."[97]

Another SS pamphlet, intended for the ideological indoctrination of the troops, implicitly picked up on the same theme. A concise, illustrated paradigm of Nazi racism, the booklet dedicated its lengthy opening chapters to an exposition on the history of the race—its origins and the evolution of its world view and history under Nazism. Its version of *ex septentrione lux* tellingly stated: "We don't claim, as science once insisted, that 'light came from the East,' but rather that 'strength comes from the North.'"[98] This creative might, builder of civilizations, resided in the blood, which, through regular waves of migration, had preserved and renewed an endangered Nordic culture whose only pure and rightful contemporary inheritors were the SS themselves. This argument was pushed even further in an article published in the journal *Die deutsche Polizei*, which reiterated the Nazi historical and racial-genetic party line with admirable consistency and supporting documentation, offering a chronological examination of the three great waves of Nordic migration: those which took place in 5000 BC, 500 BC, and AD 300, "after which German blood circulated throughout all the European nations,"[99] beginning, of course, with the German heartland itself. In essence, Germany "is not only the center of the European world, but it has also always been the source of its blood and its strength."[100]

European unity thus "[rested] on the strength of its kinship of race and blood." It was good, then, that "the Nordic race throughout the millennia [shaped] Europe and the world." The presence of Nordic blood across the continent was in fact "the first cornerstone of Europe."[101]

A third educational pamphlet reiterated this concept. Designed to provide a tutorial on the Nazi struggle to reorganize Europe, the booklet rooted this project within the immemorial history of the aforementioned waves of Indo-Germanic migrations and conquests. Titled *Deutschland ordnet Europa neu!* (Germany reorganizes Europe!), the 1942 pamphlet examined various potential definitions of the continent in order to highlight the shortcomings of formal geography. "The quarrels of geographers do not interest us," it declared, since their criteria—mountains, land, and water—were powerless to discern the *Wesen*, or "essence," of Europe, which could be understood only in terms of race: "When we speak of Europe from a political point of view, we refer to not a geographically bounded continent but the living space of a family of peoples who share biologically related, if not identical, roots."[102]

The first power to unify all of Europe, from a military or legal point of view, had been Nordic: the Roman Empire. The Romans, whom the pamphlet considered to have been originally made up of "Indo-

Germanic countrymen," were "good jurists" and "good soldiers," two qualities that had allowed them to create a model empire, strong, peaceful, and centrally organized, a product of laws that were the expression of the Indo-Germanic will to organize the cosmos and establish order: "Just as Aryan India gave the world its most profound mysticism, Aryan Persia its most beautiful mythology, and Ancient Greece its highest art, Rome gave the world its most sophisticated legal system."[103] The first empire (*Ordnungsmacht*) of Europe, Rome had then passed the torch to another imperium, a new Reich: Germany.

The German Reich had almost always been the primary organizing power of Europe: in the Middle Ages, the Reich had fought against the church and its universalist message, in favor of a "politics of empire against the papacy"[104] that had constituted its medieval raison d'être—the Christian universalist message signifying a degeneration of Roman law, which had been contaminated by a reprehensible egalitarianism introduced by "Negroids"[105] like Caracalla. The booklet could thus conclude that "ideologically, we see our battle for the reorganization of Europe as a capstone ending two thousand years of world history, and as the beginning of a new era."[106] Nothing new here under the sun: Europe, since the dawn of time, had only extended as far as the conquering spirit, military valor, and courage of the Indo-Germans had allowed it; that is to say, all the way to the distant reaches of the Far East. "From a purely spatial point of view, Europe depends on these vast Asian lands. Long ago, men of the European race penetrated far into the East. India and Iran were the end points of these migratory expeditions that had begun in Europe."[107]

Penetrating the East and conquering the vast Slavic lands were thus age-old problems. Europe's horizons, since at least the time of antiquity, had been set by the vast spaces of the Slavic and Asiatic Orient.[108]

GENEALOGY AND THE ORIGIN STORY: THE DESCENT OF MAN

There is a fine line between history and mythology,[109] and the science of history, as we have seen, can sometimes lend mythmaking a helping hand: the documents cited above, such as the popular or scholarly books by big-name authors, with their footnotes, indexes, and bibliographies, endowed a theoretical discourse that tended toward outright fantasy with the full intellectual imprimatur of an academic science. The universities abdicated their ethical obligation to the pursuit of truth and became the docile servants of an ideology that demanded its mythology be transformed, through the addition of a critical apparatus, conventional rhetoric, and basic formatting, into scientific truth. *Historia ancilla ideologiae:* History became the handmaiden of ideology. Rather than keep its sights set on the eternal and universal, the academy compromised itself with the contingent and sectarian, participating actively in that partisan instrumentalization of reason denounced since the 1930s by the theoreticians of the Frankfurt School[110] and, in France, by scholars like Paul Nizan.[111]

History made itself the servant of a myth and a fantasy. Nazism, engorged on its own mythopoetics, created a fable that recounted the history of a group, the race, according to the dictates of its own ideological principles.

These principles were so basic, and claimed themselves to be so self-evident, that it was as if history was rewritten in reverse: the ideologized present would redesign the nation's past (the medieval period) and then forge a new racial past (the prehistoric and ancient eras), in order to demonstrate certain basic concepts and answer its own immediate contemporary political needs. The principles that governed the Nazi world view were thus crudely imposed upon thousands of years of history, reread, reinvented, and rewritten to demonstrate the validity of the principles themselves. History thus had to serve and retrospectively validate the very ideological principles that required history itself to be rewritten. This thoroughly false empirical validation *ab historia* completed a vicious epistemological circle in which falsehoods gave birth to lies and, in return, the fabrications built upon them engendered further deceit. In essence, the message conveyed by Nazi rewriting of history was this: "What we claim to be the truth is true because we say it is, and furthermore, history shows that it has always been." What this circular logic neglected to state, of course, was that Nazi "history" had already been assigned the very specific task of validating the Nazis' claims. Having lost all consideration and respect for history (*Geschichte*) itself, the historical profession (*Geschichtswissenschaft* or *Historie*) showed quite clearly that it no longer cared about the past but rather had placed itself entirely in the service of the present. Rewritten, mutilated, at best fantasized or outright invented, the past was no longer valued in and of itself: historians had abandoned their concern for the vanished past, along with their scrupulous respect for the dead.

This critique of instrumental reason applied to history is not meant as a valiant effort to break down doors that for the most part are already wide open, or as an opening statement in a trial that has long since been concluded. While it remains shocking how the entire apparatus of the academy was so eager to accept this discourse, it is far more interesting and important to understand what possessed these historians and professors to embrace the party line. Nordic theory was already familiar in Germany, since the beginning of the nineteenth century. Its radicalization in the hands of the Nazis had been endorsed without too much rancor or reticence by the academy because it filled a psychological need for self-confidence and reinforced a fragile German national identity that had been weakened further after 1918. In the context of the Aryanization of German public life within which the academy found itself immersed after April 1933, the scholarly profession witnessed a sudden flowering of opportunists, careerists, and fellow travelers, many of them among the best of their generation. "Careerist" and "opportunist" surely describe those historians who, after 1945, found it relatively easy and painless to maintain their positions and continue their work, in certain cases well into the 1970s, without ever referring to racialist discourse or repeating what they said or wrote under the Third Reich: men like Joseph Vogt[112] or Helmut Berve.[113] Only in rare cases was it a matter of fanatical conviction. Indeed, a typology of the later careers of those scholars who contributed to the abuse of the classical past would be an interesting exercise, albeit one beyond the scope of this book.

Such historiography and such teaching of history constitute clear instances of what Julien Benda called, in his famous 1927 essay, the *trahison des clercs:* instead of promoting the universal and rational, these scholars placed themselves in the service of the narrowest of particular interests, that of class or race. But then, the voluntary servitude of the modern intellectual was, in the eyes of the somewhat Germanophobic Benda, a peculiarly German phenomenon: "It must be said that the German 'clerks' led the way in this adhesion of the modern 'clerk' to patriotic fanaticism.... The nationalist 'clerk' is essentially a German invention"[114]—an invention, to be more precise, of twentieth-century Germany.

It is important to keep in mind that the Nazis in fact drew heavily upon mainstream German historiography of the nineteenth century and its various associated myths: they did not invent either the concept of Helleno-German kinship or the Aryan myth. Rather, in defining and defending the race, they merely reiterated and forcibly imposed the ideas of others, such as that of the Nordic origins of all Aryan culture.

The devolution of the historical sciences, archaeology, and anthropology under the Third Reich can be seen as a logical consequence of the role assigned to and played by these disciplines in the process of constructing national identities in the nineteenth century. As Anne-Marie Thiesse has written, in order to construct a nation at the time, "it was not enough to have inventoried [one's] heritage; one had better also invent it."[115] It was this labor of invention, in the threefold sense of discovery, interpretation, and also pure and simple fabrication, that made these disciplines, alongside literature and folklore (*Volkskunde*), so ideal.

The medievalist Patrick Geary has noted that it was in Germany that a particularly zealous, ideologically driven historiography first emerged during the building of the nation, buttressing the myth of autochthony, defending the primitivity of the German tongue, and proclaiming—in a completely fantastical manner—the linguistic, ethnic, and cultural continuity of the inhabitants of German soil. Just as "the existence of European nations begins with the identification of their ancestors" and "every birth establishes its own parentage,"[116] German historiography made a fervent sacrifice to the cult of one of the idols denounced by Marc Bloch, that of origins, an "embryogenic obsession"[117] that he believed to be fundamentally German: "What word of ours could ever succeed in rendering the force of the famous Germanic prefix Ur: *Urmensch, Urdichtung*?"[118]

In Germany this constituted a pseudoscience that endowed the German nation and all other European nations with the "tools of their national self-creation," above all "'scientific' history and Indo-European philology."[119] Geary's argument challenged and chastised the nationalist historiographies of the nineteenth century: "Their notion of history is static. . . . This is the very antithesis of history. This history of European peoples in Late Antiquity and the early Middle Ages is not the story of a primordial moment but of a continuous process. . . . It is a history of constant change, of radical discontinuities, and of political zigzags, masked by the repeated re-appropriation of old words to define new realities."[120]

European nationalisms and nationalist historiographies in fact shared, in Germany as in France, a common essentialism that consisted of fixing national identity in some immutable substance immune from evolution. In the final analysis, this discourse denied the very essence of history. This was particularly marked in the case of Nazism, which displayed a deep antipathy toward and anxiety regarding the very idea of history, which is defined by change over time. The nationalist discourses of the nineteenth century, and later Nazism itself, could not accept any doubts about the past or uncertainty over the future, out of fear for the hypothetical immortality of the race.

CONCLUSION

We have thus seen how the National Socialist party adopted a discourse on the origins of the Nordic race as early as 1920. In his founding speech of 13 August 1920, Hitler described the Nordic march of civilization, raising the Aryan to pyro- and photophore, bringer of fire and light from Europe's frozen north. High antiquity thus showed its Aryan face at work: the explorer, creator of culture, builder of states, societies, and great works of art, all emanating from its original boreal home.

The idea of a single common home of all the cultures of the white race had been accorded legitimacy since the end of the eighteenth century, with the elaboration of the Aryan or Indo-European myth. A German nationalism in search of its own truth and validation simply displaced the center of gravity from India to northern Europe. This Nordification of the Indo-European thesis was brutally and dogmatically enforced as truth by the Nazis, who viewed the Orientalist notion of the Out-of-India hypothesis as an obstacle and an insult: it deprived the North of its maternal prestige and glorified an East otherwise vilified by Nazi racism. It was ideologically imperative that the traditional notion of *ex oriente lux* give way completely to the *ex septentrione lux* prevalent in nineteenth-century German thought.

This discourse possessed two functions. Above all, it aimed to flatter German national identity by extolling the virtues of its racial origins: born in large part from the humiliation and defeat of 1918, National Socialism—beginning with Hitler himself—saw itself as rearming German self-esteem (*Selbstbewusstein*), the nation's self-confidence having been badly shattered by the collapse of the empire, the diktat of Versailles, and the civic, political, and financial troubles of the first years of the Weimar Republic.

This discourse assumed such importance that it was broadcast widely, using multiple mechanisms of transmission: the speeches and proclamations of Nazi leaders, beginning with Hitler and Rosenberg, as well as the work of racial theoreticians like Hans Günther, but also art, scholarly research, teaching in the schools, and ideological propaganda distributed to the police and armed forces. Hitler argued in *Mein Kampf* that the Aryan was the Prometheus of humanity; the mimicry of this fecund theme in Nazi sculpture transformed his words into stone.

What was silently suggested in the marble or granite dotting the public sphere was also taught explicitly in the schools: the directives of 1933 on history textbooks, followed by new curricula established in

1938, expressly defined the tenor of courses on the history of the race as the glorification of Nordic genius. Professors and researchers in the nation's universities or the many research organizations of the new Germany saw nothing wrong with supporting Nordic theory in scholarly work on the swastika in prehistory or the "life rune" in Sweden and northern Italy.

The second function of this discourse on origins was to feed Germans' expansionist and annexationist imagination. If men had come from the North to create all the most prestigious civilizations of the past—if the North was really the "womb of nations," as Jordanes had trumpeted—the Nordic race could claim wherever it wanted as its ancestral home. This symbolic appropriation of the most celebrated patrimony of world history was a prerequisite and prelude to more tangible material and territorial conquests. Nordicist discourse allowed the Aryan race to claim the rich historic and artistic heritage of the great civilizations of the Mediterranean, which suddenly found itself under hyperborean skies.

CHAPTER 2

A Nordic Mediterranean

Greece, Rome, and the North, between German Cousins

A new history master, Herr Pompetzki, arrived in the middle of September. He came from somewhere between Danzig and Königsberg. . . .

"Let me tell you what this heritage [of ours] has meant in the last three thousand years. Round about 1800 BC, some Aryan tribes, the Dorians, appeared in Greece. Until then Greece, a poor, mountainous country, inhabited by people of an inferior race, was asleep, impotent, the home of barbarians with no past and no future. But soon after the arrival of the Aryans the picture changed completely until, as we all know, Greece blossomed out into the most brilliant civilization in the history of mankind." . . .

So he went on for one hour. . . . Some, mainly the duller boys, said there was something in his theory. What other reason could there have been for the mysterious rise of Greece so soon after the Dorians got there?

—Fred Uhlman, *Reunion: A Novella*

The primary effect of this new rhetoric on racial origins, a reimagining of the old Aryan myth, was to draw Greece and Rome into the orbit of the Nordic race and its civilization. The Nordicism of the Greeks and Romans was confirmed by historians and racial scientists and publicized in a number of ways, not all of them scholarly. This rhetoric was also adopted by the regime's political leaders, to a surprising degree—surprising, that is, for the level of interest they displayed in a seemingly abstract, academic subject. Yet this issue assumed a singular importance for the Nazi leadership, because it allowed them to define and promote their vision of the Nordic race, including its proprietary claims on Europe's most prestigious cultural and historical heritage, as a prelude to their other plans for territorial conquest. After all, if all civilizations originally came from the North, then the contemporary representatives of the Nordic race could assert their right to reclaim their ancestral homeland wherever they desired, to the south as well as the east.

AMBER AND SUN: THE ETHNOLOGY OF THE GREEKS AND ROMANS

In 1929, Hans Günther published (as always, with Lehmann) his *Rassengeschichte des Hellenischen und des Römischen Volkes* (Racial history of the Greek and Roman peoples).[1] That the Nazi Party's chief racial scientist felt the need to write an entire book on the Nordic roots of the Greeks and Romans was in itself a development worthy of note.

This monograph was one of two such studies, in addition to his more general works, in which Günther chose to focus on the genealogy of a specific people. In 1934, his book on the Indo-Germanic peoples of Asia[2] would aim to deal the coup de grace to the old Out-of-India hypothesis. In 1929, his *Racial History* had a different aim: to glorify the Nordic race by conferring upon it an aura of prestige taken from a Greek or Greco-Roman civilization whose triumphs he claimed as their own.

The book was structured in three parts, the first on the racial history of the Greeks, the second on that of the Romans, while a voluminous set of appendices presented numerous images of antique busts and portraits accompanied by ethnographic commentaries.

In his introduction, Günther seemed anxious to preempt any scholarly or critical attacks on his work: "The author is far from an informed expert on the history and literature of the Greeks and Romans."[3] Discretion is, after all, the better part of valor. Such caution was all the more curious given the otherwise strongly assertive, if not categorical, nature of the author's claims.

To begin his essay on the Greeks, Günther appealed to authority, citing those German historians of classical Greece who had first developed the idea of the Hellenes' Nordic roots. Among those he referenced by name were Hermann Müller, who in 1844 had published a famous tract titled *Das nordische Griechenthum und die urgeschichtliche Bedeutung des nordwestlichen Europas* (The Nordic Hellenes and the prehistoric significance of northwestern Europe), and Karl Julius Beloch, whose four-volume *Griechische Geschichte* (Greek history), published beginning in 1912, made him his generation's expert on the subject.

Günther could thus claim his place in an already long tradition. Indeed, since the nineteenth century, German historiography on antiquity had unreservedly adopted Nordicist ideas regarding the origins of the Greeks and their civilization:[4] as early as 1824, the historian of classical Greece Karl Ottfried Müller had published *Die Dorier* (The Dorians),[5] a reference work on a people who allegedly came from the North to colonize the Peloponnese and to create the famous Lacedemonian city-state of Sparta. Steeped in Nordicist theory, an entire body of literature with historiographical or anthropological pretensions picked up and popularized these ideas,[6] not just in Germany but also in France, with Gobineau and later Vacher de Lapouge.[7]

To flesh out his thesis, the author laid out evidence from several disciplines in an exhaustive, erudite manner.

Günther first examined mythography and comparative mythology: the story of the labors of Hercules, for example, was closely related to similar Scottish legends, a sure sign that there was an "Indo-Germanic spiritual heritage among the Hellenes from central and northwestern Europe."[8]

Calling on Herodotus and Diodorus of Sicily, Günther then turned to the legendary Hyperborean peoples, whom the two ancients had claimed were the antecedents of the Dorians and the god Chronos, as well as Leto and her twins Apollo and Artemis. "Hyperborean," Günther wrote, means "those who live beyond the north wind" or, "according to recent discoveries in historical lexicology," those "who live beyond the mountains"[9]—that is, beyond the Carpathians, which in Greek eyes marked the border between the Mediterranean basin and the Germanic North.

Günther also employed the science of linguistics (*Sprachwissenschaft*) to bolster his argument, citing his colleague Otto Reche (1879–1966),[10] a professor at the University of Leipzig and the author of the entry on the Greeks in the authoritative *Reallexikon der Vorgeschichte* (Dictionary of prehistory): "One short Greek word constitutes irrefutable proof: the name of the contour of the pupil, *iris,* which signifies 'rainbow.' Never could a people with brown or black eyes come up with the peculiar idea to compare the color of the eye with a rainbow, because a rainbow, of course, does not contain brown. This name could only make sense to those with light-colored eyes—blue, gray, green, or blue with an orange rim—colors not found except among the Nordic race or its bastard offspring."[11] Such linguistic evidence occasionally involved more complex machinations of thought. Richard Walther Darré argued, for instance, that the word for "steppe" in Sanskrit was the same as that used by the Greeks for "field." A field, of course, is a space that has been cleared or deforested in order to make room for agricultural activity. The inhabitants of India could not possibly have conceived of *steppe* to mean a land without trees, except as a space they had previously subjected to deforestation. The Indians thus must have originally come from a heavily forested country! That country, needless to say, must have looked much like northern Germany or the south of Sweden.[12]

Moving from linguistics to onomastics, the study of names, Günther remarked upon the frequency with which *chrysos* (gold), *pyrhos* (fire), and *xanthos*—"which represents the color of mature grain"—were used in proper names: "The oft-recurring *pyrhos,* also often used in proper names (*pyrhotrix,* etc.), derived from *pyr* (fire), clearly shows that their hair was golden, blond, or reddish brown."[13] Such linguistic evidence was deployed in more ambitious fashion by Hans-Konrad Krause, who in 1939 published an article on comparative onomastics in Greece and Germany.[14] If the Greek and German languages were not intimately related in their semantic flesh, if the latter did not descend directly from the former, at the very least they nevertheless demonstrated an indubitable spiritual kinship: the same Nordic spirit was clearly at work in both languages, constructing proper names according to the same roots and the same laws. Upon first glance, for example, *Gottlieb* and *Theophilos* share nothing in common. Closer examination, however, reveals homologous structures and a common semantic inspiration: *Gott = Theos* and *Lieben = philein.* There was thus indeed a love of god in each of the two languages; the same word existed in both Greek and German. It's not too surprising, of course, that the article carefully avoided acknowledging that the German *Gottlieb* first appeared in the seventeenth century through the simple transliteration of the Greek *Theophile,* already previously Latinized into *Amadeus.*

Several other examples followed, including those of the names Diether and Demostratos: *Diether < diot* (= *Volk*) + *Heer,* and *Demostratos < demos* (people) + *stratos* (army). What could be less surprising for two populations made up of peasant-soldiers?

In addition, the author noted, reverse symmetrical constructions existed in both Greek and German: *Nikokles* and *Kleonike, Gangolf* and *Wolfgang* each reflected the same chiastic structure between the two languages. For Krause, these simple examples, suggested as exercises for instructors of Greek, also held significant pedagogical value. They allowed teachers to show schoolchildren that "from the fact of their common Aryan blood, the Germanic and Greek intuition demonstrated a kinship, I would call it a likeness, that, in its absence, would be inexplicable." These homologous structures are, in fact, undeniable. But even though they were used here as unassailable proof of Nordic origin, they could just as easily be mobilized in defense of the original Asian migration hypothesis: the first Indo-European linguists had, in fact, done just that.

Racial scientists also drew upon a new array of culturally based arguments. The emergence of racial psychology around Ludwig Ferdinand Clauss in the 1920s furnished several avenues for consideration. Locating the spirit of a people in their blood, directly linking race and soul, Clauss constructed a psychoracial typology that assembled the various branches of the Nordic race into the same type.[15] The various Indo-Germanic peoples were assigned the same psychological identity—that of the *Leistungsmensch*, or "man of achievement"—in contrast to the Oriental or Semitic *Darbietungsmensch*, a man of mere execution (and thus submission). Inspired by Clauss, the historian of antiquity Hans Bogner pontificated on the Hellenes' Indo-Germanic roots in *Der Seelenbegriff der griechischen Frühzeit* (The concept of the soul in early Greece).[16] Drawing a pristine hermeneutic circle, Bogner explained that in order to understand the Greek soul, one must "first begin with the German soul."[17] In return, the study of the Greek soul permitted an exploration of the German soul in its original, Indo-Germanic form and thus in its purest state: "This racial kinship . . . gives us hope that we might, despite all our differences, grasp the fundamental features of our primordial stock, from which we have become estranged by foreign infiltration and which is now inaccessible to us without the assistance of the Greek, which, clear and distinct, returns us to an epoch that our own direct ancestors could not bequeath to us but for a few scattered, mute traces."[18] One of the cardinal traits of this Greek soul, Bogner wrote, was demonstrated by the behavior of Ulysses in the *Iliad:* finding himself face-to-face with the enemy, Ulysses did not prevaricate; rather, "he realized that his choice had already been made, and he could not retreat from it." His choice, to attack, was dictated to him by "his birth, his blood, his essence."[19]

The Greek soul thus bore a striking resemblance to the German spirit, whose image was depicted as if reflected in a gilt-edged mirror: courage, the will to power, a sense of community. Bogner did not hesitate to portray the Homeric Greeks as *Herrenmenschen*,[20] a master race out to conquer the Mediterranean world. Plumbing the depths of the

Greek soul was thus anything but an academic pursuit. Such study was rich in lessons for a present steeped in talk of Indo-Germanic determination and will: "And if we must bow before the fundamental principle of all Greek politics, the knowledge that the whole is greater than the sum of its parts, that the community trumps the individual in dignity and essence, then this lesson from antiquity cannot be ignored in this decisive hour of world history, when a genuine community is once again on the verge of coming into being."[21]

BLONDS IN ANTIQUITY: THE TRIALS AND TRIBULATIONS OF THE "LONG SKULLS" IN THE MEDITERRANEAN

While psychology had its virtues, the queen of sciences remained racial anthropology. Günther, as we have seen, was willing to use any means necessary to prove his point, but it was primarily from paleontology and historical anthropology that he drew his strongest evidence: the Greek body was the epitome of the Nordic ethnic type.

Günther initially deplored the scarcity of extant human remains from ancient Greece, since the Greeks observed the regrettable custom of burning their dead. Even in the absence of skulls, however, it was still possible to study Greek warriors' helmets—of which the Altes Museum in Berlin maintained an important collection—which contained proof of their "long, thin cranial shapes."[22] The Greeks, then, possessed the same dolichocephalic skull structure[23] characteristic of the Nordic race: the Frenchman Vacher de Lapouge,[24] closely read and cited by Günther,[25] had already contrasted the dolichocephalic Northern man with the vulgar brachycephaly[26] of the other European, Asiatic, and Semitic races.

Lacking direct anthropological evidence, Günther next turned to ancient literary sources. The entire Greek canon was mobilized to support his argument, most notably the twin masterpieces of Homer: "The gods and heroes of the *Iliad* were blond, as were those of the *Odyssey*."[27]

Homeric heroes and gods possessed the exact same physiology, pigmentation, and anthropometric characteristics as the Nordic race. Only a Nordic beauty like the incomparable Helen of Troy could have driven the Greeks so mad as to precipitate a decade-long war, Günther proclaimed, enthusiastically paying homage to the face that launched a thousand ships: "Helen's beauty has been abundantly described: her hair, blond and fine as silk; her eyes, almost diaphanous; her rosy cheeks and red lips; her skin, a blinding purity of white; her hands, pale and fine—all characteristic traits of the Nordic race."[28] It was not just the color of their skin or of their hair that indicated the Greeks came from the North, but also their size. "The heroes of ancient Greek history . . . were of tall stature,"[29] Günther noted, citing a number of canonic texts and authors in addition to Homer: Herodotus, Pindar, Lucian, Aristotle, and several others were all called upon to bear witness.

Günther was not yet able to refer to another useful source, which only appeared a few years later (as always, published by Lehmann), the work of a colleague, Wilhelm Sieglin, an anthropologist and professor at the University of Berlin. In 1935, shortly before his death, Sieglin finally completed his book *Die blonden Haare der indogermanischen Völker des Altertums: Eine Sammlung der antiken Zeugnisse als Beitrag zur Indogermanenfrage* (The blond hair of the Indo-Germanic peoples of antiquity: A survey of antique evidence as a contribution to the Indo-Germanic question).[30] After opening with a sixty-page introductory essay on the question of the Nordic origins of the Indo-Germanic peoples, Sieglin then devoted some ninety-two pages to an "index of gods and heroes in antiquity whose hair color has been determined and persons whose hair color has been passed down to us." He thus claimed to have compiled all the figures—real, rumored, or fictive—known to be blond or brown haired in classical literature. The index listed each person's name and identity and the source used by the author, a considerable (and exhaustive) labor when one considers that the book included nearly seven hundred entries.

This in-depth prosopography was rigorously divided into critical categories. All the peoples of antiquity were examined as a group: the Hellenes, Italics, Gauls, and Germans and Swedes, as well as the Jews and Egyptians. The Greek and Roman peoples, which made up a disproportionate number of the entries, were divided into subcategories: "Blond Gods," "Blond Heroes," "Blond Historical Figures," "Blond Fictional Characters," and so on for their less-fortunate, brown-haired brethren.

The conclusion was obvious, if not overly surprising: The Greeks, Romans, Germans, and Swedes were overwhelmingly blond. The Jews were brown haired—another race, another color. With its mania for categorization and extreme concern for precision and erudition, Sieglin's book was perhaps the most fascinating work that the racial science of the era produced in its obsessive and pedantic attention to detail.

The book received a long, adulatory review in the 15 May 1935 edition of the SS weekly *Das Schwarze Korps*. The paper even called it recommended reading for the wider public outside narrow academic circles.

The article's title unmistakably indicated the primary reason for interest in the book: it furnished anthropological proof that "the Nordic race conquered the world" and illustrated evidence of a "war of blond against brown."[31] The review enthusiastically endorsed the idea that "the master race that was the Greek people were mostly blond" and that, in Rome, "the race of patricians and lords were distinguished from the plebeians by their blond hair." The practice of mixed marriages between the two castes had been the reason why the (unfortunately recessive) blond gene had ceded its place to "the brown hairs," to the extent that the decadent Romans had been forced to color their hair with saffron to recall the original purity of their ancestors, or resort to wearing wigs made from the hair of their slaves. One finds an echo of these notions in Hitler's table talks when the führer held forth on the Romans' hair color.[32]

In addition to Sieglin, the greatest names in racial anthropology brought their expertise to bear on the archaeological record, coming to the assistance of those historians and racial scientists who were studying antiquity. Thus was the case with Eugen Fischer, who collaborated with Günther in editing a 1933 volume titled *Deutsche Köpfe nordischer Rasse* (German profiles, Nordic race),[33] an anthology of images of impeccable Germanic faces. The same Fischer, who prided himself on his knowledge of ancient history and would later tackle the question of the Jews in antiquity,[34] also collaborated with German archaeologists on another 1933 work, lending his perspective as an anthropologist to the question of human remains recovered in Mycenae,[35] which he subjected to a detailed raciological exegesis.

After having availed himself of the wisdom of linguistics, historical anthropology, mythography, and literature, Günther turned—as the legacy of Winckelmann demanded—to the history of art.

Throughout the book, the author laced his text with images of busts, statues, and portraits from antiquity, subjecting them to his racial diagnoses: each illustration was accompanied by a lapidary caption summarizing his unhesitating and ruthless racial verdict. These pictures primarily captured the face, either frontally or in profile or occasionally in three-quarter view, similar to the concept of the mug shot invented by Alphonse Bertillon to assist in forensic identification. Illustration no. 18 on page 34, for example, described an "Anonymous Greek woman (poetess). Nordic"; an image of a statue of Sophocles, who also successfully passed the racial test, read simply, "Sophocles. Nordic."[36]

The voluminous appendices that concluded the book presented assorted portraits with more detailed commentaries, veritable exegeses of facial texts. Günther's ability to extract scraps of racial scientific knowledge from a casual glance at a sculpture occasionally leaves the reader speechless at the scope of his imagination. In one of his great bursts of physiognomic enthusiasm over a particular bust, Günther remarked: "Representation of the clearheaded, powerful Nordic man. A constant tension hangs over him regarding man and the world, a sorrowful experience betrayed by his expression, a sort of serene resignation, a kind of disappointment with the weakness of the men who surround him—a tension that never goes away, the pain omnipresent, transmuted into a serenity that can appear as kindness to others; the strength and profundity of his Nordic spirit is typically enveloped in a discriminating consciousness of his own superiority."[37] At times, Günther's inductive analytic powers bordered on necromancy; the statues of the dead revealed themselves, in dialogue with him, to be inexhaustibly loquacious. However, what to us appears to be nothing less than intellectual delirium was for Günther a logical consequence of his racial theories: the phenotype was the expression of an intrinsic property, the blood, whose qualities shaped not just the body but also the psyche. The blood shaped the physical materiality, the spirit, and the artistic and cultural expressions of a civilization. The identification of the body with the spirit, and vice versa, was thus entirely legitimate, since these two elements were both reflections of the blood. The three entities together jointly defined a unique, binding identity, that of the race.

While Greek men and Nordic virility remained the primary topic of discussion, women were not neglected altogether. Günther happily argued that the women represented in Greek art possessed masculine characteristics.[38] There was something undeniably manly about the fairer sex in Greek epic. This predominance of animus over anima was, it was believed, a trait typical of Germanic women, which once more provided evidence of the Greeks' Nordic roots. To illustrate this idea, Günther cited the case of Ulysses's wife Penelope and the warrior goddess Athena: "Penelope was a Nordic figure of the seventh century BC. . . . Personages of Penelope's type, which appeared equally in Persian and Germanic epics, recall figures from Germanic epic poetry, such as the Valkyries. . . . Athena, Pindar's 'blond-haired, blue-eyed goddess,' was armed for war just like a Valkyrie."[39] Thus Valhalla annexed Olympia without firing a single shot, in a neat and tidy mythological anschluss: the two mythical heavens were the expression of the same race. The Amazons were similarly likened to Kriemhild of the *Niebelungenlied*.[40] Biological determinism, the tracing of the spirit to the blood, was thus used to create a sort of mythological structuralism *avant la lettre*.

On the other hand, Günther did not appeal nearly as often to the comparison or assimilation of architectural styles, a defect partially offset by his colleague Carl Schuchhardt in a 1933 article, "Die Indogermanisierung Griechenlands" (The Indo-Germanization of Greece):[41] the existence of circular drystone megaliths, dolmens, and beehive tombs in Ireland, England, Bretagne, and Greece was proof of the Greeks' Nordic origins. As Schuchhardt wrote, these Greek constructions had their "brothers and cousins or, more precisely, their fathers and uncles in Spain, in the north of France, in Ireland."[42] Pedagogically inclined, Schuchhardt provided his readers with a clear chronology of the Indo-Germanic migrations to Greece, which had injected Indo-Germanic blood into the preexisting autochthonous population, much like those found in the educational materials prepared for the SS: "The first, the Achaean (because this led to the appearance in Greece of Homer's Achaeans)," occurred "around 1800 BC."[43] The second, "the Doric migration," took place "around 1200 BC."[44]

Günther, like all those authors who discussed the Greeks' racial history, never failed to specify that different racial types coexisted in Greece, divided between the mostly Pelasgian natives and the conquering Nordic race.[45] In fact, Greek art included examples of not only the Hyperborean racial type but also its Eastern counterpart. Racial categories and hierarchies also manifested themselves in a distinction between types of art, which distinguished between "noble" art, such as marble sculpture, and "crude" art, like pottery. Superior, or high art (*hohe Kunst*) "looked to the North and depicted the physical and spiritual characteristics of the Nordic man," while low art (*Kleinkunst*) and artisanal crafts (*Kunstgewerbe*) were inspired and practiced by lower racial types, by "strangers to the race (Metics and slaves) . . . of Oriental or Asiatic origin."[46] Different racial stock produced different art, just as it was true, of course, that differences in physical appearance reflected intellectual or spiritual otherness.

APOLLO AND DIONYSUS: THE COLLISION OF TWO RACES

This dichotomy in the arts was paralleled by a dichotomy among the gods. In a short book published by Lehmann—a satirical attack on Nietzsche, eviscerated for allegedly glorifying the Dionysian ideal[47]—

the philosopher and art historian Karl Kynast compared Apollo and Dionysus side by side. The earthy (chthonic), Oriental Dionysus, the god of the body, of the senses, of ecstasy, was the antithesis of celestial, Nordic Apollo, the god of rational intelligence and self-control. The Dionysian cult, founded on the loss of self-consciousness produced by excitation of the senses, was the product of a nonnative race incompatible with Greek Nordicism, even if Nietzsche had wrongly described the union of Apollo and Dionysus as a factor leading to the emergence of Hellenic culture.[48]

Dionysus was a dark, opaque deity, the god of the bacchanalian night, while Apollo was the sun god, *phoibos,* "pure, bright, luminous":[49] "Dionysus was a nocturnal god, the god of savage, exuberant excess, while Apollo was the god of wisdom, of order, of harmony."[50]

The bacchanalian cult rested on an explosion of feeling, a confusion of the body brought on by a disorder of the affect and by ecstatic excitation. It was "born from non-Nordic blood and spirit"[51] and belonged to a type of man completely dominated by his passions, in thrall to his natural instincts and impulses, especially those of the libido; these were the characteristics of the inferior races of the South and East, who more closely resembled animals and were defined by their excessive emotions, whereas the Nordic man was a master of self-possession. In essence, the Dionysian cult was feminine, passive, a cult of wanton self-abandon and unbridled passion (*thymos*). The bacchanalians were infested with "women and slaves! Completely the opposite of the Hellenic man, who belonged to a people of Nordic lords."[52] The races of the South and the East, furthermore, devoted themselves to matriarchy and the "motherland" (*Mutterland*), while the peoples of the North were patriarchal and spoke of their "fatherland" (*Vaterland*),[53] a point also made by Richard Walther Darré.[54] The Nordic god Apollo, in contrast, stood for masculinity and logos, active self-mastery, and not the servile or feminine abandonment of the self to one's emotions.

The Apollonian-Dionysian dichotomy thus rested securely on the antithesis of two races and paralleled the distinction between "culture and barbarism"[55] or man and animal: if Dionysus was the god of self-expression—in the form of ecstasy, of orgasm, and of "orgiasm"—then Apollo was the god of song, the living embodiment of harmony and of mathematical precision.[56]

Kynast's thesis, which essentially consisted of an axiology of gods and races, was picked up by both Ludwig Schemann[57] and Günther. Reiterated and cited by Rosenberg in *The Myth of the Twentieth*

Century,[58] it was also cited in party ideological propaganda materials,[59] giving him a much wider audience.

Rosenberg, in fact, considered the polarity between Apollo and Dionysus to be a consequence of the racial and spiritual schizophrenia of the Greeks, who were torn between faithfulness to their Nordic roots and an upwelling of nonnative peoples that had insinuated itself into their blood after their emigration south: "The Greek was already divided within himself and vacillated between his own natural values and those of alien and exotic origin."[60] On the one hand were the gods of light and wisdom, embodying the principles of goodness, beauty, and truth, the "glorious race-soul which once created Pallas Athena and Apollo";[61] on the other, diametrically opposed to the *Lichtgott,* "golden-haired" Apollo,[62] stood Dionysus, the god of the night—"Everything Dionysian in Greek life appears as something racially and spiritually alien"[63]—his psychic and physical foreignness incarnating "the attenuation of the Nordic blood."[64]

While Athena and Apollo, the gods of light, represented the harmony and self-mastery that governed the Greek psyche and polis, Dionysus introduced barbarism within the walls of the city-state. Rosenberg painted a pompously outrageous portrait of Dionysian savagery, decrying in histrionic tones the orgiastic, orgasmic rush of the bacchanalian rites: "By the flickering light of torches, to the clang of cymbals, accompanied by thumping on drums and the shrilling of flutes," the dancers abandoned themselves to the tyranny of their senses, falling upon the sacrificial flesh with their teeth bared. Such impulsive explosions of savagery were antithetical to Greek self-control, a virile demonstration of freedom from the tyranny of the senses: "All such rites were diametrically opposed to the ethos of the Greeks. They represented 'that religion of frenzy' (Frobenius) which dominated the entire eastern region of the Mediterranean world and was evolved from the African–Near Eastern races and race-mixtures."[65]

ROMAN *COLLUVIUM*: NORDIC RACIAL STOCK IN NONNATIVE SOILS

The second part of Günther's book, which covered the racial history of the Roman people, followed the same pattern established in his discussion of Greece.

The Romans, of course, were "also of Nordic racial origin." Günther, citing the work of a handful of linguists, took it as established fact that "the foundations of the Italic and Germanic languages are closely related." Nordic Italics, he argued, came from "the region of the upper and central Danube,"[66] which did not in fact make them pure Nordics. Indeed, while everything that made Rome great was obviously due to the predominance of the Nordic type among the old Roman patrician class, one "must not believe that they were purely Nordic"; it was more likely that "on their route across the eastern Alps, they acquired a few minor Oriental traits."[67] Günther thus demonstrated a degree of caution in his description of the nature and racial characteristics of the first Romans, a restraint picked up on by his readers and fellow German racial scientists of the era.

Ludwig Schemann, a scholar of Roman history and professor of racial anthropology at the University of Freiburg,[68] Gobineau's German translator and biographer, was severe in his judgment of the muddy racial mixture of the original Romans, who were guilty of not being as pure as Dorian Sparta.

He called the founding of Rome a "*colluvium,* a mixture and a mess, an accumulation of human masses, who really had no better option,"[69] citing Quintus Tullius Cicero, a magistrate and the brother of the famous Latin orator: "Rome is a state formed by a gathering of nations" ("Roma civitas ex nationum conventu constituta").[70] It was a multicultural city from its very beginnings, a "completely artificial creation"[71] in contrast to the Nordic perfection of the Greeks and defined by such "motley stains" (*Buntscheckigkeit*), a characterization vigorously refuted by Italian racial scientists after 1938.[72]

The presence of these many different cultures did not stop the Nordic element from coming to the fore. It alone guaranteed and defended the greatness of Rome and the empire: "The historic grandeur of the Romans is inextricably linked to their Nordic stock. . . . The most prominent and decisive figures in Roman history plainly display evidence of their origins. Despite the mist of legend that surrounds them, the founders of Rome are plainly reminiscent of the first Nordic peoples." A gallery of blond-haired, blue-eyed ancestors followed: "Cato, a redhead with blue eyes (Plutarch)"; Sulla, who "was golden blond with blue eyes"; and, of course, Caesar, "a Northern man of only slightly mixed blood"; indeed, for the most part, "the truly farsighted emperors were all of Nordic blood."[73]

Günther's thesis on the Nordic origins and character of the Greeks and Romans was repeated in a number of works that happily helped to spread the new racial vulgate. Otto Reche, for example, simply paraphrased and reiterated Günther's ideas in his *Rasse und Heimat der*

Indogermanen (The Indo-Germanic race and its homeland),[74] published by Lehmann in 1936; similarly, two chapters of a multiauthor magnum opus published the following year, under the title *Europas Geschichte als Rassenschicksal* (Europe's history and racial destiny),[75] parroted Günther without a second thought.

Occasionally one finds microscopic debates in these texts, splitting hairs regarding the geographic provenance of the first Hellenes. In contrast to Günther, who proposed northern Germany and southern Scandinavia as their original homeland, the historian of antiquity Fritz Taeger contended that they came from around the Danube.[76] The common consensus that they belonged to the wider Indo-Germanic racial community, however, was not up for debate.

ATHENS, ROME, BERLIN: *TRANSLATIO STUDII ET IMPERII* UNDER NATIONAL SOCIALISM

Nazi Party leaders repeatedly emphasized the Nordic characteristics of the Greeks and Romans, giving this seemingly abstruse issue a surprising degree of political relevance. Why did leaders at the highest levels of both the party and the state demonstrate such an interest in questions that, upon first glance, appear quite abstract and academic?

It is shocking to see the amount of attention they paid to the subject, shocking to learn of Rosenberg or Hitler himself perorating and pronouncing such disquisitions on the Nordicism of Greece and Rome, both in private and in public.

Rosenberg saw the common racial essence of contemporary Germans with the classical Greeks in their natural affinity for everything Greek and rejection of all that bore the hallmark of the East: "Our awareness of our European origin and distinction between the old and the new meaning of history has allowed us to sort out, to select and reject with certainty and for all time as foreign that which comes from Syria and Babylon. At the same time, the veneration of Greek antiquity throughout German history shows us that our instinct was never fully dormant, despite the existence of other doctrines. This instinct allows us to recognize ourselves as spiritually and physically related to all that which is associated with the word *Parthenon*."[77]

Rosenberg did not forget to include Rome: "'Old Roman' is synonymous with *Nordic*."[78] The Nordic-Germanic race was not content just to create civilizations; it also periodically rejuvenated and reawakened them. Greece had regularly been reinvigorated with injections of fresh

Nordic blood from periodic waves of Aryan migration, reinforcements in its battle against Asia Minor: "The Nordic strength, though reduced by chronic warfare, was continually refreshed by further immigration. Dorians, and then Macedonians, protected the creative blond blood." Greece, in Rosenberg's eyes, marked the apogee of Nordic racial and cultural excellence: "Most beautifully of all was the dream of Nordic man made manifest in Hellas. Wave upon wave came from the Danube valley and overlaid the earlier population of mixed Aryan and non Aryan immigrants, bringing fresh creative powers. The ancient Mycenaean culture of the Achaeans was predominantly Nordic in character."[79]

Rome had also been rejuvenated by an influx of fresh blood from Germany. Rosenberg described the Teutonic invaders as a regenerative factor in the resurrection of the original, Aryan Rome; their pure blood strengthened a Nordic element weakened by a shameful spirit of tolerance for foreigners: "In later times, when the Germans offered their services to weak, degenerate emperors who were surrounded by impure bastards, the same spirit of honor and loyalty lived within them as had once lived in the ancient Romans."[80]

This wave of Germanic immigration, which would subsume the Roman Empire, was for Rosenberg the equivalent of a refounding of the Eternal City. The revolution, so to speak, of 753 BC was driven entirely by the arrival of Germans from the North. The German soldiers who began to populate the empire and constitute its auxiliary legions were the foundation of the empire and its power: "In campaign after campaign the military skill of the Romans proved ineffectual against the rude strength of a young people. Giant blond 'slaves' began to appear on the streets of Rome, and the Germanic ideal of beauty became fashionable among a decadent people bereft of all ideals of their own. Free Teutons also were soon no rarity in Rome. More and more the Caesars came to depend for support on the loyalty of the Germanic soldiery.... By the time of Constantine, the 'Roman' army was almost entirely Germanic."[81] The presence of these Germans brought the city back to its Nordic origins, after a long racial decadence: "Set apart from the indigenous population by their adherence to the Aryan denomination and by laws prohibiting intermarriage, the Goths and the later Langobards played the same character-forming role as had the first Nordic immigrants for old Republican Rome."[82]

German historiography was still loath to acknowledge that what the French called the "barbarian invasions" were, in fact, just that: the invasions of barbarians who were nothing less than the gravediggers of the

Roman Empire. Significantly, German historians referred to them not as "great invasions," as did the French, but rather as *Völkerwanderungen,* "migrations of peoples." The term *invasion* carried hostile overtones: barbarians—swarthy men dressed in animal skins—had sacked Rome, raped its women, and pillaged its temples, leaving an easy target for the derision of painters of academic art (*art pompier*). German historiography had focused instead on the consistency and progressive nature of the long, slow wave of Germanic migration: the peoples of the North had joined the empire through a series of federations (*foedera*), assimilating themselves gradually. The Nazis carried this rehabilitation of the Germans to its logical extreme. Far from being the destroyers of empire, they were the source of its biological regeneration. The empire had naturally decamped from Rome and moved farther north, with Charlemagne and later Otto I. This racial regeneration of the empire, however, didn't last: Rome had also succumbed, like Greece before it, to the assault of hostile races, as we shall see later on.[83]

The Nazi reimagining of the Aryan myth thus established that the Greeks, Romans, and Germans shared a common racial essence. All three were branches of a common Nordic race. Though the Germanic branch of the family tree had remained in the ancestral lands to protect the soil of the fatherland, there remained a sort of parental relationship between Greeks, Romans, and Germans: Germanic peoples from the North had given birth to the Greeks and Romans, who, in return, had sown the seeds of *Germanentum* (Germanicness). It was all empirically verifiable. In one of his table talks, Hitler declared, "When we are asked about our ancestors, we should always point to the Greeks."[84]

SUNLIGHT, SOPHISTICATION, AND THE PARTHENON: ENVIRONMENTAL DETERMINISM VERSUS GERMANIC BACKWARDNESS

How then to explain the shocking chasm in the level of civilization between Athens and Rome on the one hand and the primitive Germans of the *Urwald* on the other?

Hitler spent a great deal of time developing an answer to this question. In *Mein Kampf,* he vigorously disputed the idea that the Germans had been completely culturally backward—an idea he did not entirely dismiss in private but one that he could not, for obvious political reasons, state frankly in public (although he did allow himself to come rather close in his table talks, as we shall see). In *Mein Kampf,* however, he virtuously declared: "It is an unbelievable offense to represent the Germanic peoples of the pre-Christian era as 'cultureless,' as barbarians. That they never were. Only the harshness of their northern homeland forced them into circumstances which thwarted the development of their creative forces. If, without any ancient world, they had come to the more favorable regions of the south, and if the material provided by lower peoples had given them their first technical implements, the culture-creating ability slumbering within them would have grown into radiant bloom just as happened, for example, with the Greeks."[85]

Hitler thus seized upon the theory of environmental determinism so dear to classical ethnology from Aristotle to Montesquieu. Aristotle had explained how the Greeks, who inhabited a more temperate part of the world, possessed a balanced and harmonious nature far from the extremes characteristic of northern climes; a couple of centuries later, Posidonius of Apamea[86] set out an entire typology of peoples by climatic zone. For both of these writers, as for Montesquieu much later, atmospheric conditions were decisive in determining a people's level of cultural development. A botanical analogy constituted irrefutable intuitive proof of the theory's validity: a plant will grow far taller under the warm Tuscan sun than in the cold mists of the North.

In one of his table talks in 1942, Hitler expounded on this idea: "We know to-day why our ancestors were not attracted to the East, but rather to the South. Because all the regions lying east of the Elbe were like what Russia is for us to-day. The Romans detested crossing the Alps. The Germanic peoples, on the other hand, were very fond of crossing them but in the opposite direction."[87] Eastern Europe thus appeared in a rather unflattering light. In ancient times, it was a repugnant land, which explained why the early Germans, in contrast to the Nazis, did not think twice about where their version of lebensraum led them: their predilections pointed them south, not east.

It was not unusual for Hitler to describe Germany itself in that manner, as in one of his table talks from January 1942: "The soil we live on must have been so desolate that our ancestors, if they passed that way, certainly continued their journey,"[88] to which he added a derogatory porcine metaphor that left little to the imagination.[89] To listen to Hitler, a trip to eastern Prussia would have thrilled the Romans about as much as a transfer to the eastern front did the soldiers of the Wehrmacht during the Great War: "For any Roman, the fact of being sent to Germania was regarded as a punishment—rather like what it used to mean to us to be sent to Posen. You can imagine those rainy, grey regions, transformed into quagmires as far as the eye could see.... The countryside was cold, damp, dreary."[90] The image of Germany in antiquity, then, was the exact opposite of the Mediterranean, that warm and sunny land where the Nordic spirit blossomed in all its fertility, power, and grace.

Hitler had read Tacitus's *Germania*, which he occasionally cited in his speeches and table talks,[91] and readily accepted its various depictions of geography and climate. Tacitus, who never set foot in Germany even once in his life and knew the country only through the descriptions of intermediaries—primarily merchants and legionnaires—described a harsh and inhospitable land completely lacking in beauty or charm to either visitors or natives. He recoiled at "Germania ... with its wild scenery and harsh climate ... pleasant neither to live in nor to look at,"[92] concluding his aesthetic and meteorological harangue with the following judgment: "There are some varieties in the appearance of the country, but broadly it is a land of bristling forests and unhealthy marshes; the rainfall is heavier on the side of Gaul; the winds are higher on the side of Noricum and Pannonia."[93]

Hitler unquestioningly accepted the ancient Roman's aversion for primitive Germany. In his eyes, Germania thoroughly resembled the same desolate portrait that contemporary Russia, disfigured by Soviet tyranny, presented invading German soldiers: "I'd like to remind those of us who speak of the 'desolate Eastern territories' that, in the eyes of the ancient Romans, all Northern Europe offered a spectacle of desolation. Yet Germany has become a smiling country. In the same way, the Ukraine will become beautiful when we've been at work there."[94] Hitler's table talks from fall 1941 and winter 1942 reflected the positive reports coming from the eastern front and were full of hope that the Nazi colonization of the East would be crowned with success. While German soldiers fought on Soviet soil, however, Hitler saw the war in terms of Roman conquest and domination.

The colonization of the East would improve the countryside, for while racial determinism was fixed and permanent, the environment was susceptible to a degree of manipulation. It was only a matter of creative will. The force of destiny was always welcome, however—in the form of climate change, for example. In the past, Germany had finally been able to develop, Hitler sagely proclaimed, because the more temperate climate of the South had moved north over the Alps thanks to medieval deforestation. Without the soft, warming effects of the foehn wind, Germany would still doubtlessly remain that harsh, inhospitable, cold land that so repulsed the Romans: "We owe the present fertility of our soil to the deforestation of Italy. If it weren't for that, the warm winds of the South would not reach as far as here. Two thousand years ago Italy was still wooded, and one can imagine how our untilled countries must have looked."[95] Now we know the secret to Germany's cultural lift-off: the Germans were able to overcome their backwardness with respect to the Greeks and Romans thanks to the beneficial effects of the winds, previously blocked by dense Italo-Alpine forests.

Other representatives of the Nordic race had experienced such good fortune much earlier. Having had the felicitous idea to migrate south, they had been able to create flourishing, radiant civilizations. Much like a plant, the Indo-Germanic type needed sun to facilitate its cultural photosynthesis: "The Germanic needed a sunny climate to enable his qualities to develop. It was in Greece and Italy that the Germanic spirit found the first terrain favourable to its blossoming." An unfavorable climate had retarded the development of the Germanic genius in the North: "It took several centuries to create, in the Nordic climate, the conditions of life necessary for civilized man. Science helped there."[96]

Hitler's notions of climate and environment were designed to provide an excuse for a cultural backwardness that stung contemporary Germans. Others, like the art historian Paul Schultze-Naumburg, tried to come up with less hazy arguments for why such a gap existed between the great peoples of antiquity and their German cousins. For him, the question was not Why had there been such a cultural chasm between apparently related peoples? but rather Why were there so few extant examples of Germanic cultural greatness? That is, why had German works of art not been preserved in the same manner as those of the Greeks? For him, "the answer [was] . . . purely material":[97] the Greeks had worked in marble, the Germans in wood, which was sadly perishable, or in iron, which was subject to rust.[98]

CLASSICAL TASTES VERSUS GERMANOPHILIA: HITLER AND THE SS

Hitler's severe judgment of Germany's ancient history might seem shocking; for all his fascination with antiquity, and Rome in particular, he appeared to feel nothing but disdain for German prehistory, so lacking in culture, so bereft of art. The führer could become rather deeply frustrated with the Germanophilic obsessions of Himmler and the SS: German history, in his eyes, did not become truly interesting until the Holy Roman Empire, the building of great cathedrals, the rise of the

Prussian state. The history of pre-Christian Germany—Himmler's love and obsession—was worthless. Studying it further only proved another humiliation for German national pride.

Nevertheless, Himmler launched entire regiments of SS archaeologists in an assault on the forests of Germany. Their mission was to dig up all traces of Germanic civilization and to bolster the reputation of the young discipline of German prehistory, which its founder, Gustaf Kossina, deemed the "eminently national science."[99] The SS outfitted itself with an impressive-looking journal, *Germanien*, which proudly published regular reports on various prehistoric excavations.[100]

This research was viewed with a deeply negative and critical eye by a lover of antiquity like Hitler. The results of the excavations disturbed the führer, who saw them as an embarrassment rather than a glorification of *Germanentum*. The Germanomania of Himmler and the SS prompted a rather uncharitable streak of sarcasm on his part: "A skull is dug up by chance, and everybody exclaims: 'That's what our ancestors were like.' Who knows if the so-called Neanderthal man wasn't really an ape? . . . When we are asked about our ancestors, we should always point to the Greeks."[101] Hitler clearly did not appreciate the SS victoriously brandishing the bones of some pithecanthropus.

It was useless and even deleterious to disinter skulls in Germany in an effort to better understand the ancestry of the race, because it was in the marble of Greek statuary that such traces could be found: "The ancient Greeks . . . were also Germanics,"[102] Hitler calmly asserted, conflating Hellas and *Germanentum* without even bothering to trifle with the concept of their common Nordicism, revealing a surprising, if consistent, degree of amateurism on racial matters,[103] as well as his pronounced taste for intellectual shortcuts and crude synthesis.

Everything that Himmler's archaeologists succeeded in bringing to light left the führer cold, prompting this exercise in historical criticism: "As regards the archaeological discoveries made in our part of the world, I'm skeptical. The objects in question were doubtless made in entirely different regions. Their presence would indicate that they were articles of exchange, which the Germanics of the coast obtained for their amber." Even worse, the results of their research provided overwhelming proof, in his eyes, of the incurable backwardness of a culture that was hardly worthy of the name: "In the whole of Northern Europe, the level of civilisation cannot much have surpassed that of the Maoris."[104] In any event, even if we attribute the polemical exaggeration of the preceding examples to the aggravation caused by the SS and its Germanomania, it is clear that the Germans, for Hitler, simply could not compare to the ancient Greeks and Romans, who had his full attention: "People make a tremendous fuss about the excavations carried out in districts inhabited by our forebears of the pre-Christian era. I am afraid I cannot share their enthusiasm." His very next sentence perfectly summarized the führer's opinion:

> I cannot help remembering that, while our ancestors were making these vessels of stone and clay, over which our archaeologists rave, the Greeks had already built an Acropolis.[105]

For Hitler, there was no doubt that it was Mediterranean Greece and Rome, after their founding by Nordic peoples, that had been the creators of all European culture: "The real protagonists of culture, both in the thousand years before Christ and in the thousand years after Him, were the peoples of the Mediterranean. This may appear improbable to us to-day, because we are apt to judge these people from present-day appearances. But that is a great mistake."[106] Beyond evocative parallels between crude stone and clay vessels and the Acropolis, the more mundane aspects of the comparison between the Greeks and Germans were equally striking: "At a time when other people already had paved roads, we hadn't the slightest evidence of civilisation to show. Only the Germanics on the shores of the rivers and the sea-coasts were, in a feeble way, an exception to this rule. Those who had remained in Holstein have not changed in two thousand years, whilst those who had emigrated to Greece raised themselves to the level of civilisation."[107]

This civilization would, in turn, nourish a Germanic spirit imprisoned in the cold mists of the North. Through its contact with Rome, Germania refreshed itself with the creative genius that had blossomed in southern soils. For Hitler, the only Nordic peoples with intrinsic value were the Greeks and Romans; the primitive Germanics found grace in his eyes only through what they had learned from Rome. He saw the heroic Teutonic figure of Arminius, for example, not as the glorious incarnation of pure *Germanentum* but rather as a particularly gifted disciple of Rome and Latin civilization. The German leader, the vanquisher of the general Publius Quinctilius Varus at the Battle of Teutoburg Forest in the year 9 CE, was celebrated by Hitler not as the destroyer of legions but instead as a German who had decided to study and emulate Rome, learning its tactical and cultural wisdom, thus making himself a symbol of Latin-Germanic fusion: "If the Romans had not recruited Germans in their armies, the latter would never have had the opportunity of becoming soldiers and, eventually, of annihilating their former instructors. The most striking example is that of Arminius, who became Commander of the Third Roman Legion. The Romans instructed the Third in the arts of war, and Arminius afterwards used it [sic] to defeat his instructors. At the time of the revolt against Rome, the most daring of Arminius' brothers-in-arms were all Germanics who had served some time or other in the Roman legions."[108]

Arminius (or Hermann, as he was later renamed) was thus not a remarkable figure in and of himself. Hitler saw him not as the fierce German warrior eternally prepared to meet the Roman invasion, as in the Hermannsdenkmal monument at Detmold—the embodiment of a free, courageous German standing in defiance of all comers. Arminius and his comrades-in-arms were more like a cultural conduit, a relay between Rome and Germany, similar to what the Roman Gauls represented for France.

It is thus not surprising that Hitler found the unrestrained celebration of *Germanentum* on the part of Himmler and the SS to be so irritating. Indeed, he displayed a vicious wit in making fun of their Germanophilia, which he ridiculed in both public and private, chiding them for their love of crude, retrograde folklore that glorified a group of primitive idiots. In one of his public speeches, dripping with sarcasm, he declared he had no desire to take up "a bearskin to retrace the path of Germanic migrations": "We are National Socialists, and we have nothing in common with this *Völkisch* idea . . . nor with petit-bourgeois *Völkisch* kitsch, or with heavy beards and long hair. We have all cut our hair quite short."[109] Long hair equaled savagery; the shaved heads of the Romans and the SA equaled civilization.

Hitler thus echoed, in private as in public, the most humiliating prejudices about the early Germans, prejudices that the young discipline of German prehistory tried to combat with the assistance of the SS: the clichés about Teutonic hair and dress repeated by Hitler were even made the subject of an article in *Das Schwarze Korps,* which reacted against "a tendentious image of our ancestors in animal skins, with horned helmets and long flowing beards. German science has disproved all of this after a very long time."[110]

It is impossible to count just how many articles the SS weekly published to discredit and disprove all the clichés about presumed Germanic backwardness.[111] Several of these articles seized the opportunity to critique those ancient texts that had established the clichés about barbarians and animal skins in the first place, including a series of four articles published in 1935 and titled "Greuelpropaganda im Altertum-Fortsetzung" (Hateful propaganda in antiquity): classical sources themselves were thus mobilized to overturn these pejorative stereotypes and rehabilitate the early Germans as victims of an almost systematic campaign of denigration on the part of Greek and Roman writers. If Strabo mentioned the Germans in connection with human sacrifice, for instance, neither Caesar nor Plutarch repeated the claim. Pursuing such philological debate further, the author disputed the translation of Tacitus's *Germania:* In chapter 39, the Roman had written of human sacrifice. Translating *caedere* as "sacrifice," the article claimed, "was incredibly casual, to say the least"—the verb could signify "to beat, to whip, to hurl," among other things. If he had wished to write of human sacrifice, Tacitus had innumerable other Latin verbs at his disposal, such as *necare, interficere, occidere,* and *interimere.*[112]

Another article in the SS periodical thought it useful to relativize the Roman perspective on the Germans, by specifying that "the Romans, who are the source of Christian discourse on German savagery, had made contact only with an avant-garde of migrants and fighters. It is thus not surprising that the Germans appeared to them to be valiant combatants but pathetic builders. It was left to contemporary historical science to go and exhume the traces of our forefathers where our countrymen had created a high culture, and to sweep away all the old prejudices, in order to finally see the Germans for what they were: the enlighteners of the West[!]"[113]

"WHY DO WE CALL THE WHOLE WORLD'S ATTENTION TO THE FACT THAT WE HAVE NO PAST?": MUSSOLINI'S ROME AND THE NAZIS' CULTURAL INFERIORITY COMPLEX

There being no doubt about the overwhelming cultural superiority of Greco-Roman civilization, Hitler completely discounted the reactionary views of the SS, which attempted to resurrect Germanic cults, customs, and traditions, following Himmler's lead. Not only were these cults and traditions culturally the equivalent of the Maoris' gris-gris, but they had naturally disappeared over time because they were destined to perish: "It seems to me that nothing would be more foolish than to re-establish the worship of Wotan. Our old mythology had ceased to be viable when Christianity implanted itself. Nothing dies unless it is moribund. . . . It's not desirable that the whole of humanity should be stultified."[114] Hitler fulminated against those ideologues hell-bent on resurrecting ancient Germania, as in this conversation with Hermann Rauschning: "These professors and mystery-men who want to found Nordic religions merely get in my way. Why do I tolerate them? Because they help to disintegrate, which is all we can do at the moment. They cause unrest. And all unrest is creative. It has no value in itself, but let it run its course."[115] The same could be said for the Germanic obsessions of the SS and all those running around searching for horned helmets.

In a private conversation recorded by Albert Speer in his memoirs, Hitler directly attacked Himmler by name for his excessive Germanophilia. According to Hitler, all the archaeological excavations and studies conducted by the SS proved only one thing: that the Germans had no past worth remembering so long as they restricted themselves to searching on German soil. Reclaiming their Greco-Roman heritage was the only way to give Germany a long and prestigious genealogy:

> Why do we call the whole world's attention to the fact that we have no past? It isn't enough that the Romans were erecting great buildings when our forefathers were still living in mud huts; now Himmler is starting to dig up these villages of mud huts and enthusing over every potsherd and stone axe he finds. All we prove by that is that we were still throwing stone hatchets and crouching around open fires when Greece and Rome had already reached the highest stage of culture. We really should do our best to keep quiet about this past. Instead Himmler makes a great fuss about it all. The present-day Romans must be having a laugh at these revelations.[116]

Recalling a past of such barbarity and backwardness helped only to humiliate Germany rather than to glorify it. The goals and research of the SS were thus completely, idiotically counterproductive. Each stone or clay vessel they uncovered was like another slap in Germany's face delivered from on high, from the heights of the Parthenon or Colosseum.

As an unconditional admirer of Roman antiquity, Hitler was particularly sensitive to any comparisons involving Italy, all the more so because he retained a kind of inferiority complex with respect to Mussolini. His forerunner in fascism had successfully led the March on Rome in 1922, whereas Hitler had failed in his Beer Hall Putsch of 1923 and was forced to wait another ten years before seizing power. A portrait of Il Duce graced the führer's desk in Munich, but his first official visit to see the Fascist leader—in Venice in 1934, amid rising tensions over Austria and the Brenner Pass—had been a disaster for Hitler's image.

Before he irreversibly hitched Italy's fate to that of the Third Reich in 1936, Mussolini had proudly played the role of mentor and frequently recalled Nazi Germany's debt to Fascist Italy. Indeed, in a speech given at Bari on 6 September 1934, he attacked the Nazis' racism and notion of the master race, delivering a scathing rebuke:

> Thirty centuries of history allow us to look with supreme pity upon certain doctrines which are preached beyond the Alps by descendants of those who were illiterate ... when Rome had Caesar, Virgil and Augustus.[117]

The same contempt eviscerated the Third Reich's architectural pretensions, which Mussolini looked upon with disdain,[118] a sentiment Hitler would return years later when he called the Fascist EUR outside Rome a pale imitation of the Eternal City's monumental architecture, "a meaningless copy without any impact."[119]

Any discussion of the origins of the Nordic race could not be limited to Germania alone, for this would fail in its mission to glorify Teutonic and German national identity. The Nazi vision of history could well claim the prestige of the Middle Ages or a more modern era made glorious by Frederick the Great, but pre-Christian Germany was positively offensive in its lack of culture and ambition. It was thus vitally important to celebrate its Nordic identity in order to claim the prestige of the civilizations of ancient Greece and Rome.

With regard to Mussolini's Italy, Hitler displayed shades of a "historical inferiority complex"[120] common to Germans ashamed of their ancient history in comparison to classical antiquity. The symptoms of this complex were obvious: repeated reassessment and rumination on the past, which stood omnipresent as a both a reminder and a challenge. Hitler gave voice to this neurosis not out of some sense of racial masochism but in order to provoke a reaction: the führer wanted to transcend this inferiority complex both materially, with neoclassical architecture and imperial expansion, creating an empire capable of rivaling Roman precedent, and temporally, by giving the Indo-Germanic race a glorious heritage as conquerors from the North and creators of culture, sensitive to the Germans' easily wounded pride regarding their lineage.

We can thus see how the appropriation of Greek and Roman antiquity by the self-proclaimed defenders of the Indo-Germanic race was consistent with their desire to rehabilitate their ancestors by crowning themselves with all the laurels rightly due to the builders of the Colosseum. As one SS ideological propaganda booklet put it, arguing that the Germans had been wronged by depictions of their forefathers living in a backwater: "We now know today that all decisive cultural progress has come from our original Nordic living space. What's more, the ancestors of the Greeks and Romans, who long ago created the powerful empires and great civilizations of the Mediterranean basin, came from our Nordic fatherland. To those who proclaim, 'Light comes from the South,' we say: the North is the cradle of Aryan man, who has shaped the face of the planet."[121]

OVERCOMING THE FEAR OF ANTIQUITY: THE CREATION OF THE DEPARTMENT OF CLASSICAL ANTIQUITY IN THE AHNENERBE

From the perspective of those obsessed with an immortal *Germanentum*, classical antiquity suffered from one fundamental problem: its prestige threatened to eclipse the history of pre-Christian Germany itself. Its links with humanism and the *Bildung* of the Enlightenment also made its heritage ideologically suspect. Antiquity could easily be misinterpreted as the cradle of the universal humanist ideal, which the Nazis reflexively hated.[122] Rosenberg, who was more of a Germanophile than a lover of antiquity—although he obsequiously mimicked Hitler's taste for the classical world—noted this in one of his speeches criticizing the abstract accumulation of knowledge in the eighteenth and nineteenth centuries, with its universalizing assumptions and pretensions to transform humanity in blatant disregard of biological determinism. This enlightened (*aufklärerisch*) humanist education, thoroughly steeped in the classics, was based on the muddleheaded dream of an abstract humanism that celebrated belief in men's fundamental equality.[123]

For Germanophiles, particularly those in the ranks of the SS, Greco-Roman civilization competed unfairly with early German history. Himmler disapproved of classical antiquity for the way it had been celebrated throughout the centuries to the detriment of the Germans' own ancient heritage.

Initially, Himmler forbade looking for evidence of the Nordic race beyond the Reich's borders. Himmler was the high priest of a mysticism inspired by light and blood, earth and death: all that was truly German had been born and created on German soil, watered by the blood of their ancestors. Germanic blood (*Blut*) and the Nordic body (*Boden*) were inextricably linked as part of one common organism. Himmler encouraged philological research into runic writing and invented mystic rites from whole cloth out of old Teutonic legends, indulging in all sorts of fantastical ideas about the blood and the race.[124]

If Hitler's concept of history was open and integrative, Himmler's was hermetically sealed, obsessed solely with the Nazis' Germanic heritage. Whereas Hitler annexed Greco-Roman antiquity as part of Germans' racial and cultural patrimony, Himmler secluded himself within the narrow confines of the Germanic soil and its dead. A fanatical partisan of the Nordicist Aryan myth, Himmler convinced himself that the cradle of the race could be found in that Ultima Thule proclaimed by the Greek geographer from Marseille, Pytheas[125]—a sort of long-vanished Nordic Atlantis.[126] Himmler, then, discounted everything that came from the South as racially impure and ideologically suspect. In his eyes, the Mediterranean was a racial sewer.[127] Worse, it was the birthplace of Judeo-Christianity, which he abhorred. The SS, which took great pains to re-create the cult and mystique of *Germanentum*, sought to eradicate all of Christendom: "That which is Christian is not Germanic, and that which is Germanic is not Christian."[128] The Black Order had to prepare itself for the final confrontation with Christianity, which it would have to strike down:

> We live in the age of the final confrontation with Christianity. One of the missions of the SS, in the fifty years to come, is to give the German people their own anti-Christian ideological foundations to live their lives.[129]

Das Schwarze Korps also published a large number of articles that vilified Rome in all its historical, imperial, Christian, and pontifical glory.

It was precisely to study and promote the heritage of the Germanic race that, on 1 July 1935, Himmler founded the Deutsches Ahnenerbe e. V., the German Ancestral Heritage Society. Himmler sought to encourage historical and philological research on *Germanentum*, launching it into a race to catch up with the study of antiquity in terms of its institutional prestige and scientific discoveries. In essence, the Ahnenerbe was initially conceived as a mechanism with which German archaeologists and prehistorians could make war on their classicist counterparts, along with Rosenberg's Sonderstab Vor- und Frühgeschichte (Special task force for pre- and early history), created in 1940 and directed by the prehistorian Hans Reinerth.

The stated mission of the Ahnenerbe was to create a body of Germanic studies (*Germanenkunde*) endowed with all the gloss and prestige of antiquity, if possible going back to or beyond the history of ancient Rome. For the scholars of the SS, this meant supporting and scientifically validating the thesis of their *Reichsführer*, which Himmler recapitulated on the occasion of the 1935 Julfest,[130] the celebration of the winter solstice commemorated annually by the Schutzstaffeln: "Germany is more ancient and eternal, yes, more eternal and ancient than Rome itself."[131] Himmler's projects ran headlong into the führer's derision and even his public reproach, forcing the head of the SS to make concessions to Hitler's mania for all things classical. In autumn 1937, Himmler made an official trip to Italy, where he publicly rallied in support of Hitler's vision. Captivated by the runic inscriptions on the Lapis Niger in the Roman Forum, which he had photographed and copied, and fascinated by the recurrent use of the swastika as a decorative motif in Roman mosaics, Himmler decided to comply with Hitler's pet project by creating a new department within the Ahnenerbe, whose mission would be to study Greco-Roman antiquity for signs of Germanic symbols or heritage.[132] Klaus von See, the historian of Germanic myths, has noted how the political and military alliance between Germany and Italy helped reorient the SS in its study of antiquity and allowed it to move past the traditional antagonism that saw Hermann's Germans in opposition to the Romans of Varus. If the image of the German had been defined by his defiance of the Romans after the rediscovery of Tacitus in the fifteenth century, it was redefined again, beginning in the nineteenth century,[133] in contrast to the Jews:[134] the dichotomy between German and Roman was replaced by that opposing the Indo-Germanic Aryan and the Semite. This paradigm shift, solidified by the Pact of Steel between Berlin and Rome, occasioned additional exchanges, in the course of which the Nazi leadership discovered Italy's prestigious classical heritage, and led to German archaeological expeditions in Italy.

Until then, Greco-Roman antiquity had held only middling or tangential interest for the SS and the Ahnenerbe. The institute's charter, which dated from April 1937 and was titled "Plan zur Erschliessung des germanischen Erbes" (Plan for the exploration of Germanic heritage),[135] required classicists to review and comment only on ancient texts that made mention of the Germans. A few months later, however, the interest of the Reichsführer was piqued, and the Ahnenerbe had to acquire a legitimate degree of classical expertise in order to better explore the spirit and body of work produced by the Indo-Germanic race. On 10 December 1937, Himmler wrote a three-page letter to Walter Wüst, the director of the Ahnenerbe,[136] relaying his impressions from his tour of Roman antiquity, wresting the intellectual joy of their discovery, if not their ownership, from their Italian custodians: "The museums in Italy contain countless items that interest us, from the point of view of Aryanism. The Italians, they have no interest in those things."[137] Such a poor opinion of the Italians—or of all that belonged to the Mediterranean in one way or another—was a constant with Himmler, who violently expressed his anger and disdain at Italy's abandonment of the Axis in July 1943, attributing their change in sides to the Italians' fundamental lack of courage, due to a "defect in the blood and the race." Only Mussolini, who was subsequently liberated from prison by an SS commando raid, "upheld and incarnated the great Roman tradition."[138]

His newfound scientific and ideological interest in antiquity, however, justified the creation of a completely separate department of research within the Ahnenerbe, as he explained to Wüst: "I see the possibility here to really dig into this issue. I order you to create a department within the Ahnenerbe, whose task will be to study the Indo-Germanic and Aryan aspects of Italy and Greece. . . . This is a very important task: it will require the review and study of all past and future archaeological discoveries." He then specified the department's future missions: "[Acquire] precise proof that the Romans, as well as, naturally, the Samnites, the Umbri, the Volsci, the Latins, etc., but also doubtlessly a segment of the pre-Roman peoples, like the Etruscans and the Sicels, all came from the North, that they were part of a migration of Aryan and Indo-Germanic peoples who came from our lands on the North Sea. The same must be shown of the Greeks, in all their forms."[139]

The charter thus called for a systematic effort aimed at gathering together all the extant evidence that would allow the Nazis to attribute Greek and Roman culture to the work of the Indo-Germanic race. To that end, it organized ad hoc archaeological and philological research missions to glorify Indo-Germanic genius: "The goal of the operation is to furnish precise proof that Nordic and Aryan humanity, which came from the heart of Germany and the North Sea, had been present throughout almost the entire world and that, today at least, this Aryan and Germanic humanity has established universal spiritual domination."[140] It was a question, as Himmler noted in another letter, to Education Minister Bernhard Rust, of "emphasizing the Indo-Germanic contribution to Greek and Roman civilization."[141]

Ideally, the archaeological research undertaken by the Ahnenerbe would finally allow the SS to recapture its own Indo-Germanic material heritage that had been hijacked by the zealous vandalism of Christianity so long ago. If the Germanic lands no longer offered any evidence of that great Nordic culture that had left so many relics in the South, then this absence drove them to a fanatic iconoclasm: they would have to take "all of the objects from the Aryan past that have been preserved in

Italy and in Greece, which were relatively spared from Christianity while they were destroyed in our homeland, and be able to understand and explain [each of them]."[142] The patrimony of Greece and Rome was also that of Aryan culture. In order to legitimately and proudly claim this for its contemporaries, the Ahnenerbe would have to exhaustively explain and illustrate, with rigor and material evidence, the connection between Germans, Greeks, and Romans.

In practice, the Ahnenerbe revealed itself to be far less ambitious than the program outlined by Himmler, and it restricted itself primarily to philology. Walther Wüst named a Latinist, Rudolf Till, the head of the Lehr- und Forschungsstätte für Klassische Philologie und Altertumskunde (Teaching and research institute for classical philology and antiquity), where he was soon joined by the Hellenist Franz Dirlmeier. The historian Volker Losemann has noted the poverty of means allocated for the study of classical philology under the Ahnenerbe, whose greatest accomplishment was a critical edition of the *Codex Aesinas*, the oldest surviving manuscript containing Tacitus's *Germania* and *Agricola*, rediscovered during the Renaissance, which ultimately constituted the only volume in the institute's series Works in Classical Philology and Antique Sciences.

Archaeological research was entrusted to one of the Ahnenerbe's trusted collaborators and confidants, Franz Altheim, whose work fulfilled the commandments of the Reichsführer to the letter. From 1937 to 1942, Altheim undertook a series of excavations—at the expense of the SS and with the benediction of the Italian government—in Val Camonica, an alpine valley located south of Lake Garda (northwest of Verona) in northern Italy.[143] There he discovered a number of rock paintings, several of which were adorned with runic inscriptions, which he compared to those discovered in Bohuslän and Östergötland in the south of Sweden. Drawing on his comparative studies, he published two books, *Vom Ursprung der Runen* (On the origins of runes)[144] in 1939, and *Italien und die dorische Wanderung* (Italy and the Doric migration)[145] in 1940, which unveiled the rather unsurprising results of his research: the people who had originally civilized the Italian peninsula came from an Indo-Germanic migration from northern Germany or southern Sweden. He republished his findings in a 1941 article for the magazine *Die Antike* titled "Indogermanisches Erbe im Rom" (The Indo-Germanic heritage of Rome).[146] The evidence he used to support his arguments displayed a rather unusual methodology: the recurrence of wall drawings of a man armed with a spear in both Sweden and northern Italy,[147] as well as the semantic relationships demonstrated by the Latin *sibi* and the Old High German *selb*,[148] proved that Val Camonica, and thus all of the Italian peninsula, had witnessed "a wave of Indo-Germanic migration from northwest Europe."[149] Nordicist ideas remained the motor driving all archaeological research and discourse on racial origins, while their discoveries could equally have nourished theories about a completely different Indo-European relationship, based on a completely different geography, like the French philologist Georges Dumézil's notion of a common central Asian homeland somewhere in the region of the Black Sea, which today forms the basis of consensus opinion among modern-day Indo-Europeanists.[150]

In the journal *Germanien,* Franz Altheim and Erika Trautmann published a detailed study of the *Elchrune,* found in both Sweden and northern Italy, to support the same Nordicist idea: "The examples from the south of Sweden and north of Italy are close to the point that mere chance can be safely excluded. They form part of the same trail south as all other examples of wall art [*Felsbildkunst*]."[151]

These dense studies were simplified for consumption by a broader public acquainted with the classics by the review *Neue Jahrbücher,* which devoted a two-part article to "the Indo-Germanization of Italy,"[152] largely reiterating the conclusions of Altheim's earlier works. The Ahnenerbe journal *Germanien*—which, as we have seen,[153] commissioned several studies to flesh out the connection between the Indo-Germans and the great civilizations of antiquity, particularly in the East and in Asia— also published an article on the "Indo-Germanness" of the Greeks, titled "The Lion Gate of Mycenae, a Nordic Cultural Symbol."[154]

Other archaeological excavations took the SS as far as Mount Olympus. To puff up Berlin's credentials in the eyes of the International Olympic Committee (IOC), which was being tempted by the pressure of international public opinion to withdraw the games from Germany, Hitler had hastily ordered a renewed series of digs at the site that had given the Olympics their name.[155]

In addition to the Abteilung für Klassische Archäologie (Department of classical antiquity), the Ahnenerbe contained the Lehr- und Forschungseinrichtung für indogermanisch-arische Philologie und Kulturwissenschaft (Teaching and research unit for Indo-Germanic-Aryan philology and cultural studies). Its most notable contribution came in the form of a study of the relationship of the belief systems of the Italic and Germanic peoples. The historian Werner Müller, who published a detailed study of the symbolism of the circle and the cross in the two peoples' cultures,[156] noted the omnipresence of these two symbols, which, when melded together, resulted in a form of crooked cross, the sun cross, a representation not only of the poles of the globe and the four cardinal directions but also of the sun and the universal cycle of the cosmos. The cross, the circle, and their combination were thus signs of an orderly universe and of a cult of sun worship, fundamental characteristics of the Indo-Germanic imaginary and an expression of the spiritual and racial community that linked the Italic peoples who came from the North with their Germanic cousins who had remained in their original Nordic homeland.

The Ahnenerbe was not the only body within the SS that demonstrated an interest in antiquity. Himmler had been well and truly convinced of the Greeks' racial greatness, and he gave free rein to his penchant for amateur racial-anthropological sorcery by demanding, in 1942, that the pronatalist Lebensborn e. V. select certain German infants who displayed a Greek nose for an experiment.[157] The study consisted of observing the children as they developed before amassing them together in a special battalion of the Waffen-SS in order "to evaluate their performance, their capabilities, and their limits through a series of further tests."[158] Himmler, like some latter-day Philip of Macedon or Epaminondas of Thebes, thus sought to reconstitute a sort of Macedonian phalanx or sacred band of brothers with a living, breathing racial experiment: was not the Greek profile, indeed the entire Greek body, the gold standard of physical fitness and military valor? Such research questions happily blended racial philhellenism and a love for the occult with zootechnical ambition.

GERMANY LEARNS ITS NEW HISTORY: SS PROPAGANDA IN THE SCHOOLS

Nordicist theory on the Indo-Germanic roots of the Greeks and Romans wasn't restricted only to the cloistered, at times almost confidential, world of professional scholars. A much wider readership awaited and was targeted in a variety of ways.

SS ideological propaganda, for example, repeated the point incessantly. One booklet illustrated the Nordic origins of Greco-Roman civilization with a series of blueprints retracing the evolution of the Germanic house in comparison with the Greek temple: "It was from the Germanic house, with its vestibule at the entrance, that the Greek temple developed, copying and perfecting its form. . . . We see here a proud trace of classical architecture. The Greek temple is thus additional proof that the great civilizations did not come from the East, but from the North."[159] Another of these SS pamphlets[160] presented a portrait of a young recruit side by side with the profile of "a Roman head of state." The virile pose of the young SS soldier apparently displayed a familial echo of the Roman's masculine gravitas: "The SS soldier, son of a German countryman, carries the same Nordic blood as the men we are about to see. We will show him side by side with a Roman statesman, to remind us that the Roman Empire itself, like that of the Persians, the civilization of the Greeks . . . [was] built by the creative force of the same Nordic blood."[161]

Party pamphlets spoke equally about the glorious ancestry that contemporary Germans could claim from antiquity. A booklet titled *Materials for Ideological Development* presented the profile of a Greek woman and a reproduction of a bust of Augustus in order to provide a visual demonstration of what the caption called "the Nordic Race among the Greeks and Romans."[162]

Teaching in the schools was no different. We have already seen how the directives of 1933 and 1935 and the subsequent reform of 1938 imposed a radical revision on the accepted narrative of the origins of European civilization. It was thus only logical that the Greeks and Romans found themselves Aryanized in school textbooks.

A 1937 work of pedagogy titled *Geschichtsunterricht als nationalpolitische Erziehung* (The teaching of history as national political education),[163] by Dietrich Klagges, was designed as a manual to guide schoolteachers in the principles of the new history promoted by the party-state according to the instructions laid down by the Ministry for Science and Education. After a few opening epistemological considerations, the book outlined a summary of the history of the Indo-Germanic race in nine chapters, from its origins to the Parousia of the Nazis, passing through the times of troubles both medieval and modern. The chapters titled "On the Tracks of Our Fathers"[164] and "Men from the North Conquer the South"[165] were intended as a vade mecum for instructors encouraged to promote a new vision of Indo-Germanic racial development that reconciled pre-Christian German history with classical antiquity.

The directives of Frick and Rust to reform the teaching of history did not immediately lead to the publication of new textbooks. Publishing houses showed themselves very eager to get rid of their remaining stock, so instructors and their pupils continued to use texts dating back to the Weimar Republic that were simply amended with hastily compiled inserts to complement or update the older texts. Such was the case with the pamphlet written by Karl Schmelze, a professor of history at a realschule in Munich, titled *Rassengeschichte und Vorgeschichte im Dienste nationaler Erziehung* (Racial history and prehistory in the name of national education),[166] published in 1936 as a forty-page "complementary booklet"[167] to cover the entire prehistoric and antique period. After a quick presentation on the Nordic race, Schmelze took a few pages to discuss the "diffusion of the Nordic race" (*Indogermanisation*), recounting the first Indo-Germanic migrations as a result of "overpopulation"[168] of the original homeland to the North.[169] Schmelze carefully outlined "four migratory routes," leading to Iran and India, Greece, Italy, and the West (France, Great Britain, Spain), a textual explanation of the accompanying maps. These migrations, thanks to the "creative force of the Nordic race,"[170] had led to the great civilizations of antiquity, in Greece and Rome, "which owed their grandeur to the Nordic race":[171]

> Without these Nordic invaders and without this influx of Nordic blood that periodically rejuvenated Italy, there would have been no Roman civilization.[172]

Such textbooks visibly strove to prove how both the Greeks and the Romans were Indo-Germanic: their culture, but also their physical appearance and their moral values, provided ample demonstration of their kinship and the roots of their origins in a common Nordic homeland.

Schmelze then summarized all the "traits belonging to the migratory peoples of the Indo-Germanic tongue." Their emphasis on the group over the individual, their sense of honor, and their worship of heroism and courage all led to the memorable exploits celebrated in "the heroic songs of the Indians, the Persians, and the Greeks": "Magnanimity, nobility of soul, love of truth, and pride all separated them"[173] from other peoples, as did their vigilant protection of the "purity of the race," enforced through the prohibition of all interracial procreation and the elimination of impure or half-breed children. The holistic and heroic ethos of the Indo-Germanic peoples, particularly the Greeks and Romans, made it desirable that young Germans should study them and the humanities: the Hellenist Otto Regenbogen suggested that Greek *arete* and Roman *virtus* were the ideal guidelines for the political education of the youth of the new Germany.[174]

Later—especially after the curricular reform of 1938—publishers began releasing new textbooks, like the one by Walther Gehl that was designed for use in the first year of university.[175] His text opened with a keynote of some thirty pages on the origins of the Indo-Germanic race (what he called "Nordic prehistory"), then dedicated almost one hundred pages to the history of Nordic Greece and Rome. A quick perusal of its table of contents reveals his desire to instill in young readers the Nazis' symbolic annexation of Greco-Roman civilization. The titles of the various chapters were in essence branded with the systematic use of the adjective *Nordic,* like a form of rhetorical carpet bombing. The chapter dedicated to "the area of Helleno-Nordic civilization in the eastern Mediterranean" was thus subdivided, in its discussion of archaic Greece, according to the following phenomena:

> The Aegean civilization of the Nordic Achaeans
>
> The protection of the race in the social life and warrior state of Dorian Sparta
>
> Nordic attitudes toward the Greeks
>
> Racial and religious unity among the Greeks
>
> The spiritual conquest of the world through free thought and inquiry

"Classical Greece" was also defined by whatever was the most Nordic, as in the following chapters:

> The War to Defend against the Asiatic Race and the Nordic Leaders during the Greco-Persian Wars
>
> Greek Art under Pericles: The Oeuvre of Nordic Creativity
>
> The Attic Peoples under Nordic Leadership in Democratic Athens

The chapters devoted to the Roman Empire, meanwhile, itself a "Nordic creation," displayed traces of having been translated directly from the ministry's directives:

> The Victory of the Nordic Tribes over the Etruscans of Asia Minor in Italy
>
> The Romans' Nordic State
>
> Race Struggle and Racial Equilibrium
>
> The Unification of Italy through Roman Power Politics

The Nordicist dogma of the Indo-Germanic origins and nature of the Greeks and Romans was not the sole preserve of history textbooks. It was also on proud display in textbooks on ancient languages, whose teaching and lessons constituted a very effective pedagogical tool by virtue of their declarative simplicity. The first words of one Latin textbook from 1942, for example, contained a brief and trenchant summary of the Greeks' original migration and their kinship with the Germans and Romans: "The Greeks did not always live in Greece. In ancient times the Greeks, who shared blood with the Germans and Romans, migrated to their new homeland."[176]

"INDO-GERMANIC STUDIES" IN THE UNIVERSITIES

While we can draw certain conclusions from the titles of individual courses, the programs in history and philosophy offered by German universities did not display overt signs of outright revolution after the change in regime in 1933. Certainly, the universities were profoundly affected and transformed by the Aryanization of the professoriate in accordance with the law of 7 April 1933. The introduction of obligatory military exercises, in the form of the *Wehrsport,* also demonstrated the spirit of the times. Nevertheless, the fact remains that the courses offered in history and philosophy were not marked by an openly ideological stance; the Nazis' ideas about the Indo-Germanics appeared to be applied more explicitly to the study of linguistics. Yet despite the course listings of university catalogues (*Vorlesungsverzeichnisse*) or the purported content of courses themselves, this appears to be a classic case of how the teaching of history could be more ideologically fraught than first impressions might lead one to believe. We need look no further than the universities of Jena and Heidelberg. In 1933, Heidelberg offered a summer semester course in ancient history titled "Völker, Sprachen, Rassen der alten Welt als Grundlage ihrer neueren Geschichtsentwicklung" (The peoples, languages, and races of the ancient world as the foundation of contemporary development).[177] This weekly one-hour lecture course was delivered by Friedrich Bilabel (1888–1948), a papyrologist and epigrapher specializing in Greek history and philology. At Jena,[178] the academic fief of Hans Günther, students selecting a seminar in history could choose from two of the master's offerings, on "the Orient and the Occident" and "Aryans and Semites" in antiquity. They were also offered a cycle of courses titled "History of the Nordic-Indo-Germanic Peoples in Antiquity," which integrated all of Germanic, Greek, and Roman history into a single field of study.

Philosophy departments offered courses that were largely consistent with those prior to 1933. The universities of Vienna and Prague planned to offer courses such as Introduction to National Socialist Ideology[179] and National Socialist Pedagogy[180] among their introductory-level philosophy offerings, but here too these were relatively isolated examples. Nothing too exotic stood out from among the offerings on Greek philosophy, Plato, or Roman Stoicism.

While departments of history and philosophy remained relatively modest, seminars in linguistics were all too happy to commingle Latin, Greek, and Old High German under the heading of *Indogermanische Sprachwissenschaft* (Indo-Germanic languages). In summer 1942, for example, the university at Würzburg grouped together its courses on the grammar of "Historical Latin" and "Historical German"; classes such as Exercises in Germanic Runic Inscriptions and Sanskrit for Beginners completed the department's offerings.[181]

Other universities, like Christian-Albrechts-Universität in Kiel, went further, explicitly turning linguistics into a prerequisite for the racial sciences. During the summer semester of 1935, it offered Introduction to the Prehistory of the Germanic Peoples and History of the Latin Language, as well as a course on "ancient Italic dialects." Also offered were Exercises in Indo-Germanic Linguistics and a course on "Greek, Latin, and Germanic heritage," plus a seminar on "the relationship between race and language."[182] This linkage among the three languages, and between linguistics and racial anthropology more broadly, was standard, as demonstrated by the programs of countless other universities that conflated the identity of the Greeks, Romans, and Germans in the eyes of the public and the academic community.

The widespread publicity given to the Nordicist idea that the two great peoples of antiquity came from the North also transcended the schools and universities. In addition to the relatively limited fraction of the German people engaged in the educational system—at least in terms of age or social class—the party was able to reach a much wider public through its many social and cultural organizations, as well as an array of popular media that were only superficially neutral. Its ideas made their way into the salons and libraries of German families through widely accessible and affordable reference books, like an encyclopedia, for instance; the 1937–38 edition of the *Brockhaus* informed readers in its entry on Greece that "the Indo-Germanic Greeks of the Nordic race had migrated from the North to the southern part of the Balkan peninsula around two thousand years before Jesus Christ," where they had "encountered a native population from Asia Minor, of mixed Western-Asiatic provenance."[183] But such propaganda could also take on much more spectacular forms.

ATHENS ON THE ISAR, OR PANATHENAEAN MUNICH: THE DAYS OF GERMAN ART

The Germanic essence of the Greeks was put on display in grandiose fashion at the 1936 Berlin Olympics, as we shall see,[184] but a similarly gaudy demonstration occurred as early as 1933, during the *Tages der deutschen Kunst* (Days of German art) celebrated in Munich. The first of these days took place in October of that year, to commemorate the ground breaking of the *Haus der deutsche Kunst*—a massive Doric temple erected as a monument to the race—followed by days to celebrate the inauguration of the museum in July 1937 and again in October 1938 and 1939.

The Bavarian metropolis, which held the honorary title of *Hauptstadt der Bewegung* (Capital of the movement)—it had welcomed Hitler in 1913, witnessed the founding of the party, and been the site of the Beer Hall Putsch in 1923—retained a special place in Hitler's heart:[185] having already commissioned Paul Ludwig Troost to build the Braunes Haus for the party's headquarters, Hitler entrusted the architect after the seizure of power with creating a neoclassical monument to the Doric form that would confirm Munich as a cultural capital. Under Ludwig I of Bavaria, Munich had been conceived as a tribute to German philhellenism: the king had built his Königsplatz full of neoclassical monuments, just as he had built a temple to German genius with the Walhalla, outside Regensburg, in the form of an exact replica of Athens's Parthenon set in the middle of the Danube River valley.[186] Ludwig I had thus made Munich a sort of Athens on the Isar, just as Berlin, under Friedrich Wilhelm III, had plainly become the Athens of the North, celebrated by Voltaire under the reign of Prussia's Frederick the Great. In Munich, then, Nazi classicism was grafting itself on to a rich, long-standing philhellenic tradition: the Königsplatz would find itself flanked by two open-sky temples conceived by Troost to house the bronze sarcophagi of the "martyrs" of 1923. The Doric columns and marble of the Ehrentempel conferred upon the final resting place of the heroes of the putsch a sense of grandeur and a timeless aesthetic that flattered Hitler's tastes. The centerpiece was Troost's Haus der deutschen Kunst, whose imposing colonnade immediately acquired the nickname "Athens Station" among the citizens of Munich. Its Doric architecture plainly communicated the purpose of the "temple"[187] to German art that Hitler so dearly desired.

In October 1933, Hitler's ceremonial laying of the building's cornerstone took place with a series of solemn rituals. The führer sought to give the ground breaking a deeply symbolic meaning: the construction of the Haus der deutschen Kunst would mark the beginning of a renaissance of authentically German art, free from Jewish interference and influences. The choice of Munich was anything but casual. It was in this prewar bohemian capital of the avant-garde (supplanted by Berlin only in the 1920s), the birthplace of the Die Brücke group, that the "purification of the temple of art" would begin: defiled by degenerate art, both "negroid" and Semitic, German *Kunst* would henceforth enjoy the patronage and protection of the state.

To mark the occasion, antiquity took to the streets. The link between Hellas and Germania would no longer be just a sophisticated topic for scholarly conversation but would become the subject of a very public display that would allow it to be seen and understood by the German people, who would bear witness to an unprecedented spectacle. Drawing on the long German tradition of historical reenactment (*historische Festzug*),[188] the Day of German Art parade[189] on 15 October 1933 was given the name "The Golden Centuries of German Culture." The organization of the parade and selection of its motif were entrusted to Josef Wackerle, who decided—at Hitler's personal request—to declare the theme to be antiquity. All along the parade route, from the Ludwigstrasse to the site of the future museum, various floats allegorically depicted the diverse genres and epochs of German art, led by the *Hoheitsadler*, a Romanesque eagle designed by Hitler himself to represent the Nazi Party and the state, a symbol of the German spirit and ideal. The second float represented architecture, in the form of an Ionic capital, the third float painting, through "antique wall paintings"[190] by the artist Richard Klein. Sculpture followed, in a reproduction of a bust of Hercules preserved in the Vatican Museums.

Then came the eras of German art, the first of which, Greek art, was represented by a float of Pallas Athena. Indeed, Athena was everywhere, not only on her float but also in the form of a giant medallion suspended between two pylons that marked the beginning of the parade route on the Ludwigstrasse.[191] The official symbol of the Tage der deutschen Kunst, which would also ultimately become that of the official review *Die Kunst im Dritten Reich* (The art of the Third Reich), was a profile of Athena with a torch, set against a background of columns.

Four years later a second parade took place, this time for the museum's inauguration. The event took on epic proportions: on 18 July 1937, the route stretched some three kilometers (two miles) and employed five hundred cavalry, twenty-five-hundred foot soldiers, and some two thousand women, all of whom were outfitted in historically appropriate costumes befitting the eras they represented. The motif, similar to that of 1933, was Two Thousand Years of German Culture—a title that carried over to the follow-up edition of 1938.[192] Here too, Greek art, in the form of Athena, was portrayed as a period of German art history.

The organization and materials for the procession thus made art and antiquity roughly equivalent: the monumental figure of Athena, the mock-up of the Haus der deutschen Kunst in 1933, the medallion, the architectural framework of Munich, between the neoclassicism of Ludwig I and the neo-Doric mimicry of Troost, conferred upon the celebration of German art a stiff, highly stylized solemnity that Hitler, with his petit bourgeois tendency toward a vaguely kitschy imitation of culture, freely associated with high art.

The Nazis' antique kitsch was on plain display during these *historische Festzüge* in Munich, just as it was in the regime's highly staged propaganda, an orgy of flags and Roman eagles that—to borrow a couple of well-worn catchwords—engendered fascination (*Faszination*) and incarnated terror (*Gewalt*).[193] This artificial kitsch was the subject of scorn from the likes of Heidegger, who criticized the Nazis' inauthentic relationship with antiquity,[194] but also of parody, in the form of a musical comedy composed by Reinhard Schünzel.[195]

This musical, which is believed to be the only thing of its kind shot in Germany between 1933 and 1945, was interpreted upon its release in 1935 as a satire of the regime's great displays of propaganda, like the Tage der deutschen Kunst or the party rallies at Nuremberg. The story of Amphitryon—already well trod by Plautus and much later by Molière and Jean Giraudoux,[196] as well as Heinrich von Kleist, whose 1807 piece Schünzel adapted—told of the subterfuges employed by Zeus to conquer and subjugate mortal men. Smitten by the Theban Alcmene, Zeus disguises himself as her husband, the king Amphitryon, and makes her the mother of Hercules. As a comedy, the tale rescues Alcmene from her adultery by revealing Zeus's deception, which Schünzel broadened into a satire of the gods in all their ridiculous excess: the film, which tended toward the burlesque, portrayed a lazy and libidinous Zeus, deciding the fate of man's battles on a whim, completely submissive to the tyranny of an aging Hera and a timid, weakly Hermes. The burlesque nature of the comedy, and the simple fact that it dethroned the gods and gave them a human (indeed, all too human) face, amounted to a savage criticism of power. In a totalitarian regime, such a film was notable in and of itself; because the film appeared to belong to the genre of German light comedy, it was even approved by Goebbels for its cheap laughs and unending silliness, which, in the context of the times, possessed an obvious potential for escapist thrills.[197] Schünzel's comedy was punctuated with subtle references to the power of the Third Reich: a *Halbjude* himself according to the Nuremberg Laws, Schünzel would have to receive one special permit (*Sondererlaubnis*) after another in order to continue his film career. They were granted, almost solely because of his popular success as an actor and director,[198] before he finally decided to emigrate across the Atlantic in 1937.

SYMBOLIC APPROPRIATION AND TERRITORIAL ANNEXATION: THE BLITZKRIEG OF 1941, OR THE FOURTH INDO-GERMANIC MIGRATION TO GREECE

This racial-historical discourse, the teaching of history in the schools, and the ideological indoctrination of the troops, all embedded a simple chronology of north-south migration in the hearts and minds of the German people. After the two initial waves of prehistoric migration came the third, that of the great invasions, in the late antique period.

In this context, the German blitzkrieg into Greece was presented and interpreted as a fourth wave of Nordic migration to defend and rejuvenate Greek soil after a long period of racial decay.

The symbolic appropriation of ancient civilizations into the history of the Aryan race thus legitimized and justified the Nazis' territorial claims: the conquest of Greece in 1941 was rationalized in reference to the Greeks' Indo-Germanic past. From 22 to 25 April 1941, the Wehrmacht and the Waffen-SS stormed the pass at Thermopylae, forcing the British aside and opening the road to Attica and Athens.[199] The event was hailed by the *Völkischer Beobachter,* which dedicated a significant amount of space in its daily editions to the success of the blitzkrieg. On 28 April 1941, the party daily celebrated "Der Siegeslauf nach Athen: Der deutsche Sturm über die Thermopylen" (The triumphant race to Athens: The German assault on Thermopylae) with a long article that filled the second page: "The circle of world history has been closed today, at Thermopylae. Some 2,500 years ago, the Greek people under Leonidas held out against a numerically superior foe. They were later forced to surrender to the English. Today, with our powerful blows, we have chased the English out of Greece and out of Europe."[200]

The closing of a circle: German soldiers were the worthy descendants in a line of Nordic-Germanic heroes that began with Leonidas. Whereas the three hundred Spartan heroes had only delayed the Persian advance, German divisions had expelled their distant English successors. It was thus entirely racially and historically legitimate that the soldiers of the Reich should take possession of those distant, unredeemed Indo-Germanic lands that the unworthy and racially degenerate modern-day Greeks had abandoned to their enemies. Once again, a wave of Nordic heroes had brought an influx of fresh blood to civilize and save a Greece threatened by inferior Asiatic peoples, including its own citizens, bastards of mixed Greek and Turkish blood.

The 1936 Olympics had been a major opportunity to celebrate not just the relationship between ancient Greece and modern Germany, as we shall see later on,[201] but also the beauty and dignity of the Greek people: Leni Riefenstahl's film *Olympia*, poorly versed in racial orthodoxy, showed numerous images of trim, bronze young Greeks, their complexions somehow nothing short of diaphanous, and the official ceremonies paid homage to the first winner of the Olympic marathon of 1896, the Greek shepherd Spiridon Louis.

In 1941, the invasion initially prompted some disillusionment and confusion, until the Nazis' awareness of their Nordic superiority swept it away and cleared their consciences. The contemporary Greek people were a population of half-breeds that had degenerated through long centuries of promiscuity and racial mixing with their Asiatic and Turkish neighbors; accordingly, all sexual relations between German soldiers and Greek women were strictly forbidden. Little by little, such haughty disdain would nourish and legitimate the Nazis' practice of almost genocidal terror upon the Greek civilian population, beginning in 1942, as Mark Mazower has shown.[202]

The Greek people were thus less native to their own country than the Germans themselves, who were the legitimate, pure descendants of the Indo-Germanic race that had come from the North in the first place to bring civilization to the Greek peninsula. While the official communiqué of the Wehrmacht's High Command (Oberkommando Wehrmacht, or OKW) proudly and insistently repeated that "the flag bearing the swastika has been raised over the Acropolis,"[203] this declaration of possession was, in the end, nothing more than a return to racial and historical normality.

This was Hitler's own line of thinking, fully consistent with a distinguished pan-Germanist tradition: wherever there were people with

German blood in their veins, the land they lived on belonged in a greater German Reich; thus any political or military policy to conquer and annex those lands could be justified by racial-historical right. Indeed, before the war Hitler had declared on several occasions that he wanted to bring into the Reich the peoples of Scandinavia, Holland, and Britain, since they were all Germanic, as well as the Greeks, who were also Germanic at least in origin. Marveling at the resistance of the Greek army, which had booted the Italians out of the country and held off German advances, Hitler confided to Goebbels that "perhaps there is still a touch of the old Hellenic strain in them."[204] This was only a hypothesis, because it had been a very long time—since at least the late Hellenic period[205]—since Nordic blood had been diluted and lost through fatal miscegenation. The Reich's claims to the Greek peninsula resided not in the living, pulsing, spilling blood of its contemporaries but rather in what the blood had created and left behind before being shed in the distant past. The modern Greek people, a mongrel race of half-breeds, were but the contemporary despoilers of a land and a heritage of which the Nordic peoples, its true creators, remained the owners by biological right.

One year after the victory of April 1941, in two articles commemorating their triumph, the SS "leadership magazine," the *SS-Leithefte*, recalled the glorious military feats of the Wehrmacht and Waffen-SS by comparing their deeds to the Nordic heroism of the Spartans.[206] These two short articles offered an opportunity to recount the battles but also to place the conquest of Greece and the resistance of Leonidas in the broader context of the racial Gigantomachy between the Nordic West and the Asiatic Orient. Leonidas's brave three hundred thus "became the first blood witnesses in the battle against the global power coming from the East."[207] The Spartans' sacrifice had "broken the wave" of Asiatic invasion, just as, much later, Henry II the Pious had thrown himself and his men in front of the Mongol hordes at Legnica in 1241 or Hitler had opposed the Communists and national decline on 9 November 1923 or, even more recently, the Freikorps saboteur Albert Schlageter had proudly offered his breast to the criminal firing squad of the French troops stationed in the Ruhr. All these acts of sacrificial heroism were marked by a disdain for death and thus a love for life, which was "the heart of the Nordic-Germanic spirit":[208] the truly Nordic heroism of Leonidas and his men was dictated by an intrepidness that sacrificed the corruptible for the good of the essential, the defense of the fatherland, the Greek civilization, and the race.

The German occupiers were equally willing see the legitimacy of their Greek conquest based on a curious historical precedent. The Greeks, they claimed, in an odd chiastic logic, welcomed the Reich's divisions like those hordes of Germanic barbarians who, at the dawn of antiquity, washed over Greece on their way to sack Rome: a positive souvenir from antiquity was thus used to counteract a negative one. While Giorgos Theotokas awaited the imminent arrival of the Wehrmacht's first motorized units at the end of April, along with the rest of the Greek people, he recorded in his journal this snippet of verse from the poet Constantine Cavafy:

> What are we waiting for, gathered in the market-place?
> The barbarians will come today.
> Why is there no activity in the senate?
> Why are the senators seated without legislating?
> Because the barbarians will come today.
> What laws can the senators pass now?
> The barbarians, when they come, will make the laws.[209]

On the German side, the press coverage of this triumph in the spring of 1941 created a deceptive impression of what Greece and its people had become: Greece appeared, in the eyes of its German conquerors fed on classical illusions, to be a dusty, filthy, completely backward country; the Greeks, far from resembling Winckelmann's statues, were nothing more than a hodgepodge of scruffy Levantines. A long article published in the paper *Der Angriff* on 19 April 1941 testified to the disillusionment that awaited the German soldiers who expected to find in Greece the country of their history textbooks or of the German philhellenic tradition. Instead of this fantasy, they would discover a poor country, dominated and ruled by the stereotypical "Greek merchant,"[210] a Levantine type similar to the German Jewish *Krämer*. The 1937 edition of the *Brockhaus* encyclopedia nevertheless made it a point to state that the influx of Slavic and Albanian blood into what had been Nordic Greece had led to a lamentable degree of miscegenation, and that "modern Greeks demonstrate, from the point of view of the race, several essentially Western, Balkan, and Asiatic characteristics, while those of the Nordic race, to which the ancient Greeks once belonged, have receded."[211]

This deception was thus both economic and aesthetic but also racial. The Nordic Greeks of the time of Pericles had become spiritually bankrupt as the result of a long history of miscegenation and racial degeneration.[212] The magazine *Volk und Rasse,* which was published by

Lehmann and counted among its contributors all the biggest names in racial anthropology, including Günther, Baur, and Fischer, devoted two articles to a fine-grained racial analysis of the modern Greeks with the goal of showing that, despite the vicissitudes of history, the Greek population could still be partially included in that Nordic bloc whose genetic material still flowed in their veins. A 1939 article titled "Greek Racial Profiles" compared the Greeks of Laconia, the chosen land of the Nordic Dorians, with the more diverse inhabitants of Athenian Attica:[213] while in the land of the old Indo-Germanic Sparta, re-created by Otto I of Greece, "blond hair, blue eyes, and tall height are common," the Athenians were just a "people of mixed race."[214] The author of the article described this conflict between the two halves of Greece in his description of people representing these two racial types in a café in Laconia: "Here the contrast reveals itself. On one side the Greece of the ancients, on the other the Greece of today!" The former had preserved its Nordicism, while the latter had sold itself off to the highest bidder. For the author, there was no doubt that "these blond-haired, blue-eyed men" of fierce, proud Laconia were the direct "descendants of the ancient Greeks,"[215] miraculously preserved from miscegenation.

It was this predominantly Nordic population that allowed the possibility for Greece to be welcomed into the Nazis' Europe. An article published in 1941 aimed to demonstrate how German intervention in Greece was not, from a racial perspective, immoral or unethical: the German armies were welcomed in the Mediterranean as though returning home; a southern anchluss to form a Nordic bloc was entirely legitimate. Certainly, as the title of the article suggested, Greece remained a "Land of Contrasts."[216] The phenomenological evidence highlighted the miscegenation and foreignness of a thoroughly Orientalized people. Nevertheless, "nothing could be more false than to say that the Greek people as a whole have been Balkanized. Curiously, we tend to hold the Greek people to a higher racial standard than we do other people," as if their glorious Nordic past and the olden days of German philhellenism had created an expectation that the contemporary Greeks could not fulfill unless they resembled an exact replica of their classical forefathers. Now, the author argued, the Greeks were often pro-German and anti-Semitic[217] and also displayed a mental disposition that tended to indicate a common racial descent with those from northern Europe: "An unconscious recollection of their Nordic roots from deepest antiquity seems to reverberate through the veins of the Greek people."[218] Their roots, still visible in the two racial types described in the article of

1939, demonstrated that the recovery of the Greek body through rejuvenation by Nordic blood was still possible: after Turkish, French, and English domination, Greece found itself as a result of the Germans' invasion "finally included in the circulatory system of European blood."[219] Once again, Greece had been resuscitated by a wave of Nordic migration and an injection of its pure, fresh blood. The three prehistoric and ancient waves of migration had been joined by a fourth: that of the Reich triumphant.

CONCLUSION

During the Days of German Art organized around Munich's Haus der deutschen Kunst in 1933 (and again in 1937, 1938, and 1939), the image of Athena watched over the parade of the different periods of German art. Her presence clearly signaled to the public that the Greeks were also German and that their art belonged to the Nordic race.

This was vitally important. Where else could one find expressions or confirmation of the genius of the Nordic race? Examples abounded from the Middle Ages, with its cathedrals, and then again during the modern era, with Bach, and, finally, with the German philosophers of the contemporary period. The preceding eras, however, offered noting of worth: fragments of vases or remnants of lakeside settlements, which Himmler, a passionate inventor of the German past, had exhumed by his squadrons of SS archaeologists. Hitler hated such excavations: what point did they serve, if not to show "that we have no past," such mediocre relics providing proof of the backwardness of the Germans living on German soil?

Hitler turned his sights to the South, citing the difference in climate between Germany and the Mediterranean: the common Nordic origins of the occupants of both lands left no doubt that the gap in development between North and South was due to the disparity in sunlight and differential in temperatures between the two regions.

In Hitler's view of antiquity, we can thus see traces of a cultural inferiority complex that frequently afflicted those from north of the Alps when confronted with the prestige of the great Mediterranean civilizations. It was not enough, however, simply to explain away German backwardness. Hitler proposed to give the Greeks and Romans a Nordic genealogy, backed by an academic body of knowledge inherited from the nineteenth century and explicitly formulated to support this very notion. Racial scientists, anthropologists, and historians found themselves in unison with Nazi leaders when hailing the blond hair of an Augustus or the blue eyes of a Pericles. Their message was not confined to the closed world of professional scholars: it was paraded through the streets of Munich and taught in the nation's schools, barracks, and party organizations. This discourse on the racial anthropology of the Greeks and Romans was designed to base German pride on the appropriation of a Mediterranean heritage that would not oppose the Germans but welcome them. Nordic-Germanic blood would be known not solely for the creation of a heap of pottery shards or wooden huts but rather for its more sublime expression under the more clement skies and on the more fertile soil, in the building of the Parthenon and the creation of prestigious civilizations.

The discourse that the Nazi Party and state put forward on the subject of Greco-Roman antiquity was soothing and self-satisfied, designed to reassure a national pride gravely wounded by defeat in 1918: the Greeks and Romans were flattered to be considered part of the Pantheon of Germanic culture, in that Walhalla built out of the founding rhetoric of Nazi ideology, as well as the teaching of German schoolmasters and the publicity given to all its cultural and artistic manifestations.

As important as this metaphorical appropriation was, it was not solely symbolic in nature. In April 1941, such discourse on the Indo-Germanic roots of the Greeks was used to justify and legitimize the invasion of Greece by the soldiers of the Reich, called down into the Mediterranean by the weakness and foibles of Germany's partner in the Pact of Steel, Fascist Italy. Allied to the English and racially degenerate, the Greek people were clearly no longer fit to rule or enjoy their own country, their own patrimony, or their own culture, which they had managed for two thousand years but which they had lost through racial and political degradation. German soldiers were only restoring a land and its culture to their rightful Indo-Germanic owners.

That said, as we have seen in the case of the SS, the promotion of Mediterranean antiquity did not occur without conflict or discussion. The Nazi seizure of power had also legitimately raised the hopes of Germanophiles in love with runic alphabets and Saxon prehistory. In order to have their ideas heard, they would force a debate on the teaching of the humanities.

CHAPTER 3

Mens sana

Antiquity, the Humanities, and German Youth

The beginning still is. It does not lie behind us, as something that was long ago, but stands before us.
—Martin Heidegger, "The Self-Assertion of the German University"

Everything was all there just as it should be: the ancient Greek warrior, resplendent and formidable, plumed like a cock; and there along the staircase wall—yellow oil paint here—they all hung: from the Hohenzollern rulers down to Hitler. . . .
 No doubt there's some regulation requiring it to hang there. Rule for Prussian High Schools: *Medea* between VIa and VIb, *Boy with a Thorn* on that wall, Caesar, Marcus Aurelius, and Cicero in the corridor, Nietzsche upstairs where they're already taking philosophy. . . .
 It was still there, the Thermopylae inscription we had had to write, in that life of despair I had known only three months ago. . . . Seven times I had had to write it: in Antique, Gothic, Cursive, Roman, Italic, Script, and Round. Seven times, plain for all to see: "Stranger, bear word to the Spartans we . . ."
—Heinrich Böll, "Stranger, Bear Word to the Spartans We . . ."

The National Socialist movement that came to power in 1933 was full of new ideas regarding education, so much so that we might even talk of a pedagogical revolution. Nazi anti-intellectualism, which rejected the pursuit of knowledge for its own sake, disdained abstract thought in favor of decisive action. This approach flew in the face of the entire Western tradition, which, since the time of Plato and Aristotle, privileged the *bios theoretikos,* or "life of contemplation," as the fullest expression of one's humanity, a concept bequeathed to posterity in the Latin, Christian, and medieval tradition of the *vita contemplativa.* The Nazis also completely dismissed the notion that education should take the development of the individual as its starting point and ultimate goal. Modern individualism, as canonized in the Declaration of the Rights of Man and of the Citizen in 1789, was cast aside in favor of a holistic view of man: not a fully autonomous, self-sufficient atom but an inseparable member of a group, without which the individual would wither and die.

This two-pronged revolution was backed, with consummate political opportunism—and perhaps occasionally genuine conviction—by respected scholars of the ancient world, professors of classics and history, who sought to promote the study of antiquity as a paradigm of proper values for the youth of the new Germany. Their self-appointed mission in the new Reich was nothing less than to save the humanities.

HISTORIA MAGISTRA VITAE: HITLER AND HISTORY

In *Mein Kampf,* Hitler confided that as a schoolboy he had been passionate about history, thanks largely to one particular instructor, who had excelled at bringing the past to life in front of a class of enthusiastic disciples: "This teacher made history my favorite subject."[1]

The passages that Hitler devoted to his favorite mentor are too important to be overlooked, for they allow us to grasp the significance that the führer attributed to the study of history. In his magnum opus, Hitler expounded upon his view of history twice: first in the chapters devoted to his autobiography, where he discussed the importance of Dr. Leopold Pötsch's history course at the realschule in Linz, which he attended from 1900 to 1905, and again in his description of the program for educational reform that the Nazi state would implement once the NSDAP had come to power. As the German historian Eberhardt Jäckel has noted, "The world of Hitler's political thought was heavily influenced by history."[2] Speer, for his part, recalled that Hitler "saw himself and his role from a historical angle."[3]

Hitler conceived of history as both a subject for instruction and a mode of instruction in its own right, reflecting the German linguistic distinction between *Geschichte*, the facts and events that constitute all of human development, and *Historie*, the narration of this development, more frequently understood in English as historiography. History was ultimately about lessons, lessons of such fundamental importance for the führer that understanding them was like a sort of sixth sense—the ability to view events in temporal perspective—as indispensable in its own right as any of the other five:

> A man who is indifferent to history is a man without hearing, without sight. Such a man can live, of course—but what a life?[4]

History, the narrative of humanity's past experience, existed to serve as a compass for the present. This pragmatic, utilitarian notion of history as lesson was a concept inherited directly from antiquity.

Cicero defined history as the mistress of life, the teacher of men and states: "Historia magistra vitae."[5] To the ancients, history was full of morals from both an ethical and a political point of view, instructions that guided man on the path toward a just life and showed rulers how to govern well. All ancient historians prefaced their works with self-aggrandizing introductions promoting their utility and significance.[6] Thucydides, one of the two paradigmatic historians of antiquity (along with Herodotus), went so far as to boldly declare in his introduction to *The Peloponnesian War* that his work would stand as a "possession for all time."[7]

A few centuries later, Polybius composed his *Histories* to illustrate the reasons for Rome's greatness, telling the triumphal story of a small city in Latium that had subjugated the known world and built an unprecedented empire: "As for the reasons why they excelled in everything, these will become clearer from what I have written, and it will also be seen how many and how great advantages accrue to the student from the systematic treatment of history."[8] For Polybius, like all ancient historians, there was nothing either trivial or objective about history. History dispensed lessons, and the historian conceived of his work as a course in systematic history[9]—that is, history written with an eye toward contemporary decision making and action. In a certain sense, then, Polybius intended to compose a how-to manual for imperial hegemony. That suited Hitler's interests precisely.

After the Renaissance, which witnessed the rediscovery of the ancients and their concept of history, these ideas were shared with and passed down to generations of educated Europeans. In the Germanic world, the *Gymnasien*—not coincidentally named after the Latin *gymnasium*, itself transliterated from the Greek—as well as all the other schools, including the realschule in Linz,[10] perpetuated this tradition of the teaching of history as an introduction to political theory and practice. In the opening pages of *Mein Kampf*, Hitler deplored how, all too often, history was force-fed to students as the sterile repetition of facts and dates: "Few teachers understand that the aim of studying history can never be to learn historical dates and facts by heart and recite them by rote." Far from such dry recitation, the teaching of history should evoke the people who lived in the past, an almost magical resuscitation of the men and forces that had shaped human development, plunging to the heart of the desires and intentions of history's actors, who were a source of inspiration:

> To "learn" history means to seek and find the forces which are the causes leading to those effects which we subsequently perceive as historical events.
> The art of reading as of learning is this: *to retain the essential, to forget the non-essential.*[11]

In virtually every one of his remarks regarding education and culture, Hitler criticized the "ballast" with which the schools weighed down their pupils. In history, the dead weight to be thrown overboard consisted primarily of those bothersome facts and dates whose rote memorization was perfectly useless: "What matters is not whether the child knows exactly when this or that battle was fought, when a general was born, or even when a monarch (usually a very insignificant one) came into the crown of his forefathers. No, by the living God, this is very unimportant."[12]

This critique of the gymnasium and its formulaic method of instruction formed part of a much broader climate of vigorous anti-intellectualism that extended well beyond the Nazis. The historian Fritz Stern brilliantly demonstrated how critiques of cultural modernity in imperial and Weimar Germany frequently shared a blanket condemnation of the educational system in the secondary schools and universities.[13] For the writers studied by Stern[14]—dissidents exiled from the academy, who suffered personally as a result of their institutional marginalization—the methodical labor privileged in the gymnasium stifled imagination and extinguished the flame of individual genius, celebrating mediocrity at the expense of the true intellectual aristocracy: "Much of the irrationalism and hatred of 'system' which characterized German youth sprang up in opposition to these schools."[15]

The last avatars of a Germany hostile to rationalism and the Enlightenment since the end of the eighteenth century, these men, whom Stern called "cultural Luddites,"[16] sublimated their ferocious anti-intellectualism into a heroic vitalism, a romantic glorification of pure instinct that fulminated against rationality and abhorred academic routine.

Often deliberately aphoristic and little inclined to respect the architecture or principles of logical reasoning, they "wrote with great fervor and passion. . . . They condemned or prophesied, rather than exposited or argued, and . . . their writings showed that they despised the discourse of intellectuals, depreciated reason, and exalted intuition. Humorless and murky, their prose was fitfully lit up by mystical but apodictic epigrams."[17] They cared little, then, for factual evidence. It is striking to note how easily this same judgment could be applied verbatim to the writings and speeches of the Nazi leaders themselves, especially the führer.

Hitler remembered his old teacher at Linz, Dr. Pötsch, as though he were a magician who knew how, quite literally, to conjure up the past, to breathe new life into it and give it rebirth through the inspiration and education of his students. His "good fortune" to have such a teacher, he confided to us in *Mein Kampf,* "affected my whole later life": "This old gentleman's manner was as kind as it was determined, his dazzling eloquence not only held us spellbound but actually carried us away. Even today I think back with gentle emotion on this gray-haired man who, by the fire of his narratives, sometimes made us forget the present; who, as if by enchantment, carried us into past times and, out of the millennial veils of mist, molded dry historical memories into living reality. On such occasions we sat there, often aflame with enthusiasm, and sometimes even moved to tears."[18]

Following Pötsch's example, the teacher should thus know how to make history come alive and, with his eloquence, convey a sense of emotion to make the past *feel* real and familiar to the students. But imbuing past lives and events with intense feeling was not an end in and of itself; it was but a means to a far more profound end, that of making students aware of the lessons that history had to offer: "What made our good fortune all the greater was that this teacher knew how to illuminate the past by examples from the present, and how from the past to draw inferences for the present. As a result he had more understanding than anyone else for all the daily problems which then held us breathless."[19]

These remarks would become the basis for official dispositions in the text of the 1938 educational reform for secondary-school instruction:

"History, in its unfolding, should appear to our youth not like a chronicle, which recounts all events indifferently, but like a story"—the implication being that the teacher should not "renounce value judgments" but rather, to the contrary, should do away with the impotent objectivity of an abstract positivism.[20] Dramatization and axiology were to be the new cardinal rules.

The "daily problems" that Hitler referred to were above all of a political nature. History, with all the rhetorical weight and depth it holds for readers and listeners and the fascination it possesses for political and military "deciders," frequently constitutes a justification for political action. Hitler noted in *Mein Kampf* that history nurtured his development as the political man he had become and that it taught him far more than those other subjects he had been so assiduously forced to study: "The habit of historical thinking which I thus learned in school has never left me in the intervening years. To an ever-increasing extent world history became for me an inexhaustible source of understanding for the historical events of the present; in other words, for politics. I do not want to 'learn' it, I want it to instruct me."[21]

History, unshackled from its ballast of facts and dates, reduced to minimalist purity, became little more than a collection of political maxims always at the ready for the political man—that is to say, he who was making history in the present. Politics, in essence, was "history in the making,"[22] *werdende Geschichte,* history in the present tense. The substantive connection between past and present made the learning of such lessons an important and legitimate activity. Politics, as the history of the present, must thus be guided by the history of the past, which was useful only and precisely for the guidance it provided to the present day: "The aim of studying history is not to forget its lessons when occasion arises for its practical application, or to decide that the present situation is different after all, and that therefore its old eternal truths are no longer applicable; no, the purpose of studying history is precisely its lesson for the present. The man who cannot do this must not conceive of himself as a political leader."[23]

Hitler wanted nothing to do with history as an aesthetic or nostalgic contemplation of the days of yore. The ultimate goal of history instruction was not the past but the future, less about the accumulation of knowledge about the past as such and more about the possibilities for political action in the present and their consequences for the building of the future. This was not art for art's sake: "For we do not learn history just in order to know the past, we learn history in order to find an instructor for the future and for the continued existence of our own nationality."[24]

Even less than a collection of maxims or morals for policy making, history was reduced to a skeleton upon which to hang proof of simplistic logic about the nature of people and states. Hitler hammered this point home repeatedly: the duty of the teacher was to divine the "great lines of development [of the nation]"[25] ("die grosse Entwicklungslinie der Nation"), the tendencies or trends that would define the future of the nation, a blueprint unencumbered by any excessive detail that obscured meaning, clouded the intellect, and caused the individual to lose sight of the essentials. The teaching of history in the *Völkisch* state would have to become the mirror image of its social and racial policy: selection, elimination, purification. But the teaching of history was still bogged down in details: "A few facts, dates, birthdays and names remain behind while a broad, clear line is totally lacking. The essentials which should really matter are not taught at all; it is left to the more or less gifted nature of the individual to find out the inner motives from the flood of dates and the sequence of events."[26]

The harmful character of such instruction directly reflected the political state of the country and the quality of its ruling class, which was politically incompetent, either because it was ignorant of history or because it was lost in the details and thus unable to generalize effectively—both extremes equally detrimental to the development of a clear vision. Hitler denounced what he saw as a veritable perversion that had resulted in the confusion of means and ends. "The continued existence of our own nationality" was, as we have seen, Hitler's ultimate goal. "That," he declared, "is the *end*, and historical instruction is only a *means* to it. But today the means has become the end, and the end disappears completely." History, in terms of the knowledge of facts and dates, should be restricted to the bare minimum that would ensure "that measure of historical insight which is necessary for [a man] to take a position of his own on the political issues of the nation."[27] Only those who wanted to become history professors should be compelled to study "all and even the smallest details."[28]

This purging of history to suit Hitler's tastes was woven into the Nazis' education reform. The "ballast" that was thrown overboard would no longer cloud students' minds nor take up their valuable time; Hitler wanted to cut a chunk of hours out of instruction to free up room in the school calendar for physical education, the primary pedagogical priority of the future National Socialist state: "The school as such in a

Völkisch state must create infinitely more free time for physical training."[29] The reform of history curricula would also be swept up by this reformist spirit.

SAVING CLASSICS, SAVING HISTORY: ON THE REFORM OF HUMANITIES EDUCATION

Did these new pedagogical concepts threaten the prestige and even the future of ancient history and classical literature? If history instruction was to be completely oriented toward understanding the present, the fate of that "ballast" so derided by Hitler—which was supposed to be thrown overboard to make way for the teaching of sport—seemed a foregone conclusion.

At the same time, however, Hitler's taste for ancient history was well known, as demonstrated by *Mein Kampf,* which classicists and scholars of antiquity would hold up as the final word on the issue in order to try to preserve their own status.

For their part, historians proved unquestioningly obedient. Pedagogues and professional teachers of history bent over backward to fulfill Hitler's wishes. Political changes demanded "a complete makeover of the curricula," a "radical redefinition," a "revolutionary reform of the schools," proclaimed one history journal in 1933: "We must do away with liberal ideology and its anemic, hypocritical objectivity once and for all"[30] and make a clean break with an antiquarian historicism that "cultivates the past for the past."[31] Such phrases could have been copied virtually word for word from *Mein Kampf.*

The new history, particularly that of the ancient world, would bury those "utopian dreams of fraternization" and "blissful internationalism" that had all too often contaminated minds with irenic liberalism. They "must disappear,"[32] pure and simple.

The study of the classics, however, faced a very real threat in the form of *Völkisch* nativists, so classicists took it upon themselves to sound the alarm and rally around their field: their task was nothing less than to save the teaching of literature, Latin, and Greek from extinction in the imminent curricular reform (though ultimately the reform would not in fact go into effect until 1938). To do this, it was necessary to demonstrate all the benefits that a Nazi education could draw from their discipline. In 1933, instructors of ancient history and Latin, led by the historian Fritz Schachermeyr[33] and the Latinist Hans Oppermann,[34] published a special issue of the journal *Neue Wege zur Antike* dedicated to "humanist education in the National Socialist state."³⁵ This self-serving plea was designed to head off criticism of the classics by demonstrating, in eight pieces that addressed a wide range of potential attacks, how old-fashioned subjects like Latin, Greek, and ancient history could still help shape the best Nazis. The pieces included recommendations for "the modern gymnasium,"³⁶ the "return of humanism,"³⁷ "paths to humanism for the Third Reich,"³⁸ and "the humanities as a German weapon."³⁹

Their initiative was joined by that of the Deutscher Philologenverband (Association of German philologists), which, on 30 September 1933, published a manifesto signaling the classicists' stance on the state's new ideas for education and the need to reorient the schools toward the formation of a new man, which they based on the model of the ancients: "The goal of all German education is the German man as a member of the people's community [*Volksgemeinschaft*]"⁴⁰ and not as an abstract individual or example of the allegedly universal man. It was thus only right that "the education of the individual," understood in this sense, was rejected. In this context, antiquity offered a reminder that "man is a political being par excellence, and that the state comes before the man."⁴¹

MANIFESTOS FOR A NEW HUMANISM:
HOLISM AND THE POLITICAL MAN

The new humanism promoted by scholars of antiquity was thus both holistic and political, focused not on man as an individual but on the group to which he belonged. As the professor of classical literature Fritz Bucherer forthrightly declared in an article on the humanities in the new Germany: "Subjects, professors, and schools exist for the students, but the students, both boys and girls, exist for the state."⁴²

The idea was no longer to educate the individual as such but to shape the individual according to the needs of the state—in other words, the formation of what 1930s theorists called the political man, *der politischer Mensch*, a man who, as Werner Jaeger wrote, could not exist without the catalyzing spark of antiquity.

Jaeger, who tried to reconcile himself and his "third humanism" (*dritter Humanismus*) to the spirit of the times before emigrating to the United States in 1936, had defended his ideas in a 1933 article that, through its cautious phrasing and place of publication—the journal *Volk im Werden*, edited by the Nazi intellectual Ernst Kreick—appeared to be an attempt at a pledge of allegiance or, at the very least, a genuine effort to accommodate Germany's new masters.

But Jaeger's article also engaged in a delicate battle, explicitly defending the humanities and the *Gymnasien* in the context of the political winds apparently blowing in favor of the Germanists and prehistorians. He conceded there was "an ambiguity in the very concept" of humanism, which was subject to two definitions, and immediately clarified that he dissociated himself from the first of these. The "critique" of humanism that came "from the point of view of National Socialism" likewise addressed only the first of these two meanings—the humanism inherited from the Enlightenment, which was clearly out of step with the political and ideological context of the times: "The humanism which has come under attack and which might seem incompatible with the historical and intellectual premises of National Socialism is a very particular ideology, albeit one not necessarily well defined, whose roots can be traced back to the civilizing system of Western Europe in the eighteenth century, that is to say the Enlightenment."[43] This was an apolitical humanism that disregarded the supremacy of the polis: "There is no connection with the path of the community, or if a link exists it is very loose. The real reason certainly lies not in the ancient components of that humanistic education but—jumping ahead—in the completely apolitical character of German culture under Weimar classicism."[44]

This second, Weimar humanism was just as guilty as the first humanism of the Renaissance, both of which Jaeger dismissed in a single blow. Similarly, the historian of religion Wilhelm Brachmann would argue that it was "necessary to distinguish between humanism and humanism," taking aim at that universalizing liberal Erasmus, a rootless cosmopolitan whose motto could almost be seen as an advertising slogan for statelessness: "Home is where it is good" ("Ubi bene, ibi patria"). This universal humanism directly contradicted its more exclusionary counterpart, just as Erasmus could be contrasted with Plato or Ulrich von Hutten.[45]

The third humanism, Jaeger argued, had to be sharply distinguished from the *aufklärerisch* humanism of the Enlightenment. The latter had as its goal "the aesthetic and formal education of the sole individual." With respect to antiquity, that humanism betrayed its own essence through "its completely apolitical character," which obscured how man was "a political creature . . . , a social being that existed within a state." The second humanism, of Weimar classicism, could similarly be dismissed without fanfare, condemned for its visceral individualism and consubstantial liberalism: "German classicism, which is and must remain the foundation of our national culture, is (as I have already stated earlier) the product of a completely apolitical culture, so much so that we might think of Weimar, which represents the summit of our culture, as the opposite of the spirit of Potsdam, which has been so decisive for the future of our state."[46] Potsdam here stood for Prussia and its willful construction of German political power, as well as a reference to the Day of Potsdam, 21 March 1933.[47]

To defend against the criticisms aimed against humanism, it was necessary to show that "the political man," *der politischer Mensch*, could best be molded through exposure to his ancient heritage and that the bridge leading to this antiquity was called "humanism."

Jaeger parried arguments that denigrated the humanities as passé or foreign to German culture, in the name of the race or revolutionary innovation: "The historical elements of the spiritual constitution of a race change little over the course of centuries, much less than its essential properties as a race."[48] It was precisely because of such biological solidarity, the very identity of the German race, that the humanities of antiquity—the spiritual product of a common blood—should be spared from the intellectual firing squad of the German national revolution and its state-sanctioned racism. Humanism, from a racial perspective, was nothing less than a special connection to the spiritual heritage of the Indo-Germanic race. What's more, Hitler's seizure of power was driven by ideals whose roots lay hidden deep in the mists of ancient times: "The vitality of the ancient political and spiritual ideals in the movement making the history of our time leaves no doubt about the fact that among the fundamental forces [that drive the movement] . . . can be counted the architectonic power of antiquity, which has survived centuries and which constantly renews itself." Jaeger vowed that professors of history and classical literature had cured themselves of the historicizing or formalist abstraction that had gotten the better of them in the nineteenth century: one of the consequences of the Great War and the subsequent chaos of political life under Weimar had been the politicization of the study of the humanities. As a result, "the state had become, for all those who lived through those times, the great problem of the age."[49]

It was now obvious to all that the teaching of classical literature could no longer be undertaken solely in the spirit of a "pure grammatical formalism that exercises the mind but leaves it vacant." Henceforth, the teaching of Latin and Greek must be above all a means of instilling values: "History today imposes upon the German people a particular duty, that is the creation of the political man. . . . When the new type of political man has been created, the need for antiquity will become self-evident to all of us."[50]

In England, as in Greece, the universities linked sport and rhetoric in the form of the debating club in order to shape the elites of the realm: the classics and the humanities engaged a much wider public than just that of future philologists.[51]

In Germany, the spirit of Greek paideia had been disseminated and preserved through the institution of the gymnasium, which needed to be defended against all efforts to dismantle it: "Our *Gymnasien* are a vital linchpin in the reconstruction of a political-humanistic education. How better to nourish the minds of our youth, how better to teach them to be conscientious members of the political community, than by introducing them to the great monuments of political thought from antiquity?"[52]

Jaeger offered a list of Greek and Latin authors who should be required reading, along with a brief summary of their respective merits: Homer, Solon, Hesiod, Plato, Demosthenes, Horace, Virgil, Cicero, Livy, Tacitus—but also Tyrtaeus. Too often unjustly ignored, this Spartan lyric poet, whose martial verses were recited to the rhythm of the fife and the drumbeat of marching infantry, deserved recognition for composing the "Code of the Citizen Soldier"[53]—a political soldier who gave body and soul to the fatherland—no less than Hesiod did for describing the nobility of labor or Plato the state and the new man.

In the early years of the Weimar Republic, still reeling from the war and Germany's defeat, Jaeger had written: "We hope that our youth will produce leaders [from our humanist *Gymnasien*] who will not be taught to be pure scholars or library rats, mere technicians or specialists, in letters or aesthetics, but who will be taught to be steadfast and self-assured in their ideas and their future paths, through exposure to the greatness of Hellenism."[54] The Nazification of classical literature, ancient philosophy, and ancient history had thus blossomed in rather amenable soil, already fertile with hopes for national revolution and the military regimentation of its youth since the birth of Weimar, a bastard child of a hasty armistice and an ignominious peace.

The development of the political man was thus consonant, indeed inextricably linked, with that of engaged humanism—a humanism renewed, in the eyes of its defenders, by its political commitment and goals. Wilhelm Brachmann even insisted on the idea that this new humanism was a warlike ideology, vigilantly watching over the heritage of the Indo-Germanic race. Political humanists eliminated any trace of the conceptual or the ethereal, speaking of their mission in terms of flesh and blood. As Brachmann explained: "Where contemporary humanism speaks of literature, political humanism speaks of blood or the race."[55]

The abstract, universalizing humanism of the Renaissance tradition—which had gone against the original exclusivist, hierarchical conception of the Greeks—was a cosmopolitan humanism, the product of a stateless mentality, and needed to be consigned to the same dustbin of history as Erasmus: "This discourse on 'humanism' must be replaced by a discourse on the spiritual history of the Indo-Germanics, which will express more clearly than any other discourse the particular nature of German political humanism. This humanism stands guard to protect the spiritual heritage, determined by blood, of Indo-Germanics in general and thus also, and above all, preserves the heritage of classical antiquity."[56]

NATIONAL SOCIALISM AS HUMANISM

Political humanism in contemporary Germany thus encompassed anything that involved the *politischer Mensch,* the political man—a creature that Alfred Bäumler, an expert on Nietzsche, made it his mission to define in a series of lectures and articles.

Bäumler too objected to classical humanism, which he believed conflicted with National Socialism: "Humanism is no longer the dominant force in this country: the only spiritual force in Germany is National Socialism."[57]

The two terms were not, however, mutually exclusive. Nazism was irreconcilable with only the variant of Latin humanism that was the hallmark of a bastardized Rome, whose heritage had subsequently been claimed by the French, which Bäumler unconditionally rejected, along with the Latin language and its descendants. Such humanism was native "to Italy and France"[58] but not to Germany. French was humanist, as the blood of the French dictated it to be: "For the French, humanism is not only a part of their history but a part of their soul. . . . The Latin tradition belongs in their blood. Defending humanism is thus, for the French, like defending themselves."[59]

The gaping chasm that existed between "the humanist and racist conceptions of history" thus dictated an emphasis on the heritage of the Greeks if one wished to avoid closing off all access to the classical tradition. Only the expression of a more purely Nordic blood could help redefine a more rigorous form of humanism that, in contrast to the decadent Romans or the French and more in line with the thought of the Greeks themselves, "thought not in terms of individuals but in terms of races and peoples. This is the true humanism."[60] This true humanism implied a more precise concept of "true" humanity, which the Nazis explicitly redefined in harmony with their version of Greek thought, based on the concepts of hierarchy, race, and eugenics. The German effort after Winckelmann to dust off the Acropolis and return to Greece was "a search for a Greek model, independent of the Roman tradition," the refusal to accept a "secondhand"[61] Greek heritage deformed by its passage through Roman hands.

All this talk of humanism from those of a political sensibility not frequently associated with that term might sound surprising. Yet in the works of Bäumler and a number of other classicists, there was clearly a very real desire at work to define what seems to us to be a blatant oxymoron: a Nazi humanism. This was not just a question of salvaging the salvageable; rather, it was a more profound attempt to place the cardinal principles of Nazi ideology within the broader normative order of the Western tradition and to assert a heritage and prestige that it could draw upon for legitimacy. Arguing that the party's principles were ultimately the same as those of Sparta,[62] for example, amounted to a demonstration that their worth and nobility, if not their precise content, stemmed from their privileged rapport with ancient history and the link to their Indo-Germanic roots, as manifest so spectacularly in Greece and Rome. It is evident that the Nazis took great care to avoid being seen as parvenus in terms of either ideology or concrete policy, ennobling their principles and burnishing the brutality of their slogans with the patina of long centuries of tradition, giving their ideas a prestigious pedigree.

In the face of opposition to their anti-Semitic policies or their treatment of the mentally ill—a particular source of consternation to religious leaders, who viewed this as a symptom of a disregard for human life, which was a gift from God—the Nazis appealed to the classical tradition, in this case one that was even older than the Judeo-Christian tradition itself. They claimed to derive their ideals from the earliest history of their race: that is, from the Indo-Germanic peoples of antiquity. The "slave morality"[63] of the Judeo-Christian Ten Commandments—a morality at once both Jewish and Bolshevik—was an infectious disease imported by a foreign and destructive race. Masculine Indo-Germanic decisiveness, their treatment of foreigners and the sick, eugenic selection, and the elimination of the different or the weak: these were all Greek and Roman ideas before they were the Nazis'—one could cite Seneca, for example, as an advocate for the gassing of the mentally ill.[64] Such a strategy allowed them to follow through on their ideas with a clear conscience despite their patent extremism, since their actions responded to ethics rooted in a long-standing ancient tradition. Their most abnormal, aberrant activities could be relativized, the exceptional or unacceptable made legitimate.

One sees similar care at work in Himmler's desire to placate the potentially guilty consciences of the men under his command by proclaiming their actions to be those of a superior morality that, though purely formal,[65] could be judged not by Judeo-Christian standards—the morality of the weak, a suicidal folly for the elite—but only by a racial morality, which restricted its categorical imperative solely to members of the race. The construction of a Nazi humanism, like that of the categorical imperative to race murder, proceeded according to the same logical scheme: in both cases, the group to whom its principles applied (and were indeed universal) was tightly constrained. The radical Nazi critique of cosmopolitan, liberal humanism and the denigration of its false conception of humanity led to a restricted use of the term: yes, there was a Nazi humanism, but it was a humanism that applied only to those who were truly human. *Humanism* was a word that had been cheapened with overuse and thus needed to be reclaimed and employed more rigorously: humanity was the community of all human beings— that is, the community of Indo-Germanic people, the last remaining elements of the true human race, surrounded by a false, universal humankind that could more appropriately be called subhuman. Elements foreign to the Nordic race were indeed subhuman, in the sense that they no longer belonged to humanity. The underlying logic was undeniable: such subhumans could no longer possess any claim to the rights or principles of humanism.

The *politischer Mensch* was thus the rediscovery of the ancient Greek, who drew his sense of identity from his belonging to the polis, in the guise of a reinvigorated humanism. We should note that the term is a nearly literal translation of the Greek *zoon politikon,* the definition of a man as a "political animal" proposed by Aristotle in his *Politics.* Alfred Bäumler made clear that his conception of the *politischer Mensch* did indeed draw upon Aristotle but that it was also much broader: the term "does not signify only that which Aristotle's old definition proposed, according to which man is a political—that is to say, social— being." Bäumler constructed his notion around a series of binary oppositions between politics and theory, action and contemplation, activity and passivity. For Bäumler, politics entailed "activity, labor, productivity, oriented toward some end"[66] and not "observation, comprehension, contemplation."[67] A political being is one who is engaged in the life of the collective group, which gives meaning and purpose to his existence and which he nourishes, develops, and protects in return. He is active in his defense of the group, whose life, like his own, is defined by struggle—the shadow of the First World War being omnipresent in Bäumler's work. The *politischer Mensch* was thus the self-actualization (through entelechy) of the *politischer Soldat*, or "political soldier," whom Bäumler lauded during his inaugural lecture of 10 May 1933 at the University of Berlin, where he equated "the fighting man, the political being, the soldier, the farmer, the worker" as types completely opposite from the "learned man."[68] In fact, just as he began his inaugural lecture before an auditorium full of brownshirts, several battalions of these *politische Soldaten* in SA uniforms began their assault on the university's libraries, gathering books for an auto-da-fé held later that same night.

Bäumler disdained abstraction, rejected theory, and virtually denied the existence of the abstract intellectual: "The man of theory is . . . a fiction," since "man is fundamentally a political being."[69] This political being, a Greek and thus Nordic creation, must be trained in the Greek fashion in order to maximize his utility in the service of the community. This was the mission of the humanities. In a 1933 speech leading up to his official instructions for the teaching of history in the schools, the Prussian interior minister Wilhelm Frick declared that if Germany's mission was to "train members of the political community,"[70] then this was the role of the humanities. Of similar inspiration and significance, the curricular reform of 1938 actually used the original Greek term *zoon politikon*, whose education and formation was the job of the humanities: Latin and Greek must "contribute to training and educating the German youth in order to make each of them, in both body and mind, a *zoon politikon*."[71]

The glorification of ancient heroism, training in self-denial and sacrifice, holistic thinking that privileged the group over the individual, and the renunciation of the self—these were all values aimed at hardening a steely German youth, tempered in a cold bath of Indo-Germanic propaganda.

FROM DIVIDED MAN TO TOTAL MAN: THE PARADIGM OF GREEK PAIDEIA

All this talk about the *politischer Mensch* naturally led to a celebration of the classical Greek system of education, which was aimed at cultivating the total man, a complete, harmoniously proportioned being fully developed in all his faculties—in contrast to the "humanist" man, a wan, bleary-eyed intellect lacking physical strength.

The Reich's pedagogues and classicists, following Nietzsche, execrated what they saw as a divided man, castrated or incomplete, and celebrated the Greek *volle Mensch,* or "total man," defined by his complete possession of all his physical and intellectual attributes. The Greek was a true man, one who had mastered himself and his faculties: his body was not separate from his mind, nor was his mind divorced from his body—a masculine paradigm promoted and celebrated with great fanfare, perhaps most notably at the 1936 Olympic Games.[72] The new German educational system would follow the Greek way, as Alfred Rosenberg proclaimed in a wide-ranging speech of 15 March 1934, in which he sarcastically denigrated the muddleheaded dream of the "humanization of mankind" ("Humanisierung der Menschheit") à la Schiller.[73] This was a noble and generous idea in theory but one that was in reality "antibiological, and completely contradictory to all the laws of race,"[74] because it had been inspired by a seductive, sentimental universalizing humanism. Against this emphasis on universal human reason, "German education must not be formal and aestheticizing; it will aim not at the abstract development of reason but rather at the formation of character,"[75] through a return to nature and the training of the body, too frequently neglected by a desiccated and overly cerebral rationalism. In addition to their racial ties that bound them to the new Germany, the Greeks offered the proper model to imitate:

> It is only thus that the body and the soul can unite in common action. It is only then that this organic union can become what was once a reality, in complete freedom, among the Nordic peoples in Greece. The secret of Greek civilization lies in the fact that the Nordic tribes long ago subjugated another country and that, moved by an aesthetic ideal, they trained and educated their body and their soul in beautiful unison. This is why Greece is not just a simple example that we have made out of a foreign people . . . , but ancient Greece shows us how a Nordic people could freely educate themselves while, for a one and a half millennia, German history has been oppressed by universalist dogmas and the political-military imperialism that they brought with them. This is why the renaissance of antiquity that we see at work in the soul of today's new Germany is also in essence a renaissance of the free Germanic man, and the only true task of the National Socialist movement is to reinforce these values of our character . . . in order to forge a common destiny that conforms to the laws of nature and of life and the eternal exigencies of the German racial soul.[76]

The glorification of the Greeks' education of the total man in this vein fell largely to Ernst Krieck—one of the chief pedagogues of the Third Reich and a professor at the University of Berlin—who wrote a book based on the idea that the Hellenic paideia had constituted a fusion of the physical (*gymnisch*) and the lyrical (*musisch*) that transcended the sterile opposition of mind and body, which was a fundamentally Oriental and Judeo-Christian notion. Krieck welcomed the political revolution of 1933, which finally permitted "the German people to turn away from the civilization of pure rationalism,"[77] a trend initiated at the end of the nineteenth century by the back-to-nature movement known as the *Lebensreform*. The Greeks, the fathers of logos (logic), had also been wise not to amputate man's *thymos* (spirit) and *epithymia* (desire), to borrow Plato's terms for his tripartite topography of the soul. According to Krieck, the importance given to music in a Greek education revealed their attentiveness to developing the total man. Music played a vital role, since it allowed for the organic development of the instinctive and the irrational by impressing a spiritual form, stimulated by song, on the physical body. With the importance it placed on music, paideia took into account the dual nature of man, the spiritual and corporeal, a duality that recalled the bipolarity of the Dionysian (trance) and the Apollonian (harmony) in a being that was at once full of both passion and reason. Krieck, it should be noted, accepted the Nietzschean theory of the felicitous merger of the bacchanalian and Apollonian, in contrast to someone like Kynast, who saw this duality instead as a sign of irreconcilable racial conflict.

Greek paideia, which was originally all about enlightened, harmonious dualism, had been subsequently clouded by the reductive focus on strict rationalism with the arrival of Aristotle. Later, during the Hellenistic period, the Greek blood and spirit were perverted by the entirely foreign distinction between mind and body, a perversion that came from below and beyond, in the form of an ascetic, mutilating Orient that wormed its way into the heart of the Nordic Greek body. The disappearance of the Greek musicogymnastic ideal helped fossilize classical culture as though it were a lifeless body, stuck in a museum for cold, rational contemplation: with the great desiccation of the Hellenistic era, "living Hellenism was petrified, only to become a death masque."[78] The Hellenistic age "of individualism and sovereign reason" signaled the death of "the Athenian spirit, which became a stateless cosmopolitanism."[79]

Nazi humanism thus required a very careful selection of just which humanities it ought to emphasize. It could not canonize all of the classical tradition but rather needed to separate the Indo-Germanic wheat of archaic and classical Greece from the Semitic chaff of the Orientalized Hellenistic era.[80] The latter was dismissed as a symbol of the twilight of racial decadence by historians like Fritz Schachermeyr: "Until now, we have accepted all of antiquity as a sort of sublime revelation.... But instead the humanist, who was once the preserver of the most noble Nordic spirit, became the vehicle of an anti-Nordic spiritual heritage," which "caused the dissolution of the Nordic peoples of antiquity" and still remained a "destructive poison"[81] in the modern world.

The alpha and omega of all humanism, and the ultimate goal of a humanistic education, was—as it must be for humanity itself—racial selection, the choice of which texts and which peoples to privilege. The historian of Greece Hans Bogner argued firmly that "our place can be found with the Greeks and Romans, whenever and wherever they were not yet alienated from us by racial miscegenation. Our natural racial kinship with them is a living bond and makes it possible for us to understand Greco-Roman antiquity . . . , while such a genuine understanding of the foreign peoples of antiquity must remain elusive, for they are far too exotic." Bogner argued that traditional humanism erred when it naively believed that "the Greeks wanted to create a man of ideas through paideia," pursuing a universal, abstract ideal unbound by any blood ties or racially determined characteristics. For the Greeks, culture was not supposed to be emancipated from nature, nor was it unconstrained by blood; indeed, it was defined and reinforced by it. Greek culture was a racial culture, meant only for the Greeks, to educate and elevate their innate, superior Nordic humanity: "In Greece they wished to educate pure Hellenics and not man in general." For the Greeks, as for the Germans, other peoples were "foreigners of the highest degree," who, contrary to what the false humanism that degenerate idealists would have the world believe, "could not and did not want to be assimilated."[82]

Bogner's attack on this seductive humanism was virulently racist, coming as it did from an article denouncing the *Assimilationsjude* of antiquity—the Jew of the diaspora who dressed in Greek robes to hide in plain sight in the Hellenistic world, then later donned a Roman toga and learned to speak Latin under the Roman Empire.[83] It was this open, welcoming, even universalist notion of paideia, the learning of languages, myths, and customs exclusive to the Greek Nordics, that encouraged assimilation and even the transcendence of natural selection through the crude application of cultural knowledge. Culture was thus merely cosmetic, as in the appropriation of a style of dress, and language simply a mask to conceal or disguise one's nature, hiding the Jew and making him invisible. Only the late, decadent Hellenistic Greeks had sought to promote a concept of education aimed at the universality of mankind or the universal in the individual man: High Greek culture, which was fundamentally selective and elitist, had been sold off to the highest bidder by degenerate Levantines, who had imposed their idea that "it was not their roots but their culture (paideia) that made the Greeks." They reduced an exclusively Nordic Greek culture to the diluted lingua franca of "universal civilization" (*Weltkultur*), a deracinated, stateless expression of "the universal spirit of Hellenism."[84]

The historian Karl Georg Kuhn leveled an equally sharp accusation against paideia regarding the Jewish diaspora and its assimilation, which he encapsulated as having "falsified" all of Greek culture: "They dressed up their speech with classical citations. They also practiced the art of Greek rhetoric,"[85] draping themselves in fashionable words and concepts to obscure the obstinate reality of their otherwise inescapable otherness.

ARETE, ARISTOI, FÜHRER: TRAINING SOLDIERS AND LEADERS

The Greeks' education of the total man was closely connected to the military duties and primary vocation of the *Männerbund*, the "band of brothers" that made up the polis.

The paideia of body and soul, which embraced the dual nature of man, cultivated a harmonious blend of poet and athlete, philosopher and gymnast, and, finally, citizen and soldier—a political soldier who would defend the city-state. A physically fit body was a warrior's body, that of a hoplite or soldier on horseback; practicing sport was not about individual fulfillment but rather was thought of as a form of service to the community and the state. As Ernst Krieck put it: "The Greek man educated in the Greek manner appears to us as a model and illuminating example for our own path, a man educated in the science of the Muses as well as that of arms, in the context of the ancient Greek polis."[86] It was in order to provide the state with the best citizen-soldiers that Plato—who, "in a time of decline, appealed one last time to the idea of the state locked in mortal combat"[87]—argued for education in music. Since life exists "between the two poles of irrational instinct and rational structure,"[88] it was important to take both into account in educating and building a state, imposing upon Dionysian instinct the harmonious structure of Apollonian reason instead of compartmentalizing or constraining them in ascetic repression of an Asiatic or Christian type, which was a negation of the body.

The fully formed man of Greek paideia was thus a political soldier, a soldier who defended his city and his race, a combatant of the eternal Occident against the eternal Orient. As Krieck noted: "This race forever appears to us full of eternal virtue and imperishable beauty, she who victoriously preserved Europe from Asiatism."[89]

In modern Germany, these Indo-Germanic soldiers would be commanded by officers who would be expected to possess a thorough knowledge of Greek antiquity. In 1932, the historian of Greece Hans Bogner published an essay for the training of officers with the self-explanatory title *The Training of a Political Elite*. Taking Greece as an example, the essay examined the conditions for the emergence of a political elite in Germany, the "biological and historical"[90] prerequisites for the creation of the führer's leadership caste. To build this political elite for the German polis, it was first necessary to turn to antiquity[91]—skipping the modern era, with its hostility to elitism—in a sort of "great leap inward," since "between the German and the Greek there is a secret inherited bond."[92] In his strongly worded but on the whole rather banal national-conservative view, Bogner railed against contemporary democracy, which could never "train, offer, or even abide a true leader."[93] Liberal democracy, imposed on Germany by the Weimar constitution, was antithetical to the development of political leadership (*politische Führung*) worthy of the name: "The system of popular sovereignty and representation, the philosophy of identity"[94]—in short, equality and liberal democracy itself—killed any nascent elite within.

True equality was possible only in a group assembled in the spirit of a proud, vigilant elitism that was jealously guarded from all external influence or penetration, as in Sparta. Bogner lauded the Spartan system of education,[95] a mixture of sport and military drill, as well as *Musik*, the art of the Muse understood in its broadest sense; the Spartan oligarchy was thus clearly preferable to Athenian democracy, which sank beneath the weight of an oppressive, incompetent egalitarianism in the absence of any hermetic seal to protect the purity of the group.[96]

Martin Heidegger, himself wishing to break with the disembodied abstraction of traditional humanism, argued that the Greeks' system of knowledge was anything but theoretical. Everything in Greece was oriented toward the ultimate goal of praxis, of action, and especially political action, foremost in the minds of all Greek thinkers. In his famous address upon assuming the rectorate at Heidelberg, Heidegger saw the Greek θεορια not as "pure contemplation," as had so often been the case in the past, but rather as the supreme form of ενεργεια, or "man's 'being-at-work.'"⁹⁷ For the Greeks, "theory was itself to be understood as the highest realization of genuine practice," since for them knowledge was not a simple "cultural good" but "the innermost determining center of all that binds human being to people and state."⁹⁸ As a rector, Heidegger, who wagered his term and the renaissance of the German academy on the revival of interest in Greece and Greek thought, made the hours devoted to the *Wehrsport* obligatory for all students and even organized a camp for reflection, a sort of outdoor philosophy class, at his home at Todtnauberg, where the master's cabin was soon swarming with brownshirts and swastikas.⁹⁹

The Greek (and more specifically the Spartan) model was of interest not only to Heidegger or the Reich's minister for science and education Bernhard Rust; it also appeared in the writings of the SS general August Heissmeyer, the inspector general of the Napola, the Nationalpolitische Erziehungsanstalten (National political institutes of education), which had been conceived as training academies for the crème de la crème of the future Nazi elite. According to the general, the training academies needed to follow the Greek example, a model of "community education," or *Gemeinschaftserziehung*, a harmonious and balanced education on the cultural, political, and military greatness of the state.¹⁰⁰

A PLEA FOR CLASSICAL HISTORY

The cry to save the classics also applied to classical history, its intellectual status and institutional position equally threatened by a growing wave of Germanists and prehistorians all too happy to knock their colleagues off their pedestals—and take their prestigious chairs and tenured appointments.

The quarrels between Germanists and classicists, prehistorians and scholars of antiquity, were echoed in the concepts behind the new history. The June 1933 directives of the Reich's interior minister Wilhelm Frick specified that the teaching of history must no longer commence with the ancient Mediterranean civilizations, as had previously been the case. Henceforth, Germanic prehistory would be restored to its proper importance and given pride of place.¹⁰¹ There was thus a sense of some urgency if the status of the antiquities was to be preserved. A radical modernization of the discipline was desperately needed.

In 1933, the ancient historian Fritz Schachermeyr published a call for such revision in an article fittingly titled "Die Aufgaben der Alten Geschichte im Rahmen der Nordischen Weltgeschichte" (The mission of ancient history in the framework of Nordic world history). In what he considered "a quarrel [*Streit*] for or against antiquity,"[102] it was necessary to defend and justify research on ancient history and the teaching of the humanities by recalling that *Greek* and *Roman* were synonyms, if not for *Germanic,* then certainly for *Nordic.* Any legitimate, comprehensive understanding of the history of the Nordic race and its cultural heritage could not ignore Greece and Rome without falling prey to the myopia of Germanophilia, a shortsighted view of the Germanic peoples that rejected the greatest heritage of the Aryan race.

The author nevertheless conceded that the scholarly study of antiquity was guilty of a lack of enthusiasm for the racialized restyling already under way in other disciplines. This was perhaps a harsh assessment,[103] but we must recall that Schachermeyr was comparing ancient history to racial anthropology and prehistory, both among the vanguard of such revisionism in the arts and sciences. Ancient historians—prisoners of routine, susceptible to the inertia induced by the veneration of their field and overconfident in its intrinsic worth, given its own long history and august body of work—were unsure about how to integrate this new framework and address themselves to the service of the National Socialist revolution, "which absolutely demands a change in the social sciences."[104]

The inertia gripping ancient history was all the more regrettable since the historiography of antiquity "contained, like no other discipline, the optimal material to provide a historical foundation for National Socialism"[105]: racial anthropology and Nordicist thought were limited to making sterile predictions in a vacuum without the empirically legitimating evidence that only the ancient historian could provide.[106]

Scholars of antiquity had thus far remained creatures of habit, born of classical philology, which had kept the classics confined to the strict orbit of the Greco-Roman world and completely lacked the global Nordic dimension that such studies would henceforth have to provide.[107] The future health of their discipline thus required the conversion of ancient history to incorporate a much broader Nordic perspective. As Schachermeyr proclaimed:

> The time is over when ancient history could confine itself to the contemplation of ancient sources without concern for its place in a more general historical framework. It is now necessary ... to tell the history of the two peoples of classical antiquity with Nordic fates and to consider them from the point of view of the community of Nordic peoples to which they belonged.[108]

In order to do this, the study of antiquity would have to imitate racial anthropology and prehistory, which had both quickly "provided National Socialism with the appropriate intellectual tools"[109]—by which he meant race, a concept equally dear to Schachermeyr's heart. Race was not just the fruit of the imagination of racial scientists but an undeniable reality, as the author strikingly declared with a bit of circular reasoning: "Race was not invented by racial scientists or National Socialists; it is an established historical fact."[110]

Thus reformed and reinvigorated with racialist ideas, ancient history would reassume its rightful place in the academy through the creation of a National Socialist body of thought and the construction of the new Germany. Even better, it would help take the full historical and cultural measure of the Nordic race. Privileging the medieval or modern to the detriment of the ancient, in the name of some strictly defined *Germanentum*, was a gross error: "If, in the future, our historiography remains limited to prehistory, the Middle Ages, and the modern era, we will have been spinning our wheels going around and around the same Germanic circles. It is only through comparison with the other Nordic peoples of antiquity, with the Hittites, the Persians, the Greeks, and the Romans, that we can see how the Nordic race possessed a global reach."[111] This "global reach" could not have what was undoubtedly the most prestigious part of its heritage amputated. Ancient history had a duty to obey to memory: "The Nordic heritage from antiquity [must not] succumb to forgetting. We cannot ignore that the Nordic cultural heritage imposes upon us a sacred duty, that it can only continue to live on and be preserved by us Nordics."[112] Hans Bogner also pleaded for greater scholarly engagement: "the sciences of antiquity" had been timid for too long, stuck in a cautious neutrality that bordered on culpable negligence. The *Realenzyklopädie*, for instance, and especially its entry for *Antisemitismus*, amounted to a "masterpiece of Jewish propaganda" for its omission of any discussion of "racial stock," which would have constituted "an effective justification for that anti-Semitism"[113] present in antiquity.

In this heavyweight battle to save their status and their jobs, classicists and scholars of antiquity could count on the support of a genuine champion: Hans Günther. The high priest of the Nordic race, pope of scientific racism, and thin-skinned ideologue of the most rigorous Nordicism (that of the SS) wanted nothing to do with Germanomania. While he had made the Nordic race and its provenance in Germanic soil the basis of his intellectual career, he nevertheless remained quite attentive and open to the classical culture so dear to the erudite German academic of his time, which of course he had helped to define. After all, the Greeks and Romans—like the Persians, Indians, and Iranians of whom he wrote—were each examples of the greatness of the Nordic race.

THE ATTIC AND THE RUNIC: THE CREATION OF THE INDO-GERMANIC HUMANITIES

In this open combat between the partisans of everything Germanic and the avatars of the classical civilizations of antiquity, Hans Günther plainly sided with the latter: "The cultural value of these [primarily Nordic] peoples, for us Germans as for all Germanic peoples, resides in their Indo-Germanic spirit, in the Persian, Hellenic, and Roman civilizations, as well as in the primitive culture of the Germanics." The peoples of Greco-Roman antiquity belonged to the same race as contemporary Germans; it was idle and foolish to pretend otherwise, dismissing Latin and Greek culture in favor of some hypothetically pure *Germanentum*. Scholarship on classical antiquity was racially just as legitimate. It produced knowledge of the history of the race, a single race that reassembled peoples which only an absurd pseudoscience could wish to keep separate: "The unity of our culture is held together by Indo-Germanic spiritual values. This conviction should put an end to the quarrel between those for whom our culture needs Greece and the Romans, needs classical antiquity, and those who defend 'Germanic antiquity.' For our culture . . . , a purely Indo-Germanic spirit is precious, for it to have come into being and for it to remain in existence. Each of the great Indo-Germanic peoples expressed, in remarkable and exemplary fashion, the specific virtues of the Nordic racial soul."[114]

Günther took a more extreme stance while plunging into the debate over the new curricula for secondary-school education and the place assigned to Latin, Greek, and ancient history. In a short, multiauthor volume designed to win support for the so-called dead languages, Günther put his name on what amounted to a warning to avoid an overly narrow Germanophilia. Understanding Indo-Germanic heritage, of which he was among the greatest supporters, required the mediation of the humanities:

> We, the Germans, cannot expect to have a full appreciation of the values that elevate our life and culture through *Germanentum* alone; we can hope to achieve the proper, reverent contemplation of all that is Indo-Germanic only by first including Persia, the Greek people, and the Roman people, with and alongside *Germanentum*. Ancient Hellenism and *Romanitas* . . . offer the

younger generations an exciting image of the grandeur of being Nordic and Indo-Germanic, which the study of *Germanentum* alone cannot. . . . All our love for *Germanentum* must not mean we can turn our backs on the greatness of the Greeks and Romans.[115]

The racial solidarity between contemporary Germans and the Nordic peoples of antiquity thus overrode any irreducible, frontal opposition between antiquity and *Germanentum*, a point also made by Wilhelm Brachmann in an article in the *Nationalsozialistische Monatshefte* (a monthly Nazi scholarly journal) on the heritage of the Greeks. For this historian of religion, "the binary opposition between the Hellenes and the German peoples disappeared" thanks to the racial ideas put forward by National Socialism, which included both peoples within a common race: "National Socialism was able to show, thanks to its racial ideas, the close proximity that exists between the Germanic or German and the Greek, both Nordic worlds."[116]

If it was still true that "culture is an expression of the blood" and "their blood is our blood,"[117] the cultures of antiquity must be considered expressions of the same Nordicness: ancient languages encouraged a knowledge of "the antique branch of the tree of Nordic essence,"[118] since they were "eloquent evidence of the Nordic essence, Nordic blood coagulated into language." As there was a "community of the same blood," he repeated, the encounter of the "Teutonic-German world with the ancient world" actually "reinforced Nordic racial thought and ideas." The apparent otherness of ancient civilizations was misleading; studying an antiquity previously believed to be racially foreign could ultimately prove to be a better and more reliable way to understand the most profound essence of the Indo-Germanic spirit: "The creative forces of antiquity, the forces that held out form and realization, built in sun and blood the cathedral of the spirit and the soul . . . , the Nordic spirit and the Nordic soul, as an expression of the Nordic body."[119]

The humanities were thus important in the educational curriculum of Indo-Germanic youth, not because humanism mattered in and of itself but because it was the primary means to understand their racial identity: what mattered was "thus not the humanist idea itself but the Nordic essence."[120] The author dramatized the seemingly rather innocuous issues at stake—the role of ancient languages in the reform of secondary-school curricula—by turning his concern for antique heritage into a weapon in defense of an Indo-Germanic essence eternally threatened by Jewish subversion, currently incarnated in the form of Bolshevism. Defense turned to offense, however, when he argued that the abandonment of Greek and Latin heritage would amount to losing the war for the race itself:

> We must realize that Germany, aware of its Indo-Germanic substance, is, at a time when the Indo-Germanic peoples are still spellbound by imperialism and liberal thought, the last determined defender of Indo-Germanicness itself. Germany is on the front lines of the war for the Indo-Germanic race. It is incumbent upon us to develop all the strength of our blood and our Nordic soul to assure the future of the Indo-Germanics, faced with an Asiatic destroyer in the form of Bolshevism, faced with racial subversion from the East in the form of the Jew, faced with spiritual uprooting by the liberalism of Western democracy. . . . The forces we see at work in Hellenism and *Romanitas* are particularly important from this point of view. Appealing to antiquity is thus nothing other than in the best interest of the racial heritage of the Indo-Germanic world.[121]

It was thus "a historical responsibility" to "preserve the Nordic strength . . . of ancient Hellas and *Romanitas*."[122]

Reservations about the role of antiquity fundamentally derived from material interests: the promotion of scholarship on German prehistory and the creation of chairs, museums, and research institutes—and the prestige that accompanied them—did not possess any intellectual value in and of themselves. From a purely intellectual perspective, Rome and Greece were far more easily included in any paean penned to the glory of the Nordic-Germanic race.

Ultimately, everyone shared an interest in Mediterranean antiquity: classicists, for their own professional reasons, and Germanists, for their ability to use it to demonstrate the intrinsic qualities of the Nordic race. For the latter, however, the reference to antiquity was a temptation to be avoided at all costs, for it showed the Germanics as nothing but pale imitations of the Greeks and Romans, a condescending stance that humiliated the German people by forcing them to swallow the fact that their historical-cultural legacy was irremediably tainted by shameful backwardness. But the converse was also true: everything began as the result of Nordic genius, hence—racial causality already having been established—the Greeks and Romans could be portrayed as incarnations of that racial genius and its virtues. Interest in the Greeks and Romans was therefore focused on highlighting their racial qualities, the antique model being essentially designed to help educate German youth.

Classicists defended themselves against the attacks of Germanophiles and prehistorians by proudly vaunting the merits of ancient history and languages for the political and ethical education of their young German pupils. If the mission of the German schools was, as Wilhelm Frick had proclaimed in his speech announcing the official instructions for the teaching of history, to "train members of the political community"[123] (the *politischer Mensch* yet again), then ancient history and languages would indeed retain a prominent role.

The introduction of German youth to the old Indo-Germanic values that had allowed Rome to build its empire could only be of benefit to the new Germany. As an article published in a journal aimed at classicists under the title "The Virtues of the Old Romans" argued:[124] "We Germans as well, we must work today toward the regeneration of values that will reshape the life of our people; we must also reinforce our faith in the highest values of Germanic-German humanity, the values of honor, loyalty, courage, that dominate our views, our thought, and our activities in all areas of life." The Thousand-Year Reich could only be built in the image and values of its glorious predecessor, the Roman Empire: "Only then will the German state, the German Reich, be able to survive for millennia."

A LATIN *QUERELLE*

In France after the defeat of 1870, "le querelle du latin" was an expression used to describe a series of debates around the place of classical literature (both Greek and Latin) in secondary-school education, both prior to and immediately after the reform of the *baccalauréat* in 1902.[125] Germany also hosted two major conferences on the future of the schools, once in 1890 and again in 1900. Both were convened by Kaiser Wilhelm II, who stood on the front lines with the modernists against the traditionalists, calling for a greater emphasis on the teaching of German as opposed to the Greco-Latin classics, in order to establish a "national standard" and "train young Germans and not young Greeks or Romans."[126] In the end, the German reform of 1901 did succeed in reducing the hours devoted to the teaching of Greek and Latin, much to the chagrin of scholars like Werner Jaeger's mentor, Ulrich von Wilamowitz-Moellendorff.

While the French and German debates of the 1890s lumped together both Latin and Greek, the debate that took place in Germany beginning in 1933 concerned Latin only, even if both Latin and Greek were ultimately linked in the eventual reforms and equally affected by the reduction in teaching hours.[127]

Walter Eberhardt, a professor at the University of Münster,[128] opened the hostilities against Latin in an accusatory 1935 article published in

Nationalsozialistische Wissenschaft, a Nazi academic journal.[129] The classical scholar agreed with the need to study the values of antiquity in order to revive them in practice, but only Greek antiquity—not Roman. While Rome had been the favorite of sixteenth-century French and Italian Renaissance humanists, Greek antiquity had been rediscovered in the eighteenth century by the Germans. This was not an accident: "They rediscovered it at a moment when, locked in combat against French classicism (which is, ultimately, Roman and Latin), they needed an ally."[130] The Germans had thus constructed their own version of antiquity, which conflicted with the Latin and Roman heritage claimed and manipulated by the French, an old nation of Gallic Romans and a legitimate heir of Roman imperialism. Interestingly, the author used the word *Kulturkampf* to describe the German struggle against French classicism, epitomized in the eighteenth century by the Sturm und Drang movement of Lessing and his peers, who refused to adopt and imitate the conventions of classical theater *à la française.* There was thus a sort of transhistorical solidarity, a common organic identity, shared by the German combatants against the three Romes: the Rome of antiquity (Arminius), the Rome of the Catholic Church (Luther and Bismarck), and the Rome of France, that is of Latinate cultural and military imperialism.

According to the author, the hostility of Rome and its imitators toward *Germanentum* was amply demonstrated by the aggression of its legions, from the "expeditions of Drusus and Tiberius to the punitive expeditions of Germanicus."[131] In a rather startling historical comparison spanning millennia, Eberhardt likened Varus's Roman legions to the Latinate hordes of French poilus in the trenches of 1914, all of them animated by the same contempt for the Germans, whom they presumed to be barbarians and treated with presumptuous arrogance: "If we move to the present, we see that it is that very same ideology of civilization that, supported by the ideas of the French Revolution, raised the banner and, 1,500 years later, began the First World War against us, the barbarians from across the Rhine."[132]

The French were worthy perpetuators of this anti-Germanic imperialism, inheriting from Rome the same contempt for imagined Teutonic savagery and the same pretensions to universal hegemony. They insisted that they were "the legitimate heirs of Latin civilization (Paris as the capital of the modern world, as Rome was of the ancient)," a pretension that "underlay all French intellectual life" and "at the same time constituted a justification of French hegemonic ambitions," which had already caused Germany so much suffering under the reigns of Louis XIV and

Napoleon, not to mention the wars of the Revolution. The Pax Romana had thus given birth to a presumed Pax Franco-Gallica; the imperialism of Rome and that of the French were each adorned with the glittering hypocrisy of a false peace.[133]

Eberhardt saw this never completely forgotten cultural and political antipathy as a sign of otherness, a fundamental racial incompatibility between *Germanentum* and *Romanitas:* "Rome as a global phenomenon is foreign to our race,"[134] and what was all too easily subsumed under the much-abused term *antiquity* was in fact not a unified and coherent entity.[135] It was important to distinguish between Rome and Greece. "Our reticence toward Rome . . . comes from the depths of our being," for "the worlds of Hellenism and *Romanitas* were two very distinct entities."[136]

Alfred Bäumler also joined in on this racially based aspersion, renouncing Rome in the name of the purity of the Nordic blood: "In Greece," at least, "we find a pure Nordic blood, which was not mixed with Etruscan or any other Oriental blood as in Rome."[137] Germany's great cultural nostalgia for Greece was dictated here by the laws of biology and racial kinship.

While the affirmation of a spiritual or racial relationship between Hellas and *Germanentum* was a constant from Winckelmann to Heidegger, the vehemence and violence of such attacks on Rome remain surprising: it is as if Rome, Latin, the French, the Enlightenment, and the church were all indiscriminately tarred with the same brush—a brush that would soon be used on Fascist Italy as well. Indeed, anti-German contempt was voiced not solely "from across the Rhine" but also from "across the Alps." The primacy of the French was now being "contested by Fascist Italy,"[138] Eberhardt noted, an interesting remark that betrays the timing of the article, written and published in 1935, when tensions with Italy were still high. Before the Italian invasion of Ethiopia soldered together the Fascist and Nazi dictatorships in the Pact of Steel that created the Axis, Italy seemed to look down upon its transalpine cousin, disparaging the Germans for their views on Austria and exploiting the crisis over the Brenner to enjoy the spotlight at Stresa in the company of the international diplomatic elite. In July 1934, Mussolini made a show of force by massing Italian troops in the Brenner Pass to intimidate Hitler and dissuade the Germans from any effort to annex Austria[139] and subvert international order; in a scathing speech,[140] Il Duce lambasted German pretensions to racial superiority, flaunting from on high Italy's two thousand years of Latin culture and civilization. After the Brenner

Pass incident, 1935 began as the year of the Stresa Front, uniting Italy, the United Kingdom, and France.

Rome—the Rome of the emperors, of the popes, of Il Duce, and of Gallo-Roman France—was thus the eternal, irredeemable home of Latin and the source of a profound and perennial hostility to the Germans and Germania. This view was symptomatic of the state of Italo-German relations in the first half of 1935. Only later, after June 1935, would an alliance with Italy begin to take shape.

TEACHING LATIN: THE VIRTUES OF THE OLD ROMANS FOR THE NEW GERMANY

The rapprochement with Fascist Italy and the constitution of the Rome-Berlin Axis in November 1936 helped ease the burden on defenders of Latin, as demonstrated by Hans Oppermann, a professor of Latin literature at the University of Freiburg and an indefatigable proponent of the teaching of classical literature in the schools and universities.[141] The author of several articles on "the educative value of Latin instruction,"[142] Oppermann responded immediately to Eberhardt in a review, choosing an appeal to authority as his best defense. In this case, the authorities were none other than Rosenberg—the editor of one of Eberhardt's pamphlets—and Hitler himself: "Rosenberg shows us a Rome of Nordic people who demonstrated exemplary obedience to their state. . . . And as the führer has said, Roman history is the best teacher of politics."[143]

The authorities themselves joined in at the ministerial level. Bernhard Rust, the Reich's minister for science and education, also defended the teaching of Latin in a January 1935 article on sport titled "Die Grundlagen der nationalsozialistischen Erziehung" (The foundations of National Socialist education). The minister drew the analogy of Latin as a sort of mental gymnastics, restating Latinists' classic argument in favor of their subject: "Sport is a prodigious means of shaping character in the system of National Socialist education. With Latin grammar, we have a prodigious instrument for shaping the intellect. With this, we can make the mind agile and strong, as though we were exercising at the gymnastics bar. We will not sacrifice this bar, but rather we will remedy the unilateral character of intellectual formation [through the rehabilitation of physical education]."[144] Despite the existence of a *querelle du latin* in specialist circles, the teaching of classical literature appeared to remain a sanctuary, protected by the education minister himself, who was, after all, an old professor of Latin at the high school level.[145] Still, a lobby made up of professors of history and ancient languages, brandishing a few choice quotes from *Mein Kampf* as their last resort, flooded his office with countless letters, a great many of which remain preserved in the minister's archives.[146]

The existence of classical literature as a field was preserved, but while instruction continued, the hours devoted to its teaching were drastically cut back and its content modified. The curricular reform, Rust's own initiative, went into effect on 29 January 1938. His decree on the "reorganization of secondary education"[147] reduced the hours allotted to Latin and Greek in order to make way for sport and physical education, following the principles Hitler had outlined as far back as *Mein Kampf*. In reducing the time devoted to teaching the classics, the reform also required a review of all course offerings: classes in Latin and Greek needed to be rethought to determine just what could and should be taught in the time allotted. Pedagogical experts decided to shift the focus of attention from the rules of grammar to the content of civilization, from philology toward a version of history heavily tinted with moralistic overtones.

In a 1938 article commenting on the Rust reform, Oppermann recognized that the new schedule did not allow for the same depth of philological study as in the past, but chose to look on the bright side, arguing that this presented a new sort of challenge for professors, who would now be called upon to initiate their disciples into the essentials of ancient civilizations.[148] Oppermann strongly defended the Rust reform to his readership of fellow educators. He condemned what they deplored as a drastic cutback in hours, but relativized the damage this caused by noting that similar reductions affected all the disciplines that had been forced to make room for sport: "Complaining about the loss of a year and a reduction in hours compared to other subjects risks missing the point . . . , that physical education is now the favorite son in all the schools." Such a reform indeed followed the National Socialists' new conception of man (*Menschenbild*), which "no longer separates body from mind dualistically but [sees] man as a single entity"—thus conforming, in the final analysis, to the spirit of antiquity itself, which might be taught differently but would be reflected in students' actual lived experience.

This spirit of antiquity could not be understood or transmitted by the systematic learning of conjugations or declensions. Tellingly, in 1938, the *Neue Jahrbücher für Antike*—a venerable review for professors of classical literature and the German journal of philological record—was renamed after 113 years of existence, becoming *Neue Jahrbücher für antike und deutsche Bildung*. The theme of "German education" was simply added to "antiquity" in the title, as if the former could possess meaning only in relation to the latter. Refounded by a historian of Greece, Helmut Berve, the review saw itself as faithful to the spirit of the Rust reform. Berve's note to readers stated it loud and clear: the time of philological and grammatical arts for arts' sake was over. Instruction in classical literature had to devote itself to the teaching of the values and works that had established ancient civilization.[149] A glance at the articles published in the review between 1938 and 1943 demonstrates the importance accorded to history over questions of language and philology: of the 122 articles published, some 70 discussed political or racial questions, and only 18 matters of strict philology.

The backlash against grammar and the teaching of languages as such seemed thus to be fully under way. What two classical literature instructors, Ludwig Mader and Walter Breywisch, called "Grammaticism" (*Grammatizismus*) in their plea to save ancient languages in the new Germany was hopelessly out of fashion. The traditional motto of Latin instruction, "Grammatica facit miracula" (Grammar works miracles),[150] no longer applied; Werner Jaeger, along with many others, sought to bury "pure grammatical formalism."[151]

Teachers of classical literature, in an effort to save what they could through professions of loyalty to Nazism, unleashed a charm offensive and, with remarkable spontaneity, offered up the old way of teaching dead languages to public vilification: instructors agreed to let go of their grammatical ballast to save the sinking ship of the field as a whole. As the minister, who since 1933 had received and read their memoranda, declared in a set of "directives for ancient languages" on 21 July 1937: "The goal [of teaching the Latin language] is not to speak Latin. . . . We must consider the language as an expression of the character and will of the Roman leaders; scholars can talk all they want about Latin as a means of communication, [but] the German schools will have nothing to do with that."[152]

To help teachers in their quest to save classical literature by making a thorough pedagogical and ideological readjustment, the league of Nazi professors (Nationalsozialistischer Lehrerbund, or NSLB) published a periodical beginning in early 1937—during the reform's final phase of drafting and debate—helpfully titled *Toward the National-Political School: Contributions toward a National Socialist Orientation in the Teaching of Ancient Languages*.[153] This effort, which had a whiff of the union sheet, with its survey of the rank-and-file and industry gossip, as well as being an informational bulletin and an academic-pedagogical journal, enlightened its readers on the proper way to teach the third declension or the appropriate reading of Cicero and Horace from the perspective of race and the German national revolution.

HORACE, POET OF WAR

If the highly politicized rereading of Plato's oeuvre and curtailing of Platonic exegesis was, as we shall see, an entirely predictable example of the new direction in the humanities, the new reading of Horace and his work was far more surprising: in Germany, the ethereal, delicate author of gallant elegies gave way to the manly poet of the people, the lyric poet of Augustan power, the resurrector of ancient cults and traditions.

Six articles—two by Hans Oppermann and four in the *Neue Jahrbücher*—promoted this evolution, the mutation of the lyric poet into the composer of odes to the *Volksgemeinschaft* and supporter of Augustan *Führertum*.[154] Oppermann gushed over "Horace, the poet of the community" and "Horace, poetry and the state."[155] The sin committed in many "erroneous judgments" on the oeuvre of the Latin poet was that of confining this "creator of sublime lyric, the great artist" to the realm of contemplative aestheticism: that is, a poet of individualism and hedonism. Countless hackneyed critics had established a "liberal and individualist" reading of his work, which had retained only a handful of sound bites—the various "odi profanum vulgus" (I hate the unholy rabble), "carpe diem" (seize the day), and "procul negotiis" (far from the madding crowd)—while depicting his work as bourgeois and mundane, or "Byzantine, polite art."[156] Certainly, the young Horace was a poet of existential questioning, but that, which originated in anguish at the limitations of the individual, had subsequently been converted into a love of community, the *Männerbund*,[157] a holistic civitas, a city reborn through the decisive action of Augustus—on whom Oppermann wrote an essay to celebrate the two-thousand-year anniversary of his birth.[158] Far from aestheticism and art for art's sake, Horace became the poet of state, race, and people, as well as of their führer Augustus, to whom Horace had pledged his life and his talents after the Battle of Actium. According to Oppermann, Horace had understood the historical and racial significance of the battle in 31 BC, which he perceived as "the decisive and final battle in a long struggle between East and West, like the liberation of the Roman nation from the threat of encirclement by the East, incarnated by Antony, Cleopatra, and their hordes of barbarian slaves, defiled by unnatural vices."[159] Such devotion to the fatherland and the emperor made Horace the political poet par excellence. The author of the *Carmen saeculare* rose from the depths of neurotic individualism and sublimated or surmounted his anguish at the limits of the self by joining his being with that of the *Volksgemeinschaft*. Death was no longer something to be feared, since civic heroes would survive in and through the group, which would make them immortal: "Dulce et decorum est pro patria mori" (It is sweet and fitting to die for one's country) was true, because "death for the community transcends all endings."[160] In the *Neue Jahrbücher*, the author of one article on "ideological questions in Horace's oeuvre" interpreted the poet's proud "non omnis moriar" (I shall not wholly die) as a wish to "die for the fatherland."[161]

The *Neue Jahrbücher* saw this as the evolution of the hedonist understood "in a Cyrenaic-Epicurean sense,"[162] which shared some traits with the Cynic and Stoic schools, toward the abnegation and "patriotic sacrifice" of a poet who became the voice of his leader and his race, the *vates romanus*[163] of civic religion.

The article concluded with "the importance of Horace's poetic legacy for the present day":

> "We see how our community and our state find themselves in the process of reconstruction, beginning from the source of their strength and racial substance. Horace allows us to see the renovation of the Roman order from the inside . . . as a similar phenomenon." One could see "the Horatian need for a rigorous state power, the moral renaissance of the people, and the tough, strict education of youth" as elements "particularly dear to our new ideal": "The poetry of Horace . . . is thus for us, and particularly for our youth, who must be introduced to it through scholastic instruction, a positive example. It is by reliving the resurrection of the Roman state, in its ideals and its successes, that we can better comprehend the imperatives of our own age."[164]

The importance of Horace as the poet of the city and the Augustan revolution was only emphasized by the reforms of 1938: the "political poetry"[165] of the Roman lyricist was made compulsory in all Latin classes.

MEMORANDA FOR REFORM

This radical restyling of the canon and its interpretations flattered the nationalist-conservative bent for the classics as a discipline, with the exception of the racist discourse that it was compelled to accommodate. It was also apparently welcomed by professors of classical literature themselves—at least by a very active minority of them, who, believing the new regime hostile to their field, strove to save the humanities by demonstrating their usefulness in the new Germany.

This is demonstrated by an interesting source in the archives of the Reich minister for education containing letters addressed to Berlin by teachers who, either on their own or in the name of their school, tried to prevent the removal of classical literature from the new curriculum by emphasizing all the benefits of regular instruction in Latin or Greek for the national-political education of German youth.

Written by teachers with strong nationalist-conservative views—or, at least, those endowed with enough literary skill to mimic the rhetoric of their new political masters—these letters defended the teaching of Latin and Greek, both Nordic languages, as an education in political virtue by example, through exposure to the heroic models and holistic ideals contained in ancient texts. These missives appealed to National Socialism's own hagiography but also provided pragmatic advice on the course schedule (*Stundenplan*) and the short program of books and themes to be studied:[166] the potential victims of the curricular reform offered their counsel to their prince, suggesting their own ready-made reforms in addition to restating their own indubitable utility.

Such letters frequently insisted on the "relationship of race and space," that *Rassenverbundenheit* that linked Greeks, Romans, and Germans and thus made texts written on Mediterranean shores some 2,500 years earlier immediately familiar, legible, and comprehensible to German youth: "The works of antiquity are the authentic racial expressions of the same spirit . . . ; cultural creations based on their fundamental racial identity."[167] If race legitimized the study of the classics, it followed that there should be some criteria by which classical literature, philosophy, and history were selected for use in class: "Only a racially pure Hellenism and *Romanitas,* in which Nordic blood still clearly circulates, have a place in the schools today."[168] Another memo argued that "the literature of a period of degeneracy must no longer be included, except for rare examples, and then only on the margins."[169]

A meticulous process of selection was thus needed, to distinguish between that which was most purely Nordic and that which was the expression of racial decadence: "Writers who wrote in Greek or Latin but were not of the Greek or Roman race must disappear, since they themselves were foreigners or of mixed blood [*Mischblut*]."[170]

Purity of blood was the only guarantee of an education in the model of the original, undiluted spirit of the race. Bastards and half-breeds could produce only a pernicious, morally decadent literature, to match their biological degeneracy. At most, such types could serve only as examples to illustrate the decadence of the race: "Greeks and Romans who were intellectually sick must also be tossed out, as living proof of the racial degeneracy of their blood community. One might use them strictly as dissuasive countertypes."[171]

The criterion of racial purity thus strictly delimited the appropriate time period for young students. For Latin, "the literature that interests us belongs to the era that stretches from around 100 BC to around 100 AD."[172] Authors of pure Nordic blood were to be particularly emphasized, such as, for example, a "poet as rooted in his race as Virgil."[173] A memo from Mecklenburg used the same phrase to explain the importance of such rooting: "The poet rooted in his race incarnates the most noble, the racially highest and most fully developed values present in his people. He represents them in the purest form and encourages his most intimate companions as a model."[174] Their common Nordic roots formed the basis of all interest in Greek and Latin, which would serve as a catalyst for the development of the younger generation's racial consciousness and increase their awareness of their Indo-Germanicness through exposure to ancient texts: "Knowing that Greco-Roman civilization was the product of the Nordic race gives the teaching of ancient languages a new definition and can help to awaken and later reinforce the consciousness that the young possess of their race."[175]

If, in essence, "the German race finds itself at the center of the German schools," if the mission of those schools was to sound "the depths of the essence of our people," then the "creative forces of antiquity" helped to accomplish this, since "these creative forces were ultimately nothing other than the force of the race, that is the Nordic race, which long ago gave birth to these two ancient peoples and which constitutes the heart of our own people."[176]

The awakening of their racial consciousness would allow German youth to join the community of blood, which would provide them with a legitimate source of pride. This rooting in their racial group was also an admission into the body politic. Greeks and Romans having both been deeply political peoples, reading their texts and immersing oneself in their civic culture was a way of forming the *politischer Mensch:* "The Greeks and Romans are closer to us today than ever before. The man of antiquity, the Greek, was in essence a self-consciously political soldier; the new Germany also trains and requires the political man (the Reich interior minister, Dr. Frick, declared before the conference of education ministers on 9 May 1933: 'The German school educates the political man')." There was no better way to educate the political man than to introduce the young to the civic thought of the ancients:

> How better to nourish the minds of our youth, how better to make these young people conscious members of our community of people than by offering them these unique monuments to the political spirit of antiquity? Just as the Greeks and Romans of the classical era were communal beings, working with their texts will allow us to better integrate the individual into the community, in the community of the state and the people, which today is more important than ever.[177]

From this point of view, turning to antiquity was a tool that would allow German youth to better understand and be aware of their belonging to a state, a people, a racial community: "The goal of all German education is the German man as a member of the *Volksgemeinschaft*. The culture of antiquity is, for the student of humanities in high school, a springboard toward a real, living consciousness of his belonging to a people."[178]

THE 1938 CURRICULA AND THE TEACHING OF CLASSICAL LITERATURE

The reform's statement of its rationale exposed the goals and principles of the new teaching of ancient languages. This teaching was supposed to elucidate all that was "Nordic-Hellenic" and "Nordic-Roman" in the ancient civilizations of the Mediterranean: "Thus we will shape ... not young Greeks or young Romans, but rather we will purify and reinforce the Nordic character of young Germans, by broadening their historical horizons through the culture of the two Nordic peoples that shaped the face of Europe." Traditional German sentiments regarding their affinity for Greek culture were confirmed by "the knowledge that we now possess of our common Nordic origin."[179]

The Latin program specifically named which certain classical texts or passages were to be made obligatory, primarily those of historians or first-person narratives with a political or moral bent: among those included on the list were Caesar's *The Gallic Wars*,[180] Livy's *The History of Rome*,[181] Suetonius's *Live of the Twelve Caesars,* and the works of Cato. The program also outlined a suggested approach to each work for instructors. Sallust's *The War with Jugurtha* and Cicero's *Catiline Orations* each showed how "the forces of decomposition of the empire and the dangers run by the people were visible, as were the appeal to a savior and the racial strength that remained in the era of the old Rome."[182] As for Cicero, he was recommended less for his philosophical banter or virtuous plaints than for his *Republic*—in German titled *Der Staat*—which was considered "indispensable" for "its national-political orientation on the reading of Latin," since it showed "the end of the *libera res publica* and the transition toward the principate," which Augustus vigorously seized from a dying regime.[183]

The seventh grade would focus at length on Augustus, to whom an entire semester would be dedicated, through the writings of Virgil—particularly the famous sixth book of the *Aeneid*, which obsequiously flattered the founder of the empire—as well as the "political poetry" of Horace.

The program made one concession to the Germanophiles, dictating that "the reading of Latin is capped off by the description of Germania provided by Caesar and Tacitus"[184] in the middle of the eighth grade.

In Greek, the *Anabasis* of Xenophon was deemed particularly appropriate for the "national-political education" of young pupils. The reading of his *Hellenica* was to focus closely on the heroic figure of Alcibiades, the defeat of Athens, and the success of the Spartan model in the Greek world of the end of the fifth century BC. Herodotus would be used to illustrate "the Greek fight for freedom"; the episode of "Solon and Croesus,"[185] to exemplify the racial, cultural, and ethical contrast between East and West. In addition to the epic, with Homer, and the Athenian tragedies, the program made compulsory the reading of Plato's *Republic* and his *Seventh Letter*.[186]

FROM GERMAN PHILHELLENISM TO GRECO-GERMAN RACIAL KINSHIP

The Helleno-German special relationship was a constant theme of the Nazi period and was proudly reaffirmed in a variety of ways, most visibly, perhaps, in the 1936 Berlin Olympics.

But the notion of a unique cultural proximity—whether spiritual or racial—between Germany and Greece was much older. The Aryan myth that had been adopted as the founding principle of German identity in the nineteenth century established a kinship, subsequently determined to be parentage, between the Indo-Germanic racial stock and the civilizations of antiquity, believed to have all come from the same Nordic roots. But among the many varied Indo-Germanic peoples, it was the Greeks who were closest to the heart of the contemporary German nation. In the European great game to find the source of national identities in the heritage of ancient civilizations, Rome had already been claimed by Italy and, even worse, the haughty France of Louis XIV, the Revolution, and the Napoleonic Empire. From the devastation of the Palatinate (1689) through the War of the League of Augsburg (1688–97) and up to the Confederation of the Rhine (1806–13), French threats to German soil all pursued the same imperial ambitions as the Roman legions turned back by Arminius at the Battle of Teutoburg Forest (9 CE). For the Germany of the *Befreiungskriege,* or "wars of liberation," at the dawn of the nineteenth century, Rome was synonymous with Napoleon, whose political and artistic neoclassicism usurped the place of revolutionary Sparta and its austere virtue.

Roman imperialism, identified with French territorial aggression, was not just military but also cultural. Before the conquests of the Revolution and the empire, an entire generation of German artists rose up in defiance of French classicism, from Lessing to the young preromantics of the Sturm und Drang movement.

Going further back in time, another source of German antipathy toward Rome could be traced to the sixteenth century and the Protestant schism led by Martin Luther, who fought against a greedy, parsimonious Rome symbolized by the sale of indulgences, which he virulently depicted as a satanic Babylon: just as in biblical times, the people of God would have to shake off the papal yoke imposed by the Roman Antichrist, a modern Nebuchadnezzar. This denunciation of Latin imperialism, which drew largely upon ancient sources, also contained political implications, illustrated by the quarrel over investitures between the pope and the emperor—a battle between men of the cloth and the crown that Bismarck cleverly echoed in the Kulturkampf (1871–78) when he declared that he would not go to Canossa.

The idea of Rome was thus historically charged with negativity. An appendage of Gallic-Latin France, imperialist and classicist, Rome held no positive connotations in Germany. To German eyes, France and its culture were Roman—as the German language demonstrated, designating the study of French language and literature with the word *Romanistik.*

The Germans thus chose to be related to the Greeks. The adoption of Greece and the glorification of the Helleno-Germanic relationship would counteract and nullify the claims to prestige and universality of the French cultural and political project.

Nineteenth-century Germans took as their starting point the works of Johann Joachim Winckelmann (1717–68), particularly his *Geschichte der Kunst des Altertums* (*The History of Ancient Art,* 1764), which formed their passageway to ancient Greece. For Winckelmann, interest in Greek art obeyed a logic of "constant regression toward the archaic" and was a "quest for the primordial": "Interest in Greece, for Winckelmann, took the form of an obsessive quest for origins."[187] His readers shared this quest, which was transposed epistemologically to the cultural and political realm by a German public seeking an identity and thus searching for origins and archetypes. In art, as in all other spheres of human expression, Winckelmann endowed Greece with a "maternal dignity"[188] that made everything Greek both source (*Quelle*) and model (*Urbild*): chronology became confused with axiology, and the fact that the Greeks came first became a sign of their sacrality and normative superiority. After the Greeks, there could be nothing but clumsy or pale imitations, whose faults were measured in contrast to the perfection of Greek genius.

Winckelmann's glorification of the primordial Greek was a rarity in the eighteenth century, when most eyes turned to Rome following the discovery of the exceptionally well-preserved sites of Pompeii and Herculaneum (1709). The educated Europe of the Enlightenment did not appear to pay much attention to Greece as such; at least, it did not enjoy close academic or scholarly attention. Rather, it was subsumed under the general term "antiquities," a broader category that, as in the French *Dictionnaire de Trévoux* of 1752, encapsulated everything from China to Rome. Greece was simply one part of a much wider time and place called antiquity. Only Winckelmann's work, and the sheer force of his argument, conferred upon it a degree of singular respect.

The German literary class thus claimed to have rediscovered Greece and to possess a special ability to understand it. Only a German could exhume poor ignored and misunderstood Greece—or, as Wilhelm von Humboldt put it, in a letter to Goethe: "We Germans don't understand very clearly just how distinguished we are, to be so closely related to Homer and Sophocles."[189]

Cultivated elites in Goethe's Germany were absolutely smitten with the Hellenes. The humanism of the *Deutsche Klassik* found its model in the physical perfection of man as represented in Greek art. Beginning with Prometheus, "sui ipsius plastes et fictor,"[190] Greek art was an appeal to human perfectibility, celebrating the autonomous, self-made man, which Goethe commemorated in his famous poem.[191]

The greatest representatives of Weimar classicism—Goethe and Schiller, Novalis and Hölderlin, the Schlegel brothers—all found common ground in the cult of worship of Greece and defended the idea of an elective affinity or συμπαθεια between the Greek and the German spirit.[192] "Noch lebt, noch waltet, der Athener / Seele, die sinnende, still bei Menschen," Hölderlin wrote—"The soul of Athens still lives, still prevails, / pensive, peaceful in men"[193]—*Menschen* in this case surely referring to the German people. The German educated elite celebrated the perfection of the Greeks and the kinship between Germans and Hellenes to create a national identity that would soothe the humiliation inflicted upon them by that French Caesar, Napoleon. In this regard, "faith in Hellenism is ultimately nothing but a metaphor . . . for faith in *Germanentum.*"[194]

Greek perfection illuminated a path to follow in the construction of German identity. One phrase in Winckelmann's *Gedanken über die Nachahmung der griechischen Werke in der Malerei und Bildhauerkunst* (*Reflections on the Painting and Sculpture of the Greeks*) held particular resonance for a Germany at war with France: "There is but one way for the moderns to become great, and perhaps unequalled; I mean, by imitating the an[c]ients."[195] According to the literary historian Walther Rehm, who published his study *Griechentum und Goethezeit* (The century of Goethe and Greece) in Dresden in 1936, "the memory of Greece was, in Goethe's era, nothing other than an introduction to a possible Germanic humanism. When they spoke of the Greeks, in reality they thought of the Germans."[196]

With the Greeks, Germany found the cornerstone of its own identity, in polar opposition to Romanized France. Rehm told the story of how, during their meeting at Erfurt in 1808, Napoleon asked Goethe to write a tragedy about Caesar—an implicit request for a bit of personal propaganda. Goethe, like any good lover of Greece, refused the Romanesque Napoleon's proposal.[197]

The affirmation of Helleno-Germanic kinship and the glorification of Greek genius continued unabated in Germany throughout the nineteenth century. As one contemporary of the Third Reich, Eliza Butler, a British specialist in German literature, wrote in her detailed 1935 examination of the subject, *The Tyranny of Greece over Germany,* "Germany is the supreme example of [Greece's] triumphant spiritual tyranny."[198] For Butler, the essence of the German spirit was rooted in an incorrigible idealism, "a hopeless passion for the absolute."[199] This quest for the absolute had been appeased by Christian myths and symbols until Luther "destroyed the mythological element of Christianity"[200] by advocating the intellectualization of faith through the reading and personal contemplation of scripture. The subsequent search for a usable myth invested itself in the reclamation of the Nordic heritage and the rediscovery of Greece. The Germans made the Greeks "an absolute standard of perfection, solemn, statuesque, and unreal; ... and the prayer 'give us a mythology' was uttered by more than one as they looked with dazzled eyes at [these] mysteriously impressive beings."[201]

While we might rightly look skeptically upon such a reductive dismissal of all German culture to a fatally flawed idealism, the idea that modern Germany suffered from a mythological vacuum is a seductive one: the pursuit of national identity was enveloped by a quest for physical and poetic self-representation that the Germans sought in Greek and Nordic sources. The absolute perfection of the Greek archetype made it a permanently distant and unapproachable ideal, as Rehm noted, citing Hölderlin—"Gehöret habe ich / von Elis und Olympia" ("Of Elis and / Olympia I have heard")[202]—the poet carefully avoiding all direct contact, since "reality and the ideal must remain distinct, just as the legend, the dream of Greece remains serene."[203] In fact, neither Goethe nor Winckelmann before him nor any of the philhellenists in German literary circles of the time had ever visited Greece.[204] Doing so "threatened to shatter their own myths"[205] and provoke a "postmortem shock."[206] Greece became the hidden God of the new faith for the German man in the age of Goethe and his followers.[207]

This fascination with Greece was not a passing trend. Eliza Butler could thus rightly push her study all the way up to include Stefan George and his circle,[208] which imitated the literary schools of the Italian Renaissance and attempted to revive antiquity not only by penning eclogues but also by performing costumed rituals; George himself, for instance, dressed up as Caesar to canonize a young boy who died prematurely, as if to resuscitate Hadrian and his attempt to deify Antinous.

The German obsession with Greece appears not only in literature but also in architecture, history, and philosophy, as evidenced by the abundant historiography on German philhellenism.[209] After the Winckelmann revolution, German architecture adopted a neoclassical style obviously inspired by the Greeks. Klenze, Gilly, Schinckel, and their ilk plastered Munich and Berlin with neo-Grec edifices.

German historians of the nineteenth century virtually founded the scholarly historiography on antiquity, faithful to a tradition of philological excellence dating back to the German humanists, thus multiplying the analogies between ancient Greece and contemporary Germany. One need look no further than Wilhelm von Humboldt, and his *Geschichte des*

Verfalls und Untergangs der griechischen Freistaaten (History of the decline and fall of the Greek republics; begun in 1808 but unfinished), or Johann Gustav Droysen, who in his biography of Alexander the Great (1833) established clear parallels between Prussia and Macedonia, Greece and Germany, Europe and Asia. The unification of Germany and its conquest of Europe would occur under the thumb of a new Prussian Alexander. Philosophers, for their part, followed Jacob Burckhardt and Friedrich Nietzsche, who also genuflected at the altar of Greece.

The Germans' literary, architectural, and philosophic obsession with their Greek lineage was also encouraged by the political events taking place on the Balkan Peninsula in the nineteenth century.

The Greek war of independence from the Ottoman Empire (1822–30) became a very popular cause in the Europe of the romantic era, creating a politicized philhellenism that, in Germany, reinforced the preexisting artistic variant. While Byron died at Missolonghi (1824), Delacroix painted *The Massacre at Chios,* and Hugo composed his collection of poems *Les Orientales,* German princes maneuvered to set one of their own on the new throne with the support of the great powers (France, the United Kingdom, and Russia). This was the young prince Otto of Wittelsbach, who in 1831 would become the first king of Greece under the appropriately Germanic name Otto I.

The first ruling dynast of a free Greece, liberated from Turkish tyranny, was thus Bavarian; his successor, a Danish prince, would take a Prussian queen (the sister of Wilhelm II).[210] The Germans enjoyed an unusual degree of privileged political access in Greece as a result of their entrenchment with the royals. This could help explain the strong influence of the German scholarly community in Greece, particularly among archaeologists:[211] as the Reich's leaders and the Nazi press never tired of repeating at the Berlin games of 1936, it was German archaeologists who had uncovered the ruins of Olympus.

In 1939, the historian Hans Bogner wrote a brief volume in the series Publications of the Reich Institute for the History of the New Germany, titled *Der Seelenbegriff der griechischen Frühzeit* (The concept of the soul in early Greece). This brief tome, as we have already seen, promoted the idea that an understanding of the Greek soul offered the potential to unlock the secrets of the German soul by exploring that of its earliest ancestors: "This racial kinship . . . gives us hope that we might, despite all our differences, grasp the fundamental features of our primordial stock, from which we have become estranged by foreign infiltration and which is now inaccessible to us without the assistance of the Greek."[212] This racial identity, as defined by Hitler himself and fleshed out by historians, was logically accompanied by a spiritual identity, a proximity of the Greek and the German in soul, culture, and mind. By the 1930s, it was clear that the latter had descended from the former and that German philhellenism was a matter of their common racial origin. The sympathy of German intellectuals for ancient Greece, that elective spiritual affinity, could be traced back to their racial community. As Ludwig Schemann put it, "Lessing, Herder, Goethe, Schiller, Hölderlin, and finally Richard Wagner" had all "seen and recognized in the Hellenic Aryan an ancestral reflection of themselves."[213]

MARTIN HEIDEGGER AND THE RETURN TO GREEK METAPHYSICS

Among the greatest of the German philhellenists was Martin Heidegger, whose political engagement with the NSDAP—he became a member of the party in May 1933, before assuming the rectorate at the University of Freiburg—was symbolic of the rediscovery of Greek thought.

For Heidegger, the rehabilitation of the pre-Socratics was not solely a labor of scholarly craftsmanship. Beginning with his inaugural address, Heidegger dedicated his rectorate to reemphasizing the importance of Hellenism, because he believed the return to Greek philosophy to be an important omen for the future of Germany and the West.

Heidegger proposed a rereading of the history of Western thought in terms of de-cadence, the fall into decline of the very question of Being, which he called *Verfallen* ("fallenness" or "falling away"): the philosophy of Being had ceded its position of importance to questions of worldly existence.

The proper distinction between the ontological (Being) and the ontic (being) held for Heidegger a historial significance—that is, one that was not merely historical (*geschichtlich*) but also anticipatory (*geschicklich*), holding the key to the destiny (*Geschick* or *Schicksal*) of the West. The question of being was not simply a matter of language or etymology. At stake was nothing less than the future of Western civilization, which could either persist in forgetting its Being, with all the attendant consequences—that is, the destruction of the earth through the mechanistic, commercial logic of material existence—or return to the primordial questions of Greek ontology. In 1935, Heidegger distinguished Europe, where such philosophical thought was still possible, from both the Soviet Union and the United States:

> This Europe, in its unholy blindness always on the point of cutting its own throat, lies today in the great pincers between Russia on one side and America on the other. Russia and America, seen metaphysically, are both the same: the same hopeless frenzy of unchained technology and of the rootless organization of the average man.[214]

One finds in these words an echo of that siege mentality peculiar to the Germans, whose geographical position at the very heart of Europe left them vulnerable to any continental upheaval or outbreak of hostilities,[215] as the devastating impact of the Thirty Years' War had amply demonstrated.

The fate of European philosophy was thus linked to the political fate of the West, which, if it could only manage to think ontologically, might still save itself from the destruction that otherwise awaited it.

Amid the explosion of mechanization and technocratic thinking that pervaded the modern world, Heidegger proposed the following alternative to the German people: either drown in the frenzy of technology dominating contemporary life and participate in the "spiritual decline of the earth"[216] or return to the primordial philosophy of Being, beginning from its inception, with the first questions and fresh-eyed morning clarity of Greek thought.

In the first case, submitting to the vision of America and Bolshevik Russia would contribute to "the darkening of the world, the flight of the gods, the destruction of the earth, the reduction of human beings to a mass, the hatred and mistrust of everything creative and free."[217] In the second, the German people would undertake an "other inception."[218] This inception would not be the mere repetition of the past; to the contrary:

> An inception is not repeated when one shrinks back to it as something that was, something that by now is familiar and is simply to be imitated, but rather when the inception is begun again *more originally*, and with all the strangeness, darkness, insecurity that a genuine inception brings with it.[219]

Heidegger viewed the arrival of the Nazis in power as a potential "historial" rupture with technological modernity, offering the possibility of a return to the primordiality of Greek thought. It would be a matter of rediscovering the Greek essence of the German being, in order to break with the erroneous scientific and technical logic that had dominated modern philosophy. Assuming the rectorate of the University of Freiburg, where he was a professor, was his contribution to that return to Greek metaphysics. The historical mission of the German people and their universities, which educated the nation's elite, was to encourage the West to rethink its own origins. "This means nothing less than to *repeat and retrieve* the inception of our historical-spiritual Dasein,"[220] the aura of European humanity that gave birth to Greek thought.

This inception was fundamental and neither obsolete nor outdated. It was permanent and enduring, continually available to us if we made the decision to revive it, as Heidegger asserted in his rectoral address of 27 May 1933: "The beginning still *is*. It does not lie *behind us*, as something that was long ago, but stands *before* us."[221]

Heidegger intended his rectoral address to be a lucid, programmatic introduction to political practice. He emphasized that the historical mission of the German people would not come to fruition unless Germans engaged in three types of service on behalf of people and state: alongside the labor service, or *Arbeitdienst,* and the military defense service, the *Wehrdienst*—both borrowed from Nazi party rhetoric— Heidegger added the knowledge service, or *Wissensdienst*. His trinity echoed the tripartite hierarchy described by Plato in *The Republic,* where each citizen was called upon to fulfill the civic and political duty of his class, an ideal society that reflected the three parts of the human soul. The Platonic inspiration was so obvious that Heidegger, following the fashion of the times,[222] opened his speech with a quote from Plato.

In 1933, the rectoral address thus depicted a historic possibility to rethink and relive the inception of Greek philosophy, brought about by the still inchoate national revolution initiated by Nazism, and to renew a philosophic tradition buried by twenty-five centuries of neglect of Being. Reliving the Greek inception required its authentic rediscovery through philosophical, political, and civic conversion, which Heidegger sought as rector to instill in various ways: the introduction of the *Führerprinzip* in the universities, compulsory participation in the *Wehrsport,* and even the organization of a "scholarship camp"—a "mixture of scout camp and Platonic academy"[223]—at Todtnauberg from 4 to 10 October 1933, where students divided their time between sport and philosophical meditation, just as in the Greek schools of old (themselves modeled, of course, on Plato's Academy).

Heidegger very quickly became aware that he had been misled. He resigned his position as rector less than a year after his appointment, in February 1934, and distanced himself from a regime that he would subsequently criticize cogently and vigorously in his lectures, perhaps most notably in a 1937 seminar titled "The Threat to Science." Certainly, with regard to the crimes committed under Nazism, it might seem pathetic or absurd that he criticized them in but one respect—their mechanization, a symbol of their blindness to authentic Being. But for Heidegger that was the essential point.

Far from having contributed to a renaissance of metaphysics, National Socialist power had resolutely hurled Germany into a further mechanization of being, imitating Bolshevik Russia and the United States of the New Deal. Nazi Germany had even created its own plan for industrialization.[224]

Germany seemed to have renounced the "transcendence of metaphysics" that had been his ambition as rector and that Heidegger, reflecting bitterly, summed up thus: "Completely misfiring, the effort to put the German university in shape for this task; it might have been possible in the last few years, if there had been sufficient will. For the decades to come, all is lost at sea."[225]

With the unfettered domination of technology and modern science, aggravated by Nazi Germany's efforts at rearmament, philosophy—and the hard work of intellectual contemplation—was dismissed. Knowledge was no longer legitimate unless it was immediately useful to the *Volksgemeinschaft* and to the state. The party only called upon specialists it could reliably employ for concrete ends, not pure thinkers: there was "a rush, on all sides, in the direction of specialized schools. . . . What is needed now . . . are more specialists!"[226]

The specialized knowledge privileged by the regime was technical, practical, immediately actionable and usable, and thus independent of the need for any contemplation or the unbiased freedom required for abstract thought. National Socialism mistakenly thought only in terms of worldly being, and the horizons of its worldly being were limited to one thing: war.

All the sciences, not just physics or math, were judged according to their potential utility. Heidegger objected to the complicity displayed by the sciences, which were valued only for their usefulness and their usage in a vast enterprise of intellectual indoctrination. Archaeologists, philologists, historians, biologists, geographers were all engaged in the retrospective validation of ideological dogma, while mathematicians, physicists, and chemists were put to work developing weapons, ersatz goods, or fuel. Heidegger painted a somber portrait of the state of the German university: "The university . . . is without a mission, without standards, without goals. . . . Hence its eagerness to assume new tasks: geopolitical studies, the environment, etc.; autonomy in supply, armaments. Everything that can be put into the service of the world view: races, prehistory, military science. Once again there are things it can do. . . . Science, however, has been crushed in the grip of this new reality. . . . The university as an institution offers one of the saddest spectacles to be seen, . . . the forgetting of being and the destruction of truth."[227]

The crowning indignity in this canonization of science and technology was the replacement of philosophy with ideology. Heidegger virulently denounced "this tired flood of words, that speaks only of the weltanschauung," and deplored that "the temptation to externalize, to no longer think, to no longer wish to think or question, becomes ever stronger."[228]

In universities across the country, professors of philosophy were being replaced by Nazi party ideologues given free reign to use their new pulpit to spread the good word of "the popular verbiage of the weltanschauung":

> Cutting the number of chairs, eliminating positions belonging to scholars whose subject is philosophy, that is not the real damage. . . . But wanting to decide what constitutes philosophy itself, that is what is ridiculous. Philosophy cannot be suppressed with the swipe of a pen, much less defined by administrative measures, because it is not among the type of things that one can "organize," and thus one cannot expect to organize its disappearance.[229]

The historicizing duty of the German people had been betrayed. Germany had elected not to fulfill its role as savior and had thus condemned itself by refusing to realize its own essence: "The Germans and the suppression of philosophy—with the goal of acquiring a people's true manner of being!—from the point of view of world history, it is a suicide."[230]

Nazism turned out to be even more modernist and mechanized than either American capitalism or Soviet Bolshevism. The Nazism of the Four-Year Plan and the march to war aimed to create a thoroughly technological man, capable of surviving and dominating only within modernity, a mankind remade in the image of technological modernity: "The mechanistic calculation of every action and planning in its most absolute form demands a new humanity that goes beyond anything that man has been until now."[231]

The blitzkrieg and its debauched spreading of mechanical technicity were a far cry from both the reaction against technological modernity and the inception of Greek thought. Heidegger came to understand that the historicizing reality of Nazism did not lie in a return to the beginning, but rather that the Reich was the entelechy of the modern technical mentality, the fullest expression of modern technicism.[232] The relationship that the Nazis claimed to have with the Greeks was, from the beginning, inauthentic and purely superficial, nothing more than window dressing.

NAZI GREECE: SPECTACLE AND INAUTHENTICITY

In *Basic Concepts,* a series of lectures published in 1941, Heidegger showed himself to be a harsh critic of an inauthentic appropriation of antiquity that was nothing more than sterile imitation. Under Nazism, reverence for and reference to the Hellenes seemed to be an obligatory part of public discourse but one that lacked a full appreciation of their originality:

> The whole world talks about the extraordinary "cultural" significance of the ancient Greeks. But no one who speaks like this has the slightest knowledge that, and how, an inception occurs there.[233]

Heidegger deplored how antiquity was being turned into a political weapon by a servile historiography that sought "to 'paint' over the old and the bygone with the gloss of the respective present, and so to justify historiographical activity itself as indispensable."[234]

Commemorative one-upmanship and flowery, purely decorative rhetoric were simply convenient alibis to avoid any serious, authentic examination of the Greek past: "Love of antiquity is then a pretext for striving to evade every decisive reflection." Spectacular displays of commemoration were no substitute for authentic remembrance. The desire to relive the ancient past required a historicizing awareness that engaged both current thought and civilization's future: "The measure of whether remembrance of the inception is genuine can never be determined from an interest in reviving classical antiquity, but only from a resolve to attain an essential knowing that holds for what is to come."[235]

Should this be read as a criticism of the Nazi regime, which surrounded itself with the trappings of antiquity, draped not in Roman costume (as Marx claimed of the French Revolution) but in the panoply of the hoplites? Undoubtedly. Heidegger was offended by the Nazis' distasteful mania for associating the Greeks with the Germans to force home the idea of a kinship between the two peoples: "One renders no service to the knowledge and estimation of the historical unicity of National Socialism by interpreting the Greek phenomenon in such a way that one could believe that the Greeks were already all National Socialists."[236] The misleading conflation of Greeks and Nazis avoided the issue of National Socialism's historical singularity. Far from reiterating the party line, Heidegger was actually spurred to further reflection.

One can easily see in his writings between 1937 and 1942 how Heidegger distanced himself from Nazism, which he criticized for its unabashed Cartesianism and inauthentic relationship with the inception. Narrowing one's focus to include only his writings from 1933 to 1935[237] leads to a fundamental misunderstanding of Heidegger's relationship to Nazism—which was opportunistic at times, certainly, but grounded in a coherent logic that, while perhaps deplorable, cannot be simply dismissed. In 1949, he would define the Nazis' most egregious crime, the Holocaust, as the epitome of technological modernity. After the war, Heidegger clearly viewed Nazism as the fullest expression of the logic of technology. His only public remarks to reference the Shoah, which were inexcusably cavalier, made but a fleeting reference to the six million dead:

> Agriculture is now a motorized food industry—in essence the same as the manufacture of corpses in the gas chambers and extermination camps, the same as the blockading and starving of nations, the same as the manufacture of hydrogen bombs.[238]

The industrialized extermination of the Jews and Gypsies in the name of the race thus did seem to be perfectly comprehensible to the philosopher, at least in one way: as a symptomatic instance of the planetary domination of technology, the exaggeration of a logos turned *ratio*—reason turned into objectifying calculation—that sees only inanimate objects offered up for manipulation by man's labor. That labor being the reduction of the human to a mere object in the death factories, prior to the destruction of the earth.

For Heidegger, Nazism had truly seemed to represent a historic opportunity to promote a decisive reaction against mathematical-technical modernity. The Nazi movement itself, with its ambiguous relationship to modernity, seemed to possess the will to react. When Heidegger, in his 1935 *Introduction to Metaphysics*, celebrated "the inner truth and greatness of this movement," he was thinking of the National Socialist movement, which had already transformed Germany in just two years, but also of the Nazi Party itself—the word *Bewegung*, or "movement," being used throughout the text to describe the NSDAP. The phrase referring to National Socialism was never removed from any of the postwar editions of the book. Heidegger thus seemed to demonstrate that he assumed full responsibility for his past engagement with the Nazis, whom he had entrusted with his hopes for a spiritual change in Germany.[239] Nazism had offered a historic occasion to bring about a philosophical revolution in favor of an antimodernist reaction, but the protagonists of the *Bewegung* did not demonstrate themselves to be up to their historically appointed task.

The only regret Heidegger would ever admit to would be his error in judgment regarding the Nazis' historial potential, which was not as great as the "greatness of the movement" demanded. Heidegger would later, in private, speak of his *grösste Dummheit*—his "most incredible stupidity."[240]

Heidegger, who resigned from his post as rector in 1934, would slowly but surely become ever more aware of the Nazis' unsuitability to lead the return to the primordial Greek inception that he hoped for. His writings portray the gradual estrangement of the philosopher from a state and its representatives that were ultimately, from intellectual laziness or sheer stupidity, not up to the task of their self-appointed historical mission. Heidegger's *grösste Dummheit* was his having placed his trust in such vulgar thugs, not his having believed in Nazism's historical mission. Thus the philosopher reiterated in an interview with the German newsmagazine *Der Spiegel* in 1966:

> I see the task of thought precisely in this, that within its own limits it helps man as such achieve a satisfactory relationship to the essence of technicity. National Socialism did indeed go in this direction. Those people, however, were far too poorly equipped for thought to arrive at a really explicit relationship to what is happening today and has been underway for the past 300 years.[241]

CONCLUSION

The National Socialist seizure of power raised the hopes and expectations of radical, die-hard Germanophiles: prehistorians of *Germanentum* and proponents of runic Futhark hoped that the establishment of a deeply ethnocentric and exclusionary ideology like Nazi racism would have positive repercussions on the curricula in the schools and universities. The purification of the race through rigorous selection, the removal of foreigners, and the preservation of existing heritage would be accompanied, on a cultural level, by the rethinking of those subjects that were indispensable for the formation of the new German man: everything extrinsic to his race would have to be discarded. Greek, Latin, and the study of Mediterranean antiquity had no place, according to the

Germanophiles, in this new scholastic order. The advent of National Socialism would finally bring about the coronation of Germanic studies, putting an end to the "tyranny of Greece over Germany" and that of the classics in the German university: chairs and appointments of all kinds would henceforth fall to the followers of Gustav Kossina.

Classicists and historians of antiquity reacted quickly and energetically. Everyone acknowledged and deplored the errors of the past: too much grammar, abstraction, soft humanism, intellectualism ... The teaching of classical literature and ancient history had been bloated by the universalizing heritage of the Enlightenment and *Weimarer Klassik*, schools that held the study of antiquity to be the type of arduous intellectual exercise that revealed the universality of reason common to all men.

Against this dangerous vision of antiquity, which surely justified its own exclusion from a proper National Socialist education, professors of ancient history and classical literature defended the plurimillennial *Volksgemeinschaft* that linked Germans, Greeks, and Romans. The peoples of antiquity, who had come from the North, were quite conscious of the standards of their race. If they were humanists, it was because their definition of "humanity" was strictly limited to the Greeks and Romans, in opposition to the sea of subhuman peoples surrounding them, whether Persian, Scythian, Phoenician, or Jewish. National Socialist racism could thus indeed draw inspiration from ancient humanism—if it was properly understood.

Classical literature and ancient history also demonstrated a way to reconcile body and mind: whereas later, decadent humanism, corrupted with Christian principles, sought to divide man's body and soul, National Socialism, by rehabilitating the cult of the body through physical education, rediscovered the ancient notion of their harmonious union, the foundation for a man reconciled with himself. Men shaped along the intellectual and physical lines of the ancient Greek would be good citizens and good leaders; the defenders of antiquity recalled that the ancient man was nothing if he was not a citizen and that the virtues of self-denial, of devotion, of sacrifice for the polity were all traits of ancient leaders, themselves the products of an unabashed elitism. Here too the new Germany had everything to gain from exposing both its subjects and its elites to the wisdom of the ancients: the Napola, according to the SS inspector general, should imitate the Greek model.

The defenders of antiquity could count on one very important ally: Hitler himself. Citing passages from *Mein Kampf* on Rome and Greece became an obligatory exercise for those pleading to save the classics in the schools: if, as Hitler had written, the German gymnasium was a shameful caricature of the Greek paradigm, surely it was not by eliminating Greek and Latin that this disgraceful situation would be best remedied.

In a traditionally philhellenic Germany, the teaching of Latin found itself in a particularly precarious position. Latin evoked thoughts of Rome, the Caesars, the pontificate—and of France, the Revolution, and the empire. Even worse, the identity of the Romans remained suspect from a racial point of view. Rome could not flaunt the immaculate racial pedigree of the Hellenes; it had experienced miscegenation far too early in its history. To elide such dangerous arguments, the defenders of Latin invoked a wide range of Roman stereotypes: *mos maiorum, fides romana,* the virtue of the Quirites—no cliché was spared the reader of articles and memos by the classicist lobby, which also never missed an opportunity to cite the benefits of a Latin education for the formation of a strong, logical mind. Intellectually subtle arguments were given a more discreet profile: the primary selling point was the ethical value imparted by Latin and Roman history, rich in models and virtues, exemplars that had so much to teach the new German man, who was, after all, tied to the original Romans through their common race. In the memos surrounding the drafting of the curricular reforms for secondary schools, classicists went so far as to paint Horace as a combination of Tyrtaeus and the French nationalist author Paul Déroulède: the self-examination of the gallant lyric individualist was ignored in favor of the celebrant of the Roman political community, whose existence and greatness were thus freed from his existential anguish. By conscripting himself into the struggle for racial survival that was the basis of all political activity, the individual was granted immortality as a man of his race through the performance of his civic duty.

This earnest lobbying bore fruit: cuts to Greek and Latin were minimized in the reforms of 1938, which preserved obligatory instruction of those "national-political" authors recommended by classical scholars themselves.

The relationship between the new Germany and the ancient world concerned much more than just the classroom: several public spectacles and events, like the Days of German Art in Munich or the 1936 Olympic Games in Berlin, offered a much wider stage for the display of ancient kitsch—a physical manifestation of the Nazis' discourse on origins in the public sphere.

Martin Heidegger, briefly the rector at the University of Freiburg, took umbrage at what he perceived to be such a superficial spectacle: the imitation of antiquity was poor theater, similar to what Marx mocked when he described the revolutions of 1848 in France as replaying the Revolution of 1789 while draped in Roman costume. What was important to Heidegger was that the new Germany rediscover the Greek philosophy of Being, abandoned after Plato for a metaphysical dualism that opened the door for the Cartesian split between the *res cogitans* and the *res extensa,* the subject and the object. The subject, endowed with the ability to reason and calculate, dominated the being-less object and reduced it to its mere utility. The Nazi Germany of forced rearmament and the Four-Year Plan was not, however, in any way disposed to forgo the technological perversion of modern Western civilization. The regime's attempts to assert its privileged connection with antiquity and commemorate the greatness of the Greeks were for Heidegger transparently inauthentic, nothing but window dressing. His disillusionment explains why Heidegger turned away from an ideology and set of practices that, far from reviving Greek thought, limited themselves to mimicking antiquity in a most crude and superficial imitation.

PART TWO

Imitating Antiquity

Men make their own history, but they do not make it just as they please; they do not make it under circumstances chosen by themselves, but under circumstances directly found, given and transmitted from the past. The tradition of all the dead generations weighs like a nightmare on the brain of the living. And just when they seem engaged in revolutionizing themselves and things, in creating something entirely new, precisely in such epochs of revolutionary crisis they anxiously conjure up the spirits of the past to their service and borrow from them names, battle slogans and costumes in order to present the new scene of world history in this time-honored disguise and this borrowed language.... Camille Desmoulins, Danton, Robespierre, Saint-Just, Napoleon, the heroes, as well as the parties and the masses of the old French Revolution, performed the task of their time in Roman costume and with Roman phrases, the task of releasing and setting up modern bourgeois society.
—Karl Marx, *The Eighteenth Brumaire of Louis Bonaparte*

Most beautifully of all was the dream of Nordic man made manifest in Hellas.
—Alfred Rosenberg, *The Myth of the Twentieth Century*

It is ... no wonder that every politically heroic age immediately sets out to build a bridge through its art to a no less heroic past. The Greeks and Romans then suddenly seem very dear to the Germans, because their roots can be found in a common race, and therefore their racial offspring must also seek to repeat the immortal feats of these ancient peoples.
—Adolf Hitler, speech at the Cultural Conference at the 1933 Nazi Party Congress in Nuremberg

CHAPTER 4

From Stone to Flesh

The Body of the New Aryan Man between Aesthetics and Eugenics

I went to the Bureau of Verification of Aryan Descent . . . and presented a certificate attesting to my grandmother's descent, which I had obtained after months of running around. The official looked just like a marble statue and was sitting behind a low stone wall. He reached over the wall, took my paper, and tore it to bits, and threw the pieces into an oven that was built into the wall. And he remarked [condescendingly, using the familiar form of address, *Du*], "Think you're still pure Aryan now?"
—Excerpt from a dream report, in Charlotte Beradt, *The Third Reich of Dreams: The Nightmares of a Nation, 1933–1939*

That the Greeks were of Nordic origin is abundantly clear from their sculptures. The figures of the gods that they carved out of stone show, in the body, the shape of the skull, the expressions on their faces, all the traits of their Nordic descent. It is hard to distinguish them from contemporary representatives of the Nordic race. The same is true of the Romans.
—Hermann Jekeli, "Rasse ist Verpflichtung" (Race is an obligation), in *Rasse und Volk*, a party ideological pamphlet

Even the marble of ancient statues could be read as proof that their sculptors and subjects were of Nordic descent. Greek and Roman sculpture formed a sort of conservatory of ideal racial traits and Nordic beauty; as such, party members were instructed to study them carefully, as in the pamphlet cited above. The art of the Third Reich itself would similarly be required to illuminate the aesthetic perfection of the Nordic people. The nudes of a Breker or a Thorak had to cast in stone the profiles, torsos, and legs of the race's greatest specimens and to display them for public contemplation and admiration. These sculptural archetypes were so pervasive, whether in statues, cinema, or art exhibitions, that they even permeated the dreams of at least one Berliner, who described the officer charged with certifying his Aryan racial status—and thus his racial purity—as looking "like a marble statue."

Germany's relationship with the ancient Greek canon had its origins in the writings of Johann Joachim Winckelmann. The National Socialists took this established aesthetic penchant for classical art and added their own taste for eugenics and social Darwinism, turning stone into flesh and transforming a conservatory into an assembly line for the reproduction of a race whose beauty was a testament to its superiority.

THE GERMAN FASCINATION WITH THE GREEK BODY

The Nazi dream of corporeal perfection was part of a much longer history that dated back at least two centuries, to the rediscovery of classical art.

This rediscovery, which began during the Renaissance, was introduced into the eighteenth century by Winckelmann (1717–68), an archaeologist and librarian who was invited to Rome in 1759 by Cardinal Alessandro Albani, who entrusted him with cataloging his collection of antiques. He compiled the catalog at the prelate's request and in 1764 published his *History of the Art of Antiquity*.[1] This work, which glorified Greek statuary (albeit through a study of the Romans' copies of the originals), was received with immediate and widespread acclaim across all of Europe. Winckelmann's text and its accompanying illustrations presented an educated European public with an anthology of descriptions and images of calm, confident masculinity, the embodiment of virtues both physical and moral. The Greek athletes depicted by Winckelmann were strong, harmoniously proportioned, and demonstrated an air of serene composure, even in the midst of strenuous effort—like Laocoön, who seems to stretch and strain for life with every fiber of his being while caught in the grasp of malevolent serpents.

Winckelmann's oeuvre, along with the excavations at Pompeii and Herculaneum, introduced the age of rococo to classical architecture and the plastic arts of the ancients, instilling the eighteenth century with a kind of mania for the antique that would weigh heavily upon the future of Western art. The French Revolution, as we have read, was cloaked in Roman regalia, and nineteenth-century Europeans produced countless monumental edifices whose shape and proportions clearly demonstrated the return of a taste for the classical. Rome and Pompeii gave birth to the Empire style, just as the reading of Winckelmann inspired the French revolutionaries and their painter Jacques-Louis David.

This antique revival also brought with it a new emphasis on shaping and sanctifying the human body. George Mosse has shown how the eighteenth century witnessed the development of an "image of man"[2] based on new moral and aesthetic standards of virility—a thoroughly modern masculine ideal but one deeply influenced by the art and ethos of the ancients.

Educated Europeans of the eighteenth and nineteenth centuries were captivated by Winckelmann's athletes and sought to re-create them. Aesthetic ideals and moral considerations developed in synergy with contemporary advancements in medicine and hygiene, which allowed them to fantasize in new ways of shaping and sculpting the human body.

In Germany, the sport of gymnastics evolved from the writings and associations established by J. F. C. Guts Muth and Friedrich Ludwig Jahn, who published his *Die deutsche Turnkunst* ("German gymnastics"; written with Ernst Eiselen) in 1816. The entry to all *Gymnasien* in Germany proudly displayed the motto *Mens sana in corpore sano*,[3] intended to encapsulate the wisdom of the ancients, which they endeavored to put into practice. This involved developing not just the body but the entire individual. Western modernity learned the wisdom of the Latin adage *Vultus animi speculum:* "The face is the mirror of the soul." Material form corresponded perfectly with interior virtue; the physical reflected the moral. The shape of the body could divulge the contents of the mind and soul. This principle was the foundation of the Swiss-German physician Johann Kaspar Lavater's *Essays on Physiognomy*,[4] published in 1781: there was a homologous relationship between the external and the internal, and this new science claimed to possess "the ability to recognize the hidden character of a human being through his outward appearance."[5]

Born as a semiotics of the physical form, which claimed to read faces and bodies like an open book, inferring broader judgments about the individual as a whole, physiognomy employed a strict reductionism, condensing the psychological to the physical and resting upon an implicit amalgamation of moral and aesthetic categories.

It thus constructed a masculine type that linked the aesthetic perfection of the body to the beauty of the mind, or physical seduction to moral excellence; mere visual observation was sufficient to deduce the one from the other. Mosse has shown how Western modernity was deeply influenced by this idea, captured perfectly by *The Portrait of Dorian Gray*, in which Oscar Wilde describes the effects of one man's dissolute life on his face: Wilde's hero famously doesn't age a day, while his portrait bears all the stigmata of his moral vices.

The masculine ideal inherited from antiquity, the embodiment of moral and aesthetic perfection, informed German youth movements before the First World War as well as postwar monuments to the dead, which often employed representations of the ancient body in the form of gladiators or Greek ephebi sacrificed in combat.[6]

The Nazis relied upon these concepts and the resonance of the aesthetic ideal embedded in the stone of antique statuary. Greek art was an unavoidable component of all compulsory and university education in Germany, and familiarity with Greece was one of the fundamental elements in the cultural upbringing of any decent, upstanding citizen.

It is thus not surprising that, when defining their racial and aesthetic ideal, the Nazis turned to Greek statuary, the Germans' cultural inheritance brought back to life by Winckelmann. Mosse has observed how there was an undeniable connection that existed between Winckelmann's writings and the Nazis' discourse on the new man:

> This love for the body beautiful would continue to inform modern manliness: it would characterize the masculine stereotype. Indeed, the continuities are startling, as when, for example, over a century and a half later, Adolf Hitler traces what he calls the immortality of the Greek ideal of beauty to the combination of singular bodily beauty, a radiating spirit, and a noble soul. He goes on to establish the precedence of the beautiful body when he asserts that a rotten body cannot be beautified even by the most radiant spirit.[7]

Beauty of spirit could not redeem ugliness of body, since there was a strict equivalence and direct correlation between one and the other.

Greek statuary did not merely function as a simple analogy or metaphor for perfection, however; it was also a representation of the Germans' Nordic ancestors, flesh of their flesh and blood of their blood. As one party ideological pamphlet read: "That the Greeks were of Nordic origin is abundantly clear from their sculptures. The figures of the gods that they carved out of stone show, in the body, the shape of the skull, the expressions on their faces, all the traits of their Nordic descent. It is hard to distinguish them from contemporary representatives of the Nordic race. The same is true of the Romans."[8] Greek statues were thus, for the art historian Paul Schultze-Naumburg, and for Hitler himself, a sort of conservatory that had preserved and protected an image of the Nordic race with granitic solidity, enduring through the millennia. As the racial scientist Ludwig Schemann marveled, "It [Greek statuary] has come to represent in our eyes the Nordic ideal and to hand it down from century to century."[9] It thus represented the potential of the race in static form, immobile, needing the flesh and movement of life to finally be fulfilled.

THE BERLIN GAMES: THE NAZI OLYMPIAD AND THE GERMAN OLYMPIA

The 1936 Olympic games were an ideal opportunity to reinforce and celebrate Helleno-Germanic racial kinship and to put on an impressive spectacle: the athletic German body could be shown off side by side with the image of the Greek—although the grand ceremonies of 1936 hardly stopped there.

The link between Greek and German athletics had already been the subject of an entire body of literature in the nineteenth century, which likened Hellenes and Teutons in the *agonism*—the spirit of conflict and competition—common to the two civilizations.[10]

The centrality of the *Wettkampf* (αγον, sporting or martial competition) in the Greek and German cultures was also proof of the spiritual community that linked the two peoples, which could only be the result of racial kinship.

In 1856, the archaeologist and historian Ernst Curtius (1814–96) wrote a book, appropriately titled *Der Wettkampf*, exploring this idea in greater depth. He submitted the notion that the Indo-Germanics were characterized by a striving for action—conquest, defense, combat, creation—while the Semitic or Oriental peoples were paralyzed by their passions, which weakened and dominated them. Regarding the site at Olympia where he was set to conduct a major excavation, Curtius concluded, in a phrase often quoted in 1936: "What lies buried in those dark depths is life of our life" ("Was dort in dunkler Tiefe liegt, ist Leben von unserem Leben"). Nietzsche, in his "Homers Wettkampf" (1872), and later Jacob Burckhardt, in his *Griechische Kulturgeschichte*

(1898–1902), picked up on the same theme: the Greeks, like the Germans, were "competitive, colonizing peoples," in contrast to the timid, soft Orientals, depleted by their emotions, which they were unable to master. Similarly, several partisans and theoreticians of the young *Turnbewegung,* or German gymnastics movement, claimed the prestige of Greek precedent to glorify the work of Guts Muth and Jahn, underlining its fundamental Greek, Indo-Germanic, and thus German essence.[11] Such cultural similarity, and the unique agonism of its peoples, was the hallmark of their common identity as a race.

This was the racial identity that the Olympics were designed to evoke and demonstrate, in words, images, and dress, as well as the organization and decoration of physical space. An official publication of the propaganda committee for the games, titled *Olympia 1936: Eine nationale Aufgabe* (Olympia 1936: A national duty), specified that one of the tasks required of the hosts—beyond the material and technical preparation of the appropriate infrastructure and warm welcome of athletes and spectators—was the exploitation of the event in propaganda, as a historical commemoration of the race: "Furthermore, we must seek to place a spotlight on the intimate relationship of our sporting culture with the gymnastics of the ancient Greeks (the relay of the torch from Olympia to Berlin, exhibits on antiquity)."[12]

The Olympic games were first and foremost an occasion to emphasize that ancient Greece was the sole preserve of Germany. Nazi propagandists endlessly repeated variations on the theme that the rediscovery of Greek culture was the work of the German people alone. To commemorate the führer's official opening of the games, the *Völkischer Beobachter* set aside an entire page of its 2 August 1936 edition for a selection of Greek and German texts, juxtaposing Nietzsche's *Homers Wettkampf* to passages from Lucian, Herodotus, and Homer himself.[13] More generally, the paper did all it could to evoke the privileged cultural bond that existed between Greece and Germany. Hölderlin was another frequently mentioned figure in this regard, as in one article from the paper that cited his "Gesang des Deutschen" to demonstrate the nostalgic longing of the German spirit for Delos and Olympia. As the author remarked of the poem: "The unquestionable awareness that the Olympic idea of the Greeks is ... intrinsically related to us was impressed upon the great poet from the depths of a Nordic racial heritage that dates back to the beginning of time."[14]

Contrary to all the evidence—and aside from a courteous passing reference to the work of Pierre de Coubertin, who also suffered the misfortune of being French[15]—it was equally important to promote the idea that the Olympic Games themselves were a German creation. The same edition of the *Völkischer Beobachter* contained a long article titled "Wegbereiter der Wiedergeburt: Winckelmann, Curtius, und Dörpfeld, Pioniere des olympischen Gedankens" (The precursors to the renaissance of the games: Winckelmann, Curtius, and Dörpfeld, pioneers of the Olympic idea). The piece conveniently celebrated Winckelmann as "the veritable discoverer of Hellenism, who was the first to highlight the racial foundations of art and culture," and canonized Curtius ("the prophet of the Olympic idea") and Dörpfeld ("the discoverer of Olympia") to show how this extension of Olympia was a fundamentally German project.[16] During the months of July and August 1936, the German media conspired to downplay the importance of Coubertin; the *Olympia-Zeitung*, which briefly saluted the comte, preferred to linger over the figure of Curtius, who was solely responsible for the rediscovery of Olympia and all that it represented. The paper cited one German archaeologist who, like Humboldt and Goethe, argued that the Germans were uniquely able to perceive the full essence of Hellas: the Germans, because of their duty to their race, were "better placed than anyone else to understand the meaning of the modern Olympics."[17] *Das Schwarze Korps,* the SS weekly newspaper, similarly downplayed the Frenchman's role in order to celebrate Curtius.[18]

Alfred Rosenberg, in a proclamation disguised as a welcome to the peoples of the world, delivered in several languages and later published in *Völkischer Beobachter* on 17 July 1936, had set the tone: "German men have always . . . held in high regard the original culture of ancient Greece. . . . Many great figures in the German sciences, like Schliemann and Dörpfeld, have dedicated long, laborious lifetimes to bring to light the treasures of a Greece that they held particularly dear. Everything that they have done at Olympia and at Troy can justly be considered for the common good of all civilized peoples. Their work has brought the spirits of Greece and Germany closer together."[19] Even Carl Diem, an éminence grise of the International Olympic Committee and a personal friend of Pierre de Coubertin, minimized the Frenchman's role and chose to focus the spotlight on German historians and archaeologists. Retracing the history of the excavations at Olympia, he briefly mentioned an early French dig (dating back to 1829) only to clarify immediately that "it was to the newly created German Reich that this right was reserved, to achieve the sublime cultural work of the excavations at Olympia, which have brought glory to the German spirit."[20] He too paid the usual reverent homage to Winckelmann and Curtius.

After the appropriation of Greco-Roman antiquity into the history of the Indo-Germanic race, here we find a prime example of fraudulent historical subtraction. Pierre de Coubertin was conveniently and unceremoniously shoved aside to make room for the great resurrectors of the Greek ideal in Germany. No longer accorded the distinction of being the inspiration behind the Olympic idea, he had merely been the simple instrument of an essentially German project.

The proof of this unwavering Helleno-Germanic affinity lay in the grand enterprise of the excavations at Olympia, an undertaking dutifully assumed by German archaeologists. These digs and excavations on the site of the original games were conveniently celebrated in the form of a book of art photography, titled *Olympia,* the result of collaboration between an archaeologist and a reputable photographer, published promptly in 1936.[21] German excavations, reprised in 1934 on the orders of Hitler in preparation for the 1936 games, were also the subject of regular progress statements in the journal of the German Archaeological Institute in Athens, as well as more widespread publicity in the media controlled by the SS. The new Olympia excavations were entrusted to a young archaeologist, Hans Schlief, whose career and earnings, until then rather meager, benefited considerably from his acceptance into Himmler's Black Order in 1935.[22] Schlief's work was closely documented by *Das Schwarze Korps,* which in 1936 proudly published a mock-up of the Olympia site as laid out by the *SS-Unterscharführer:* "At the location where, some 3,500 years ago, to honor King Pelops, that Nordic conqueror, on that Peloponnesian peninsula that bears his name, a series of solemn games, races, and competitions were held around his burial mound, the excavation site at Olympia has been opened. As part of the *Sport der Hellenen* exhibition organized by the museums of Berlin, the SS-Unterscharführer Dr. Hans Schlief, who himself took part in the excavations at Olympia beside Wilhelm Dörpfeld, has created this model, as accurate as possible, of the site."[23] Two years later, in 1938, the weekly devoted two pages to summarizing the excavations that Hans Schlief had conducted, under the title "Olympia: The Führer's Excavations."[24]

This promotion of the Helleno-Germanic kinship was dictated by party officials, whose words were frequently simply repeated by the press. We have seen how the *Völkischer Beobachter* devoted an abundant amount of space to its coverage of the locations, ceremonies, and outcomes of these sporting events. The organizing committee for the Berlin Games also produced a newspaper, called the *Olympia-Zeitung,* which appeared daily for the duration of the games (21 July to 17 August 1936) and complemented its chronicling of the games themselves with stories on Greek art and culture, the precise route traveled by the Olympic flame (with illustrations), and the many other peripheral events associated with the games.

The *Olympia-Zeitung* encouraged readers to visit two exhibitions on the history of sport in the West in an article titled "Yesterday: 600 and 2,000 Years Ago."[25] The article promoted the exhibit *Die deutschen Leibesübungen des Mittelalters in Buch und Bild* (Medieval German physical education in words and images) alongside *Sport der Hellenen*, which opened in Berlin on 29 July 1936. These two shows, linking German medieval practices and ancient Greek culture, provided an abundant supplement of images and realia in support of the notion of Helleno-Germanic kinship. Driven by an insistent pedagogical thrust, the organizers of the latter exposition carefully curated their material to hammer home the link between ancient Greece and Nazi Germany, showing the public various reproductions of Greek cups and vases depicting athletes throwing the discus, each disk clearly stamped with a swastika. Visible proof, tangible in its symbolism, of the Indo-Germanic origins of the Greeks, whose use of the swastika made them the natural precursors of the Nazi movement, just as Theobald Bieder had demonstrated in a short 1933 essay on the hakenkreuz,[26] or as Alfred Rosenberg had claimed in *The Myth of the Twentieth Century*. These reproductions were given pride of place in the exhibition's catalog, as well as in the illustrations accompanying a volume titled *Sport und Staat* published in the run-up to the games in 1935.

The Helleno-Germanic relationship was clearly publicized and celebrated through a number of different channels: art exhibitions; the official poster advertising the games, which depicted a Greek athlete crowned in laurels looming over an image of the Brandenburg Gate; and the neo-Doric architecture of the Berlin Olympiastadion, designed by Werner Marsch.

The naming of the stadium, incidentally, became the subject of some debate for the Nazis, as the very principles behind the games themselves had been.[27] The dispute over the dedication was, among other things, an illustration of the very sensitive nature of the quarrels over the humanities for German honor and national identity. The debates that raged between classicists and Germanists after 1933—a thinly veiled power struggle that touched upon a nation's identity and cultural self-image—in many ways reflected the quarrel of the Ancients and the Moderns in seventeenth-century France. The latter began with a dispute over an inscription: should the tableaux in the Hall of Mirrors at Versailles be labeled in Latin or French? The Ancients emphasized that the sacred dignity of the king and his palace required the formal nobility of Latin; the Moderns sought to consecrate the use of the French language.

By 1936, the Third Reich had its own quarrel over an inscription. How should the Olympic stadium in Berlin, built especially for the 1936 games, be baptized: with a Greek or a German name? Wilhelm Frick, the Reich's interior minister and, as such, a member of the organizing committee, drafted a declaration "regarding the introduction of a German name for the stadium and sports forum": "This new facility was built as an arena for the elite competitors of all peoples. In addition, the stadium and sports forum will be sites where young German boys and girls will be taught how to become vigorous men and women. I consider it more worthy of that great patriotic duty to endow these facilities for exercise and competition with German names rather that Latin or Greek ones."[28] Frick proposed calling the stadium the Deutsche Kampfbahn, or "German combat arena."

He ran into opposition from Goebbels, who was more in favor of a name that drew upon antiquity. Frick then turned to the Chancellery to ask for mediation from the führer himself. In a letter dated 22 January 1936 and addressed to Hans Lammers, the secretary of state and chief of the Reich Chancellery, Frick explained his differences with the minister of propaganda, who had proposed the Greek-sounding name of Olympia-Stadion, while the stadium built at the Grunewald race course for the aborted summer games of 1916 already bore the name Deutsche Kampfbahn. Frick requested an urgent resolution, since the stadium's name would appear on official documents and tickets and the opening of the games was less than six months away.[29]

A response was not long in coming. The führer's decision was communicated to Frick two days later, in a letter dated 24 January: "The führer wishes the stadium to carry the name Olympia-Stadion,"[30] apparently opting for whatever sounded the most Greek. Hitler, as a lover of antiquity, thus came down on the side of the Ancients against the Moderns in this latter-day quarrel. The Germanizing "Moderns" did not, however, give up the fight completely: *Das Schwarze Korps* would refer to it with the expression "Kampfbahn des Reichssportfeldes" (Combat arena of the Reich sports forum),[31] a contorted if martial-sounding circumlocution that allowed it to identify the stadium without resorting to its Greek-sounding name.

GAMES IN GRECO-ROMAN DRESS: THE GRAND SPECTACLE OF HELLENO-GERMANIC KINSHIP

Hitler in essence wished that the games could take place in Greco-Roman dress. Neoclassicism was the preferred architectural style, and the stadium was flanked by a Greek-style *Freilichtbühne,* or "open-air amphitheater," described by the *Völkischer Beobachter* as an "antique theater"[32] designed to host musical theater outdoors, the latest and most prestigious example of the national program to create *Thingstätten.*[33] It was here, at the Dietrich-Eckart-Bühne, that Handel's *Herakles* was performed from 9 to 16 August 1936: an opera inspired by the Greeks, written by a German composer, about a hero celebrated for his physical prowess—one who could also be seen as the incarnation of the link between the Indo-Germanic Septentrion and the Nordic Mediterranean. Hercules was, according to the *Olympia-Zeitung,* the "most physically impressive hero of antiquity"[34]—whom Tacitus had already associated with his Germania,[35] not just as a Nordic-type hero but also as the one who "introduced the games by bringing the crown of laurels from the shores of the Danube, so that, even at the time, the Olympic festivals were linked with the Nordic lands."[36] The journalist then described the "fantastic" ambience of the spectacle: "We are transported back to Greek antiquity. We gaze past the musicians, and their music seems as if it comes out of nowhere. These are not actors onstage but Herakles himself, whose destiny we share with empathy."[37] Around the same time, on 3 August 1936, the Staatliches Schauspielhaus in Berlin staged Aeschylus's *Oresteia,* also in honor of the Greek games; the critic for the *Völkischer Beobachter* extolled the "superb Greek goddess"[38] Athena.[39]

Like the relaying of the torch, the staging of Handel's *Herakles* constituted one of those ceremonies held throughout the duration of the games that attempted to visually represent the connection between contemporary Germany and ancient Greece. Another fine example of such a ceremony was the reception held by Hermann Göring for the various national delegations at the foot of the Pergamon Altar in Berlin's Altes Museum, a reception that received heavy coverage in the *Völkischer Beobachter,* including an ample photographic layout:[40] the steps to the altar filled with young girls in antique-style outfits and young boys decked out as archers, with that consummate sense of costumed kitsch that characterized such spectacles, like the lighting and departure of the flame from the ruins of Olympia. The *Olympia-Zeitung* focused its coverage—complete with photographic essay—on the thirteen young girls dressed in ancient robes who accompanied the carrier of the flame under the Greek sun.[41]

During the reception at the Pergamon Altar, Bernhard Rust gave a speech celebrating the sacred character of the Berlin Olympiad, like a sort of funerary rite and tribute to the example of the original Greek games. "The modern Olympic Games have rediscovered their deepest roots," he proclaimed, because they constituted a form of worship of the dead from the Great War, when "life passed into a new world, that of myth, which now begins to penetrate and fertilize our own thoughts, just as the Greeks, at the height of their civilization, lived in the spirit of myth."[42]

In addition to grand official receptions and art exhibitions surrounding the games, there were many smaller symbolic demonstrations that punctually reminded visitors that the Third Reich had resuscitated ancient Greece through the games—like the temporary exhibition of two groups of antique-style nudes by the sculptor Eberhard Encke on the Pariser Platz before the Brandenburg Gate, widely publicized by the *Völkischer Beobachter*.[43]

The ultimate mechanism for depicting the sacred Helleno-Germanic kinship was, of course, the cinema. Leni Riefenstahl's film *Olympia* used its opening sequences to celebrate the bodies of German athletes as resurrections of the glorious classical form. After it acquired executive authority over the organization of the games, the Ministry of Public Enlightenment and Propaganda decided to produce two films—one on the Winter Games in Garmisch-Partenkirchen, titled *The Youth of the World*, and the other on the Summer Games, to be held in Berlin. The first was entrusted to Hans Heidemann, the *Reichsfilmdrammaturg* and vice president of the Reichsfilmkammer. The second was assigned to another prominent figure of contemporary German film, Riefenstahl, who was much admired by Hitler for her mountain films (*Bergfilme*) of the 1920s and her 1932 masterpiece *Das blaue Licht* (*The Blue Light*), which subsequently earned her the chance to produce the three *Reichsparteitagsfilme* between 1933 and 1935.[44] Given a considerable budget and some four hundred kilometers (250 miles) of film, *Olympia*—composed in two parts and released on the führer's birthday (20 April 1938)—won the highest cinematographic distinction available in the Third Reich, the Nationaler Filmpreis.

The opening scenes of *Olympia* speak volumes. Set among the ruins of Olympia, the camera films statues of Greek athletes as they come alive and begin to move, one by one, tracing a path to Berlin via the relay of the torch that brings the Olympic flame to the Reich's capital.

Riefenstahl's prologue was a clear allegory for the Nazis' relationship with Greek history; like Nazism, the filmmaker's camera breathed life into the very stone that for centuries embodied the ideal of Nordic beauty, like the *Discobolus* of Myron. "In the prologue," Riefenstahl herself later remarked, "the ideal of the classical form detaches [from its base] into the living realization of today's athlete."[45]

The pose of the discus thrower, captured in stone in a moment of intense concentration, fades into the movement of the living athlete throwing his disk: Greek marble transformed into German flesh in a celebration of Nordic continuity. To film this famous scene, Riefenstahl called upon the celebrated German decathlete Erwin Huber, whose bare, bronze, well-toned form seemingly refused to show any sign of fatigue or perspiration—and thus betrayed no indication of mere mortal humanity. Rigorously sculpted and almost like a statue itself, Huber's body was filmed from below, in the pose of the discus thrower; just as Myron's work was the model for the contemporary athlete, the athlete himself was offered up as a model for the viewer's contemplation and imitation.

In its setting and its staging, the opening of Riefenstahl's film thus captured the dialogue taking place across the centuries between the ancient Greek body of stone and the contemporary German body of flesh—but it also engaged their surroundings. The images of ancient ruins presaged those of the Olympic stadium in Berlin, a grandiose neo-classical edifice that welcomed the Olympic flame after its journey across Europe from South to North. The gigantic neo-Doric building in the German capital echoed the ruins of Olympia, its just and worthy successor in the eyes of Nazi architects. And it was precisely to link the two capitals of the Olympic spirit, Greece and Germany, that the minister of propaganda had devised the relaying of the Olympic torch.

THE OLYMPIC TORCH RELAY: LINKING HELLAS AND *GERMANENTUM*

In antiquity, a sacred flame was lit upon the Altar of Hestia at the Prytaneion in Olympia, which burned throughout the duration of the Panhellenic Games.

Following the wishes of Pierre de Coubertin, the first flame of the contemporary era was ignited at the Olympisch Stadion in Amsterdam for the games of 1928, a ceremony that was repeated at the games held in Los Angeles in 1932. But the idea of a relay bringing the Olympic torch to the host city was wholly the creation of the German organizers of the Berlin games, and especially Carl Diem, who in 1937 published a short work[46] explaining how he had wished the relay to serve as a link (*Verknüpfung*) between antiquity and modernity, Hellas and *Deutschtum*. The idea seduced Goebbels enough for him to agree to this concrete symbolism of the direct physical link uniting ancient Greece and the new Reich. Indeed, with its depiction of the circumstances of the games' birth and its weighty symbolic charge, the Olympic torch relay won over the International Olympic Committee to the extent that it was retained even after the war, remaining to this day a subject of public spectacle.

Diem's proposal was accepted by the IOC at its meeting in Athens on 18 May 1934.[47] One of its members, Jean Ketseas—a friend of Diem's—then proposed lighting the torch in the same fashion as the ancients, following the ritual described by Plutarch in his *Life of Numa Pompilius*.

And so, as the German correspondent for the *Olympia-Zeiting* crowed, the flame was lit at Olympia in 1936 "just as in antiquity": "On the holy ground of the ancient stadium, the Olympic flame was lit. . . . In imitation of antiquity, in the same manner that the ancient Greeks tended their sacred fire, according to Plutarch's description, today's Greeks lit the Olympic flame."[48] They did this by focusing the reflected rays of the sun on a concave mirror provided by the German optical firm Zeiss; the torch itself was also designed along the lines of the ancient model. Walter Lemcke, the sculptor, who also produced the bell used at Berlin's Olympic stadium, drew his inspiration from examples provided by Diem and Theodor Lewald (the longtime chair of the German Olympic Committee and Diem's superior as the president of the International Olympic Committee), torch-shaped columns from the museum at Eleusis, and an Attic bas-relief of the Palazzo Colonna in Rome. Evidence concerning the original torch was provided by Alfred Schiff, the administrative director of the Hochschule für Leibesübungen (University for physical education), who gathered it for the *Sport der Hellenen* exhibition. The actual production of the torch, in V2A Nirosta stainless steel, was entrusted to the firm Krupp.

The route for the *Fackelstaffellauf* was planned out in minute detail by the German organizing committee. The head of the Sportabteilung, Werner Klingeberg, made a survey of the sites himself in a Daimler-Benz graciously made available by the automobile manufacturer as a form of sponsorship.

The lighting of the flame in Olympia on 20 July 1936 was attended by numerous journalists, as well as a film crew for Riefenstahl, who decided to return to the scene after the fact in order to meticulously erase any bothersome, comic, or anachronistic elements that might disturb the otherwise sacred classicism of the spectacle. The press coverage was intense: the *Völkischer Beobachter* devoted one full page each day from 22 to 24 July to articles and photographs of the flame—its lighting, departure, and first kilometers of travel[49]—and followed up with daily articles on the various stages of the relay.

The Olympic flame traveled for twelve days, covered 3,075 kilometers (1,911 miles), and was carried by 3,400 couriers prior to its arrival in Berlin on 1 August 1936 for the games' opening ceremony, having passed through Bulgaria, Austria, and Czechoslovakia before entering the German borders of the so-called Altreich on 31 July—at the appropriately named frontier village of Hellendorf, a location chosen precisely for its suggestion of the close kinship between Greeks and Germans.

The route traveled by the flame, which, kindled amid the ruins of the games' original city, would ignite the Olympic cauldron in Berlin, made visible the lineage binding the Greeks of antiquity to contemporary Germans, ceremonially reaffirming the continuity linking one to the other, similar in spirit to the Tages der deutschen Kunst through the streets of Munich, which included floats embodying different eras of Teutonic culture beginning with a statue of Pallas Athena.

The material connection created by the road between these two cities, Olympia and Berlin, symbolized their indissoluble bond of blood, a bond that transcended time and space. The path of the relay positioned contemporary Germans as the pure and worthy inheritors of a blood and racial spirit embodied by the ancient Greeks of a bygone era, making their kinship one of direct descent: the Germanics had founded Greece, but the ancient Greeks were also somewhat like the forefathers of modern Germans, who would have to imitate them to rediscover their harmony and clarity of mind, as well as their perfection of body, in order to faithfully represent the Indo-Germanic spirit. The path of the flame was thus one of racial engineering on the curvilinear axes of time, a test of the racial *Geist* and *Blut* that linked Greeks and Germans.

The symbolism of the flame also recalled the figure of Prometheus, a metaphor for the Aryan in *Mein Kampf*, as well as the ancient practice of keeping a sacred fire. In antiquity, the creation of a new Greek settlement required the transportation of a flame from the public hearth of the old city to the new colony. Similarly, the fire of the Vestals had been introduced to Latium by Aeneas, who, significantly, would leave Troy only with his father on his shoulders, a torch bearing the flame of the city in his hand. National Socialism, through its elaborate staging of the torch relay, repeated the sacred ritual of *translatio igni,* a concrete material symbol of the *translatio imperii et studii* from Greece to its legitimate Indo-Germanic heir, Nazi Germany.

PAIDEIA IN GERMAN SCHOOLS: THE *VOLLE MENSCH*

The hosting of the Olympic Games thus served as propaganda in two ways: as a showcase for the regime in front of athletes and visitors from around the world and as a platform to commemorate the bond that existed between ancient Greece and contemporary Germany.

The Olympics were all the more a "national duty" in that they were meant to instill the desire and determination necessary for sport and strenuous exercise in the minds and bodies of the German people. The games' organizers aimed to create a more lasting pro-sporting movement, not just the brief glorification of a sporting competition destined to last but a single summer. As the organizers' official handbook proclaimed, "[Our] duty is nothing less significant than to encourage the permanent, regular practice of physical exercise among the entire German people."[50] A joint proclamation of Goebbels, Frick, and the *Reichssportführer* Hans von Tschammer und Osten reiterated the point: "We, the Germans, we have long been content to dominate the world of the spirit," becoming "a nation of poets and philosophers." Circumstances in the real world, however, were such that "the education of the body must take its place alongside that of the mind."[51] The country of *Dichter und Denker* (poets and thinkers), the supreme mental athletes, must become a nation of physical athletes as well.

The games were the perfect occasion to celebrate and promote the Nazi vision of human perfection, the *volle Mensch,* or "total man," who was superior to the divided or cleft man who emerged from traditional systems of education, overly intellectual and weak in body. The idea of the Greek male as a complete, fully well-rounded man was a recurrent obsession in the literature and media of the day. The "national duty" represented by the games also required each individual to perform their "task," to exercise regularly and improve or perfect their body as a member of the German people: "The young Greek from the class of free men who surrendered himself to Olympia was ideally a sportsman, singer, dancer, warrior, and farmer, all combined in one man. We doubly feel the need for such a model, for National Socialism has awakened in us the desire to rediscover the totality of life and to liberate ourselves from . . . vague intellectualism."[52] The Greeks incarnated the profoundly Nordic desire to "find the perfect unity between body and spirit,"[53] in order to ensure that "the body should be a temple for a noble, willing mind,"[54] an idea that "has long lain dormant in our blood"[55] before being awakened by National Socialism and realized through the practice of sport.

A convinced anti-Christian, Alfred Rosenberg lashed out in a proclamation of 17 July 1936 against the "old theories that tried, in past centuries, to extract the mind and soul from the body": *Seele, Geist,* and *Körper* were a healthy "trinity" that needed to be "preached"[56] anew against the so-called Holy Trinity, which was abstract and fatal to the body. In the same issue of the *Völkischer Beobachter,* another article commented in detail on the passage from *Mein Kampf* in which Hitler celebrated the "Greek ideal of beauty":[57] "Beginning with the harmonious trinity between body, soul, and mind, the Greek created the desirable ideal of the complete man. Training of the body and nobility of the soul stood on equal footing in Greece, and it is the synthesis of these three educative factors that produced the ideal figure of the *kalos kai agathos* [beautiful and good]." Greek education, like the new German pedagogy, was thus aimed at nothing less than raising youth who were "physically strong, intellectually lively, and morally healthy."[58]

The *volle Mensch* was universally celebrated by the Reich's intellectual elites and party leaders as a symbol of their rupture from and opposition to the monasticism of the eastern or late Hellenistic tradition and the Christianity of the Middle Ages. In the midst of the media frenzy surrounding the Olympics, the *Völkischer Beobachter* revisited this theme, citing the Reich education minister Bernhard Rust, who, at the opening of the International Congress on Youth Sports, hailed this "harmonious man," this "man understood as a whole,"[59] whose sublime image had been handed down through Greek sculpture. Such words contained echoes of the celebration of the Greek total man and Greek education as a synthesis of the *musisch* and *gymnisch* by two of the Third Reich's most prominent pedagogical minds, Ernst Krieck and Alfred Bäumler.[60]

This celebration of Greek paideia, which educated man in all his spiritual and physical faculties, also found a welcome forum in the SS weekly *Das Schwarze Korps* in a 1935 article on the ancient Greek Olympics: "The Greeks of antiquity trained their bodies for beauty and movement in an exemplary manner, but they did not forget to deepen the education of their mind. *Mens sana in corpore sano,* in the words of the poet Juvenal, was the key to all education in antiquity, ... [a]

double education [entrusted to the state through its] public gymnasia."⁶¹ The ultimate goal of the practice of sport—beyond the health of the individual, the beauty of the race, or the vigor of the *Volksgemeinschaft*—remained that supreme and most vital form of *agon,* or "contest": not athletics but war, the former being only a means of training for the latter. Even in Greece, the Indo-Germanic practice of sport aimed at hardening the body to prepare it for martial combat. As a 1936 publication of the German Olympics organizing committee claimed, quoting Solon, regular physical exercise ensured both "the freedom of the individual [and] the autonomy and prosperity of the fatherland."⁶²

THE GLORIOUS RACIAL BODY, AND ITS OPPOSITE

The celebration of the Greek body was not just a matter for the Olympics. The Nazis' preferred art also sought to imitate those famous Greek lines. The sculptures of Arno Breker and Joseph Thorak depicted male athletes and virile warriors, vigorous and nude, following in the footsteps of the Greek canon—sharpened, however, with a hint of the regime's bellicose aggression.

Nazi art aimed to portray a normative physical standard, with traits for the new race to strive for. These traits were not defined solely in positive terms; they were also revealed in deliberate contrast to another set of physical characteristics, those of the non-Aryan. During the exhibition *Le Juif éternel,* held in Paris in 1941, one of Breker's statues of a nude athlete stood regally amid casts and photographs of Jewish bodies, almost like a measuring stick or aesthetic and anthropometric reference point and in any event a visually striking demonstration of the clear contrast between Jewish ugliness and Aryan beauty.⁶³

To put it simply, the archetype of the Aryan body could not be envisioned without its opposite, to reaffirm and emphasize its beauty. In the absence of any knowledge of DNA or deep understanding of the mechanisms of genetics,⁶⁴ nineteenth- and early twentieth-century racial scientists and policy makers defined a race purely by observable criteria. Race was fundamentally about blood—it had to be pure, of course, and free of any admixture—or skin color and the size and shape of the body, which was a candid and credible witness testifying to its racial purity or adulteration. The crime of racial mixing was made physically manifest on the body, which expressed and furnished proof of the truth: a *Mischling,* or "half-breed," carried the stigmata of his racial shame (*Rassenschande*) and degeneracy (*Entartung* or *Ausartung*) in his flesh itself.

The countertype to the Aryan was, of course, that omnipresent other in the eyes of the Nazis: the Jew. The black was too distant. He contaminated and corrupted colonial France, which had already been ensnared in the process of "negrification,"[65] as well as the United States, but he had spared Germany. Hitler made only fleeting references to blacks, although the Nazis smothered all discussion of the question of the *Rheinlandbastarde,* the illegitimate children of the black French fusiliers stationed along the Rhine during their occupation of the Ruhr, just to be safe. The problem with the Jew, the countertype to the Aryan, was that his otherness was not necessarily immediately apparent; the Jewish body did not always display signs of its difference. The German Jew was frequently well assimilated socially and could be indistinguishable in his dress: he was invisible, undetectable. The Nazis thus set out to make him more visible, by offering the Aryan people a physical countertype that placed their own beauty and perfection into sharp relief.

The Nazis determined which anthropometric characteristics would differentiate Jews from Aryans. Nazi anthropometrics drew upon the hackneyed stereotypes inherited from Christian anti-Semitism, such as the hawkish, hooked nose in contrast to the straight, Greek type.[66] These criteria rested on an already lengthy tradition of anthropometric thinking that dated back to the nineteenth century,[67] which was dusted off and refined by the physicians of the SS Main Office for Race and Settlement (Rasse- und Siedlungshauptamt der SS, or RUSHA), created in 1931.[68]

The racial scientist Ludwig Schemann marveled and rejoiced when he encountered any sign of the Nordic phenotype in the history of Greek art: "One can ... browse through hundreds and hundreds of Greek reproductions without seeing anything other than that beauty whose opposite, in the Semitic type, has rightly become proverbial."[69] The Nazis also illustrated the contrast between archetype and countertype with images of Jews chosen expressly because they were deemed ugly. Racist Nazi propaganda films, most notoriously Veit Harlan's 1940 *Der ewige Jude (The Eternal Jew),* showed not German Jews but rather those from the Warsaw Ghetto, who wore traditional dress and were already strenuously tested by their harsh daily living conditions. Abuse, famine, and illness had scarred and deformed their bodies, leaving them a ready target for the revulsion of the viewing public. Their ravaged, starving bodies, their dirty, unshaven faces and hollow cheeks—all produced a vivid, exacting image of the corporal degeneracy that the Jews were said to incarnate and hinted none too subtly at the menace that awaited any mixing with their fundamentally subhuman race. The film explicitly compared the Jew to an animal, opening with a revolting scene teeming with rats, visually equating Jews with these hideous creatures and thus excluding them from the ranks of humanity, demonstrating the need for a thorough and redemptive act of disinfestation. More perverse and threatening than a mere rat, the Jew was just as frequently associated with vermin, as an insect or a bacterium. In the film, Jewish hideousness was juxtaposed to the perfect, harmonious form of Greek statuary, which appeared during a sequence in which the narrator enumerated the list of cultural treasures endangered by Semitic barbarity.

Against such decadence and perversion, the poisoning of the blood and the spirit, it was vitally important to protect the uncompromising standards of an art that was the pure expression of Nordic genius. Iconoclasts and burners of books, the Nazis unleashed their violence against a culture they considered immoral and contagious, in the name of a superior Nordic culture whose canon was built upon a triptych of Greek, medieval German, and Italian Renaissance art. The sequence of the film that presented "the Nordic man's conception of beauty" showed a succession of works by Greeks, medieval Germans, and Renaissance masters, all set to Bach's *Toccata,* before displaying a series of works of degenerate art, set to a piece of decidedly Oriental music.

This clash of archetype and countertype had already famously been put on display during the two major concurrent exhibitions held in Munich in 1937. On 18 July, the Haus der deutschen Kunst held its grand opening, five years after Hitler had laid the ceremonial first stone in 1933. The museum gathered all the creations of contemporary Germanic genius under one roof, in the Grosse deutsche Kunstausstellung (Great German art exhibition), whose works were chosen with ruthless selectivity by a jury officiated by Hitler himself. The exhibition, headlined by the sculptures of Thorak and Breker, focused tightly upon the beauty of the Aryan body. The very next day saw the opening of the traveling exhibition *Entartete Kunst,* or "Degenerate art." Here too an accent was placed on the body: of the fifty-seven images reproduced in the exhibition catalog, fifty-two depicted bodies—those of the disfigured and ill, deformed by anxiety, consumed by anguish. The cover, significantly, depicted a piece by Otto Freundlich titled *Der neue Mensch* (The new man). This sculpture of a head, hideous and pox ridden, with protruding lips and a flattened nose, eyes bulging from their sockets and frontal bossing of the pronounced forehead, recalled African art or a mental retardation akin to Down syndrome. The message was clear: the new man depicted in degenerate art was the polar opposite of the powerful, radiant athlete celebrated by Nazism. Degenerate art, considered a form of *Kulturbolschewismus* (cultural Bolshevism), was interpreted as a symptom of mental illness due to miscegenation. The catalog happily juxtaposed works of art and the drawings of the mentally ill,[70] inviting the reader to compare formal art with the scribblings of the mad. Two pieces by Oskar Kokoschka were placed side by side with a sketch by a hospitalized psychiatric patient: "Which of these three drawings is the work of an amateur in a mental institution? Nope. It is the first, in the upper right!"[71] Physical appearance, moral substance, and mental capacity were all intertwined. For the Nazis, ugly or repugnant works of art could have been produced only by sick minds and bodies; like their works, the artists themselves presented a risk of contamination. Conversely, the creation and exhibition of beautiful works, the product of beautiful souls, contributed to the health of a perfect race through inspiration and imitation, giving the image a performative aspect akin to magic.

For the Nazis, art was an instrument to re-create the past perfection of the race, or at least to construct a racial ideal, trying to pass on the moral and aesthetic perfection inherent in Greek stone.

THE RESURRECTION OF THE ANCIENT CANON

In his speech in Munich for the opening of the Haus der deutschen Kunst in July 1937, Hitler commended his subjects for bettering their race, as evident in the bodies of the German people themselves, who, in his eyes, now approached the ancient paradigm:

> The new age of today is at work on a new type of man. Overwhelming efforts are being made in countless sectors of life to elevate the nation's people, to make better, stronger, and more beautiful men of our people, of our youth and our boys, our women and girls. . . . Man has never been more similar in appearance and in sensibilities to the men of antiquity than he is today.[72]

The entire world had been able to see and appreciate these bodies during the Berlin Olympics, held the year before. Like a theatrical spectacle of Nordic beauty, the games had been an international showcase for the regime, a parade of the best of the German race, the annunciation of the glorious corporeal perfection belonging to a new type of man: it allowed them to exhibit this new man in his purest form, forged through the eugenicist policies and strict selectionism of the *völkisch* state.

State-sanctioned eugenics was aimed at the palingenetic resurrection of a racial canon. Antiquity played a fundamental role, since it was in Greek statuary that the image of the standard had been preserved. Hitler repeated this notion in Munich one year later, during a 1938 speech given at the reception for the *Lancellotti Discobolus*,[73] acquired by the city's museums for the sum of five million reichsmarks on Hitler's express order and with Mussolini's wary assent, the Italian state being the owner. In the speech, the führer exhorted his people to emulate what he considered to be the aesthetic standard-bearer of the Nordic race: "And may all of you take this to heart as a standard for the tasks and accomplishments of our time. May you all strive for beauty and perfection so that you shall also stand the test of time both before the *Volk* and [before] the ages."[74] It was thus also important to incarnate the Nordic physical archetype for posterity; the Germans of the Third Reich would live on for all eternity just like the Greeks, who had bequeathed them a vision of perfection. Media coverage of the event, centered on the arrival of the statue and Hitler's speech, repeatedly focused on the canonical features represented by the *Discobolus;* newsreels from 20 July 1938 devoted a long sequence to the physical beauty of the work before segueing into the contemporary practice of sport through a report on the SA's *Reichswettkämpfe* (physical fitness contests).[75]

Nazi eugenics did not limit itself to exclusion or appropriation. It also sought to train the body for the performance of beauty. Here too the Greek notion of aesthetic perfection was the ideal. In the aforementioned speech, Hitler invited the audience not merely to imitate the beauty incarnated by Myron's *Discobolus* but to surpass it. In 1937, Hitler had been happy to confirm that contemporary Germans were getting closer to the Greek ideal; by 1938, this was no longer sufficient: "May none of you who visit this house fail to go to the sculpture gallery. May you all then realize how glorious man already was back then in his corporeal beauty, and that we can speak of progress only if we have attained like perfection or if we manage to surpass this level."[76] This was an ambitious goal, but Hitler was convinced that the Nazis' policies to promote sport and racial hygiene would allow them to accomplish their aim within a century. After having glanced at a photograph of a "beautiful female swimmer," Albert Speer recalled, Hitler once remarked: "What splendid bodies you can see today. It is only in our century that young people have once again approached Hellenistic ideals through sports. How the body was neglected in earlier centuries. In this respect our times differ from all previous cultural epochs since antiquity."[77] But how could one equal, much less surpass, the idea of Greek beauty? They would have to sculpt living matter to bring out the features of a body that was of "Greek inspiration," the "Greek ideal type" taken "to exemplify a healthy mind in a healthy body."[78] The Nazis would have to become artists, to mold the flesh the way Greek sculptors had long ago carved such elegant forms from mute blocks of marble.

In the Nazi racial state, each individual was invested with a responsibility to give his or her own body the most beautiful and vigorous form possible. This responsibility transcended mere individual well-being or aesthetic beauty. The body, after all, belonged not just to the individual but to the people and the race—or, as a Nazi slogan ominously put it, to the führer. The act of physically perfecting one's body had repercussions for the race as a whole.[79]

This labor of aesthetic perfection was to be conducted under the direction, and under the thumb, of Hitler, the sculptor-in-chief. The metaphor of führer-as-sculptor, the führer-artist, was a common one in the Third Reich, as demonstrated by a famous cartoon that appeared in 1933 in the satirical weekly *Kladderadatsch*[80] depicting Hitler kneading human flesh to transform a work of degenerate art into the statue of a warrior à la Breker. With great determination, animated by their desire to change the course of history, the Nazis fully embraced the pose of the demiurge and of the creator. As Joseph Goebbels put it: "For us the masses are simply a shapeless material. Only under the hand of an artist can a people be shaped from the masses, and a nation from the people."[81] Goebbels outlined the idea even more explicitly in an open letter to the German conductor Wilhelm Furtwängler: "We who are giving form to modern German politics feel ourselves to be artists entrusted with the lofty responsibility to form from the raw masses a full and solid image of the people."[82] The führer and the state thus sought to mold the raw racial material of the German people with one eye fixed on the paradigm provided by the ancients; they wanted to cut, carve, chisel, and polish it along antique lines.

Classical beauty represented the standard of racial perfection, the apotheosis of the nobility and beauty of the Nordic body. All SS members were given a sort of ideological textbook to teach them how to evaluate the Nordicity of the contemporary body by comparing it to representations of the Greek or Roman form. As we have already seen,[83] one side-by-side pair of illustrations displayed the portrait of a young SS officer next to the bust of a Roman profile, the contemporary Nordic man shown to highlight the Indo-Germanic traits of the Roman.[84]

The same booklet showed the differences between the Nordic type and his Semitic countertype by contrasting the mug shots of two Jews—wild eyed, deliberately filthy and unshaven, both accused of *Rassenschande,* or "sexual crimes against the race," in violation of the Nuremberg Laws, which forbade Jews from any sexual relations with Aryans—with an ancient statue displaying the face and body of a young, Apollonian Greek boy.[85] The juxtaposition of these two sinister-looking types to the serene calm of the Greek ephebe in a "posture of Nordic prayer,"[86] and the simple implication of any kind of sexual activity by the former contaminating the latter, was enough to provoke disgust in the reader.

FROM GREEK AGON TO GERMAN SPORT

The primary tool to mold the body was sport, the forms of physical exertion and competition inherited from Greece, its palaestra, and the original Olympic Games. It was the Olympics, after all, that had demonstrated the greatness of the rejuvenated German body before the entire world: "Millions of young people are steeling their bodies through participation in competitive sports, contests, and tournaments and, increasingly, are putting these bodies on display in a form and constitution that has not been seen, much less imagined, in perhaps a thousand years. There is an absolutely stunning new type of man emerging. . . . This new type of man who, in all his glistening, glorious human strength, made his spectacular debut at the Olympic Games last year."[87]

In *Mein Kampf,* Hitler had stated unequivocally that the schools of the racial state needed to produce aesthetically beautiful but physically tough athletic bodies. Hitler lambasted traditional methods of teaching, which focused excessively on intellectual apprenticeship, a pedagogy that concentrated on the mind without paying attention to the body. The German schools had forgotten the Greek paradigm even while taking the name of *gymnasium* and thus claiming to perpetuate their prestigious lineage. The Greeks developed mind and body in harmony, while the *Gymnasien* turned out misshapen scholars, cultivated brains in physically weak bodies: "The institution that is called a *Gymnasium* today is a mockery of the Greek model. In our educational system it has been utterly forgotten that in the long run a healthy mind can dwell only in a healthy body."[88] The German educational system had thus forgotten the very fundamentals of pedagogy: the body must be developed at least as much as the mind. A hypertrophied mind in a sickly body was nothing other than a symptom of degeneracy: "For taken in the mass, a healthy, forceful spirit will be found only in a healthy and forceful body. The fact that geniuses are sometimes physically not very fit, or actually sick, is no argument against this. Here we have to do with exceptions which—as everywhere—only confirm the rule."[89] In the racial state, then, schools should allow more time for physical education, not "the inoculation of mere knowledge, but . . . the breeding of absolutely healthy bodies. The training of mental abilities is only secondary."[90] Hitler recommended that two hours at least be devoted to sport on a daily basis.[91] Intellectual knowledge as such was frowned upon, even rejected as an encumbrance, nothing but dead weight that paralyzed instinct and anesthetized the spirit of decisive action, plunging the individual into the passivity of contemplative abulia and the apathy of intellectual fatigue.

The championing of sport was the refrain of a hymn to the glory of the physical body, which the Nazis insisted they had unearthed after two millennia of Judeo-Christian negligence. The attention given the body and the dignity conferred upon the naked form also constituted arguments supporting the thesis of the Nordic kinship between the Greeks and the Germans: their common affinity for nature, their lack of shame over or distaste for the body, their practice of nudism.

The *Lebensreform* of the late nineteenth century had glorified such freedom of the body, closeness to nature, healthy living, and regular physical exercise in order to break with an urban and industrial civilization deemed spiritually unhealthy and physically deforming.[92] In the 1920s, an officer of the Reichswehr named Hans Surén became a tireless and eloquent promoter of nude sport, a combination of traditional FKK (*Freikörperkultur,* "free body culture," or nudism) and the gymnastics and physical education of his own military training, in the spirit of self-reform and bucolic lyricism that characterized the *Wandervögel.* He was also a successful author: his most famous work, *Mensch und Sonne (Man and Sunlight),*[93] sold 175,000 copies between the publication of the first edition in 1924 and the appearance of a revised edition with a new preface in time for the games of 1936. The book developed the idea that the Nordic man was a "solar" being who lived in close proximity to and complete harmony with nature, for whom nudity—literally shedding the artificial barriers of Judeo-Christian dress and morality—was the gateway to rejoining the *magna mater alma* (Great Mother) of all existence. Surén defined the Nordic race not only by its physical phenotype but also (here following Ludwig Clauss, the inventor of racial psychology) by its collective psyche and spirit, which made each of its members a form of Aryan-Olympian. This spirit was composed of "sun, nature, and nakedness,"⁹⁴ a synthesis of sport and nudism, the permanent exposure to the sun and the air that previously characterized the ancient Greeks, "our ancestors."⁹⁵ Throughout the book, the Greeks appeared as an example to demonstrate the proximity of the Nordic race to nature and the sun: "Friends! Remember the glorious age of the ancient Germans and Greeks! Browned skin was the first requirement to be a man; white skin was considered feminine."⁹⁶

To restore the ardor for combat to his men about to succumb to the assault of the Persians, Surén recalled, Leonidas showed them the naked bodies of Persian prisoners, "whose white skin had such an effect on the Greeks that they laughed at these effeminate men and returned to battle, full of courage, against a numerically superior enemy, whom they soon routed."⁹⁷ Unlike the delicate women of the eighteenth century, the ancients did not try to preserve the immaculate whiteness of their Nordic skin. True men exposed themselves to the sun and wind in both war and labor, disdaining the alabaster corpulence of the Persians. Since "the ancients revered the sun above all else," and since the "healing properties of the sun were well known to the peoples of antiquity (Egyptians, Greeks, and Romans)," the Greeks lived largely in the most simple, natural way possible, without the slightest sense of shame. Ancient Greeks and Germans "were never prudish. The naked form was natural to them, sacred and beautiful, a true joy."⁹⁸ The young were particularly accustomed "to nudity in public"⁹⁹ without any embarrassment or false modesty. Surén cited a long passage from Plutarch describing how in Sparta young boys and girls commingled at civic ceremonies, and also participated in sporting contests in the nude, with mutual regard and appreciation. It was then simply a question of choosing a beautiful companion with whom to procreate, replicating those beautiful bodies that made up a pure and vigorous race.¹⁰⁰

The condemnation of nudity arrived with the irruption into Greece of a new doctrine hostile to the body and to all terrestrial things, oriented toward the chimera of a hypothetical otherworld and toward the abnegation of life on earth. Asiatic, Semitic Christianity had turned the Nordic man away from his own body and its communion with the elements.¹⁰¹

This condemnation of Christianity and its disdain for the body and the world was popular among the Nazis, who attributed it in part to Nietzsche. To disarm the barbarians from the North, the Semites had found nothing more effective than the dogma of original sin and the stigmatization of everything related to the body, the powerful, beautiful body that was the foundation of the pride and identity of the blond Germanic beast. As Richard Walther Darré wrote, wistfully recalling the example of Spartan nudity: "The Nordic race has always found any negation of the body to be foreign. It was only when the immense shadow of an asceticism hostile to beauty arose in the East that it provoked the eclipse of culture in antiquity."[102] The body, alas, had become the detestable womb of sin, mere weak flesh that needed to be chastened by asceticism and corporal mortification.

The SS weekly *Das Schwarze Korps* listed its grievances in two articles dedicated to the question of nudity in art and the practice of nudism:[103] "There was a time when the opposition between body and soul constituted the cornerstone of philosophy. The dogmatic Christianity of the Middle Ages used the Eastern idea of original sin in its fight against a Nordic elite full of energy and joy for life. . . . In the end, the Nordic conception was swept away by this somber, medieval universe of guilt and sin. We know, as those fine Nordic men, the Greeks and Romans, did then, that a healthy soul can be at home only in a healthy body." In contrast to the obligatory self-hatred of the medieval Christian era, the Greeks and Romans enjoyed complete physical and mental health, thanks to their Nordic roots. It was thus essential to repair the links to the past that were broken by Christianity, a non-Germanic and fundamentally Semitic element. It was essential to recover that simple and immediate corporeal joy that had been so dear to the Greeks and that had been negated, rejected, and condemned by a morbid, Oriental-Semitic asceticism: "In their era, the Nordic people among the Greeks had already identified the only valid rules for the representation of the body of our race. Since the time of the Renaissance, when the Nordic feeling for life rose up against monastic obscurantism, the figures of the classical plastic arts have stood before the whole world as the most perfect expressions of our conception of beauty."[104]

Surén floridly described how the Greeks had inaugurated the practice of Olympic sport in the nude during the eighth Olympiad. The passage, a hypotyposis of exalted lyricism and scantly veiled homophilia,[105] is worthy of extended citation: "The Greeks arrived from all over. Their supple togas flowed gracefully over their shoulders, covering only part of their bodies. Their bare arms, turned golden by the sun, were well formed, as were those of the sage men who converged on the stadium, deep in serious conversation. The proud bodies of these young men, naked for the most part, and bronzed, made for a happy image. The boys' eyes sparkled with pride and the awareness of their developing strength."[106] Tradition held that it was during the course of these games that the courier Orsippus of Megara stripped off his loincloth midrace, beginning the practice of sporting nudity. Scenes of this type abound in Surén's book, allowing him to assert that "in Greece it was understood how the culture of the body was linked to life, and to death, with the prosperity of a people":[107] "Nudity and gymnastics were for centuries at the heart of the strength and health of the Greek people. It was naked that, every day, the Hellenes would train in their gymnasia and palaestrae."[108]

For the health of Germany and the Nordic race, of which the German people were the only, last real representatives, it was essential to rediscover "the vital spirit of Greece," which "is fundamentally a Germanic spirit. Both flow from the same Aryan source." On one point Surén allowed himself to be more Catholic than the pope, in protesting the use of the term *Olympics* for the games held in Berlin in 1936. If, in essence, "the true Olympic spirit is an Aryan spirit"[109]—the argument reflected in his book's subtitle—then "the international Olympic spirit is a contradiction in terms, since the Olympic spirit can only be Aryan" and only the "Nordic race"[110] incarnates that spirit. As a result, "it would be preferable to call these international contests not Olympic Games but World Sporting Games, since that is really what we are talking about. The Olympic Games should be reserved for peoples whose blood is predominantly Nordic."[111] Olympic hospitality was no match for hostility, Coubertin's internationalism no match for racial exclusivity.

The moment had come to rediscover the Aryan-Olympic spirit, since the political conditions were, with the Nazi seizure of power, now favorable. The renaissance of Germany required a renaissance of the Nordic body, which had long lain in the cold repose of antique marble. Surén took the Greek paradigm, which incarnated the profundity of the body and spirit of the race, and declared it the ideal for the future German people: "Our epoch today is ripe for a renaissance of *Germanentum* and *Hellenentum,* through the practice of physical exercise, [since Germany felt a] profound nostalgia for Germanic-Hellenic ennobling of our corporal selves."[112]

FROM SPORT TO WAR

Sport can sometimes shade into war, the aesthetic into the strategic, the beautiful into the bellicose. Sport was certainly aimed in part at cultivating health and beauty. It thus performed a vital function for both the individual and the race. But it also served the people and the state. For war was the ultimate goal of physical exercise. Here too for Surén, the Greek model of state-sponsored physical education served as a point of reference: "After the National Socialist seizure of power, we live in an era of action. Action demands that each National Socialist must work on their body according to the precepts of the Aryan-Olympic spirit. The great legislator Solon elevated gymnastic training to the rank of state education. Gymnastics became the duty of the citizen—today, it must become the duty of the people. It is on gymnastics that performance is built, not only that of the athlete but also that of the soldier."[113] Only this type of state-mandated physical education would encourage the body of the race to strengthen itself and prepare itself for war: "You will be heroes, just as your ancestors were,"[114] proclaimed the sportsman-officer, who wanted to see the German people become athletic, aesthetic, and heroic figures "in the mold of our ancestors from Greece and Germany."[115]

Göring used similar terms in the preface to a book on the Olympic Games of 1936: "The National Socialist man can exist only when the education of the mind is connected to the hardening of the body, which must resemble steel. . . . Let this book harangue the youth of Germany and make them see that an iron will, selfless ambition, and a group spirit are the guarantors of the honorable victory that we hope for them."[116] Sport had become an individual and political imperative. It produced healthy bodies that would be put to use for the community: in the labor force during times of peace, and in the military during times of war. It was thus important to toughen the body, make it hard, give it the strength and temper of steel, the stuff of machines—machines of war. "After his day's work," Hitler had written, a boy "should steel and harden his young body."[117] The use of steel as a metaphor was omnipresent when it came to talk of training the body. The sport that Hitler favored above all others aside from gymnastics was boxing, which encouraged endurance, quickness, and aggression, a combat sport that could be an introduction to the confrontation of war.[118] The body it produced, built through Nazi racial genetics and the practice of sport, was in the final analysis that of a warrior, chiseled, hard, and cold, sculpted not for the delight of aesthetic contemplation but for the inevitable war on the horizon.

The model for the Aryan body was the aggressive form of the imposing, menacing warrior, which Breker made his specialty, the best examples of which are undoubtedly the two nudes representing the party (*Die Partei*), brandishing a flame, and the army (*Die Wehrmacht*), recognizable by his sword, which welcomed visitors to the Reich Chancellery in Berlin after 1937. In addition to these two sculptures, Breker had sketched out several bas-relief models that were destined to grace the public offices of the monumental north-south axis that would constitute the spine of the planned future capital of the Reich, Germania. Breker conceived of a series of nude warriors, each with prominent, well-defined musculature, all based upon the ancient theme. These nudes were destined to be high profile, capturing archetypal moments of camaraderie, vigilance, departure for the front, and military action. They would function as allegories of masculine military virtue for the citizens of the new Germany, virtues cast in marble and thus eternal, drawing on the most distant past of a race that had been reinvigorated by National Socialism. Breker's plans were dominated by the figure of the hoplite: his nudes were frequently depicted in the Greek *peplos*, flowing robes that gave his figures a beautiful draping effect, as well as the *hoplon*, the round shield of the Greek infantry, and the *gladius*, a sword whose shape and scabbard were more evocative of Rome. This Greco-Roman synthesis was also evident in one of Breker's most monumental bas-relief projects, *Der Wächter*, as well as a sketch of a monumental frieze for the Soldatenhalle in Berlin, called *Auszug zum Kampf*, a blatant imitation of the frieze on the Parthenon, ornately decorated with Roman-style eagles. This sort of confusion may seem surprising, but the simultaneous presence of Greek and Roman elements was due neither to accident nor to the ignorance of the artist: blending Greek and Roman symbolized the syncretic image of a Germanic-Nordic humanity understood in terms of an ahistorical and hagiographic racial unity. Hoplites and legionnaires, Greeks and Romans coexisted and commingled to provide the image of a single, inalterable Nordic warrior that the new Germany had resuscitated. The figure of the hoplite, as an ahistorical Nordic allegory for war, was similarly featured in the work of other artists of the time, such as Willy Meller and Hubert Netzer.

THE EROTICISM OF THE CLASSICAL NAZI NUDE

With terror comes fascination. Warriors' bodies were also desirable bodies. The increasing popularity of nude sculpture under the Third Reich did not take place without debate. How was it possible to reconcile the omnipresence of the nude, both male and female, in public as well as in the museums, with the almost Victorian morality of German society and of Nazism itself, prudish in the image of its führer, who declared that the only pornography allowed by the Reich was anti-Semitism?[119] We might begin by noting that the Nazi nude was subject to a form of sexual distancing. While the genitalia were indeed depicted, the body was deprived of any real eroticism. The glabrous skin was smooth and cold, without color or hair, particularly in the pubic area; such sculpture deliberately gave the impression of being a statue, and only a statue, without a breath of life or anything that could recall a living being. The bodies were nude, but it was an idealized nudity: the white of the marble served, as David d'Angers remarked, as the "vestment of immortality,"[120] draping the figures in a sort of "costume of nudity" ("Kostüm der Nacktheit"), to borrow the felicitous expression of Birgit Bressa,[121] who also describes their "mortifying transmutation, a metamorphosis from flesh to stone,"[122] their only guarantee of immortality. In essence, if the goal of art was to represent the eternal archetype of the race, the nude—nameless and timeless, not confined to any specific era by any historical context—was the ideal form. The ancient, identified by a robe, a toga, a sword, by the frosted, achromatic patina of centuries, could itself also signify this timelessness, since its posterity spoke for itself as a certificate of its immortality.

Nazi nudes could still lack modesty all the same. Silke Wenk, who has worked on feminine nudes, remarks that contrary to conventional traditions, which refrained from showing female genitalia out of propriety, Nazi art exposed the feminine without hiding anything: "Their bodies were presented as a whole, openly, with the pubis visible and in particular with a repeated emphasis on proud, almost erect breasts."[123] There were at least a few elements, then, that carried an erotic charge in Nazi nude sculpture.

Such examples were put on display not simply to establish a physiological paradigm or to develop the viewer's racial sensibilities through the reproduction of an idealized standard. The Aryan body was also the subject of careful staging and promotion. It needed to be exhibited, exposed, and desired. The Aryan body needed to be seen and to provoke an eroticized feeling that would encourage imitation: sexual desire would feed the desire to emulate. Such was the case of *The Judgment of Paris*, sculpted by Thorak and exhibited at the Haus der deutschen Kunst in Munich in 1941. The bodies of its three Greek (and thus Indo-Germanic) goddesses were eroticized objects in the eyes of the judge Paris, whose posture as an observer explores the position of the visitor to the exhibition, inviting the visitor to look, judge, and desire the feminine form exposed before his gaze. This example of overt eroticism in the Nazi nude, encouraged and even demanded, exhibits that fascination that Nazism developed as a form of seduction and political governance, so well studied by the historian Peter Reichel.[124]

The beauty of the Aryan body exposed in this way generated emotion and emulation. As Hans Surén noted in another best-selling work, *Gymnastik der Deutschen* (German gymnastics): "The contemplation of a well-toned body has a profound pedagogical influence, not only in physical terms but also in moral matters. The nudity of a noble body is a great incitation to imitation, as the ancient Greeks knew well."[125] It was the beauty of the sculpted nude, like that of the living body itself, that encouraged anyone who gazed upon such perfection to strive to imitate such grace through sport for the betterment of the race. In this sense, the goal of sport was less physical performance than physical beauty. Performance was, all in all, merely secondary; before all else, it was vital that the body of the athlete be beautiful: "I have sometimes been repulsed by an athlete who ends up winning a race, because the man was inharmonious and ugly.... This is not Nordic body culture. Who would wish to preserve the example of this athlete for posterity by immortalizing him in marble?"[126]

The athlete must thus be beautiful like a statue, providing his contemporaries with an image of aesthetic perfection and leaving evidence of his beauty for posterity. The important thing in an athlete was his representation of a normative standard: his "browned body, as if he were a statue made of bronze, attracts the eye out of pure admiration and encourages the viewer to do everything possible to achieve such beauty."[127]

HEALTHY ART FOR HEALTHY BODIES: ART AS CRADLE AND CONTAMINATION

Bodies cast in stone, meticulously sculpted and displayed, thus informed the work of shaping bodies in the flesh: art was both a standard and a point of reference, a model and a challenge. Germans' flesh had to mimic stone, whether that of age-old Greek sculpture or that of Thorak and Breker, themselves great imitators of classical art. This was why Hitler, as we have seen, invited the German people to try to match the aesthetic perfection of the Greek *Discobolus*.

Art already possessed an active, performative function as a sort of matrix to nurture the ideal form of the body and the *Volk*. The Nazis conceived of art as a medium for the cultivation of the race through self-contemplation. An artistic image impressed itself upon the imagination, helping mold and beautify the flesh of the viewer's progeny; mediated by sight and memory, artistic depictions of the body thus cultivated the body itself, form shaping substance, the ideal making the real. This theory of artistic eugenics has a long history in the Western tradition; Éric Michaud, for one, traces it back to the Bible and to Greek antiquity.[128] It has for the most part proved to be quite tenacious: in his work *The City of the Sun,* Tommaso Campanella argued that the state should show pregnant women the images of beautiful bodies so that they would produce beautiful children. Similarly, Baudelaire wrote: "The idea of beauty which man creates for himself imprints itself on his whole attire, crumples or stiffens his dress, rounds off or squares his gesture, and in the long run even ends by subtly penetrating the very features of his face. Man ends by looking like his ideal self."[129] There was thus a dialectical relationship between art and the body: art was, in the tradition of Hegelian idealism, the expression of the spirit—or more specifically, for Paul Schultze-Naumburg, the spirit of the race—but in return, art molded the body and gave it form, as Hitler reaffirmed at Nuremberg in 1935: "Art, since it forms the most uncorrupted, the most immediate reflection of the life of the people's soul, exercises unconsciously by far the greatest direct influence upon the masses of the peoples."[130]

In his 1928 book *Kunst und Rasse* (Art and race), Schultze-Naumburg began with a bit of common sense: how could one acknowledge the existence of a diversity of aesthetic judgments without admitting that the differences between such critiques ruined the very credibility of the critical enterprise?

If one wished to accept this diversity without calling into doubt the legitimacy of all criticism, one was forced to introduce the concept of race. Artistic judgment, just like the creation of art itself, was tied to race. Critics, like artists, were necessarily locked into the strict circle bounded by their physiology, into what biological determinism had given them: "It is impossible [for the artist] to emancipate himself from the limitations of his own body."[131]

As Schultze-Naumburg noted in another work, this dependence "of the artist on his own corporality" was particularly visible in the fact that "all physical representations that an artist creates present a real resemblance with his own body. It is as if the painter or the sculptor must always necessarily produce self-portraits."[132] What was a body if not an individual physical expression of the race?

Race was the determining factor in all artistic creation. The whole physical being of the artist, sublime yet unchanged, went into a work of art. More than a self-portrait or symbolic reproduction of corporality, cultural creation was in every way similar to natural procreation and obeyed the same laws regarding the hereditary transmission of human characteristics: "The creation of a work of art is a process of spiritual childbirth that is in fact comparable to the procreation of a baby. The laws of heredity have taught us that infants necessarily possess the hereditary traits already found in their ancestors. . . . The inheritance of the moral infant, the work of art, is nothing other than the hereditary predisposition found in its creator." The essence of the race was thus embedded in a work of art. More precisely, the ideal of racial beauty found its expression in art, since a race was determined not only by the qualities present in the blood but also by "a representation, what we might call a regulatory concept of the race, a representation of complete harmony between body and spirit" that "showed the path and the goal"[133] of its physical and moral existence. For the author, blood and its aesthetic ideal possessed a material impact upon creativity: If the blood was good and pure, its ideal of beauty and the artistic creation depicting it would be sublime. If, on the contrary, the artist's blood was mixed or otherwise corrupted, its aesthetic would be morbid and its depiction similarly unhealthy.

This was the basis upon which Schultze-Naumburg founded his dichotomy between classical Nordic art and degenerate art—of which he was the first and primary theoretician.

Nordic art was the pure expression of the Indo-Germanic race and its ideal man. It had known two great periods of prominence: that of the Greeks, who had "possessed beautiful bodies,"[134] and that of the Italian Renaissance. For the Italian painters of the Renaissance were also indubitably men of Nordic descent, since the great barbarian migrations of the late antique era had left behind a vein of Indo-Germanic blood on the peninsula that had finally found a manner in which to express itself after the long medieval night. The Renaissance was, in essence, "Lombard"[135] and thus Germanic.

As for the Greeks, one could never say enough about their Nordic essence, even if, as he conceded, the idea might still surprise some readers:[136] "The extraordinary Greek people [who] created all that appears to us today to be humanly impossible . . . were a Nordic people."[137] As befitting the perfect incarnation of the Nordic race, the Greeks had cast the beauty of their bodies into marble; the representation of the Greek body had "remained the standard of physical beauty in the Western world."[138]

In chapter 10 of his book *Nordische Schönheit* (Nordic beauty), Schultze-Naumburg presented thirty-eight images of various artworks: twenty-five Greek statues and busts, seven medieval works, and six works from the Renaissance.[139] Two-thirds of the foundational works of Nordic art were thus Greek.

Quite unlike the perfection of the classical era, unfortunately, contemporary art—like that of the Weimar Republic—"prefers and emphasizes the representation of degeneracy."[140]

The humanity represented by degenerate art bore little resemblance to the well-proportioned body of the athlete but rather to "the idiot, the whore, the sagging breast. One must call a spade a spade. It is the veritable hell of subhumanity that shows itself to us. One breathes a sigh of relief when one leaves that atmosphere for the pure air of other cultures, like those of antiquity and of the Renaissance, where a noble humanity looked to its art to express its nostalgic desire [for beauty]."[141] To understand degenerate art, one had to observe the degenerate men who had produced it, "in the psychiatric wards, the hospitals for the physically handicapped, the lepers, in all those dark corners where the most degenerate types burrow themselves."[142]

Marrying description and admonition, in *Art and Race* Schultze-Naumburg placed images of contemporary art side by side with photographs of the mentally ill and physically handicapped, concluding that "we must strive so that these poor wretches suffer no more, by eliminating them and by preventing more of their kind from being born."[143] The self-appointed judge and purifier of art was also a eugenicist, for censure and artistic dirigisme were a large part of a policy of racial hygiene and purification. In the preface to the third edition of the book, published in 1938, Schultze-Naumburg rejoiced that, thanks to the advent of Nazism, "the destruction of inferiors is no longer a distant ideology but is anchored in law and thus now a reality." The iconoclastic rage of the Nazis against degenerate art, labeled *Kulturbolschewismus,* betrayed their belief that such so-called ugly art not only was the product of a biologically degraded humanity but could also nurture something monstrous.[144]

To combat this contamination of the body through its depiction in hideous and deformed shapes, it was essential not only to destroy the malignant, infectious images but also to disseminate as widely as possible the image of healthy bodies. Breker's works were accordingly destined for mass reproduction: "Breker greatly adapted his artistic production to the demands of reproduction,"[145] creating a veritable assembly line for the distribution of healthy bodies. In summer 1942 a new atelier, the Arno Breker Steinbildhauerwerkstätten GmbH, was opened in Wriezen-zur-Oder to complement his original atelier in Berlin-Dahlem, and by 1943 employed some forty-six artisans. Breker's sculptures were reproduced on a large scale, in the form of statuettes as well as portraits. Photography, which allows a sculpted work of art to be reproduced an infinite number of times, little by little became one of his work's raisons d'être in its own right. Birgit Bressa has noted that "by the end of the war, his works were being created for the sole aim of reproduction through mass media, and for their aesthetic-photographic presentation."[146] Rough models of many sculptures were reproduced on a smaller scale: tricks of photographic perspective could give the illusion of the appropriate refinement and monumentality. The goal of such mechanical reproduction was to reach the largest audience possible, not just those who visited the Haus der deutschen Kunst or made the pilgrimage to the Parteitage in Nuremberg. Such a massive distribution of the canon of imitation would encourage more rapid improvement of bodies and of the race. One is reminded of Walter Benjamin's piercing insight in his 1936 essay "The Work of Art in the Age of Mechanical Reproduction," which examined the "introduction of aesthetics into political life"[147] under fascist regimes: "Mass reproduction is aided especially by the reproduction of masses." Benjamin was thinking especially of "big parades and monster rallies" or "sports events," all "captured by camera and sound recording," in which "the masses are brought face to face with themselves."[148] The same could have been said, however, for high art, and especially this type of sculpture, which admirably served the ultimate goal of generating masses of healthy bodies through a massive distribution of images of healthy bodies.

Nazism thus pursued its idea of utopia in the production and reproduction of perfect bodies, which all conformed to a Helleno-Nordic ideal. This vision of utopia was driven by a desire to revive this ideal and to resurrect an aesthetic canon that had been preserved in stone for all eternity. The Greek body had spent millennia in its petrified gangue, representing a potential that the Nazi regime wanted to bring to fruition, in the real world and in the flesh.

CONCLUSION

We will make new men based on the model of the ancients. The Third Reich's new man was first and foremost a body, and this body could be achieved only through recourse to an antiquity that the Nazis held up as the archetype and canon of racial beauty. The Greeks and Romans were Indo-Germanic populations, their bodies fulfillments of the Nordic type, which was vital to maintain or restore in the racial present. The Greek and Roman body was preserved for us in ancient statuary, which Hitler put forward as the standard for emulation by the German people, as in his speech at the reception for the *Discobolus* in Munich in 1938. The sublime, fully realized archetype of the Aryan body would, by saturating the public with its image and continually proclaiming its perfection, nourish the same standard of beauty among its contemporary cousins.

This would be accomplished in part through contemplation. Image was performative; beauty begat beauty, just as ugliness—the product of a sick body—was an infection that pathologically spread ugliness to whoever witnessed it. The sculpted, harmonious forms of state-sponsored art were held up on high for public consumption in museums and mechanically reproduced on a large scale, just as flabby bodies and degenerate art were subjected to public vilification and destruction.

To achieve this standard of Greek beauty, however, it was not enough simply to go to a museum. One was compelled to exercise, practice sport, a duty for one's own health as well as that of the race—since, according to good holistic and totalitarian logic, the body belonged less to the individual than to the group, viewed metaphorically and biologically as one great social organism, whose members were linked by a community of blood and a common destiny. Sport was the subject of an intense promotional campaign under the Third Reich: rehabilitated by Hitler in the name of a Greek ideal that had been betrayed by an overly cerebral, rational, humanist gymnasium, the practice of sport became a priority in both scholastic and university education. It was aimed at resuscitating the Greek ideal of the complete man, the total man, the product of a harmonious synthesis of body and mind. For too long those had been kept separate, divided by an ascetic, Eastern Christianity that had malignantly fractured beautiful Nordic unity. Sporting exercise, a reconciliation of man with his body and his body with nature, the practice of nudity—this was the Indo-Germanic heritage illustrated by Greek culture, tragically interrupted by medieval Christianity, which saw the flesh solely in terms of sin and carnal temptation, worthy only of punishment.

Sport was designed not only to produce beautiful bodies whose desirability would fuel admiration and emulation: the rehabilitation of the

Greek and thus Nordic *Körperkultur* encouraged the development of hardened bodies ready for martial combat. Sport, in essence, was placed in the service not only of the body and the race but also of the community, a manifestation of bellicose intent common to those competitive civilizations that made up Nordic culture: Greek and German *Wettkampf* communicated across the centuries and celebrated their common essence and mutual origins in the grand spectacle that was the Berlin Olympics of 1936. Awarded by the International Olympic Committee in 1931 to Weimar Germany, the games were retained by the Nazis thanks to the will and activism of Hitler, who wanted to make them both a welcoming window on the new Germany and a great parade of German bodies to celebrate the privileged connection between Hellas and *Germanentum*. The Berlin Games were thus dressed up in ancient robes, surrounded by the Doric splendor of an Olympic stadium flanked by a Greek theater and the ceremonial kitsch of the peplos displayed at Olympia and the Pergamon Altar. Such pedagogy was brought to its zenith in the staging of the relay of the Olympic torch from Olympia to Berlin: a demonstration of the common blood and race that linked ancient Greece and contemporary Germany. The torch relay, the subject of intense coverage in the German media, was also immortalized by Leni Riefenstahl in the opening scenes of her film *Olympia:* the beauty of Alexander, Athena, and the caryatids here and there among the ruins giving way to a Greek *Discobolus* that slowly transformed into the real-life flesh and blood of a contemporary German athlete. At the 1936 games, the people of the new Germany, as the largest and most faithful representatives of the Indo-Germanic race, solemnly renewed their connection with Greek ethics and sporting competition. The real Western renaissance was not that of the abstract humanism of classical letters but the rediscovery of an authentically Nordic culture that had emigrated long ago to Mediterranean shores and now, in the shadow of the Olympic flame, returned to its ancestral northern home.

CHAPTER 5

The Racial State and Totalitarian Society

Plato as Philosopher-King, or The Third Reich as Second Sparta

The eighteenth century . . . has furnished us with a new example of the influence of History, and of the abuse of its comparisons. You must be aware that I allude to that mania of citations and imitations of the Greek and Roman history, which within a few years has struck us as it were with a vertigo. Names, surnames, dress, manners, laws seem all about to become Spartan or Roman. . . . They forget that at Sparta an aristocracy of thirty thousand nobles held two hundred thousand serfs under a yoke of the most cruel oppression; that of four millions of persons, which was all the population of ancient Greece, more than three millions were slaves.
—Constantin-François Volney, *Lectures on History*

Plato and the "tyranny of reason"—yes, how rightly you see that! . . . How is it that de Gruyter in Berlin could publish a book in 1933 called *Plato and Hitler*?
—Karl Jaspers, letter to Hannah Arendt

To believe the Viennese philosopher Karl Popper, "Plato's political programme [was] purely totalitarian."[1] One might well be surprised by the questionable anachronism inherent in the application of this contemporary political category to a body of work that is 2,500 years old. Popper, an Austrian and a Jew, dedicated an entire book to this idea, a volume that he began to write "on the day I received the news of the invasion of

Austria"[2] in 1938 and that was only published in 1945. A harsh critique of Plato and his philosophical followers, *The Open Society and Its Enemies* is presented as if written in abstract, rarely referring to the intellectual context of its gestation. If, in many respects, it has the air of a political pamphlet, this is because it challenges the reading of Plato offered by Nazism and consequently by a large part of the German academy in the 1930s and 1940s—a reading of Plato as the philosopher of dictatorship and the racial state.

THE MASTER PHILOSOPHER: PLATO AS NORDIC HERO AND HERALD OF NORDICISM

The Hellenist Hans Bogner boasted in 1937 that "no [other] classical Greek author is as widely read today, even by laymen, as Plato."[3] No other classical author, nor any philosopher. It is often believed that Nietzsche was the philosopher of National Socialism; a posteriori, it seems obvious that a truncated, poorly understood version of Nietzsche was indeed a significant element in the genesis of Nazism, or at least of the symbolic world and spirit of the age—the zeitgeist—that it came to dominate. Nietzsche bequeathed the Nazis several concepts that became slogans or semantic reflexes, like that of the *Übermensch,* which was interpreted in a physical and racial sense despite its author's intended description as a psychic type or ethos. Furthermore, Nietzsche had indeed been a proponent of the *Lebensphilosophie* and metaphysical vitalism that left such a mark on the youth movements and combatants of the Great War, the milieu from which many of the first Nazis emerged.[4] But, as even Alfred Bäumler—who claimed to be an expert on the philosopher from Sils Maria and had written an entire book trying to Nazify him[5]—acknowledged in his article "Nietzsche and National Socialism," while one could list several affinities between the Nazi world view and Nietzsche's philosophy, particularly their elitist, militaristic concept of life, "National Socialism, in its origins, borrowed virtually nothing directly from Nietzsche. In the years that followed the war, no one thought to attribute the new movement to Nietzsche."[6] Certainly, as Ernst Nolte has noted, there was intense interest in the figure and philosophy of Nietzsche under the Third Reich, and many commentators spent a great deal of effort trying to turn him into "the philosopher of the new Germany."[7] But while Hitler paid formal homage to the philosopher in 1935 by attending funeral services for his sister, Elisabeth Förster, he virtually never mentioned or cited him in his speeches or table talks.[8] Rosenberg mentioned him even less; he thoroughly preferred Houston Stewart Chamberlain, the son-in-law and faithful inheritor of the tradition of Wagner, whom Nietzsche had violently turned upon, sealing the rupture in their friendship with a scathing essay, a virtually unpardonable sin against a composer said to be Hitler's idol and the operatic standard-bearer of the Teutonic spirit.

The official philosopher of the Third Reich, the man who could simultaneously offer intellectual substance and political prophecy, was not Nietzsche but Plato—a Greek and not a German, although that posed little problem, since Nazi Platonists emphasized their champion's Nordic roots. They were equally quick to point out that the study of Platonism was born in Germany, where, as one of them, Kurt Hildebrandt, said, "the authentic flame of Platonic humanity was rekindled in the north, in the arid soil of the Altmark."[9] This was thanks to the work of Winckelmann above all, but also to all those eminent intellectuals who had informed German Philhellenism.

The Plato of the 1930s and 1940s was, however, read and reinterpreted in a very specific political light. The center of gravity of the Platonist oeuvre had already begun to shift under the Weimar Republic,[10] but it did so far more sharply after 1933: the emphasis was no longer on the Athenian philosopher's epistemological or gnoseological texts but on his political writings. The metaphysical Plato, the philosopher of ideas, was an acolyte of disembodied humanism and the *Aufklärung* of metastasized rationalism. He was shoved aside in favor of the political Plato, the philosopher of the ideal city-state and the regeneration of the community.

In a pamphlet aimed at teachers of Greek, Hans Bogner bluntly declared that the heart of the Platonic oeuvre was the triptych composed of "*Politeia, Politikos, Nomos*"[11]—that is, *The Republic, The Statesman,* and *Laws*—to which the racial scientist Hans Günther added Plato's *Letters*.[12] The Plato who was important now was the "philosopher of the state" and not the "representative of the theory of ideas." For Günther, Plato was not simply a thinker; he "was of the lineage of Solon and Clisthenes. This is the history of Athens: they are the great legislators and men of state . . . who make up the background of his oeuvre," not "the Ionian φυσικοι" or the "first book of Aristotle's *Metaphysics*."[13] His stature was thus due more to his place in the pantheon of lawmakers and statesmen than to his place in that of mere philosophers. As Werner Jaeger forcefully asserted in a 1933 article published in the Nazi journal *Volk im Werden,* in a vigorous attack on the individualist humanism of the eighteenth century, "The Plato of our generation is a creator of states, a legislator. He is no longer the neo-Kantian systematizer and honorable scholarly philosopher, as our predecessors saw him."[14] For Jaeger, Kant was not the saint he was assumed to be in philosophy seminars throughout German universities. Far from being the archetype of German genius, he was a dangerous avatar of a rootless, cosmopolitan Enlightenment. In contrast, so-called Platonic idealism was actually an unsparingly lucid realism, which "only a superficial reader could argue refers to the inaccessible and celestial Kantian ideal."[15]

As we have already seen, the Nazis and their accomplices in the world of pedagogy and the academy resolutely rejected the scrawny, sickly figure of the intellectual, pale and anemic from all his time spent in the dim light of the library within his ivory tower.[16] To them, Plato appeared to be the perfect antithesis of this despicable creature. He was, in contrast, the fullest expression of the "total man," at once a powerful thinker, a respected sportsman, and an accomplished warrior. Nothing surprising when one imagines, as Günther did, that Plato was a Nordic, a product "of the highest Attic nobility . . . where the Nordic blood of the original Hellenes was best preserved until a later date."[17] Günther, who also wrote a book on Plato, emphasized that he was not just the "simple logician or theoretician of knowledge" that "professors of philosophy"[18]—those incorrigible proponents of rational abstraction—had made of him.

This new reading of the Platonic oeuvre was not restricted to the closed circles of pedantic academic cut and thrust. Plato was also taught to young Germans in the secondary schools, through courses in history and in Greek. Platonists and Hellenists argued that in the Third Reich, students needed to be introduced to Plato in high school, for, as Adolf Rusch, a professor of classical literature at the Mommsen gymnasium in Berlin-Grunewald, declared, he was nothing less than "the teacher of the German man."[19] In an article with that very title, Rusch argued that the new German school must forget about the interests of the individual and focus solely on the group, the *Volksgemeinschaft*. Plato was just the man to combat "the sophistic," an expression of "outrageous individualism." Rather than "the maxim according to which man is the measure of all things," he believed that man existed "wholly within the order of the world"—that is, the order of the polis. "For the education of a young man in a state like ours today and for a state like ours today," Plato was "the surest way"[20] to reach and to raise a new generation devoted to the people and to the state.

Looking at German history textbooks, one finds that Plato was a central figure in the Nordic resistance to the racial, intellectual, and moral decadence of the Athenian city-state and the Greek world more generally, a resistance that was, despite the philosopher's entreaties, unfortunately destined to an inglorious exit from the historical stage. Courses in Greek likewise presented Plato as the final torchbearer of Nordic Hellenism. A memo composed by a teacher of classical literature argued that "one must teach Plato to students, precisely because he lifts the Nordic spirit in combat against the most deleterious decadence, against an entire era of destruction. Even if he could not prevent the degeneration of the Athenian people, his fight still resonates today in all men who belong to his race."[21] To all those who dared to see Plato as an ethereal spirit floating weightlessly in a diaphanous cloud of ideas, a memo from one teacher addressed to the Ministry for Education countered that, to the contrary, "the active Nordic spirit found its most sublime expression in Plato's philosophy. With him, the search for knowledge was placed in the service of the education of men and states. If contemplation is in the Easterner an end in itself, Platonic contemplation itself is never dissociated from action."[22]

There was an obvious element of racial determinism in the way that Plato was positioned with respect to subsequent philosophers from the East: the *vita activa,* the *bios politikos* were eminently Platonic, because the Nordic spirit was engaged, active, constructive. The *Leistungsmensch* of Ludwig Clauss's psychoracial typology[23] was once more juxtaposed to the Oriental *Darbietungsmensch,* who was submissive, slippery, and cunning. For Plato, intellectual activity could not be an end unto itself: it was always undertaken in pursuit of another goal, the construction of the ideal city-state.

In this way, teaching Plato boiled down to "practicing racial education." One thus needed to take care, as in all good racial pedagogy, to contrast Plato with "the sophistic and rhetoric as expressions of foreign influence on the race" and as "signs of decadence."[24]

The 1938 reforms took such calls into account. Plato was listed as one of four authors written into the different segments of the Greek curriculum,[25] along with Homer, Thucydides, and Xenophon, rather surprisingly preferred to other classics of Greek instruction, like Isocrates and Demosthenes, from Athens's decadent fourth century, or Aristotle and the Stoics, neither of which were included in the curriculum, for similar reasons. Plato's weight in the curriculum was further emphasized when one considers his influence on Xenophon, who was his rival and, like him, a philo-Spartan resolutely opposed to Athenian democracy.

Past teachers and scholars had frequently been mistaken about Plato, who was not merely a great theoretician of knowledge. They had failed to understand the role he imagined for philosophers in the new city-state that he sought to create to combat Athenian decadence. Plato had said that philosophers should rule, yes, but the word *philosopher* for him did not mean what we understand by the term today. Günther observed that the word *philosopher*, which for us is "but a word composed of four dead syllables that speak only to the scholar,"[26] had a completely different meaning for the Greeks. According to Günther, the philosopher is one who desires, thinks, and lives truth—a *volle Mensch*, epitomized by Plato himself, who could not be confused with his mediocre epigones, mere professors of philosophy, whom Günther so enjoyed despising.[27] Kurt Hildebrandt, an intellectual historian and expert on Plato,[28] similarly warned that one must not confuse the great philosopher with the "ivory tower intellectual"[29] or the "abstract thinker":[30] the true philosopher was one like Socrates, a soldier in the Peloponnesian War who, turning to civilian life, "fought with the weapon of dialectic wit."[31] Hildebrandt was the only one, however, who depicted Socrates in such a positive light.[32]

More specifically, the philosopher was thus a warrior, and in fact, military language structured much of the discourse on Plato. As Hildebrandt noted: "The philosopher Plato is the exact opposite of the abstract scholar: he is a man who distinguished himself in war as well as in the conduct of affairs of state."[33]

It is easy to see how the Greeks' martial perspective on the world impregnated all of Plato's work; as he was the archetypal Hellene, his work itself was proof of his Nordic character. "Plato agreed with Heraclitus: Polemos [the Greek embodiment of war] is the father of all things," which teaches that "the education of warriors is placed at the center of the politeia,"[34] since "for him being a real man means being a warrior."[35] Those whom he described as philosopher-kings were, first and foremost, warriors who were not "removed from the caste of warriors until the age of fifty," having distinguished themselves through the use of both their minds and their weapons.[36] The warrior was a sort of intellectual knight, and combat a cultural activity; accordingly, the philosopher Ernst Krieck exhorted his students to become political soldiers, while Martin Heidegger recognized the armed services and the labor service alongside his knowledge service.

RACISM AND INEQUALITY: PLATO, A FORERUNNER OF THE FÜHRER

A product of the Peloponnesian War and the crisis it provoked but also consistent with a fundamentally combative Greek warrior culture, the Platonic world view was not content with the strict confines of a "small Hellenic state without a foreign empire." According to Hildebrandt, Plato envisioned the creation of what he called a Grossgriechenland,[37] a Greater Greece that strangely recalled the Pan-Germanist and Nazi Grossdeutschland, or Greater Germany. Hildebrandt implicitly invoked the specter of a Greek *Kleinstaaterei*—what we might today call "balkanization"—and fratricidal civil discord, a state of permanent war between Greek city-states that, as Plato foresaw all too well, would lead to their destruction. The political disintegration of the Greek city-states as they split into rival camps was often compared to the extreme fragmentation of the German states before unification in 1871. In this context, Plato was a *Kämpfer*, a fighter who battled for the survival and rejuvenation of his people, bloodied and weakened from the Peloponnesian War and threatened by racial subversion within through miscegenation with Asiatic races. The Platonic oeuvre was thus given the weight of drama, held aloft like a heraldic banner in times of great crisis. Plato stood out as a redoubt in a situation of historical urgency, according to Günther, who portrayed him as the last Nordic sentry in a polluted and perverse world on the point of self-destruction.

The parallel with Hitler was so clear that Joachim Bannes, another Plato specialist, made the connection explicit in all seriousness in the title of a pamphlet he wrote comparing the führer to the founder of the Academy. In *Hitlers Kampf und Platons Staat: Eine Studie über den ideologischen Aufbau der Nationalsozialistischen Freiheitsbewegung* (Hitler's struggle and Plato's republic: A study on the ideological foundations of the National-Socialist liberation movement),[38] Bannes equated *Mein Kampf* to Plato's *Republic* and delved into a comparison of Hitler's biography with that of the philosopher, demonstrating the profound affinities shared by the two thinkers and statesmen. Hans Bogner, for his part, contented himself with merely hinting at the conflation of the führer of contemporary Germany and the führer of Athenian philosophy, remarking that the teachings of the Greek master and his vigorous prescriptions for the issues of his day were formulated in "a dictatorial tone."[39] This hardly fit with the reality of a dialogic and questioning Plato—or his frequently aporetic dialogues—a philosopher for whom the essential resided in the question, in the movements of a mind that sought to shed itself of certainty in the attempt to reach truth. But for these Nazi Platonists, there could be no doubt that Plato was the theoretician of *Führergedanke*,[40] the idea that the führer was providentially chosen and racially incorruptible.

Like Hitler, Plato was a Nordic warrior who fought to save his people from the threat of extinction. This was the reading of Plato offered up by the Hellenist Hans Holtorf in his introduction to an anthology of selected passages from *The Republic* designed for high school students: "In this era of profound shock to all moral values, the great Plato stood up and led the heroic fight against the degeneration of his people, against the disastrous spirit of absolute destruction.... This great, wise figure appealed to the grandeur of the Nordic soul.... The fight that Adolf Hitler leads today has the same sublime objective. The führer's words show in what direction the work of Plato must lead us, and must enter into the souls of German youth."[41] For Hans Heyse, a historian of philosophy who dedicated his inaugural rectoral address to "the idea of science and the German university," Plato was a model for every combatant in the service of the National Socialist ideal. The professor, who was certainly not afraid of conflating eras that spanned millennia, maintained that Plato's intention was not the development of an insipid pseudoidealism, as "classicism and an outmoded humanism believed," but "an attempt at the total renewal of the National-Hellenic Dasein."[42]

The renewal of an Athenian city-state on the road to extinction demanded a strict racial policy, of which Plato was supposedly the pre-nineteenth-century avatar. Plato's texts were accordingly reinterpreted through the prism of Nazi racism. Hans Günther, in his book on Platonic racism, made the founder of the Academy into a precursor of "Gobineau, Mendel, and Galton," none of whom "ever failed to appreciate the iron law of inequality"[43] among peoples, otherwise overshadowed by the perverted, deleterious idealism of 1789. Plato took into account the undeniable fact that not all men were created equal: *The Republic* taught that mankind could be divided into three types, each called upon to perform its duty as producer, warrior, or ruler. To expand upon this idea and identify these three types, Plato turned to parable, describing souls made of gold, silver, and bronze, which Günther claimed as a metaphor for racial difference. While the philosophers were supposed to rule, it was evident that "only men of pure blood could be philosophers;"[44] the "predisposition to philosophy" was not a question of apprenticeship or application but rather "a question of race"[45]—not something that could be read in a book and thus potentially open to anyone, but a biologically determined calling. Günther thus dismissed the universality of reason, just like Hildebrandt, who deduced that "the state depends on a pure race and the proper selection"[46] of philosopher-kings and the willingness of every person to adapt to the function that nature had assigned them. The Hellenist and historian Hans Bogner thought much the same thing: "Who has the right to be a philosopher? . . . Certainly not bastards, but only men of pure blood (*Rep.* 535c et seq.) . . . men of sound body and mind (536b)."[47] It was thus only fitting that "aptitude for philosophy was for Plato a question of race."[48]

If this eugenicist reading of Plato was not completely insane, it nevertheless certainly did violence to the text of *The Republic,* which, though it speaks of "chattel" and of selection, does not confine individuals within the strict determinism of their birth, destined to shape their entire existence. Nazi racism hermetically sealed people into the airtight bubble of their race, while for Plato, every individual with the proper qualities must be deemed worthy and eligible for entry into the castes of warriors and philosopher-kings.[49]

For our authors, however, Plato's racism logically led to eugenics, of which the founder of the Academy was also the first theoretician.[50] The biologist and anthropologist Fritz Lenz did not think twice about claiming this prestigious lineage for his own work, since Plato "was as much a eugenicist as a philosopher."[51] Richard Walther Darré, who also wrote a book on Plato, did much the same in subtly linking idealism and selectionism. How can one claim to be a man of ideas if one does not elevate the idea, at once form and object, high above mere reality? To speak of the ideal was thus to speak of hierarchy and selection: "It was Plato who gave the word *idea* its philosophic meaning, who became the first founder of idealism . . . [and] who gave the realm of the ideal an absolute value, above all others—and it was this very same Plato who, as an idealist, was led to create the idea of selection."[52]

Hans Günther, meanwhile, described the sense of historical urgency and peril that conditioned the circumstances of Plato's life: "One must recall that, in Plato's time, Attic noblesse, the eupatridae, . . . were in the process of dying out, and that this nobility of Nordic racial descent had been diluted several times over with foreign stock after the founding of Attica."[53] Plato's time "was an era of decadence" marked by "de-Nordification and . . . racial degeneration" brought about by an absurd, fratricidal Peloponnesian War that had shed the finest Nordic blood, the decimation of the great blond long skulls of the original Greece: "In

Plato's time, blonds had become a very weak minority . . . the dominant race of the era, the Nordic race, [having] come within a hair's breadth of utter disappearance during the war."[54] The natural leaders of the Athenian community, the Nordics, were decimated by the war, the capital of Attica abandoned to democracy, a cheap, populist regime that glorified the individual and lost sight of the natural purpose of a state, the *Volksgemeinschaft*. Plato thus made it his mission to restore the city-state's leadership caste, "to train führers" for the Athenian polis, which of course presumed the availability of the right human matériel. One could not create leaders out of just any group of humans; "one first had to find the stuff of which leaders are made."[55] To restore Athens's caste of superior Nordic men to the original purity and beauty of their Indo-Germanic countrymen at the time of its founding,[56] it was important to encourage marriages between racial equals, in order to foster the birth of racially pure children,[57] and to impose "the elimination of all sick or deformed children, the extermination of all who are unfit for life."[58]

Far from being a naive or innocent idealist, Plato was held up as a representative of the most uncompromising and virile realism. In a small collection of essays titled *Staat und Rasse* (State and race), the Platonist Kurt Hildebrandt reversed the common perception of the philosopher: "Plato was not a utopian but developed a genuine knowledge of [natural] reality and necessity."[59] The selectionist, segregationist, and eugenic measures extolled in *The Republic* were cited as examples of a fully developed racial policy,[60] ideas that "demanded painful sacrifices of the idealism"[61] underlying irresponsible modern humanism.

Plato was not being cruel when he gave such laws to his ideal city-state; he was merely being consistent, unafraid to espouse the design of nature: "his laws have something of natural law about them,"[62] in that they proscribe any counterselective effort to restrict the course of nature, which social organization must not impinge in any way. As Hitler had said in *Mein Kampf*, the principles of National Socialism took their inspiration from the decisive and unyielding character of the laws of nature.

Fulminating against the obstacles to such selection erected by the emerging welfare state, Hildebrandt paid homage to Plato, who had "understood perfectly that every obstacle to that which today we call natural selection" could very well profit the individual, thus coddled and protected, but it "hurt the people seen as a whole." The happiness, well-being, or survival of the individual mattered little to the Nordic statesman, legislator, or führer: Plato "always saw the totality [of the people], thus turning away from the individual case,"[63] since "leniency [toward a degenerate individual] would appear to Plato to be a cruelty against the people seen as a whole,"[64] the hard law of numbers that, for the Platonist as for eugenicists, discounted the nullity of the individual in favor of the infinity of the masses. Such a policy would seem hard to conceive for a humanist, steeped in mercy, who myopically focused only on the individual and forgot to consider that the only thing that gave an individual meaning and even life itself was his community, which a deformed or weakened person would contaminate if allowed to live and to procreate. Hildebrandt thus reiterated all the arguments deployed by partisans of eugenics and the eradication of a biological threat through a policy of neutralization (that is, sterilization) or destruction (physical elimination). To appease the fears or forestall the objections of contemporary humanists, Hans Günther magnanimously clarified that he would not advocate the application of Plato's ruthlessly severe laws. His proposals constituted a civilized, contemporary eugenics: he was content to prescribe the "sterilization"[65] of weak individuals in lieu of the death penalty allegedly demanded by Plato.

As an implacable enemy of the feeble, compassionate humanism of the Enlightenment, Günther argued that Plato's ideas had been opposed by none other than the Sophists, who were "men of the Asiatic race, as racial science has taught us."[66] A secondary-school textbook proclaimed that while the Greeks had indeed been receptive to the Sophists' individualism, it was only because their blood had already been diluted, as could be deduced by the strict determinism that governed the spirit of the race: "The sophistic is completely foreign to Nordic thought and proves to be a product of the race of Asia Minor, which habitually debates concepts and questions inherited wisdom in order to destroy it. The influence of this philosophy could grow only because the Greeks had become unfaithful to their origins. If they had remained a people of pure race, the accent that [the Sophists] placed on the exceptionality of the individual and his rights would have seemed incomprehensible to them."[67]

Part of this paragraph is a virtual copy of a passage written by Hans Günther himself.[68] Ever faithful to his racial symptomatology, Günther considered the sophistic "completely impregnated with a non-Hellenic spirit."[69]

Times had hardly changed. The struggle and the racial principles at work were the same as in antiquity; the new enemies of the Nordic race were 1789 and the man whom Günther, significantly, called "the sophist Rousseau,"[70] a worthy offspring of a mongrel France completely in thrall to an egalitarian ideology. The French radical Édouard Herriot's proposal for an *école unique*[71]—the absolute antithesis of the selective, elitist system of education established by Plato—was but a deplorable, if revealing, symptom.

Against the blind egalitarianism of revolutionary modernity, which ineptly and imprudently proclaimed "the same thing for all," it was imperative to return to a virile, Nordic, and Platonic "to each what he deserves,"[72] a *Jedem das seine* that now sounds like a sinister anticipation of the motto displayed at the entrance to the camp at Buchenwald. The democratic ideal of equality was repudiated in favor of equity, which distributed rights proportionally to each subject.

Plato was indeed a "master for our time,"[73] as Hildebrandt claimed: "modern biology would be hard pressed to propose laws better suited for the selection of the fittest than the laws of Plato."[74] Whoever wished to build an organic state for the *Volksgemeinschaft,* a state-body that relied upon "unity through blood"[75] and a strict racial hierarchy, should follow Plato's precepts. Reading the great Nordic philosopher, Hans Bogner warned, should not lead to a simple, useless "aesthetic Hellenomania"[76] but rather instill a firm desire to enact "a renaissance in our existence" as a nation, a rebirth that would rest on "the rich, diverse heritage of a thousand-year past."[77] Bogner rejoiced that Greece was the order of the day in contemporary Germany: "The presence and predominance of the Hellenic in the new Germany is clear to every observer; one need only think of our new buildings, of the games and the Olympic idea, of sport, of the rediscovered unity of the body and the spirit, of a state now seen as an institution for the education and selection of men, of our fine arts. At public events, the fundamental kinship and elective affinity that exists between Germany and Hellenism is frequently visible."[78]

CHORAL THEATER AND GREEK AMPHITHEATERS: THE REPRESENTATION OF A HOLISTIC *VOLKSGEMEINSCHAFT*

Bogner had reason to rejoice: the holistic community of the new Germany was built not just with imitation architecture but also with Greek dramaturgy, one source of the "public demonstrations" that it enacted. The ancient Greek theater and its chorus would also help construct the national community. One of the Nazi Party's many cultural initiatives, the Reichsbund für deutsche Freilicht- und Volksschauspiele e.V. (Reich league of open-air and people's theater), established on 23 January 1933, assumed the task of sponsoring theatrical performances with an overt political message. As part of its mission, the league, formally part of both the party and the Reich's Ministry for Public Enlightenment and Propaganda, promoted an initiative to build some four hundred open-air theaters, called *Thingstätten* (of which some sixty would eventually be built); this ambitious public works project, which fit perfectly into the economic policy of countercyclical pump priming through public works, was entrusted to the Reichsarbeitdienst (Reich labor service), headed by Robert Ley.

Terms like *Thing, Thingplatz,* and *Thingstätte* were borrowed from German translations of Tacitus, who used such terms to describe the legislative and judiciary assembly peculiar to the Germanic peoples,[79] an assembly that until Boulainvilliers and Montesquieu had nourished the fantasy of a Germanic democracy amid the freedom of the forests.[80]

These buildings, which were destined to host festivals and political and cultural demonstrations for the *Volksgemeinschaft,* were meant to resound "with Germanic prehistory" and with "the deepest racial roots"[81] of the German people. The *Thingplatz* at Heiligenberg,[82] overlooking the Neckar River valley at Heidelberg, was inaugurated by Goebbels himself on 22 June 1935 upon a hilltop that preserved archaeological traces of what were supposedly Germanic cults. All such *Thingstätten,*[83] however, presented an architecture that was a strict copy of the Greek amphitheaters of antiquity; the semicircle of raised stone steps was taken directly from the theaters of the Attic peninsula or Asia Minor. In Heidelberg as in Greece, this section reserved for spectators—the *koilon*—was dug into the hillside at a natural gradient. The rows descended toward an orchestra, circular like at Epidaurus, where the chorus was to be assembled. Acoustics were provided by a wall in the back that combined elements of the Greek skene and thymele, the altar of Dionysus.

The *Thingstätten* were in essence conceived to host outdoor performances of choral theater in the Greek style, a new dramatic genre promoted by the regime's cultural politics. These *chorische Dichtungen,* composed by authors handpicked by the regime, which offered them wages, stage time, and SS uniforms, borrowed their themes from medieval German history or the present day: the tragic fate of Albert Leo Schlageter[84] and the seizure of power in 1933[85] were adapted to contribute to the political education of the masses through theater. The form of these pieces, in which the protagonist rattled off a litany of appeals, each answered by the chorus, imitated the Attic theater of Thespis, who created the Greek tragedy when he added an actor to the tragic chorus of Dionysian liturgy. This form was thus ideal to depict the allegorical scene relating the führer (the protagonist) to the *Volk* (the chorus).

The pedagogical program of the *Thingstätten,* which ultimately proved too costly to build and maintain, was abandoned in 1936. The regime quickly determined that the skies over Germany did not offer the same benevolent climate for outdoor theater as those of the Mediterranean. The clumsy scenography and heavy-handed didacticism of the *chorische Dichtungen,* which failed to win over the public, gave way to demonstrations, parades, and torchlit gatherings organized by the party. The idea of publicizing the link with antiquity through theatrical performance was abandoned, and the party instead entrusted such activities to the Tage der deutschen Kunst in Munich, as well as the various demonstrations surrounding the Olympic Games in 1936.

ARISTOTLE IN PURGATORY

The contrast between the Third Reich's avid interest in Plato and its relative neglect of Aristotle is shocking but instructive.

The volume of Platonic studies far exceeded the number of books and articles devoted to Aristotle, who, from a quantitative perspective, sank into virtual oblivion and, in qualitative terms, was as derided as Plato was exalted.

At first glance, one might think that Aristotle would be an ideologically pivotal figure for National Socialism, given the recurrent use of the term *politischer Mensch* by Nazi intellectuals and ideologues.

The expression *politischer Mensch,* which can be traced back to Alfred Bäumler, was in essence a calque of Aristotle's *zoon politikon,* which appeared in book 1 of his *Politics*—"man is by nature a political animal"—and which Bäumler, as a good Philhellenist, knew quite well. As we have seen, however, he reformulated the Aristotelian concept to turn this essentially and ultimately sociable being into a political soldier in the service of the new Reich.[86] Still, Bäumler returned to Aristotle, discreetly and without attribution, in an article in which he defined the political man as "a man in a community"[87] and reminded readers that "*politics* is a Greek word."[88]

The fact that Bäumler, a man intimately acquainted with Greek philosophy and letters, mentioned Aristotle's name only once while appropriating his most basic ideas is revealing of the poor esteem in which the Stagirite was held by Nazi intellectuals. Aristotle was condemned to philosophical disgrace because of his poor historical timing and his racial corruption.

Alfred Rosenberg liquidated Aristotle in just a few pages in *The Myth of the Twentieth Century*, calling him a "systematic diffuser [of the Socratic method],"[89] stigmatized for being a heavily cerebral logician in the lineage of the Oriental Socrates, the polar opposite of the Nordic integrity of a Plato, who was agile both physically and intellectually.

Ernst Krieck carried this dismissal of Aristotle even further, making him responsible for the entire decline of traditional Greek education. Aristotle had encouraged the emergence of a dry, disembodied rationalism, overly literary and abstract, which had lost all sense of proportion between body and spirit. He depicted the philosopher as "the great master of this system of [Hellenistic] education," the perverse humanism of pure rationality, having lost sight of the organic wholeness of the human being. Living during the height of Hellenistic civilization and the decline of the Athenian city-state, Aristotle was little valued, since his oeuvre dated from an era of racial and intellectual decadence, the physical and spiritual de-Nordification of Greece. Aristotle was interesting only, Krieck suggested, as a preserver of the Greek wisdom that he had patiently accumulated in his scrupulous encyclopedias. He revealed himself there, as in other places, to be a simple "curator," in contrast to a true Nordic creator like Plato, and in any case, he remained a pure "rationalist"[90] and complete foreigner throughout his life.

Positive remarks about Aristotle were brief and rare. A few could be found in the work of Ludwig Schemann, who deemed the disowning of Aristotle, as a theoretician of slavery and racial hierarchy, to be "incomprehensible."[91] Another could be found in a secondary-school textbook: there Aristotle—the teacher of Alexander the Great—appeared to be a figure of wisdom, warning against "disruptions of the blood" and "the mixing of Greeks with peoples foreign to the [Nordic] race."[92] Despite these two points in his favor, Aristotle nevertheless remained a thoroughly marginal figure.

STOICISM, OR THE ANTI-PLATO

Even more harmful than Aristotle were the Stoics. The doctrine of Stoicism, a school of thought that emerged in the fourth century BC, marked a break with the ancients' traditional conception of the world and man. Traditional Greek cosmology looked out upon a finite world, ordered and permanent, where every being and every object tended to find its natural place. It followed that, like the cosmos, the world of men was hierarchical and unequal, with every individual occupying its assigned place in the inherently objective, inegalitarian order of nature—the two worlds, natural (cosmos) and civic (polis), possessing the same structure.[93]

In contrast to this hierarchical, pluralistic vision of the cosmos, the Stoics possessed a unified, monist conception of mankind and its universe, in which all possessed reason equally.

For the Nazis, the Stoa—the site of late Greek philosophical education—was an expression of the eclipse of the race; it marked the passage from luminous Hellenic Nordicism to crepuscular Hellenism, the antithesis of a pure and heroic Hellas that had persevered until Plato, its final incarnation taking the form of the great Academician.

A product of the Asiatic-Semitic immigration that had subsumed Athens and diluted its blood through racial miscegenation by the end of the fifth century BC, the Stoic school promoted an egalitarian doctrine that destroyed all sense of racial hierarchy, as the racial scientist (and follower of Gobineau) Ludwig Schemann remarked: "We have long felt and stated that blood played an essential role in the foundation and development of the Stoic school. It arose almost exclusively from Semitic circles."[94] The Viennese historian of antiquity Fritz Schachermeyr agreed and vehemently denounced Hellenism: "Hellenism reveals to us a Greek people in complete dissolution in cosmopolitanism and thus in full de-Nordification. The most remarkable product of Hellenism, the Stoa, points in the same direction. It had been developed by Semites and bastards, becoming a pseudoideal good only for the arguments of the stateless and the racial enemies of later eras."[95] Schachermeyr extended his racial punctiliousness so far as to detail, with meticulous precision, the geographic origins—and thus the racial identities—of the leaders of the Stoic school: "Among the scholarchs who came before Panaetius, only one came from a village where the majority were of Greek blood. . . . The others came from Cilicia, from Cyprus, and from Babylon. Zeno, the founder, came from the Semitic village of Citium, on the island of Cyprus."[96] In another text, Schachermeyr generically provided all Hellenistic philosophers with a "Levantine background."[97] Max Pohlenz, a great expert on the Stoic period and the author of several works on Stoicism definitive up until the 1970s, wrote of Zeno as a *Vollblutphöniker*, a "full-blooded Phoenician":[98] "We find in the Stoic doctrine a good many traits that remind us that its founders were not Greeks." The Stoics were *unhellenisch*[99]—"un-Hellenic," and thus definitely not Nordic, either in their ideas or in the blood that produced them.

No Nordic mind would have imagined that all men could be considered equal, called to membership in some universal fellowship of the human race (*universi generis humani societate*) as imagined by the Roman Stoic Cicero,[100] an unrecognizable χοσμοπολις devoid of all hierarchies based on racial values. Here Schachermeyr picked up on a theme dear to racial theorists and proponents of scientific racism, who, since Gobineau, attributed all egalitarian, individualist, or democratic ideas to blood ruined by miscegenation and shorn of all its unique qualities, blood that had thus lost all concept of greatness and racial hierarchy. According to strict biological determinism and simple physiology, any truly pure blood that was free of racial mixing and aware of its own precious value could think in terms of only elitist and not egalitarian ideals.[101] The Stoa thus appeared to Nazi historians and racial scientists as the anti-Plato par excellence. Ludwig Schemann, the disciple of Gobineau, denounced the Stoa and the complex of "cosmopolitan and egalitarian ideas"[102] that made up the heart of its doctrine as a Semitic poison.

A symptom of Greek racial degeneration, Stoicism was also subsequently a powerful instrument of Roman decadence: after the battle of Cynoscephalae (197 BC) and the Roman conquest of Greece, Stoicism was in essence a part of the conquerors' spoils. Books, prisoners of war, and the *graeculi* brought back in the train of Rome's legions imported what would, little by little, become the preferred philosophy of the republican and imperial elite. They found in Stoicism a rigor compatible with the *mos maiorum* and a universalist ideology well suited for Roman imperialism and its project for global hegemony. The Stoics' view of a unified mankind found fertile ground in Roman imperial domination and its unification of the ecumene, which became a true cosmopolis, a unitary *civitas maxima* that encompassed all of humanity under one single leader and authority.[103]

The emperor Caracalla was inspired by Stoicism, as well as obvious fiscal motives, when he granted Roman citizenship to all residents of the empire in 212 through the *Constitutio Antoniniana*,[104] which Rosenberg decried as the root cause of "Roman race-chaos."[105]

Hans Günther averred that "Stoicism has been considered one of the most racially destructive forces in Roman history": the original, strictly hierarchical Nordic republic of the old Romans had been undone by Stoic notions of "individualism" and "cosmopolitan citizenship."[106]

What truly disqualified Stoicism was that "on the one hand it looked only at the individual in isolation and on the other at the community of betters from all peoples and all races, not as a member of a lineage or a clan or a people or a race. As a doctrine, Stoicism eliminated all blood differences."[107]

Like Sophism a few centuries later, Stoicism was an intellectual starburst that presaged the Revolution of 1789. Fritz Schachermeyr asserted, deploringly, that "the result of man's fundamental equality was the notion of the dignity of man, the rights of man, the need for tolerance." In short, because of Stoicism, "humanity now means leveling,"[108] the most deleterious individualism associated with the most dissolute universalism.

This diabolical convergence led to the disintegration of the racial body through the infiltration and admixture of foreign ideas that brought with them a new vision of man and his relationship to the collective. Once upon a time, when the Nordic body of Greek citizens was still uniform and whole in its initial purity, the mutual and spontaneous belonging of its members was a given: the homogeneity of blood expressed itself intellectually through an organic and holistic conception of the body politic, and the individual held no meaning and enjoyed no dignity except as a member of the racial body.

The mixing of blood had muddied this unitary conception of the racial body. Detached from his belonging to a blood and a soil, the figure of the cosmopolitan who emerged with the advent of later Hellenism could be defined only as an atomic individual, an isolated monad absolved of any ties to a group that, in any event, simply no longer existed: Hellenistic bastardization dissolved the binds of the polis to privilege the individual.[109] This, according to the author of a manual for teachers of history, explained the antipodean opposition between the Platonic conception of the state, which was strictly holistic, and the individualistic sensibility of Hellenistic philosophers: "In the place of the common good, of belonging to a community defined by blood, the unrestrained domination of the individual, of the cosmopolitan who recognized no other bond other than that of reason, imposed itself. The Greek no longer had a fatherland; the world was his country."[110] The advent of the individual, "detached from the state and his people, alone at the center of the world," the fragmentation of the Greek people "into an infinity of atoms, each of which existed only for itself," was the work of racially degenerate philosophers like "the founder of Stoicism, Zeno, a Hellenized Semite."[111]

Others based their arguments not on race but on opposition to the Enlightenment and the humanism of modern natural law, lamenting a caricatured, biologically degenerate and intellectually decadent version of Hellenism in contrast to its original Nordic variant. Nineteenth-century German romanticism and its French idols, such as Maurice Barrès, juxtaposed the natural, holistic coherence of a gemeinschaft, a community of birth, soil, and blood, to the cultural fragility of a gesellschaft, an artifact constructed by the willful decision of free individuals to join a social contract that they supposed to be preexisting: the holistic gemeinschaft of blood, fate, and nature opposed the individualistic gesellschaft of choice, free will, and culture.

A high school textbook explained how Plato's ambition was the resurrection of a holistic racial principle, a society conceived as a biologically unified body—that is, of the gemeinschaft: "The true state was not, in Plato's eyes, composed of individuals. . . . It was, rather, an organism, a unique entity. The citizen was but a member or a part of the whole and found purpose and meaning only in the group."[112] Another text took two pages to depict Plato as a sort of Don Quixote of the Attic period, a hero of the sublime and "vain struggle against racial decadence."[113]

Stigmatized as a philosophy of individualism and withdrawal, a doctrine of private happiness and ataraxy far from the affairs of the world, Stoicism was a philosophy of dissolution of the polity and disintegration of the racial and political community. Stoics were destroyers of the state because their doctrine came from a vandal blood that destroyed cultures: in the tripartite typology of race offered by Hitler in *Mein Kampf,* such Orientals and Semites belonged to the destructive species of *Kulturzerstörer,* in contrast to the creative *Kulturbegründer,* the Aryans.[114]

Nevertheless, both Günther and Schemann made clear that Stoicism had been able to seduce fundamentally Nordic ancient Romans like Seneca and Marcus Aurelius only because they no longer felt any connection with a racially miscegenated Roman people and thus sought to retreat into the every-man-for-himself ethos of private happiness, where they could while away the time meditating on the *fatum* and waiting for ataraxy.[115] Their estrangement was a choice dictated by the racial mediocrity of the Roman people.

THE PHILOSOPHER WITH THE UNLOVABLE FACE: SOCRATES THE SATYR AND DECADENT METIC

The Asiatic maggot of the Stoics had been concealed within the philosophical fruit of the Greeks since the time of Socrates. The man that Plato—perhaps because of his slight racial deficiency, an ounce of

Dinaric blood[116]—had chosen as his master, a seducer and corrupter of Athenian youth, was in many respects presented as the antithesis of Plato, in both race and ethos.

The repudiation of Socrates by scholars of Plato under the Third Reich was virtually universal. Only Hans Bogner recommended that his Greek class read Plato's *Apology,* which celebrated the figure of a master of whom it could be said Plato was "the most faithful disciple"[117] or even an "evangelist."[118] Bogner presented an image, as positive as it was rare, of Socrates taking up the sword of dialectic against foreign Sophists who were corrupters of the polis, in an uphill battle against the decline of Athens.

He was truly the only one. In his take on Platonic racism, Günther completed his tour de force without mentioning Socrates one single, treacherous time in more than a hundred pages.[119] In his other works, he made not a single passing reference but rather lingered virulently, like many others, on the trial of the subhuman Socrates.

To begin with, Socrates was ugly—of an ugliness that clashed dreadfully with the Nordic stereotype: "Xenophon described Socrates as a short, stocky type, with a thick neck and a pot belly," Günther recalled.[120] As any semiotician of the human physiognomy could tell, such hideousness of the body could only correspond to a similar hideousness of the spirit. Günther proposed an original interpretation of the Socratic dialogue and maieutics, which became "vulgar and anti-Nordic familiarity": "This lack of restraint and distinction . . . is betrayed by how it functions, for it assails strangers with questions on the street and inserts itself into the conversations of others," something foreign to Nordic propriety and reserve. Faced with such a bundle of damning symptoms, the verdict, implacable, was clear: Socrates was, according to all the evidence, of "an Eastern race,"[121] inferior, miscegenated, and foreign, a man who tried to impose his ideas at a time of Athenian decadence, when the Nordic racial element was in decline.[122] Others, like the art historian Paul Schultze-Naumburg, saw in him "a perfect example of the Alpine type."[123]

The harm posed by Socrates was not limited just to inopportune intrusions into the private conversations of his contemporaries. For Rosenberg, Socrates heralded the advent of the Stoics, in that he established the basis for Greek philosophical individualism. By teaching that virtue could be learned, Socrates undermined the elitist foundations of Greek inegalitarianism:[124] Socrates proposed a new conception of humanity, "a new human classification, not according to races and peoples, but according to individual man. With the collapse of Athenian social democracy, Socrates became the international Social Democrat of his day."¹²⁵

This deleterious individualism had produced as its monstrous offspring the Western individualistic humanism of more recent centuries, which, "like Socrates, looked toward man, not the Greek, the German, the Jew, or the Chinese,"¹²⁶ and which Günther denounced with the vigor of a Joseph De Maistre.

This unitarian conception of the human community, which destroyed the strictly hierarchical and inegalitarian vision that traditionally characterized the Greeks, was taken up by Antisthenes, the true disciple and continuation of Socrates and his legacy.¹²⁷ Alfred Rosenberg accordingly absolved Plato of any accusations of Socratism: "It was his disciple Antisthenes, the son of a Hither-Asiatic slave woman, who then drew so many conclusions from Socrates' ideas and ventured forth to preach the destruction of all barriers between races and peoples in the name of human progress."¹²⁸ Like the Stoics but well before them, Socrates—who lived in an era when Athens was demographically exsanguinated by war—was at once cause and symptom of the decline of the Greek spirit and the Hellenes' racial degeneration: "The greatest symbol of this new, hostile, racially unconscious chaotic group—the antithesis of the Hellenic race-soul—was Socrates."¹²⁹

Plato neither promoted nor disseminated Socrates' teachings. In fact, he presented his pupils with a Platonic version of the great philosopher, putting "the words of his own soul in the mouth of Socrates,"¹³⁰ who became a supporting actor in his dialogues, reduced to a mere spokesman for Plato's own message. Plato was thus not a disciple of the devil. This beautiful Nordic specimen was not the dupe of an Eastern *Untermensch* but, quite the contrary, the desperate defender of the race, who, "at the end of his life," according to Rosenberg, "wished to save his people racially by enacting a powerful constitution. None of this was Socratic; it was the last great flowering of the Hellenic spirit."¹³¹

One sees, then, that the figures of Socrates and the Stoics were exposed by denunciation and repudiation: Socrates and the Stoics had undermined and threatened the inegalitarian, hierarchical, holistic edifice of the traditional Greek community through their deliberate promotion of individualism. From the moment that Socrates, and later the Stoics, proclaimed that the individual was the source of all value, the notions of people and race necessarily lost theirs.

Vigilance, according to Fritz Schachermeyr, was thus necessary for the scholar of the humanities, classics, or antiquity if they wanted, as the author emphasized, to preserve their role and their place in the new National Socialist state. Experts in antiquity would have to teach racially valid and spiritually pertinent material: "Until now we have accepted everything that came from antiquity as a sort of sublime revelation. . . . This is how the humanist, who was on the one hand the conservator of the most noble part of the Nordic spirit, has become the vehicle for all anti-Nordic spiritual patrimony." Only a starry-eyed humanism, a blind adoration for antiquity that did not separate the Nordic wheat from the Asiatic-Semitic chaff, could have preserved the "destructive poison" in a culture that had "eliminated the Nordic peoples of antiquity"[132]—and that still remained an active threat in the contemporary world. Not all of antiquity was ripe for the eating; any self-respecting humanism thus required a very selective approach to the humanities.

The Platonic project of the renewal of the Athenian state and Attic civilization had adopted the model of Sparta, of which Plato was a fervent admirer: the infatuation with the "philo-Spartan would-be Dorian" ("spartafreundlich-dorisierend")[133] under the Third Reich was inseparable from the renewed interest in the history of Lacedaemon and the organizational model exemplified by the Laconian city-state.

Like Plato, Sparta found new favor among Hellenists and pedagogues after 1933. Helmut Berve, a specialist in Greek history and the author of a monograph on Sparta first published in 1920, used the preface to a 1937 edition to highlight the attention that Sparta now received: "Little in the antique world enjoys such general and lively interest as the Spartan state. Its education of its young, its communitarian spirit, its military way of life, its discipline and heroic submission of the individual—its duties and virtues, then, which we have rediscovered, appear to us to be designed with total clarity and fulfilled with an absence of compromise that compel us to dive into this unique community."[134]

THE MYTH OF SPARTA: FROM ANTIQUITY TO THE THIRD REICH

The Lacedaemonians had cultivated discretion and secrecy. Their laconicism has been proverbial since antiquity: not content just to speak little, they wrote little and built little as well, leaving nothing to posterity that could attest to their political and military might in the Greek world of the fifth and sixth centuries BC. The Athenian Thucydides himself was moved by this discrepancy between their parsimony with symbols and their very real power; Athens built the Parthenon and created the tragedy, but Sparta built nothing and contented itself with exercising its troops to the rhythm of the fife and the poetry of war, the crude pen of Tyrtaeus, while it dominated the Hellenic ecumene.[135]

Spartan silence left a vacuum quickly filled by myth. In the absence of the Lacedaemonians' own self-representation, their image was created by their contemporary allies and enemies. Admirers and detractors alike forged the myth of Sparta, a legend draped in black or gilt with gold, excessive in admiration or damnation, but always largely imaginary, deprived of any essential sources left behind by the subjects themselves. The Spartan image, somewhere between idealization and caricature, derived from the curiosity this strong, silent people piqued among the historians, philosophers, geographers, and doxographers of antiquity, who turned Sparta into an archetype that served as both a measuring stick and a lightning rod for political debate, as for instance in fourth-century BC Athens. In this way, the image of Sparta itself became a subject of study for subsequent historians, who have interested themselves in the birth of the myth[136] and its legacy—as it was in a sense performative and an actor in history in its own right.

Elizabeth Rawson, a historian and the author of *The Spartan Tradition in European Thought*,[137] mentioned National Socialism on the very first page of her book, considering it the apex of popular fascination with Sparta in Europe. But the German interest in Sparta did not date from 1933, even if this was not immediately obvious. In her chapter on Winckelmann, Rawson demonstrated how the art historian established a philo-Athenian tradition that viewed Sparta and Laconia as the poor, pitiable cousin of culturally brilliant Attica. In his wake, the great names of early nineteenth-century German Philhellenism glorified Athenian culture and freedom: Attic democracy was trumpeted by Hegel as a further step in the march of the *Weltgeist* toward liberty, while Sparta in this view consisted of little more than a dead end in the great historical epic of the world spirit. For Weimar classicism and the German idealists, Sparta was a mere foil, a tyrannical and militarist state that Humboldt, a liberal individualist, criticized for its omnipresence in the education of its youth, torn away from their families and stripped of their own personalities through intensive communal drills.

The second half of the nineteenth century and the creation of the Reich by Bismarck raised a few timid comparisons between the Prussia of the chancellor and Sparta, a continental power that managed to unify the Greek world of the fourth century BC through the force of its arms and the constitution of the Peloponnesian League after its defeat of Athens.

Thus wearied, Sparta was defeated by Philip, and only the Macedonians were able to revive the Greek city-states, in a league devoted to them. After the eighteenth century, comparisons between Frederick II and Philip of Macedon became more frequent and popular; it was in this tradition that Johann Gustav Droysen published his 1877 biography of Alexander, under the immense, looming shadow of Bismarck. Sparta remained the redheaded stepchild of German Philhellenism: Burckhardt and Nietzsche encouraged this *damnatio memoriae,* portraying Sparta as a restive, backward state devoid of all refined culture and hostile to freedom.

Sparta would owe its subsequent symbolic health to Aryanist racism. Supporters of the Indo-Germanic myth had already produced a positive appreciation of Sparta, by the historian Carl Ottfried Müller, who had dedicated a lengthy 1824 monograph to the Dorian people,[138] in which it turned out that the Spartans, whom he called *die Preußen der Antike*— "the Prussians of antiquity"—were paragons of Nordicism for their racial purity and martial valor. Müller's thesis was picked up by one of the early twentieth-century founding fathers of German racial anthropology, Ludwig Woltmann, whose 1903 tome *Politische Anthropologie* (Political Anthropology) depicted Sparta as the archetype of the Indo-Germanic state in its eugenic policies and exemplary militarism, which tended toward conquering expansionism.

In Nazi eyes, Sparta was doubly interesting: Sparta was the archetype of an elitarian, racist, militarist Nordic state, protototalitarian in its conception and practice of education, but also the most elegant illustration of the virtues of obedience and military self-abnegation. This aspect of the Spartan myth would be mobilized, as we shall see, during the Battle of Stalingrad.[139]

The historian Karl Christ, an expert on the historiography of antiquity, has noted that "there is no other subject in ancient history that has been so politically and ideologically abused as Sparta under Nazi Germany." As a result, the subject "became taboo"[140] in postwar Germany, and it would take until 1983 before German historiography could once again contemplate Laconia and publish the first scholarly work on the subject since 1933.

"SPARTANISM" BETWEEN TOTALITARIANISM AND THE REBIRTH OF THE WEST

In an article on the importance of ancient history for the schools of the new regime, the historian of Greece Helmut Berve defended the value of studying Sparta, the subject of his professional expertise, and the example set by the Spartans. He warned that the amateur aesthetes of belles lettres and high art had misunderstood Sparta's grandeur and significance if they viewed it simply as a cultural desert of verse and lyres. But even those who saw it as a "poor and crude" city-state must not forget that the richest part of its heritage resided in "the creation of a perfectly communitarian way of life," to the point that the "greatest philosopher of the Greeks"—by which he meant Plato—"saw there, more than anywhere else, a way of life that was dignified,"[141] if not happy. Juxtaposing Ionian individualism to Dorian communitarianism, he portrayed Sparta as a source of great wisdom for the construction of a racial and civic community.

In fact, when viewed from the outside, the Third Reich itself was perceived to be a sort of second Sparta. Back in the eighteenth century, Voltaire had quipped that Prussia was Sparta in the morning and Athens in the afternoon; in Potsdam, a barracks city and the site of the Sanssouci palace, the mornings revolved around troop exercises, while the rest of the day was left to the Muses and to philosophy.

Even more than its militarism, however, it was its apparently totalitarian character that seemed to make Sparta the precursor of the Third Reich. Viktor Ehrenberg, a social-democratic historian in exile since 1933, gave a radio address from Prague in 1934 in which he recalled that Sparta was the first state to interject itself into all aspects of an individual's life, just as the Nazi dictatorship was now doing centuries later: "It is for this reason that the modern representatives of totalitarianism have claimed Sparta as the model or the ideal for their own actions."[142] Drilled in communal life and self-denial for the health of the community and the state, the Spartans were, in Ehrenberg's eyes—drawing on a Nazi concept—"the most consistent type of political soldier."[143] After having stigmatized the suffocating coercion and unchecked militarism of the Lacedaemonians, Ehrenberg concluded with a warning: "Sparta did not leave us a model for us to imitate; rather, it signaled to us the dangers that we must avoid."[144]

A more distant observer who suffered less at the hands of the Nazis, the French Germanist Henri Lichtenberger devoted a whole chapter of his 1937 reedition of *L'Allemagne nouvelle* to what he called Nazi "Spartanism." A professor at the Sorbonne, he interpreted this Spartan rigor as the emphatic and logical outcome of a lazy approach to culture (*Kulturkritik*) brought on by the selfish materialism and individualism of Western civilization, which had been dying for some time. Hitler and the Nazis, Lichtenberger argued, hoped to revitalize the German community through the vigorous restoration of civic mores and self-denial, to combat what he called "economism," the "mentality primarily oriented toward the acquisition of wealth and comfort through the spread of urban forms detached from nature and the land, the bourgeois haunted by worries over the future, imbued with class prejudices, stuck in shortsighted egoism, the intellect scornful of manual labor and full of illusions regarding the power of reason, the aesthete enamored of a sterile vision of beauty and culture." Hitler sought to "break violently with the errant ways that threatened to bring about a crisis of Western culture, and advocated the organization of a new society, founded on a strict national solidarity, on the raw virtues of the peasant, the artisan, the soldier, on the practice of a strict discipline and the willing sacrifice of the individual for the community, on these civic qualities, in a word, virile and robust like those that in Greek antiquity founded the glory of Sparta."[145]

The Nazis' ambition for a rebirth of Western civilization demanded a "Spartan breeding policy for the new generations."[146] The term "breeding," *Züchtung* in German, with its unpleasant animal coarseness, was used in similar fashion by the expressionist poet Gottfried Benn, another of National Socialism's fellow travelers (before he turned away in 1936). Benn saw Sparta as the great organizing force of Greece, the Apollonian principle that gave form and order to the creative passion of its people. In a chapter of his 1934 book *Kunst und Macht* (Art and power) titled "Dorische Welt" (The Doric world), Benn wrote: "Between intoxication and art must enter Sparta, Apollo, the great force of breeding and learning."[147] Benn waxed poetic about the Greek city-state, "a Northern place"[148] that rested on the twin pillars of holism and imperialism: "It had but one internal moral, the state, and one external moral, victory," based on a "radical racism, a racism of state."[149] This moral was entirely directed toward the production and breeding of "beautiful bodies":[150] "Their dream was breeding and eternal youth, the imitation of the gods through will and fire, a thoroughly aristocratic racism, concern for the race above the self."[151] It's worth remembering here that Benn was trained as a physician; at the time, he saw in National Socialism a historic opportunity for Germany's physical renewal as well as the cultural renaissance of the country. He seemed to combine the clinical gaze of a Louis-Ferdinand Céline with the ontological aspirations of a Heidegger when, extolling the rediscovery of

Doric culture, he hoped that by following its example the new Germany would once more temper its men in a bracing bath of virility and pure will, which would break with the swooning, errant ways of a nervous, decadent, feminine modernity.

A SPARTAN EDUCATION: AN *AGŌGĒ* FOR THE NEW MAN

That the Spartan example possessed special didactic value was further confirmed by the project entrusted to the archaeologist Otto Wilhelm von Vacano, who had written his thesis on Olympia and his *Habilitation* on Sparta[152] and was charged with putting together a history textbook on the Lacedaemonians for use in the Adolf-Hitler-Schulen. First published in 1940, Vacano's textbook was composed of a selection of texts from ancient sources, accompanied by a brief, relatively anodyne history of the Dorian city-state. Vacano's tone was moderate or even neutral in comparison with other textbooks of the era. Of course, Vacano was happy to repeat the vulgate of the time regarding the origins of Sparta, whose founding was attributed to "a migration of peasants from the North" chased out of their natural home by "a demographic surplus."[153] Directly tracing a parallel with the medieval Germanic occupation of the East, he specifically instructed young readers to "understand these migrations as similar to their countrymen's colonizing expeditions to the East in the Middle Ages."[154] Naturally, he recounted the Spartans' healthy sense of horror for all forms of democracy, an individualistic and egalitarian destroyer of the hierarchical and holistic cosmos of their forefathers[155] and a source of irreconcilable conflict with Athens. Vacano indulged equally in the contemporary rhetoric that used the word *blood (Blut)* as a synecdoche for the people (*Volk*), attributing Sparta's ultimate ruin to a hemorrhage (*Ausbluten*)[156] of good Nordic blood, spilled all too generously on fields of battle throughout Greece and Asia: "The strength of this [Nordic] blood was consumed in [military] engagement."[157]

Yet only the title made plain that the history of Sparta amounted to a "life-and-death struggle of the Nordic elite" (*Lebenskampf einer nordischen Herrenschicht*), a point reinforced less by Vacano himself than by the exhortation contained in the preface, written by Kurt Petter, the *Kommandeur* of the Adolf-Hitler-Schulen, who vigorously emphasized the lessons to be learned from the Spartan example by the latest generations of the Nordic race:

> *Kamaraden!*
>
> In reading this book I realized once more how much we can learn from Sparta for our work as National Socialists. Many of the conclusions and principles that guided the Spartans in the creation of their state and the education of their elite are valid for us as well. However, we must not repeat the mistakes that led to their ruin. We want to help the führer build a Great Reich: Sparta must serve as both an example and a warning![158]

The visions of Sparta offered in other secondary-school textbooks were just as explicit as those of Petter's preface.

A textbook by Walther Gehl devoted three pages to explaining "the defense of the race in the socialist, warrior state of the Dorian Spartans." The author began by recalling the Spartans' origins in a "new wave of Nordic peasant-warriors [*Bauernkrieger*]"[159] who conquered and reduced to servitude the preexisting population, natives with whom "Nordic Achaeans" from an earlier migratory wave "had become miscegenated." The Lacedaemonians had had to build a state capable of preserving the strength and the purity of this small ruling class of conquering Nordics, who were far inferior in number to the indigenous population of Laconia: "In the Spartan state, the social hierarchy was also a racial hierarchy," its duties and functions being distributed among the people according to their degree of racial purity. This racial principle was enforced by an almost totalitarian coercion: "The entire life of the Spartans was dominated by the idea of a racial state," the author noted, specifying that physical education was mandatory, celibacy forbidden, and childless marriages annulled. These strict eugenics policies were not, however, an end in themselves, since "an aptitude for war was the goal of the state's education of the community," a harsh, rigorous education in which "the only art cultivated was that of music ... which was needed for marching and combat." Eugenics and militarism converged in the enterprise of defending a Nordic elite proud of its race and concerned with preserving its natural dominion over an abundant slave population. As a prototalitarian state, Sparta subjected its people to a barracks lifestyle for the good of the whole: "Beginning from the age of seven, young boys were subjected to a life of permanent military service and drilled in physical exercises, armed combat, hardening of the body, obedience, and self-mastery." No topos was ignored in constructing this edifying tableau of a Sparta where self-mastery and self-sacrifice for the good of the *Volksgemeinshaft* served as the cornerstones of a barracks state. These concepts were even reflected in their language, for, like music and the rhythm of the infantry march, "responses, in the land of Laconia, had to be short, sharp, and to the point—that is to say, laconic."[160] Indeed.

When Hitler, in the chapter of *Mein Kampf* dedicated to education, wrote that "*loyalty, spirit of sacrifice,* and *discretion* are virtues that a great nation absolutely *needs*, and their cultivation and development in school are more important than some of the things that today fill out our curriculums,"[161] he did not name Sparta. But it was indeed the Lacedaemonian *agōgē* that he was describing, from the perspective of one who, as we have seen, knew and appreciated Sparta as a model Nordic community.

The Spartan *agōgē* was glorified by Helmut Berve, who saw it as the only proper way to educate a master race called upon to exercise total control over themselves in order to conquer and subjugate vast territories and large populations: "The constraint exercised upon the impulses and their integration into a community that channeled them into a single direction created in Sparta, as it would elsewhere, the model of a superman . . . [both] used to obedience and called to command."[162] The Reich's education minister Bernhard Rust also reveled in the myth of Sparta, as here in 1933: "I would leave no one with any doubt: we must raise a Spartan youth, and those who would not be ready to enter into this Spartan community should forget about ever becoming citizens of our state."[163] The minister was glad that German youth had "a new and vibrant rapport with the reality of the Greek polis [after] they had freed themselves from the alienation of a culture that was not their own [and had] opened their minds to the profound points of commonality that link them . . . to the heroic youth of Sparta"[164] from an ethical—but especially racial—perspective.

In his inaugural address for the exhibition *Medieval German Physical Education in Words and Images*, Rust recalled "that we know Greece not because of humanism but because, quite to the contrary, Sparta was well and truly German."[165]

HOLISM, SOCIALISM, EUGENICISM

Like Sparta long ago, Nazi Germany offered an example of a community without class distinctions united in a common goal, a *Volksgemeinschaft* made possible by patriotism, civic participation, and racism. In the regime's economic and social propaganda, the term *Spartan* possessed a positive connotation. A book celebrating the workers of the Deutsche Arbeitsfront (DAF), the Nazi trade union, whose members spent day after day building the German autobahn network, proudly and floridly described the "small Spartan garret"[166] of the foreman, who was the führer of his workers yet remained the humblest of the humble. The idyllic description of soothing irenicism, the shared life of a *Bauarbeiterlager*, glorified the easygoing camaraderie, functional socialism, hard work, and joy of a national community in which the specter of class conflict had been abolished.

The memory of a community of *homoioi*, Spartan equals, was dusted off and invoked by Goebbels in a speech on 18 February 1943, two weeks after the German surrender at Stalingrad. The gauleiter Goebbels, who had wrested Berlin from the German Communist Party, the KPD, in the early 1930s thanks to an egalitarian, pro-worker message straight from the far left wing of the NSDAP, where he had gotten his start, returned to this so-called brown-red Nazism in a proclamation of total war that fired on all demagogical cylinders: the time for genteel, white-gloved promenades on horseback through the forests outside Berlin had passed. Total war demanded the complete solidarity of a community of equals, racial comrades, united in resistance to danger: "The German people want to lead a Spartan life, and want the whole world to live like Spartans, the powerful as well as the weak, the rich as well as the poor."[167] The notion of Sparta as a Nordic community was repeated ad nauseum in appeals to history and a propagandistic discourse that never failed to recall the Spartans' and Germans' shared racial roots. For Helmut Berve, "the history of Sparta possesses an eternal value for all peoples who belong to the same family as the Greeks, a family to which we know we belong now more than ever."[168]

Berve also justified the practice of eliminating deformed or unviable children at birth. The Spartans had simply turned a "process of selection at work in nature"[169] into a social custom. Faithful to natural law, they had watched closely to make sure that the cultural and historical order of the state did not impede the work of nature through any counterselective measures.

Fritz Lenz, in his summa on eugenics, also cited the Spartans as a model: "It is well known to all that the exclusion of weak infants was practiced among the ancient Spartans. According to Plutarch, the legislator Lycurgus had very specific selective goals in mind." This Spartan custom was part of a much broader shared racial and cultural tradition common to the Indo-Germanic peoples: "The elimination of infants was widely practiced in classical antiquity, and the practice was open. This custom appears to have been a trait of the Indo-Germanic race."[170]

In Rome, "even sweet Seneca" had made himself a resolute advocate of the euthanasia of weak or deformed children: "We drown the weak and the deformed. This is not fanaticism but logic, that we separate the viable from the nonviable."[171] Natural law was harsh, but it was the law; any *Gegenauslese*,[172] any counterselective measures of support or assistance that artificially kept racially sick elements alive in a compassionate society, were "more grave"[173] than outright barbarism.

Hans Günther, meanwhile, praised Plato, the "guardian of life" according to the title of one of his books,[174] for having been conscious of the "laws of heredity and selection" and having "explained this apparently paradoxical truth: there was more philosophy in Sparta than in Athens"[175]—the quality of a state's philosophy being measured by its ability to act in accordance with the laws of biology. Philosophy was common sense, and that meant not getting in the way of nature but rather scrupulously supplementing it.

The immortal heritage of Sparta was, in the eyes of Ludwig Schemann, encapsulated by the words of Leonidas, drawn not from his famous address at Thermopylae but from his farewell to his wife—"this quite laconic testament," a mark of elevated self-denial, which he made "to his wife: 'marry a good man and bear good children,' a phrase that summarized the canonic law of the heroic, aristocratic eugenicism"[176] of Sparta.

Hitler himself seized upon the same theme. In his unpublished *Zweites Buch* of 1928, Hitler made Sparta the model for the Third Reich to come. Sparta, "the first racialist state" in history, was the archetype of the Nordic state. A racially superior but numerically inferior Indo-Germanic elite had been able to establish its uncontestable domination over a horde of Helots and Perioeci thanks to its aggressive policy of selective racial eugenics, which mercilessly eliminated all weak and deformed elements:

> The Spartans were once capable of such a wise measure, but not our current dishonest, sentimental, bourgeois-patriotic crowd. The subjugation of 350,000 Helots by 6,000 Spartans was possible only because of the racial superiority of the Spartans. This, however, was the result of systematic racial preservation, so we see in the Spartan state the first racialist state. The abandonment of sick, frail, deformed children—in other words, their destruction—demonstrated greater human dignity and was in reality a thousand times more humane than the pathetic insanity of our time, which attempts to preserve the lives of the sickest subjects—at any price—while taking the lives of a hundred thousand healthy children through a decrease in the birth rate or through abortifacient agents, subsequently breeding a race of degenerates burdened with illness.[177]

Hitler referred here to the culling of viable infants at birth by the city-state, which could either decide to retain them or order their expulsion down a ravine on Mount Taygetus. The fate of those infants deemed weak or nonviable was dictated by the military imperatives of the city-state, which required its citizens to be physically vigorous and fit for service. Hitler's meditations on the history of Sparta, pronounced in such shockingly premonitory tones, foreshadowed the T4 euthanasia program, in which Nazi eugenicists transformed themselves from prophylactic sterilizers into mass murderers. The reference to Sparta, the Nordic city-state par excellence, in the 1920s thus helped establish the mentality in which the idea of state-sanctioned murder and a eugenicist policy of the destruction of human beings deemed inferior was indeed possible.

Such ruthless selectionism made Sparta, in Hitler's eyes, the model of a eugenicist state, the "most clearly racist state in history,"[178] just as the Third Reich demanded. While the *Zweites Buch* was never published, the führer also called upon the example of Sparta, leaving little to the imagination, in his public speeches: "World history gives us the example of a state that employed the selection of its progeny. This state was Sparta. . . . The Spartans purely and simply destroyed all that lived that was not perfectly healthy. This was, it must be recognized, a cruel practice. But through this selection, they spared future generations from many maladies, and the Spartans who passed the selection enjoyed a much more pleasant existence."[179] The public promotion of Spartan-style eugenics returned once again to traditional arguments about state-sponsored biological eradication: the sacrifice of a corrupt minority would assure the health of the greater number, a method that required nothing more than the zealous and obedient application of nature.

The history of the Nordic race thus taught, through the Spartan example, how to create a strong aristocratic elite capable of subjugating numerically superior populations. Through an aggressive policy of selective eugenics and the destruction of weak or corrupt elements, the surviving racial nucleus could then concentrate its strength on the domination of other peoples, without being overwhelmed by the burden to care for the sick.

The SS, whose vigorously selective, elitist ideology persuaded them that they were the racial elite, the Nordic aristocracy, of the German people, appropriated this concept of Sparta. It was precisely among the German people themselves that the new Spartans, the blackshirted *homoioi* of the SS, constituted an elite called to dominate a racially questionable majority, crossbred with Dinarics and Alpines, as one high-ranking officer confided to Eugen Kogon in 1937: "What we trainers of the younger generation of Führers aspire to is a modern governmental structure on the model of the ancient Greek city-states. It is to these aristocratically run democracies with their broad economic basis of serfdom that we owe the great cultural achievements of antiquity. From five to ten per cent of the people, their finest flower, shall rule; the rest must work and obey. In this way alone can we attain that peak performance we must demand of ourselves and of the German people."[180] Active selectionism and uncompromising eugenics practiced upon one's own people were the prescription for the ultimate goal of conquest and domination by a racially elite minority over vast spaces and numerically superior populations.

Hitler marveled in private at the manner in which this Nordic racial aristocracy had been able to reduce, control, and impose its will upon the Greek world, colonizing a swath of the Mediterranean. The fact that "six thousand [Spartan] families" had conquered "over three hundred and forty thousand Helots, and, on the other hand, reigned over Asia Minor and Sicily . . . for several centuries" was "proof of the greatness of this race."[181] Hitler's words, along with those of Kogon's SS officer, show how Sparta presented the Nazis with a model for domination that seemed easily transposable to a Europe and its eastern territories under their yoke.[182]

The unstinting advocate of "blood and soil" Nazism Richard Walther Darré also seized upon the Spartan example. In keeping with his aim to demonstrate that the Indo-Germanics not just were about great migrations and martial exploits but were primarily a peasant people, Darré reversed the traditional perspective on the history of Sparta, unjustly remembered by posterity solely for its military virtues, when such wars were actually peripheral to the Spartans' working the soil as peasants. The agronomist relativized the warrior culture of Sparta by showing them as a paradigm of his *Blut und Boden* utopia. If Sparta was a *mahnendes Beispiel*, a "cautionary tale" for its ultimate ruin, this was due to the notion less that the Spartans had demonstrated an excessive lust for war and had been profligate with their blood than that they had gradually lost touch with their essentially agrarian nature.

For Darré, Sparta was not just the "warrior state par excellence"[183] that its contemporaries and posterity were so certain it had been. Sparta had become a military state despite itself, had been forced to take up arms, train, and obey an iron discipline to protect its racially superior but numerically inferior Nordic elite, encircled by overabundant masses of lesser racial value, the famous Helots and Perioeci. The essence of Sparta was thus not military but primarily agrarian: the Spartans were an Indo-Germanic people and thus a population of farmers. Like all of Greece, Laconia had been colonized by a "great Nordic peasant migration"[184] in search of land to cultivate. Surrounded by racially inferior and hostile peoples, Sparta found peace only in a "military state and unbelievably severe discipline," but this was not an end in itself or the expression of a fundamentally militarist Nordicism but rather a simple "organization for the defense of an open peasant state, that is an organization of military defense such as Prussia developed in German history"[185] of more recent times.

This perspective led Darré to advance a reading of the ruin of the Lacedaemonians that contested the traditional interpretation. The author devoted some fifteen pages of his book to showing that the Spartan state had not been brought down by the hemorrhaging of its Nordic blood through an endless series of wars, an error of interpretation that rested on "a fundamental error of calculation," a foolish mistake that ignored the fact that a man fallen in battle could be replaced by the calling up of sufficient reinforcements, which were provided by the remarkable fertility of the Indo-Germanic race. Contrary to the frequently hasty assumption, Sparta "was de-Nordified not by war but by economic questions linked to ownership of the land." The decline in the number of Spartan citizens, or *oliganthropia,* was less important for him than the division of plots (*klēroi*) among descendants, which parceled out land to the point that it became less profitable and was thus gradually left to the Helots and Perioeci. Darré thus killed two birds with one stone. War was not evil in and of itself; it would be "foolish" to believe this was the cause, since the Nordic people themselves never started wars. Rather, it was the land question and the Indo-Germanic peoples' attachment to the soil that was "the central question of the fate of the Nordic race":[186] "Wars did not de-Nordify Sparta," but rather it was the abandonment of their "healthy peasant foundation"[187] that was their original sin.

CONCLUSION

What value could this noble ancient literature possibly hold for a regime that made such a point of flaunting its anti-intellectualism? The previous two chapters have shown how the glorification of the body and the total man were part of a Greek tradition that National Socialism took it upon itself to revive. We have seen how, from Rosenberg, Darré, and Günther to German historians of antiquity and scholars of Greek philosophy, the entire history of Hellenic thought was refracted through the prism of racism. There were noble, elitist, racialist, or eugenicist thinkers, and then there were the half-breed or mixed-race philosophers, whose ideas about miscegenation and human equality were products of their own muddied blood, whose ignorance of racial genius sadly infected the blood of superior peoples with the illness of the inferior. Even worse, like a germ or a microbe, they introduced racially foreign concepts into Greek philosophy, extolling mankind's fundamental equality, based on the possession of reason common to all individuals, despite the overwhelming mass of evidence to the contrary. This contrast was made readily visible by comparing Socrates and Plato: the Asiatic Socrates, whose ugliness was a constant source of derision, stood for equality, while the Nordic Plato, true to the greatness of his race, aimed to protect its eminence through fundamentally inegalitarian policies. Other foreign racial and intellectual concepts were introduced into Greek thought by the cabal of Orientals and Semites known as the Stoics, who made dangerous claims about a global community of man, each individual equally endowed with reason and dignity under the law, a cosmopolis of interbreeding and undifferentiation.

There could obviously be no question of such ideas taking root under the Third Reich: nature had its unbending laws, and inequality was an obvious fact. The foundation of Nazi racism was based on a strict hierarchy of races that could not be allowed to mix or miscegenate under any circumstances. Plato and his theory of the three races, the tripartite state of philosopher-kings, soldiers, and producers, was the Helleno-Nordic precursor to National Socialist racism and its conception of society. This was the view employed by scholars of Greek philosophy, concerned as always about proving their worth in a new Germany where blatant anti-intellectualism seemed to leave little future for Platonic studies.

In fact, Plato was viewed very favorably under the Third Reich, and he was frequently and widely cited. In Athens he had been known for his philo-Spartanism; his uncle Critias, one of the infamous Thirty Tyrants, had been a collaborator with the Lacedaemonians. Between 1933 and 1945, Plato remained strongly linked to Sparta, the Laconian city-state enjoying the favor of political theorists and leaders like Günther, Darré, and Hitler, as well as those professional historians who carefully sought to portray the subject of their expertise as a model and source of inspiration. A racist, eugenicist, military state, Sparta received Hitler's seal of approval for its biological selectionism as the first truly racist and Nordic state, a legitimate precursor to the Third Reich. Descriptions of the violent disposal of undesirable Spartan infants helped to create a cultural climate favorable to theories of eliminationist eugenics, which would become very real policy between 1933 and 1939. The scrupulous care given to the construction of a racial elite that compensated for its numeric inferiority with its biological purity, clearly demonstrating the contrast between the *homoioi* and the surrounding populations of Helots and Perioeci, offered a model of racial hierarchy and domination that Darré and the SS applied to contemporary race relations within Germany and subsequently in the conquered territories of a vastly expanding Greater Reich.

Sparta, the first racist, militarist, Nordic city-state, was thus invoked as a model for the new Germany—its greatness akin to that of the Roman Empire.

CHAPTER 6

From Empire to Reich

The Lessons of Roman Rule and Classical Colonialism

Aut Caesar, aut nullus [Either a Caesar or a nobody].
Emperor of the world!
—Adenoid Hynkel (Charlie Chaplin), *The Great Dictator*

For if the city of the Lacedaemonians should be deserted, and nothing should be left of it but its temples and the foundations of its other buildings, posterity would, I think, after a long lapse of time, be very loath to believe that their power was as great as their renown. . . . As Sparta is not compactly built as a city and has not provided itself with costly temples and other edifices, but is inhabited village-fashion in the old Hellenic style, its power would appear less than it is. Whereas, if Athens should suffer the same fate, its power would, I think, from what appeared of the city's ruins, be conjectured double what it is.
—Thucydides, *History of the Peloponnesian Wars* 1.10.1–4

—Henceforth, o living flesh, you are no more!
You are of granite, wrapped in a vague dread . . .
—Charles Baudelaire, "Spleen (II)," *The Flowers of Evil*

It was in Latin that Charlie Chaplin chose to parody National Socialist megalomania in his famous scene from *The Great Dictator* (1940): anxieties over the ultimate ends of Nazi expansionism are laced throughout the film—which was well received in the United States in the wake of Pearl Harbor—depicting Hitler as a power-hungry potentate out for world domination, a worthy successor to the Caesars and all their subsequent imitators.

There was a tension in Hitler's approach to antiquity, torn between mere imitation and forthright defiance, a desire to eclipse the past, which required following in its footsteps, repeating the same actions and choices. Rome showed the meaning of history—that is, it simultaneously constituted the ends of history itself and the means to achieve those ends. Roman history was, as Hitler wrote in *Mein Kampf,* "die beste Lehrmeisterin"—"the best teacher,"[1] the ultimate school for would-be world conquerors. The art of war and domination could be understood and learned by reading up on Roman history, a veritable academy for princes and soldiers since the Middle Ages.

A source of infinite lessons and precise instructions, the history of Rome showed not only how to build empires but also the tangible symbols of that empire. National Socialism would thus have to pursue its imperial pretensions by imitating and eclipsing the shadows of the ancients in the granite of Nuremberg, where once the living, breathing mass of the *Volksgemeinschaft* met and rallied in congress, now only a desolate wasteland haunted by the devastation of the Nazi Walpurgisnacht.

THE GLORY THAT WAS ROME: THE SOVEREIGNTY OF A GERMANIC ARISTOCRACY

The Roman Empire was, for Hitler, both precursor and pedagogue to the greater Nazi Reich. The study of Rome's history was all the more critical since the Romans had also pursued their own project for global hegemony; they had done it well, and their conquest had established a dominion that lasted several centuries. There was thus much to learn from them, even from the most trivial details. Hitler's writings, speeches, and table talks are full of numerous, diverse lessons drawn from Roman history, almost like some kind of profuse, eccentric inventory.

Rome, the source of all Western law, and especially public law, was above all the creator of the principle of sovereignty. It was Rome, Hitler declared, that had created the modern concept of the state: "Italy is the country where intelligence created the notion of the State. The Roman Empire is a great political creation, the greatest of all."[2] Rome, a city of soldiers and jurists, had bequeathed to the West an idea of the state as a creative body, setting norms and constraints and endowed with sovereignty and power. For the führer, the existence of a strong state was a necessary condition for the emergence of culture, a fact, he claimed, that was borne out by antiquity: "Now, the example of the ancient world proves that civilisation can flourish only in States that are solidly organised. . . . Without organisation—that is to say, without compulsion—and, consequently, without sacrifice on the part of individuals, nothing can work properly."[3] Hitler was only repeating what he had already written on more than one occasion in *Mein Kampf*: the state alone, as the political form of social organization, could foster the emergence and production of culture. The work of cultural production was unthinkable except within a structural framework that assigned each individual their duty and coordinated—that is, enforced and managed—the efforts of all. The establishment of a state, like all acts of cultural creation, could only be the work of Aryans, the only people capable of transcending their self-interest to work toward the construction of a unified community. Culture and the state were thus patent signs of a generous Aryan idealism, diametrically opposed to the selfishness and sordid materialism of the Jews,[4] a greedy individualism that knew no sense of self-denial nor any concept of political community.

Sovereignty demands that the state be perfectly free and autonomous with respect to the outside world. Rome could have taught this lesson to the Weimar Republic, a state whose sovereignty was amputated by the Treaty of Versailles, especially Articles 231 and 232, which, in attributing responsibility for the war to Germany alone, forbade the country from maintaining an army and imposed financial reparations. Within the concert of nations, Germany was thus not *gleichberechtigt*: it was deprived of its equal rights, shackled in chains that prevented it from exercising its full and rightful sovereignty. The lesson of ancient history, both Roman and Greek, was that a state's freedom—or, in terms of international law, its sovereignty—is a prerequisite for its cultural development, as Hitler argued in *Mein Kampf*:

> The cultural importance of a nation is almost always bound up with its political freedom and independence; therefore, the latter is the presupposition for the existence, or, better, the establishment, of the former. Therefore, no sacrifice can be too great for the securing of political freedom. What general cultural matters lose through an excessive promotion of the state's

implements of military power, it will later be possible to restore most abundantly.... From the hardships of the Persian Wars arose the Age of Pericles, and through the cares of the Punic Wars the Roman state began to dedicate itself to the service of a higher culture.[5]

Once free of the threat of Persian or Carthaginian domination, Athens and Rome were able to concentrate completely on the development of a culture that would not admit any subjection or submission to a foreign power. Contrary to the conventional wisdom that held militarization and culture to be opposites—the former drawing resources, attention, and energy from the latter—Hitler established a direct causal link between war, liberty, and political power on one side and the vigor of cultural creation on the other. The cultural apogees of Western history, Pericles's Athens and classical Rome, had logically and chronologically followed periods of total war that had affirmed their states' complete sovereignty.

In addition to representing this paradigm of sovereignty, the Roman state centralized and delegated power in a way that made it ripe for imitation. Even before the Augustan principate, which saw Rome resurrected in another form, under a monarchy, which had not been seen on its soil for five centuries, the Roman res publica was, according to Hitler, anything but a republic in the contemporary meaning of the word. In a speech on the Weimar chancellor Gustav Stresemann delivered on 2 May 1928 in Munich, Hitler burnished the *Führerprinzip* of his party and future state with a patina of noble Roman origins:

> Roman democracy possesses approximately the same rapport with German democracy that National Socialism has with your democracy. Roman democracy was in truth an elitist oligarchy [*Führeraristokratie*] of the most extreme kind.[6]

Though I have used the word *oligarchy*, which is the consensual definition of the Roman *res publica* among historians and political scientists,[7] Hitler's term *Führeraristokratie* designated more of a pyramidal aristocracy crowned at the top by a führer. This was, in theory, the organizational power scheme of the NSDAP after 1919, as it would be of the National Socialist state after 1933.

Hitler in essence imposed the *Führerprinzip* on top of the centralized state, on the länder—commanded, after the Gleichschaltung, by the gauleiters of the NSDAP's administrative districts (gaue)—as well as upon the municipal administrations. In one of his table talks, Hitler raised the question of local government in reference to the example of the Roman *coloniae* and municipia: "In this respect, too, we can learn a lot from the Romans."[8] The Roman res publica thus offered a fully developed example of that "Germanic democracy" so lauded by Hitler as the natural, spontaneous, organicistic form of decentralized executive power exercised by the natural leaders of the community, who were designated and elected by a mysterious and providential but utterly necessary annunciation.[9]

THE WEHRMACHT IN THE FOOTSTEPS OF THE ROMAN LEGIONS

A model state and creator of the principle of sovereignty, the Roman Empire was also a wartime conqueror. The *Gröfaz*,[10] as a modern field general, had much to learn from its use of force and military success. Rome was a military state and could teach the art of war to anyone who wished to learn its lessons. For Rosenberg, Rome's mastery of war demonstrated "that formal state discipline with which a threatened community must fashion and defend itself."[11] Its teachings were many, even touching on the details of military procurement and lines of supply. Roman history showed how to feed an army, for instance, which in the context of the stalemate on the eastern front in 1942 developed into a legitimate concern for the regime's leaders. Take this exchange during a luncheon at the Reich Chancellery on 25 April 1942:

> Dr. Goebbels asked whether a pound of potatoes had the same nutritive value as a pound of meat. The Führer replied:
> As far as we know, the food of the soldiers of ancient Rome consisted principally of fruit and cereals. The Roman soldier had a horror of meat, and meat, apparently, was included in the normal rations only when the difficulty of obtaining other supplies made it inevitable. From numerous pictures and sculptures it seems that the Romans had magnificent teeth, and this seems to contradict the contention that only carnivorous animals have good teeth.[12]

The rations for the soldiers of the Wehrmacht could thus very well skip the meat, for it would neither fuel their ardor for combat nor promote good dental hygiene. Hitler found in Roman history confirmation of his own prejudices as a militant vegetarian accustomed to hurling invectives at the first *Leichenfresser,* or "corpse eater," who had the poor taste to order meat at his table.

In terms of tactics, ancient history taught that the vanquishing general was always the one who possessed the most advanced weaponry.

Since antiquity, generals and strategists had paid particularly close attention to technology, a point Hitler liked to emphasize to his dining companions:

> It is astonishing to note to what a degree the ancients succeeded in adapting technology to the needs of war.
>
> The victories of Hannibal without his elephants, or of Alexander without his chariots, his cavalry and the technique of his archers are impossible to conceive.
>
> In war, the best soldier—that is to say, the soldier who achieves the greatest success—is the one who has the most modern technical means at his disposal, not only in battle itself, but also in the field of communications and supply.[13]

In another conversation, one month later, Hitler returned to these questions and meditated on the importance of armored vehicles, comparing them, mutatis mutandis, to Hannibal's elephants: "During lunch, the führer spoke of military matters. He remarked, among other things, that just as the use of elephants as an offensive weapon in Hannibal's time had been most judicious, so tanks constituted the most advanced and important offensive weapon today."[14] One Panzer model, the SdKFz 194—a sixty-five-metric-ton (seventy-one-short-ton) mechanized pachyderm—even bore the nickname "Elephant."[15]

From Caesar, Hitler the military leader took only one thing: his political prudence, a form of *phronesis* highly valued in antiquity. A general, like any man of power, had to have his ear to the ground and have a feel for the morale of his soldiers, respecting their beliefs and not dismissing their feelings, even if they were irrational: "It is precisely in time of war that people become most superstitious. The Romans, including Julius Caesar, were a superstitious people; although it is quite possible that Caesar was not really superstitious, but simply bowed to public opinion. I myself would never launch an attack on the thirteenth, not because I myself am superstitious, but because others are."[16] A general must thus possess an understanding of the humble backgrounds of his men and be guided by a Machiavellian spirit that takes the driving sentiments of his people into account without necessarily sharing them.

More fundamentally, perhaps, Hitler had learned from the Roman art of war that wherever force was employed, it should be employed totally, to destroy as much as possible the adversary's material capacity to retaliate, and to eliminate any vague psychological impulse to respond through the language of terror. The Romans' undeniable will to destroy

Carthage and the taking of both the Phoenician capital and Jerusalem—razed to their foundations and, it was said, cursed to the infernal gods, the soil sown with salt—undoubtedly influenced Hitler's totalizing conception of the use of military force. Both the war in the east and the violence of the SS in central and—toward the end of the war—western Europe could not fail to evoke thoughts of the pitiless *delenda* of Scipio's legions.

The German will to power and the focus with which the Nazis pursued their bellicose politics of annexation certainly recalled Rome in the perceptive eyes of Simone Weil, who could not help thinking of the Roman Empire when she dreamed of Hitler: "What resembled Hitler's Germany two thousand years ago was not the Germans; it was Rome."[17] Weil thus inscribed the Third Reich within a line of continuity stretching back to a violent, predatory Roman Empire, the empire that Tacitus denounced in a famous passage of prosopopoeia through Calgacus: "To plunder, butcher, steal, these things they misname empire: they make a desolation and they call it peace."[18] For Simone Weil, who wrote several articles on the subject in 1938, "the analogy between the systems of Hitler and of ancient Rome is so striking that one might believe that Hitler alone, after two thousand years, has understood how to copy the Romans."[19] There was definitely a peculiar similarity in their ends, conquest in the name of empire, but also in their means, an "unlimited and shameless brutality"[20] for which she criticized the Romans, otherwise all too easily absolved of their military aggression because of their self-proclaimed mission as benevolent civilizers.[21] The positive aspects of colonization would always be celebrated in any history written by the victors: "In any case, everything that disgusts and also everything that shocks us in his methods is what he has in common with Rome. Neither his objective, which is to impose peace by enslavement and subdue the nations by force to a pretended superior form of organization and civilization, nor the policy by which he pursues it, [is] different from the Roman." Weil summed up her opinion with a cutting remark on the depth of Hitler's appreciation of the classical and Germanic traditions: "Any specifically Germanic frills that Hitler has added to the Roman tradition are pure literary and mythological patchwork."[22]

After conquest, made possible by meatless rations and a few minor concessions to humor the troops, there would come the time for hegemony. The empire would have to be secured and kept firmly under control if the conquerors wished to establish a lasting dominion. Once again, Roman history had shown Hitler the way: "If we wish to preserve the military power of the German people, we must be careful not to give arms to the peoples of the countries we have conquered or occupied. One of the secrets of the might of ancient Rome was that throughout the Empire only Roman citizens were entitled to carry arms."[23] The territories of the Reich would thus remain under the jurisdiction of a fighting elite, that of the German army, following in the image of the Roman Empire. The rest of humanity, the masses of men and women bent under the yoke of Nazi domination, could not be allowed the right to bear arms. Hitler reiterated his firmness on this point in another conversation: "A people cannot lay claim to mastery of the world unless it's ready to pay with its blood. The Roman Empire had recourse to mercenaries only when its own blood was exhausted. In fact, it was only after the Third Punic War that Rome had legions of mercenaries."[24]

The reference here to Rome could be bolstered by turning to Greece. The notion of a racialized military state evoked Sparta, or at least the image of the Lacedaemonian city that Hitler had in mind in his 1928 statement on the principles behind what would become Nazi foreign policy, later published in 1961 as *Hitlers zweites Buch*.[25] Having lauded Sparta, Hitler returned to Rome to express his conviction that an empire could be founded only on a strong, racially homogenous core. This was, in his eyes, one of the greatest lessons offered by the Roman conquest. The Roman Empire could not have been built without its foundations in a union of racially related peoples, the populations of Latium, thrust under the yoke of Roman conquest. This racial union had been the indispensible prerequisite for the conquest of Italy and the Mediterranean: previously weak and divided peoples had, under Rome's iron fist, achieved the critical mass necessary to build the military might that allowed them to conquer the world. Hitler saw this Latinate union, forged by the will and the sword of Rome, as analogous to Prussia's much-needed union of the German "tribes," or *Stämme,* a prerequisite for any future foreign adventures: "We know from past experience that lasting unions can only take place when the peoples in question are of equal racial quality and related, and second, when their union takes place in the shape of the slow process of a struggle for hegemony. That was how Rome once conquered the Latin states, one after the other, until finally its power sufficed to become the crystallization point of a world empire. But this is also [through] the history of the emergence of the English world empire. Furthermore, Prussia ended the fragmentation of the German states in the same manner."[26] It only followed that it was imperative to preserve this powerful, racially unified core. The state would thus have to stand guard and encourage the fecundity of its people through adequate pronatalist measures.[27]

FROM ROMAN ROADS TO *REICHSAUTOBAHNEN*: BUILDING AN IMPERIAL INFRASTRUCTURE

After conquest it was time to build, to construct the infrastructure that made empire politically, militarily, and commercially possible: an ambitious network of lines of supply and communication. An empire simply could not exist without roads, to connect territories and integrate space. Hitler freely associated the concept of empire with that of the road—the former built the latter, and the latter gave structure to the former. Empires were different from all other types of territorial domination because of their ability to transform and shape space, creating a lasting form of organization for the *longue durée:*

> The Roman Empire and the Empire of the Incas, like all great empires, started by being networks of roads.[28]

The civilizing virtue of an empire could be seen in its construction of such infrastructure, as Hitler remarked in a conversation of 27 June 1942: "The beginnings of every civilisation express themselves in terms of road construction. Under the direction of Caesar, and during the first two centuries of the Germanic era, it was by means of the construction of roads and tracks that the Romans reclaimed the marshlands and blazed trails through the forests of Germania. Following their example, our first task in Russia will be to construct roads."[29] In the summer of 1942, with German armies retaking the initiative on the eastern front, the conquest of such vast spaces seemed possible once more.

Roads were thus accorded the status of cultural monument. In 1937, Fritz Todt, the *Generalinspektor für das deutsche Strassenwesen* (General inspector for German roadways), commemorated the construction of such a network in similar terms, in a text produced by his office, titled *Deutschlands Autobahnen: Adolf Hitlers Strassen* (The German autobahn: Adolf Hitler's roads).[30] Todt's preface eloquently explained his roads' cultural significance: "Roads are cultural goods. Every road that we take has its own ancient history and meaning. A road is a work of art. It comes from the creative force of its engineer."[31] A road was not just a strictly utilitarian commodity. It was not a banal, modern fact of life, as one might be led to believe. It was nothing more or less than the objectification, in the Hegelian sense, of an idea, a spirit, within the broader context of the imperial project: "In every epoch, the road has always been the expression of the history of its time, and the traces it has left behind bear witness to this past. . . . In its method of construction, in its design, it is not just the techniques of different centuries that is on display but also the spirit and will of its creators."[32]

As if testifying to the cultural dignity of roads, Todt invoked ancient history. The modern road dated back to ancient world, and Herodotus himself had deemed roads worthy of mention in his works, a sign of their historical and cultural sacredness in antiquity: "Herodotus himself spoke of the first paved road. He reported that this road had been built three thousand years before our era, on the occasion of the construction of the Pyramid of Cheops. Herodotus put the completion of this road on the same plane as the construction of the pyramid."[33] The product of an artistic, creative spirit, the road was also the physical manifestation of the imperial idea: "The road must be the expression of the German essence. It is in this sense that we work on the gigantic project of Adolf Hitler's roads. Our program for their construction is a striking expression of the German will to live and the unity of the German Reich."[34] The Reich's roadways, integrating its territories, joining its various parts, were an expression of political unity: "The lines of these new roads firmly emphasize the new unity of the Reich."[35] The political meaning of a system of roads had been evident since Roman times: "Ample work on the construction of roads has always been the sign of particular effort. Enormous roads have been built to ensure the conquest of vast empires."[36]

In its logistical role, the road, which facilitated troop movements, was in essence a tool of conquest. Significantly, Todt also indicated that the Reich's motorways were oriented largely toward the east: "They lead toward India and the Far East. The Nordic man has always, throughout his history, taken the road pointing toward India. Alexander the Great treaded this path, and along this route we can find countless cultural documents that testify to the presence of the Nordic race."[37] The routes that led to the east were "the same routes that guided the German political and cultural conquest of the East," a reference to the *Drang nach Osten* of the Germanic Middle Ages. The Reich's roads were also inspired by another imperial model, that of Napoleon, himself a great admirer of the Roman Empire and its lines of communication. Following the example of Rome, "the roads of Napoleon I expressed, in their orientation and their merciless layout, the brutal will to power of a great conqueror, and so they also bear witness to the grandeur of his ideas."[38] The manifestation of a political will to power, the führer's roads, vectors of a project of military conquest like those of the Romans or of Napoleon, were as straight and sure as the barrel of a cannon, *ultima ratio regum* (the last argument of kings). This rectilinearity was the product of the strategic imperative to save time, as Hitler confided to his companions at table: "All strategic roads were built by tyrants—for the Romans, the Prussians or the French. They go straight across country. The other roads wind like processions and waste everybody's time."[39]

Military roads, built for conquest, were not just rectilinear. They were also designed to provide for resupply and refreshment. Hitler cited how Roman roads had been equipped with resting posts, *mutationes* that allowed travelers to relax and change their clothes, and punctuated at regular intervals by military encampments. The führer marveled at the Roman model: "The speed with which the Roman legions moved is truly surprising. The roads drive straight forward across mountains and hills. The troops certainly found perfectly prepared camps at their staging areas."[40] Beyond conquest, roads were the arteries of civilization. As Fritz Todt declared, "Roads also serve a benevolent, peaceful civilization." In fact, it was on these roads that "traffic flows, beating with the pulse of life."[41]

The Romans had perfected the road, from both a technical and a political point of view: "The uncontested masters of road construction in antiquity were the Romans. Their immense empire was unthinkable without its vast network of strategic and commercial routes. The Roman road network extended a length of eighty-five thousand kilometers [fifty-three thousand miles] and stretched from Scotland to Jerusalem and from the Pyrenees to the Danube. On these ancient Roman roads there were first-class rest stops, which were ultimately of equally great importance for governing and commerce. The construction technique employed on Roman roads was very advanced. Today we still admire its blueprint."[42] Like a work of art or an idea brought to life, however, the roadways of the Reich emerged from a peculiarly monumental vision. As Todt had noted, Herodotus celebrated roads just as much as the pyramids; unfortunately, the Third Reich and its contemporaries could not boast of similarly outrageous achievements to glorify the work of the führer, as implicitly admitted by the official journal *Die Strasse* in 1938: "The roadways of the Reich must, like the Great Wall of China, the Acropolis in Athens, or the pyramids of Egypt, become a monument on the landscape of history."[43] In 1941, the Austrian poet Josef Weinheber published "Ode an die Strassen Adolf Hitlers," in which he elevated the roads,

> similar to so few of man's works
> To the eternity of the pyramids, perhaps
> To the monuments of ancient Rome."[44]

It is difficult, however, for a road to assume the status of a monument on the landscape of history. The monumentality of a road is two dimensional, not three; it sits inscribed on a map and does not rise off the ground to occupy space. To make the enormity of this work of infrastructure stand out, Nazi propaganda compiled figures and photomontages that juxtaposed an immense heap of rubble, meant to represent the debris from construction, to the peaks of great mountains. But the road as monument still suffered from its unspectacular nature. The vast extension of its two dimensions lacked the third, vertical dimension of a true icon, as Ernst Bloch remarked humorously from his London exile in 1937: "A singular work of architecture, millions of kilometers long, but as a monument it's a bit flat."[45]

This plane and nearly invisible work of art thus needed to be adorned with other artful feats of engineering, bridges and viaducts especially, whose style deliberately mimicked Roman imperial monumentality.

The construction of viaducts was inspired directly by Rome. The Third Reich copied its arches and imperial stonework even though more modern construction materials, like concrete and iron, and techniques rendered the resurrection of these architectural dinosaurs completely useless.

But roads and bridges were signifiers of the Nazis' imperial ambitions. Hitler and Todt, as we have already seen, viewed roads as symbols of empire. Roman-style bridges were given a similar association, as clearly illustrated by the rapid spread of the word *Reichsautobahn*. The now common neologism *autobahn* was originally inseparable from the word *Reich;* its roadways could be conceived only in terms of the Reich and thus as imperial roads. An examination of the Nazis' projects and achievements in infrastructural architecture provides a concrete demonstration of just how discourse was transformed into action, from imperial idea to empire on the ground. The journal *Die Kunst im Deutschen Reich,* the official art revue of the National Socialist regime, published numerous photographs, sketches, and blueprints of bridges. Friedrich Tamms,[46] the architect in charge of road bridges under the Organisation Todt, sketched plans for a project that, while never fully completed, nevertheless constitutes a striking example of the Nazis' guileless imitation of Rome. Tamms appropriated the classical design of overlapping arches and drew a structure that was three levels high, interrupted by a massive central arch, which was unnecessarily expensive and purely decorative. His goal was apparently to be more Roman than the Romans and not to satisfy any technical necessity whatsoever.

Not to be left behind, in 1937 his friend and colleague Albert Speer developed plans for a roadway in Salzburg. A giant shrine that resembled the Augustan Ara Pacis was flanked by two monumental columns that evoked the Pillars of Hercules, or perhaps the two legs of the Colossus of Rhodes, one of the wonders of the world, both columns topped by the Nazi eagle. The columns marked the border crossing with an Austria not yet attached by the anschluss to the Altreich.

IMPERIALISM AND IMPERIAL ARCHITECTURE: PUBLIC ARCHITECTURE AS CULTURAL MONUMENT AND SYMBOL OF POWER

The influence of Roman architecture under the Third Reich went far beyond a few sketches or major roads and bridges. Hitler's general tastes in art, and architecture in particular, are well known through both the table talks and Albert Speer's writings. As early as 1925, Hitler began sketching plans for a future arc de triomphe and several other monuments in a notebook (preserved today in the Kunstgeschichtliches Seminar of the University of Göttingen),[47] later confiding in his architect in chief how he had been thwarted in his pursuit of his true artistic vocation:

> Speer, you are my architect. You know that I always wanted to be an architect myself. . . . The World War and the criminal November revolution prevented that. Otherwise I might today be Germany's foremost architect, as you are now. But the Jews! . . . The Jews made me go into politics.[48]

The importance attributed to art—and above all to architecture, the representational art par excellence, the art of inscribing power in space—was thus in part the product of a widely recognized personal penchant, but it was also the product of an idea of politics conceived in terms of persuasion, an appeal to the passions through the expression of aesthetic feeling.[49] Hitler believed that any self-respecting state must outfit itself with the architectural trappings of power. Sovereignty was expressed in stone, and a strong state had to mark its territory rather than allow an unchecked proliferation of private spaces.

In a long passage from *Mein Kampf,* as in a number of his speeches, Hitler deplored the disproportionate gap between the number of private and public buildings, the latter having been reduced by the triumph of commercialism and the consequent relegation of the state to whatever space was left over. Hitler lamented that "what recent times have added to the cultural content of our big cities is totally inadequate." Many of them "possess no monuments dominating the city picture, which might somehow be regarded as the symbols of the whole epoch. This was true in the cities of antiquity, since nearly every one possessed a special monument in which it took pride."[50] In contrast to the cultural deficits of the contemporary era, antiquity appeared to be a paradigm of political decisionism (*Dezisionismus*) and architectural fecundity.

The public monuments of ancient cities were the product of the architectural and civic will of the state, reflections of the community and not of private interests: "The characteristic aspect of the ancient city did not lie in private buildings, but in the community monuments which seemed made, not for the moment, but for eternity, because they were intended to reflect, not the wealth of an individual owner, but the greatness and wealth of the community."[51] The state's strength would thus muffle and silence any manifestation of inopportune or ostentatious individualism through a sort of tacit compromise that gave preference to public structures: "The few still towering colossuses which we admire in the ruins and wreckage of the ancient world are not former business palaces, but temples and state structures; in other words, works whose owner was the community. Even in the splendor of late Rome the first place was not taken by the villas and palaces of individual citizens, but by the temples and baths, the stadiums, circuses, aqueducts, basilicas, etc., of the state, hence of the whole people."[52]

The same was true of the Germanic Middle Ages: "What in antiquity found its expression in the Acropolis or the Pantheon now cloaked itself in the forms of the Gothic Cathedral," which stood out among the "swarming" small dwellings of a medieval town, a "conception which in the last analysis was the same as that of antiquity." The modern state lacked such signs of culture and power; "even the sum of money spent on state buildings is usually laughable and inadequate."[53] Urban space had been conquered and occupied and was now rotting from its gangrenous infection with too much private space, a mark of cultural decadence defined by rampant individualism and the worship of money. Tellingly, it was while framing his fury in antithetical categories like public versus private or commercial versus civic that Hitler disparaged the Reich Chancellery, which he had occupied since 30 January 1930. Speer, who would be tasked with building the new palace of the chancellor, recalled that Hitler "described the Chancellery ... as 'fit for a soap company.' It would not do for the headquarters of a now powerful Reich." This was why, in assigning Speer responsibility for the new building, Hitler "demanded an architectural stage set of imperial majesty."[54] The word *imperial* was never casual nor innocent when it came from the mouth of the führer.

Once in power, Hitler did not hesitate to dedicate considerable sums of money to the construction of gigantic monuments, sweeping aside the reservations of the Reich's finance ministers regarding the size and number of the projects undertaken. The building of the Deutsche Stadion in Nuremberg, for example, estimated by Speer to cost 250 million reichsmarks, was for Hitler "less than two battleships of the Bismarck class. How quickly a warship can be destroyed, and if not, it is scrapiron anyhow in ten years. But this building will stand for centuries."[55]

Financial considerations were thus summarily dismissed in favor of a desire for immortality, a hard desire to endure that was similar to the Roman mentality, an ancient ethos that framed Hitler's self-perception, as his historical disquisitions and glorification of the hero demonstrated. Hitler was constantly preoccupied with the view that posterity would have of his era if the situation remained as it were.[56]

The preference for an imposing architecture to represent the state and "establish its authority"[57] was a characteristic of the ancients, as classicists did not fail to point out; among them was Joseph Vogt, a professor of Roman history at the University of Leipzig, who was happy to see that the relationship between Nazism and antiquity was no longer limited to the lifeless words of bloodless intellectuals but rather constituted an authentic renaissance, as he saw the architecture of the new regime. Vogt rejoiced in the revival of an "architecture understood as the monumental self-representation of the community." As in antiquity, architecture would once again be the "expression of a conception of community guided by the state." The Third Reich would follow in the footsteps of the First Reich, the Roman Empire, whose edifices were "achievements related"[58] to those of the new Germany: "In this way the Olympic complex looks more like the Roman forum than a Greek sanctuary; the Königsplatz in Munich, with its temples in honor of the heroes of the movement, recalls the temple of heroes in a Greek or Roman capital."[59]

Architecture as an expression of a holistic community was also, in this way, a demonstration of the state's power. Joseph Vogt cited his colleague Gerhart Rodenwaldt, a historian of art and architecture who, some years later, would provide a contribution to the multiauthor volume *Das neue Bild der Antike* on "the state architecture of Rome." Rodenwaldt compared Hitler to Augustus, who, according to Suetonius's *Vita Augusti* and the *Res gestae divi Augusti*, had found Rome in brick and left it clad in marble: "Like all great statesmen, he considered architecture . . . as a means to express power." He made sure the *maiestas imperii* was made tangible though the "authority of public buildings,"[60] thus giving birth to an "architecture *pro maiestate imperii*."[61] In this way Hitler, for Rodenwaldt, revealed himself to be a worthy heir to the Augustan tradition: "The buildings of the present time evoke, in their composition, their planning, and their size, the state architecture of Rome. In the great projects to redesign the capital of the Reich *pro maiestate imperii*, we find the intersection of two axes, the intensity of orientation, the coordination of monumental streets, plazas, and interior spaces. . . . We also resemble the Romans in that we confront ourselves anew with the principles and bases of European monumental architecture that the Greeks erected with the temples that they dedicated to their gods."[62] The dominant trait of this state architecture was its blatant classicism, even if the style remained poorly defined, somewhere between the imperial Romanesque so dear to the Austrian Hitler and the severe Doric preferred by Troost and Speer.

Paul Ludwig Troost was Hitler's first architect. Before his premature death in 1934, he was responsible for providing the leader of the *Bewegung* with his first success as a contractor by building several projects for the führer in Munich. Troost was responsible for the construction of the party headquarters, the Braunes Haus, and after the seizure of power he also built the Ehrentempel, in memory of the Nazi "martyrs" from the putsch of 1923. He was also responsible for the design of the Haus der deutschen Kunst, so dear to Hitler's artistic pretentions. Speer deemed his predecessor's style to be "Spartan traditionalism."[63] Hitler's relationship with Troost was such that, upon the master architect's death, Hitler actually mentioned the possibility of taking over his office himself, a notion that in retrospect, as Speer remarked sarcastically, "was no stranger than his later assuming supreme command of the army."[64]

Speer professed respectful admiration for Troost. Confessing to having had ambitions to be "the legitimate heir of the Berlin classicists"[65] or "a second Schinkel,"[66] he possessed a love for Greek and classical architecture that he would never relinquish, as demonstrated by the various etchings that decorated his cell in Spandau after the war. The twenty years he spent in prison were only just brightened by a "bronze head by Polyclitus, Schinkel's sketch of a palace on the Acropolis, an Ionian capital, and a classical frieze. The first thing I see from bed every morning is the Erechtheum on the Acropolis."[67] Speer described his own style as "neoclassical, for I thought I had derived it from the Dorian style,"[68] having made several voyages to study Doric buildings: "Because of my fondness for the Doric, when I went on my first trip abroad in May 1935, I did not go to Italy to see the Renaissance palaces and the colossal buildings of Rome"—an obligatory rite of passage for all German intellectuals after Winckelmann—"instead, I turned to Greece."[69] There, Speer recalled, "my wife and I sought out chiefly examples of Doric buildings"; this was also the goal of a second trip he took, in March 1939, through Sicily and southern Italy, the colonial lands of Magna Graecia, where Speer particularly admired the "Doric temple ruins in Segesta, Syracuse, Selinus, and Agrigentum," which were "a valuable supplement to the impressions of our earlier journey to Greece."[70]

Hitler thus felt comfortable delegating authority for his classical monuments to his new architect in chief. In addition to his pretentions to immortality, Hitler's taste for antiquity meant that he "appreciated the permanent qualities of the classical style."[71] The aura that surrounded such ancient architecture, particularly anything connected with the Roman Empire, made it almost like a metaphor for eternity. A man so obsessed by time and so concerned about longevity[72] as Hitler could hardly help being profoundly moved and seduced by it. His idea of classical style was fundamentally Greek and more specifically Doric, Speer noted, since Hitler "thought he had found certain points of relationship between the Dorians and his own Germanic world"[73] and since he "believed that the culture of the Greeks had reached the peak of perfection in every field."[74]

Speer tempered his appreciation of Hitler's aesthetic sense with the observation that the führer's tastes remained bloated by what he had seen of the imperial Vienna of his youth, "the world of 1880 to 1910," marked by the "inflated neobaroque"[75] of the Viennese Ringstrasse and the Parisian Palais Garnier, which Hitler adored and which he tended to revert to after 1937. According to his most favored architect, the führer then began to distance himself from the Dorian style to espouse an overwrought neo-Empire style that resembled less the strict severity of Doric temples than the "show palaces of Oriental despots."[76] In hindsight, Speer saw this as a regression toward an "art of decadence" that, upon reflection, heralded the descent of a Reich that had become as bloated as its architecture, just as the French Empire style, which had come after the Spartan gravity of the Revolution, had accompanied the rise and fall of Napoleon.[77] In these passages, Speer developed a philosophical critique of art that saw its evolution in proportion to the political context, of which it was both sign and symptom. The former architect of the Nazi imperium distrusted the Empire style and what it foreshadowed: after the excesses of late rococo, the French Revolution had managed to restore a more strict, spare aesthetic, visible in the designs "of Boullée, Ledoux, and Lequieu,"[78] utopian architects whom Speer admired. The Directorate had enriched this classical severity with some decoration in the years 1789–94 before the empire arrived to exaggerate everything with its wealth and ornamentation. The period 1789–1815 thus offered "compressed within the span of twenty years ... a phenomenon that ordinarily took place only over centuries: the development from the Doric buildings of early antiquity to the fissured baroque façades of Late Hellenism," an evolution compressed further still by Nazism, into four years of severity followed by eight years of imperial exaggeration in both the ornamentation and the proportions of the buildings involved—something that, as Speer admitted, was "hidden from me at the time."[79] Speer was arguing, in essence, that with the growth of German power and the emergence of progressively more grandiose imperial ambitions came not just a tendency toward outrageous opulence but also and especially a gigantism that resembled that of Oriental despotism, while simultaneously recognizing that the Greeks too had suffered from similar "megalomaniacal notions."[80]

HYBRIS: MEGALOMANIA IN STONE

Speer deemed Hitler's imperial tastes to be a case of *gebaute Megalomanie,* or "architectural megalomania,"[81] and recalled that his own father, aghast at the disproportionate size of his son's designs, said to him: "You've all gone completely crazy."[82] Such was the spontaneous reaction of an outside observer. Speer's plans for the reconfiguration of Berlin were truly demented in scale. The dome of the proposed Grosse Halle was supposed to reach 250 meters (820 feet) in height, or the height, minus the antenna, of today's Fernsehturm (Television Tower) near Alexanderplatz. The eagle that was going to perch atop the dome was to reach some 290 meters (951 feet), or roughly the same elevation as the Eiffel Tower. "The element he loved in classicism," Speer wrote, "was the opportunity for monumentality. He was obsessed with giantism."[83]

In his book *Architekt der Weltherrschaft* (Architect of world domination),[84] the historian Jochen Thies read this architectonic grandiosity as a sign of imperial ambition on a global scale, an ambition so unprecedented that its designs beggared belief: their size was commensurate with the enormity of the führer's strategic ambitions. Thies argued that there was a singular logic connecting this grandiose architecture to the Nazis' military plans for the construction of long-range bombers capable of striking the United States. Imposing imperial edifices and flying fortresses were both expressions of the same drive for world domination.[85] There could thus be no doubt that Hitler's expansionism would not content itself with the conquest of vital living space to the east. His fight was on a global scale, against a Jewish conspiracy of world-historical proportions. Hitler was, Thies noted, obsessed with the example of the British Empire, a successful contemporary model of global hegemony, in addition to that of ancient Rome, which remained, in architecture as in politics, the führer's standard and challenge,[86] the historical absolute against which all grandeur must be measured.

Any self-respecting empire must defeat and surpass not only its contemporary rivals but also those of the past. In the same way, the architecture of this empire must transcend anything that might stand in comparison or opposition to it. Hitler formed his aesthetic judgments in terms of quantitative rather than qualitative categories: *Wucht* (force), *Gewalt* (violence), *Monumentalität* (monumentality), *Riesenhaftigkeit* (hugeness) were the coordinates orienting his personal vision and the attributes that he admired in buildings, which he frequently evaluated based solely on their size, their gigantism signaling their crowning virtue in the führer's hierarchy of values.

Hitler's avowed taste for the monumental was not the expression of a personal pathology, some kind of aesthetic elephantiasis, but rather an affect that drew upon a precise political symbolism. The gigantism of monuments under the Third Reich was part of a deliberate effort to give the German people a renewed sense of dignity and greatness, sentiments violated and vanquished by the shameful diktat of Versailles and the interminable years of repeated crises during the *Systemzeit* of Weimar. For the führer, in essence, "it is only through such works that one can give back to a people their sense of self-confidence."[87] At the inauguration of the new Reich Chancellery on 9 January 1939, he declared:

> It has always been my goal to restore this self-confidence to the German people, on all levels. Certain people perhaps might ask why the führer proclaims that this thing is the largest, why our roads are the widest, why does

he want them to be the biggest.... Why must everything always be the biggest? My German comrades, I do this to restore self-confidence to the German people.[88]

On multiple occasions Hitler declared in no uncertain terms his desire to surpass all the great monuments around the world. The hymn of the old Reich, which remained (along with the "Horst-Wessel-Lied") that of the new Germany, exhorted a "Deutschland über Alles in der Welt"—an injunction that Hitler took literally in his architectural designs, an early foreshadowing of the political ambitions that would follow soon after.

The contemporary reference point for Hitler was America: everything in the new Germany had to outdo its American counterpart. Hitler wanted Hamburg to build "the largest bridge in the world" rather than a more practical tunnel, because technological convenience was far less important than it was to

> make the Germans aware of it...: what is it about America and bridges? We can do exactly the same thing. This is why I make them build skyscrapers of the same height as the largest skyscrapers in the United States. This is why I make them build an imposing capital in Berlin. This is why I make them build giant factories in Nuremberg or Munich and these immense roadways throughout the German Reich, not purely for reasons of transportation but because I am convinced that it is necessary to give the German people this confidence in themselves that, though once great in the past, has been wounded.[89]

The führer-architect orchestrated an incredible symphony of superlatives: Berlin would have the longest and widest avenue in the world, running along its north-south axis, the largest airport in the world, the most powerful radio transmitter in the world;[90] Nuremberg would host the largest stadium in the world.[91] "Why always the biggest? I do this to restore to each individual German his self-respect."[92] However, while America, with its suspension bridges and skyscrapers, was the contemporary reference point, Hitler's gaze was above all turned toward Rome, "our only rival in the world,"[93] the sole historical power against which Hitler, sub specie aeternitatis, deigned to measure himself. As Speer later remarked, "His megalomania applied to time as well as to space."[94]

ROME: MODEL AND CHALLENGE

It remains to be said at this point to what degree Hitler's idea of Rome constituted a model for or a challenge to his own political labors to build an empire. For all the great conquerors of posterity, the Roman Empire—

its network of roads; its many cities, built like so many little Romes; its state, law, and army, which dominated virtually all of the known world—this empire, which vanquished the resistance of all save the distant Parthians to the east, appeared to be the paradigm of universal hegemony. It combined the strength of its military with the eloquence of its language and civilization, which sent legions and proconsuls everywhere from Africa to Britannia. It was thus hardly surprising that Charlemagne, Otto the Great, and later Napoleon had all wanted to display their might clothed in ancient rags and replay history in Roman robes. For Hitler, as for all conquerors, Rome was sign and symbol of hegemonic power and global domination. In a symbolic language in which signifiers were reduced to their most basic salient characteristics, the name of Rome functioned as a symbol of power, in the same way that *Athens* signified philosophy or *Prussia* stood as a synonym for discipline and organization. Hitler himself explicitly subscribed to this type of linguistic analysis, remarking upon the legacy of Caesar's name: "The destiny of a word can be extraordinary. For two thousand years the expression 'Caesar' personified the supreme authority."[95] Just as the word *Rome* was equated with imperial might, the name *Caesar* signified a military commander in chief and the incarnation of power itself. The superlative exemplarity of the Roman model could thus be read like a language, and both Caesar and Rome, immortalized for their unprecedented exploits, survived in the common memory as the very definitions of glorious accomplishment, since they were at once archetype, model, and symbol. The very words themselves had become monuments.[96]

Rome was both the symbol and archetype of military conquest and the creation of a global power, a power that set deep roots by imposing its language and culture, cultivating and shaping both spaces and peoples. Rome was the superlative, never again equaled—not even, or at least not yet, by the Greater German Reich: "The Roman Empire never had its like. To have succeeded in completely ruling the world! And no empire has spread its civilisation as Rome did."[97] In his table talks of November 1941—when the Wehrmacht patrolled the suburbs of Moscow—Hitler, admiring yet unsatisfied, believed that Rome was still without parallel, *nicht seinesgleichen*. Hitler's ambition was to create an empire on the Roman scale: the *imperium romanum, das römische Weltreich*, would soon have its counterpart in the Reich, which was on the verge of subjugating the entire European continent and of imposing its own race and culture. In 1941, the war against the Soviet Union was explicitly defined as a racial war of extermination against the Slavs and the Jews, who had to be displaced to make room for German colonizers. The racial homogenization of imperial space would be the modern counterpart to Rome's imposition of its language, law, and culture.

If Rome was so prominent in Hitler's mind and ideas, this was undoubtedly because Roman history made it seem possible to do what was patently impossible, and truly megalomaniacal—that is, to rule the known world. Basing a political project, no matter how insane, on real-life past events and eras meant inscribing these ideas in the realm of the possible, in a past that was real and thus could be achieved again. In referring to Rome, Hitler found the precursor and preceptor for that which, in its absence, could have been seen only as foolish and vain. By referring to Roman antiquity, Hitler's imperial folly found the slightest of anchorages in reality, which made his myth just a little more viable and credible. In Hitler's eyes, Rome essentially foreshadowed the Reich.

For Nietzsche, such inscription in the real was one of the functions of history, one of the ways in which it served life. In the second of his *Untimely Meditations* (1874), in fact, Nietzsche argued that "history belongs above all to the man of deeds and power, to him who fights a great fight, who needs models, teachers, comforters and cannot find them among his contemporaries."[98] History thus performed the function of helping this man discover past grandeur to inspire and encourage him in his task, showing him that no matter how unlikely it might seem in the present, such greatness remained possible, because it had in fact occurred in the past. Nietzsche called this type of history "monumental history." History became a sort of pilgrimage to the source of historical grandeur, through the discovery of the monuments of bygone eras, the great deeds and works of the past that presaged those of the present, or at least remained as evidence of their possibility. The man of action, the great man of the present could take courage from this contemplation of the monuments that history offered up to him, as well as determination and consolation in the face of the incomprehension of his contemporaries: "He learns from it that the greatness that once existed was in any event once possible and may thus be possible again; he goes his way with more cheerful step, for the doubt which assailed him in weaker moments, whether he was not perhaps desiring the impossible, has now been banished."[99]

BIGGER THAN THE COLOSSEUM

The monument that was Rome thus served as an example, a model to imitate, and a challenge to overcome, the only one worthy of the Reich in terms of its territorial expansion, its military power, and the memory of posterity. The images of the Germans' ancestors, preserved on the familial altar, always possessed the twin functions of counsel and injunction, example and challenge.[100] Hitler described the significance of his plans to rebuild central Berlin in one of his table talks of October 1941: "It's only thus that we shall succeed in eclipsing our only rival in the world, Rome."[101] The führer pronounced these words in an atmosphere of military and geostrategic euphoria, at a moment when the blitzkrieg in the East appeared to be a success and plans for a Greater German Reich seemed on the verge of realization.

If Hitler wanted essentially to build his way to unsurpassed greatness, Speer understood that it was really a matter of outclassing the masters of antiquity. Hitler was enthusiastic when his favored architect "could show him that at least in size we had 'beaten' the other great buildings of history":[102] the comparison mattered less in terms of absolute space than in terms of time; the reference point was not the United States but Rome. Speer's memoir is buried in an avalanche of units and measurements, specifying, for example, that the platform at the Zeppelinfeld at Nuremberg "had a length of thirteen hundred feet and a height of eighty feet. It was almost twice the length of the Baths of Caracalla in Rome."[103] To avoid cost overruns, it was built not in granite but in travertine, a less noble material but one that had been used for the Roman Colosseum. The platform was supposed to be crowned with an allegorical statue some sixty meters (197 feet) tall, which immediately led Speer to draw up certain specifications, employing historical and geographical examples from America and Rome: "In A.D. 64 Nero erected on the Capitol a colossal figure 119 feet high. The Statue of Liberty in New York is 151 feet high; our statue was to be 46 feet higher."[104]

Back in Nuremberg, Hitler's Deutsche Stadion was supposed to be able to hold four hundred thousand spectators. "History's largest precedent was the Circus Maximus in Rome, built for between one hundred and fifty and two hundred thousand persons. Modern stadiums in those days"—including that of his colleague Werner March, the Olympiastadion in Berlin—"contained about a hundred thousand seats."[105] These capacities were deliberately proportioned to keep pace with the geographic and demographic expansion of Germany, which was swelling into a Greater Reich whose population, according to Hitler's predictions in *Mein Kampf*, would in time reach some 250 million individuals. This demographic inflation impacted not only Nuremberg but also the Reich's capital. In Berlin the imperial project made it imperative to replace the 1939 Chancellery with a new Führerpalast on the Adolf-Hitler-Platz. This too would dwarf the ancient model and eclipse "even Nero's legendary palace area, the Golden House, with its expanse of more than eleven million square feet"; with some twenty-two million square feet, Hitler's palace would "outstrip" the competition.[106]

The dead had also earned their just homage in Hitler's architectural megalomania. The *Totenburgen,* those "gigantic funerary complexes" whose construction was entrusted to the architect Wilhelm Kreis, would resemble "tumuli from the ancient world"[107] but, once again, hypertrophied beyond recognition, with dimensions of one hundred square meters (1,076 square feet) or more.

This deluge of figures and waltz of comparisons in Speer's memoir palpably demonstrates the heady intoxication of the Reich's leaders, who were clearly convinced of their own historical exceptionalism. The buildings of imperial Rome—the Baths of Diocletian, the Circus Maximus, the Domus Aurea—were all cardinal reference points for this Nazi gigantism. It was Rome, as the very definition of an imperial metropolis, that offered the only model fit for the Reich to imitate and surpass.

GERMANIA, *NOVA ROMA:* A MANIFESTO SET IN STONE

The naming or renaming of a city is an assertion of power, the inauguration of a new era. This, according to Suetonius, was the ambition of Nero when he sought to remake the old capital of the imperium and to rebaptize it in his own name as Neropolis.[108]

In wanting to reshape his capital city with new buildings and new instruments of power—like the Soldatenhalle for the Oberkommando der Wehrmacht, the Army High Command—as well as novel social amenities, like the baths to be built along its north-south axis, Hitler followed in the path of two Roman traditions: that of the princeps, the ruler-as-builder, which led each new emperor of any ambition to endow Rome with a new forum, and that of the *euergetes,* the benefactor who, prince or otherwise, gifted the city with the necessary tools for social life.[109]

Hitler wanted to give Berlin a facelift. The rebirth of the Reich's capital would be accompanied by a new name, a performative semantic act that would herald the city's renaissance and the beginning of a new era. Berlin would henceforth be known as Germania, a title that, ironically, was not at all German.[110] *Germania* was a purely Latin word, popularized by Tacitus in the book so closely linked to his name since the Renaissance. Its German derivatives, *Germanen* and *germanisch,* had their own Nordic cognates, which derived from the legitimately Saxon root *teutsch*, Latinized as *tuidisc, tedesco,* or *tudesque* (and in the modern English term *Teutonic*). The Latin character of *Germania* was accented still further by the feminine ending *-a*. It is interesting to note that the SS did not follow Tacitus's lead when it came time to name its journal for anthropological and architectural research; rather than *Germania*, it preferred the more traditionally Nordic *Germanien*.

Its nomenclature echoing its status as the new Rome, Germania was conceived by Hitler to be the capital of a world empire. Like all of the regime's new architectural contributions, the new global metropole was an explicit manifestation of Nazi imperialism, an inscription of power not only in space but also in time, the millennia-long arc of posterity. This monolithic architecture would bolster the power of the führer and his successors, the future führers to come, leaving a monument in granite that would secure their place in history for all eternity.[111]

In order to support this ambitious comparison and remain worthy of its idol, Hitler's new world empire would have to speak the language of imperialism—that is, that of Roman monumentality. In fact, the new capital would have to reproduce all the signs of imperial *Romanitas* and possess all the architectural elements that defined Rome to make the city—through the projection and diffusion of those elements in the cities of the *provinciae*—the capital of the empire.

And so Germania needed to possess its own triumphal arch, a central element of the Roman military and urban landscape that recalled and made permanent through stone the portal to the battlefield.

Germania's arc de triomphe, designed by Speer after a sketch by Hitler, needed to be taller, larger, and longer than that of Napoleon, the other resurrector of European empire, in Paris: Hitler's arch would measure 117 meters (384 feet) in height—double that of the Champs-Élysées (50 meters, or 164 feet)—170 meters (558 feet) wide, and 119 meters (390 feet) long. As drawn by Hitler himself in his *Skizzenbuch* in 1925, the arch was "the heart of his plan" and "the classic example of the architectural fantasies he had worked out in his lost sketchbook of the twenties."[112] The monument would be situated at the end of two rows of cannons that began at the southern gate and led all the way down to the Grosse Halle.

The great hall would be the centerpiece of the new capital. Designed to be the future site of the führer's major speeches to the German people, it was to be set in an immense quadrilateral with an open colonnade, capped by an enormous dome, and capable of holding some

180,000 spectators. The greatest monstrosity of Nazi architectural megalomania, the Grosse Halle, its walls stretching some 315 meters (1,148 feet) in length, would occupy some 100,000 square meters (1,076,391 square feet), its cupola some 250 meters (820 feet) in diameter. Other than its unprecedented size, the Halle, with its columns and its dome, had obviously been inspired by Rome: "The Pantheon in Rome had served as our model," Speer admitted.[113] The Pantheon was very familiar to Hitler, a self-taught historian of art since his youth, who had already realized one lifelong dream in viewing some of Rome's antiquities during an official state visit to see Mussolini in May 1938. Having arrived in Ostia on 3 May, Hitler was bound by protocol and official obligations only through the sixth; on 7 May, a providential rain spared him the lengthy military parade organized by the Italians, allowing him the time to tour ancient Rome at his leisure. After making a return trip in private to see the Mostra Augustea della Romanità, which he had visited officially the day before, he went to the Capitoline Museums, the Baths of Diocletian, and the Pantheon, which he requested to enter alone. He remained there awhile in contemplation, admiring the dome that Speer's plans had copied and enlarged by a factor of twenty.[114] The stairs leading to the building were to be flanked by two sculptures, "each fifty feet high." Hitler, Speer later wrote, "had already decided on the subjects of these sculptures when we were preparing our first sketches of the building. One would represent Atlas bearing the vault of the heavens, the other Tellus supporting the globe of the world."[115] Hitler thus sought to allegorize his power in Greco-Roman terms: the master of earth and sky, whose weight he carried on his shoulders and whose fate he held in his hands.

Beyond these military and political edifices, which reproduced and transposed the classical elements of Roman imperial architecture, Germania also needed to have baths, the ultimate symbol of classical *euergetism* and further evidence of the Nazis' concern for hygiene and the body.[116] Speer noted that "even an indoor swimming pool, built in Roman style and as large as the baths of Imperial Rome, [was] deliberately included in [Hitler's] plans."[117] Hitler knew the Baths of Diocletian from his private archaeological tour of the ruins on 7 May 1938 in Rome. His own baths would be situated on the north-south axis, to the east of the southern gate and next to the Reich Postal Ministry.

The buildings of Germania needed to be distributed along a great north-south axis, which Berlin had never previously possessed. The traditional axis of Berlin, the Prussian royal axis, led from the royal house to the statue of Frederick II, the Brandenburg Gate, and the Siegessäule (Victory Column) in an east-west direction; this was the line followed by Unter den Linden, which extended beyond the gate in a long avenue toward Charlottenburg—the Siegesallee, or "Road of victory" (a line that, despite the Cold War, still structures the urban space of central Berlin today). Hitler wanted at all costs to create a north-south axis, by superimposing a monumentally broad boulevard over a large number of railway lines that ran from the southwest to the northeast, which would have required decommissioning the Potsdamer Bahnhof and the Anhalter Bahnhof. In addition to this impressive railway network, the planned new axis required the destruction of hundreds of hectares of existing residences and streets. The scale of this act of urban planning and the enormous sums it would have required are scarcely comprehensible without an appreciation of the führer's determination to give the city a *cardo,* a north-south axis, the primary orientation of the classical Roman city. Roman urban planning, largely of military origin, was a carbon copy of the orthogonal plan of a legionnaire's camp: four gates, two axes, square barracks, with intersections at right angles of the two axes, the *cardo* and the *decumanus,* which ran east-west. While Rome itself was an older city, built through archaic synoecism and in which the Hippodamian plan was scarcely visible, it nevertheless frequently characterized the new *coloniae* and their outposts.

The capital that Hitler inherited was not Roman enough for his taste: with two axes crossed at close to a right angle near the site of the current Soviet monument at the Tiergarten, the capital of the Reich would have its new *cardo* along with its traditional *decumanus* and thus become fully imperial.

The general structure and number of specific buildings were of overtly Roman inspiration. Their ornamentation also had to evoke Rome, in a sort of architectural homage: along the east-west axis of Unter den Linden, the regime built new columns designed by the architect and *Reichsbühnenbildner* Benno von Arent to mark the occasion of Mussolini's visit in September 1937. These were columns with Doric capitals, topped by *Hoheitsadler,* or "eagles of sovereignty." Initially meant to be only temporary, the columns suited Hitler's tastes so well that he decided to keep them. Once Il Duce had left, the columns were fixed in stone permanently. In *The Great Dictator* (1940), Charlie Chaplin makes fun of this spectacle *à l'antique* in the midst of Berlin in a scene depicting the return of the dictator Adenoid Hynkel to his palace after one of his speeches. The avenue he travels down in his giant black convertible is littered with antique and pseudoantique works of art, such as the *Venus de Milo* with her arms restored in the position of a Nazi salute and a copy of Rodin's *Thinker,* his head resting heavily on one of his two arms while the other performs the same *Hitlergruss.*

ROMAN AND CLASSICAL MYTHOLOGY IN THE DECORATIVE ARTS

As we have seen, Hitler paid particularly close attention to the design of party uniforms, symbols, and insignia, following the lead of his onetime Italian Fascist patron, whose neo-Roman tastes he very much appreciated. Hitler, who professed a sincere, long-standing admiration for Mussolini and who admitted to his close associates that "the brown shirt would probably not have existed without the black shirt,"[118] borrowed from Italian Fascism anything that hinted at the venerable majesty of ancient Rome, like the party insignia that decorated the National Socialist dress uniform. The eagle that adorned party standards, threatening to take flight, talons clenched and wings spread wide, was inspired by Rome, as were the banners themselves, the famous *Standarten* that filled party assemblies with flags, eagles, and iron crosses. Hitler designed them himself in the image of the Roman legions, accompanied by a telling annotation in his sketchbook: "Caesar by way of Mussolini."[119] Hitler conscientiously researched the subject, which made his imitations of Roman standards all the more convincing. They summarily assembled all the constituent elements of Roman military symbolism: the vexillum, the square red flag that served as the legions' banner, which in the Nazi version was adorned with the hakenkreuz on a white background and the motto *Deutschland Erwache!;* the *aquila,* or eagle; and finally, the standard, or *signum,* adorned with discs and crescents. Nazi *Standarten* displayed the swastika inserted in a *corona civica* of oak leaves, with a badge indicating the geographical provenance of the unit represented (city or gau), corona and badge also representing Roman military symbols. The "civic crown" possessed particular significance, for it was the distinction given to those who had saved the life of a fellow citizen in battle. Augustus saw fit to award himself a similar crown for having saved the state from civil war and chaos. Undoubtedly, Hitler, the true *pater patriae* who had saved Germany from the chaos of Weimar and communist subversion, thought that the party merited the same. The swastika, omnipresent like the eagle, was depicted not only on the flag (in the white circle on a red background) but also as an architectural motif, surrounded by the famous corona of woven oak leaves.

Other elements of Nazi decorum were also borrowed from Rome. The supreme power of the Reich dressed itself in Roman robes not only in the form of its buildings but also in their interior decoration.[120] The iconography of the new Reich Chancellery, unveiled in January 1939 by Speer, whose efficiency impressed Hitler to the point that he would give him a ministerial promotion three years later, was saturated with references to antiquity, in the choice of materials as in the themes depicted. A marble hall in regal crimson contained numerous mosaics, the Roman art par excellence, depicting eagles, crowns of laurel, olive branches, flaming torches, and thyrsi. Mosaics were everywhere, not just in the Chancellery. The ships of the Kraft durch Freude (KdF), or "Strength through Joy" organization—floating palaces for the worthiest members of the working class—were equipped with swimming pools whose decorative motif adopted similar classical materials and themes. The baths of the *KdF-Schiff Wilhelm Gustloff* (1938)[121] were decorated with mosaics depicting Neptune reigning over the waves and waterways. In the Chancellery, other materials, like mural tapestries and large-format tableaux, hewed closer to the tradition of the absolute monarchs of the seventeenth and eighteenth centuries, but their subjects too were borrowed from antiquity: twenty-one tapestries from the seventeenth century in three series depicted the life of Alexander the Great (eight), the history of the Roman consul Decius Mus (five), and the acts of Dido and Aeneas. The Alexandrine symbolism, an allegory of imperialism, was blatantly obvious. The figure of Decius Mus, the Roman consul who devoted himself to the gods and found death on the battlefield to achieve victory for the Rome of the Latins (third century BC) symbolized the heroic sacrifice of the leader who gave his life for his city,[122] and that of Aeneas evoked a leader who, like the führer,[123] refused to let his love for a woman, or any other personal sentiment, turn him away from his sacred mission. Aeneas, of course, left Dido to go found the colony of Latium, the birthplace of Rome.

Hitler's office also spoke in an allegorical language plucked from antiquity. Hitler's worktable was inlaid with three marquetry panels that faced visitors, who were seated in deliberately lowered chairs.[124] Hitler believed that visitors to the new Reich Chancellery should be compelled to realize that they were meeting with the master of the world: seated facing his desk, all were invited—journalists, ministers, or foreign plenipotentiaries—to recognize that they were speaking to a king at war. The marquetry on the desk depicted Mars at the center atop a crossed javelin and a sword emerging from its sheath, flanked to his right by Medusa and to the left by Minerva. The Gorgon, with the fangs of a great cat and hair of live serpents, had a stare that would petrify her enemies. After she was defeated by Perseus, her head was eventually given to Athena, who placed it on her aegis, a practice imitated by the Greek hoplites, who depicted Medusa's head upon their shields—a ritual at once apotropaic and expiatory, since Medusa's gaze was supposed to freeze their adversaries and root them to the spot. Minerva (Athena), the virgin warrior goddess, conveyed the same message: the era of the Reich was at hand, and the brutal (Mars), atrocious (Medusa), and supremely intelligent (Minerva) violence of the German war machine was simply waiting to be unleashed.

ANTIQUE GIGANTISM AND HIERATISM, FROM NUREMBERG TO PARIS: THE IMAGE OF THE NEW GERMANY

The capital of the Reich was not the only city subjected to the führer's architectural solicitude. Munich, which maintained the status of *Hauptstadt der Berwegung,* or "capital of the movement," and the *Reichsstadt* of Nuremberg were also supposed to be redesigned in antique and monumental terms. In Nuremberg, the stand for the Zeppelinfeld, which would host the huge gatherings of the party congresses, was "undoubtedly . . . influenced by the Pergamum altar,"[125] the imposing, prestigious masterpiece of the Pergamonmuseum of Berlin.

The Nuremberg *Reichsparteitagsgelände* also had to be endowed with a vast staging area to accommodate the Wehrmacht's parade maneuvers, which typically took up one whole day of the congress. Significantly, this area was known by the name *Märzfeld,* a nod to Rome's Campus Martius, the gathering place for citizens at arms where the various legions would present themselves upon hearing the call and form their comitia to vote, outside the pomerium, or city limits, within which no arms were allowed. Speer noted, however, that the name carried a double meaning, since "the name was intended not only as a reference to the war god Mars, but also to the month in which Hitler introduced conscription,"[126] March 1935, when the Nazis reorganized the Wehrmacht and reinstituted conscription in violation of the Treaty of Versailles.

The great complex at Nuremberg would be crowned by the construction of the great stadium, which Hitler entrusted to Speer. The stadium had to be able to host some four hundred thousand spectators, in order to be a worthy theater for the party congress speeches as well as future Olympic Games, which, after the war was won, would always be held in Germany. The stadium was inspired, of course, by the Roman Colosseum, from which it borrowed the large galleries, but also by the Athenian stadium of Herodes Atticus, which had been restored for the inaugural modern games in 1896. Speer recalled having been "overwhelmed . . . by the reconstructed stadium of Athens. Two years later, when I myself had to design a stadium, I borrowed its basic horseshoe form."[127]

Some informed contemporary observers fell prey to the effect of this neo-antique architecture, seeing the Third Reich for what Hitler wanted them to see: the resurrection of the most powerful, dominant, and striking elements of antiquity. Robert Brasillach, who compiled a celebrated anthology of Greek poetry, described his impressions of the Nuremberg Congress in these terms: "At the *Zeppelinfeld*, outside the city, an immense stadium had been built, in this almost Mycenean architecture that the Third Reich was so fond of. Its stands could hold 100,000 people seated, and the arena itself 2 or 300,000."[128] The strikingly powerful effect was such that Brasillach actually recalled the archaic, preclassical Greece of the cyclopean architecture of Mycenaean royalty. Pierre Drieu La Rochelle saw Nuremberg in the image of the Athens of Pericles, who had been the führer-architect of his time: "It is the most beautiful thing I have seen after the Acropolis," he declared, after having attended the *chorégies* of the Nuremberg Congress in 1935.[129]

Contemporaries thus took notice of this show of strength, admiringly—or disdainfully, like the French ambassador to Berlin, André François-Poncet, who sniffed contemptuously that the Nazis built "a giant stadium [for] one hundred thousand spectators. From the outside the façade is deceiving. It lacks the imposing majesty of the Colosseum in Rome."[130]

In addition to these model cities of Reich and party, other towns and provincial capitals of the various gaue were also encouraged to imitate the *Reichshauptstadt* Germania: "The Berlin model had become a rigid pattern,"[131] Speer noted, whose reproduction evoked the Roman tendency to build miniature versions of the *urbs* throughout the empire, each endowed with its own forum, baths, basilicas, temples, and markets. A bemused Speer observed how the gauleiters, those pint-size führers of the provinces, developed a sudden passion for architecture, including their own fervent imitation of the Berlin blueprint: "The plans for Berlin inspired a host of designs for other urban programs. Every

Gauleiter henceforth wanted to immortalize himself in his own city."¹³² Similarly, in the new gaue of the territories conquered in the East, Hitler dreamed of the exact replication of the Berlin model, with typically German monuments that would foster the Indo-Germanicization of the newly conquered countryside, imitating the *coloniae* of the Roman Empire as well as the Greek colonies.¹³³

To a foreigner, the image of the Reich was wrapped up in the Doric style, not only in the *Repräsentationsbauten* of Berlin and Nuremberg but also in the construction of the German pavilion at the Paris International Exposition of 1937. Its predecessor, at the 1929 Barcelona Expo, had been designed by Mies van der Rohe as an ode to functionalism, a monument of the *Neue Sachlichkeit* in the finest Bauhaus style. Now pilloried as an example of degenerate art, such modernist architecture could no longer be allowed to furnish Germany's window to the world. A cold, strict Doric style would dominate the pavilion, designed jointly by Speer and Hitler. The impassive hieratism of this tall structure, supported by columns capped with Doric chapters and topped by a Nazi eagle, erected an insurmountable wall in front of the ardent, restless curves of the Soviet worker and kolkhoznik on the march toward a radiant tomorrow. The placement of the Soviet pavilion directly opposite that of Nazi Germany in the Trocadéro was due to the fact that "the French directors of the fair had deliberately arranged this confrontation"—or at least that's how it seemed to Speer, who added that he had "accidentally" stumbled upon a sketch of the Soviet pavilion, which was supposed to have been kept secret, and had accordingly positioned the eagle to look down upon the proletariat striding confidently toward a happier future.¹³⁴

There can be no doubt that this neoclassical architectural style was a manifesto carved in stone, speaking to the inhabitants of towns and cities across the Nazi empire in the language of imperialism. It was, however, also part of a broader contemporary trend: returning to architectural forms and styles that borrowed from a venerable hieratic Western tradition. From Stalinist structures to the federal buildings of Washington DC in the 1920s and 1930s, passing through the Parisian Trocadéro of 1937, neoclassicism caught on everywhere and was not solely the prerogative of totalitarians nor, a fortiori, of Nazism.

Speer readily relativized the originality of his own oeuvre and many of his projects, rejecting the idea that Nazi classicism was new or unique: "It has often been asserted that this style is characteristic of the architecture of totalitarian states. That is not at all true. Rather, it was characteristic of the era and left its impress upon Washington, London, and Paris as well as Rome, Moscow, and our plans for Berlin."[135] Speer's obvious attempt at self-exoneration has been refuted by Miguel Abensour, who rejects the idea that such architecture was politically neutral or indifferent. There can be no "autonomy in architecture's relationship to the political," since "the institution of space" through architectural creation is part and parcel of "the logic of the totalitarian institution of the social."[136] What was truly specific to Nazi architecture was its crushing monumentality, which aimed to herd the people and overwhelm or stun the subjected masses, as Speer later realized.[137] The gigantism that characterized Nazi architecture seemed to aim to crush the individual and bear down upon the people through its disproportionate size, compressing them into a compact mass so that every interstitial space that distanced or differentiated one person from another disappeared into the greater whole of an organic totalitarian entity. The political space of the democratic agon, a space "paradoxically linked to division,"[138] was destroyed.[139] Nazi architecture created sites for the fusion of the masses and for compressing them into a single, unified subject. It was stagecraft in granite, the physical orchestration of a new type of rapport between the individual and the state in terms of the mass, whether the compact mass of stone or the more malleable mass of humanity that, gathered into columns, made the pillars and lines of this architecture even more monumental.

A similar argument could be applied to Stalinist architecture and what it borrowed from neoclassicism. In the case of the Soviet Union, however, the dimensions were smaller, and neoclassical architecture was not a vector for the transmission of a genetic discourse on race. Speer's architecture used monumentality to shape a mass of people subjugated to totalitarian power and borrowed classical grammar to signify the racial relationship that linked Dorians, Romans, and contemporary Germans. The return to classicism in the USSR was not exclusive and admitted coexistence with other styles;[140] the Soviet Union acknowledged its multiethnic character and the multiplicity of its peoples. Official Soviet art never sought a primal, original, nativist style that served as the basis for a canon, whereas in the Third Reich neo-Doric and neo-Roman were meant to express the original artistic essence of a race that did not change through the millennia. The adoption of this neoclassical style demonstrated their link with the distant antiquity of the race and proclaimed their desire to restore and preserve its original purity.

THE FIGURE OF THE LEADER AND
FÜHRERPERSÖNLICHKEIT IN ANTIQUITY

Nazi architecture was an allegory of the *Führerprinzip* and its relationship to the *Volksgemeinschaft*. To speak of empire or an authoritarian regime with imperialist aspirations was to speak of the princeps, or führer. A series of articles and other publications in the Third Reich explored the figure of a Nordic leader inspired by the models of antiquity.

The seemingly unavoidable Fritz Schachermeyr, for example, wrote a piece dedicated to "the personality of the Nordic leader in antiquity." After a long passage on the value and utility of the humanities for any truly National Socialist education, the author defined the Nordic leader as "that exceptional individual"[141] who manages, through sheer force of will, to transform his environment in line with an idea—an inspired idealist, then, who succeeds at turning his ideas into reality, a definition reminiscent of Hitler's numerous tirades against the vulgar materialism of Marxists and Jews in contrast to the elevated idealism of the Nazis. The Nordic leader in antiquity was like an artist who, in working with the materials of his métier, gives form to his sparks of genius and overall vision and who, through charisma and sheer force of will, unifies a social body that in his absence would become "a conglomerate of autarkic individuals . . . , an atomized mass."[142] Such writing strictly espoused the mystique of the chosen leader. Hitler had previously described the soteriological and redemptive figure of the führer, the savior of Germany and guarantor of its unity, in *Mein Kampf*. Reading between the lines—though one need not read too deeply, as the reference was fairly obvious—shows that Schachermeyr was drawing a portrait of the actual führer by developing a rather unsubtle comparison between Pericles and Hitler.

Pericles had appeared at a time when Athenian democracy was in crisis, "precisely similar to that which we experienced before the appearance of Adolf Hitler." But Pericles's desire to reform the Athenian state became bogged down by "the Mediterranean substrate foreign to the [Nordic] race" of Pericles and the Indo-Germanic Athenian elite. Schachermeyr pursued this parallel between Greek and German leaders further, comparing Aristides, Cimon, Cleisthenes, Themistocles, Pericles, and Peisistratus[143] to Frederick the Great, Bismarck, and Hitler. These German leaders had to be understood both "in terms of their Germanic character" and "in terms of their Nordic identity,"[144] an identity they shared with the Greeks, who themselves had to be studied, not solely out of love for ancient Greece but to educate and train a new generation of National Socialist leaders.

The imposing figure of Pericles, so fascinating to Hitler, was also the subject of a talk given by Helmut Berve, his inaugural lecture after assuming the rectorate at the University of Leipzig. The title given to all rectors after 1933 was *Rektor und Führer der Universität*; the modern führer and historian of antiquity thus aligned himself with a führer from antiquity. Berve began by recalling that Pericles's name had become synonymous with the Greek fifth century, which represented "a singular height of Indo-Germanic humanity."[145]

Pericles's democratic politics were not mere demagogic clientelism; he strove to allow every Athenian to participate in the life of the city, to make it a real community with a genuine consciousness of itself as such. According to Berve, Pericles wanted "to make all levels of the Athenian people active politically and to make them part of a real community of political life,"[146] a holistic interpretation that made the democratic sensibilities of the great Nordic leader more comprehensible and acceptable.

The great works policy set in motion by Pericles, which included the building of the Acropolis, was primarily intended to provide work and subsistence for all, a goal strangely consonant with the Nazis' *Arbeit und Brot* (Work and bread) campaign and their policy of countercyclical state intervention in the economy. To gather the means for this policy, he needed to find financing: since he was prevented from overwhelming the Athenians with an excessive fiscal burden, he had been forced to resort to imperial conquest. Athenian imperialism was thus fully justified as the foundation of a domestic political project: the creation of a unified *Volksgemeinschaft*, the grand Periclean design.[147] Berve remarked that "the spirit with which the planning for war was undertaken and soon applied leaves no doubt about the fact that a compelling and driven will was at work,"[148] Pericles being an "imperturbable führer," without fear and above reproach. The war, as Hitler himself noted in *Mein Kampf*, was thus a positive one. The power and sovereignty of a state, acquired through war, allowed him to build and leave to posterity the cultural trappings of such power: "It was thus the brute strength of Athens and the unbending will of its führer that allowed for the creation of those wonders that are the Parthenon and the Propylaea on the Acropolis, which still today, even as ruins, present the most sublime evidence of man's creative energies."[149] It was not very difficult to find the contemporary equivalent of this courageous man, the bringer of a political project of national unity underpinned by a necessary imperialism, indispensable for financing an ambitious and generous great works policy, a tireless, fascinating man, incorruptible and bold, faithful to his companions and to his ideals.

The analogy became even more explicit when Berve presented the reader with Pericles as führer-artist, the great architect of a new Athens: "Pericles's immersion in the construction of the Acropolis" was total;[150] the great strategist cultivated "a close relationship with Phidias, to whom he entrusted the supervision of the whole," redesigning a new Athens commensurate with its empire, a conquering thalassocracy, powerful and self-assured. The parallel between the relationships of Pericles and Phidias and of Hitler and Speer was obvious, as was the delegation of the projects for the new Athens and Germania. Pericles, like all great Nordic leaders, had been put to the test by war. The Peloponnesian War had been his "hour of truth,"[151] just as the Seven Years' War was much later for Frederick II. Pericles, for whom "life was a battle until his final breath,"[152] also awed his contemporaries, both friends and foes alike, with his incredible charisma.[153] This edifying portrait of the Nordic leader was made complete with the inevitable tirade regarding the lessons of Indo-Germanics from ancient history for the modern era.[154]

A few other exceptional figures from Greco-Roman antiquity were similarly rebuilt into paradigms of the Nordic führer in the Third Reich's version of history and state-sponsored propaganda. Such was the case for Augustus, much like Pericles, although judgment was reserved or suspended—and at times even openly negative—with regard to Alexander and Caesar, who both suffered for their unabashed imperialism:[155] the problem with the great world empires of antiquity was that they had enabled racial miscegenation and allowed themselves to serve as platforms for the expansion of the Jewish diaspora. As a result, Caesar, who granted Judaism some privileges, was seen as too close to the Jews;[156] Alfred Rosenberg did not mention his name even once in *The Myth of the Twentieth Century*.

Biographies of Pericles, like those of Augustus, in the context of the fifth and first centuries BC, respectively, functioned as allegories for the political predicaments of Weimar Germany. In the case of Augustus especially, historians of antiquity found the parallel with Hitler simply too good to pass up: a climate of civil war and delinquent behavior by a state threatened by the prospect of a global war between East and West—until the appearance of a savior sent by providence saved Rome and in so doing revived its most profound traditions.[157]

ANTIQUITY AND THE CULT OF THE LEADER:
PROVIDENCE, THE PAST, AND THE GREAT MAN
THEORY OF HISTORY

Hitler, as we have seen, loved history, doubtless in virtue of his narcissism as a political animal who happily identified with the great figures of the past. The history he grew up on was dominated by the Great Man theory: a sort of portrait gallery of notable leaders, their biographies tending toward outright hagiography, whether of king, statesman, or military commander. These were the men who made history: an endlessly quoted phrase that was stolen from Treitschke[158] and stripped of its original meaning. Treitschke was arguing that the human world was not subject to natural law and that man, as a creature of reason, possessed free will—not that history was made only by great men in positions of power. But of course this was the interpretation put forward by the Nazis, in keeping with their elitist and providential conception of history: "We, my Party comrades, co-leaders of the *Volk* and the Army, have been chosen by Fate to make history in the loftiest sense of the word. What millions of people are deprived of has been given to us by Providence. Even most distant posterity will be reminded of us by our work."[159] This heroic Great Man theory was subject to very little opposition or criticism, for it glorified the willpower and individual drive that Hitler claimed to incarnate and that he expected of every German. What's more, the Great Man theory of history magnified the role of the contemporary man who was making history in the present: the führer. The Nazis developed a cult of personality around the führer that added to the pantheon of political heroes commemorated by the party: figures such as Albert Leo Schlageter, the young Nazi shot by the French during the occupation of the Ruhr; or the fallen revolutionaries of the failed putsch of 9 November 1923, remembered every year in Munich, where after 1933 an Ehrentempel housed their bronze sarcophagi; or Horst Wessel and Wilhelm Gustloff, among the many figures chosen to populate the indispensable gallery of martyrs to the cause.

At the summit of this hierarchy of heroes sat the führer, the great man of present-day Germany. Hitler made history, he gave it form and substance, just as the great men of the past had shaped their own times, as Goebbels noted in his journal:

> Great men make great eras, but great eras do not make great men. What does it mean for an era to be great? There are times of calm and times of agitation. Our time is of the latter. But an era cannot become great without a man: Alexander, Caesar, Barbarossa, Napoleon, Frederick, Bismarck . . .[160]

The last name on the list, the seal of the prophets, was obviously Hitler, just as the election posters of 1933 depicted Frederick the Great, Bismarck, Hindenburg, and Hitler—that is, the king, the chancellor-prince, the marshal, and the corporal[161]—as incarnations of an eternal Germany and supreme leaders in the national pantheon.

In a 1926 speech, Hitler attempted to justify this cult of personality, for which the Nazis were frequently reproached. It was entirely legitimate to celebrate the great man in the form of the leader, he argued, since it was the great man, sent by providence, who made history: "They criticize us for celebrating a cult of personality. This is not true. In the course of all the great eras of history, one great personality has emerged from within a movement. It is not the movement that history remembers, but the individual. Today we still speak of Caesar, of Constantine, but not of the Roman movement. Similarly, in two thousand years they will still speak of the leaders of the National Socialist movement."[162] Hitler enjoyed seeing himself as the culmination of a series of great men not only nationally but globally. Speer recalled that the führer, on his fifty-fourth birthday (20 April 1943), "drifted off into lengthy expatiations on the role of the individual in history. What had counted had always been the will of a single individual: Pericles, Alexander, Caesar, Augustus, and then Prince Eugene, Frederick the Great, Napoleon. . . . His relationship to history was sheer romanticism and centered around the concept of the hero."[163]

Unlike the dialectical materialism of Marxism, which made the so-called great man a creature brought about by the necessities of historical laws, a superficial dollop of foam atop the rising tide of class conflict, Nazism celebrated the hero's will and genius, the force of his outsize, Promethean will, falling in line with the ancient tradition that viewed history as a celebration of great, illustrious men as *bona exempla*[164] to revere and imitate. History was above all the compilation and comparison of their biographies, as in Plutarch, whose *Bioi paralleloi* was composed of the parallel lives of illustrious Greeks and Romans.

Great men and heroes thus had to be revered for their valor and dignity, because they were models of action and virtue and because they all paved the way for the hero among heroes, the führer. In *Mein Kampf*, Hitler suggested that the professor of history should pay particularly close attention to the great Germans, illustrations of the country's valor, who were thus appropriate to stoke feelings of national pride: "Our admiration of every great deed must be bathed in pride that its fortunate performer is a member of our own people. From all the innumerable great names of German history, the greatest must be picked out and introduced to the youth so persistently that they become pillars of an unshakable national sentiment."[165] History had to be presented as the pantheon of the nation's glories and proudest moments, of the great men who had shaped their time, as the Nazis aimed to do in the present. Hitler made this part of his programmatic instructions for the teaching of history, as he outlined in a speech before the Reichstag on 23 March 1933: "Heroism is coming forward passionately and will in future shape and lead political destiny.... Respect for the great men of the past must once more be hammered into the minds of our youth: it must be their sacred heritage."[166] These instructions were mechanically reproduced in a circular by the Reich's interior minister Wilhelm Frick, who on 20 July 1933 issued his "Directives for History Textbooks." The circular began with an outline of general principles, among them the strengthening of units devoted to Germanic prehistory, the principle of race, and the "idea of the hero ... coupled with the idea of the führer in our time," the last two notions "arousing with their own strength the power to mobilize hearts, an enthusiasm without which history too easily becomes, for the majority of students, a boring compilation of facts."[167]

The Great Man theory of history came from the teaching of the subject as it had long been practiced in the schools. Generations of students had been raised on the cult of the great man. The Finnish historian Vappu Tallgren has written on Hitler's view of this heroic myth.[168] At the same time that it called upon myth, Nazism also called upon the hero, the unambiguously ideal type, who incarnated virtue and galvanized those who understood the significance of his heroic act. Tallgren explores the genealogy of the heroic myth for Hitler by examining its origins in the history instruction that the schoolboy Adolf Hitler received alongside all the other Germans of his generation. The texts used by his teachers spoke volumes, including that used by the instructor to whom Hitler paid homage in *Mein Kampf*, Dr. Leopold Pötsch.[169] "It was a determining factor in Hitler's career that the conception of history at work in the textbooks of his generation of young Germans ... possessed an essentially heroic concept," Tallgren wrote, adding that they were put together "following the principle: it was men who made history."[170] The ancient history text used by Pötsch accordingly showed Pericles in a positive light, as the resuscitator of Athenian power and builder of its most beautiful monuments, a man of almost superhuman exceptionality, a Jupiter who, according to the text, actually rained down "thunder and lightning" when he spoke.[171]

When we recall that, in Hitler's own words, Pötsch presented world history as the heroic saga of the Indo-Germanic race, it is easy to understand the determinism of the heroic portraits contained in these textbooks and in classroom instruction: Hitler conceived of his cult of the hero because, like other students of his generation, he was steeped in the teaching of history as a tribute to the great man, who was supposed to be lionized. Tallgren suggests that Hitler, in *Mein Kampf*, consequently composed his autobiography by following—no doubt unconsciously—the set stages of the heroic trope: in his youth he displayed signs of predestination; in war he received his first test, tasting initial defeat; then he bounced back and finally discovered his mission. All under the extraordinary protection of a mysterious and divine providence.

AN AUSTRIAN AUTODIDACT'S TASTE FOR THE ANTIQUE

Like many students of his generation, Hitler absorbed from his elementary school history courses both a heroic vision of history and a pronounced taste for antiquity. It was in terms of his memories of his primary education that Hitler expressed his admiration for Pericles, who was glorified in the textbook and lessons employed by Dr. Pötsch—and who was Hitler's boyhood hero, according to Ernst Hanfstaengl, foreshadowing Hitler's later characterization as Pericles's modern reincarnation.[172] As Joachim Fest noted, Hitler the architect "considered himself a ruler in the mold of Pericles and was wont to draw parallels; Albert Speer recalls that he regarded the Autobahnen as his Parthenon."[173]

His interest in the heroes of antiquity was reinforced by the many books that the young, unemployed Viennese Hitler of 1907–13 devoured in his ample spare time.[174]

Josef Greiner, who lived alongside Hitler at the men's dormitory on Meldemannstrasse in Vienna between 1910 and 1913, was critical of the lack of interest he demonstrated for learning a craft that would allow him to earn a steady living: "Instead, he would bring back books by the kilo from the lending library. He immersed himself in translations of Greek and Latin literature, like Sophocles, Homer, and Aristophanes, or even Horace and Ovid."[175] But more than literature, it was history that fascinated the young Hitler: "He threw himself into the history of ancient Rome,"[176] which he interpreted as the achievement of a branch of a Nordic race profoundly hostile to Judaism.[177] All the evidence of the period, like that of his first friend and flatmate in Vienna, August Kubizek,[178] confirms the young Hitler's considerable taste for reading, as a young man whose grip on reality occasionally seemed weak and who turned every conversation into a long-winded monologue pontificating on his latest literary discovery. A passionate autodidact and barroom orator, he had an appetite for the written word that never entirely left him. Hanfstaengl recalled that in the 1920s in Munich, the young führer of the nascent NSDAP remained a *Bücherfresser*,[179] or "bookworm," whose library, in addition to books on German history and biographies of Wagner, also contained an anthology of Greek myths, Gustav Schwab's *Gods and Heroes of Ancient Greece*,[180] which remains a classic to this day. Hitler's mental universe was formed early through this passion for antiquity. Classical figures frequently served as cultural reference points: Caesar, Pyrrhus, and Cato were his friends, as well as Herostratus and Ephialtes, who were like household names in his writings. Hitler labeled the ministers of Weimar—guilty of having negotiated and ratified the Young Plan—so many "Ephialtes"[181] and called one particular police commissioner a "Herostratus"[182] who was destroying Germany because he was too severe in his treatment of the SA.

Time only accentuated Hitler's predilection for this type of history, the reading of which made him feel closer to those great men with whom his delicate ego identified, great men whose lives and deeds presaged, heralded, and anticipated his own and who were like a promise of immortality. His interest in ancient history, the history of Western civilization, was focused more intently on Rome than on Greece. The historian Alexander Demandt has noted how this tendency was a function more of Hitler's personal idiosyncrasies than of a broader German cultural trend. Since the eighteenth century, German culture had celebrated Hellas more than *Romanitas,* which had been left to France, which proclaimed itself (not without reason) to be more Roman than Germany. In his choice of Rome as a model, Hitler's admiration for Mussolini and Catholic education, such as it was, undoubtedly played a determining role,[183] as did his Austrian nationality. We must remember that Hitler left Austria for Munich only at the age of twenty-three, after having spent his entire youth in Linz and Vienna. He thus had plenty of time to absorb the Austrian genius loci, which, as Jacques Le Rider has noted, was Catholic and Roman: the government of Metternich and then that of Franz Josef maintained a healthy distrust of the Philhellenism that Weimar classicism adored, given the danger inherent in celebrating the democratic principle (in Athens) or the national idea (in anti-Turkish pro-Greek sentiment),[184] a double threat for a neo-absolutist and multi-ethnic empire.

Hitler's fascination with Rome even extended to his rejection of Gothic script, which was replaced by Roman typography.[185] A decree by the Reich's minister of economics, dated 29 January 1941, banned Fraktur script and ordered the use of the Latin font Antiqua for all party and state documents. The archives of the Reich Chancellery are full of letters from upset Germanophiles who expressed their outrage in no uncertain terms;[186] many, especially those in the venerable Allgemeiner Deutscher Sprachverein, protested vigorously to officers of the Chancellery. Before responding, Hans Lammers turned to Martin Bormann, who outlined the führer's thoughts in writing: "The so-called *Deutsche Schrift*" must "be considered, in the führer's mind, an un-German [*undeutsch*] form of writing, a Jewish script."[187] For the führer, only Latin characters, clear and direct, unsullied by their medium or muddied by association with the ghetto, could express Indo-Germanic thought in all its purity. It was this kind of attention to the smallest details that distinguished the greatest leaders.[188]

Hitler's taste for the antique would never fully leave him. As Goebbels noted in his journal entry of 8 April 1941, when the Wehrmacht had to come to the aid of Mussolini's armies in Greece and the Balkans, the führer refused to bombard Athens, in order to preserve its architectural and archaeological treasures: "Piraeus has been mined. The Führer forbids the bombing of Athens. This is right and noble of him. Rome and Athens are his Meccas. He greatly regrets having to fight the Greeks."[189] Goebbels continued, commenting: "The Führer is a man totally attuned to antiquity."[190] This version of antiquity was, as it was for a number of German lovers of antiquity—like gentlemen courting a portrait without ever daring to approach their beloved beauty in the flesh—an idealized version of reality, far more exquisite as a dream than it could ever be in real life. As Speer noted: "Of course he was sentimental about classical antiquity; at least once in his life, he said at the time, he wanted to see the Acropolis."[191] His prayers would be answered regarding Rome and Paris—but never, however, for Greece.

The heroes in Hitler's personal pantheon could be found predominantly among the ancients. Speer remarked that Hitler "drew all his heroes from two historical periods: antiquity and the eighteenth and nineteenth centuries. The only exception was Charlemagne, whose empire he occasionally called a prelude to his own plans for European power,"[192] and the Carolingian *renovatio imperii* a resurrection of the Roman Empire. Hitler never invoked any of the great figures of the Middle Ages or the Renaissance. As for the regal house of Hohenstaufen or the great kings of France, like Louis XIV, it was as if "they did not exist in his eyes."[193]

Why did Hitler profess such a marked taste for antiquity and—all the more notable and surprising in Germany (albeit less so in his native Austria)—for ancient Rome in particular? From *Mein Kampf* and his table talks one might infer a number of reasons.

First, as we have seen, ancient history presented itself in the form of a gallery of severely stylized busts, heroic and paradigmatic representations that retained only the most prominent features of those persons deemed worthy of being cast as models for posterity. Ancient history may have been a teacher, but it was a slightly shortsighted headmistress who didn't worry too much about the details, celebrating the noble, civic rigor of Lucius Junius Brutus, who allowed his sons to be executed for their participation in a plot against the state; the virtue and self-denial of Cincinnatus; the assertiveness of Cato; or the strategic and tactical exploits of Caesar. The marble profiles of ancient history were thus two-dimensional, a simplification accentuated by the pedagogical practice of history or of Latin and Greek, which aimed above all to convey an immediate message and edify its pupils.

Transfigured by this heroic makeover, the characters of ancient history became archetypes, which erased all complexity and any ambiguity from the life of the actual person. The production of such archetypes suited Hitler, who happily welcomed such clear-cut ideas and boasted in *Mein Kampf* of knowing how to distill everything down to its essence, making this ability to oversimplify into an eminently political art.[194]

The virtues celebrated in ancient history and the historiography of antiquity were those that Hitler emphasized wanting to instill in the German people: self-denial, sacrifice for the community, a sense of duty, physical fitness and a fighting spirit, respect for one's word, and a sense of camaraderie, all elements that constituted obligatory passages of the *laus* and the *epitaphios logos* (studied by Nicole Loraux),[195] the praising of the hero in historical narration or in funeral oration, respectively. Such masculine virtues, which had characterized the valorous Lacedaemonians and the first Romans, had to be brought back to life in the present day by the Germans.

Hitler's artistic and architectural tastes, as an amateur watercolor artist and architect by vocation, seemed always to lead back to antiquity.

Artistic education of his day very much followed the classical model. As for architecture, Hitler admired all the monuments that Rome bequeathed to posterity, like the Colosseum or the Pantheon, from the time of his youth. Josef Greiner recalled that Hitler loved all "the buildings of ancient Rome" and that "if he had had the money, he would have gone to Rome in a heartbeat."[196] The young Hitler was furious about the destruction caused by the iconoclasm of the first Christians in attacking the idols and traces left behind by paganism.[197] In his memoirs, Speer authoritatively confirmed Hitler's unchanging tastes in architecture,[198] later writing that his monologues to his guests were more like "endless tirades" on his many obsessions, such as "the Catholic Church, diet recipes, Greek temples, and police dogs."[199] The young bohemian of Vienna would realize his dream of a Roman holiday only some twenty years later, on an official state visit in May 1938:

> I've seen Rome and Paris, and I must say that Paris, with the exception of the Arc de Triomphe, has nothing on the scale of the Coliseum, or the Castle of San Angelo, or St. Peter's. These monuments, which are the product of a collective effort, have ceased to be on the scale of the individual. There's something queer about the Paris buildings, whether it's those bull's-eye windows, so badly proportioned, or those gables that obliterate whole façades. If I compare the Pantheon in Rome with the Pantheon in Paris, what a poor building—and what sculptures! What I saw in Paris has disappeared from my memory: Rome really seized hold of me.[200]

It is remarkable that Hitler recalled nothing of Paris except the Arc de Triomphe, built *à la romaine* by a French emperor who saw himself as the successor to Charlemagne and thus in the line of the Caesars. What drew Hitler to Roman architecture, in addition to its colossal scale, was its expression of exorbitant power, its defiance of time, and its endurance over the *longue durée,* as we have seen. Like Rome, Hitler was fundamentally obsessed with standing the test of time and leaving his mark on the world through monuments bequeathed to posterity.[201] The architecture of Rome, with its hint of immortality that appeared to defy, if not transcend or negate, time itself, was the perfect model to emulate.

Hitler's taste for antique kitsch was similarly typical of a rising Austrian or German petite bourgeoisie that wanted to assume the appearance of possessing great culture. The Nazis—including Ribbentrop, who put on great airs and was accustomed to moving in society circles—were great parvenus who, intimidated by the customs of cosmopolitan society, nevertheless desperately wanted to embrace its conventions, the *Handküsser* Hitler and his adopted, outré Viennese manners first and foremost among them.[202] Hitler even had Gerdy Troost (the wife of the architect Paul Troost, who died in 1934) make a full set of silver with a frieze from the Parthenon and various other Greek decorations etched on the spoons, forks, and knives. In sharing the pious memory of ancient Greece with his table guests, Hitler sought to express his affinity for antiquity and proximity to a historical period that he called "the light of humanity."[203] To go along with the silverware, two bas-reliefs by the sculptor Josef Wackerle were placed, on Hitler's express orders, in the Mooslahnerkopf Teehaus at Obersalzberg: the figures depicted Pan, with his goat and his flute, and Artemis (the Romans' Diana, the huntress), with a doe and a quiver of arrows on her back.[204] Untamed nature and the hunt, two allegories not out of place in a country house.

Ultimately, one might think that this taste for antiquity, which led Hitler to look to Hannibal to understand the developments unfolding in the Russian campaign,[205] was a manifestation of a clear tendency to withdraw from reality in order to take refuge in fantasy, to retreat into the land of myth.[206] Living and perceiving the world through allegory was a way of sublimating the trivial or disappointing details of reality. Hitler, as we know, was a great lover of cinema, which he watched in private viewings at the Chancellery, but he was also a lover of the work of Karl May. The führer would occasionally cite his favorite author to his flabbergasted generals, who must have had to pinch themselves and rub their eyes when a staff briefing took a detour into the land of exotic tigers and American Indians created by the prolific author of adventure novels, just as when Hitler invariably became wrapped up in some monologue on the Punic Wars. Hitler was not the only one to constantly use and abuse antiquity in this manner, however, as a look at the subject of colonization demonstrates all too well.

BUILDING AN EMPIRE THROUGH COLONIZATION: NORDIC *LANDSHUNGRIGE BAUERN* AND THE SEARCH FOR LEBENSRAUM IN ANTIQUITY

The Indo-Germanic race was both morally reserved, modest and discreet, and yet in action rather extroverted: it expressed itself through the creation of artworks that expressed its spirit and it sought to increase its lebensraum. Its essence was inextricable from the will to power that animated it, which on a geographical or spatial plane took the form of colonial conquest. The Greeks, of course, had been fervent colonizers, as the historian and Hellenist Hans Bogner reminded his readers: "The men of the master race that we find in Homer were conquerors free in the lands that they colonized."[207] Richard Walther Darré (1895–1953) was the NSDAP's proponent of a colonized agrarian utopia that he saw as an alternative societal model to industrial, urban modernity, one that aimed to restore the preexisting harmony that linked the blood and the soil of the race.[208] An agronomist by training, he was the primary intellect behind the antimodernist ideology encapsulated by the phrase *Blut und Boden* and at the same an important figure in the development of the Reich's racial policies, in his roles as the head of the Rasse- und Siedlungshauptamt (RUSHA, the Race and Settlement Office), under the SS, from 1931 to 1938,[209] and later as the agriculture minister from 1933 to 1942. Darré had published his summa on agrarian racism in 1929, the georgically titled *Das Bauerntum als Lebensquell der nordischen Rasse* (The countryside as source of life for the Nordic race).[210] This long, pedantic book, dense in style and laboriously erudite, aimed to be a historical biography of the Nordic race as well as a prospective treatise on the measures to take in order to preserve its future existence. Its fundamental thesis was that the Indo-Germanics were not simply a race of warriors, as had long been believed, much less conquering nomads, but rather an essentially sedentary race of farmers, deeply rooted in their original home soil and later that of the provinces they conquered through war or migration. The number and success of these wars had falsified views on the Nordic race, which too often was seen simply as a "people of warrior-heroes."[211] Because the figures of the hero and the farmer are hard to reconcile in the collective imagination, only the conquering exploits of the Nordic race were remembered, at the expense of the peaceful and creative work of settlement and cultivation of the lands it conquered. If, according to Hitler's definition, the Nordic race was the only creator of culture,[212] one could not be satisfied with a conception of Aryan culture as purely violent and nomadic; nomadic warriors do not create anything durable. Of course the Indo-Germanics were conquerors. They came from a home in the north of western Europe, "a point of light that we suppose was situated somewhere south of Sweden"[213] or, "as is equally plausible, in the north of Germany,"[214] and had conquered the lands of the Mediterranean, where they founded Greek and Roman civilization.

The Indo-Germanics had thus established a lasting presence in a land where they had sunk their roots. The traditional image of bellicose

Reiter (horsemen) and bandits uniquely suited for war and plundering expeditions was thus false: the predatory, parasitic nomadism of a warrior horde in perpetual motion more closely exemplified the Semitic and Asiatic races. The Semitic or Asiatic nomad came, took, destroyed, and spread like a virus to new prey after having exhausted the resources of its victims: "The Semitic spirit has never, at any time in the history of the world, possessed the least interest in the peasantry. A nomad is simply not capable of it . . . [, since he lives] a parasitic existence."[215] Darré sought to reconcile the two sides of the Janus-faced Nordic race, the conqueror and the peasant. The sword and the plow were tightly bound in the Nordic ethos, since "peasant" and "freedom" went hand in hand: an enslaved peasant was no longer a peasant but a "valet" or a "farmer" in the pay of another, so the peasant needed to know how to defend himself. Darré's goal was to demonstrate that migration and conquest were not, for the Nordic race, ends in and of themselves, as they were for the nomadic Semites, but rather means in the service of a social project to settle and till the soil. If the Indo-Germanics had launched armies and chariots on the road to conquest, it was not out of some taste for battle or to satisfy a spontaneous, bellicose impulse. The first Indo-Germanic expeditions and conquests were "peasant expeditions"[216] in search of land. The early Indo-Germanics were "peasants starving for land,"[217] who had been subjected to the penury of a soil insufficient to nurture a dynamic, fertile people in the midst of a demographic explosion.

As proof, Darré provided some erudite comments on the Roman (originally Sabine) ritual of the *ver sacrum*.[218] For the Sabines, living in a state of perpetual peril, this ritual consisted of a vow to the god Mars regarding all animals, vegetables, and children born by the following spring. The children so consecrated, *sacer,* the sole property of god, were later sent off to colonize a new land and found another city. Darré turned this *ver sacrum* into a rite of spring migration among the first Romans, those of an archaic Nordic Rome, sending their excess population to found the colonies. This spring migration was for Darré at once the heritage and the reiterative commemoration of the first migrations that the original Nordics undertook "along the banks of the Tiber,"[219] which he deduced from elaborate calculations of the calendar: "If one considers the period that seemed the most favorable for migration in the eyes of a peasant people from the north of Europe, in particular Sweden, one sees that the winter, which extended from September to March, was discounted of necessity." Equally discounted was the period that ran from June (planting season) to August (harvest time), inevitably sedentary for a people of peasants who lived off the fruits of their agriculture: "There can be no doubt that the months of March through May were the only ones available for migration. One can thus accurately predict the migratory period of the Roman *ver sacrum*."[220] These reflections on the *ver sacrum* once again confirmed the Nordic character of the Romans, tracing the origins of their rite of spring migration and colonization back to their most distant Indo-Germanic ancestors, who used the practice to relieve the demographic pressure of excess population by sending people off to new lands for them to conquer and colonize: "Thus the rough outline becomes clear: a colonized space fills up, little by little, and from time to time a portion of the families move . . . [when] the situation becomes critical." Malthusianism being viscerally foreign to the life-affirming spirit and fertile loins of the Nordic race, the only solution to lower population density was, and remained, emigration through colonization.[221]

Darré thus traced the eternal problem of lebensraum deep into history, as the cardinal explicative factor of a Nordic geopolitics that was at once retrospective (the search for land by an overly abundant Nordic population explained the whole of Indo-Germanic history) and programmatic: if "the existence of a people without sufficient space is the original problem of all history since the existence of the Indo-Germanic peasantry in northern Europe" and if this lack of land "continued up to the present day,"[222] it was predictable that contemporary Germans, as the worthy heirs of the original Indo-Germanics, would sooner or later strike out on the road to military conquest and colonization. Darré thus used history to bolster Nazi pretensions regarding the expansion of the Germans' vital living space, the expression of profound frustration at having been kept on the margins of European colonization and having had an important part of the old Reich amputated by the Treaty of Versailles. Claims for vital living space in order to maintain the survival of the German people were one of the fundamental leitmotifs of Nazi discourse from the very creation of the NSDAP; they implied both the revision of the Treaty of Versailles and the acquisition of additional land for Germany by negotiation or extortion, peaceful means or brute force.

The perennial demographic fertility of the Nordic race made insufficient land a perpetual problem throughout its long history. By explaining why the first Indo-Germanics had conquered Greece and Italy and why the Romans had adopted the *ver sacrum*, Darré justified and sketched out the prospective politics of military conquest and agrarian settlement that he would later promote when, as the head of the RUSHA, he would envision the initial plans for the conquest and colonization of the Russian lands to the east.

Darré's inquiry into the essence of the Nordic race, the historical biography that he put forward, was based exclusively on a long and fastidious exposé of Greek and Roman exemplars as the paradigmatic Nordic peoples. To prove the profoundly sedentary character of the Nordic race, Darré produced a long study of the topography and semiotics of the Greek and Roman house. Built around a main foyer, the antique home revealed a "stunning similarity" to the typical "Germanic house,"[223] both medieval and modern. The importance given to fire as the center of topographic and semiotic gravity in the home was the expression of a world view that was both hierarchical and deeply rooted, which rested on the burial of the dead and on the dominance of a paterfamilias whose authority derived from strictly patrimonial rule. "These brief considerations of the Greek and Roman home are undoubtedly sufficient to prove" their proximity to the "Germanic home" and to show that "despite an interval of at least 5,500 years, the essential core of the Indo-Germanic and Germanic family has remained unchanged."[224] Darré similarly offered multiple arguments based on historical anthropology to support his thesis that the Greeks and Romans were Indo-Germanics, even counseling the reader to turn to the work of his Nordicist colleague Hans Günther for further information.[225]

The Nordic conquerors of Greece and Italy planned to establish sedentary, agricultural colonies in the lands they had conquered militarily. The warrior-peasants from the North established fields on open land suited for agriculture rather than retrenching themselves in urban fortresses from which they might make foraging raids for sustenance or demand a share of the harvest from exploited or enslaved native peoples: "While the populations that found themselves there [before the conquest] remained in their towns, the Dorians and the Eleans established open villages in the *komes* and the demes."[226] In fact, if the Indo-Germanics "had been concerned only with conquest, they ultimately would have had to do nothing more than dethrone the princes they found there and take over the conquered fortresses themselves." But quite to the contrary—and like the Germans of the barbarian invasions much later, who "left the Roman cities alone and occupied the farms and villages"—the Nordic conquerors of Greece "paid no attention to the towns they found there, and settled in the countryside,"[227] to work the land and create lasting agricultural settlements.

278 | Imitating Antiquity

Contrary to all the preconceptions about the supposed warrior nomadism of the Indo-Germanics, "the conquest of Greece reveals upon closer study to have been a purely agrarian matter."[228]

VER SACRUM, HELOTIZATION, AND *WEHRBAUERNTUM*: ANTIQUITY AND THE EAST IN THE NAZI COLONIAL IMAGINARY

Richard Darré was not a direct participant in the conquest and colonization of the East. After 1936, he appears to have been marginalized within the Nazi state apparatus for his antimodernist posture and intransigent agrarianism at a time when the Four-Year Plan was launching Germany on the path to rearmament. Stripped by Himmler of his position as the head of the RUSHA in 1938, he was also dismissed as the minister of agriculture in 1942. Despite his personal fall from grace, he remained intellectually influential, and his agrarian myth, wrapped in ancient history, helped inform the Nazis' colonial imaginary in the East: their discourse on colonization in the East reflected the same themes, ideas, and concepts present in Darré's work on the Indo-Germanic colonizations of antiquity.

The colonization of the lands to the east was conceived primarily in agrarian terms. *Ostkolonization* would permit a "sociobiological refoundation" of the Nordic race,[229] through the creation of an agrarian society free from the plagues of urban, industrial modernity. The image of a conquered, pacified, and settled East drew heavily upon the agrarian ideal espoused by Darré. The plans of the SS, made public during an exposition held in Berlin at the end of 1941, depicted a well-ordered peasant society living in renewed harmony. As Christian Ingrao has pointed out, the plans to redefine the boundaries of communal farmland and build villages did not mention the presence of any repressive state apparatus, police, or justice system, since "the community was imagined to be free of all conflict."[230] This was a pure agrarian utopia, cleansed of any retrograde nostalgia through the explicit use of scientific and technical modernity, which outfitted the newly colonized countryside with machinery and automobiles.[231]

The construction of this utopia implied that the Nazis intended to follow in the footsteps of their ancient predecessors, even if the comparison with antiquity was not exclusive. The Nazi colonial imaginary was in fact also informed by and constructed around other overlapping historical examples. The first, the most obvious and resonant, was medieval:

that of the *Drang nach Osten*[232] of the Teutonic Knights, the conquerors of pagan Prussia (1230), whose thrust into the vast expanse of Russia was ultimately broken on the banks of Lake Peipus by Prince Alexander Nevsky (1242), whom the filmmaker Sergey Eisenstein would so memorably salute in his eponymous 1938 film.[233] As we have seen, the Reichsführer-SS was happy to see himself as the heir or reincarnation of Henry the Fowler (the king of Germany from 919 to 936), of whom the Black Order made a cult imbued with the sort of pseudomedievalism that so enraptured their leader. This figure frequently blended together with that of another Henry held in the same high regard by the SS, Henry the Lion, the duke of Saxony (1129–95), who, in addition to also sharing the same first name as Himmler, was credited with having undertaken intensive colonization in the east at the same time that his cousin the emperor Frederick Barbarossa fell prey to the siren song of Italy. This "cult of Henrys" fostered by the man sometimes known as *Reichsheini*[234] only drew further scorn from Hitler, whose historical preferences were of course quite different from those of his chief of police.

Himmler's notorious love of the German Middle Ages, as conveyed in the ideological indoctrination of his troops and cadres, led the SS to portray the war in the East as the continuation or repetition of a preemptively forestalled medieval quest. While the Middle Ages may have predominated, the imaginary of war and colonization was also informed by the memory of the agrarian warrior conquests of old, those of the Roman *ver sacrum* and the Spartan city-state, references to antiquity bequeathed to the SS by Darré and Günther. Second without being secondary, this imagery was always present. Dorians and Teutonics blended together in the same desire for territorial might. Drawing a parallel between the migrations of the first Nordic peasant-soldiers and the medieval Germanic colonization of the East, Otto Wilhelm von Vacano, the author of a famous history textbook on Sparta, declared that "we must view these migrations as comparable to the peasant colonizing expeditions to the East in the Middle Ages."[235] In these two movements, the same race displayed the same drive to expand its living space, which was perpetually too small to contain a fertile people in constant demographic growth.

PEASANT-SOLDIERS AND SLAVES: SPARTAN COLONIZATION AS MODEL

Despite Darré's institutional fall from grace, remnants of the classical paradigm remained in the vocabulary employed by the active players in the colonization efforts of the SS, and in its discourse surrounding internal promotion: *Wehrbauern, ver sacrum, Kolonien, Sklaven, Versklavung, Heloten.* A reference to antiquity also bubbled up to the surface in the notion and ideal of the peasant-soldier (*Wehrbauerntum*). The Teutonic Knights were warrior-monks, aristocrats who prayed and fought, not peasant-soldiers, who wielded the plow to work the earth.

The notion of the *ver sacrum* was not discarded along with Darré. In a 1942 speech, Himmler called the colonization of the eastern territories a *neuer Frühling*,[236] a "new spring," for both the earth itself and the Indo-Germanic race, picking up on the theme of the sacred spring so dear to the agronomist.[237]

The enslavement of the subjugated populations of the East was another recurrent central theme. The numerical disproportion between victors and vanquished made the exploitation of such vast territories impossible without a massive auxiliary labor force. Rather than the more benign Nazi euphemism *Zwangsarbeiter*, or "compulsory worker," the SS preferred *Sklaven*, "slave," which echoed antiquity and with its casual cruelty hinted at the brutality of its leaders' vision for their future empire. As Himmler declared, "If we do not fill our camps with slaves—I say these things very clearly—with slaves that we force to work, without worrying about waste, to build our cities, our towns, and our farms . . . ,"[238] . . . it only followed that the colonization of the East would be extremely difficult, since the conquering race was in the minority.

The terms *slave* (*Sklave*) and *enslavement* (*Versklavung*) themselves led to two other, more explicitly Greek (and specifically Spartan) notions, those of the Helots (*Heloten*) and Helotization (*Helotisierung*), which were particularly wont to come from the mouth of Reinhard Heydrich. In a speech of 2 October 1941 on the occupation methods to be used in the vast conquered lands to the east, Heydrich stated that the slave population was to be used "like a crude commodity, as workers who must build the great projects of our culture, like Helots, if I must put it bluntly." In the autumn of 1941, the blitzkrieg in Russia remained unchecked and the success of Operation Barbarossa made the question of the colonization and lasting exploitation of the East particularly acute: the Wehrmacht had conquered immense swaths of land, where it would take generations to establish anything more than the thinnest "German surface layer,"[239] a weak racial elite that would have jurisdiction over vast territories and large populations.

This image of the Helot was deeply rooted in the culture of the SS, which, in keeping with its racial elitism, did not employ mere slaves, as we saw previously in Eugen Kogon's 1937 conversation in Vienna with a high-ranking SS officer. Just as in the "ancient Greek city-states" of old, a racial aristocracy would reign over "a broad economic basis of serf[s]"[240] who were not Nordics and whose inferior racial stock would be recruited from both within Germany and without. Racial hierarchy would in fact determine social organization and a political pyramid, whose summit would be occupied by a tightly restricted Nordic elite, who would disseminate orders down to a Germanic helotry composed of Dinaric, Alpine, and Westic factions among the German people. At the bottom would be the mass of subhumans, mostly slaves, whose only use would be forced labor; just being in the service of a superior culture would honor this crude, animalistic subhumanity.[241] As a result, after June 1941 the *Generalplan Ost* foresaw the enslavement of some fourteen million people in the East, slaves destined for the construction of the Reich in the conquered territories.[242] These notions were shared by Hitler, of course, for whom there was no doubt that the conquest of the East would lead not simply to exploitation but to settlement: "But in contrast to the English, we won't just exploit, we'll settle. We are not a nation of shopkeepers, but a nation of peasants,"[243] similar to the Dorians who conquered the Peloponnese.

Everything would be carried out in their image, and the Spartan example of colonization by a Nordic elite of vast territories occupied by a numerically superior population would be repeated. Hitler, as we have seen, was fascinated by the Spartan miracle of lasting domination by a slight racial aristocracy over a mass of inferior beings, the empire of "6,000 Spartans" over "350,000 Helots."[244]

Nazi colonization, the new *Bauerntreck* of peasant-soldiers to the East, marched in the steps of the Teutons as well as the Greeks. Embedded in the very principle of Eastern colonization, the Greek model also informed the practicalities of its realization. In order to ensure their permanence, the layout of colonized territories would happen along the lines of the practice of ancient metropoles that, whether Greek or Roman, reproduced their own architectural forms to appropriate colonized spaces through a projection of their symbolic patrimony. In his diary, Speer recalled Hitler's thoughts on the subject: "It was perfectly all right for us to copy familiar buildings, so that even in Russia a feeling for the homeland could develop. In antiquity, Hitler would say, no attempt was made to develop new forms of temples for, say, the colonial cities in Sicily."[245] Urban plans were designed for a population of peasant-soldiers who would be undertaking the drive to the east, both a frontier and an *Ostwall* at the same time. This simultaneous frontier and fortification, the front lines of the Reich in the East, would be peopled and cultivated by SS veterans and constantly refreshed troops.

For Reinhard Heydrich, the establishment of the frontier meant securing a border, the front line and point of contact of Aryan colonization; the legions of SS veterans had to be entrenched in their battle stations and form "a wall of protection composed of peasant-soldiers [*Wehrbauern*] . . . against the Asiatic tidal wave."[246] What blood and sword had conquered, plow and sweat would make into a fertile land to nourish the Nordic race. A sword and a plow even illustrated the cover of an SS pamphlet titled *Die Sicherung Europas* (The securing of Europe).[247]

These SS veterans were thus at once the sharp point of the sword of conquest, the plow of Aryan colonization, and the shield of empire. After having nobly served the Reich, they would be given plots of land in the model of the Roman legionnaires, set up in their *coloniae* as a projection of the Eternal City over the vast expanse of the empire, serving also as so many watchtowers or bridgeheads in defense against the barbarians.

The SS based its promotional message on this promise of land in the East. A recruiting brochure for the Waffen-SS proudly proclaimed, "This is how the SS ensures the future of its men!"—volunteers were promised the status of a "free farmer in the East." In the words of the brochure, the *Ostsiedlung* offered a comfortable future to SS soldiers who proved themselves in combat and, having served their time, set down their weapons, scarcely concealing the military and racial function of this massive establishment of farmer-warriors at the frontier of the empire: "*Kamaraden* of the SS at the front are creating a new German peasantry, a living wall in the East, whose strength and stability is guaranteed by the peasant-soldiers of the SS."[248] This retirement in the colonial countryside thus constituted a sort of reserve service, but one that strongly resembled active duty. Before a more exclusive audience, in a speech of April 1943 permeated by post-Stalingrad anxiety, Himmler did not hide the fact that the job of the peasant-soldiers placed on the Reich's front lines would be anything but a sinecure: everyone knew there was more to being in the SS than just parading around in that becoming black uniform.[249]

CONCLUSION

All the empires of Western civilization that followed have been conceived and thought of as copies of the original Roman imperial model.

Charlemagne, who openly pursued a *restauratio imperii*, Otto I, Charles V, and Napoleon each sought what Hitler himself planned: to equal the expanse, power, and prestige of the empire of the Caesars. In the case of the Nazis, this ambition was grounded in a racial scientific logic that to a greater or lesser degree established the common racial identity shared by the original Romans and contemporary Germans: Rome was, in the beginning at least, a racial oligarchy, whose laws and spirit the Third Reich imitated. As we have seen, the resurrection of the Roman Empire was trumpeted through historical analogy: for historians of antiquity, as always desperately concerned to defend the utility of their field, a Berlin at war with London resembled the Rome of the Punic Wars, Carthage and England both being maritime and commercial powers thoroughly controlled by the Jews.

To build an empire, one had to destroy Carthage, and to do that, one needed the appropriate military instruments. The power and success of the Roman legions made them the proper logistical and strategic model to emulate. The lessons of history could be found in the vegetarian diet of the legionnaires and the charisma of their visionary leaders: Hitler, the self-styled Gröfaz, saw himself as a Caesar and forced his guests at table to listen to his own version of the *Commentarii*, a series of rambling thoughts on the Roman art of war. For their part, professional historians preferred to glorify the figure of Augustus, whose rule was longer and more fecund than the abortive reign of his great-uncle. The period lent itself to such thoughts; in 1938, Italy celebrated the second millenary of Augustus's birth with an exhibition that Hitler visited on two occasions. The resuscitator of the original Rome, its values and its strong state, Augustus was the best classical analogy for a führer who had also been compelled to rescue his state after civil discord and a crisis without precedent.

Rome was not only a source of military and political inspiration: it was also copied architecturally. To build an empire, one had to endow its capital and its major cities with monuments that sufficiently conveyed its ambition, expanse, and power. These symbolic structures had to convey this through their size and their neo-Roman style; Speer's projects and Hitler's sketches for Germania abounded with monuments that were, in terms of their stylistic imitation, immediately obvious signifiers of imperialism.

Yet National Socialist symbolism in architecture was neither pristine nor precise: the most important thing was that the buildings constructed gave off a *feeling* of Romanness, making them seem Roman or at least ancient. Thus, the neo-Roman sat side by side with the neo-Doric, the two styles representing the two pillars of official state architecture. One might see this as an all too visible sign of basic incoherence. Hitler, after all, was a self-taught man whose understanding of the ancient world was passionate but crude, as any reader of his table talks could attest. This was not, however, the case for Speer or Troost, accomplished architects trained in classical art. The coexistence of Doric and Roman was thus the product more of an assertion than of a fundamental confusion: Greek and Roman were blended together, as in Breker's nudes or the mosaics in the Reich Chancellery, as a sign of the common racial identity of Nordic, Greco-Roman, and Germanic peoples and the progression from one to the next. Romanesque architecture conveyed a will to power and an imperialism faithful to the Nordic-Roman tradition, while the Doric style recalled the spirit of the Nordic race made tangible in the temples of Segesta or Syracuse, the sole creator of all culture since the dawn of time. The truest and purest contemporary representatives of that race could find their ancestral home wherever this spirit had been at work, further legitimizing an imperialism written in the stone of such symbolic classical architecture.

There was thus an organic link between the monuments of modern Germany, the distant history of the race, and its imperial future. This link could be traced all the way back to the first migrations, those of the great conquering agrarian peoples, to see the work of a Nordic race hungry for land, victory, and fields to sow. Richard Walther Darré popularized this history, describing a race that, through migration and conquest, created a people of peasant-warriors, conquerors because they were agrarians, equally bound to the plow and the sword. Darré was not given, however, to elegies or panegyrics. He wrote to advocate a vision of an agrarian Nordic civilization that, if it were to abandon its millennia-long bonds to the earth and fail to preserve the purity of its blood, was destined to disappear.

Greco-Roman antiquity was an inexhaustible source of exemplars, of virtues, and of models to imitate. But it was also a graveyard of civilizations that no longer existed, whose vestiges, bleached white as bone, served as a melancholy warning to a present at times all too ready to forget that no civilization is immortal.

PART THREE

Reliving Antiquity

Aryan races—often absurdly small numerically—subject foreign peoples, and then, stimulated by the special living conditions of the new territory (fertility, climatic conditions, etc.) and assisted by the multitude of lower-type beings standing at their disposal as helpers, develop the intellectual and organizational capacities dormant within them. Often in a few millenniums or even centuries they create cultures which originally bear all the inner characteristics of their nature, adapted to the above-indicated special qualities of the soil and subjected beings. In the end, however, the conquerors transgress against the principle of blood purity, to which they had first adhered; they begin to mix with the subjugated inhabitants and thus end their own existence; for the fall of man in paradise has always been followed by his expulsion.

—Adolf Hitler, *Mein Kampf*

This passage from *Mein Kampf* perfectly encapsulates the biography of those culturally creative peoples, the Indo-Germanics: Born in their womb in the far north, they emigrated in search of land and adventure, subjugating native populations to build great civilizations. Authoritarianism and slavery made the creation of such historical and cultural monuments possible. What followed, alas, was blood sin. Succumbing to the temptation to "transgress against the principle of blood purity," they threw away their Aryan greatness through destructive racial mixing.

The history of antiquity marvelously exemplified this tragic fate. The great Indo-Germanic peoples of antiquity, the Greeks and the Romans, fought to establish the reign of their pure blood before opening the veins of their race to infiltration by inferior types, fatally weakening their racial essence. Hitler, particularly after 1942, repeatedly remarked that he thought often of the causes behind the disappearance of the ancient world, a historical and civilizational agony that intrigued both historians and biologists who, through the will of the state, sought to respond to the Spenglerian fatalism of cyclical rise and fall or the passive Gobineauian resignation of a fatal miscegenation.

Annexed and imitated, the history of Greco-Roman antiquity also resounded as an insistent, funereal echo in the thousand-year Reich, a racial and cultural death knell that, as defeat approached ever more clearly, sounded more and more like the strident ringing of an alarm bell.

CHAPTER 7

History as Racial Struggle

The Clash of Civilizations between East and West in Antiquity

"All the same . . . ," he adds wistfully, his face lighting up, "war can be fine, you know! Think of the ancient Greeks!"
—Christopher Isherwood, *Goodbye to Berlin*

We are deeply convinced that, out there in the East, Germany and its allies today are defending Homer and Augustus as well as Hohenstaufen, Beethoven, and Goethe.
—Alfred Rosenberg, "Innere und äussere Freiheit des Deutschen" (Internal and external freedom of the Germans)

HISTORY AS A THEATER OF RACIAL CONFLICT

Hitler argued in *Mein Kampf* that the discipline of history and its teaching had to follow a "broad, clear line"[1] amid the sound and the fury of human deeds and activities. For Hitler, the basic, most fundamental lesson of history that overruled all others was rooted in an unshakable law: the history of mankind was the history of racial conflict.

This idea rested on three core principles. The first, of course, was the very existence of different races, a widely held belief in the wake of nineteenth-century scientific racism.[2] The second was that these races engaged in combat for territorial domination and for their very survival, an eternal struggle that was finally entering a decisive phase. The history of the entire world could be reduced to the story of this racial conflict, the universal principle that was the driver of all human affairs, as Hitler had written in *Mein Kampf*: "All occurrences in world history are only the expression of the races' instinct of self-preservation."[3] In a finite world, races were locked in a ruthless struggle for control of a planet that could guarantee their survival but could not hold them all. Hitler revealed this Darwinian side to his racism in a 1942 speech before a class of Wehrmacht officers ready for deployment to the eastern and western fronts:

> We are all creatures of a nature that, as we understand it, knows but one, hard law: a law that gives the strongest the right to live and takes away the life of the weakest. We, mankind, cannot emancipate ourselves from this law. The planets revolve by following an eternal law governing suns, moons, and planets; over the infinitely large and the infinitely small, only one principle rules: the stronger determines the course of the weaker. On earth itself, we see that all living beings struggle with one another. An animal lives only insofar as it kills another. One might say that it is a very cruel, terrible world, since the existence of the one is linked to the destruction of the other. We can abstract ourselves in our mind from the world, but in reality we live in it.[4]

In the real world, nature provided land for races and species the way that states provided an arena for gladiators. The surface of the earth was simply the "field where they must prove their strength."[5]

The third principle behind this idea was that the most cunning weapon available in this struggle was miscegenation, the mixing of races via interracial coupling. As Hitler proclaimed while musing about the disappearance of the ancient civilizations of antiquity that so intrigued him:[6] "All great cultures of the past perished only because the originally creative race died out from blood poisoning."[7]

Ancient history was particularly well suited to teach young Germans about the race question. Hitler's proposed reform of history education would give pride of place to ancient history, particularly that of Rome, as the führer explained in *Mein Kampf*: "Especially in historical instruction we must not be deterred from the study of antiquity. Roman history correctly conceived in extremely broad outlines is and remains the best mentor, not only for today, but probably for all time. The Hellenic ideal of culture should also remain preserved for us in its exemplary beauty. We must not allow the greater racial community to be torn asunder by the differences of the individual peoples. The struggle that rages today is for very great aims. A culture combining millenniums and embracing Hellenism and Germanism is fighting for its existence."[8] Hitler's emphasis on the importance of ancient history was accompanied by a reverence for Latin and its instruction in the schools; learning Latin was akin to "training in sharp, logical thinking,"[9] which produced a pure, clear intellect similar to that of the ancients. With the history of Rome and its language, Hitler was privileging instruction in the Latinate humanities, as Goebbels noted in his diaries in 1940: "He lauds... classical and humanistic education. Classical antiquity contains everything a young German man should know."[10] Part of what one needed to know about antiquity was the havoc wreaked by the Jew, the destroyer of Aryan states and cultures: in an outline of world history titled "Die germanische Revolution" (The German revolution), Hitler noted that he would begin his future book with a history of Athens and Rome to illustrate the opposition between "the Jew and the Aryan"—the increasing prevalence of the former being "the cause of the decadence"[11] that doomed the great ancient civilizations.

After 1933, a vast library of books was written to provide theoretical heft in support of this transformation of the teaching and writing of history based upon the cardinal notion of race and the theme of racial conflict. We might cite the essays of the historian Rudolf Benze,[12] among many others, or the work of the doctor Walter Gross, the director of the NSDAP's Office of Racial Policy, who convened a lengthy 1936 conference on "the idea of race in the new conception of history."[13] The historian and pedagogical specialist Dietrich Klagges, who also wrote several textbooks, devoted a chapter of his imposing treatise on the teaching of history to the race question under the title "The Racial Question Is the Key to World History,"[14] a phrase drawn more or less word for word from *Mein Kampf*.[15]

With regard to ancient history, it was Fritz Schachermeyr who most forcefully exhorted his colleagues to fully integrate the new racist paradigm into their research. To assist them, he composed a sort of introductory essay that constituted an epistemology of the new history. Published in 1940 as *Lebensgesetzlichkeit in der Geschichte: Versuch einer Einführung in das geschichtsbiologische Denken* (Natural law in history: An attempt at an introduction to biological-historical thought),[16] Schachermeyr's racist magnum opus was a manifesto on the application of biological concepts and racialist discourse to historical research and writing. The laws of nature needed to be fully understood by the historian, he argued, if one were to claim to present a truly scientific discourse. A fundamentally conservative discipline with an astonishing tendency toward inertia, history had to enter the modern scientific era and recognize racial factors in order to "give the young Germany a new science, a science that is suited to it."[17] Dense, hastily written, and full of half-baked ideas, Schachermeyr's essay blended analytic exposition of biological concepts (race, miscegenation, degeneration) with historical examples drawn from across eras and geographical regions.

One of his colleagues, Fritz Geyer, put together an overview of ancient history from the racial perspective to complete and expand upon the work of Hans Günther on the Greeks and Romans, receiving the benediction of none other than Günther himself. The thesis of Geyer's 1936 book *Rasse, Volk und Staat im Altertum* (Race, people and state in antiquity) is simple: the author sought to reframe ancient history "in a radically new way" by showing how ancient civilizations, once the bastions of Nordic culture, had been threatened and brought low by blood miscegenation until only an influx of "fresh Nordic blood" had been able to "save the heritage of antiquity."[18]

The teaching of history in the schools was synchronized to be in harmony with this approach. The table of contents of an aforementioned textbook by Walther Gehl from 1940 speaks volumes in this regard.[19] To introduce students to "the racial decadence of Hellenism"—the title of one section—the text explored the idea of the "spiritual decadence caused by the deleterious effects of the Enlightenment," which was itself attributable to "the weakening of the Greeks' racial strength through the fratricidal war in the Peloponnese" combined with the "destruction of race, society, and state by unrestrained democracy"; the efforts of Plato and the Thirty Tyrants were but a "vain struggle against racial decadence." These fifth-century BC phenomena were only precursors to the racial catastrophes of the fourth century BC and the later Hellenistic era, which witnessed the "definitive uprooting of the blood from the soil" and the construction of the "Greco-Oriental empire of Alexander," who created an "urban Hellenistic civilization" that was no less than a "culture of racial miscegenation." Rome was not spared either; an entire chapter lingered upon the "disappearance of the ancient world into racial chaos" and the end of the Roman world.

FESTUNG EUROPA: FROM THE CATALAUNIAN FIELDS TO STALINGRAD

In this millenary struggle between East and West, the final refuge of the Indo-Germanic race was Festung Europa, or "Fortress Europe," a seemingly omnipresent theme in Nazi discourse after the defeat at Stalingrad and subsequent retreat of the German lines.

An SS pamphlet traced the lines of racial, cultural, and moral continuity in this pan-European battle, comparing the soldiers of Marathon and the legionnaires of Rome with the Teutonic Knights as part of the same war against the East: "An enormous historical process began, which we understand as the battle of West against East, a battle that continues to this day. The soldiers of Marathon and the conquerors of Carthage are the same as the warriors of Poitiers and Vienna, the same as our soldiers in the East, combatants in defense of the values that we call European."[20] The final battle in this racial war to the east would at last inaugurate the construction of a new Europe: "Ideologically, we see our battle for the reorganization of Europe as a seal closing two thousand years of world history and as the beginning of a new era."[21]

The continuities of race, of the enemy, and of the values at stake made these wars, which were otherwise separated by centuries, all part of the same struggle, as Hitler himself explained in a speech before the Reichstag in December 1941, at a time when the probability of victory against the Soviet Union made the creation of a Greater German Reich and a new Festung Europa along the lines of the Roman Empire into an almost tangible reality:

> In the Battle on the Catalaunian Field, 554 Romans and Teutons joined together for the first time to defend that civilization in a struggle of unforeseeable significance. Starting with the Greeks, this civilization first cast its spell on the Romans and now finally on the Germanic people.
> Europe grew. Hellas and Rome developed into the Occident. For many centuries, its defense was the task not only of the Romans, but also in particular of the Germanic peoples. The term *Europe* experienced a spatial expansion. The degree to which the Occident, enlightened by Greek civilization and inspired by the mighty heritage of the Roman Empire, expanded its space through Germanic colonization ... was always the struggle of the developing Europe against a profoundly alien, surrounding world. ... It was not Rome that the Greeks [*sic!*] once defended against Carthage. It was not the Occident that the Romans and the Germanic people defended against the Huns. ... Instead, it was Europe that all of them defended. In the same way today, Germany does not fight for itself, but for the continent that belongs to all. ... While Rome had earned undying merit in the creation and defense of this continent, the Germanic people now took over the defense and protection of a family of nations.[22]

Hitler hailed the victory of the Nordic ideal in the Battle of the Catalaunian Fields (451 CE) as a triumph for its containment, even if only for a time, of the assault from the East: "If, for instance, the battle of the Catalaunian Fields (in 451 of the Common Era) had not ended with the victory of Rome over the Huns, the cultural rise of the West would have been impossible at that time, and the civilized world would have gone into a decline, like that which threatens us because of the Soviets."[23] He returned to the topic on more than one occasion in his table talks:

It was the destiny of all the civilised States to be exposed to the assault of Asia at the moment when their vital strength was weakening.

First of all it was the Greeks attacked by the Persians, then the Carthaginians' expedition against Rome, the Huns in the battle of the Catalaunian Fields. . . . And now we're facing the worst attack of all, the attack of Asia mobilised by Bolshevism.[24]

The Battle of the Catalaunian Fields was not merely part of Hitler's personal mantra. This halting blow delivered against the Asiatic horde, the barrage unleashed by the Romans and Germans against a tidal wave of Oriental subhumanity, was also turned into part of a much broader propaganda campaign. After Hitler spoke of it in his speech of 11 December 1941, the Reichsführer-SS imitated him in making reference to the battle of 451 on several occasions, in his speeches to the young Junkers of his Black Order[25] or in those before the Waffen-SS: "While you, my men, fight out there in the East, you are pursuing the exact same battle that our fathers and forefathers pursued for centuries, again and again. It is the same battle, against the same subhumans, against the same subraces that long ago went by the name of Huns. . . . Today they attack under the name of Russians and under the political banner of Bolshevism."[26]

The internal ideological propaganda of the SS picked up on the same topic, employing the battle of 451 in an identical manner. A famous, widely distributed pamphlet titled *Der Untermensch* portrayed the Asiatic assault on Europe in simplistic terms: it depicted three Horsemen of the Apocalypse, their obvious savagery matched only by their hideousness, mounting a charge against European civilization, trampling women and children under the hooves of their horses. Their dress and visages blended the features of the Huns, Hungarians, Tatars, and other Mongols whom the West had contained to one degree or another from the time of Rome to the Third Reich.[27] Another pamphlet designed for the ideological education of the Waffen-SS fighting in the East contained a page listing the major blows landed against the Asiatic assault: the first, decisive strike of course was that of 451.[28]

The idea of a millenary struggle between East and West—the East, parasitic and destructive, the Indo-Germanic West, the creator of all culture, beauty, and valor—was constantly reiterated in the Nazi historiography of the period, which hammered home the direct confrontation between two irreconcilable peoples and ideas. Schachermeyr put together a volume titled *The Indo-Germanics and the East: Their Political and Cultural Confrontation in Antiquity* (1944), while the historian Fritz Taeger wrote *East* and *West in Antiquity* (1936), which linked battles both past and present—the wars of the ancient Greeks and Romans, "who were of our same blood,"[29] were part of the same conflict that, in 1936, was depicted as a much-needed storm ready to burst: "The East, in modified form, attacks the West once more. In our people, the eternal might of the West gathers to face this foreign world. We fight for our future, and it is vital to all of us that this fight not be lost."[30] Taeger's work, published in 1936, was hardly that of an objective, dispassionate scholar. In its wide distribution and the intransigence of its racial discourse, it and others like it performed an important social function by mobilizing the manpower of the Indo-Germanic race for its impending final showdown against its eternal foe.

DELENDA EST CARTHAGO, DELENDA EST HIEROSOLYMA: LIKE CARTHAGE, JERUSALEM MUST BE DESTROYED

Historians of antiquity brought together as part of "the war effort of the German human sciences"[31] certainly did their part by publishing *Röm und Karthago* (Rome and Carthage; 1943), a metaphor for racial conflict between the Semitic East, represented by a Jewish Phoenicia, and a Nordic West, defended by classical Rome.

In the book's preface, Joseph Vogt suggested that the binary opposition between Rome and Carthage served as a racial-political allegory: "Rome and Carthage are among those names bequeathed by history that have become concepts, symbols of bottomless racial hatred and a war of extermination.... Four generations [were] dragged into the struggle between these two peoples of opposing races."[32] Rome's victory in a race war that was "saturated with hate" possessed a singular consequence "of the utmost importance": "The Semitic people were removed from any position of domination [in the Mediterranean]."[33]

The war between Rome and Carthage has long been interpreted as a war between two powers seeking domination of the Mediterranean basin. But this book posed the issue in resolutely racial terms: "One question that has scarcely been asked until now comes to the fore: was this conflict, so full of portent, predetermined by the blood of the peoples involved, with Rome, which was fundamentally Nordic, facing a rebellion from Carthage, whose otherness stemmed precisely from its Punic essence?" This was thus a "racial confrontation," since the people of Carthage could be "characterized as fundamentally Semitic."[34]

Vogt begrudgingly acknowledged that "antiquity did not possess the modern concept of race," which obviously posed a methodological problem, a conceptual transposition that could lead to an overdetermined reading of the source material. The modern scholar of history and the human sciences needed to include an etiology of race in the behavior of individuals and peoples, however, to trace how race served as an explanatory principle in historical events: "The contemporary researcher tries to relate the character traits of peoples to their racial structure. One must thus ask the question of whether the famous absence of a Punic faith can be attributed to Armenoid, Arabic, or Hamitic elements among the Punic people."[35]

Having thus framed the central question, the book revealed its research agenda in its table of contents. The titles (and authors) of the essays provided ample confirmation of the intentions laid out in the preface: Fritz Schachermeyr offered his "racial-historical considerations on Carthage";[36] Matthias Gelzer contributed a study of "racial difference as a historic factor in the outbreak of the Roman-Punic wars"'[37] Fritz Taeger reflected on "wars of the peoples and races of the western Mediterranean";[38] and Joseph Vogt's conclusion anticipated the later decadence of the Roman Empire in its study of the relationship between "the Punic people and the dynasty of Septimius Severus."[39]

This volume, a perfect example of classical scholars' contributions to the *Kriegseinsatz der deutschen Geisteswissenschaften* (German historians' war effort), was not the only text to read the Punic Wars as a racial conflict: Alfred Rosenberg, following the lead of Houston Stewart Chamberlain, had already drawn attention to the *rassengeschichtliche Bedeutung*—"racial-historical significance"—of the struggle between Rome and Carthage in *The Myth of the Twentieth Century*. It was only after the defeat of the Greeks, who sank under waves of Asiatic invaders, that the Romans entered the fray to confront the enemies of the Nordic race, enemies who in this instance appeared in a guise that was more African and Semitic than Asiatic. For Rosenberg, Roman history repeated the same script as that of Greek history, magnifying it until the battlefield of racial struggle encompassed nearly the entire known world under the control of the Roman Empire: "The history of Rome essentially parallels that of Hellas, although it is set against a greater expanse of territory and a larger political power structure."[40]

The Romans' racial nemesis took the face of the Carthaginian conqueror. Carthage was Rome's great rival in the third and fourth centuries BC, and Rosenberg made the conflict between these two powers for the military and commercial domination of the Mediterranean into a clash of antagonistic races:

> Encircled by the maritime races of the Near East, Rome was often compelled to defend itself ruthlessly with the gladius.
> The destruction of Carthage was a deed of superlative import in racial history: by it even the later cultures of Central and Western Europe were spared the infection of this Phoenician pestilence.[41]

Cato the Elder's famous phrase *Delenda est Carthago* (Carthage must be destroyed) thus possessed a racial-historical meaning: Rome destroyed a Phoenician civilization with both African and Asiatic roots, which would have smothered a nascent Western civilization in the cradle if Hannibal or any other Carthaginian general had managed to take Rome. The Romans had saved the Nordic race from Phoenician infection and preserved their superior racial essence from being overrun once again. Chamberlain had previously commemorated Rome's battle against Carthage in *The Foundations of the Nineteenth Century*, an important book for Rosenberg, who in many ways was content to simply paraphrase or rewrite it verse for verse:

> If the Phoenician people had not been destroyed, if its survivors had not been deprived of a rallying-point by the complete destruction of their last city, and compelled to merge in other nations, mankind would never have seen this nineteenth century....
> These are the men, this the fatal branch of the Semitic family, from which we have been saved by the brutal *delenda est Carthago*.[42]

Rome's victory over Carthage was, for the Nazis, a fundamental landmark in the history of racial conflict. After a conversation with Hitler, Goebbels noted in his diary on 28 February 1945 that "the Punic War was more decisive [than the Seven Years' War] in a world-historical sense and its effects were felt over several centuries"[43]—which without Rome would not have included either Western civilization or the survival of an Aryan race now threatened once again by a new Hannibal in the form of Joseph Stalin.[44]

In his book, Rosenberg lamented only that Rome had not been able to press its advantage further. The Romans had rid the world of the Punic menace, but then they had stopped in their tracks when they could have continued the war and extermination all the way to Palestine and reduced Jerusalem to rubble:

> World history might well have taken a very different course had the obliteration of Carthage been accompanied by a total annihilation of all the other

Semitic Jewish centers in the Near East. The act of Titus came too late. By then, the Near Eastern parasite was no longer centered in Jerusalem but had already spread its strongest tentacles from Egypt and Hellas to Rome itself.[45]

Titus, the conqueror of Jerusalem (along with his father Vespasian), had acted too late: the siege of the city and destruction of the Temple, in the year 70 CE, should have taken place much earlier. Furthermore, to contain and prevent the infectious spread of the Semitic parasite throughout the empire, the Romans should have exterminated the defeated Jews as well: if strategic considerations alone did not suffice, then biology demanded it. Their fatal error had been Rome's downfall and led to its ultimate disappearance.

With the Roman war in Palestine, the Jew made his debut in the racial conflict. The enemy of Greece had been the racially inferior Asiatic peoples. The first enemy of Rome was a bastardized Phoenicia, which had been both African and Asiatic.[46] The leaders of the Semites never joined in battle themselves against the master race—except in the first century of the Common Era. The Jews' direct military confrontation with Rome and its legions, however, was an exception to the rule in their war against the empire: open war, combat at arms, was rare. Contrary to the Greeks' nemesis Persia or Hannibal's Carthage, which both fought in the open field, the Jews struck from the shadows, cloaked in the darkness of conspiracy. But in their war against the Roman Empire, the Jews would wield one particularly insidious and cunning armament, their secret weapon: Pauline Christianity.[47]

THE MORTAL STRUGGLE BETWEEN EAST AND WEST IN IDEOLOGICAL PEDAGOGY AND THE CLASSROOM

The school textbooks and ideological education materials produced by the party and its various organs also helped disseminate this racial reading of the Punic Wars. Thus, a Nazi Party pamphlet titled *Dieser Krieg ist ein weltanschaulicher Krieg* (This war is an ideological war),[48] published in 1942, elaborated on the concept of "six thousand years of race war":[49] "After a brief clash with the Greek people, Carthage threw itself once again into combat with the rural Nordic world, this time in ancient Rome. It is hard to imagine a greater contrast than the one between the luxury, wealth, and decadence of that land of merchants and the simplicity, modesty, and devotion of Rome. Conflict between that mercantile state and the racial republic of ancient Latium was foreordained.

These two worlds were fated to confront each other, and so it was that the greatest and most decisive war of races in the history of antiquity came to be." Carthage, being a cunning, mercantile nation, sought to attack Rome through "infiltration," but the Romans were determined to take the fight to the more honorable open battlefield: "this was a war of soldiers,"[50] the type of war one might expect of the honest, true, warriorlike Nordic people, the enemy of all such cunning or deception.

Textbooks lingered proudly upon this fantastic example of racial conflict between the Nordic and Semitic worlds; Walther Gehl's tome devoted a whole chapter, some eight pages, to "the racial war against the Semitic people":[51] it was this victory against an enemy race that had allowed the seemingly modest capital of Latium, once confined within Italy, to strive toward a global empire—because it had needed first to confront the overt opposition of its eternal Semitic nemesis. The Hohmann and Schiefer textbook, meanwhile, explained the stakes of the conflict in simple terms: "The Romans were Indo-Germanics, the Carthaginians Semites. The war to come was a war between races that would determine which of the Nordic or Eastern civilizations would dominate the shores of the Mediterranean. The Nordic will to power squared off against the Semitic mercantile spirit."[52] After narrating the twists and turns of the conflict, the authors awarded the victory to Rome: "The decision had been won by the Aryan race, and Europe escaped any danger of domination by a Semitic people."[53] Yet both Greece and Rome had eventually succumbed to the East in this clash of racial civilizations. The two Nordic civilizations had perished less from direct combat, however, although the wars had indeed hemorrhaged the best Nordic blood, than from the surreptitious, insidious, infectious, and ultimately fatal infiltration of foreign blood.

The curricular reforms of 1938 resolutely presented the history of the ancient Indo-Germanics in terms of the conflict with the East. As Nazi-approved textbooks and teachers taught their pupils, "the history of the Indo-Germanic peoples in their southern lebensraum was that of the conflict with foreign influences over their patrimony."[54]

The Greco-Persian Wars, which Fritz Schachermeyr called "a war of giants for Greek liberty against their hereditary Persian enemy," were described as a further example of this racial gigantomachy: "The wars against the Persians were a struggle for Greek freedom from the threat of enslavement of both their state and their spirit by the East."[55]

As for Rome, the 1938 reforms declared that teachers should present "the Punic Wars as a war of races" in which the Romans had emerged victorious before subsequently succumbing to those they had vanquished: the instructor had to elucidate "the fatal consequences of Roman imperialism ('the Punicization of Rome'),"[56] the empire's global expansion having led, through a deplorable lack of vigilance, to moral decadence and the dissolution of Roman blood. The text by Hohmann and Schiefer followed these instructions to the letter. In their telling, the fanfare heralding Rome's racial victory over Carthage had scarcely began to play when the hammer fell: "But the victory cost them dearly. The Roman peasantry was drained [*ausgeblutet*] from the horrible loss of life and the systematic devastation of the Italian campaigns. The Roman people were wounded to their core. Profound disruptions in society and the economy rattled the state to its foundations. It was ultimately fatal to Rome to allow itself to be dragged into the Hellenistic East."[57]

An article in the journal *Volk und Rasse* on "Roman history from a racial perspective" affirmed that Rome had conquered the East but that "the East had its revenge. Rome paid for its political victory with the extermination of the old Roman people, the total mutation and dilution of its racial and spiritual essence. Rome perished because of the East. In the place of the seemingly dominant Nordic race, there was now a mélange of races, made up of all the different bloods under the empire."[58]

WELTREICH AND WELTJUDENTUM: THE JEWISH QUESTION IN ANTIQUITY

At the heart of this racial confrontation between East and West stood the war of the Jews against Nordic civilization. The cause of the East and the cause of the Jews were one and the same, for it was the hostility of the Jews toward the Nordic race that gave birth to the clash of East versus West. The inferior races and bastardized racial amalgamations of the East had spread throughout the ancient world via the diaspora. In a pamphlet on the question of "the Jew in Greco-Roman antiquity," Hans Oppermann described how "the contribution of the Jews to the general Orientalization of the ancient world is clearly visible. The Jews thus played a very special role in the global advance of the East." Orientalization and the "Jewification of the ancient world"[59] were synonymous. In Nazi anti-Semitic discourse, Jewishness and Orientalism were frequently interchangeable: the Jews were no longer just a race but rather a mixture of inferior peoples. Oppermann wrote of the Jews as an "Eastern race" and a "race of Asia Minor,"[60] while Ferdinand Fried identified the three components that made up the original, impure Jewish racial blend as the Israelites (*sic*), the Babylonians, and the "Punics and Phoenicians."[61]

In the battle to the death between East and West, Semites and Nordics, all these writers agreed without a shadow of a doubt that it was the Jews who struck first. The Jews, we learn, were spiteful and bellicose by nature. Their way of life was based on hatred of all that was different, of the goyim who did not possess the good fortune to be similarly chosen, as Fritz Schachermeyr wrote: "Hatred, that is the Jew's primary business."[62] The notion of Jewish hate was even the subject of an NSDAP political education booklet, opportunely titled *Three Thousand Years of Jewish Hate*. The booklet was a masterpiece of inverted reality characteristic of so much Nazi propaganda, which transposed the definitive traits of Nazi hatred on to their enemies.[63] Anti-Semitism, put into practice first as a form of prophylactic persecution and later as extermination, was thus plainly justified as legitimate racial self-defense: the race war conducted by the Nazi Party and its Praetorian Guard, the SS, depicted as a preventive war. This inversion of reality and causality was captured perfectly in the chiasmus of its opening line: "The Jew hates us because we fight him, but we fight him because he hates us." The authors proceeded to elaborate an interesting etiology of Jewish hate, which they attributed to the chasm between the megalomaniacal self-regard of a people that believed themselves to constitute an elect and their real-world weakness. Positively Nietzschean in its analysis of resentment, this reading linked hatred and impotence, the frustration of desire without corresponding ability—the harmonious blending of will and power being a prerogative of the superior Nordic peoples: "It is the hatred of the inferior and the incapable, born of the tension between a disproportionate self-regard and complete political impotence" that led the Jew to feel a ferocious hatred toward the "great powers of the times,"[64] whether Babylon, Egypt, or the Persian Empire, all Nordic in their essence.

Numerous writers, like Hans Bogner, emphasized that the Jews hated Rome, fighting the empire and ultimately subverting Roman law and order, since, as vandals and fierce individualists, they were hardly faithful to themselves and only at best to their "tribe," while the Indo-Germanics defined themselves by the superior reality of the "state"[65] that they constructed.

Being fundamentally destructive, the Jews hated any ambitious state-like structure, as Oppermann noted: "The Jews hated Rome and never ceased dreaming of its destruction. . . . The hatred of the Jew for Rome was the innate hatred of the parasite for any power that creates a statist order, the hatred of an asocial race for the order imposed by power, represented here by the Roman Empire. This hatred was born of a feeling that the Jew could thrive only where the state was weak."[66] The Jews had no ambition toward the "creation of a state" of their own but instead relied on the "spread of individuals and their dispersal throughout already existing states."[67] Their essence and their parasitic existence were based on unproductive, vampiric consumption, whereas the Nordic race aspired to build states and cultures.[68]

The SS manual remarked that their hatred was insatiable, as the Bible itself attested: "For the Jews, war had always been synonymous with a war of extermination,"[69] a fact demonstrated by the "Aryan pogrom" perpetrated by the Jews in Persia, which resulted in the deaths of seventy-five thousand Nordic Persians, as celebrated in the book of Esther (9:5–16) and to this day commemorated by the Jewish holiday of Purim. One can easily see again in this example how the traits of Nazi anti-Semitism itself were turned around and used against those who were its victims: the terms used to describe the victims are the same as those used to describe anti-Semitic violence—pogrom, extermination—while the role of the butcher or executioner is ascribed to the Jewish people. This massacre of Aryan Persians was not, however, enough to satisfy the Jews' lust for Nordic blood, which reared its head once more against the new dominant power and sought to "defy a global empire like the Roman Empire." The Jews' war on Rome was extreme in its methods and presaged the depths to which they were willing to sink: "The battle was fought with incredible fanaticism and as a consequence resulted in unthinkable cruelty. This was a most appalling Jewish revolt, littered with mass killings, of the kind to which only Bolshevism has inured us."[70] The historian Ferdinand Fried, in his essay *The Rise of the Jews*, returned to this aspect in his discussion of the suffering of the Indo-Germanic peoples of antiquity: "It was with great hatred that the Romans and Greeks were persecuted and bloodily exterminated,"[71] an "unquenchable Semitic hatred."[72]

Only through the ruthless and resolute action of Hadrian's Roman legions was the Jews' revolutionary subversion finally defeated, but Hadrian, like Titus, failed to push his advantage all the way to the necessary end, the destruction of the Jewish people, their complete biological eradication: "The plow worked over the site of the Temple to demonstrate that it should never be rebuilt. Thus the dream of a Jewish state was ruined, but not that of Jewish world domination. . . . The Jewish state had disappeared, but not the Jewish people."[73]

Since then, the Jewish people had survived, dispersed throughout the empire, their bonds of solidarity unbroken, their overt war replaced by the surreptitious and cunning activities below the surface, subterranean sapping, "mining and working from within"[74] through racial infiltration, curial intrigue, and financial subterfuge.[75] The Jews were still possessed by their "racial hatred." They were a population of rabid dogs that dreamed only of death and devastation, which thoroughly justified a preventive racial war and the attendant radical measures of confinement and isolation, even extermination, of an enemy that had to be destroyed before it was allowed the time to strike: as the tragic example of Rome showed, "there could be no peace with them; they could only be destroyed"[76]—without half measures or similar weakness that had so hobbled the Romans' repression of this fundamentally destructive people.

The Jews had first chosen the path of open, violent war against Nordic mankind. The vigorous response against the Jewish rebellion by the legions of Titus and Hadrian had led the Semites to seek other, more subversive paths in a battle that was now subterranean and concealed in the darkness of a racial conspiracy.

THE DIASPORA AND THE ASSIMILATION OF JEWS IN ANTIQUITY

The Jews revealed their lack of racial purity through their nomadism, their urbanity, their complete disconnection from any land and its soil: "The link with the soil of the country plays, for the Jews, a role that to us is unbelievably minimal," the historian Hans Oppermann noted.[77] The Jews were a people of merchants, an essentially urban people that invaded the great cities of the Hellenistic world and later the Roman Empire to establish trading posts and shops, like a thousand meeting points in a global network. A people of money and material goods, a people without any link to the land—and thus hardly a people at all, and certainly not a race.[78] This absence of any connection to the land, this geographic nomadism, was like the absence of a faith, a moral nomadism: *fides romana*, the Germanic ethic, rooted in sincerity, was met by Punic and Jewish cunning. The Jews were traitors, as demonstrated by the figure of Flavius Josephus,[79] the Romanized historian of the Jewish wars, a double perjurer, a traitor to everything and everyone.[80]

Nomads, immigrants, diaspora, the Jews chose the surreptitious path of assimilation, a deleterious form of racial corruption for the body that hosted them: "The Jewish diaspora rapidly and greedily took the path of assimilation into the Greek people," Georg Kuhn wrote in an article on "world Jewry in antiquity" for the Institute for the History of the New Germany.[81] The Jews, he charged, had insinuated themselves everywhere in antiquity, making themselves invisible. Having abandoned their native language and soil, they imitated Greek ways while remaining Jewish on the inside: "The Jew preserved his Jewishness while abandoning his mother tongue[s]"[82]—Aramaic and Hebrew—"abandoned"[83] in favor of Greek and then Latin, the two universal languages of an ecumene homogenized by Alexandrine Hellenism and later the Roman Empire. "The linguistic assimilation of the Jews limited itself to these two languages, which were the global languages of international importance," the Jews not bothering to learn demotic Egyptian or any other language that remained confined within the borders of a single polity. Not content simply to renounce their language, they also renounced their traditional names, Oppermann noted, adopting Greek names to better blend in with the Hellenized masses of the Greek world: "It was thus that a Jew named Jesus took the Greek name Jason, and a Jew called Joseph was known as Justus to the Romans, just as in the modern era a Levy calls himself Löwe and a Salomonsohn becomes Solmsen."[84]

These Jewish strategies of infiltration and assimilation perfected in antiquity would resurface much later in other Indo-Germanic lands: "Just as the Jews took old Germanic names in Germany, like Siegfried or Siegmund, so did the Jews of the diaspora assume Greek names."[85] Names in Greece and in Rome, as in Germany, served as camouflage and allowed the Jews to mask themselves in the face of their host population. The villages of antiquity suffered from Jewish infection in a prefiguration of the same sort that afflicted modern urban areas: Gerhard Kittel compared the fate of Minorca in 418 to that of Vienna in 1934, both infiltrated by the Jews.[86]

Whereas Hans Oppermann waxed ironic on the Jews' remarkable "faculties of adaptation,"[87] Eugen Fischer and Gerhard Kittel studied the Jews' entire repertoire of assimilation techniques in their 1943 volume for the series Research on the Jewish Question, titled *Das antike Weltjudentum* (World Jewry in antiquity): the biologist and the historian congratulated themselves for their "cooperation between the sciences of man and the sciences of nature"[88] in the context of this "decisive battle"[89] that Europe faced against "a world Jewry that is neither new nor modern," since its first appearance in Greco-Roman antiquity. They thus sought to "draw out the lessons offered by antiquity," since history was, following Hitler's lead in *Mein Kampf,* the "great teacher."[90] History taught that the Jews' rise to power was accomplished not through the traditional means of conquest or taking possession, in the virile Nordic manner, but through trickery, since the Jew was an expert at blending in, simulating and dissimulating. It was not the "conqueror or the colonizer but the wandering Jew of antiquity"[91] who had ultimately conquered the world, through relentless assimilation:[92] "The assimilated Jewry of antiquity, who adapted to their environment by assuming its language, its names, its lifestyle . . . , and took pride in appearing, with education and culture, completely Greek or Roman,"[93] had infiltrated a world to which healthy Nordic blood should have denied it access.

The diasporic diffusion and assimilation of the Jews across nations led to the creation of an international Jewry, which took advantage of the existence of imperial infrastructures (routes and ports) and the Pax Romana, both of which helped eliminate borders and homogenize space. In this context, international Jewry wove its web: "One can observe time and time again where Jewish communities of the ancient world worked to preserve themselves, openly or secretly, and how this nascent Jewry forged its solidarity."[94]

The great minds of antiquity cried out against Jewish infiltration. The still healthy elements of Nordic blood had been repulsed by the spread of the Semitic peoples. Martial[95] and many others, among them "the finest representatives of Roman literature, Cicero and Tacitus, Seneca and Quintilian, but also poets like Persius and Juvenal, were all unsparing in their fulminations"[96] and anti-Semitic recriminations. These great Roman minds had clearly perceived what Mommsen noted about his contemporary world much later; the abundant citation of these Roman authors proved that these men were Indo-Germanics and that they had been deeply hostile to Jewry. An ideological training pamphlet for the party and the Wehrmacht, titled *Der kampf um unsere Weltanschauung* (The struggle for our world view), contained an entire chapter on this subject, "The Jew as Universal Parasite."[97] Presented as a set of condensed notes, like a list of simple directives, the text required educators to speak to their public about the nefarious and lethal role played by the Jews in antiquity: "Intrusion into the Greek and Roman world. Undermining of the Roman Empire. Mommsen: "The Jews as effective ferment of decomposition." Hatred of Jewry for the universal empire of Rome."[98]

Yet again, the example of the ancients was scarcely confined to the publications of scholars but rather made the subject of widespread propaganda designed for combat units, whose ardor for battle had to be stoked by the historical importance of the menace they were fighting.

The volume also referred to a quote from the third volume of Theodor Mommsen's *Römische Geschichte* (*The History of Rome*): "In the ancient world also Judaism was an effective leaven of cosmopolitanism and of national decomposition."[99] Mommsen's phrase, an intellectual indictment that was appreciated far more than the historian of liberal tendencies himself, was the subject of two essays, the first by the historian Eugen Täubler, in a volume that essentially republished Mommsen's chapter on the Jews in antiquity,[100] and the second by Richard Fester, who repeatedly cited and commented on Mommsen's work before launching into a global history of "Judaism as an element in the destruction of peoples."[101]

In 1935, Mommsen's line on the Jews in Rome was picked up by the Nazi leadership. Hitler himself repeated it in his closing speech to the party congress at Nuremberg that year,[102] before Goebbels liberally adapted it in his famous speech at the Berlin Sportpalast on 18 February 1943: "International Jewry is the devilish ferment of decomposition."[103] In such a grave hour for the Reich, in the immediate aftermath of Stalingrad, the example of Rome remained ever present, and the similarity of the situations faced by Rome and Germany in terms of Jewish subversion was blindingly obvious.

The Jews had been able to expand into all nations thanks to the infrastructure of empire. The Jews had dispersed throughout the ecumene because the imperial powers of antiquity had provided them with means of communication, relative peace, and trading networks: the empire of Alexander the Great was thus just as culpable as the Roman Empire, both perpetrator and victim of the racial mixing that would be their downfall, the ambiguous laws of the Roman legislative infrastructure a reflection of the ambiguous racial status of Rome itself.

A sequence in the film *Der ewige Jude* (1941)[104] used maps and animation to show how the Jewish people spread across the four corners of the globe: "We probably would never have been bothered by them had they stayed in their Oriental home. The cosmopolitan empire of Alexander the Great . . . and especially the boundless world empire of the Romans,"[105] with its peace, infrastructure that favored travel and exchange, and integration of different lands, allowed the diaspora to exist. The global empire had as its avatar "the international Jewry that we know today."[106] This sequence immediately preceded the infamous jump cut to a teeming swarm of rats—a creature that the film claimed also emerged from the East and Asia Minor and followed the same migratory routes as the Semitic peoples. The implicit suggestion of the 1940 film was that, in contrast to the unhappy precedents of Alexander's Greece and its Roman successor, the new Indo-Germanic Empire would not make the same mistake of allowing Jewish populations to live under its jurisdiction and freely permeate its imperial territory at their leisure.[107]

Fritz Schachermeyr also emphasized the affinities between "world Jewry and global empire,"[108] remarking that the Jews were feverish partisans of Caesar and his imperial aims and that the "global power" of the Jewish "hydra"[109] was indissolubly linked to a global empire that allowed it to spread around the world. Soon enough, the Jews had tried to circumvent the imperial authority of Rome by insinuating themselves into the heart of the capital city: Titus had displayed a soft touch with Palestine and had not exterminated the Jewish people as he should have, because, in the historian's judgment, he had been seduced by that "Herodian Berenice,"[110] a woman of Jewish blood whom the Roman people had rightly seen fit to ship back where she came from in the East.[111]

By virtue of this primacy of the spiritual over the physical and the systematic reduction of the spiritual to the biological, this battle of racial archetypes was also a sort of "war of ideologies," a *Weltanschauungskampf* between Eastern perversion and Western genius, which Joseph Vogt described in a dense scholarly essay in 1939.[112]

THE JEW PAUL AND THE SUBVERSION OF THE EMPIRE

For Hitler and the Nazis, Christianity meant Judeo-Christianity, a Judaized Christianity, promoted and spread throughout the entire world to bring down the Roman Empire.

While he chose to remain relatively cautious and moderate on this subject in *Mein Kampf* and his public speeches, the führer did not hold back from expressing what he truly thought about Christianity in his table talks: "But if I were to die to-day, it would shock me to know that there's a single 'sky-pilot' within a radius of ten kilometres around me."[113]

Hitler was at once resolutely anti-Christian and profoundly agnostic, all the while believing in the existence of some form of divine providence and the laws of nature, a perpetual race war in which only the strongest would survive. In his private conversations, providence and the law of nature were frequent subjects, and on the question of metaphysics and what lies beyond, Hitler displayed a nonchalant agnosticism.[114]

His only real, tangible certitude was the existence of blood and race and their submission to the laws of nature, which subjected all races to the strongest among them and condemned a race that welcomed interbreeding to ineluctable degeneration. The race itself had to survive, from generation to generation, and each individual that belonged to it was but a means to that end: "I dream of a state of affairs in which every man would know that he lives and dies for the preservation of the species."[115] Hitler thus viewed existence and transcendence as a function not of external divinity but of the blood. The Nazi religion was thus a curious synthesis of transcendence and immanence: the transcendence of a race that had to preserve and perpetuate itself, and the immanence of a blood that was the most intimate part of each individual.

This healthy worship of nature was the polar opposite of Christianity, which for Hitler was a religion of Jews—with the exception of Jesus, for "Christ was an Aryan":[116] "It's certain that Jesus was not a Jew. The Jews, by the way, regarded Him as the son of a whore—of a whore and a Roman soldier."[117] Hitler thus exempted him from the law defining Jews and imagined that, as a result of his paternal Roman ancestry, Jesus had narrowly escaped Judaism.[118]

The figure of Christ was singularly absent from Hitler's countless fulminations against the Christian religion. Christ's message had, in his opinion, been perverted by his disciples and apostles, most notably the former Jew Paul, a late convert and neophyte zealot who appeared in Hitler's mind to represent Jesus's malevolent twin. Paul was the most heinous demon of Christianity, the man who put the religion in the service of the Jews and in doing so perverted its fundamental message: "The decisive falsification of Jesus's doctrine was the work of St. Paul. He gave himself to this work with subtlety and for purposes of personal exploitation." Hitler argued that Jesus's original Christianity was actually an Aryan revolt against the Jewish domination of Palestine: "For the Galilean's object was to liberate His country from Jewish oppression. He set Himself against Jewish capitalism, and that's why the Jews liquidated Him."[119]

Alfred Rosenberg made a similar distinction between the first Christianity, that of Christ himself, and later Christianity, which was degenerate, contaminated by the Jewish element that had appropriated and corrupted it. He denounced and stigmatized "this collective bastardization, orientalization, and Judaization" of Jesus's original Aryan message. The Nordic character of this original message could yet be found, he claimed, in the Gospel of John, which "still retains an aristocratic spirit."[120]

The Jew Saul, who later converted and took the name Paul, was in his heart an implacable enemy, a zealous tormentor of the Christians, as Hitler explained in a 1941 conversation against the backdrop of the war with the Soviet Union: "Paul of Tarsus (his name was Saul, before the road to Damascus) was one of those who persecuted Jesus most savagely. When he learnt that Jesus's supporters let their throats be cut for His ideas, he realised that, by making intelligent use of the Galilean's teaching, it would be possible to overthrow this Roman State which the Jews hated. It's in this context that we must understand the famous 'illumination.'"[121] The torturer Saul thus became Paul, the faithful, the proselyte, the apostle. In Hitler's eyes, his conversion was clearly insincere. There was no mystical encounter with the divine, as Paul would have it; it was merely a cold political calculation. The Jews hated the Romans, who had conquered them and taken all their gold: "Think of it, the Romans were daring to confiscate the most sacred thing the Jews possessed, the gold piled up in their temples! At that time, as now, money was their god." Hence Saul's unquenchable resentment: "St. Paul discovered that he could succeed in ruining the Roman State by causing the principle to triumph of the equality of all men before a single God."[122] Paul was like the Bar Kokhba of the Gospels.

Paul had perceived the revolutionary and eminently subversive nature of the Christian message: if all men were creatures of God, all equal before him, a political system founded on hierarchy and discrimination like the aristocratic Roman Empire would be doomed to extinction. In fact, it was precisely this politically subversive aspect of Christianity that Paul so capably exploited in winning over the dregs of the empire with the message of their equality before God. Christianity would successfully unite all the losers, the weak and the enslaved, of an empire that reserved its aristocratic superiority for a racial elite:[123] "Whilst Roman society proved hostile to the new doctrine, Christianity in its pure state stirred the population to revolt."[124] Christianity had been the weapon of the oppressed and the inferior, the banner of a vile, teeming horde that wished only to rise up against the Roman racial aristocracy and overthrow the empire: "Paul used his doctrine to mobilise the criminal underworld" and unleashed it against the Roman Empire. Paying no heed to chronology, Hitler turned

Paul into a precursor—or even a protoagent—of Bolshevism. The political subversion he had introduced in Rome was comparable, indeed identical, to that of contemporary Bolshevism: "St. Paul ... organise[d] a proto Bolshevism."[125] This conversation occurred on 13 December 1941, just as Hitler had given the oral order to exterminate the Jews of Europe.[126] At the very moment when the policy of extermination was being decided, Hitler was making frequent and sustained references to the destruction of the Roman Empire by Pauline Christianity, which was nothing other than an ancient manifestation of the Jewish conspiracy. The use of the Christian-Bolshevik/Rome-Reich analogy was unsettling and anxiety provoking, giving a feeling of world-historic urgency that could help the imagination acclimatize itself to the idea of extirpation and the suggestion of the Final Solution: at the very moment when a counterattack had grounded the invasion of the East to a halt, a moment when the Wehrmacht—for the first time since 1939—found itself on the defensive, it was essential to do everything possible to prevent the Reich from succumbing to the same fate as Rome. Throughout these days and weeks that were so decisive for the evolution of the extermination order and the subsequent Wannsee Conference, Hitler was also developing his ideas on the "downfall of the ancient world."[127]

This anti-Pauline discourse was not the sole province of the führer. For Rosenberg too, the Semitism that had rapidly corrupted Christianity was subversive and anarchic, the destroyer of all aristocratic principles. It had infected the original Christianity of the elite through "the Semitic conception of a capricious god who exercised a boundless despotism."[128] Semiticized Christianity was in effect egalitarian, which would lead right to revolution, to democracy, to the destruction of a healthy social and racial hierarchy.

The downfall of the Roman Empire was thus, for Rosenberg and Hitler, directly imputable to the Judeo-Christian revolution, the insurrection of inferior masses rallied by its subversive egalitarian message against their Nordic masters: "The sensational event of the ancient world was the mobilisation of the underworld against the established order. This enterprise of Christianity had no more to do with religion than Marxist socialism has to do with the solution of the social problem."[129] Rosenberg's thoughts were completely in line with Hitler's: "Paul accomplished something which is never admitted in churchly circles. He made the suppressed Jewish national rebellion *internationally* effective, thus paving the way for the further spread of racial chaos in the ancient world. The Jews in Rome knew very well what they were about when they placed their synagogues at his disposal as places wherein he could make his proselytizing speeches."[130]

Christianity was the form that the Jewish conspiracy took in the ancient world. What the Jews could not attain by outright, open revolt, through armed insurrection against Rome, they had done by introducing into the empire an egalitarian monotheism that undermined the Roman state, destabilizing the foundations of its society and civilization.

Hitler and Rosenberg thus reversed the terms of our common understanding of this history. Christianity is generally perceived as a phenomenon that helped to regenerate and transform the Roman Empire, whose decline is attributed to the later barbarian invasions, which the Germans called *Völkerwanderungen*. Hitler tried to clarify this as a misconception and show that it was false: "It was Christianity that brought about the fall of Rome—not the Germans or the Huns."[131] All the anti-Semitic literature of the era agreed that, weakened by Oriental and Jewish blood, Rome had been revived by a happy influx of German vitality and not destroyed by what was too often depicted as a destructive wave of invasions: Rome was killed by an assault from the East and the South, not from the North, by an Eastern and Semitic tidal wave and not by the penetration of the Germans, eternal scapegoats in the story of the grandeur and decadence of the Romans.

After the pollution of the Tiber by the Orontes, Rome no longer resided in Rome, in the eyes of the raciologist Ludwig Schemann, but rather farther north: "What existed in Rome and Italy, not to mention throughout the empire, was Roman in name only. In truth, beneath the surface of a name, two gigantic communities of blood fought against each other, two historical principles, two visions of the world," "the original Nordic element being in its death throes."[132]

Nazi propaganda and pedagogy incessantly spoke of the beneficial re-Nordification of Rome through Germanicization.[133] The phenomenon that pedants regrettably referred to as the "barbarian invasions" was in fact a healthy process of *Aufnordung* (re-Nordification), the antithesis of and antidote to *Entnordung* (de-Nordification), a criminal, destructive enterprise that diluted Germanic blood with an influx of weaker, mixed blood. This Nordic topos was repeated in numerous works, like that of Ferdinand Fried: "While the German [*sic*: not 'Germanic'] soldiers of the Roman Empire could not help but take up a domination that had long been falling to them, in order to avoid complete dissolution and total chaos—and, in the final analysis, to create a new order, a new world order even—these savages, these Semitic animals did nothing but destroy, kill without mercy and without reason, moved by the desire for vengeance, race hatred, and religious fanaticism, thus destroying a world order without being able to replace it with something new of their own."[134] An SS ideological education pamphlet spoke of this notion of the *ver sacrum*,[135] a metaphor to designate the regeneration of a Roman Empire that was moribund, of mixed blood, by the injection of pure, fresh German blood: "This was truly a 'rite of spring' for an old civilization that desperately needed it,"[136] a veritable racial renewal, a biological reblossoming thanks to the influx of Nordic blood that once more flowed with vigor through the veins of a sullied empire.

CHRISTIAN OBSCURANTISM VERSUS ANCIENT PURITY

For Hitler, the advent of Christianity signaled the triumph of obscurantism, of deep ignorance and shadowy fanaticism, over the brilliant purity of ancient thought. The führer had developed a thoroughly idealized image of Roman antiquity, which he frequently summarized with two words: *intelligence* and *tolerance*. Christianity represented the complete opposite, the victory of the darkest and most morbid side of man, a crass, zealous hatred of intelligence and knowledge, and murderous intolerance: "The notions represented by Jewish Christianity were strictly unthinkable to Roman brains. The ancient world had a liking for clarity. Scientific research was encouraged there."[137] Ignorant, obscurantist, and criminal, Christianity had destroyed antique culture. The vengeful iconoclasm of the Christians who had knocked down temples and statues and burned libraries had reduced the treasures of human wisdom and knowledge to smoking ash—a body of knowledge of which Christianity constituted the absolute antithesis: "When, in ancient Rome, the plebs were mobilised by Christianity, the intelligentsia had lost contact with the ancient forms of worship. . . . We can be glad that the Parthenon is still standing upright, the Roman Pantheon and the other temples. It matters little that the forms of worship that were practised there no longer mean anything to us. It is truly regrettable that so little is left to us of these temples."[138] Christian vandalism was proof enough of Christianity's obscurantism: "What a certificate of mental poverty it was for Christianity that it destroyed the libraries of the ancient world! Graeco-Roman thought was made to seem like the teachings of the Devil."[139] Christianity systematically, relentlessly attempted to wipe out ancient culture, a meticulous work of erasure that left virtually nothing behind: "Christianity set itself systematically to destroy ancient culture. What came to us was passed down by chance, or else it was a product of Roman liberal writers. Perhaps we are entirely ignorant of humanity's most precious spiritual treasures. Who can know what was there?"[140]

If the contemporary era understood antiquity so little and so poorly, the fault lay entirely with Christianity, which was guilty of a heinous cultural crime. In their rage, Hitler fulminated, the Christians had destroyed the wonder of wonders, the monument to ancient culture that was the Library of Alexandria. The library, however, was first reported to have been burned half a century before the birth of Christ, some 450 years before the iconoclastic savagery imputed to the Christians by the Nazis. Here, yet again, we can see an example of the Nazis' propensity to attribute their own acts to their declared enemies: the Christians were denounced as barbarous book burners and destroyers of culture, even though the bonfires of 10 May 1933, a ritual of spiritual purification, were the symbolic essence of most National Socialism. There was a further perverse irony to Hitler's lamentations about moderns' poor understanding of ancient culture, which might well have given him joy—the void left by this lack of knowledge gave free rein to fantasy and imagination and provided space for any and all forms of fictional deformation of the past, including the grossest errors: "If nowadays we do not find the same splendid pride of race which distinguished the Grecian and Roman eras, it is because in the fourth century these Jewish-Christians systematically destroyed all the monuments of these ancient civilisations. It was they, too, who destroyed the library at Alexandria."[141]

Once ancient culture had been destroyed, the reign of Christian obscurantism began. Hitler often rhetorically wondered how someone with even the slightest hint of culture could believe all the foolishness and harebrained nonsense that Christianity presented as revealed truth:

> Christianity is an invention of sick brains: one could imagine nothing more senseless, nor any more indecent way of turning the idea of the Godhead into a mockery. A negro with his tabus is crushingly superior to the human being who seriously believes in Transubstantiation.[142]

The incoherence of the Christian religious message was, in his eyes, the surest indication that it must necessarily disappear: "Christianity, of course, has reached the peak of absurdity in this respect. And that's why one day its structure will collapse. Science has already impregnated humanity. Consequently, the more Christianity clings to its dogmas, the quicker it will decline."[143]

For Hitler, who was fascinated by the timelessness of the Catholic Church, the only political institution to exist continuously for two thousand years,[144] Christianity's time had come: "What's to be done, you say? I will tell you: we must prevent the churches from doing anything but what they are doing now, that is, losing ground day by day. Do you really believe the masses will ever be Christian again? Nonsense! Never again. That tale is finished. No one will listen to it again."[145]

This frenetic, fiendish obscurantism shaded into another dimension of Christianity, another of its darker aspects: this intolerant religion of fanatics had led to the creation of a regime of terror throughout the West. Hitler first made this accusation in *Mein Kampf*: "Christianity could not content itself with building up its own altar; it was absolutely forced to undertake the destruction of the heathen altars. Only from this fanatical intolerance could its apodictic faith take form; this intolerance is, in fact, its absolute presupposition."[146]

An "apodictic" creed—that is to say, a faith that would countenance no opposition nor any doubt—went hand in hand with fanatical intolerance, which could not accept the coexistence of any other form of belief or religiosity. Christianity had thus created a reign of terror that stood in stark, grievous contrast with the liberty, wisdom, and tolerance of the ancient world: "The individual may establish with pain today that with the appearance of Christianity the first spiritual terror entered into the far freer ancient world."[147] Greco-Roman antiquity was in this way a lost paradise of knowledge and tolerance, a world that in retrospect seemed pure and luminous. As Goebbels noted in his diary on 8 April 1941, during the invasion of Greece:

> [The führer] hates Christianity, because it has crippled all that is noble in humanity. According to Schopenhauer, Christianity and syphilis have made humanity unhappy and unfree. What a difference between the benevolent, smiling Zeus and the pain-wracked, crucified Christ.... What a difference between a gloomy cathedral and a light, airy ancient temple....
>
> The Führer cannot relate to the Gothic mind. He hates gloom and brooding mysticism. He wants clarity, light, beauty. And these are the ideals of life in our time.[148]

Antiquity, pure, tolerant, and free as a consequence of the Apollonian liberty and wisdom that were its hallmark, had of course been the epoch when the full physical and intellectual capabilities of the Nordic man had blossomed. Christianity, regressive, oppressive, and obscurantist, had contaminated and mutilated him like a contagious pandemic; the smiling, sovereign Zeus of the Greek temples had given way to the macabre Christ on a cross, while the Nordic man, a natural ruler and conqueror, had become ill, his conscience gnawed upon, learning of sin. The belief in sin and the notion of self-flagellation, a product of the Christian revulsion at man's depraved nature, were both symptoms and aggravating factors in his racial degeneration, as Rosenberg explained in *The Myth of the Twentieth Century*:

> Into this raceless stew which was now Rome came Christianity. Its success is largely to be explained by its concept of a sinful world and redemption through grace, which was its natural compliment. The doctrine of original sin would have been incomprehensible to a people whose racial identity was unadulterated. In such a people there dwells a secure confidence in itself and in its will, which it regards as Destiny. The concept of "sin" was as alien to the heroes of Homer as it was to the ancient Indians, the Germans of Tacitus, or the epics and sagas of Dietrich von Bern. An oppressive sense of sin is a sure symptom of racial bastardy. Race pollution shows itself in a number of stigmata; in an absence of clear direction in thought and action; [and] an inner self doubt.[149]

Racial mixing thus entailed a perversion of a previously healthy and pure soul. Self-confidence gave way to self-hatred; reason crumbled before madness. Rosenberg's biological determinism was clear: physical and racial degeneration necessarily led to the perversion and impoverishment of the spirit. The Christian doctrine of sin provided evidence of this degeneration, which it nourished and amplified in return. Christianity, through the self-hatred and disdain for the physical world that it preached and elevated into dogma, destroyed not only souls but bodies as well, bodies that it denied and repudiated as the source of sin. In his most important work, Richard Walther Darré—the chief ideologue of the SS and Himmler's close friend—denounced man's destruction by Christianity as the product of an insidious and dangerous form of asceticism: "The negation of the body was originally foreign to the Nordic race. It was only when the shadow of asceticism crept into antiquity as the enemy of beauty, an asceticism that came from the East and took the shape of the monastic way of life, that cultural decadence set in, beginning an inversion of moral values that ultimately viewed the body as nothing more than the incarnation of sin."[150]

CHRISTIANITY: BOLSHEVISM UNDER A TINSEL OF METAPHYSICS

Christianity, which was thus so damaging to man, aimed at nothing more or less than the destruction of life and the eradication of mankind.

Hitler turned Christianity into an exterminating angel in a conversation the very day after he gave the oral order to Himmler to put into action the Final Solution to the Jewish question: "Pure Christianity ... leads quite simply to the annihilation of mankind. It is merely whole-hearted Bolshevism, under a tinsel of metaphysics."[151] After having destroyed the Roman branch of the Nordic race, Christianity had anesthetized and immobilized the German people. Without this religion, "the Germanic races would have conquered the world. Christianity alone prevented them from doing so."[152] The Christian faith deprived life of all substance, paralyzed will and aggression through its message of love and the doctrine of sin, the source of ill conscience and self-hatred. It was a politically toxic element. It sapped pride, vitality, and forceful, warriorlike self-affirmation, devaluing life in favor of an imaginary beyond: "It was necessary for the Jew to appear on the scene and introduce that mad conception of a life that continues into an alleged Beyond! It enables one to regard life as a thing that is negligible here below— since it will flourish later, when it no longer exists."[153]

Jewish Christianity ruptured the immediacy and self-evidence of the ancients' relationship with the natural world, which was all light and divinity, turning the world into a somber universe of death and terror and destroying all of life and creation. It was ideologically and politically dangerous to tolerate the kind of message that placed all hope for man in the afterlife. As Hitler stated flatly on another occasion: "We don't want people who keep one eye on the life in the hereafter."[154] Like the ancients, the Germans found fulfillment in the here and now of the world that surrounded them and refused to take refuge in sick, hollow dreams. But the Christian message of death had imposed itself through violence and terror; its intolerance had led to horrific carnage: "In the ancient world, the relations between men and gods were founded on an instinctive respect. It was a world enlightened by the idea of tolerance. Christianity was the first creed in the world to exterminate its adversaries in the name of love. Its key-note is intolerance."[155] Christianity, morbid and macabre, had killed the joy of life through terror: "There are towns in Germany from which all joy is lacking.... Clearly, one must not forget that these areas are still feeling the weight of several centuries of religious oppression. Near Würzburg, there are villages where literally all the women were burned.... One cannot succeed in conceiving how much cruelty, ignominy and falsehood the intrusion of Christianity has spelt for this world of ours."[156]

Such fanatical terror could be met only with terror and fanaticism, as Hitler had declared previously in *Mein Kampf:* "A philosophy filled with infernal intolerance will only be broken by a new idea, driven forward by the same spirit, championed by the same mighty will, and at the same time pure and absolutely genuine in itself. . . . Coercion is broken only by coercion, and terror only by terror."[157] Once again, then, National Socialism was only using aggression to answer oppression.

In contrast to the terror and intolerance of Christianity, antiquity—Rome above all—was characterized by confessional freedom and absolute tolerance: "In this sphere, the Romans were tolerance itself. The idea of a universal god could seem to them only a mild form of madness—for, if three peoples fight one another, each invoking the same god, this means that, at any rate, two of them are praying in vain. Nobody was more tolerant than the Romans. Every man could pray to the god of his choice, and a place was even reserved in the temples for the unknown god. Moreover, every man prayed as he chose, and had the right to proclaim his preferences."[158] Hitler, who was a self-proclaimed agnostic, foresaw the opportunity for a return to the tolerance of antiquity: "It's probable that, as regards religion, we are about to enter an era of tolerance. Everybody will be allowed to seek his own salvation in the way that suits him best. The ancient world knew this climate of tolerance. Nobody took to proselytising."[159]

Hitler here claimed to simultaneously represent a paragon of Roman virtue and Frederick II of Prussia, his other great historic idol, who said, "Jeder kann nach seiner Façon selig werden" (Everyone has the right to find salvation in their own way).[160]

Generous, liberal, and tolerant, the Romans had been tricked by that cunning apostle of political subversion whom they had allowed into their midst. Paul had taken advantage of their religious tolerance to preach his message, rallying the proletariat against the empire: "St. Paul knew how to exploit this state of affairs in order to conduct his struggle against the Roman State. Nothing has changed; the method has remained sound. Under cover of a pretended religious instruction, the priests continue to incite the faithful against the State."[161] Hitler despaired that this politically and socially subversive message had found culpable accomplices in the person of certain emperors. Hitler admired the imposing figure of Julian, whom Christian posterity had ignominiously labeled the Apostate. Julian had been true to the faith of his fathers and his people and had tried everything to halt the triumph of Christianity: "When the Crown sees the throne totter, it needs the support of the masses. It would be better to speak of Constantine the traitor and Julian the Loyal than of Constantine the Great and Julian the Apostate. What the Christians wrote against the Emperor Julian is approximately of the same calibre as what the Jews have written against us. The writings of the Emperor Julian, on the other hand, are products of the highest wisdom."[162]

Hitler had evidently read the letters of Julian the Apostate, which he spoke about on several occasions: "I didn't know that Julian the Apostate had passed judgment with such clear-sightedness on Christianity and Christians. You should read what he says on the subject."[163] This was a book to be read and passed on, to enlighten the masses who had been radicalized and made superstitious by Christianity. For the führer, Julian was a model of purity and wisdom, and his writings could be a source of highly effective political propaganda: "The book that contains the reflections of the Emperor Julian should be circulated in millions. What wonderful intelligence, what discernment, all the wisdom of antiquity! It's extraordinary."[164]

FROM ROME TO THE REICH: JUDEO-CHRISTIANITY, JUDEO-BOLSHEVISM, CHRISTO-BOLSHEVISM

It was not by accident nor a slip of the tongue when Hitler belittled Christianity as metaphysical Bolshevism or Saul as a "commissar."[165] In the context of 1941, of course, the use of the word *Kommissare* could only conjure up the image of the political commissars of the Communist Party of the Soviet Union (CPSU)—the very same commissars whom Hitler commanded the Einsatzgruppen to execute without mercy during the Russian campaign, in an order issued on 6 June 1941. Hitler frequently associated Christianity with Bolshevism. More than a comparison, it was an identification, a deliberate effort to convince the world that the two were one and the same. The Christianity of antiquity and the Bolshevism of the modern era were separated by roughly two thousand years, but to Hitler they were both substantially part of the same movement. The comparison between the two fulfilled a legitimating function of fundamental importance: the vigor of the Nazis' political and military engagement against Bolshevism was justified by the harm done in the past by its Christian ancestors, those levelers of the Roman Empire, whose contemporary descendants now threatened to prove fatal to the new Indo-Germanic Reich. Christianity and Bolshevism were in essence both ideologies that mobilized the dregs of humanity against the state and the rule of born leaders. Christianity and Bolshevism both contained subversive political messages and sought to sow revolution and anarchy. The one presaged the other—"Christianity is a prototype of Bolshevism:

the mobilisation by the Jew of the masses of slaves with the object of undermining society."[166] Bolshevism and Christianity were identical in principle and in essence. Both offered a message of equality that aimed to mobilize the oppressed against their betters, those who held the power of the state.

Worse than just the early symptom of a full disease, Christianity was fundamentally the same thing as Bolshevism, only dressed in rags and clothed in different words. Christianity had offered a cultural and spiritual reign of terror; the terror created by Bolshevism was physical and material: "What Bolshevism does today in the material and technical sphere, Christianity already did in the theoretical and metaphysical realm."[167]

The two phenomena were biologically related, both sharing the same cultural matrix—that of Jewish hatred:

> The heaviest blow that ever struck humanity was the coming of Christianity. Bolshevism is Christianity's illegitimate child. Both are inventions of the Jew.[168]

Just as the Christian faith could be understood only in the context of Judeo-Christianity, so Bolshevism could only be framed as part of a Judeo-Bolshevist plot. The two ideologies were both subversive revolutionary weapons forged by the Jews for use against the rest of Nordic-Aryan mankind. In Rome, Christianity had brought down the state built by Nordic man and caused a cultural regression with an unprecedented wave of vandalism. The revolution that followed this regression was repeated in Russia, where the Bolshevik menace now threatened to swallow the entire world unless the Reich stepped in to set things right: "Rome was Bolshevised, and Bolshevism produced exactly the same results in Rome as later in Russia"[169]—destructive results that Hitler learned of with the first reports from the SD regarding the hasty executions and scorched-earth tactics employed by the NKVD in the summer and autumn of 1941.

The Jewish conspiracy was thus not born with *The Protocols of the Elders of Zion*. It dated back far beyond the modern era. The Jewish conspiracy was a two-thousand-year-old enterprise, a war of cunning that the Jews had first unleashed with the advent of Christianity against the Roman Empire before attacking the Aryan with Bolshevism. Hitler expressed this delusion in the most terse manner imaginable, with this striking analogy: "Saul has changed into St. Paul, and Mardochai into Karl Marx."[170] Saul the Jew had become, through cold calculation and political pragmatism, Saint Paul the apostle; in the exact same way,

Mardochai—the family name of Karl Marx's father—had disguised himself as Marx, the prophet of communist revolution. This message was transmitted and disseminated in an SS pamphlet that attacked the Judeo-Christo-Bolshevik conspiracy by comparing the "Jew Paul" with the "Jew Marx," confronting the spirit of "Proletarians of the world, unite" inherent in Paul's words in Galatians 3:26–29 (KJV):

> For ye are all the children of God by faith in Christ Jesus. For as many of you as have been baptized into Christ have put on Christ. There is neither Jew nor Greek, there is neither bond nor free, there is neither male nor female; for ye are all one in Christ Jesus. And if ye be Christ's, then are ye Abraham's seed, and heirs according to the promise.

The parallel between the universalism of the Pauline message, which was truly revolutionary in that it transcended all borders between peoples and nations, and the internationalism of the Marxist maxim led the SS ideologues to proclaim that Paul and Marx "were one and the same thing."[171] The notion seemed so self-evident that someone like Ferdinand Fried could write that the revolt of the Jews against Rome—that "nascent Jewish world conspiracy"—was clearly "proto-Bolshevik."[172]

Hitler repeated this point in a conversation from February 1942: "The Jew who fraudulently introduced Christianity into the ancient world—in order to ruin it—re-opened the same breach in modern times, this time taking as his pretext the social question. It's the same sleight-of-hand as before. Just as Saul was changed into St. Paul, Mardochai became Karl Marx."[173] Christianity and Bolshevism contained such striking similarities that it was all too easy to see them as the exact same thing. Both were revolutionary ideologies, egalitarian and destructive of the current order. Both contained messages that claimed to be universal, seeking to unite and organize the oppressed of the world against their masters, who naturally belonged to the Nordic race. Communism was an avowedly internationalist doctrine that aspired to throw the entire world into global darkness, an octopus whose tentacles stretched across the five inhabited continents. The Christian faith too was a supranational ideology. Led by Paul, Judeo-Christianity opposed the Roman idea of a sovereign racial nation-state in favor of a universal spiritual empire, thus claiming that all races, masters and slaves alike, were equal before God: "If the Jew has succeeded in destroying the Roman Empire, that's because St. Paul transformed a local movement of Aryan opposition to Jewry into a supra-temporal religion, which postulates the equality of all men amongst themselves, and their obedience to an only god.

This is what caused the death of the Roman Empire."¹⁷⁴ The Judeo-Christian revolution aspired to be global, universal. To fulfill that aspiration, it had to bring down the Roman national and racial state.

We find ourselves confronted with the overarching, driving principle of history: racial conflict. The all-out race war between the Jew and the Aryan pitted Christianity against the Roman Empire. History was only repeating itself two thousand years later in the Nazi fight against Bolshevism. The times might have changed, but the actors stayed the same. The Reich picked up the torch from Rome, just as Rome had once received it from Greece. In the same passage of *Mein Kampf* where he talked about Roman history as "the best teacher," Hitler also argued: "We must not allow the greater racial community to be torn asunder by the differences of the individual peoples. The struggle that rages today is for very great aims. A culture combining millenniums and embracing Hellenism and Germanism is fighting for its existence."¹⁷⁵ Rosenberg faithfully repeated this mantra: "We see that fundamentally the same struggle by the Greeks and Romans has fallen to the Germans. They can just as little escape this struggle as the other two great Nordic folk waves."¹⁷⁶

Rosenberg then issued a clear warning, foreseeing that "a complete triumph of this 'humanity' would have the same consequences as once the victory of Hither Asia over Athens and Rome."¹⁷⁷ A defeat in the race war against inferior peoples would mean miscegenation and drowning in a flood of impure blood, a fatal mistake that would bring with it the vengeance of a blood personified by its god:

> It is through this desecration of the blood that personality, people, race and culture perish. None who have disregarded the religion of the blood have escaped this nemesis—neither the Indians nor the Persians, neither the Greeks nor the Romans. Nor will Nordic Europe escape if it does not call a halt, turning away from bloodless absolutes and spiritually empty delusions, and begin to hearken trustingly once again to the subtle welling up of the ancient sap of life and values.¹⁷⁸

Hitler, Rosenberg, and their imitators thus put forward a reading of history based on oversimplification that functioned on two levels. The first consisted of consolidating all the contingencies and chaos of human choices and intentions into a single explanatory law of history that was also a law of nature—the idea that races struggled against each other for their survival; the second, that despite the long arc of time, history's actors were fundamentally all the same and history was fundamentally reducible to the confrontation between two races in many different guises.

The permanence of this confrontation, despite the passage of centuries, flattened out differences in historical eras and even in the evolution of time itself, in events that happen in chronological succession, in facts and people that were and are historically unique and not strictly comparable with one another. When Hitler called Christianity "proto-Bolshevism,"[179] he demonstrated his teleological sense of history, of course, but he also made a distinction between a before and an after: ancient Christianity had bequeathed Bolshevism to posterity. But more often, Hitler obliterated any differences in time and ignored all distinctions between eras. The identification of Christianity with Bolshevism blended phenomena and eras into a single history that was no longer based on a linear time-space continuum, unidirectional and irreversible, but rather on a continuum that was three-dimensional, circular or cyclical, a sense of time appropriate to his mythical sensibility: "Originally, Christianity was merely an incarnation of Bolshevism the destroyer."[180] Time was rejected, reduced to a singular eternal present. Significantly, Hitler raged against "the Bolsheviks of their day" when he decried the cultural vandalism of the Christians and communists and behind them the Jews, the destroyers of all culture: "In the old days, as now, destruction of art and civilisation. The Bolsheviks of their day, what didn't they destroy in Rome, in Greece and elsewhere? They've behaved in the same way amongst us and in Russia. One must compare the art and civilisation of the Romans—their temples, their houses—with the art and civilisation represented at the same period by the abject rabble of the catacombs. In the old days, the destruction of the libraries. Isn't that what happened in Russia? The result: a frightful levelling-down."[181] The Nazi philosophy of history thus eviscerated history itself. Time disappeared into a homogenized mass under the weight of a uniform interpretation.

The diversity of real life was compressed to obey a single law, its actors reduced to only two. History was read as a series of recurrent engagements in the same war, fought by unchanging racial antagonists. Nordic man was willing to engage in open combat, like honorable warriors on the battlefield, as he had been in the Greco-Persian Wars or the taking of Jerusalem by Titus. But the Jews took to battle with silence and cunning, hidden in the shadows. The Jews fought using the trickery of conspiracy, a universal Jewish plot that stretched across time and space.

The myth of a Jewish conspiracy possessed two distinct virtues: First, it was universally valid and could be used to explain anything and everything. It was born of a desire to simplify complex problems, a simplification that Hitler credited with his political success, as he confided to Bertrand de Jouvenel: "I will reveal to you what it is that has made it possible for me to rise to my position. . . . Our problems seemed complicated. . . . I however have simplified the problems and have reduced them to the simplest formula. The masses recognized this and followed me."[182] This simplicity was its second virtue. The myth of conspiracy possessed the enormous advantage of subsuming a wide range of enemies into a single figure. In *Mein Kampf,* Hitler coldly explained the propagandistic and political utility of reducing multiple opponents into a single common denominator: "It belongs to the genius of a great leader to make even adversaries far removed from one another seem to belong to a single category, because in weak and uncertain characters the knowledge of having different enemies can only too readily lead to the beginning of doubt in their own right."[183] Doubt could easily corrode faith when one was unanimously rejected by the Social Democrats, the Communists, the Christian Democrats, the churches, and the foreign ministries. It was hard to maintain belief when it appeared that everyone was always against you. Knowing that all such opposition was due to the malice of the protean Jew, who manipulated, owned, or infiltrated everyone and everything, however, was reassuring: one's enemies were not numerous and diverse but solitary and alone. The two sides were not so unequal after all; they formed part of a frontal collision between two forces. The history of antiquity was perfect to validate the transhistorical principle of race war.

CONCLUSION

Nihil novi sub sole: "There is nothing new under the sun." This phrase from Ecclesiastes 1:9, expressing a notion of time repeating itself in cycles, also captures the National Socialist vision of history. The class conflict of material determinism was simply replaced by the racial conflict of biological determinism. Social Darwinism and the racism of a Galton, Chamberlain, or Vacher de Lapouge converged in an unending binary dynamic of two peoples locked in mortal combat. The ideological training materials of the party and its various organs described six thousand years of race war and three thousand years of Jewish hatred for the Indo-Germanic master race. After the great dispersion of 70 CE, the Jews of the diaspora had insinuated themselves within the Nordic West, infiltrating and undermining it from within, but they had also attacked from the outside, raining blows upon the Far East, where they subjugated the

Asiatic and Slavic peoples—a vile, amorphous mass of subhumanity—and used their undeniable Jewish cunning to make these groups serve the Jews' own ends: the Roman Empire was a target of Attila's invasions, while the Reich, Rome's distant successor, was forced to initiate a preventive war against the Soviet Union, the latest wave of a Judeo-Oriental threat that had cloaked itself in the guise of Bolshevism.

And it was a guise: the Jewish menace, protean and ever shifting, had already adopted several others in the past. The Third Reich's propagandists and historians catalogued the genealogy of the Jewish threat since antiquity: Punic Carthage was the Semitic nemesis of Rome before Jerusalem, rebelling against Roman rule, had picked up the banner of the Jewish assault against the Nordic race. Scipio Africanus and later Titus had restored order, but they had unfortunately called off their dogs rather than exterminate the Jewish people, which, spared, had been allowed to wander and settle among the nations. The vast and unsettling reach of the diaspora, even before the destruction of Jerusalem, had profited from the existence of global empires that had built roads and lines of communication throughout the known world and had fostered a peace and security that allowed Jewish traders to move about freely and weave their web. Since antiquity, the Jews' cunning ability to assimilate wherever they went had made itself felt: this foreign body had inserted itself into and blended in with its host organism and become virtually unrecognizable through its cosmetic and vernacular concealment.

The activities of this foreign body were not limited, alas, to mere assimilation. The Jews, faithful in this sense to the essence of their race—defined in *Mein Kampf* as the subversion and desolation of all culture—also aimed to destroy. Little given to open combat under the open sky and further discouraged from such a frontal assault by their defeat on the battlefield at the hands of Rome, the Jews henceforth counted on the clandestine deceit of conspiracy, a tactic developed by the apostle Paul: a Semite converted to Christianity for pure self-interest, Saul/Paul seized upon the Christian message and turned it into a weapon for use against the hierarchical, racial state of the Roman Empire. To shatter and destroy this cultural edifice, he had to mobilize the racially and socially inferior masses, subjugated by the empire, through the use of an egalitarian ideal—if God, as Christ had said, loved all his children equally, then the emperors would be seen to be wearing no clothes. Pauline Judeo-Christianity thus brought down Rome, unleashing his destructive rage and iconoclastic fury against the greatest works of antique civilization, turning the world into an artistic and cultural desert and throwing the world into darkness for a thousand years—the darkness of the Christian Middle Ages.

The strong, harrowing drama of this rewriting of ancient history, particularly that of Rome, was perfect for the construction of the racial enemy as a monstrous terror.

The creature that had successfully brought down Rome now threatened to repeat its triumph against the Reich: the Judeo-Christian conspiracy had transformed into a Judeo-Bolshevik plot. Marxism possessed the same power of eschatological mobilization and promoted the same message of radical egalitarianism that, once again, threatened to unite the inferior rabble in revolt against a Nordic elite.

There truly was nothing new under the sun, then, in this vision of history that rejected a three-dimensional, Heraclitean, unidirectional passage of time. Just as the Jew Saul had become the apostle Paul, the Jew Mardochai had become the communist prophet Marx: the Judeo-Christian conspiracy and the Judeo-Bolshevik plot shared a permanent racial bond in their eternal war. Nazi racism and its biological determinism thus proposed a vision of history that was profoundly ahistorical, at once the permanent, cyclical repetition of itself and a stuttering, narrow-minded hermeneutic principle of race war.

CHAPTER 8

Volkstod or *Rassenselbstmord*

How Civilizations Die

We later civilizations . . . we too now know that we are mortal.

We had long heard tell of whole worlds that had vanished, of empires sunk without a trace, gone down with all their men and all their machines into the unexplorable depths of the centuries, with their gods and their laws, their academies and their sciences pure and applied, their grammars and their dictionaries, their Classics, their Romantics, and their Symbolists, their critics and the critics of their critics. . . .

And we see now that the abyss of history is deep enough to hold us all. We are aware that a civilization has the same fragility as a life.

—Paul Valéry, "The Crisis of the Mind"

Eight days after the Wannsee Conference, en route to Berlin on the evening of 28 January 1942, Hitler queried his entourage: "Do you know what caused the downfall of the ancient world?"[1] Ancient history easily lent itself to idle reflections on grandeur and decadence, rise and fall. As early as 1933, in fact, the National Socialists developed a clinical etiology of the root causes responsible for the deaths of the great civilizations of antiquity, whose symptoms and sources served as warnings and lessons for the present.

Such seemingly idle thoughts touched upon the Nazis' palpable anxiety in the face of a truly terrifying historical event: the demise of two civilizations that seemed destined to last for all eternity. Their recurrent references to antiquity to explain the various causes of *Volkstod*—the "death of a people"—attest to the degree of world-historical importance that they attached to the disappearance of these great and powerful Indo-Germanic civilizations: the spectacle of their sun-bleached ruins, the dusty bones of a decayed racial body, resounded in the Nazi imaginary like a thunderclap, a solemn warning reminding them to remain ever vigilant.

DENATALISM: THE MALTHUSIAN LESSON OF GREECE AND ROME

The Nazis possessed firm pronatalist convictions, even while lamenting the geographical straitjacket of a country they deemed too small for the powerful masses of the German people. Following the example of Jean Bodin and contra Malthus, they believed there was no wealth or strength but in men: a powerful state, with all the economic and political means at its disposal, still required an adequate supply of manpower. Besides, if the Nordic race was truly the foundation of human civilization, it needed to demonstrate this in the flesh, by procreating to produce a large number of fecund people. Finally, the Nazis, in their complete adherence to social Darwinian principles, believed that a numerically inferior people was destined sooner or later to be overrun by a foreign race or fatally infected with its blood. In either case, denatalism was tantamount to signing one's own death warrant.

A population that no longer produced children was a dying population, and history was all too generous in offering up examples that validated this thesis. Most often, it was precisely the most superior peoples and civilizations, those with Nordic blood, that had gradually become too parsimonious with their own seed and thus disappeared. The Nordic civilizations of antiquity that had vanished—historic events of unprecedented size and significance—owed their disappearance in part to their declining birthrates. One SS statistician made something of a cottage industry out of studying ancient birthrates, producing five articles and one short book on the subject between 1935 and 1939. Richard Korherr, who would later be placed in charge of keeping statistics for the Final Solution, published his brief tome in 1935 under the title *Geburtenrückgang: Mahnruf an das deutsche Volk* (Denatalism: A warning to the German people),[2] in which he offered a detailed exploration of the cases of ancient Greece and Rome—a subject he would return to in a statement before the 1937 Congrès international de la population (International Congress on Population Problems) in Paris. In his statement, he argued that the Greeks and Romans, by restricting family size and the number of births, had committed a form of *Rassenselbstmord,* or "racial suicide,"[3] that could not be reversed by the pronatalist policies enacted by the republic and later by Augustus and Tiberius. The establishment of tax breaks for particularly fertile couples, together with penalties for celibacy or sterility in marriage, unfortunately proved ineffective in the face of this Malthusianism *avant la lettre.* Korherr followed that up with a series of four articles in 1938 and 1939 grouped under the collective title "The Death of Ancient Civilizations: An Annotated Statistical Analysis,"[4] which explored these examples in greater depth.

One of Korherr's most attentive readers was Heinrich Himmler, who personally wrote the preface to his 1935 book. The statistician, the Reichsführer-SS wrote, presented "a history and funeral oration for these great peoples that are now dead."[5] Since it was clear that a declining birthrate led inevitably to *Volkstod,* it was essential that the victory of National Socialism also be a victory of German children. Himmler thus recommended the book, as its title suggested, as a warning to the present: history shows us how dominant, self-assured civilizations collapsed in the past because they had failed to pay sufficient attention to propagating and perpetuating their race.

Himmler also made reference to Korherr's work in several of his speeches on the question of German birthrates. In one 1942 speech, he proselytized in favor of a more comprehensive pronatalist policy than anything that had ever been tried before, despite what was admittedly a checkered past for such measures: "It is not enough to say: We will create assistance, tax breaks, good housing, etc. Gentlemen, these measures are as old as the world itself! We find them as far back as Babylon and Rome, before the Roman Empire disappeared, and in Greece, in Sparta and Athens."[6]

The ideological propaganda of the SS also echoed Korherr's ideas. One pamphlet published in 1943, titled simply *Rassenpolitik* (Racial policy), explained over two whole pages how the death of Sparta and that of Rome were both due in large part to declining birthrates that ultimately struck them down.[7]

Hitler himself, in one of his table talks, observed to his companions that the Roman Empire had declined because of a paucity of children, imputable to the spread of a deleterious ideology of materialism and individualism, whose antinatal effects had the gravest political consequences:

Do you know what caused the downfall of the ancient world?
The ruling class had become rich and urbanised. From then on, it had been inspired by the wish to ensure for its heirs a life free from care. It's a state of mind that entails the following corollary: the more heirs there are, the less each one of them receives. Hence the limitation of births.[8]

DEPOPULATION: *SELBSTZERFLEISCHUNG* AND HEMORRHAGING OF THE BLOOD

More than birthrates, it was the phenomenon of depopulation that so vexed the Nazis.

The founders of German scientific eugenics, the biologists and anthropologists Fritz Lenz, Eugen Fischer, and Erwin Baur, were haunted by the deaths of ancient civilizations. How could one explain such unprecedented historical developments as the demise of these powerful cities and states, their huge populations, their flourishing arts and culture? How could one explain the silence of the ruins? The passing of great civilizations resonated like the echo of an apocalypse coming from the depths of time, calling out to the moderns to heed their warning and take all necessary action: the ruins screamed of the need for a state eugenics policy that would allow Germany to avoid the fate of prior dead civilizations. The funeral litany and memory of Greece and Rome emerged as a recurrent obsession in their writings: Fischer possessed an inclination to the Jewish question, while Baur meditated on the biological factors behind the ruin of entire populations, and Lenz packed his work full of references to Greek and Latin history.

In a 1932 article, Erwin Baur investigated "the death of civilized peoples in a biological light":[9] how could one explain the mortality of civilizations that seemed to possess such intimate knowledge of the eternal truths? What did this mean for a present that was all too certain of its immortality? The premise of his study, the event that prompted his central question, was the "collapse of such dramatic rapidity" that beset the great Indo-Germanic peoples of antiquity, "Assyria, Egypt, Greece, Rome."[10] The causes of these peoples' deaths were undoubtedly "of a biological nature."[11]

In his treatise on eugenics, Fritz Lenz outlined its principles with abundant references to Greek and Roman examples. War—especially the countless Roman civil wars or the fratricidal conflicts between the city-states of Greece—had bled these Mediterranean Nordic elites to the bone: "In ancient Greece, the cultural and political elite paid a severe price for their civil wars, which contributed significantly to the disappearance of Hellenic culture."[12] The same could be said for the Roman Empire;[13] "suicidal wars" of that magnitude had also brought down Rome,[14] which lost "a great amount of its best blood": "The population of central Italy was reduced considerably, only to be replenished by the descendants of slaves and emancipated freemen, who came largely from Asia Minor or Egypt."[15]

The idea that these populations lost their life-force to war, particularly the Greek civil wars between racial kinsmen, permeated Nazi-era literature on the ancient world. As Fritz Geyer wrote of the Peloponnesian Wars: "This fratricidal war proved fatal to Greece. It had been conducted with such cruelty and disdain for the lives of their compatriots that its impact on the Nordic elite was thoroughly destructive"[16]—a view shared by Hans Günther[17]—while this "Thirty Years' War in the Peloponnese" was depicted in secondary-school textbooks as "a suicidal massacre"[18] of the Nordic race, comparable only to the conflict that left Germany exsanguinated and devastated in 1648. Ludwig Schemann, meanwhile, wrote of Roman social tensions and subsequent civil wars as forms of "self-extermination." These conflicts were always due to "the same demon that slithered among the Aryans' ranks," the demon of internal division, which took the "unprecedented form of a Nordic civil war during the world war."[19] Richard Walther Darré proved to be the rare exception, perhaps unsurprisingly attributing the depopulation of the ancient world primarily to the Aryans' abandonment of the fields: a Nordic state always recovers from war, thanks to the fertility of its blood, but it perishes when its people fail to tend their land.[20]

For the majority of these writers, war, especially civil or fratricidal war, was destructive to the race. It was always the finest blood that was spilled upon the sands, since only the most valiant and capable of freemen were sent into combat. War, which tore open a "gaping wound"[21] in the racial body, thus had a counterselective effect: "While the elite destroys itself at war, slaves and inferiors ... are able to prosper."[22] We can find a striking echo of these ideas in Hitler's instructions to Speer when giving him the task of developing the Nazis' scorched-earth rearguard tactics for the defense of Germany. Speer, taken aback by such nihilism, delicately attempted to protest but was quickly dismissed by the führer: "In any case only those who are inferior will remain after this struggle, for the good have already been killed."[23]

Not content with just making war and thus withering away through combat, the Nordic elites of Greece and Rome also adopted contraceptive policies that reduced their number and potency even further. As Lenz declared, in a form of indictment: "It was voluntary contraception that delivered the real coup de grace to the Greek people, contraception that, as in modern societies, affects the superior classes above all others."[24] The problem of contraception, which was the product of rampant individualism and a lust for luxury, did not spare Rome either, despite Augustus's pronatalist efforts:[25] "The causes of the death of the Roman Empire [were] in fact similar"[26] to those that were fatal to the Greeks. Civil wars and contraception created a vacuum, Lenz argued, a void that was filled by racially mixed and inferior elements: "In place of the ancient Romans, we see the arrival of emancipated slaves and their descendants, mostly from Asia Minor." The Romans thus shed their best blood and conquered the known world "not for their own people, whom they let die, but for foreign immigrants and the children of their slaves. A racial tragicomedy!"[27]—the tragic extinction of the finest of their race followed by the atrocious burlesque conducted by a people of inferior blood.

War, especially the absurdity of civil war, thus led to a mutation of Roman racial identity. In the place of its original Nordic element, which was decimated, a servile and inferior race managed to impose itself through immigration and social mobility. A 1943 article in the journal *Volk und Rasse* described the phenomenon this way: "They thought they could compensate for the loss of Roman blood by importing massive numbers of slaves—most often from the East. In the beginning, they placed limits on their slaves' ability to procreate, but then gradually they began to accept their progeny as a cheap source of manpower,"[28] before conceding the ultimate generosity of emancipating them. Granting freedom, and then citizenship, to these former slaves "from Asia Minor, Syrians, Punics," as Fritz Geyer charged, created a "massive influx of slaves" that left Rome "thoroughly Easternized."[29] In much the same way, Athenian citizenship had, in its time, been sold off to pay for the Peloponnesian Wars, the Attic city welcoming anyone who would take up arms on its behalf, due to a critical lack of men.[30]

While it was true that, given the wars and consequent weakening of Nordic racial primacy, one could trace the beginning of Roman decline to the Second Punic War, the Nordic race had nevertheless been forced to confront an inferior people much earlier. In essence, the Italian peninsula had never really "housed a pure race,"[31] and the Nordic Italic peoples who settled there had of course come upon a preexisting indigenous population. These two races had cohabited in early Rome, separated into social classes that were, according to the racial scientist Ludwig Schemann, actually racial castes: "Despite some miscegenation, the patricians belonged primarily to the Nordic race, while the plebeians, descendants of the indigenous peoples, had all been Westics. The contrast between patrician and plebeian was thus of a racial nature"[32]—a concept reaffirmed by Fritz Lenz when, citing Vacher de Lapouge, he wrote that "the class struggle is a race struggle."[33] The real war was thus the one that took place between the races, while the Nordic elites had, all too often in the course of their history, wasted their bellicose impulses in fratricidal, intraracial conflicts, the inversion of a healthy martial spirit that should have been directed externally, toward their miscegenated biological enemies.

IN TIBERIM DEFLUXIT ORONTES: THE FALL OF ROME

The carnage of war had numerous consequences. The loss of men and blood, and the changes in Roman custom due to their acclimatization to an Eastern way of life, led the hardy original Romans to turn their backs on working the fields, in order to enjoy the riches of their conquests.

Late Rome witnessed a shift from agriculture based on small landholders to the formation of large capitalistic latifundia, a development that heralded the death of the old Roman peasant identity. Richard Walther Darré's publisher, Verlag Blut und Boden (Blood and soil publishers), put out a book that specifically addressed this phenomenon,[34] exploring the catastrophic consequences of this shrinking dedication to agriculture in the later Roman Empire and echoing the orthodox interpretation of Darré, whose magnum opus, *Das Bauerntum als Lebensquell der nordischen Rasse* (The peasantry as the life-force of the Nordic race), attributed de-Nordification less to the hemorrhaging of Nordic blood on the battlefield and more to the Nordics' abandonment of the fields.[35] This other book, written by Ferdinand Fried and titled *Latifundien vernichteten Rom!* (Latifundia destroyed Rome!), exposed the dramatic consequences of the concentration of land in the hands of a few in the era of the great Roman conquests.

In Fried's account, the price of Rome's wars to conquer Italy and the Mediterranean world was paid largely in the blood of the *Altrömer*, the older Indo-Germanic peasant people. The loss of this original population led to a decline in the inheritance of traditionally cultivated land, which was now left abandoned by peasant-soldiers sent to roam the world carrying the banner of their legions. When the legionnaires were fortunate enough to return home, they came back to a profoundly changed landscape, which had been thoroughly corrupted by the riches accumulated through war: the plundering of the soldiers and their acquisition of loot, as well as the legions' contact with the mercantile East, had infected the virtuous original Romans with a taste for wealth and luxury that led them to see their own soil as property for capitalistic development and not as their hearth and home, fields needing to be plowed, a connection to the memory of their dead—it was now a commodity to be exploited rather than a sacred bond with their race. This culture change led to both the concentration of vacant lands in grand estates, fostering the creation of economies of scale, and a shift in the nature of production.

A food-producing culture, Fried argued, had been overtaken by a culture of speculation; wheat and grains were replaced by wine and oil because the latter had a far higher monetary value and required an equal or lesser amount of labor: "The result of this unscrupulous business practice was a massive overproduction of wine and oil, while at the same time there was a paucity of grains, leading to famine in the towns and cities."[36] These large estates, the latifundia, were run through the exploitation of an army of slaves brought back to Italy by Rome's legions, since the Romans themselves, suffering from the gangrenous effect of luxe and lucre, had lost their taste for hard work and now sought a life of easy gain and speculation. The virtues of the old Romans surrendered to those of an East that had been defeated on the battlefield but ultimately won the war by vanquishing Roman culture. As Juvenal wrote in *Satires* 3.62, "In Tiberim defluxit Orontes"—the Syrian Orontes had polluted the Tiber, a fluvial metaphor perfectly suited for an infection of the blood, the revanchism of a defeated people that took revenge upon their conquerors. Foreign blood now flowed through Rome's veins, corrupting its customs, as seen in the Orientalization of its literature, with hints of overheated Asiatic rhetoric inflecting its formerly strict Attic clarity, as well as in the evolution from the pure Nordic *Lebensbejahung* (affirmation of life) to a thoroughly Eastern pessimism, paving the way for Christianity, a spiritual crime against a healthy racial body now destined for mortification.[37] An entire series of articles expounded upon this moral decadence—the inevitable consequence of racial degeneration—in the *Neue Jahrbücher,* the classics scholars' journal.

One of these articles, titled "The Beginning of Roman Moral Decadence,"[38] blamed the Romans' triumphs in the south and east and the subsequent perversion of the victors by the vanquished: the *mos maiorum,* or "ancient customs," celebrated by Ennius ("Moribus antiquis res stat romana virisque," "The commonwealth of Rome is founded firm on ancient customs and men of might"),[39] which allowed Rome to build its impressive state and conquer the world, those old Roman values of discipline, patriotism, and devotion to the common good—in short, their gravitas—were corroded, warped, or eviscerated by their encounter with the East and a Greece that had been Orientalized over the centuries and had lapsed into the louche pleasures of individualism and immediate gratification. Only the reign of Augustus managed to instill a brief redress of balances, but that was quickly swept away by an inexorable wave of racial mixing and the arrival of emperors who were either Semitic, Eastern, or African. Cato the Elder, who embodied resistance against this decadence for his spirited defense of the traditional values of *Romanitas,* was the subject of another of these articles, in the same issue.[40] The historian Fritz Geyer did not want to be left out, joining in the chorus of lamentations when he wrote: "The age-old idea of the empire in decline. Until then, there was nothing more noble in Roman eyes, whether patrician or peasant, than the res publica: the public was placed above the private, the common good before sectarian interests. . . . But then came the arrival of Eastern materialism."[41]

For Ferdinand Fried, the deserting of the fields and the abandonment of a vigorous rural mentality and food-producing culture, a product of the Romans' renunciation of a healthy and hardy way of life, that of their peasant-soldier ancestors, resulted in nothing more or less than the "destruction of the blood"[42] and all that was Nordic in Rome. The pleasure-seeking mentality fit ill with a spirit of sacrifice and was a parasite that was due precisely to the goodwill of a Nordic race that set out to build states and cultures. Infected by miscegenation, the old blood of the North had been beset by a fatal dose of tetanus: "They soon lost all taste for working the earth" and "became all too quickly accustomed to the idle life of the parasite, which fulfilled all the needs of the Southern man."[43] History instruction in the schools saw scholarly historians and racial scientists fall into lockstep denouncing the fatal results of this contact with the East. The Hohmann and Schiefer textbook lamented the "collapse of morals"[44] in Rome after the victory of the *Urbs.* An SS ideological education pamphlet obediently described how, while the superior character of the Greek and Roman civilizations was due to the purity of their Nordic blood, miscegenation had led to their decadence and ultimate decline.[45]

There is a peculiar physics of space and blood common to all these writings: in the racial body, disruption of a stable demographic blood pressure and what we might call racial hemodynamics meant that any void in this metaphorical vascular system created by the loss of Indo-Germanics was filled by nonnative blood. Greek and Roman population decline thus necessarily led, according to the principles of fluid mechanics, to a fatal process of infiltration and infection.

Hitler, who as we have seen was preoccupied with the demise of ancient civilizations, reduced the story of their disappearance to a single biological cause. As he wrote in *Mein Kampf*, "All great cultures of the past perished only because the originally creative race died out from blood poisoning,"[46] a truth he validated with Greek and Roman literature, as we shall see.

THE DE-NORDIFICATION OF THE ROMAN PEOPLE

Blood poisoning also happened to be the subject of another intriguing article in *Volk und Rasse,* titled "The De-Nordification of the Roman People."

Its author reinterpreted Roman history as the story of inevitable racial decline due to the slow and inexorable dilution of its Nordic blood, which could not be inoculated against the infusion of inferior foreign substances. In a curious but certainly convenient reduction of an entire population to its rulers, the article condensed the history of Rome to that of its succession of imperial dynasties, tracing the evolution, the ebb, and finally the disappearance of their Nordic essence through a careful reading of their facial features as they were cast in stone. While Augustus and Livia were "still of Nordic blood,"[47] the Flavian dynasty seemed to display a shift in the racial center of gravity toward the Phalian (or Dalic) side; the face of Vespasian "could be that of an old peasant from Westphalia." The Flavians nevertheless remained "the last Roman dynasty to be essentially Nordic." Hadrian betrayed "important markers of a non-Nordic mixture," which seemed almost acceptable in comparison to the "strong features foreign to the Nordic race" that belonged to Septimius Severus, a "native of Africa," whose son Caracalla, that great collector of nicknames, was described as a "disgusting bastard" for having "officially legalized racial chaos inside the Roman Empire."[48] The regent who eventually succeeded him, Julia Mamaea, was explicitly depicted as the racial antithesis of "Livia, who was fundamentally shaped by her Nordic essence":[49] the comparison between the two women was tangible evidence of the Romans' loss of racial purity. The reign of Maximinus Thrax (the son of a Goth peasant) offered a brief respite from the slippery slope of degeneration before the inexorable decline resumed with the accession of Philip the Arab—a *Vollblutsemit,* or "full-blooded Semite,"[50] and the son of a bedouin—who owed his reign to the army.

The author, who made frequent use of the observations and categories of Rosenberg and Chamberlain, concluded that "an attentive examination of these ten portraits and a comparison of the traits of Augustus and Livia with those of Caracalla, Julia Mamaea, and Justinian II, for example, shows more clearly than any words could what racial chaos, the chaos of peoples, truly means."[51]

The regrettable degeneration of the Roman people—the ebbing of their Nordic essence—while being hounded, cornered, and driven back on all sides in an unprecedented racial maelstrom, began very early. The article argued that "the first step toward this chaos of peoples, as Chamberlain called it, was taken with the law of 443 before the Common Era, which authorized marriages between patricians and plebeians"—and which could conveniently be compared to "the law of 1823 that sanctioned unions between Germans and Jews."[52] Here the author was following Rosenberg, who had previously argued that the first cases of mixed-race marriage dated back to those between patricians and plebeians. The latter, he declared, were a mass of racially inferior slaves who had been subjugated by a Nordic aristocracy. The borders between social classes aligned with those between races; social marginalization originated with racial inferiority: "By the middle of the fifth century B.C., the first step towards chaos had been taken. Mixed marriages between patricians and plebeians were made legal. Race-mixing thus became for Rome, as it had for Persia and Hellas, the seed of ultimate decay of *Volk* and state." The irreversible decline of Roman civilization and the downfall of its empire thus had very early roots. In this sad history there were only a few, rare exceptions of racial purity: "In these chaotic times, a few men still held true: The powerful, blue-eyed Sulla, the pure Nordic Augustus. But they could not turn the tide."[53] Rome thus lived out the destiny of all empires, all civilizations that violate the laws of nature. Racial degeneration and the dilution of Roman blood led ineluctably to the demise of an entire world. Rosenberg hammered away at the idea that Rome perished because it had forgotten the eternal laws of race and racial struggle. Though it had been the most prestigious creation of Nordic humanity, Rome had defiled itself by tolerating racial miscegenation and become fleeting by forgetting the iron laws of nature. Rome had welcomed the seed of foreign blood with culpable negligence, even to the point of accepting emperors with African blood, like Caracalla. In Rosenberg's eyes, the Syrian Caracalla was guilty for having conferred citizenship upon all the inhabitants of the Roman Empire, in 212 CE, putting an end to Rome's tradition of racial aristocracy, which dated back to its very foundation:

> Influenced by his Syrian mother (daughter of a priest of Baal in Asia Minor), Caracalla, the most loathsome bastard ever to sit on the throne of the Caesars, declared that all "free" inhabitants of the Roman empire were citizens of Rome (212 A.D.).
> So perished the Roman world.[54]

All hierarchies and distinctions based on race disappeared, and the Roman world, once racist and inegalitarian, witnessed the waning of its power, which had been based on the strict and attentive preservation of its racial purity.

The glory of Rome before its "Semiticization" and "negrification" offered a cruel contrast to the degeneration in race and thought via bastardization by the emperors of the middle and late empire.[55] The creation of a model empire was undone by the extension of rights not only to Aryans but to all the inhabitants of the realm. The Indo-Germanic rule of law decayed into flawed universalism with the "race bastard"[56] Caracalla and subsequently with the adoption of Christianity.

The emperors of the late empire "represented all the races of the Mediterranean basin, the Negro race, the Semitic race, the African race, and the Germanic-Roman race":[57] Elagabalus, for instance, was "a Syrian scoundrel" ("ein syrischer Schandbube")[58] to Fritz Taeger and "a repugnant fool" ("ein widerlicher Narr")[59] to Schachermeyr. The son of "half-nomadic Syrian fellahs," Elagabalus made a mockery of Rome and *Romanitas*. He "remained a Syrian"[60] and sought to impose the cult of Baal (Elagabal), of which he was a priest, over all the empire.

The perversion of the Roman legal tradition through racial miscegenation ultimately meant that "ink was stronger than blood"[61]—a dash of a pen, and no longer their blood, determined a person's status. The simple tools of convention and freedom of choice were more important than biological necessity. Schachermeyr made his indictment sharper and more specific by naming two jurists of the late empire, Ulpian[62] and Papinian,[63] both Levantine North Africans, who had left their nefarious mark on a thoroughly Judaized Roman law. Ferdinand Fried followed

Schachermeyr's lead, berating the "Phoenician-Semitic" Ulpian and the "Syrian" Papinian, as well as Salvius Julian, originally from "Africa," and Julius Paulus, "the most important among them, who was in all probability of Semitic origin."[64]

Caracalla, the mastermind of this great racial-legal upheaval, was nothing but a "repulsive bastard."[65] He was, in Fried's words, "of the Oriental-Asiatic race, with the blood of blacks and God knows what other murky mixture coursing through the veins of this horror."[66] For once, Schachermeyr—who wrote that "Caracalla resembled a beast of prey from the African desert"[67]—was outdone for pure invective.

For all these classical scholars of the period who turned to a racial reading of history, and Roman history in particular, the Severan dynasty came in for especially harsh judgment. In his 1943 book on the war between Rome and Carthage, Joseph Vogt included a section on the "Punic people and the Severan dynasty,"[68] in which he interpreted the advent of the African reign of Septimius Severus as the racial revanchism of a Punic people defeated in battle but nevertheless conspiring, underground and in the darkness, while the Romans, who had razed their city to the ground, neglected to exterminate its people. Just as the Orontes polluted the Tiber, Punic blood had stained the imperial purple and corrupted the Palatine Hill.

This analysis was repeated in a more radical (and invective laden) form by Ferdinand Fried, who, in a work titled *Der Aufstieg der Juden* (The rise of the Jews), set aside several pages to discuss the decay of Rome under its Semitic emperors, beginning with Septimius Severus.[69] He described this period, which lasted roughly two centuries, as an "era of terror,"[70] a "dictatorship of terror"[71]—a racial terror created by the unleashing of "Semitic hatred"[72] that had been restrained and repressed for too long by Jews lusting for an opportunity to confront their Nordic superiors.

The range of reasons put forward to explain Rome's decline thus all included the concept of race. Fritz Geyer pointed out that the debate over the root causes of the end of antiquity had plagued the Western mind ever since 476,[73] the many hypotheses offered for the rise and fall of the Roman Empire all being linked by a connection to the racial principle:

> To conclude, one might say that all efforts to explain the end of the ancient world contain an element of truth: intellectual and physical exhaustion (Burckhardt), the destruction of the ancient world's best (Seeck), the clash of civilizations between urbanism and rural barbarity (Rostovtzeff), the struggle with Christianity (Gibbon); all these effectively contributed to the end of

antiquity. But they were but symptoms and not root causes. The cause was the wasting away of the Nordic racial elite that had originally created ancient civilization.[74]

Fritz Schachermeyr, always anxious to turn ancient history into a racial science, was no less categorical: "Racial scientists have established after long study that the decline and dissolution of the Greek and Roman peoples was due to the influence of non-Nordic blood and thus a spirit foreign to the race."[75] Germans had to learn their lessons from history and be ever vigilant to preserve their Nordic blood from any miscegenation: "No one can argue that the Greek people dissolved among the non-Nordic, Aegean blood that interbred with them, or that the Roman people were fatally wounded by the influx of blood foreign to the race: as a result, we must reject all that is not Nordic and refuse to be drawn down into the same history as the Greeks and Romans."[76]

The thesis of decline through miscegenation was not just the product of a young generation full of ambition and the desire to become the masters of the moment or ride the fashionable new wave of the times. It was promoted just as vigorously by established scholars and eminent academics, like the venerable Ernst Kornemann, who was already emeritus when he organized a 1940 conference on the grandeur and decadence of the Roman Empire, the predecessor and precursor to the Greater German Reich in its reshaping of the political geography of Europe. For Kornemann, the decline of the empire was the result of "miscegenation and the degradation of the race, which replaced the old Roman peasantry of the imperial era with a mishmash of peoples."[77]

A WARNING TO GERMANY

Historians of antiquity and party ideologues were interested in creating a version of the death of ancient civilizations that confirmed the Nazi vulgate concerning racial and cultural degeneration through miscegenation. This was the message that teachers of history were supposed to convey to German youth. The 1933 "Directives for History Textbooks" specified that the death of Greek civilization had to be read as an example of racial decline as a result of the Greeks' failure to protect their Nordic roots. It stated that the Nordic conquerors who had established Greece were but a "minority" who had been forced to deal with masses of indigenous peoples, and subsequently slaves, who were largely of "Asiatic origin." The line separating superior from inferior had been breached by the advent of democracy and its deleterious egalitarianism: "With the suppression of distinctions between the castes through democracy and the rapid, increasing racial miscegenation that it caused, accentuated to an even further degree by population decline (see Polybius!), the fate of the Nordic race in Greece was sealed, and the decline of Greek civilization metastasized so rapidly that in hardly two hundred years the Greek people were reduced to the most utter insignificance." The pronouncements contained in the Prussian official bulletin made explicit reference, as we have seen, to the work of Hans Günther on the racial history of the Greeks and Romans: teachers were to recite the sad story of death by blood poisoning. The history of Rome was little other than a long funeral dirge for a race that neglected the reason for its greatness and died as a result: "The Nordic element of the Roman people was soon completely destroyed by incessant wars. Under the reign of Tiberius, there remained no more than six of the old patrician lines! The overwhelming majority of the Italian population was composed of descendants of Eastern slaves. The desperate nature of the situation was a source of the ferment that led to the Stoic ideology of the Romans. Thus, by the beginning of the millennium, the de-Nordification of southern Europe was virtually complete."[78]

The curricular reform of 1938 went one step further than the directives of 1933. Textbooks and teachers had to show how "contempt for the unforgiving law of race led these peoples to the ruin of their blood and their soul and thus to degeneration and death."[79] The facts had to demonstrate that "the Peloponnesian War was a fratricidal war that exterminated the race," leading to "the racial estrangement of Athens." The de-Nordification of the Attic city-state was the subject of some resistance from "a few isolated voices, notably that of Plato," whose message was to be taught despite its ultimate failure. After the fifth century BC, when the Nordic race committed suicide through a fratricidal conflict and the hemorrhaging of its finest blood, the subsequent centuries were defined by deplorable miscegenation, a "Hellenism [that] is the very definition of a culture of interbreeding." With this interbreeding, the Hellenistic era foreshadowed the Roman Empire, which was characterized by "Hellenistic, Eastern, and Jewish influences," the "power of capital, the emptying of the fields, and cosmopolitanism"— in sum, a "deracinated imperial civilization, as opposed to the peasant civilization of the North."[80]

Textbooks followed these instructions to the letter. A brief look at the table of contents of Walter Gehl's tome discussed earlier speaks volumes:[81] one lengthy chapter discussed "the racial degeneration of the Greeks," including sections on "spiritual contamination by a supercilious Enlightenment" and the "weakening of the Greeks' racial force through the fratricidal massacre of the thirty-year Peloponnesian War" before "the destruction of a race, people, and state by unchecked democracy" and "failure in the fight against racial decline." The story remained the same for the fifth century BC, a harbinger and cause of the final destruction of Nordic Greece through Hellenism. One chapter discussed the "complete decoupling of blood and soil in Hellenism," particularly in the cities, which received special treatment: "the urban and cosmopolitan civilization of Hellenism as a culture of racial interbreeding." As for Rome, various sections addressed "the de-Nordification of the Roman elite in a constant struggle for power," which occupied republican Rome before the empire washed away its Nordic blood in a flood of peoples: "The Dissolution of the Ancient World into Racial Chaos" was the title of one chapter, presaging another, titled "The Orientalization of the Blood and Spirit of the Empire."

The educational propaganda furnished to the Hitlerjugend also helped popularize this reading of antiquity. In one pamphlet, Walter Gross, the head of the Office of Racial Policy, informed German youth about the imperative to display loyalty to two concepts: loyalty to the führer and loyalty to the idea of race were the surest ways to guarantee the survival of the German people and ensure their victory.[82] In the text—whose title, *Deine Ehre ist die Treue zum Blute deines Volkes* (Your honor is loyalty to the blood of your people), recalled the motto of the SS[83]—Gross presented his young readers with Greek history as tragedy, the abandonment of their race, an act of treason committed by an Indo-Germanic people against their own blood. While Indo-Germanic immigrants had long refused to interbreed with the indigenous population, "their racial conscience weakened, little by little, [and] interbreeding with the contemptible peoples they had subjugated became more frequent until it became the rule and, instead of a pure-blooded Nordic elite, there were more and more bastards. Hand in hand with this development came the weakening and degeneration of their old spirit and energy." Interbreeding was a tragic historical and racial error, accepted by those Greeks who had previously been careful to preserve their racial purity and who ended up losing their Nordic essence, diluted and ultimately drowned in a tidal wave of foreign blood: "Here too the story ends with the decline of a great people and the loss of their superior culture, which Greece still bears traces of today in its ancient stone, while its inhabitants no longer possess anything in common with that fierce race of long ago."[84]

The SS were also trained by a racial scientist who drew upon the history of the ancients. Thus, the story of Jason and Medea also imparted a lesson about the danger of Nordic blood being infected by inferior foreign substances, in an article published in the organization's "leadership magazine," *SS-Leitheft*. It is hardly surprising that the SS should take an interest in the Argonauts, those Greek heroes who set off in search of the Golden Fleece in distant Colchis, a fabulous and far-off land situated on the eastern shore of the Black Sea. The expedition of the Argonauts became a metaphor for the *Drang nach Osten* of the Indo-Germanic armies of the Reich, and the myth of Jason resonated with them as a warning to SS soldiers deployed to the eastern front, where they were strictly prohibited from any sexual relationship with the women they encountered there.

As told by the SS for the SS, the tragedy of Medea became in essence a tragedy of racial interbreeding, of "interracial marriage," as the title of the magazine article indicated.

The article began by recalling how the Greeks, "that ancient civilized people of Nordic blood,"[85] were conscious of the value of their blood. Their mythology condemned any racial mixing outright, just like the "laws of the führer"[86] in contemporary Germany. The Argonauts were led by Jason, a true hero, "healthy and handsome as a god," his shoulder-length hair "a shining blond splendor,"[87] an Apollonian figure of Indo-Germanic racial purity. But even this Nordic hero could unfortunately be tempted by and succumb to the charms of a foreigner, the Caucasian Medea, "a barbarous foreigner to the race." After two years of apparent happiness, the couple were torn asunder when Jason, increasingly aware of "the difference between their races," turned to "a woman of his own kind," Creusa. Medea then unleashed all the violence and perversion inherent in her blood, poisoning Creusa and killing her own children. What for Euripides was the tragedy surrounding the death of a great love became for the SS a tragedy of racial interbreeding and its horrific consequences, symbolized in the myth by the killing of Jason's sons—and thus the extinguishing of his line—and the murder of a spouse from his own race, the womb of his future pure blood: "The marriage between Jason and Medea was thus a union between two people of different races, a blood sin, according to not only our customs but also those of the original Greeks."[88] With this story, "the ancient legend of Nordic conquerors,"[89] the Greeks sought to "depict the consequences of a racial intermarriage."[90] But they did not heed the laws of nature or their own myths; the fate of Jason was also the fate of their entire people.

The same fatal racial mistake also brought down Rome. An SS pamphlet illustrated such physical differences in images—for visual learners—portraying the visage of Augustus side by side with that of an anonymous "bourgeois Roman during the empire's decline." The text accompanying the illustration commented: "This image shows two Romans from antiquity. The first still bears pure Nordic blood, like those who built the Roman Empire. The second presents without a shadow of a doubt all the symptoms of blood miscegenation, the penetration of blood from Asia Minor into the once Nordic body of the people."[91]

The party helpfully also provided a summary of Nazi thought on the causes of the rise and fall of Greece and Rome in other propaganda materials. One of these pages explained that for a long time the Greeks had "applied the strictest racial laws and most radical measures of selection"[92] and had thus been able to maintain the quality of their blood and the fecundity of their culture—but that their fate was sealed when they lowered their guard: "Absolute foreigners became Athenians, and democracy entrenched itself.... The death of this precious Nordic blood in a sea of peoples meant that those who once were capable of maintaining a certain cultural greatness became ossified and consumed the last of their precious reserves of pure blood." Its author applied the same formula to Roman history—"The same unfolded in Rome, as in Greece"[93]—before summarizing the sad but edifying racial history of the Roman people.

ON DEMOCRACY AS RACIAL BASTARDIZATION

In this racialized historiography, everything could be seen as a sign of either biological health or decay. From this perspective, democracy was viewed as both a symptom and a catalyst of Athens' racial bastardization.

There was one variant of true, sane democracy—the Nordic variety, of course, described by Tacitus in his book on the Germanic peoples as an assembly of the *Stamm*, or tribe, called simply the *Thing*. An oligarchy of social betters in the strictest sense, an aristocratic gathering, this version of Germanic direct democracy was appropriated by Hitler in *Mein Kampf*[94] and later by Joseph Goebbels in the special edition of the *Völkischer Beobachter* devoted to Greece and the Olympic Games. There, in the same space used to welcome the people of the world to the opening of the games, Goebbels proclaimed that Nazi Germany was actually a true democracy—for the fundamental principle of democracy is that "what is good for the people should be carried out. . . . The best among the people are called upon to fulfill this mission. They are the sponsors of an aristocratic democracy that, through a process of continual selection, raises the elect to positions of authority, since they possess the will and the art of leadership."[95] After this semantic parlor trick, it was all too easy for the Nazis to repudiate Athenian democracy as a false conception of the ideal: the government of a free people that voted on its own laws was a far cry from the censorious and highly exclusivist model of Germanic democracy.

In the same vein, the Hellenist and historian Hans Bogner used an essay on the grandeur and decline of Greek democracy[96] to describe how the Athenian model, created in the spirit of a true *Adelsherrschaft,* or "aristocracy" (the subject of his first chapter), had degenerated into a demagoguery that had ultimately proved fatal to the Attic power after the gradual widening of the electoral body and the triumph of political clientelism, with demagogues pandering to the people by encouraging all-out war—a practice that enriched themselves while leaving the city-state in ruins. Bogner frequently cited and commented upon the comedies of Aristophanes, particularly *The Wasps* and *The Knights,*[97] in which the Athenian playwright mercilessly mocked the class-based politics of Cleon, whose popularity was based on a war that provided the miserable class of serfs, the *thetes,* with money and loot by prolonging a conflict in which the fleet and its masses of proletarian rowers played a primary role. Bogner was simply repeating and elaborating upon the almost sociological criticism of previous detractors of democratic Athens, who had pointed out the fundamental ambiguity in the term *demos*—which could mean either a sovereign people, in all their Rousseauean majesty, or an entire populace in the widest sense, the vile and teeming masses that a demagogue capably flattered in both word and deed. Hohmann and Schiefer's history textbook described Athenian democracy as a simple "question of food and pleasure,"[98] while its counterpart by Walther Gehl dedicated several pages to the various vices of the Attic democracy.[99]

In another of his essays, this one on the formation of a political elite, Bogner fused democracy and mesocracy, or the rule of the middle classes; in this reading, democracy was fundamentally based upon a hatred of power, its compulsory egalitarianism seeking to demolish the figure of the leader, incapable of tolerating the concept of individual or group superiority:[100] "The ever present opposition to Sparta, whether noble or common, was simply eliminated by fiat, as if each individual were equal to everyone else. The commoners were eager to believe this, out of pride or ambition."[101]

Bogner noted that, in an era characterized by the decadence and disintegration of Athenian power, only one man, Alcibiades—a dignified representative of the old nobility—could have saved the ancien régime, but democracy would not allow this, for the very greatness of his character stood as an insult to the mediocrity of the masses: "It was everyone's opinion that [Alcibiades] could have saved the state," but "he never had the chance, for the common man took umbrage at his greatness."[102] Full of envy, "the masses could only be wary of him," and so Alcibiades saw this mediocre majority form a coalition against him, the spiteful *vulgum pecus* getting the better of him through the grotesque farce of accusing him of sacrilege in the Hermes affair, which ultimately sent this great Athenian on a mission out of the city. The crime of the democratic regime was thus to rid itself of its natural führer for the mere fact of his superiority compared to the middling masses, who as a last resort abused their suffrage to impose their will: "The power of the mass tolerates no leader nor suffers any man who unmistakably distinguishes himself from the mass and thus blatantly contradicts the fiction of equality."[103]

This union of the weak constituted a force capable of bringing down and destroying the strong: democracy as a *Massenherrschaft* (mass rule) and not a proper, healthy *Adelsherrschaft* (aristocracy) thus revealed itself to be counterselective. The friend of mediocrity and foe of the born leader, democracy was to Fritz Geyer little more than a movement toward "leveling, that rejects any dominant personality, that promotes the ideal of absolute equality before the law and in the practice of government (*Isonomia* and *Isegoria*)." The institution of ostracism, which originally came about to prevent any efforts to establish a tyranny, "revealed itself to be a weapon in the class struggle, in which it devolved into the rejection of any man who raised himself above the level of the vulgar mass."[104] What had originally been a democracy in the Nordic-Germanic sense, a racial oligarchy, had degenerated into the "tyranny of the mass,"[105] the ochlocracy described and deplored by Aristotle in book 6 of his *Politics*.[106]

This critique of democracy's main drawback, its unerring tendency to find the lowest common denominator, can be traced back, as one might expect, to a racial scientific reading of the past.[107] Emerging from the thoughts and pens of the Frenchmen Joseph Arthur de Gobineau and Georges Vacher de Lapouge, this interpretation of democracy was picked up and popularized by Alfred Rosenberg, who argued that the triumph of democracy over the monarchical or aristocratic forms of governance that had characterized archaic Greece was a sure sign of racial degeneration. The advent of democracy marked nothing less than the victory of the mass of slaves and undesirables over the racial elite of the leadership class: "This democracy was not the rule of the people but the dominion of the Near East over the Greek tribes, whose manpower and strength were being rapidly dissipated."[108]

For Rosenberg, democracy was not simply a political system but a symptom of a racial pathology, miscegenation and degeneration. Democracy, in promoting the ideal of equality before the law and freedom of speech, was the antithesis of a healthy aristocracy based upon the racial greatness of the few. He got this notion from an author to whom he affectionately paid homage in a speech given in Paris in late 1940: Joseph Arthur de Gobineau.[109] For Gobineau, nineteenth-century France was a theater of racial miscegenation without precedent. Truly pure races (whether white, yellow, or black) had not existed for a long time. But France suffered from racial mixing on a level never before seen. The symbol of this miscegenation, after the French Revolution, was its democratic government.

Gobineau's theory was deterministic: when blood mixed, all grandeur and order disappeared, along with purity and nobility; miscegenation left mankind "stunted, abased, enervated, and humiliated in the persons of its noblest sons."[110] All that was racially superior vanished in a sea of mixed-race blood.

The disappearance of blood nobility and superiority was reflected in a people's political, legal, and social ideas. A mixed-blood society that no longer possessed any nobility could hardly conceive of the notion of inequality: "When the majority of the citizens have mixed blood flowing in their veins, they erect into a universal and absolute truth what is only true for themselves, and feel it to be their duty to assert that all men are equal."[111] Egalitarian democracy was thus the political ideology of interbred peoples, who exalted and concealed their impure and miscegenated nature under a cloak of universal normativity. Equality and democracy were vital ideals for a miscegenated, degenerate portion of humanity. No one of pure race could have feverishly conjured up the doctrine of the republic or the equality of man, the ideas of what Gobineau called a *raisonneur métis*, or "mixed-race thinker."[112]

Gobineau thus displayed a symptomatic reading (*lecture symptomale*) of democracy, turning it into a sure and terrifying sign of mankind's ineluctable march toward nothingness.

This theory would be reprised in the work of Georges Vacher de Lapouge, another of Rosenberg's favorites. Vacher de Lapouge wrote that "contemporary democracy corresponds to the appearance of new ethnic groups, brachycephalous masses that strive for power.... The tendency toward uniformity is an unmistakable sign of regression."[113] The principle of human equality espoused by democracy signified the death of any racial elite and its submersion into the confusion of miscegenation: "Mass politics is the flattening of all that is superior and the enslavement of all that is independent."[114]

His ideas were well encapsulated by Karl Kynast, in his *Apollon und Dionysos:* "We know well that men of inferior race, like bastards, deny all distinctions between the races of man and, at the same time, the differences of caste that rest upon these differences of nature. As soon the miscegenation of races and empowerment of the inferior begins, no principle is as widely preached and encouraged as the democratic principle, by which all mean are supposedly created equal."[115] In this racial and political debacle, which afflicted Republican France just as it had ancient Greece, Rosenberg portrayed Plato as a noble, pure representative of Nordic Hellas trying to oppose the triumph of democracy over aristocracy through the ferocious critiques contained in his writings. Rosenberg was not, in fact, mistaken about Plato's general intentions: he was opposed his whole life to the type of Athenian democracy that had killed Socrates. Plato's political writings, like those of Xenophon, rest within a tradition of aristocratic philo-Spartanism, a reaction against and resolute opposition to the democracy of Athens that had culminated in the rule of the Thirty Tyrants toward the end of the Peloponnesian Wars. Rosenberg went so far as to align Plato with the views of Callicles, Socrates's opponent in the *Gorgias:*

> In the *Gorgias*, Plato vainly makes Callicles proclaim the wisest of messages: "The law of nature demands that the higher breeds rule over the lower."[116]

Rosenberg's scripting of the end of classical Greece contained an unequivocally racial reading of events. To him, the Greeks had forgotten all too quickly that they had a race to maintain in the fullness of its purity and beauty, superior blood that required protection against any mixing with inferior, Asiatic species. They were thus unable to escape the vengeance of this Asiatic blood, anthropomorphized into a terrible avenging angel at the outset of Rosenberg's work: "None who have disregarded the religion of the blood have escaped this nemesis—neither the Indians nor the Persians, neither the Greeks nor the Romans."[117] It was a case of blood vengeance: the Greeks, who had accepted interbreeding, were irremediably bastardized and had succumbed to an inexorable decline. Thus miscegenated, the Greeks became Levantines, who were no longer truly Greek but for their peculiar semantic abuse of the term. The very name *Greek* became worthless, and what had once designated the most beautiful offshoots of the Nordic race now assumed a pejorative connotation: the "deceitful Hither Asiatic trader entered [the polis]," making it so that "lies and falsehood later formed the constant background of 'Greek' life, which occasioned Lysander to the words that one cheats children with dice, men with oaths."[118]

Their slow disappearance would not, however, be completely in vain. Before becoming interbred, the Greeks had valiantly fought against Asia, as the Greco-Persian Wars could attest. It was only after reinforcements from the North, those waves of immigrating Nordic peoples, had dried up that the Greeks had finally fallen. Nevertheless, they had, at least for a time, kept the subhuman Asiatics at bay; without them, these hordes would have washed over European soil far earlier. In the Nordics' great battle against their enemies—in this instance, Asia—the Greek era had thus had a dilatory effect: "And yet even in his deepening twilight, the Greek had stemmed the incursion of Asia and scattered his own brilliant gifts all over the world, gifts which inspired the Nordic Romans and later became the greatest heritage of the Germanic West." Even at the hour of their retreat, the Greeks had slowed the Asiatic advance and passed the torch of civilization to the Romans. Rosenberg here repeated the ancient and medieval idea of *translatio studiorum et imperii*, the "transfer of power and knowledge" from Greece to Rome, and later from Rome to the Germanic West. Rome had succeeded Greece as the historical incarnation of Aryan-Nordic mankind and as the defender of the purity of its blood: "Rome had, with its sword, long held off the scourge from Asia Minor, which was only growing stronger."[119]

De-Nordification was thus the key concept to understand and accept the otherwise inconceivable decline of such great ancient civilizations. The deaths of Greece and Rome were a veritable racial Götterdämmerung, a thoroughly Germanic twist on tragedy. According to Schachermeyr, Greek history was pregnant with "the same Nordic tragedy that, later, the Germanics would express in their myth of the end of the world and that, much later, Richard Wagner would capture in *The Ring of the Nibelung*. It thus constitutes a subject that invites us to reflect and places us on guard against the fatal destiny of de-Nordification."[120]

The reign of Alexander the Great and the Hellenistic period following the era of Athenian democracy in the fifth century BC showed in greater detail the nefarious consequences of this de-Nordification.

ALEXANDER AND THE HELLENISTIC PERIOD: THE GREAT RACIAL MAELSTROM

The Hellenistic period was despised and condemned for having been a sort of counterantiquity, the antithesis of the Nordic miracle in all its cultural and racial greatness. Presented as an early era of globalized migration, exchange, and culture, it opened the floodgates—and the veins of the racial body—to mixing with foreign blood. But there could be no Hellenistic period without Alexander and the integration of different lands under the aegis of the Alexandrine Empire, later divided among the Diadochi, who left their successors with the same Greek culture, or close to it. The figure of Alexander, like the era of glory that now bears his name, thus posed a fundamental conundrum: How should Alexander be depicted? Should he be celebrated as a Nordic conqueror or condemned as the man who permitted the kind of racial miscegenation that proved fatal to the Hellenic world, leading to a decadent and deleterious Hellenism? On the one hand, Alexander the Macedonian was a perfect Nordic specimen, with blond hair and blue eyes; on the other, he dreamed of a universal kingdom and enjoined his lieutenants to marry young women from just-conquered Persia to fuse together the elites of the two cultures. Furthermore, he left behind a world primed for unfortunate racial and cultural globalization.

The Alexander conundrum was the focus of much discussion among historians of antiquity. For Fritz Schachermeyr, "Alexander was an Indo-Germanic endowed with predominantly Nordic blood, there can be no doubt."[121] His racial superiority and the quality of his blood as a Nordic man explained the greatness of his many successes in combat, a campaign still unequaled, and meant he could be deployed as a positive example of the Indo-Germanic race: his wars were, as Fritz Taeger wrote, an "intoxicating victory for the West,"[122] and the echoes of his many triumphs resounded "to this day."[123]

But his project of universal rule through the fusion of races proved to be "dangerous for the race."[124] He made the creation of a world empire his ultimate goal, when it should have been but a means to defend and strengthen his race: "World empire represented in his eyes a cardinal value; everything was subordinate to it." This was the classic error of the

Nordic conqueror, given over to hubris and lured by the ideal of unifying the known world under a single power. He thus forgot about the dignity and preeminent importance of his Nordic blood, which was reduced to the same rank of all other blood types, as a mere building block for the creation of an empire: "For him it was all just pliable material,"[125] leading him to treat the Greeks, the Persians, and all other peoples as though they were of the same rank and level. Since "the idea of race" had "ceased to represent a positive value" in his eyes, Alexander resorted to the "fusion of peoples"; as Schachermeyr wrote, "It was the *raison d'état* of world empire that dictated his idea for interbreeding."[126] Taeger commented that it was hubris, in wresting him from his native land and setting him off on the route to world conquest, that had caused Alexander to forget his duties to his blood: "The conqueror uprooted himself from the soil that nourished him and gave him victory. He became the successor to the Achaemenids, a great Asiatic king, a master of the world who sought to don the royal costume of the Medo-Persians and who tried to introduce the custom of *proskynesis* [prostration before superiors], which caused the otherwise penitent Spartans sent to greet him to object."[127]

Beyond the Alexandrine example, it was the very notion of a world empire neglectful of racial hierarchy that seemed deleterious. Schachermeyr reproached Caesar just as he did Alexander; the Roman, who was also a Nordic, had had a similar leveling project for world empire—but fortunately he had been stopped in his tracks, also like Alexander, by his premature death.[128] Augustus would prove to be more cautious in preserving Roman racial superiority.[129]

The general opprobrium was such that the *Brockhaus* encyclopedia published in 1937 went so far as to contrast the Nordic father Philip—the proud, beautiful archetype of a Greek Indo-Germanic king—with the degenerate son Alexander: "His son Alexander the Great unified all of the Hellenic world against Persia and established an immense empire. But that also marked the beginning of the dissolution of the Greeks' racial superiority. The cultural and racial fusion of the Greeks and Asiatics led to an alteration of the Hellenic spirit."[130] The same contrast between Philip and Alexander appeared in one of Schachermeyr's essays on the figure of the leader in Greek antiquity.[131] Philip of Macedon resuscitated the ideal of the Nordic führer after a period of democratic egalitarianism caused by the racial decline of Athens. The Macedonian king was rehabilitated and exalted, particularly in comparison to Demosthenes; Philip was "a soldier-king of the purest type, in every respect the true offspring of the Nordic Macedonian people."[132]

His son, however, although endowed with "personal potential beyond [that of] the ordinary human," had betrayed the "Nordic *Führerprinzip,*" or cult of the leader, for he had "removed himself from his own people." Alexander had become "the representative of the idea of world domination," which "was foreign to the Nordic race and came primarily from the Asiatic East."[133] Alexander had betrayed his race, even though it had fought valiantly against Asia during the Greco-Persian Wars. The weddings at Susa—his attempt in 324 BC to conjoin the Greek and Persian elites—were roundly and unanimously condemned. The intermixing of blood occurred, as always, to the detriment of the biologically superior. One secondary-school history textbook commented bitterly that "this merger was less a Hellenization of the Persians than an Orientalization of the Greeks."[134]

In *The Myth of the Twentieth Century,* Rosenberg put forward a more nuanced reading of Alexander's venture, in an effort to rehabilitate this hero of the race. He emphasized that the Macedonian was trying to intermarry not the entire population but rather just the Greek and Persian elites. The nobility of the Persian Empire, of course, had also come from the Nordic race. The Alexandrine project was thus not a repugnant attempt at interbreeding so much as a means to rejoin the Persian elite to their original people: "Through Alexander, a more disciplined idea of late Greek life, primarily aesthetic, once again predominated. . . . Alexander did not unconditionally pursue the aim of a world monarchy and the mixing of peoples, but wished only to unite the Persians and Greeks, recognized as racial kindred, and to bring them under one rule, so as to avoid further wars." As proof of Alexander's racial bona fides, Rosenberg pointed out that he "only placed Macedonians or Persians in leading posts, whereas Semites, Babylonians and Syrians were deliberately excluded."[135] In addition, he made the Asiatic subjects of his empire kneel to address him, whereas "with his Macedonians he acted as with comrades,"[136] having quickly given up on Orientalizing pretensions such as the idea of introducing *proskynesis* among the Greeks. Rosenberg conceded, however, that the overall balance sheet of the results of Alexander's ambitions was negative: the Alexandrine Empire and his project of world domination by a Nordic-Macedonian elite did not last, for their "cultural offshoots . . . were not permanent enough. . . . The subjugated alien blood triumphed, the time of clever but characterless Hellenism began."[137]

For the racial scientist Ludwig Schemann, the Alexandrine era, which led to the Hellenistic period, was one of "racial destruction,"[138] an "era of imitators and half-breed bastards—bastards in both blood and culture."[139] Schachermeyr, in *Indogermanen und Orient,* described this later Hellenistic period as one of "fusion and interbreeding between the Greeks and the East,"[140] a "marriage (or one should say a crossing) of East and West."[141] At first glance, one might think that the Alexandrine conquest had led to the lasting establishment of Greek culture in a global ecumene united under the ferule of the Diadochi and their followers. In reality, however, this apparent triumph of Greek Nordicity was but an illusion. While it seemed that Nordic-blooded Greeks and Macedonians had ruled the world through Hellenization, Taeger retorted that "this Nordic layer was oh so fine":[142] this "superficial Hellenization" was but a "thin skin"[143] that masked the reality of a new racial balance of power. Under the surface of Hellenization and the apparent domination of the world by Nordic blood, "the opposition forces of oppressed peoples and races were at work,"[144] for the Greeks had entered into contact with the "foci of Semitic subversion," cunning and malignant peoples from the East who sought to infiltrate the Greek ranks surreptitiously: "They unlearned their maternal language and were, apart from all that they could not similarly acquire, hard to distinguish from the Greeks."[145] Schachermeyr agreed that this interbreeding lumped what remained of "Nordic culture" in the same gallimaufry with "signs of Westic-Mediterranean culture and, later, Armenoid subversion." Anything that was good in that unhappy era of racial interbreeding was due to the creative strength of Nordic blood: "The Nordic force still expressed itself through Hellenistic arts and sciences." In this Hellenistic culture, however, it was the "Westic-Mediterranean" blood that predominated, engendering a "sophism" and a "rhetoric"[146] that belonged more to the *esprit*—Schachermeyr used the French term, understood in a pejorative sense—than to a philosophy that was fundamentally Indo-Germanic, Greek, and German:[147] "*L'esprit* alone remained on the page; the old Greek way of thinking became more and more rare."[148] Hans Günther shared Schachermeyr's racial-cultural condemnation. Hellenism, the criminal denaturalization of Nordic Greece, was essentially the work of imposters: "The Hellenistic civilization sterilely imitated the old Greek culture, destroying or disowning it." There was no doubt in the racial scientist's mind that "Hellenistic and Alexandrine culture were the intellectual creations of a de-Nordified and degenerate era."[149] The product of criminal miscegenation and an exsanguinated Nordicity, this culture was the sublimated expression of a very real physical mutation as well. The mixing of blood led to the physical deformity of the beautiful Greek archetype, as demonstrated, for example, by the darkening of their hair.[150] This mutation of the phenotype corresponded to a change in the Greek mind, which lost its sense of perspective that stemmed from its Nordic, Apollonian spirit. The Asiatic and Semitic influence distorted the now degenerate Greek, leading him toward belief in an imaginary beyond[151] and an immoderate love of the intellectual and abstract: "The Hellene had become the *graeculus* of the Romans, a slave to study . . . , which for the traditional—that is to say, the Nordic—Romans was something ridiculous and a terrible shame."[152]

THE PROPHECY OF THE APOCALYPSE: LESSONS FROM THE DEMISE OF ANCIENT CIVILIZATIONS

National Socialist eschatology foresaw the coming of a decisive battle and prophetically anticipated the abominable consequences of defeat. The Nazis' eschatology was apocalyptic: they prophesized complete and utter chaos should the Aryan race suffer the ultimate loss.

Rosenberg's warning in *The Myth of the Twentieth Century* left no doubt; if the Aryan were to lose, the world would plunge into turmoil: "If it [the Aryan myth] does not triumph in the great struggle which is coming, the west and its blood will perish just as India and Hellas are dissolved forever in chaos."[153] The demise of Athens and Rome offered terrible warnings: "A complete triumph of this 'humanity' would have the same consequences as once the victory of Hither Asia over Athens and Rome, so that the latter, once the deadly enemy of the Etruscan-Pelasgian-Syrian world, became virtually the chief representative of these same forces after the original values of ancient Rome had collapsed."[154] In his table talks, Hitler also backed this notion with examples from ancient history: "It was the destiny of all the civilised States to be exposed to the assault of Asia at the moment when their vital strength was weakening. First of all it was the Greeks attacked by the Persians, then the Carthaginians' expedition against Rome. . . . And now we're facing the worst attack of all, the attack of Asia mobilised by Bolshevism."[155] A fate like that of Rome awaited the Reich and all of Nordic-Germanic mankind if they did not react and fight with all their might against the Jewish menace in its present form: the rampant Asiatic hordes under Stalin's iron rule.

Nazi racial discourse was also apocalyptic. It was all revelations, end times, the imminence of the final battle, and the terrible prophecy of utter devastation and disarray in the event of an Aryan defeat.[156] The Nazis kept repeating that the hour of the decisive battle was at hand, that it would settle the question once and for all, annihilating one of the two combatants and leaving the victor finally triumphant. The hour had come for the Aryans and the Jews to end their millennial race war. In *The Myth of the Twentieth Century,* Alfred Rosenberg forewarned that "with the increasing dilution of this Germanic blood . . . the entire culture of the West must perish," adding that "today, we have the terrible awareness that we are face to face with a final decision."[157] In a 1935 speech to the members of the Nordische Gesellschaft (Nordic society), he situated the Nordic race in steadfast opposition to the Judeo-Bolshevik destroyer that threatened to overrun the world. These two giants were sharpening their swords and preparing their weapons for the final showdown, a *Schicksalkampf,* as Rosenberg proudly declared:

> We are today, in the present circumstances, perfectly aware that a decisive battle, that concerns our destiny, our substance, and our essence, is at hand, a battle on a scale never before seen.[158]

This battle would be without mercy: "The Nordic idea, as the renaissance of all creative forces, and international communism are now spiritually face to face in a terrible and ruthless battle."[159] This exhortation in favor of mobilizing the country's full energies toward the destruction of its racial enemies found its apogee in Joseph Goebbels's proclamation of total war in a speech at the Berlin Sportpalast on 18 February 1943. Given at a time of crisis, sixteen days after the surrender of *Generalfeldmarschal* Friedrich von Paulus at Stalingrad, the speech proclaimed the total mobilization of the German people for the final battle, which would be a matter of life or death. This battle would not leave victors and vanquished, like other wars, but only "those who survive and those who are destroyed."[160] Goebbels repeatedly stressed that "Stalingrad was and is fate's great alarm call,"[161] that mobilization was "the task of the hour,"[162] that total war was "the demand of the hour."[163]

In *Mein Kampf,* Hitler had evoked the terrifying image of a deserted planet, void of all humanity, which was guilty of having forgotten the laws of nature: "At this point someone or other may laugh, but this planet once moved through the ether for millions of years without human beings and it can do so again some day if men forget that they owe their higher existence, not to the ideas of a few crazy ideologists, but to the knowledge and ruthless application of Nature's stern and rigid laws."[164] Nourished by natural providence, the führer could see and predict the future, assuming at times a prophetic air. According to J. P. Stern, he "[hid] behind the metaphor of 'the prophet,' turning the fiction into an active political myth."¹⁶⁵ What was only fiction could, through his prophetic posture and language, acquire the status of myth—a myth that, more than mere fiction, could help shape reality. The most famous of Hitler's prophecies can be found in his speech of 30 January 1939, pronounced amid swelling international tensions, on the sixth anniversary of the *Machtergreifung* (seizure of power):

> I have been a prophet very often in my lifetime, and this earned me mostly ridicule. . . . It was primarily the Jewish people who mocked my prophecy that, one day, I would assume leadership of this Germany, of this State, and of the entire Volk, and that I would press for a resolution of the Jewish question, among many other problems. The resounding laughter of the Jews in Germany then may well be stuck in their throats today, I suspect.
>
> Once again I will be a prophet: should the international Jewry of finance (*Finanzjudentum*) succeed, both within and beyond Europe, in plunging mankind into yet another world war, then the result will not be a Bolshevization of the earth and the victory of Jewry, but the annihilation (*Vernichtung*) of the Jewish race in Europe.¹⁶⁶

Nazi racial discourse abounded with promises of complete havoc and images of destruction and devastation, depicting what would surely befall mankind should the Aryan race be defeated. Just as the fall of Rome plunged the West into the darkness of the Middle Ages, the fall of the Reich would leave chaos and desolation, as Hitler reaffirmed in a 1942 speech: "The collapse of the antique world brought a thousand years of chaos. The collapse of Europe would probably bring two to three thousand years of chaos. Those who have seen what the East is like know what would take the place of Europe, not to mention our fatherland."¹⁶⁷ Worse than chaos, Hitler foresaw utter nothingness: "The result of the collapse of the Roman Empire was a night that lasted for centuries."¹⁶⁸ This nothingness was a medieval darkness, an unprecedented cultural regression that had plunged the West into shadow and ignorance, fanaticism and terror, that lasted for ten centuries. The pure light of antiquity had been snuffed out by a terroristic Judeo-Christianity.

The collapse of the Reich would have consequences even more dire than those of the fall of Rome. Hitler evoked them in the agonizing nights of the Wehrmacht's retreat in the East during the winter of 1942: "Christianity is the worst of the regressions that mankind can ever have undergone, and it's the Jew who, thanks to this diabolic invention, has thrown him back fifteen centuries. The only thing that would be still worse would be victory for the Jew through Bolshevism. If Bolshevism triumphed, mankind would lose the gift of laughter and joy. It would become merely a shapeless mass, doomed to greyness and despair."[169] For Hitler, the destruction of Rome and the extinguishing of the ancient world by Judeo-Christianity were but a pale and partial foreshadowing of what awaited mankind should Judeo-Bolshevism emerge triumphant. The Bolshevik terror surpassed in violence and atrocities anything that the Judeo-Christians had done when they had ravaged the world in antiquity. Significantly, Hitler's anguishing over history and repeated references to the death of Rome in the winter of 1942 came at the exact same time as the elaboration of the Final Solution, the practical and administrative details behind the extermination of European Jews.

Messages of hope were far less frequent. Hitler seldom envisaged the final act of the race war in terms other than the darkest despair of defeat and devastation. Only very rarely did he discuss the alternative possibility, that of victory,[170] as he did at one critical moment. In his table talks from November 1941, when the advance guard of the Wehrmacht was just reaching the suburbs of Moscow, Hitler, feeling confident, imagined Germany actually expanding beyond the borders of the ancient world, which at one time were reduced to Greece and which at that moment, in the plausible scenario of a German victory in Russia, could cover a gigantic swath of land that would surpass even the farthest reaches of the Roman Empire: "In old times Europe was confined to the southern part of the Greek peninsula. Then Europe became confused with the borders of the Roman Empire. If Russia goes under in this war, Europe will stretch eastwards to the limits of Germanic colonisation."[171]

Hitler often wallowed in his hallucinatory visions regarding the coming end of the world. He foresaw death and devastation, imagining the coming destruction of the race and the planet should the Reich be defeated, like an obsessed collector of dark threats and crepuscular imagery. Nazi eschatology evolved over time toward the promise of an exterminatory apocalypse. The Roman Empire had been swallowed up by a racial catastrophe brought on by a Jewish conspiracy employing Christianity to get the dregs of mankind to rise up against their Roman masters. The Reich seemed ineluctably destined for a similar fate, and Hitler gradually became less and less capable of imagining any other end for his empire other than one like the cataclysmic death of Rome. In a table talk from 1942, he flashed a bit of dark humor regarding his lack of an heir: "If one hasn't a family to bequeath one's house to, the best thing would be to be burnt in it with all its contents—a magnificent funeral pyre!"[172] A ritual cremation dressed up in the style of the old Roman patricians.

CONCLUSION

While any death is hard to comprehend, the demise of a lost civilization defies the imagination. An individual death leaves those who survive speechless in the face of the absurd; the disappearance of ancient cultures left posterity dumbfounded, bereft of answers in the absence of evidence and of all sense, a bewilderment scarcely palliated by melancholy meditations over the motionless poetry of their ruins. For a Germany that sought to erect a political empire and create a new racial and cultural canon, ruminating on the causes of the greatness and decline of the Romans and Greeks presented an even more pressing necessity. Hitler admitted that he often wondered about "the downfall of the ancient world." Racial scientists and historians developed their responses within the context of a racialized world view and preoccupations about the end and death of an entire people. If there was no wealth but in men, the proximate cause of the end of the ancient world had to be sought in the trend of a declining birthrate. The harm caused by contraception had already made itself felt among the Greeks and Romans. In addition to this morbid Malthusianism, which only a vigorous pronatalist state policy could effectively combat, the depopulation of Greece and Rome was due to the incessant fratricidal wars that beset Nordic elites in the Mediterranean: the loss of blood through these fratricidal conflicts between Spartans and Athenians, Greeks and Romans, created a need for fresh transfusions, a call for more men that was, alas, answered only by the arrival of Asiatic and Semitic prisoners and slaves, who infected the finest Nordic blood—or what was left of it.

The case of Rome offered a masterly if terrifying portrait of de-Nordification: the hemorrhaging of Nordic blood, of course, but also the desertion of the fields in favor of the profit to be gained by conquest, the rupture of an old peasant people's ties to the soil, small landholdings cultivated by peasant-soldiers replaced by the filthy lucre of great capitalistic latifundia bursting with imported slaves—all these things altered Roman blood and its culture, the old Roman mentality of the *mos maiorum* and its masculine virtues supplanted by an individualistic thirst for money and personal pleasure. This moral decay and racial degeneration were visible in the succession of imperial dynasties. What could Augustus, a blond-haired and blue-eyed Nordic emperor, possibly have in common with the Oriental Semite Caracalla, the gravedigger of the Nordic racial aristocracy with his extension of citizenship across the empire in 212 CE? As Juvenal had written, "In Tiberim defluxit

Orontes"—"The Syrian Orontes disgorged itself into the Tiber"—the vanquished East had emerged victorious over a West that had been hailed as a conqueror only to crumble into ruin.

In Greece, the pollution of Nordic blood through interbreeding had taken place with the advent of democracy, made biologically and intellectually feasible only through the mixing of races, the miscegenation of inferiors with their betters, castrating those who were superior and leading to a philosophy of equality that was nothing other than racial leveling. The democratic fifth century, denounced by Plato, preceded the century of Alexander, the age of the first global empire that, in the absence of a segregationist and racially elitist mentality, had encouraged such exchange and miscegenation.

None of that was lost on contemporary Germany. The lessons of the past constituted an unmistakable warning in bold print: complacence, miscegenation, fratricidal war, neglect of the superiority of Nordic blood had all cost the Indo-Germanic race dearly, leading to the deaths of Greece and Rome, its two finest and most beautiful expressions before National Socialist Germany. The Nazis could not afford to make the same mistakes, for this time it appeared that the race would not receive a second chance. National Socialist discourse left itself no way out, prophesizing that the war between the races, this time against Judeo-Bolshevism, had entered its final and decisive phase, which could lead only to annihilation or total victory. The encroaching possibility of defeat after the bloodletting at Stalingrad encouraged this reading of events and such discourse. When Hitler declared on 1 September 1939 that there would not be another November 1918 in German history, he was making a forceful statement: not that Germany would never again lose but that any future defeat would be nothing less than total.

CHAPTER 9

The Choreography of the End

Aestheticism, Nihilism, and the Staging of the Final Catastrophe

> I saw, too, the pediments of the pillared temples gleam in the red rays, and from their lofty pedestals the images of the gods with shield and spear bowed down, to sink without a sound into the raging flames.
> Before this sea of fire . . . I heard, too, the pack drawing incessantly nearer, with the rabble at its heels.
>
> —Ernst Junger, *On the Marble Cliffs*

> "I know your character," he said to me. "His name is Erostratus. He wanted to become famous and he couldn't find anything better to do than to burn down the temple of Ephesus, one of the seven wonders of the world."
> "And what was the name of the man who built the temple?"
> "I don't remember," he confessed. "I don't believe anybody knows his name."
> "Really? But you remember the name of Erostratus? You see, he didn't figure things out too badly."
>
> —Jean-Paul Sartre, "Erostratus"

The absolute intransigence of German soldiers up until the almost complete destruction of the Reich's capital deeply troubled contemporaries and continues to mystify in the present day: what could possibly lead an army of conscripts to continue to fight until the very last man? It was the stated will of Nazi leaders to fight until the bitter end in a war without mercy, and that will was largely borne out through the absurd battle for Berlin, which left the German capital in ruins when surrender could have easily avoided such a tragic and useless mess. What type of discourse, what kind of imaginary thinking about war encouraged such unrelenting resistance, causing the German armed forces to sustain roughly half of their total casualties in this final phase of the war? The elements we have discussed so far constitute one part of a response: this war was a war of races, and the radical prophecy of total victory or complete annihilation was widely disseminated to the German public, in speeches, pamphlets and propaganda, films and classroom instruction. The National Socialist image of war was meticulously styled, at the very highest levels, by the Nazi leadership, out of a desire to see their prophecies of chaos and racial and civilizational destruction borne out in reality. Nazi Germany would go down in a blaze of glory, leaving behind a myth that was both terrible and eternal.

EXITING THE STAGE: THE TERROR AND THE PITY

Did Nazi leaders—particularly Hitler and Goebbels—actually aspire to victory? Their intransigence has long, and often all too conveniently, been ascribed to madness. Goebbels seemed, however, to proclaim quite the opposite in his last press conference, held in his residence, on Saturday, 21 April 1945, the day after Hitler's birthday: "When we step down, let the world tremble!"[1] During the somber days of Stalingrad, Goebbels was already commenting that events in Russia were a "drama," not in the formal definition of "a tragedy" but in the more general sense of "a spectacle." The semantic turn to the world of the theater, of entertainment, of a visual display to be described shows quite clearly that what mattered most was less the events themselves and more the manner in which they were seen, perceived, and narrated—a memoir bequeathed to posterity, to be told and retold for generations. Stalingrad was thus significant less as a real battle than as a "heroic drama"[2] of the German army, "a spectacle of truly antique grandeur" that "eclipses the *Nibelungenlied* and . . . that will live on down the centuries."[3]

The siren song of defeat: why lament Paulus's surrender, since the actions of the Sixth Army reached such heights of ancient glory that they equaled and surpassed them, leaving an indelible mark on history, the mark of a giant? Perhaps therein lies the ultimate meaning of combat, of that *Kampf* that the Nazis loved to exalt as natural law, the ennoblement of man and the alpha and omega of his existence: combat was undertaken less to achieve victory than to fight in such a manner that one created an example. Defeat mattered little if it meant enacting a myth that would lead to ferment and renaissance and the resumption of combat in a distant future. Rome mattered only because it was dead; its ruins moved humanity and set an example. Those of the Reich, and the script of its heroic end, would similarly demand respect and sacred terror and exhort future generations to combat.

Consequently, the Nazis' departure from the stage would have to be managed carefully, to make the event as catastrophic and terrifying as possible. The fall of the Reich was perceived as a sort of screenplay for a catastrophe, leaning upon the precedents set by the great declines of antiquity, and fully intended to match them in signifying force and symbolic impact. Antiquity, the very definition of cultural prestige and empire building, became a paradigm for a memorable, spectacular, heroic ending, an end that would generate its own myth and live it to the full, haunting the world for centuries to come. The memory of a fanatical and suicidal resistance would live on forever, creating a heroic myth comparable to that of Leonidas's three hundred at Thermopylae:

> A desperate fight retains its eternal value as an example. Think of Leonidas and his three hundred Spartans. In any case it does not suit our style to let ourselves be slaughtered like sheep. They may exterminate us, but they will not be able to lead us to the slaughter.[4]

Goebbels and Hitler were in perfect harmony with respect to the meaning to be attributed to their defeat, as indicated by these remarks by Goebbels in his diary for 11 March 1945: "[The führer] emphasises that the great prototypes are the men on whom we must model ourselves today. . . . It must be our ambition to set an example today on which later generations can model themselves in similar crises and times of stress, just as today we must take our cue from the heroes of past history."[5] Or, as Hitler dictated to his secretary Traudl Junge on the night of 29–30 April 1945, only a few hours before he committed suicide: "Centuries will go by, but from the ruins of our cities and monuments of art, hatred for the people who are ultimately responsible will always renew itself; against those whom we have to thank for all this: international Jewry and its helpers!"[6] This taste for ruin seemed to be the external manifestation of a self-fulfilling prophecy that could be traced back to the very beginning, a desire to make history that found its absurd completion in the final catastrophe that they now accepted, if not outright welcomed. Hitler, of course, loved the mantle of the prophet, which he had donned to foresee that the disappearance of the Aryan race would leave the earth to drift like a dead star through the cold wastes of outer space. Such a prophecy left no other choice than to sow the seeds of death and desolation. It was both easy and tremendously important for Hitler to pose as the prophet: Nazi racism possessed the pretension to have understood the laws of history; the National Socialist intellect could foresee what, conforming to the logic of history and condensed into a knowable and predictable nature, would come to pass. Consequently, prophecy was less the oracular obscurantism of a Pythia or the delirious ravings of a Sibyl than a scientific or virtually apodictic prediction, a necessary reality. The Nazis' pretention to a complete hermeneutics of the real, founded on their conviction that they had unlocked the secrets to the laws of history—which were no different than those of nature—created what Hannah Arendt called "totalitarian lawfulness,"[7] a lawfulness that was at once epistemological, since it knew with absolute certainty the movement of natural development, and practical, since totalitarian terror was but its auxiliary, the secular arm of these necessary laws of nature. The best means to see a prophecy come true is to make it come true oneself, even a prophecy of devastation and destruction. As Kant wrote, "history *a priori*" is possible "when the soothsayer himself shapes and forms the events that he had predicted in advance."[8] The intransigent nature of the battle of Berlin and the order to destroy the Reich of 19 March 1945 were one final way for the führer to be right.

RIENZI: THE DEATH OF A ROMANTIC HERO IN THE FLAMES OF ROME

By April 1945, 70 percent of Berlin had been reduced to rubble, like the Roman capital in a Wagnerian opera. The führer's decision to inter himself in an encircled bunker can perhaps be traced in part to the fascination the young Hitler felt for the hero—perfect in his chosenness, his solitude, his idealism, and his sacrifice—of Wagner's *Rienzi*.

This work, which so captivated the young unemployed provincial man from Linz, made a lasting impression on his view of politics and history. The tragedy, written and composed by the young Wagner in the manner of a pure romantic drama, had everything to appeal to the young idealist, who betrayed his loneliness in dreamy sentimentalism and the desperate conviction that he was chosen, a feeling that was only confirmed in his mind by his dereliction and isolation. Rienzi is a noble, solitary hero.

Devoted completely to the resurrection of ancient Rome and its faded grandeur, he remains chaste: the only woman in his circle, representing his only relationship with the feminine, is his sister, Irene. Rienzi seeks to recapture the nobility of the virtuous, glorious Rome of a bygone era, "das alte Rom, die Königin der Welt" ("ancient Rome, the queen of the world"), his only consolation for the mediocrity of a present rife with quarrels, injustice, and division. Its ruins are the only evidence of its glorious past:

> Seht, jene Tempel, jene Säulen sagen euch:
> es ist das alte, freie, grosse Rom,
> das einst die Welt beherrschte, dessen Bürger
> Könige der Könige sich nannten!
>
> See! Yon proud temples, yonder columns, say to you:—
> This was the ancient, mighty, glorious Rome,
> That once rul'd all the world; whose citizens
> Could call themselves the Kings of Kings![9]

But Rienzi's world shows no signs of such past grandeur; his contemporaries do their ancestors no honor. Rienzi laments the decadence of the Roman people and their morals. He thus takes it upon himself to lift up the city:

> Nun denn! Rom mach' ich gross und frei,
> aus seinem Schlaf weck' ich es auf . . .
>
> Know then! Rome shall be great and free!
> I will arouse her from her sleep . . . .[10]

The parallels with Hitler, his future biography and his carefully crafted self-representation, are striking. Initially hailed and given a plebiscite by his people, Rienzi is subsequently shunned by the public, brought low by the treasonous intrigues of a corrupted nobility: he is chosen but betrayed, for such is the fate of the elect when faced with the petty cowardice of man.

Rienzi's self-appointed mission is lofty and sublime: to restore Rome to its old greatness and to free the people from the venal and tyrannical oppression of a disgraceful nobility that had taken control of the city after the pope's retreat to Avignon. A hero who is one of the people, convinced that he has been elected by divine providence,[11] Rienzi is fully committed to his battle, completely devoted to his idea of the grandeur of ancient Rome and of justice. As beautiful as one of the ancients, he speaks words that seem as if they could have been lifted straight out of a *De viris*, and he stands with a pride that even a statue could envy.

His selflessness is evident when, like Caesar, he refuses the title of king in favor of that of tribune, that of the Gracchi. A romantic hero, as characterized by the young Wagner—a revolutionary liberal who stood, quite literally, in defiance of the reactionary Holy Alliance, helping man the barricades of Dresden in 1848—the Rienzi of the opera is hardly anything like his historical counterpart. His passionate pleas for freedom, his idealism and ultimate sacrifice made him a hero of romantic liberals and nationalists everywhere, inflamed by Wagner's work as they were in Italy by Verdi.

Such an opera could easily persuade Hitler, who had loved Werther as a schoolboy, nourished on the mystique of the solitary genius and the plebiscite, being chosen or cursed, fully convinced that politics was sublime only if it was sacrificial, that one's fate could not be truly heroic unless it culminated in the flames of a capital collapsing in a chaos of sparks and timbers. Rienzi seeks to restore the ancient grandeur of Rome in spite of its people, who betray and abandon him, incapable of following their heroic leader in his historic mission:

> Furchtbarer Hohn! Wie! Is dies's Rom?
> Elende! Unwerth eures Namens!
> Der letzte Römer fluchet euch!
> Verflucht, vertilgt sei diese Stadt!
> Vermod're und verdorre, Rom!
> So will es dein entartet Volk!
>
> This is your thanks! What! Are ye Romans?
> Degenerate folk! Unworthy of that name!—
> The last of Romans—curses you!
> Accurs'd, destroy'd be Rome again—
> Let death, yes, death and destruction come!
> So wills the Roman folk once more![12]

Rienzi's nobility is made sublime within the flames of his self-sacrifice; his death marks the definitive end of ancient Rome, for he dies crushed beneath Rome's fall.

In his first-person account of his youthful friendship with the future führer, August Kubizek—one of Hitler's few close friends—devoted an entire chapter to the impression that *Rienzi* made upon his then seventeen-year-old companion on a trip to the opera in Linz one evening in November 1906. The chapter, titled "'In That Hour It Began . . . ,'" recounts how an evening at the local theater sparked and shaped the young Hitler's calling to politics. Though given to exaggerating the importance of those years they shared together, Kubizek firmly believed that "it was then that his future life was decided."[13] Hitler had been moved by Rienzi, a man of the people, chosen by providence to be the liberator of his oppressed people. The singularity of his fate, the atrocity of his death as a man betrayed and consumed by flame, provoked a shudder of fear and pity in the two boys: after "living breathlessly through Rienzi's rise to be tribune of the people of Rome, and his subsequent downfall," Hitler was uncharacteristically "silent and withdrawn,"[14] rudely dismissing his friend's attempts at conversation. Despite the cold and damp of a November night, the two friends walked and walked, climbing up to the summit of the Freinberg, outside town. Suddenly, Hitler gripped his friend's hands and launched into a long and feverish monologue in which the timid and fragile young man dreamed of a life like Rienzi's, his own special destiny, a romantic fantasy that transcended his feelings of insignificance and failure. Kubizek had always thought his friend had dreamed of being an artist, but that was clearly no longer the case: "Now he aspired to something higher, which I could not yet fully grasp. . . . Now he was talking of a mandate which, one day, he would receive from the people, to lead them out of servitude to the heights of freedom."[15]

It is quite possible that this is an overly deterministic recollection, an a posteriori interpretation of what actually happened on that evening; the author certainly seems to be taking credit for having witnessed a moment of illumination that would go on to change the face of the world. This is the danger with all autobiographical testimony, particularly one recounted in such detail, although no less an authority than Ian Kershaw has deemed Kubizek's writings generally credible on the whole. "Many years had to pass before I realised the significance of this enraptured hour for my friend,"[16] Kubizek claimed, recalling that Hitler curtly dismissed his friend before returning to the mountains to think in solitude beneath the stars on the Freinberg. Much later, the führer would invite his childhood friend, whom he had not seen since he left Linz, to Bayreuth, in 1939. In his telling, Kubizek recounted to Hitler his memories of that night, which Hitler remembered in exactly the same way: "After a few words, I sensed that he recalled that hour vividly and had retained all its details in his memory." On a subsequent occasion, when the pair were hosted by the great composer's daughter-in-law, Winifred Wagner, the führer is supposed to have said: "In that hour it all began."[17] This was not the only time when Hitler recalled *Rienzi*'s decisive impact upon him; four years later, in April 1943, during a visit to Linz, he led an

Areopagus of Nazi leaders to the Landestheater, where, Speer later recalled, the führer showed them "with visible emotion ... the cheap seat in the top gallery from which he had first seen *Lohengrin, Rienzi,* and other operas."[18] *Rienzi,* a youthful work that Wagner later repudiated, fit perfectly within the contours of the führer's political imaginary, in which politics meant heroic sacrifice and ultimate catastrophe: the political resurrection of lost grandeur was achieved only through the suicide of the hero, engulfed in the flames of his failed mission.

That the theatrical spectacle of a Roman hero who, animated by a desire to re-create the greatness of ancient Rome, dies in a conflagration that consumes him in his home should be the tale that compelled Hitler to embrace politics is no coincidence. Hitler's aesthetic fascination with the ultimate sacrifice of the tragic hero was deeply rooted in his interest in antiquity.

BEQUEATH, NOT BUILD

Portraying Nazism as an ideology or attitude essentially concerned with death, especially its own, might seem to contradict the self-proclaimed life-affirming nature of the party and state, in particular with respect to the importance it accorded to the arts and architecture, as we saw at the outset. How is it possible to see such a fundamentally destructive logic at work in Nazism when the regime spent so much in time, energy, and resources to design and to build? Hitler demanded the use of the best and most expensive materials, whatever the cost, despite suggestions to the contrary from his finance minister, whom Hitler instructed Speer to deceive.[19] Hitler had a passion for architecture, and after 1933 the German state contracted the same infectious enthusiasm for the trowel and the chisel under his iron rule. Reading and listening to Hitler and Speer, however, one might doubt that Nazi construction projects were actually designed for use by their contemporaries. Hitler seemed less interested in building for the present than in leaving a mark on the future:

> Hitler liked to say that the purpose of his building was to transmit his time and its spirit to posterity. Ultimately, all that remained to remind men of the great epochs of history was their monumental architecture, he would philosophize. What had remained of the emperors of Rome? What would still bear witness to them today, if their buildings had not survived? ... But when after a long spell of inertia a sense of national grandeur was born anew, the monuments of men's ancestors were the most impressive exhortations. Today, for example, Mussolini could point to the buildings of the Roman Empire as symbolizing the heroic spirit of Rome. Thus he could fire his

nation with the idea of a modern empire. Our architectural works should also speak to the conscience of a future Germany centuries from now. In advancing this argument Hitler also stressed the value of a permanent type of construction.[20]

Even in public, Hitler stated bluntly that he sought to build more for posterity than for contemporary Germans: "The gigantic works of the Third Reich are a token of its cultural renascence and shall one day belong to the inalienable cultural heritage of the Western world, just as the great cultural achievements of this world in the past belong to us today."[21] The architectural patrimony created by Hitler was essentially designed to be part of a heritage, a testament in stone to the Germans' glorious ancestors, the victims of their sacred mission and their struggle. What mattered most, then, in the construction of these monuments was less the function of these structures in the present than what they would leave behind for the future. What contemporaries thought mattered far less than the opinion of future generations. Hitler was far more eloquent when describing how his buildings would be regarded by posterity than he was in discussing how they were perceived by the Germans of the present, for whom he cared only that they were not completely dwarfed and overwhelmed by the imposing masses of Nazi stone. Here too one can see how Hitler's frame of reference was diachronic and projective rather than synchronic, given more to history than to geography.

This systematic projection into the future, a corollary of the Nazis' obsession with the past, is evidence of an impulse to make themselves into the past and of a striking propensity to envision their own death, with a morbid fascination haunted by a desire for a heroic apotheosis. There is abundant evidence that Hitler was an unrepentant hypochondriac, a man who genuinely, and with a pronounced taste for theatrics, spoke with anguish of his little digestive worries and turned a bothersome case of aerophagia coupled with insomnia into a diagnosis of stomach cancer. Speer later wrote that Hitler was especially eager to complete the new Reich Chancellery because he was convinced that he did not have much longer to live. He supposedly confided to Eva Braun that he thought he would soon die—before he was even fifty years old—and kept to his strict vegetarianism by eating a virtual starvation diet.[22]

Hitler's personal obsession with his own death was tied to his almost willful intuition that the Nazis were headed to defeat and to their doom—an intuition, curiously, that dated back to the beginning of the war: "At some time, probably during the first weeks of the war—I no longer remember the context—I heard Hitler speak hypothetically of a *finis Germaniae,*"[23] Speer wrote, an anecdote corroborated by several other sources.[24] Hitler's visions of his own defeat, the annihilation of a *finis Germaniae,* were undoubtedly the logical outcome of his conception of war in radical, all-or-nothing terms. Nevertheless, this complacent acceptance, bordering on relish, of imagining the end poses some questions. Contrary to what the unmoving, unchanging ruins might leave one to imagine, the granite and marble left behind for posterity was not mere dead stone, cold and inert minerals. They were a fecund seed for the renaissance of the Bewegung, a source of inspiration for future generations, a monumental exhortation to take up the fight.

In the end, the Nazis built things precisely to be destroyed; an edifice meant nothing if it did not end in ruins. Hitler provided direct testimony of this hallucinatory concept when he laid the first stone at the Kongresshalle in Nuremberg, already earmarked for destruction and ruin. He imagined future generations walking in the sacred forests littered with titanic ruins of party buildings, finding in that edifying spectacle a sacred respect and ardor for resuming the struggle:

> Should the Movement ever be silent, even after millennia, this witness shall speak. In the midst of a hallowed grove of ancient oak trees will the people then marvel in reverent awe at this first colossus among the buildings of the German Reich.[25]

The specter of ruin was thus also a site of Nazi self-mythologization: the ruins of titans sang of heroes at arms, telling the story of glorious battles and calling upon future generations. Such monuments, in the manner of the great edifices constructed by the emperors of Rome, were called upon to create epic and myth; just as the ruins of Rome were the fount of the Italian Renaissance and the renewal of the West, inspiring the Reich, so the ruins of National Socialism would form a call to arms in future battles.

PLANNED OBSOLESCENCE: THE *THEORIE DER RUINENWERTE*

Hitler, who was so concerned with staging and self-representation that he choreographed the Nuremberg rallies himself and personally helped design party uniforms and banners, could not just leave care for his future image in the hands of Father Time. The Nazi will to power, which as we have seen was articulated in a totalitarian present and actively sought to rewrite the past, also sought mastery over the future, in the "pastification" (*passéification*) of its own present. Hitler carefully crafted the image that he would bequeath to posterity, by attempting to exercise control over the disintegration of his own monuments. Nazi monuments were not to be left passively abandoned to their own decay but rather were to be subjected to a process of planned obsolescence. It was critically important to leave behind ruins capable of stirring mythology—or, to put it another way, ruins that more or less possessed the appearance of those Roman ruins that preserved within themselves the glorious deeds of the empire.

Modern materials, particularly reinforced concrete, would seem ill suited to leave behind ruins as powerful and majestic as those of Rome. Speer wrote that during the grading of land for the Zeppelinfeld, they had to tear down Nuremberg's old metropolitan railway depot that had occupied the site: "I passed by its remains after it had been blown up. The iron reinforcements protruded from concrete debris and had already begun to rust. One could easily visualize their further decay. This dreary sight led me to some thoughts which I later propounded to Hitler under the pretentious heading of 'A Theory of Ruin Value.'" This idea, which resonated with Hitler's interest in aesthetics and memorial stagecraft, greatly enthused the führer:

> The idea was that buildings of modern construction were poorly suited to form that "bridge of tradition" to future generations which Hitler was calling for. It was hard to imagine that rusting heaps of rubble could communicate these heroic inspirations which Hitler admired in the monuments of the past. My "theory" was intended to deal with this dilemma. By using special materials and by applying certain principles of statics, we should be able to build structures which even in a state of decay, after hundreds or (such were our reckonings) thousands of years would more or less resemble Roman models.[26]

A picture being worth a thousand words, Speer presented a sketch to Hitler like a new Hubert Robert (an eighteenth-century French painter who made a career out of painting ruins):

> To illustrate my ideas I had a romantic drawing prepared. It showed what the reviewing stand on the Zeppelin Field would look like after generations of neglect, overgrown with ivy, its columns fallen, the walls crumbling here and there, but the outlines still clearly recognizable. In Hitler's entourage this drawing was regarded as blasphemous. That I could even conceive of a period of decline for the newly founded Reich destined to last a thousand years seemed outrageous to many of Hitler's closest followers. But he himself accepted my ideas as logical and illuminating. He gave orders that in the future the important buildings of his Reich were to be erected in keeping with the principles of this "law of ruins."[27]

This account is corroborated by the führer's own speeches on the question of art and architecture during the relevant sessions of the Nuremberg Party Congress and at the opening of the House of German Art in Munich: "What would the Greeks be without Athens and the Acropolis; what Rome without its buildings; what the lines of our German Emperors without their cathedrals and their palaces . . . ?" he asked in one speech, justifying his great works projects. They would probably be nothing, since a sort of commemorative Darwinism or natural selection of remembrance dictated that "there is hardly a people which history finds worthy of a mention for its positive achievement which has not in its cultural values raised its own memorial."[28] Clearly, for Hitler the fear of mortality could be assuaged and overcome only through the certainty that his empire would live on in its own ruins, just like the ruins that so impressed him and that spoke so eloquently of the "radiance of these giants."[29]

Hitler, like some kind of new Heraclitus, was afraid of the incessant, destructive flow of beings and things. Only monuments that were built to last all eternity could offer any resistance to the test of time, leaving a melancholy yet glorious reminder of an empire of giants for ever and ever, the only "indestructible witnesses"[30] of a people's historic greatness destined to go the way of all fleshly things: "But the great evidences of human civilization in granite and marble, they stand through the millennia, and they alone are a truly stable pole in the flux of all other phenomena."[31] If, as the führer maintained, "no people lives longer than the evidences of its civilization,"[32] art and architecture were naturally destined more for posterity than for their contemporaries; it was a question not of providing facilities for the present but of creating a stage suitable for memory, taking an example from "the great models of the past." The Reich itself had to learn from the Greeks and Romans to speak "the eternal language of great art."[33] Ancient monuments spoke the language of immortality, for they had warded off the finite and lived on through the centuries: "Yes, and even if the last living witnesses of such an unfortunate people have closed their mouths in death, then the stones will begin to speak."[34]

One gets the feeling from all of this that what mattered most to Hitler, from the very beginning, was not life but death: not real life, not the actual work and (relatively short) stewardship of a Thousand-Year Reich but memory and the ruins of an empire, an aesthetic, memorial, and even metaphysical concern more than a political reality. What mattered from the outset was stagecraft and the memory of the Reich's downfall: just as the Roman Empire mattered only for the heroic mythology proclaimed by its ruins, the Reich was worth more dead than alive. Hitler was concerned less with creating an empire than with planting signs and traces, leaving behind a still life of scattered ruins in imitation of the ancients, crumbling columns, blocks of marble crawling with ivy, powerful arches and walls of roughhewn stone, just like the Roman Empire. This lover of Wagnerian Gesamtkunstwerk, a passionate fan of opera, theater, and cinema, worked deliberately and persistently on the architectural staging of his own death. Hitler was preoccupied with this stagecraft from the time of his compulsory sojourn in Landsberg Prison, where in 1924 he wrote *Mein Kampf:* "If the fate of Rome should strike Berlin, future generations would some day admire the department stores of a few Jews as the mightiest works of our era and the hotels of a few corporations as the characteristic expression of the culture of our times."[35] In a certain sense, then, Nazism looks like the wistful contemplation of or even a yearning for death. It contained both a utopian philosophy of the will and a feral, desperate eagerness to envision its own demise, for what mattered was not so much victory in real life as the symbolic triumph of sublime, heroic defeat in memory, which would survive through the power of myth. "If the fate of Rome should strike Berlin" was not a rhetorical hypothesis but a real desire, not dread but a genuine wish.

One can see in Nazism an idealism that, faced with the mediocrity of the real, turned to nihilism out of spite. There was in Nazism from the beginning a fundamental drive toward death, a desire for death that, through a surprising rhetorical somersault, passed itself off as the fullest expression of a desire for life: a bizarre amalgamation of Eros and Thanatos, as in several articles meant for the SS that explained in lengthy historical-metaphysical treatises the significance of the *Totenkopf,* or "skull and crossbones," which they wore on the front of their uniforms.[36] Curiously, this death drive married with Nazi voluntarism and vitalism without any hint of irony. Architecture framed it this way: what is built into the edifice is the destruction of the edifice itself. The act of building is the act of building ruins, destruction being the fulfillment of construction. This was a nihilistic vitalism, a vitalism that gave birth to a mythology of death.

FINDING IMMORTALITY IN DEATH: THE NAZI *STEHEN UND KÄMPFEN* MENTALITY

The propaganda of perseverance (*Durchhalten*) created a fictive world perfect for the pursuit of combat to be fought to the last man and the last drop of blood. Such propaganda made it so that in the East it was all but unthinkable to lay down one's arms. This type of combat was depicted and seen as the final Armageddon in a race war that had lasted millennia. If the Reich were to lower its guard, it would be swallowed up by the repeated assaults of the eternal East. Operation Barbarossa was not a historically singular act of aggression: it was the latest undertaking by the West to destroy the Judeo-Asiatic subhumans who lay in wait to the east.[37]

We have seen how the strong eschatological charge of Nazi discourse set the stage for a final showdown and prophetically foresaw the horrific consequences of a defeat.[38] This eschatology[39] was apocalyptic: the Nazis prophesized absolute chaos should the Aryan race suffer defeat. In essence, Germany, just like "India and Hellas," faced the risk of being "dissolved forever"[40] if the Nordic ideal did not triumph in the face of its implacable, eternal enemy.

It was thus the very conception of the war in the East as a racial and civilizational *Endkampf* (final battle) or *Schicksalskampf* (battle for destiny) that forbid any capitulation, all the more so as the violence of the Red Army's reprisals began to validate a posteriori all of Nazi propaganda's most alarmist warnings. An *Endkampf* could be settled only in the either-or fashion so dear to Hitler and so common in Nazi discourse:[41] either the smashing, total victory of the Indo-Germanic race or its dramatic vanishing from the historical stage—with, perhaps in the background, the secret desire for a spectacular exit and the hope that future generations would take up the struggle, driven by the demise of their elders.

But why could the two fronts not be treated differently? If the East represented the vital, final showdown, why not ensure peace to the west in order to fully pursue the battle to the east? Why did the Nazis not attempt to procure a separate peace with the Allies in the West to turn and fight the war to the east, as Hitler contemplated only at the very end?

The first explanation is obvious: the Nazis knew that the Allies demanded an unconditional surrender, that they considered the National Socialist regime an essentially criminal enterprise, and that they would never negotiate with a state that had been so deceitful before the war and had committed so many war crimes after 1939. This explanation—which isn't really an explanation at all when one considers that as late as March–April 1945 Himmler himself believed in the possibility of a separate peace and sent out feelers to the Americans—immediately raises another question: why do everything in their power to cover up the level of violence and forbid any step backward? It is undeniable that the Nazis' genocidal violence was the product of a ratchet effect. As Joseph Goebbels wrote in his diary on 2 March 1943, still reeling from the shock of Stalingrad and contemplating defeat: "On the Jewish question in particular we are so committed that there is no escape for us at all. And that is good. Experience shows that a movement and a *Volk* that have burned their bridges fight much more unconditionally than those who still have the chance of retreat."[42] Burn all bridges: Hitler used this very metaphor only a few weeks later, saying he preferred "to burn all bridges behind him since, in any event, the Jews' hatred was so great anyway."[43] The Germans had to fight as if their backs were against the wall, all lines of retreat cut off. That was, as Goebbels noted, a "good" thing. But was this stance of obstinate resistance, this manic insistence on refusing to give ground until the last man was overrun, supposed to lead to victory? One might certainly believe that the Nazis believed this, for they certainly shouted it quite loudly and repeatedly.

The prevailing image of the Supreme Command of the Wehrmacht has long been that they were cut off from reality and that Hitler was a fanatical believer in ultimate victory: his own ideas, the nature of his orders, and the intransigent message of Nazi propaganda all converge to produce an image of a group united in blind, suicidal folly. While there were of course moments of complete irrationality, while the high command occasionally nursed their own illusions (regarding the *Wunderwaffen* V-1 and V-2, the Tiger tank, jet fighters, the atomic bomb), and while they occasionally invoked the destiny of Frederick II of Prussia to fuel hopes of a miracle like that of the House of Brandenburg in 1762, Hitler possessed a clear-sighted awareness of Germany's inevitable defeat that was far more rational and calculating than is often acknowledged. According to the historian Bernd Wegner, Hitler and the Supreme Command of the Wehrmacht knew that the Allies' disproportionate advantage in men and matériel would ultimately lead to the Reich's defeat—at least, after Stalingrad. In that case, then, how can we explain their relentless prosecution of the war? How can we explain the headline of the official party organ, the *Völkischer Beobachter*, in its issue of 28 March 1945, "Das Gebot der Stunde: Stehen und kämpfen!" (The order of the hour: Stand and fight!), when one of the goals of the Second World War was to avoid at all costs a repeat of the result of the first, in November 1918, as Hitler proclaimed in his declaration of war on 1 September 1939?

One must undoubtedly take this phrase truly seriously to understand that when Hitler said that "there shall never ever be another November

1918 in German history,"[44] he meant not that there would be no more defeats but that there would be no more humiliating defeats, defeats that, as in 1918, left a bitter aftertaste of shame and failure for an entire generation of combatants. It was less about winning the war than about dreaming of an end to the war as one works to develop an exit from a stage. The reigning mentality among Hitler's entourage in May 1943 was, according to his state secretary Ernst von Weizsäcker, dominated by the "reasoning [that went] as follows: We are going to win. If not, we will die with honor down to the last man. That was the motto of Frederick the Great as well."[45] Fantasizing about an exit from the war that would transform military defeat into moral victory meant being able to exercise mastery over combat morale until the very last instant. In this sense, the contradiction between a lucid understanding of the inevitability of defeat and the intransigence of discourse in Nazi propaganda appears less distinct: this lucidity and this blindness were two sides of the same desire to not spoil the end of the war, as had happened in 1918, which was a humiliation not because it was a defeat but because it was pitiful and did not provide the chance to die with honor. The defeat of 1918 was the tragicomic humiliation of treason, the stab in the back: the Judeo-Bolshevik plot and then the diktat of Versailles had sullied German military honor.

Hitler thus appeared to be a rock of unwavering optimism, because he had no other choice. Even in his one-on-one conversations with his closest officials, he had to maintain this inflated and unrealistic belief in the possibility of an ultimate victory: as Bernd Wegner noted, "any admission of hopelessness or helplessness was completely incompatible with his conception of his role"[46] as the führer. Any wilting of his own will or of boisterous confidence in his speech would have robbed the Nazis of all or most of their means to continue fighting the war, by sowing the seed of doubt: "What kind of devastating impression would it make if a company commander explained to his men, in the midst of a difficult situation, that he did not know what to do?"[47] Hitler once asked rhetorically.

After 1942, "Hitler's thoughts and actions were focused no longer on the final victory but on the staging of his own defeat,"[48] the "choreography of this powerful history making collective downfall."[49]

This intransigent logic has often been imputed to the führer's supposed madness, since in strictly military terms this scorched-earth defense made absolutely no sense; if the purpose of military engagement is victory, or at the very least the advance or fortification of a front,

Hitler's edict *Stehen und kämpfen* (Stand and fight) did not possess any strategic or tactical significance. When Speer composed a memorandum on 30 January 1945 to inform the führer of the imminent collapse of the wartime economy so that he might spare the cause and put an end to the conflict—since, in Speer's eyes, it no longer made sense—his ideas were met with simmering anger by Hitler, who saw in the continuation of hostilities something that a man like Speer could never see: the minister was thinking of Germany's fate in the postwar world, while the führer was dreaming of nothing but smoldering rubble. Speer was concerned with the lives of the German people, while Hitler thought of nothing other than an epic end. Specific symbolic means were employed to galvanize the troops and preserve their mental and emotional resources for the final struggle. Beginning in 1943, just when it seemed the gods of war or fate had turned a cold shoulder to the Reich, Nazi propaganda started to encourage a spirit of resistance and sacrifice by deploying three iconic examples from history: first and foremost that of Frederick II of Prussia during the Seven Years' War, but also those of Sparta and Rome, confronted like the Reich by the devastating strength in numbers of surging waves of Asiatic-Semitic hordes. The contemporary struggle against Asiatic Bolshevism and its plutocratic Jewish allies was a struggle for world domination, just as were the Greco-Persian Wars and the Punic Wars, ultimately won by Nordic elites when confronted by a racially inferior enemy.

DURCHHALTEN: PERSEVERANCE, OR THERMOPYLAE AT STALINGRAD

The myth of Sparta that was deployed in the service of a racist state and totalitarian society[50] was also mobilized in another way, for its glorification of the fallen warrior, after the Nazi defeat at Stalingrad. The memory of Leonidas's three hundred men at Thermopylae in 480 BC, already celebrated in happier times during the German occupation of Greece,[51] was pressed into service once more. Goebbels's infamous 18 February 1943 "total war" speech at the Sportpalast in Berlin[52] exalted the hardness and self-sacrifice of a people who threw themselves completely into the war effort. His reference to the Spartan way of life was reflected in his depiction of Frederick II during the Seven Years' War, a figure who stood out in Goebbels's propaganda up until the final hours of May 1945 as a source of consolation and courage by virtue of his stubbornness and ultimate victory. Goebbels invoked Sparta[53] to describe a community united behind a war effort, a society of *homoioi*, complete "equals" and champions of a national unity that obliterated class barriers, which the gauleiter of Berlin—here, at least, recalling the "red-brown" accents of his political beginnings—wanted to melt away in the fires of total war. The example of Sparta was also mobilized in a context of military defeat, to represent, along the lines of Frederick II, the unbending will, courage, and spirit of self-sacrifice of soldiers who refused to lay down their arms.

Goebbels's speech also reflected an earlier appeal by Göring, from 30 January 1943. On that occasion, celebrating the tenth anniversary of the Nazi seizure of power, Göring had sought to rouse the spirits of the Wehrmacht by making an appeal to the courage of the German divisions held prisoner at Stalingrad, which were on the verge of surrendering to the Red Army after a long and ruthless battle against a Soviet enemy that was superior in number and amply assisted by General Winter, who had been more merciless than ever. When, on 30 January, a day of official celebration for party and state, the Reich's greatest military defeat was consummated and Paulus's official surrender was but a question of hours, Göring sought to show above all that the Germans' fight had not been in vain: their defeat was undeniable, it was heavy to bear, but it was sublimated by a strategic gain of time that would allow the German armies to organize a defense of the Greater Reich. His speech returned to the notion of a disaster in the short term that was transformed into victory over the long haul: "Had the fighters at Stalingrad not taken upon themselves this heroic struggle against some sixty or seventy Bolshevik divisions, these divisions would already have broken through: the Bolshevik would have undoubtedly achieved his goal. Now he is too late."[54]

The German divisions at Stalingrad had upheld the cardinal virtues of the soldier: camaraderie, faithful pursuit of duty, and above all personal sacrifice for the defense of their fatherland. The central and most famous passage of Göring's speech compared the sacrifice of the Wehrmacht in the great Russian winter with that of Leonidas and his men at the pass of Thermopylae. The heroic stand at Stalingrad was just like that of Leonidas's three hundred: their stand had wilted, yes, but just as Leonidas's acts had allowed the Greeks to respond quickly and decisively at Salamis, where the Persian king Xerxes was finally defeated, the heroic sacrifice of the German divisions had allowed the high command to gain a significant amount of time to prepare its defense and subsequently its counterattack that would lead to the final victory.

Thermopylae was a heroic defeat, like Stalingrad, both Pyrrhic victories of sorts for the Persians and the Soviets, who had been held back just long enough by the sublime self-sacrifice of a few hundred men and a dozen or so divisions, respectively:

> My soldiers! Most of you will have heard of a similar example from the great and formidable history of Europe.
> Even though at that time the numbers involved were small, ultimately there is no difference in the deed as such. Two and a half thousand years ago, an infinitely brave and daring man stood in a narrow pass in Greece with three hundred of his men; Leonidas stood with his three hundred Spartiates—men from a race famed for its courageousness and daring. An overwhelming majority, ever renewed, constantly engaged this small troop. The heavens darkened from the number of arrows that were shot. Then too, it was an onslaught of hordes that crushed the Aryan men here. A formidable number of warriors were at Xerxes's disposal, but the three hundred men did not yield or tremble; they fought and fought a futile battle—yet one far from futile in its significance. Finally, the last man fell. In this narrow pass there stands now an epigraph: "Stranger, when you reach Sparta, tell them that you have seen us lying here, as the law commanded!" [Wanderer, kommst du nach Sparta, so berichte, du habest uns hier liegen gesehen, wie das Gesetz es befahl!]
> They were three hundred men, my comrades. Millennia have passed, and today that battle and that sacrifice there still hold good as heroic, as the example of the highest warriorhood. And once again in the history of our own days will it be said: when you reach Germany, tell them that you have seen us fighting at Stalingrad, as the law, the law of the safety of our people, commanded [kommst du nach Deutschland, so berichte, du habest uns in Stalingrad kämpfen gesehen, wie das Gesetz, das Gesetz für die Sicherheit unseres Volkes, es befohlen hat].[55]

The heroic reference to Sparta was deployed to encourage the Wehrmacht to hold fast and persevere (*Durchhalten*), into the wind, against the Asiatic hordes that had forced their way through Stalingrad just as they had so long ago at Thermopylae. The reference to Leonidas, in addition to being sufficiently recognizable to be immediately understood, contained the hope of subsequent victory and belonged to that type of forced self-confidence with which the Nazis faced the unavoidable prospect of retreat. To illustrate Göring's thesis, on 7 February 1943 the *Völkischer Beobachter* reprinted a photograph of a bas-relief by Hermann Hosaeus: a nude armed with a sword facing a field of spears, echoing Herodotus.[56]

Leonidas thus became an allegory for the ultimate heroic sacrifice that in the long run paved the way for victory by containing and keeping the enemy at bay. The SS and the Luftwaffe would even join forces to create a unit, made up of fighter pilots who volunteered to fly suicide missions, called the Leonidas-Staffel, the "Leonidas Squadron."[57] This unit of Spartan fliers was to be equipped by the aircraft manufacturer Fieseler with a new model, the Fi 103 Reichenberg—which was in essence a V-1 rocket (the Fi 103) equipped with a rudimentary cockpit and joystick.

The Luftwaffe KG 200, otherwise known as the Leonidas-Staffel, was established at the end of 1943 as a commando unit for carrying out virtual suicide missions, headed by the SS colonel Otto Skorzeny—who made his name by freeing Mussolini from captivity in the fall of 1943—the elite pilot Hanna Reitsch, and the Luftwaffe officer Heinrich Lange. Some sixty Luftwaffe pilots volunteered, along with thirty of Skorzeny's SS commandos. The missions flown by the Leonidas Squadron were apparently limited to a few documented suicide missions from 16 to 17 April 1945 in a last-ditch effort to save Berlin by slowing down the inexorable Russian advance; the pilots wore their full dress uniforms with all their medals and were equipped with helmets that played recordings of women's voices and classical music—a taste of the Valhalla that awaited them.

HANNIBAL AT THE GATES: THE *ENDSIEG* OF THE ROMANS AGAINST CARTHAGE

The decisive engagement checking the German counterattack in the West took place in the Ardennes in January 1945. In the face of the inexorable advance of the Allies and the Red Army, the Reich, caught between the two pincers, began to simply shrivel away. Faced with such a desperate situation, Nazi propaganda tried to keep alive the flickering flame of faith in the regime and ardor for combat through the use of several carefully selected examples from history. It sought to show that the current difficulties were nothing new and that historical actors in situations that were similar if not worse saw their unshakable resolution repaid unexpectedly with their ultimate triumph. The embodiment of this attitude was, of course, Frederick the Great, who, faced with a numerically superior adversary and a series of military defeats, benefited from cracks in his opponents' alliance and, in particular, a stroke of good fortune in the sudden death of Empress Elizabeth of Russia on 5 January 1762. The miracle of 1762 seemed perhaps to be repeating itself when the president of the United States, Franklin Delano Roosevelt, died on 12 April 1945: Hitler had hopes, for a few hours, that the death of this resolute enemy of the Reich would permit the creation of a new grand alliance of the West to face Asiatic Russia, but Harry Truman was not a new Peter III, and those in the bunker were merely indulging themselves in a joy that was as vain as it was fleeting. The distinguished figure of Frederick the Great remained, even up until the Reich's final hours, its preferred icon for the propaganda of perseverance.[58] Yet although he admirably embodied all the necessary virtues for this dark hour, he was not the only historic example ripe for remobilization to symbolize the unflagging resolve that the Nazis demanded of the German people. Other desperate times also provided models of uncompromising courage and heroic endurance.

Hitler thus ordered Goebbels to use the example of Rome during the Punic Wars, as the Reichsminister confided in his diary entry for 28 February 1945:

> The Führer has instructed me to publish long articles on the Punic Wars in the German press. In addition to the Seven Years War the Punic War was the great example which we can and must follow today. In fact it fits our situation better than the Seven Years War since the Punic War was more decisive in a world-historical sense and its effects were felt over several centuries. Moreover the quarrel between Rome and Carthage, just like the present-day dispute over Europe, was not settled by a single war; the question whether the resulting ancient world was to be led by Rome or Carthage depended upon the courage of the Roman people and its leaders.[59]

The führer, of course, got his wish, in the form of a series of articles printed in the Reich's various newspapers. This full-on media blitz was orchestrated by Goebbels himself, who opened the series with an editorial in the weekly *Das Reich* on 1 April 1945. For that issue, the paper splashed the banner headline "Die Beweiskraft des Vorbildes" (The demonstrative power of example), while Goebbels titled his article "Die Geschichte als Lehrmeisterin" (History as teacher). He contested the notion that the current war "had no parallel" by noting that one could easily compare it to the "Second Punic War or the Seven Years' War." Certainly, the conditions in the field were different, but these historical examples proved that it was simply a matter of "courage" whether a "people threatened with their very lives either gives in to the peril and succumbs, or resists with all its might and ... overcomes." As the Reich's propaganda minister, Goebbels thought it important to cite these examples, to "reinforce and revive our morale as fighters": reminding the German people that Frederick the Great had been forced to confront three different coalitions or that the Romans had been forced to fight three Punic Wars before becoming masters of the universe—just read "the chapter of Mommsen's *History of Rome* on the Second Punic War"—all of this "gives us more strength in the critical phase of our war than the reading of lies in the Anglo-American press." History not only offered instruction and encouragement; it also compelled one to take a necessary step back to understand and interpret the meaning of contemporary events: "The war that we must now wage cannot exhaust itself in current events." Its meaning was not comprehensible in "the face inundated with blood and tears" of the present: the meaning of the historical examples he cited "took shape over two centuries or two millennia."[60]

Just as in the time of Rome or Frederick's Prussia, victory would lead to the birth of a new world: "From this war a new world will emerge, for better or for worse," for that was the meaning of the war, which, like the Punic Wars, was a "clash of peoples" for world domination, the term *Völkerringen* reappearing in every article on the subject.[61]

How could the German people avoid the odious enslavement that Goebbels promised his compatriots if they were to lose? They had to take their example from the Romans and from Frederick: take stock, gather all their strength and will, never lose hope, and never surrender:

> In the course of eighteen years, the length of the Second Punic War, Rome suffered many defeats that could have plunged it into the abyss, and, in the eyes of the cowardly souls among its people and on more than one occasion, it seemed the hour had come to negotiate surrender with Carthage. It was telling, however, that such voices did not find any welcome ears either in the Senate or among the Roman people, and that the men of Rome, naturally cursing and swearing under the weight of defeat, and the women of Rome, crying for their fallen heroes, returned to the field of battle and to their work. Some might retort that they did not have tanks at that time. We know. But Hannibal crossed the Alps against all odds, and his sudden appearance in northern Italy provoked in the world of that time the same grief and the same horror that the arrival of Anglo-American or Soviet tanks do today in places where no one expected them. The feeling is fundamentally the same, and that is why we are of the opinion that our reaction must be identical if we want to survive.[62]

It mattered not whether the war was fought upon the backs of elephants or in the belly of a T-34 tank. Modern wars, like those of the past, would be won by "courage and firmness of soul," by "men of strong hearts," and not by "matériel or [mechanical] power": "We vigorously contest the notion that the mechanization and motorization of war have changed war in its fundamental essence."[63]

For two years, Goebbels emphasized, the Reich's enemies had made every effort to convince the Germans surrender, to see their situation as desperate. That is not what Rome would have done! Goebbels explained that "in the exterminatory Battle of Cannae, Rome lost seventy thousand men, almost all of its army. The Romans had every reason to despair, since the road to the Eternal City was now laid open to Hannibal, for the Roman command could no longer put up any real resistance. But Rome did not despair, and its obstinacy was the decisive factor in the creation of the Roman world empire." The Roman Empire was but a pale foreshadowing of the German Reich to come. In the size of its sacrifices and the losses it suffered, as in the harshness and ruthlessness of the battle it faced, the Reich had surpassed its ancient idols: "It is our deepest conviction that the heroic struggle of our people will precede the proudest birth of a Reich that history has ever known."[64] Goebbels's editorial was only the first salvo in a propaganda barrage that unfolded over the two following issues of *Das Reich,* on 8 and 15 April, before the *Völkischer Beobachter* took up the baton in its issue of the latter date.

In *Das Reich,* the rest of the job fell largely to the historian Walter Frank, who wrote a long, two-part essay titled "Hannibal von den Toren: Senat und Volk von Rom in den Punierkriegen" (Hannibal at the gates: The Roman Senate and people in the Punic Wars).[65] Frank's work provided a much more detailed narrative than Goebbels's editorial or the articles in the *Völkischer Beobachter.* He went back to the origins of the Punic Wars, which he ascribed to a long period of patient empire building by Rome and to its rivalry for domination of the Mediterranean basin. He also explored the alternating fortunes of Rome's triumphs and defeats in battle, suggesting that destiny could be capricious and that a war was never over until one of the two belligerents was completely and definitively extinguished. With studied pathos, he told the story of the arrival of Hannibal's armies in Italy, to the surprise of all those who thought that the Alps were impregnable to an imposing army riding on the backs of elephants: "His black Numidian horsemen descended upon [the Romans] like the Horsemen of the Apocalypse: fire and pillage, violence and death traced the path of the Punics into Etruria."[66]

The disaster at Lake Trasimene led the Roman Senate to appoint a dictator, Quintus Fabius Maximus, who, Frank noted, "was not a brilliant intellect" but who embodied one of the great virtues of the Roman people, "hard, unwavering stubbornness."[67] The author retraced in detail the history of Fabius's two dictatorships, the turning point after the defeat at Cannae, and his return to power, when he was respected, after having earlier been criticized for his passive and cautious defensive strategy. With great energy and firmness, he organized the defense of the city, smiling and confident as he walked its streets, prohibiting any display of public mourning and limiting private periods of mourning to only thirty days. "'Es war schon ein Verdienst nicht zu verzweifeln' [It was a merit not to despair], Ranke said,"[68] and it was not easy for the Romans to keep their hopes up against the winds and the tides of the *longue durée,* since "four generations came and went before Rome's war with Carthage was decided."[69]

The Romans had, against all odds, emerged victorious, because "Rome never committed the fault that world history can never forgive of great peoples: at no time did Rome cower" or "lose faith in its own strength and its own destiny." Rome's victory was not built in a day; it "reconquered position by position," patiently, until "the eagles of its legions once again stood proudly, victorious, under the sun."[70] Having made that clear, Frank concluded that "Rome became great when its fortunes were at their lowest. Rome became great when the space where it fought seemed to be tighter than ever," never relinquishing "its faith in its gods and in its destiny": this was how Rome pushed open the weighty door of history to become "the center of the world." The parallel with the heroic struggle of the German people turned out to be much more than just a question of the same racial essence that joined Rome and Berlin. Calling upon the spirits of the Roman dead, Frank addressed them with these words: "You are alive, oh shadows; you live again in the men who share your blood and your spirit."[71] The founder and director (after 1935) of the Reichsinstitut für Geschichte des neuen Deutschlands (Reich institute for the history of the new Germany), Walter Frank would commit suicide one month later, on 9 May 1945.

The propaganda offensive continued on 15 April 1945 with the appearance in the *Völkischer Beobachter* of an article titled "Roms Triumph über Hannibal: Die Widerstandskraft einer Soldatennation entschied den zweiten Punischen Krieg" (Rome's triumph over Hannibal: The resilience of a nation of soldiers decided the Second Punic War),[72] which contained fewer details but was far more explicit in its comparison with the contemporary context than the articles by Walter Frank. The article shared space on page four of the paper with another piece, titled "Volk in der Entscheidung: Ungebrochener Kampfgeist in Schicksalsstunden der Jahrhunderte bewährt" (The *Volk* at the decisive moment: Unbroken fighting spirit in the fateful hours of past centuries), which examined the reversals of military fortune in medieval and modern German history: "Our ancestors, forefathers, and fathers found themselves in the same decisive, inevitable, unforgiving moments that we find ourselves in today."[73] The first words of the former article, following Frank, recalled the terrible fear of the Romans—whose land had always been, with but one exception, their sanctuary—before the approaching Carthaginian forces. "Hannibal ante portas!," Rome's "cry of horror," resonated like an echo of the fear the Germans now felt before the advancing Red Army, which Nazi propaganda had promised after Stalingrad would bring nothing but violence, fire, and desolation. The author recalled the Romans' desperation. Their defeats and broken alliances represented a striking, albeit implicit, parallel with the circumstances facing the Reich. The article went through the entire litany of the Romans' trail of tears: Ticinus, Lake Trasimene, and finally Cannae, "the most famous charnel house in history,"[74] a kind of Roman Stalingrad.

The Battle of Cannae was also the subject of a 1944 article in the *SS-Leitheft*.[75] This article told the story of how Rome picked itself up from the worst military defeat in its history. At a moment that seemed "to be the end of Rome,"[76] Publius Cornelius Scipio, seized by righteous anger at the defeatists eyeing a return to the service of Oriental potentates, galvanized Rome's energies and reconstituted its army, which, routed at Cannae, recovered to claim victory at Zama: "It was the veterans of Cannae who landed the final blow against the Carthaginian center." Against all historical appearances and any resignation to fate, Roman might, seemingly mortally wounded at Cannae, "sat fifteen years later, and for half a millennium, in domination over all of Europe." These were words of warning: the vanquished at Stalingrad now knew the moral of history. Only resignation could mark the end; only defeatism could lead to defeat. "The test of fate is bloody: before its judgment, the number of dead is insignificant. But its verdict is always just."[77] The article then cited a few of Goethe's more martial verses,[78] the literary equivalent of Wagner's arias that German radio played after every speech by a party dignitary. After the worst of its defeats, and with its allies beaten or bypassed one after the other, "Rome's existence was hanging literally by a thread." But happily there came a man who, "with an unwavering firmness of soul and in defiance of all ideas of strength held by the Roman generals," saved Rome. Alone against everyone and in the face of his own generals' derision and disbelief, the consul Quintus Fabius Maximus opted for a tactic never before attempted in Roman history. Aware of the Carthaginians' numerical superiority, he refused to engage in battle on the open field, as at Lake Trasimene or Cannae, which had ended with the smashing of the Roman legions, and opted instead to employ delaying tactics, avoiding direct confrontation and reconstituting Rome's forces while waiting for Hannibal, seduced by the delights of Capua (*les délices de Capoue*), to rest on his laurels and lower his guard. Holding his line with "a stubbornness never before seen," he bravely accepted criticism and mockery from his own camp. Expressing their desires to return to the Roman tradition of "audacious attack," his soldiers and generals mistook the Fabian strategy for hesitation or cowardice. But they "misunderstood the true meaning of his intentions," for Quintus Fabius was pursuing a "strategy for crushing defeat conducted in an admirably steadfast way,"[79] which would earn him his famous nickname of Cunctator, "the Delayer."

The dictator had to accept and tolerate—and get the Roman people to accept and tolerate—all the implications of such a dilatory strategy, the "devastation of the soil of the fatherland, the prolonging of the war and all its horrors, the unbelievable test that this war represented for the Romans' nerves." All this required superhuman effort from both him and his people, not to mention "sangfroid and a complete lack of fear." The Roman *Volk* finally rallied around their leader, "in whom they recognized the brute strength that originally belonged to their race," reviving the sublime virtues of the earliest Romans, now embodied by Fabius: *prudentia, constantia, animus invictus* (prudence, steadfastness, unyielding bravery).[80] This was the portrait of a führer at war: just as Fabius had been able to master the panic of the Romans and lead his people to victory despite the apparent inconsistency of his decisions, so too did Hitler—who had also run up against the incomprehension of traitorous generals, those involved in the attempt on his life of 20 July 1944—remain unyielding and farsighted in the middle of the storm. Although Frank remained reserved about Fabius, preferring the young Scipio,[81] his article painted an equally heroic portrait of the Roman dictator.

Frank's article compared the two years of suffering after Stalingrad to the *longue durée* of the Punic Wars, a "seventeen-year crisis"[82] that Rome patiently endured until, having finally brought down its hereditary enemy, it found itself "on the threshold of world domination" that was, as the volume *Rom und Karthago* had argued in 1943, the natural result of the confrontation between Rome and Carthage. The article concluded by offering up the moral of the story: "Rome never forgot—and those who find themselves in a similar situation, those who fight the decisive battle in world history must never forget—that it was firmness and unwavering stubbornness, unyielding courage and faith in the high mission of its people that made Fabius Cunctator the victor in such a desperate situation."[83] This concerted propaganda campaign orchestrated around the example of Rome, Goebbels's topicalization of the fight to the death in this series of historical examples, also included publications aimed at more specialized audiences. The last issue of the magazine *Die Deutsche Polizei,* for instance, contained an article titled "Sind Kriege Rechenexempel? Eine historische Untersuchung" (Are wars simple arithmetic? A historical study).[84] The author showed that a numerical disadvantage, even in overwhelming proportions, was in no way decisive and had nothing to do with the outcome of a conflict. The examples used to back up this argument were Leonidas's Spartans at Thermopylae, the victors in the long run despite the fact that they were no more than a handful of men compared to the Persians, and Fabius's Romans against Hannibal. The Spartans ultimately won because "they were ready to make the supreme sacrifice"[85] and the Romans because they were "unyielding" and led by "the spirit of sacrifice,"[86] admirable virtues that were characteristic of their blood and their race: race and willpower could thwart the darkest omens and evade the seemingly most unavoidable of fates.

The Nazi propaganda of perseverance smacked of willful illusion and repeated celebration as much as of a cynical effort to mislead in order to encourage the German people to continue the fight to the point of collective suicide, rising up in a massive *Volkssturm* to face the final battle.

The article on Fabius in the *Völkischer Beobachter* lauded the dictator for having resisted the will of his people and his army, who would have preferred "an end in horror rather than a horror without end."[87] Fabius had courageously chosen to endure the misery of war in order to leave the enemy spent, even when the Roman people, fearful and rash, would have preferred a heroic final charge that would have flattered their military tradition but irremediably led to their defeat. Unlike Fabius, however, Hitler—for lack of a better idea and in the inescapable face of defeat—chose to orchestrate precisely such an "end in horror."

QUALIS ARTIFEX PEREO, OR THE DESTRUCTION OF CARTHAGE

The Reich's new Rome would suffer the fate of Carthage: an irony of history, which showed Hitler to be little more than a latter-day Herostratus (or Erostratus, as in this chapter's second epigraph).

Herostratus was the antihero of Greek antiquity, remembered for having burned down one of the crown jewels of human achievement, the Temple of Artemis at Ephesus. He became the archetype of the nihilistic antihero who sought eternal fame through destruction—and self-destruction—while Sartre turned him into a metaphor for the absurdity of man. In a series of writings on political warfare over the years, Hitler often turned to the example of Herostratus, whom he used to insult the leaders of Weimar—the signatories of the diktat, the gravediggers of the true Germany,[88] and "cultural Bolshevists," supporters of degenerate art—whom he called "Kulturherostraten" (cultural Herostratuses).[89] But in reality, this figure, whom Hitler employed as a rhetorical foil, actually seemed to incarnate the ideals of Nazi nihilism.

In a supreme irony of history, Hitler's Germania—which, with its Great Hall modeled on the Pantheon, its proud, wide boulevards, and its Arch of Triumph, was designed to inaugurate a new Rome—was crushed beneath a carpet of bombs, much to Hitler's and Goebbels's delight, for the destruction wreaked by the Allies' Flying Fortresses would spare the regime from having to preemptively tear down the existing buildings. Hitler's new Rome, razed to the ground—the capital of the Greater Reich reduced to a mound of rubble and sections of charred walls pockmarked with bullet holes—looked more like Carthage after the arrival of Scipio than like the glorious capital of a new imperium.

Hitler's decision to commit suicide demonstrated his refusal to capitulate or to allow himself to fall into the hands of the Russians and thus be displayed as a curiosity or the centerpiece of a Roman-style triumph parading through the streets of Moscow before being hanged in the Tullianum of the Lubyanka prison. The fate of Mussolini and Clara Petacci, summarily executed and left to hang on meat hooks from the roof of a filling station in a public square in Milan,[90] certainly contributed to his refusal to be an object in the hands of the victors. The Italian example and the precedents of Rome undoubtedly present in the mind of a great enthusiast of antiquity like Hitler led him to avoid the fate of a Vercingetorix or a Boudicca, whether dead or alive, since Hitler greatly feared the profanation of his body, which he ordered to be cremated.

Throughout, one sees Hitler's desire to sculpt his own myth, to let reality burn to the ground if that sacrifice would possess an aesthetic value and mythological purpose. Joachim Fest has written of a "will to destroy"[91] that possessed the most fanatical of the Nazis in the final days of the war and marked the fermata of that "profound desire for destruction"[92] that for Fest constituted the essence of Nazism, for which "there were no ... alternatives; there were merely different forms of destruction":[93] the fruit of the "boundless destructive drive that motivated Hitler and his sworn followers."[94] National Socialism was a form of nihilistic revolution,[95] the fulfillment or political manifestation of a contemporary nihilism born of a profound sense of indifference or of the absurd that enveloped contemporaries after the death of God—the phenomenon of which Nietzsche and Heidegger were the philosophers, Malraux and Camus the artists.[96] Hitler had never truly been a politician, because he was not a builder, a creator. His horizons had always been shaped by a view of the final catastrophe. Fest cites Sebastian Haffner, who argued that "what ... he lacked totally was the constructive imagination of the statesman."[97] But was this really the case? We know that Hitler the watercolor artist and *Freizeitarchitekt* (amateur architect) claimed to be building a Reich that would endure the test of time, constructing new cities and monuments for all eternity. But Hitler never seriously envisaged an end to the war if not in the form of nothingness, the radical either-or. He could conceive of only the ultimate war of annihilation, refusing to indulge in the kind of diplomatic or political solutions that the smashing triumphs of 1940 had opened up for him to establish and consolidate a new European order. The escalation of war, the unchecked pursuit of an omnipresent enemy, and a binary eschatology led him to see only one extreme solution, an either-or that could all too easily turn into a neither-nor, fully justifying this diagnosis of nihilism.

Rome's warning to the Reich from the depths of history, Hitler's prediction of total and utter defeat as a result of any weakness in the face of Judeo-Bolshevism, was in fact a self-fulfilling prophecy.

Hitler took Germany down the road to a war that, for him, could end only in a radical manner. The führer's simplistic, binary logic applied to both the conduct of the war and its outcome. Hitler's rhetoric was based on "total questions ... with their entirely predictable Yes or No answers,"[98] J. P. Stern has written. "The answer to a total question, and thus the amount of deliberation required, is minimal, no more than a Yes or No"[99]—"the hard: either-or," as Hitler wrote in *Mein Kampf*.[100]

Hitler decided to fight to the very end, and to turn Germany into a field of rubble, in order to validate his prophetic ravings. Like Rome, like Sparta, like Hellenic Greece before the Hellenistic period, Germany would vanish for its failures and its negligence of the laws of race, for its inability to uphold the *Lebenskampf* that set races against one another. Germany's final vanishing act, the suicide of the Reich through war without compromise or capitulation, constituted proof by default of Nazi racial theories, in which the world was the theater of a racial struggle for survival in which the weakest were exterminated. What mattered in the final analysis, then, was that Germany should vanish like Rome, in a racial and civilizational collapse that would resonate down the centuries and whose echo would inspire terror and pity until the end of time.

Hitler and Goebbels stated their intent to die with sound and fury, fighting to the last man and the last breath, to create a heroic myth whose memory and echo would vibrate for eternity. Instead of creating a Thousand-Year Reich, Nazism staged a thousand-year death. In his last press conference, Goebbels said so explicitly:

> If we go down, then the German people will go down with us, and they will do it so gloriously that even after a thousand years the heroic defeat of the Germans will be at the forefront of world history.[101]

The proclamation of a Thousand-Year Reich amid the ecstatic chiliasm of the seizure of power in 1933 had by 1945 mutated into a declaration of a thousand-year death. This desire to stage a spectacular demise signaled yet again Nazism's vocation for devastation and cataclysm, bent less on creation than on destruction.

The Nazis' intent to vanish in a blaze of glory demonstrated their desire to dignify their historical predecessors, those other combatants of the Nordic race who had been swallowed up in a final cataclysm. Hitler claimed his place alongside these grand ancient exemplars when, in February 1945, he confided to Martin Bormann that he wanted to re-create the "desperate fight" of "Leonidas and his three hundred Spartans."[102] He sought to prove himself worthy of the other great combatants of the Nordic race, like the Spartans of Leonidas, massacred at Thermopylae to slow the Persians' advance, provide cover to the retreating Greek forces, and thus allow them to claim the final victory. Anxious not to break this bond with his glorious Greco-Nordic precursors, Hitler steadfastly refused to leave a besieged Berlin, to abandon his post and thus lose his honor as a warrior, preferring to go down in history as the Leonidas of his bunker.

But rather than a hope for victory in the face of extreme odds, Hitler's ideas betrayed another desire, to become an exemplar himself, in the image of his glorious predecessors, whose memory endured through the ages. He sought no more or less than to create his own myth, following the model of the myths of the past that had informed his own thoughts and actions. This was the meaning of Goebbels's pronouncement that it was his wish to see Germany fall so gloriously that the clamor of its suicide would echo for another thousand years. When it came to history and the resounding echo of the cataclysm, the difference between victory and defeat was blurred. All that remained was the din of battle, the terrifying memory of the desperate heroism of the combatants. The war ending in total disaster did not bother Hitler. Despite defeat, or perhaps even transfigured by it, the führer would rapidly become myth. Goebbels was certain: "If things don't go well and the Führer finds in Berlin an honourable death and Europe were to become bolshevized, then in five years at the latest the Führer would be a legendary personality and National Socialism would have attained mythical status (*ein Mythos*)."[103] The ruins of the Reich would give proof for a thousand years to come, and the fall of Berlin would acquire the status of a new sack of Rome or a new twilight of the gods.

This conflagration, however, remained the terminus ad quem of Hitler's war. The mythologized history of antiquity inundated the Germanic apocalypse with recurrent images of the end of Greece and the fall of the Roman Empire, followed by millenary chaos. Before defeat had become plainly inevitable, in the spring of 1945 Hitler transformed into a modern-day Nero in making the decision to burn down a world that had failed to live up to the grandeur of his expectations. Buried in his bunker in March and April 1945, Hitler ruminated on his rancor toward the repeated betrayals he believed he had discovered taking place around him. The supreme betrayal was that of the German people, who had let him down with their defeat in the racial struggle. A defeated and vanquished Germany must disappear. Hitler decided to unleash a great fire by ordering a scorched-earth policy that seemed designed to target less the Nazis' enemies than the German people themselves. On 19 March 1945 he signed a *Führerbefehl* titled "Destruction Measures within Reich Territory," otherwise known as the *Nero-Befehl*, or Nero Decree. The order gave the party gauleiters responsibility for the destruction of all communications infrastructure, roads and bridges, industrial plants, and silos.

Hitler thus drew the ultimate consequence from the Nazi retreat, the retreat of the German army before the USSR, by applying the pitiless laws of nature to his own people. In a private conversation, Hitler confided to Albert Speer that the order of 19 March 1945 was nothing less than the death warrant of the German people and the Nordic race, their rightful punishment for a shameful defeat, the logical consequence of their retreat. The Nordic-Germanic race, defeated, must vanish and make room for the victorious peoples of the East, a powerful, barbarous mass, the instrument of the Jews. The iron law of nature forbade the German people from surviving their defeat. Hitler sought to lead them to their suicide and so unleash the havoc of complete collapse. As he described the Nero Decree to Speer, his minister of armaments, who did not approve, "If the war is lost, the people will be lost also. It is not necessary to worry about what the German people will need for elemental survival. On the contrary, it is best for us to destroy even these things. For the nation has proved to be the weaker, and the future belongs solely to the stronger eastern nation. In any case only those who are inferior will remain after this struggle, for the good have already been killed."[104] This was the meaning of *scorched earth:* Germany and its people would have to burn to the ground, under Allied bombardment and in the sapping and suicide mining of SS units that received orders to destroy everything—blow it all up, bridges, roads, factories, dams—and to execute all traitors and defeatists. The final weeks of the regime would thus witness Hitler ordering and choreographing an apocalyptic end to it all, carrying the nihilistic impulse deep within National Socialism to its ultimate extreme.

In the event, the Nero Decree would be applied only in part, and rather poorly, with the exception of a few battalions of truly lost soldiers, the most fanatical of the SS, those who operated rolling tribunals and summarily executed all the defeatists they came across. Speer, who did not share Hitler's destructive rage and who, obeying a political rather than apocalyptic calculus, was anxious to preserve a viable country for after the war, stripped the party gauleiters of responsibility for the execution of the order and took it upon himself to save what he could.

The figure of Nero comes up only once in Hitler's table talks, in a 1941 conversation in which, rambling on about the devastation of the patrimony of antiquity by Christian vandalism, he defended the Julio-Claudian emperor, who he claimed was unjustly incriminated for the burning of Rome in 64 CE: "I don't believe at all in the truth of certain mental pictures that many people have of the Roman emperors. I'm sure that Nero didn't set fire to Rome. It was the Christian-Bolsheviks who did that, just as the Commune set fire to Paris in 1871 and the Communists set fire to the Reichstag in 1932."[105] Hitler thus rehabilitated the figure of Nero, wresting him from the *damnatio memoriae* that befell him after his suicide in 68 CE. Nero had been tried and convicted in public memory for having deliberately burned the city, or at least not having taken the necessary measures to more rapidly extinguish a conflagration that, razing the old *urbs,* had hastened and facilitated its reconstruction. One can find a curious echo of this cynicism elsewhere in the table talks, as when he rejoiced at the destruction wreaked by Allied bombing.

Hitler undoubtedly appreciated the theatricality and megalomania of this ostentatious, solitary, artistically inclined emperor, who died while supposedly whispering one last "Qualis artifex pereo!" (What an artist dies with me!),[106] taking credit for the stagecraft of his own demise. Nero, a willing musician, gladiator, and singer, just as Hitler was a watercolor painter, architect, and corporal, had burst into song while Rome was in flames, sharing the same "aesthetic thrills from the images of destruction"[107] that Fest attributed to Hitler while scrutinizing photos of the bombing of Warsaw in 1939, or the almost sexual gratification of his imagining the skyscrapers of New York transformed into giant flaming torches under bombardment by German Messerschmitt Me 240s.

Like Hitler, Nero had held grand ambitions to inaugurate a new era through the creation of a new capital, a temporal regeneration opening a new golden age that contained as an implied prerequisite the destruction of the ancien régime. Nero's Nova Roma would be called Neropolis, a word that harked back to Greece, just as the name *Germania* promised that Hitler's new Berlin would recall the example of Rome, explicitly referring to Tacitus's Latin name for his people.

But aside from a few early achievements, Hitler's Germania would never see the light of day. Hitler and Goebbels compared the Reich to Rome during the Second Punic War, seeing in a Berlin besieged by the Russian army an echo of Rome threatened by the hand of Hannibal before the Romans' sudden and unexpected reversal of fortune. The war would make the capital of the Reich, shattered by Allied bombs and devastated by fighting in its streets, into a city that looked much more like Carthage after Scipio than the Rome that it was supposed to imitate and reproduce. Arriving in Berlin shortly before the Postdam Conference of August 1945, Truman's adviser Harry L. Hopkins immediately thought of Carthage,[108] besieged and destroyed by Roman legions, its fields plowed with salt, cursed by the gods to remain forever sterile: in the end, it was Roosevelt who was Cato and Hitler another Hannibal; the new Rome had arisen on the other side of the Atlantic. *Carthago deleta.*

CONCLUSION

Hitler had predicted on 1 September 1939 that there would never be another November 1918 in German history. That disgraceful exit, a cowardly surrender, had left the German people with the bitter taste of failure in their mouths, the scandal and weighty frustration of immense resentment: neither victory nor defeat, the outcome of the Great War did not live up to the grandeur of the titanic epic lived by the German soldiers in the trenches and the sacrifices they made. The end was as mediocre as the experience of war had been sublime.

When the Wehrmacht descended upon Poland, Hitler swore that this would never happen again: the eschatological war he unleashed would be resolved by the annihilation of one of its two combatants, the total victory of one over the other. It is striking, however, to see how Hitler envisaged the possibility of defeat and acquiesced so early to the idea of a *finis Germaniae*. It was certainly preferable to emerge victorious, but if that should prove impossible, one had to be able to shift focus, to envisage and even to welcome absolute defeat, and to actively contribute to that defeat through an absurd tactic of unyielding resistance before the enemy's advance.

For this deliberate welcoming of death, this surrender by suicide, to possess real meaning, the Nazis' end would have to be so spectacular that it would resound for all eternity, giving birth to a heroic myth comparable to those left behind by their glorious Indo-Germanic ancestors, Leonidas and the bleached skeletons of the ruins of the Parthenon and the Colosseum. If time is a chasm that avidly swallows everything before it, it was still possible to brave traversing it by inscribing a heroic image in the memory of man. The Thousand-Year Reich of 1933 had become an obvious impossibility by 1945. All that remained was to leave behind a thousand-year death. Vanquishing time through heroic memory was a preoccupation that easily predated 1945; since the creation of the monuments in Nuremberg, Hitler had demonstrated his anxiety to give the future ruins of the Reich a Romanesque appearance so that they might enter into eternity by imitating the canon left behind by the Germans' glorious Nordic ancestors. One can easily see how, beginning from at least the construction of Nuremberg, the present and the past mattered far more than the future and the fear of death; Nazism was more about bequeathing than building. The Nazis' relationship to time betrayed a profound anxiety about the end, an anxiety that could be assuaged only by the certainty of being able to master the image and the memory they would leave for future generations.

This image had to speak the eternal language of art—that of classical art, particularly the art of Rome, and of the monumental ruins that still inhabit mankind's thoughts and physical space. This monumental image was also a heroic image, leaning upon the inspiration that came from Greece and Rome. For the catastrophe to be total and for it to resonate with sufficient vigor, Nazi leaders had to ensure that the Reich held out to the end, by mobilizing the glorious, and very high, standard set at Thermopylae by Leonidas—who would lend his name to a squadron of kamikaze pilots—and the Rome of the Fabii, who, besieged by a Hannibal strangely resembling Stalin, gave no quarter before finally winning the day, a Roman miracle that prefigured that of the House of Brandenburg during the Seven Years' War. After March 1945, when the German press feverishly rehashed the story of the Second Punic War and its happy conclusion, there could be no question of victory in the field: the examples of antiquity were mobilized to galvanize and radicalize a resistance against an enemy that was designed less to save Germany than to wipe the country off the map, so that the *finis Germaniae* would eclipse even those great civilizational collapses that the tragic history of the Nordic race, since the age of Greece and Rome, had grown accustomed to.

Conclusion

The profusion and wealth of references to Greco-Roman antiquity in Nazi discourse amply demonstrate its importance to the construction of the totalitarian subject.

The Nazi Party, engaged in the project of creating a new man, sought when it seized the reins of state power to endow this man not only with a new body but also with a new personality: his character forged by the leitmotivs of Nazi propaganda (serve the führer and the state), his mind guided by ideology (that of racial struggle), his identity defined by the history of the race to which this new man belonged. This history was not only taught through school textbooks but also drew upon ceremony and commemoration, architecture, sculpture, and film, illustrating that the postulates of National Socialist ideology were real and verifiable in the study of the past. Nazism as an ideology thus depended upon its view of history, a discourse that claimed to tell the true story of the past of the race and to elaborate a system of proofs to validate its premises.

This racialized history has often been perceived as exclusively Germanocentric. Given the exclusionary nature of National Socialist racism, the Nazis were to a degree obligated to embellish the history of Frederick's Prussia and the Holy Roman Empire and to illustrate the family tree that connected Hermann der Cherusker (Arminius the Cheruscan) to Hitler. But references to classical antiquity were legion in public discourse, while the regime's official architecture revived Rome's monumental classicism and Nazi sculptors rediscovered the Greek nude. The reinvention of history, the fabrication of an origin myth, and the many alleged trials and tribulations of the Indo-Germanic peoples helped create the Nazi subject, whose racial identity and history were inflated by the annexation of a culturally prestigious past.

The annexation of antiquity gave the new man an identity he could truly be proud of. The prestige of his predecessors required and commanded that his contemporary exponents work to build a future that would be equally glorious. The past showed that despite the vicissitudes of a mediocre and unpredictable present, the inherent potential of the race remained and demanded to be fulfilled.

The building of the present and the construction of the future would lean upon the great achievements of the Nordic peoples of antiquity, just as the great Greek and Roman thinkers would be read, contemplated, understood, and followed.

One corollary of imitation was vigilance. The Greeks and Romans, despite being great Nordic peoples, had nevertheless vanished from the historical stage, because they had committed sins against their race: fratricidal wars, opening the veins of the racial body to inferior elements, and repeated poisoning of the blood had ultimately led to their demise. The Third Reich would have to do everything in its power to avoid this gruesome fate. If it could not—and if there was no longer any doubt about the impending defeat of the Nordic-Indo-Germanic ideal in the final showdown between the races—then it was better to die with honor and to leave behind a heroic myth worthy of Leonidas's Spartans and the ruins of Rome. If total victory in the decisive battle of this plurimillennial race war was to prove impossible, the Reich's defeat had to be equally uncompromising, a cataclysm of such spectacular sound and fury that it would remain lodged in the memory of all mankind as a terrible and tragic legend.

While the history of the West is full of renaissances and restorations of empire (*renovationes imperii*), the singularity of National Socialism's approach to antiquity resided in its concept of race. The Nazis' claim to represent a bridge between past and present was not spiritual or abstract, symbolic or nationalistic; it was purely material, inscribed in the flesh and blood of contemporary Germans, who possessed the same racial essence as the ancient Greeks and Romans. This continuity of race justified the Nazis' territorial conquests: if the Greeks and Romans had originally come from the North, then the Mediterranean basin—as well as the Russian East, colonized long ago by the Greeks of the Black Sea—rightly belonged to the legitimate heirs of the North.

This notion of the ancients' Nordic descent was not new: nineteenth-century Germans, with their inversion of the Aryan myth, shifting the cradle of Aryan civilization from India to Germany, had already lent credibility to this idea.

From the supposed Nordic migrations toward the Mediterranean to the dissolution of the Roman Empire, the history of antiquity was reinterpreted through a racial lens. Everything great that was made, created, or thought was a product of Aryan genius, while the decay of morals and states was caused by the dilution of their blood, tragically or criminally subjected to miscegenation. This discourse was so flattering to the German people and so satisfying from a pedagogical perspective that it could not help but receive a warm and welcoming reception. National Socialism mobilized antiquity to shape, speak to, and educate its society, its empire, and its bodies.

The fate of antiquity in the Nazis' interpretation likewise demonstrated not only their metastasized totalitarian will to claim the ancient dead in order to ensure their hold over the present but also a deep affinity for death itself, and perhaps even an urge to cross over to the other side. National Socialism, particularly as explained and described by Hitler himself, was characterized by a profound anxiety about mortality that was paradoxically sublimated into a welcoming of death, a fear of dying that could be assuaged and overcome only by suicide. Killing oneself was the ultimate act of will and demonstration of mastery over one's own demise, the staging of one's legacy for all eternity.

Not everything, of course, was directed toward death. As we have seen, Nazi discourse on antiquity also served several other vital purposes: the classical world provided reassurance, good counsel, a model for emulation, and a prophetic warning, all functions necessary for the life of a Thousand-Year Reich under construction.

The use of the classical world, however, also reveals the Nazis' ambivalent relationship to time. National Socialism sought to preserve history as myth while denying time's unidirectional linear movement. This denial took the form of radical transcendence through a racial and civilizational sacrifice that, in the present, allowed the Nazis to escape reality by destroying it and then, through the amplitude and echo of their actions, to leave behind a mythology of death that could outlast death itself. This urge toward mythos and death, visible in the use of antiquity in the choreography of the final cataclysm, was already present in utero in Hitler's desire to build monuments that would ultimately resemble Roman ruins.

The Nazis thus believed in a kind of time that, in the end, negated the notion of time itself. As we have seen, the National Socialist concept of time was based on an eternity of identical repetition, time that stood still, transcended and abrogated by the immortality of the race, its deeds, and its struggles.

And so began a time without a future, sacred time, in Mircea Eliade's brilliant formulation, the negation of time as an unfolding, linear flow of consciousness, the definitive characteristic of the mythic imagination and its perception of the real.[1] The Heraclitean passage of time is bent into a circle, a temporal repetition of experience, the "eternal return." *Nihil novi sub sole:* for the Nazis, there truly was "nothing new under the sun,"[2] for the repeated assaults of the East upon the West were the expression of a timeless racial conflict between the Oriental-Semitic and the Indo-Germanic peoples; the Greco-Persian Wars, Hannibal's attack upon Rome, Attila's assault upon the Roman Empire, and the threat of Stalin's Red Army were but different forms of the same plurimillennial hatred.

The National Socialist discourse on antiquity betrayed a profound distrust and defiance of history, which it negated as such. The laws of Nazi history, racial determinism and race war, were such that the past of the Roman Empire or ancient Greece was identical to the present of the Reich. A synchronic infinite loop took the place of the normal diachronic unfolding of time, a flattening of two-dimensional time and space into the single dimension of a perennial present: Judeo-Christianity and Judeo-Bolshevism were the same manifestation of the Jewish conspiracy against the Aryan race, Saint Paul and Mardochai/Marx identical representatives of the Indo-Germanics' eternal foe. There was nothing anachronistic to the Nazis about describing Socrates as the "social democrat of his day" or St. Paul as a "political commissar" or the early Christians as "Bolsheviks."[3]

This defiance, animadversion even, of time was matched by a similar antipathy to reality. Time is a dimension in which reality unfolds, unless it is immortalized by the ecstasy of mythic consecration. The real—imperfect, finite, prone to decadence and decay—was unfulfilling and deceptive in comparison to the ideal, and as Hitler repeatedly insisted, National Socialism was an idea. An imaginary conception of reality, of what should be, this idea could scarcely accommodate what really was. Idealistic dreams of the aesthetic richness of the real recoiled into nihilism: if the real could not live up to the grandeur of the ideal, then it had to be destroyed. This desire for the ideal demonstrated a lack of fulfillment that juxtaposed the poetry of dreams to the prose of the real world, the ugliness of reality to the beauty of fantasy.

National Socialism was concerned not so much with living, with the blossoming of reality in real time, as with dying and becoming immortal by creating an eternal myth. This mythogenesis, this desire to become myth, synergized brilliantly with the mythopoetic dimension of National Socialism, visible in the fabulation of antiquity, revised and rewritten to serve the needs of ideology.

Hitler and his associates responsible for the regime were haunted by myths, obsessed with imitating the acts of their predecessors, possessed by visions of reliving the great ancient epics. Hitler was happy to live in the self-conscious narration of his own story, whether historical or fictional; literary, cinematographic, or theatrical; the novels of Karl May, the history of Rome, or the opera of Wagner. The führer's propensity to withdraw into a purely fictional world to the point of the absurd was well known. He had to have been brought up on such fantasies to have conjured up his plans for world domination. He had to exist inside an imagination structured and governed by myth to even attempt to do things that anyone endowed with an even remotely developed sense of logic would have rightly dismissed or condemned. He needed to possess a great love of myth and a no less substantial disdain for reality to believe that the force of will would suffice for him to re-create Rome anew, for Greece to be revived once more, for his new Teutonic Knights to chase Alexander the Great and his conquest of the East.

The ultimate preoccupation of Nazi leaders was to leave behind a suitable myth for posterity. Time and power are the surest means for historical actors to reach apotheosis, to raise themselves to the status of legend: power, for the fascination it exercises and the opportunities it provides; time, for the patina and amplified perspective that it lends. The incessant repetition of names and other words and the unending recurrence of images make historical actors appear to be archetypes destined for the gilded legend of a cult or the black legend of execration, the heights of glory or *damnatio memoriae*. Once victory was clearly impossible, it became preferable to survive in the form of legend, even the negative myth of infamy, a *damnatio memoriae* that would ultimately befall the regime's architecture, the glories of the new Rome meant to become the new capital of the Reich, Germania.

The eradication of certain monuments, like the Chancellery, to desecrate a potential site of memory with the vengeful ire of Allied dynamite obeyed the same principle as the dispersal of the ashes of the men condemned at Nuremberg: there would be no physical trace of them to commemorate, no place to gather or make pilgrimage where the memory of Nazism could be made concrete.

The Allies thus revived the Roman practice of *damnatio memoriae*. In Rome, the symbolic counterpart to apotheosis was a punishment equally proportionate to deification: complete erasure from memory.[4] If the sovereign proved to be a poor emperor, he was condemned to a legal process of cancellation from memory, the ultimate form of death. The Senate would solemnly vote to wipe out his name, order his legislative and regulatory achievements to be scrubbed clean, and chisel away all traces of his name from any statues or monuments.[5] It could be argued, perhaps, that this execration fulfilled the Nazis' final wishes. In a certain sense, being damned means being remembered. *Damnatio memoriae* still implies elevation to the status of myth, albeit in a negative sense, and the void it created certainly provided ample space for the free exercise of perverse imaginations.

From the beginning, the leaders of the Third Reich abandoned the realm of history to live in the realm of myth, where everything was sign or symbol and where all chance was perceived as being of necessity. Certainly, the meaning attributed to the Nazis does not always reflect their intentions; Goebbels, paraphrasing Bismarck, said that "we [will] enter history as the greatest of heroes or the worst of criminals,"[6] which is frequently given a hyperbolic accent: Hitler as Satan and Himmler, Heydrich, and Goebbels his archangels. However, in restoring to the sad figures of the Third Reich the radical otherness of monstrosity, madness, or devilry, ceding to the temptations of demonology or a theology of absolute evil, one plays the very game that Hitler and Goebbels wanted posterity to play, as they waited for the end deep in the bunker of Berlin: that they should be shrouded in sacrality, even in a negative or evil sense, and that this aura would prohibit any rational notion of or approach to the phenomenon they represented; that their story should be wiped clean of all guesswork or venality, weakness or luck, chance or error. Hitler wanted to leave behind a myth for posterity. It would be the ultimate triumph for this eternal actor, for whom all the world was only a stage, if he should be allowed to thus choreograph his final heroic gesture: "Qualis artifex pereo!," in Nero's last words.[7]

The Nazi myth, fertile and funereal, was intended to impregnate others, to awaken the future race and urge new generations of Aryans to rise up once more, out of sacred respect for their ancestors. Strewn with their massive, glorious ruins, the party grounds at Nuremberg—to hear

Hitler tell it—would become the sacred forest of an avenging Aryan race for thousands of years to come, made fecund by the seed of these ruins and the spirit they emanated. The Nazis wanted to turn their demise into a deafening myth that would one day mobilize a new cohort of Nordic peoples to march in the footsteps of the Waffen-SS, just as they had followed the path of the Teutonic Knights and Alexander the Great, that other Aryan Greek with a fascination for the East. The *ver sacrum* and the *Drang nach Osten:* henceforth, there would be Barbarossa and the collapse of an entire world in the sputtering flames of a conflagration sparked by the Nero Decree.

Perhaps it is in this flickering light that we can see the value of the historian's craft: The historian pulls back the curtain, snuffs out the incense, pulls on the rigging, and rummages around behind the scenes. The historian interrupts the show and wrests the spectators from the trancelike illusion that if they suspend their disbelief and put themselves in the actors' hands, the play will never end. To combat a myth of death, the historian's only remedy lies in the death of myth. As Robert Antelme wrote of one of his SS guards in *The Human Race:*

> What we would like is to start by turning him upside down, to fix him with his feet in the air. And then to laugh and laugh. . . . That's what we'd like to do to the gods.[8]

Notes

INTRODUCTION

1. See Édouard Conte and Cornelia Essner, *La quête de la race: Une anthropologie du nazisme* (Paris: Hachette, 1995), 366–67.
2. Colette Beaune, *The Birth of an Ideology: Myths and Symbols of the Nation in Late Medieval France*, trans. Susan Ross Houston (Berkeley: University of California Press, 1991).
3. Claude Nicolet, *La fabrique de la nation: La France entre Rome et les Germains* (Paris: Perrin, 2003).
4. Otto Gerhard Oexle and Winfried Schulze, eds., *Deutsche Historiker im Nationalsozialismus* (Frankfurt am Main: Fischer, 1999).
5. Peter Schöttler, ed., *Geschichtsschreibung als Legitimationswissenschaft, 1918–1945* (Frankfurt am Main: Suhrkamp, 1997).
6. Alexander Scobie, *Hitler's State Architecture: The Impact of Classical Antiquity* (University Park: Pennsylvania State University Press, 1990).
7. Hannah Arendt, *The Origins of Totalitarianism* (Cleveland: World Publishing, 1958), 362.
8. Ibid., 384.
9. Ibid., 352.
10. Ibid., 350.
11. A professor of ancient history at the University of Vienna.
12. "Ein Volk lebt solange glücklich in Gegenwart und Zukunft, als es sich seiner Vergangenheit und der Größe seiner Ahnen bewußt ist."

PART I. ANNEXING ANTIQUITY

Epigraph. Paul Valéry, "On Myths and Mythology," trans. Anthony Bower, in *Selected Writings of Paul Valéry* (New York: New Directions, 1950), 201.

CHAPTER 1. ORIGINS MYTHS

Epigraphs. Nicole Loraux, *Born of the Earth: Myth and Politics in Athens*, trans. Selina Stewart (Ithaca, NY: Cornell University Press, 2000), 13; and Michel Foucault, "Nietzsche, Genealogy, History," trans. Donald F. Bouchard and Sherry Simon, in *The Foucault Reader*, ed. Paul Rabinow (New York: Pantheon Books, 1984), 79.

1. Ernest Renan, "What Is a Nation?," trans. Martin Thom, in *Becoming National: A Reader*, ed. Geoff Eley and Ronald Grigor Suny (Oxford: Oxford University Press, 1996), 52.
2. See, e.g., Hellmuth Plessner, *Die verspätete Nation: Über die politische Verführbarkeit bürgerlichen Geistes* (Stuttgart: Kohlhammer, 1959); Hagen Schulze, *States, Nations, and Nationalism: From the Middle Ages to the Present*, trans. William Yuill (Oxford: Blackwell, 1996); Schulze, *Gibt es überhaupt eine deutsche Geschichte?* (Berlin: Siedler, 1989); and Manfred Hättich, *Deutschland, eine zu späte Nation* (Mainz: Hase und Kohler, 1990).
3. Friedrich Prinz, "Der Weisswurstäquator," in *Deutsche Erinnerungsorte*, ed. Étienne François and Hagen Schulze, vol. 1 (Munich: C.H. Beck, 2001), 471–84.
4. See Klaus von See, *Barbar, Germane, Arier: Die Suche nach der Identität der Deutschen* (Heidelberg: C. Winter Verlag, 1994).
5. See Colette Beaune, *The Birth of an Ideology: Myths and Symbols of the Nation in Late Medieval France*, trans. Susan Ross Houston (Berkeley: University of California Press, 1991); and Claude Nicolet, *La fabrique de la nation: La France entre Rome et les Germains* (Paris: Perrin, 2003).
6. Tacitus, *Germania*, ed. and trans. by J.B. Rives (Oxford: Clarendon, 1999), 77 (2.1).
7. On Athenian autochthony, see Nicole Loraux, *Born of the Earth: Myth and Politics in Athens*, trans. Selena Stewart (Ithaca: Cornell University Press, 2000); and Marcel Detienne, *Comment être autochtone: Du pur Athénien au Français raciné* (Paris: Le Seuil, 2003). It is interesting to note how infrequently German historians of the 1930s and 1940s made reference to Athenian autochthony, the foundational myth of the Attic city-state—which, of course, flatly contradicted any notion of the Nordic origins of Hellenic civilization. Spartan allochthony, in contrast, was always duly noted.
8. Tacitus, *Germania*, 78 (4.1).
9. Léon Poliakov, *The Aryan Myth: A History of Racist and Nationalist Ideas in Europe*, trans. Edmund Howard (New York: Basic Books, 1974). See also Bernard Sergent, *Les Indo-Européens: Histoire, langues, mythes* (Paris: Payot, 1995), 22–25, 37–41, and 56–58.
10. See Ute Tintemann and Jürgen Trabant, *Sprache und Sprachen in Berlin um 1800* (Hannover: Wehrhahn, 2004).
11. The term was created by the German Orientalist Julius von Klaproth in 1823. See Sergent, *Les Indo-Européens*, 22–25, 37–41, 56–58.
12. Georg Wilhelm Friedrich Hegel, *Lectures on the Philosophy of World History*, trans. H.B. Nisbet (Cambridge: Cambridge University Press, 1975).
13. The 1848 German original has recently been rereleased: Jacob Grimm, *Geschichte der Deutschen Sprache* (New York: Cambridge University Press, 2009).

14. On this subject, see Uwe Puschner, Walter Schmitz, and Justus Ulbricht, eds., *Handbuch zur "Völkischen Bewegung" 1871–1918* (Munich: K. G. Saur, 1996); and Puschner, *Die völkische Bewegung im wilhelminischen Kaiserreich: Sprache-Rasse-Religion* (Darmstadt: Wissenschaftliche Buchgesellschaft, 2001).

15. See Brigitte Hamann, *Hitler's Vienna: A Dictator's Apprenticeship*, trans. Thomas Thornton (New York: Oxford University Press, 1999)—recently reissued under the title *Hitler's Vienna: A Portrait of the Tyrant as a Young Man* (London: I. B. Tauris, 2010).

16. See Nicholas Goodrick-Clarke, *The Occult Roots of Nazism: The Ariosophists of Austria and Germany, 1890–1935* (Wellingborough, Northamptonshire: Aquarian, 1985).

17. Adolf Hitler, "Warum sind wir Antisemiten?," Munich, 13 August 1920, reprinted in Reginald H. Phelps, "Hitlers 'grundlegende' Rede über den Antisemitismus," *Vierteljahrshefte für Zeitgeschichte* 16, no. 4 (October 1968): 390–420.

18. "Auf dem nördlichsten Teil dieser Welt, in jenen unerhörten Eiswüsten, ... die unerhörte Not und die furchtbaren Entbehrungen wirkten als Mittel zur Rassenreinzucht. Was schwächlich und kränklich war, konnte diese fürchterliche Periode nicht überstehen, ... und über blieb ein Geschlecht von Riesen an Kraft und Gesundheit.... Diese Rassen nun, die wir als Arier bezeichnen, waren in Wirklichkeit die Erwecker der späteren großen Kulturen, die wir in der Geschichte heute noch verfolgen können. Wir wissen, daß Ägypten durch arische Einwanderer auf seine Kulturhöhe gebracht wurde, ebenso Persien, Griechenland; die Einwanderer waren blonde, blauäugige Arier und wir wissen, daß außer diesen Staaten überhaupt keine Kulturstaaten auf dieser Erde gegründet wurden." Ibid., 401–2.

19. Ernst von Salomon, *The Outlaws*, trans. Ian F. D. Morrow (London: Jonathan Cape, 1931). Originally published as *Die Geächten* (Berlin: Rowohlt, 1930).

20. Hans F. K. Günther, *Rassenkunde des Deutschen Volkes* (Munich: J. F. Lehmanns Verlag, 1922).

21. See Sigrid Stöckel, *Die "rechte Nation" und ihr Verleger: Politik und Popularisierung im J. F. Lehmanns Verlag, 1890–1979* (Berlin: LOB, 2002), 328.

22. Hans F. K. Günther, *Herkunft und Rassengeschichte der Germanen* (Munich: Lehmanns Verlag, 1937), 11.

23. Ibid.

24. On the Nazis' relationship with the East, see chap. 7.

25. Hans F. K. Günther, *Kleine Rassenkunde des Deutschen Volkes* (Munich: Lehmanns Verlag, 1929), 101.

26. Carl Schuchhardt, "Die Indogermanisierung Griechenlands," *Die Antike: Zeitschrift für Kunst und Kultur des klassischen Altertums* 9 (1933): 303.

27. Hans F. K. Günther, *Die nordische Rasse bei den Indogermanen Asiens: Zugleich ein Beitrag zur Frage nach der Urheimat und Rassenherkunft der Indogermanen* (Munich: Lehmanns Verlag, 1934).

28. On these three figures, see Rita Thalmann, "Ploetz, Rüdin, Fischer, Lenz, von Verschuer: Pionniers et cautions scientifiques de l'"hygiène raciale,'" in

"Classer/Penser/Exclure: De l'eugénisme à l'hygiène raciale," ed. Yves Ternon and Thalmann, special issue, *Revue d'histoire de la Shoah* 183 (July–December 2005): 211–27.

29. Erwin Baur, Eugen Fischer, and Fritz Lenz, *Menschliche Erblichkeitslehre*, vol. 1 of *Menschliche Erblichkeitslehre und Rassenhygiene* (Munich: Lehmanns Verlag, 1927), 540–41.

30. Fritz Lenz, *Menschliche Auslese und Rassenhygiene (Eugenik)*, vol. 2 of *Menschliche Erblichkeitslehre und Rassenhygiene* (Munich: Lehmanns Verlag, 1932), esp. 16–17, 78–79, 88–89, 234–37, 368, and 413.

31. Walther Wüst, "Zur Erkenntnis Deutschen Wesens: Indien und Germanien," *Germanien: Monatshefte für Germanenkunde zur Erkenntnis Deutschen Wesens* 10 no. 1 (1938): 1–5.

32. Franz Altheim, "Germanen und Iranier," *Germanien* 14, no. 6 (1942): 197–208; no. 7: 239–44; and no. 8: 277–90.

33. Franz Altheim and E. Trautmann, "Hirsch und Hirschage bei den Ariern," *Germanien* 13, no. 8 (1941): 286–97; and no. 9: 349–57.

34. Ella Runge, "Zur Verbreitung nordischen Geistesguts: Nordische Kunstformen in der ostasiatischen Zierkunst," *Germanien* 6, no. 10 (1934): 305–11.

35. See Otto Huth, "Die ewigen Stammesfeuer der Germanen und Indogermanen," *Germanien* 10, no. 9 (1938): 273–78.

36. Édouard Conte and Cornelia Essner, *La quête de la race: Une anthropologie du nazisme* (Paris: Hachette, 1995), see esp. ch. 2, "Le dogme nordique des races."

37. Günther, *Rassenkunde des Deutschen Volkes*, 357. Günther cited a "Jornandes, IV"; the actual Jordanes, author of *The Origin and Deeds of the Goths*, wrote of Scandinavia: "Now from this island of Scandza, as from a hive of races or a womb of nations, the Goths are said to have come forth long ago" ("Ex hac igitur Scanzia insula quasi officina gentium aut certe velut vagina nationum . . . Gothi quondam memorantur egressi"). See *De Getarum sive Gothorum origine et rebus gestis*, 1.2.1; for the English translation, consult *The Gothic History of Jordanes in English Version*, trans. Charles C. Mierow (Princeton: Princeton University Press, 1915), 57.

38. *SS-Mann und Blutsfrage: Die biologischen Grundlagen und ihre sinngemässe Anwendung für die Erhaltung und Mehrung des Nordischen Blutes*, ed. Chef der Ordnungspolizei—SS-Hauptamt, Schriftenreihe für die weltanschauliche Schulung der Ordnungspolizei, Sonderheft, 1942, Bundesarchiv Berlin-Lichterfelde (hereafter BABL)/R 18/19, 11.

39. "Woher kommt die nordische Rasse?," *Das Schwarze Korps*, February 1935, 11.

40. See chap. 3 concerning similar debates regarding the humanities.

41. See pp. 23–24, esp. regarding Hitler's speech "Warum sind wir Antisemiten?"

42. Adolf Hitler, *Mein Kampf*, trans. Ralph Manheim (Boston: Houghton Mifflin, 1943), 290.

43. Ibid.

44. *Deutschland erwache!* was a slogan that appeared on Nazi banners after 1925.

45. "Ihr seid die Fackelträger der Nation—Ihr trägt das Licht des Geistes voran im Kampfe für Adolf Hitler." See Ruth Schmitz-Ehmke, *Die Ordensburg Vogelsang: Architektur, Bauplastik, Ausstattung* (Cologne: Rheinland Verlag, 1988).

46. Hegel's original words were, of course, "Nothing great in the world has ever been accomplished without passion." See G. W. F. Hegel, *Reason in History: A General Introduction to a Philosophy of History,* trans. Robert S. Hartman (Indianapolis: Bobbs-Merrill, 1953), 29.

47. The raciology and the destiny of these peoples can be found in a series of articles by Heinar Schilling published in *Das Schwarze Korps,* subsequently gathered into a single volume: Schilling, *Das politische Weltbild* (Magdeburg: Nordland-Verlag, 1937), esp. 9–20, on Egypt, and 21–28, on China. The series also contained articles on Iran, Asia Minor (Persia), and India, followed by Greece, Rome, and the various eras of Germanic history.

48. *Hitler's Table Talk, 1941–1944: His Private Conversations,* trans. Norman Cameron and R. H. Stevens (New York: Enigma, 2000), 248.

49. Richard Walther Darré, *Vom Lebensgesetz zweier Staatsgedanken (Konfuzius und Lykurgos)* (Goslar: Verlag Blut und Boden, 1940), 65. Heinrich Himmler appreciated Darré's judgment on Confucius's racial purity, so much so that the head of the SS even turned him into a paradigm of the Indo-Germanic conqueror: *Rede des Reichsführers-SS am 19.6.1942 vor dem Führerkorps der Division "Das Reich,"* BABL/NS/19/4009, ff. 120–21.

50. See Darré, *Vom Lebensgesetz zweier Staatsgedanken,* 65.

51. Hegel, *Philosophy of World History,* 196.

52. Ibid., 197.

53. Alfred Rosenberg, *The Myth of the Twentieth Century: An Evaluation of the Spiritual-Intellectual Confrontations of Our Age,* trans. Vivian Bird (Newport Beach, CA: Noontide, 1982), 8.

54. Alfred Rosenberg, "Nordische Wiedergeburt: Rede in Lübeck anlässlich der zweiten Reichstagung der nordischen Gesellschaft," in Rosenberg, *Reden und Aufsätze von 1933–1935,* vol. 2 of *Gestaltung der Idee: Blut und Ehre* (Munich: Zentralverlag der NSDAP, Franz Eher Verlag, 1936), 341.

55. Ibid.

56. Ibid., 342.

57. Alfred Rosenberg, "Die Ausweitung des Deutschen Geschichtsbildes," speech given to mark the Day of German Prehistory (Tag für deutsche Vorgeschichte), 29 September 1935, in ibid., 396–97.

58. Dietrich Klagges, *Geschichtsunterricht als nationalpolitische Erziehung* (Frankfurt am Main: Moritz Diesterweg Verlag, 1937).

59. For a stimulating interpretation of the Platonic myth and a history of its legacy, see Pierre Vidal-Naquet, *The Atlantis Story: A Short History of Plato's Myth,* trans. Janet Lloyd (Exeter: University of Exeter Press, 2007).

60. Founded in September 1918 by Rudolf von Sebottendorf in Munich, the Thule Society gathered ultranationalist Germans who were well versed in ancient German history and the occult. The society's intellectual cadres (Dietrich Eckhart, Alfred Rosenberg, Rudolf Hess) overlapped to some degree with the NSDAP; its journal, the *Münchner Beobachter,* would become the *Völkischer*

Beobachter, while it chose the swastika as its insignia after borrowing it from the Armanen Gesellschaft.

61. Karl Georg Zschaetzsch, *Atlantis: Die Urheimat der Arier* (Berlin: Arier-Verlag, 1922). Zschaetzsch was also the author of a phantasmagorical volume on the history of the Aryan race, *Die Arier: Herkunft und Geschichte des arischen Stammes* (Berlin: Arier-Verlag GmbH, 1900; repr., 1920 and 1938).

62. Rosenberg, *Myth of the Twentieth Century*, 5.

63. Albert Herrmann, *Unsere Ahnen und Atlantis: Nordische Seeherrschaft von Skandinavien bis Nordafrika* (Berlin: Klinkhardt und Biermann, 1934).

64. On this aspect of Himmler's personality, see Michael Kater, *Das "Ahnenerbe" der SS, 1933–1945: Ein Beitrag zur Kulturpolitik des Dritten Reiches* (Munich: Oldenbourg, 2001).

65. See the letter from Heinrich Himmler to Hermann Wüst dated 25 October 1937, in which he mentioned an "Atlantic elite," creator of states and cultures, quoted in ibid., 51.

66. Ibid., 71.

67. Ibid.

68. Albert Herrmann, "Die Nordrasse eroberte die Welt," review of Wilhelm Sieglin, *Die blonden Haare der indogermanischen Völker des Altertums*, in *Das Schwarze Korps*, 15 May 1935, 10.

69. Wilhelm Frick, "Kampfziel der Deutschen Schule: Ansprache des Reichsministers des Innern Dr. Frick auf der Ministerkonferenz am 9. Mai 1933," special issue, *Friedrich Manns Pädagogisches Magazin*, Heft 1376.

70. Wilhelm Frick, "Richtlinien für die Geschichtslehrbücher—20. Juli 1933," *Zentralblatt für die gesamte Unterrichtsverwaltung in Preußen*, ed. Ministerium für Wissenschaft, Kunst und Volksbildung, 5 August 1933, Heft 15: 197–99.

71. Frick's notes here make reference to the scholar Gustaf Kossina (also Kossinna; 1858–1931), the author of a 1910 work that would become a sort of manifesto for scholars of German prehistory (*Die Deutsche Vorgeschichte, eine hervorragend nationale Wissenschaft*).

72. Georges Vacher de Lapouge, *L'Aryen, son rôle social* (Paris: A. Fontemoing, 1899).

73. Decree (*Erlass*) of the Reich Education Minister, 15 January 1935, quoted in Helmut Genschel, *Politische Erziehung durch Geschichtsunterricht: Der Beitrag der Geschichtsdidaktik und des Geschichtsunterrichts zur politischen Erziehung im Nationalsozialismus* (Frankfurt am Main: Haag und Herchen Verlag, 1980), 26–27.

74. Bernhard Rust, ed., *Erziehung und Unterricht in der höheren Schule: Amtliche Ausgabe des Reichs- und Preußischen Ministeriums für Wissenschaft, Erziehung und Volksbildung* (Berlin: Weidmann, 1938), 69.

75. Ibid., 70.

76. Ibid.., 69.

77. Ibid., 70.

78. "Lehrgang Geschichte: In Wien-Schönbrunn vom 14–21.9.1941 für Erzieher der Volks-, Haupt- und höheren Schulen," BABL/R/4901/4550, f. 5.

79. *SS-Mann und Blutsfrage*, 26.

80. Lothar Herdt, "Geschichte Europas: Geschichte der Nordischen Rasse," *Wille und Macht*, 1933, Heft 22: 4–8.
81. *SS-Mann und Blutsfrage*, 17.
82. Kurt Schrötter and Walther Wüst, eds., *Tod und Unsterblichkeit: Aus indogermanischem Weistum* (Berlin-Dahlem: Ahnenerbe-Stiftung Verlag, 1940).
83. See, for example, Anja Heuss, *Kunst- und Kulturgutraub: Eine vergleichende Studie zur Besatzungspolitik der Nationalsozialisten in Frankreich und der Sowjetunion* (Heidelberg: Universitätsverlag C. Winter, 2000).
84. The Reichsleiter Rosenberg Task Force (Einsatzstab Reichleiter Rosenberg, or ERR) in France, the Abteilung VI G RHSA, and the SS-Sonderkommando Künsberg on the eastern front, for example.
85. See chap. 2.
86. Johannes Mahnkopf, *Von der Urzeit zum Großdeutschen Reich, Geschichtsbuch für Mittelschulen, Klasse 2: Von den Anfängen bis zum Ausklang der großgermanischen Zeit* (Leipzig: B. G. Teubner, 1942).
87. Rosenberg, *Myth of the Twentieth Century*, 99.
88. Ibid., 454.
89. Theobald Bieder, *Das Hakenkreuz* (Leipzig: Verlag Theodor Weicher, 1934).
90. Alexander Conze, *Zur Geschichte der Anfänge griechischer Kunst*, 2 vols. (Vienna: Karl Gerolds Sohn, Buchhändler der kaiserlichen Akademie der Wissenschaft, 1870).
91. Bieder, *Das Hakenkreuz*, 12, 14.
92. Ibid., 13.
93. The NSFO were created in August 1944. For more on the NSFO, see Omer Bartov, *Hitler's Army: Soldiers, Nazis, and War in the Third Reich* (New York: Oxford University Press, 1991), esp. ch. 4.
94. "Das Hakenkreuz (als Sinnbild in Gegenwart und Geschichte)," in *Stoffsammlung für die Nationalsozialistischen Führungsoffiziere*, Folge 2, Berlin, NSDAP, Nationalsozialistischer Führungsstab des Oberkommandos der Wehrmacht, undated (but likely autumn 1944), 83.
95. Carl Blümel, *Sport der Hellenen: Ausstellung griechischer Bildwerke* (Berlin: Verlag für Kunstwissenschaft, 1936). See esp. the reproductions on 55 and 61.
96. See chap. 4.
97. *Das Reich und Europa* (Berlin: SS-Hauptamt, n.d.), BABL/RD/NSD, 41/115, 2.
98. *SS-Mann und Blutsfrage*, 11.
99. "Die historischen und politischen Grundlagen der europäischen Neuerordnung," in *Die deutsche Polizei: Sicherheitspolizei und SD*, ed. Auftrag des Reichsführers SS und Chef der Deutschen Polizei vom Kameradschaftsbund der Deutschen Polizei (1933–1945), 1 January 1943, BABL/R 19/11, 5.
100. Ibid., 3.
101. Ibid., 4.
102. *Deutschland ordnet Europa neu!*, ed. Chef der Ordnungspolizei—SS-Hauptamt, Schriftenreihe für die weltanschauliche Schulung der Ordnungspolizei, 1942, Heft 4, BABL/RD 18/16, 7.

103. Ibid., p 16.
104. Ibid., 20–21.
105. Ibid., 16.
106. Ibid., 19.
107. Ibid., 7.
108. See chap. 5 and 7. See also Joseph Weisner, "Die Bedeutung des Ostraumes für die Antike," *Neue Jahrbücher für antike und deutsche Bildung,* 1942, Heft 5: 257–69.
109. It is striking to see the extent to which the Nazi philosophy of history and its historiography constituted a mythologizing of history: the quest for, and reading of, deeper meaning; Manichaeism; narrative structures built around archetypes, whether idols (the savior, the hero) or foils (the traitor, the devil), and seminal events (origins, the rise and fall, decadence, catastrophe, redemption, resurrection); and the pronouncement of moral judgments.
110. See, for instance, Max Horkheimer and Theodor Adorno, *Dialectic of Enlightenment,* trans. John Cumming (New York: Continuum, 1972); and Horkheimer, *Eclipse of Reason* (New York: Oxford University Press, 1947).
111. Paul Nizan, *The Watchdogs: Philosophers of the Established Order,* trans. Paul Fittinghof (New York: Monthly Review Press, 1972).
112. Diemuth Königs, *Joseph Vogt: Ein Althistoriker in der Weimarer Republik und in Dritten Reich* (Basel: Helbing und Lichtenhahn, 1995).
113. Luciano Canfora, "Helmut Berve," in Canfora, *Le vie del classicismo,* vol. 1 (Bari: Laterza, 1989), 169–220, available in German in Canfora, *Politische Philologie: Altertumswissenschaften und moderne Staatsideologien,* trans. Volker Breidecker, Ulrich Hausmann, and Barbara Hufer (Stuttgart: Klett, 1995), 126–78; Karl Christ, "Helmut Berve," in Christ, *Neue Profile der alten Geschichte* (Darmstadt: Wissenschaftliche Buchgesellschaft, 1990), 125–87.
114. Julien Benda, *The Treason of the Intellectuals,* trans. Richard Aldington (New York: William Morrow, 1928) 57–58.
115. Anne-Marie Thiesse, *La création des identités nationales: Europe XVIIe–XXe siècle* (Paris: Le Seuil, 1999), 13. See also Jérôme Bruner, *Pourquoi nous racontons-nous des histoires? Le récit au fondement de la culture et de l'identité individuelle* (Paris: Pocket, 2005).
116. Thiesse, *La création des identités nationales,* 21.
117. Marc Bloch, *The Historian's Craft,* trans. Peter Putnam (New York: Vintage, 1953), 30.
118. The quote does not appear in the English translation. See Marc Bloch, *Apologie pour l'histoire, ou, Métier d'historien* (Paris: Armand Colin, 1993), 86.
119. Patrick Geary, *The Myth of Nations: The Medieval Origins of Europe* (Princeton: Princeton University Press, 2002), 13.
120. Ibid., 156–57.

CHAPTER 2. A NORDIC MEDITERRANEAN

Epigraph. Fred Uhlman, *Reunion: A Novella* (New York: Farrar, Strauss and Giroux, 1997), 93–95.
1. Hans F. K. Günther, *Rassengeschichte des Hellenischen und des Römischen Volkes* (Munich: Lehmanns Verlag, 1929).

2. Hans F. K. Günther, *Die nordische Rasse bei den Indogermanen Asiens: Zugleich ein Beitrag zur Frage nach der Urheimat und Rassenherkunft der Indogermanen* (Munich: Lehmanns Verlag, 1934).
3. Günther, *Rassengeschichte*, 6.
4. See, for instance, Karl Christ, *Hellas: Griechische Geschichte und deutsche Geschichtswissenschaft* (Munich: C. H. Beck, 1999).
5. Karl Ottfried Müller, *Die Dorier*, vols. 2–3 of *Geschichten hellenischer Stämme und Städte* (Breslau: Josef Max Verlag, 1824).
6. See, among others, Georg Billeter, *Die Anschauungen vom Wesen des Griechentums* (Berlin: Teubner Verlag, 1911); Karl Penka, *Origines Ariacae: Linguistisch-ethnologische Untersuchungen zur ältesten Geschichte der arischen Völker und Sprachen* (Vienna: Teschen, 1883); and Karl Georg Zschaetzsch, *Die Arier: Herkunft und Geschichte des arischen Stammes* (Berlin: Arier-Verlag, 1900).
7. A very learned survey of this literature can be found in Ingo Wiwjorra, *Der Germanenmythos: Konstruktion einer Weltanschauung in der Altertumsforschung des 19. Jahrhunderts* (Darmstadt: Wissenschaftliche Buchgesellschaft, 2006), 280–300.
8. Günther, *Rassengeschichte*, 13.
9. Ibid., 12 (see also n. 5).
10. Otto Reche had been a professor of anthropology at Vienna in 1924 and then the editor in chief of the journal *Volk und Rasse*, published in Munich by Lehmann. He held his professorship in Leipzig from 1927 until 1945, becoming a member of the NS Lehrerbund (National Socialist Teachers League) in 1934 and a full member of the NSDAP in 1937.
11. Otto Reche, "Griechen," in *Reallexikon der Vorgeschichte*, ed. Max Ebert, Band 4 (Berlin: De Gruyter, 1926), quoted in Günther, *Rassengeschichte*, 18.
12. Richard Walther Darré, *Das Bauerntum als Lebensquell der Nordischen Rasse* (Munich: Lehmanns Verlag, 1929), 191.
13. Günther, *Rassengeschichte*, 22.
14. Hans-Konrad Krause, "Griechische und alte deutsche Namengebung," in *Neue Jahrbücher für antike und deutsche Bildung*, 1939, Heft 2: 121–27.
15. Ludwig Ferdinand Clauss, *Rasse und Seele: Eine Einführung in den Sinn der leiblichen Gestalt* (Munich: Lehmanns Verlag, 1926); and Clauss, *Die nordische Seele: Eine Einführung in die Rassenseelenkunde* (Munich: Lehmanns Verlag, 1933).
16. Hans Bogner, *Der Seelenbegriff der griechischen Frühzeit*, Schriften des Reichsinstituts für Geschichte des neuen Deutschlands (Hamburg: Hanseatische Verlagsanstalt, 1939).
17. Ibid., 5.
18. Ibid., 14.
19. Ibid., 17.
20. Ibid., 19.
21. Ibid., 33.
22. Günther, *Rassengeschichte*, 18.
23. From the Greek *dolikhos*, "long."

24. Most notably in Georges Vacher de Lapouge, *L'Aryen, son rôle social* (Paris: A. Fontemoing, 1899). For more on Vacher de Lapouge, see Pierre-André Taguieff, "Racisme aryaniste, socialisme et eugénisme chez George Vacher de Lapouge (1854–1936)," in "Classer/Penser/Exclure: De l'eugénisme à l'hygiène raciale," ed. Yves Ternon and Rita Thalmann, special issue, *Revue d'histoire de la Shoah* 183 (July–December 2005): 69–134.

25. "The racial history of Athens," Günther wrote, "has already been examined by [Vacher] de Lapouge in his *Sélections sociales* (1896)." Günther, *Rassengeschichte*, 42.

26. From the Greek *brakhys*, "short."

27. Günther, *Rassengeschichte*, 19.

28. Ibid.

29. Ibid., 20.

30. Wilhelm Sieglin, *Die blonden Haare der indogermanischen Völker des Altertums: Eine Sammlung der antiken Zeugnisse als Beitrag zur Indogermanenfrage* (Munich: Lehmanns Verlag, 1935). Much earlier, in 1901, Sieglin had given a lecture titled "Die Haarfarbe der Griechen in Altertum" (The hair color of the ancient Greeks); see Wiwjorra, *Der Germanenmythos*, 296 (and n. 468). It is, of course, important to note that Sieglin's 1935 book was published with Lehmann.

31. Albert Herrmann, "Die Nordrasse eroberte die Welt," review of Sieglin, *Die blonden Haare der indogermanischen Völker des Altertums*, in *Das Schwarze Korps*, 15 May 1935, 10.

32. See *Hitler's Table Talk, 1941–1944: His Private Conversations*, trans. Norman Cameron and R. H. Stevens (New York: Enigma, 2000), midday, 21 October 1941, 76–79, esp. 78.

33. Eugen Fischer and Hans F. K. Günther, eds., *Deutsche Köpfe nordischer Rasse* (Munich: Lehmanns Verlag, 1933).

34. Eugen Fischer and Gerhard Kittel, *Das antike Weltjudentum: Tatsachen, Texte, Bilder*, vol. 7 of *Forschungen zur Judenfrage* (Hamburg: Hanseatische Verlagsanstalt, 1943). See also chap. 5.

35. See Georg Heinrich Karo, *Die Schachtgräber von Mykenai* (Munich: F. Bruckmann, 1933).

36. Günther, *Rassengeschichte*, 35, ill. 20.

37. Ibid., 142, Tafel II b.

38. Ibid., 24–25 and 34.

39. Ibid., 34.

40. Ibid.

41. For an article with a similar title published in the *Neue Jahrbücher*, see Siegfried Fuchs, "Zur Frage der Indogermanisierung Griechenlands," *Neue Jahrbücher für antike und deutsche Bildung*, 1939, Heft 2: 165–74.

42. Carl Schuchhardt, "Die Indogermanisierung Griechenlands," *Die Antike: Zeitschrift für Kunst und Kultur des klassischen Altertums* 9 (1933): 308.

43. Ibid., 303.

44. Ibid., 304.

45. See Karl Kynast, *Apollon und Dionysos: Nordisches und Unnordisches innerhalb der Religion der Griechen, eine rassenkundliche Untersuchung* (Munich: Lehmanns Verlag, 1927), esp. 8–9: the Pelasgians were a "Western" people with "Eastern" influences.
46. Günther, *Rassengeschichte*, 27.
47. Kynast, *Apollon und Dionysos*, 5 and 112. Nietzsche was lost in "completely ridiculous self-contradiction" (112) and was later violently criticized for his stance on Richard Wagner (112–13).
48. See Friedrich Nietzsche, *The Birth of Tragedy*, trans. Douglas Smith (New York: Oxford University Press, 2000).
49. Kynast, *Apollon und Dionysos*, 81.
50. Ibid., 83.
51. Ibid., 5.
52. Ibid., 17.
53. Ibid., 18–19.
54. See Darré, *Das Bauerntum als Lebensquell der nordischen Rasse*.
55. Kynast, *Apollon und Dionysos*, 5.
56. Ibid., 101.
57. Ludwig Schemann, *Hauptepochen und Hauptvölker der Geschichte in ihrer Stellung zur Rasse*, vol. 2 of *Die Rasse in den Geisteswissenschaften* (Munich: Lehmanns Verlag, 1930), 100–101.
58. See Alfred Rosenberg, *The Myth of the Twentieth Century: An Evaluation of the Spiritual-Intellectual Confrontations of Our Age*, trans. Vivian Bird (Newport Beach, CA: Noontide, 1982), 13. Rosenberg's racial reading of the Greek pantheon on 12–21 drew directly from Kynast.
59. See Hermann Jekeli, "Rasse ist Verpflichtung," in *Rasse und Volk: Stoffsammlung für die weltanschauliche Schulung*, ed. Beauftragten für die weltanschauliche Schulung der deutschen Volksgruppe in Rumänien, November 1941, Heft 2: 3–25, esp. 16 ("The conflict between two racial souls, the Nordic soul and the Asiatic soul, is mirrored quite clearly in the religious ideas of the Greeks"). The Nordic, Apollonian cult of light and wisdom was invaded by the darkness of the night and unregulated passion.
60. Rosenberg, *Myth of the Twentieth Century*, 12.
61. Ibid.
62. Ibid., 13.
63. Ibid., 18–19.
64. Ibid., 19.
65. Ibid. Leo Frobenius (1873–1938) was a German ethnologist famous for his studies of West African art and culture; he claimed to have found an "African Atlantis."
66. Günther, *Rassengeschichte*, 69.
67. Ibid., 74.
68. Ludwig Schemann (1852–1938) defended his doctoral thesis in history, on the Second Punic War, at the University of Bonn in 1875. A noted translator and biographer of Arthur de Gobineau, he founded the Gobineau-Vereinigung in Freiburg in 1894. Between 1928 and 1931, he released a trilogy of books that

constituted an intellectual testament and learned summa of his racial philosophy: *Die Rasse in den Geisteswissenschaften: Studien zur Geschichte des Rassengedankens,* vol. 1 (1928), vol. 2, *Hauptepochen und Hauptvölker in ihrer Stellung zur Rasse* (1930), and vol. 3, *Die Rassenfragen im Schrifttum der Neuzeit* (1931).

69. Schemann, *Hauptepochen und Hauptvölker der Geschichte,* 154.
70. Ibid., 155.
71. Ibid., 156.
72. See, for instance, Giulio Cogni, "Nordische Gestalten in Italien," *Volk und Rasse,* 1939, Heft 5: 110–13.
73. Schemann, *Hauptepochen und Hauptvölker der Geschichte,* 157.
74. Otto Reche, *Rasse und Heimat der Indogermanen* (Munich: Lehmanns Verlag, 1936).
75. Werner Kulz, "Kurze Rassengeschichte des griechischen Volkes," in *Europas Geschichte als Rassenschicksal: Vom Wesen und Wirken der Rassen im europäischen Schicksalsraum,* ed. Rolf Fahrenkrog (Leipzig: Hesse und Becker Verlag, 1937), 17–57; and Bernhard Pier, "Italien," in ibid., 58–82.
76. Fritz Taeger, *Orient und Okzident in der Antike,* Philosophie und Geschichte 58 (Tübingen: J.C.B. Mohr, 1936), 6.
77. Alfred Rosenberg, "Die Ausweitung des deutschen Geschichtsbildes," speech of 29 September 1935, in Rosenberg, *Reden und Aufsätze von 1933–1935,* vol. 2 of *Gestaltung der Idee: Blut und Ehre* (Munich: Zentralverlag der NSDAP, Franz Eher Verlag, 1936), 395.
78. Rosenberg, *Myth of the Twentieth Century,* 26.
79. Ibid., 12.
80. Ibid., 26.
81. Ibid., 41.
82. Ibid., 42.
83. See chap. 7 and 8.
84. *Hitler's Table Talk,* night of 18–19 January 1942, 225.
85. Hitler, *Mein Kampf,* trans. Ralph Manheim (Boston: Houghton Mifflin, 1943), 393.
86. A Greek ethnographer and geographer who lived from 135 to 51 BC.
87. *Hitler's Table Talk,* evening of 4 February 1942, 289.
88. Ibid., night of 18–19 January 1942, 225.
89. Hitler's actual words, not captured in the English-language translation edited by Hugh Trevor-Roper, could be loosely translated as "Our country was a pigsty" ("Unser Land war ein Sauland"); see *Hitlers Tischgespräche im Führerhauptquartier 1941–1942,* ed. Henry Picker (Bonn: Athenäum, 1951), 297.
90. *Hitler's Table Talk,* evening of 4 February 1942, 289.
91. See esp. Hitler's speech at Annaberg on 17 April 1929 and the speech given to the Industrie-Klub in Dusseldorf on 27 January 1932, in *The Speeches of Adolf Hitler,* ed. Norman H. Baynes, vol. 1 (Oxford: Oxford University Press, 1942), 777–829, esp. 782.
92. Tacitus, *Germania,* trans. M. Hutton, rev. E.H. Warmington, in *Tacitus: Agricola, Germania, Dialogus* (Cambridge, MA: Harvard University Press,

1970), 131, translation of *Germania* 2.1 (130): "Germaniam . . . informem terris, asperam caelo, tristem cultu aspectuque."

93. Ibid., 137, translation of 5.1 (136): "Terra etsi aliquando specie differt, in universum tamen aut silvis horrida au paludibus foeda, humidior qua Gallias, ventosior qua Noricum ac Pannoniam aspicit."

94. *Hitler's Table Talk*, night of 2–3 November 1941, 110–11.

95. Ibid., 111.

96. Ibid., evening of 4 February 1942, 289.

97. Paul Schultze-Naumburg, *Rassengebundene Kunst*, Volk und Wissen 13 (Berlin: Brehm Verlag, 1935), 24.

98. See Paul Schultze-Naumburg, *Nordische Schönheit: Ihr Wunschbild im Leben und in der Kunst* (Munich: Lehmanns Verlag, 1937), 148–50.

99. His most important work was, in fact, titled *German Prehistory, an Eminently National Science*: Gustaf Kossinna, *Die deutsche Vorgeschichte, eine hervorragend nationale Wissenschaft* (Würtzburg: Kabitzsch, 1910). On Kossina himself, see Heinz Grünert, "Gustaf Kossinna—ein Wegbereiter der nationalsozialistischen Ideologie," in *Prähistorie und Nationalsozialismus: Die mittel- und osteuropäische Ur- und Frühgeschichtsforschung in den Jahren 1933–1945*, ed. Achim Leube (Heidelberg: Synchron, 2002), 307–20.

100. See, for instance, Hans Schleif and A. Langsdorff, "Die Ausgrabungen der Schutzstaffeln," *Germanien: Monatshefte für Germanenkunde zur Erkenntnis deutschen Wesens* 8 (1936): 391–99; and 10 (1938): 6–11.

101. *Hitler's Table Talk*, night of 18–19 January 1942, 225.

102. Ibid., night of 25–26 January 1942, 248.

103. In his speeches as well as *Mein Kampf*, Hitler was content to conflate the distinct concepts of "people" (*Volk*) and "race" (*Rasse*); a people, of course, can be composed of many different races.

104. *Hitler's Table Talk*, evening of 4 February 1942, 290.

105. Ibid., midday, 7 July 1942, 566.

106. Ibid.

107. Ibid., evening of 4 February 1942, 289–90.

108. Ibid., dinner of 16 May 1942, 486–87.

109. Adolf Hitler, speech of 12 March 1926, quoted in Frank-Lothar Kroll, *Utopie als Ideologie: Geschichtsdenken und politisches Handeln im Dritten Reich* (Paderborn: Ferdinand Schöning, 1998), 73.

110. "Statt Bärenfell und Hörnerhelm . . . Die Tracht unserer Vorfahren," *Das Schwarze Korps*, September 1935, no. 31, 5.

111. Among the many, we can cite "Greuelhetze in gelehrtem Gewande," *Das Schwarze Korps*, January 1935, 11; "Dilettanten machen Germanen," *Das Schwarze Korps*, 29 May 1935, 5; "Greuelpropaganda im Altertum," a series of four articles, *Das Schwarze Korps*, August–September 1935, nos. 26–29; "Wider die Teutobolde," *Das Schwarze Korps*, 16 January 1936, 9; "Karnevals-Germanen," ibid., 17; see also the short film titled *Germanen gegen Pharaonen* (1939), Bundesarchiv-Abteilung Filmarchiv, K-182277-1.

112. "Greuelpropaganda im Altertum-Fortsetzung," *Das Schwarze Korps*, 4 September 1935, 9.

113. "Dein deutsches Volk," *Das Schwarze Korps*, 20 January 1938, 6.

114. *Hitler's Table Talk*, midday, 14 October 1941, 61.
115. Hermann Rauschning, *The Voice of Destruction* (New York: G.P. Putnam and Sons, 1940), 51.
116. *Inside the Third Reich: Memoirs by Albert Speer*, trans. Richard Winston and Clara Winston (New York: Macmillan, 1970), 94–95.
117. "Trenta secoli di storia ci permettono de guardare con sovrana pietà talune dottrine di oltr'Alpe, sostenute dalla progenie di gente che ignorava la scrittura ... nel tempo in cui Roma aveva Cesare, Virgilio e Augusto." Quoted in Ernst Nolte, *Three Faces of Fascism: Action Française, Italian Fascism, National Socialism*, trans. Leila Vennewitz (New York: Holt, Rinehart, and Winston, 1966), 505n399.
118. See Alexander Scobie, *Hitler's State Architecture: The Impact of Classical Antiquity* (University Park: Pennsylvania State University Press, 1990), 5.
119. Albert Speer, *Spandau: The Secret Diaries*, trans. Richard Winston and Clara Winston (New York: Macmillan, 1976), 126.
120. Nikolaus Himmelmann, *Utopische Vergangenheit: Archäologie und moderne Kultur* (Berlin: Gebrüder Mann Verlag, 1976), 127.
121. *Glauben und Kampfen: Für die SS-Männer aus den deutschen Volksgruppen des Südostens* (Berlin: SS-Hauptamt, n.d.), BABL/RD/NSD 41/119, 49.
122. See chap. 3.
123. See Alfred Rosenberg, "Von der Auffassung über nationalsozialistische Erziehung," speech of 15 March 1934, in Rosenberg, *Reden und Aufsätze von 1933–1935*, 47–58.
124. See Helmut Heiber's edited collection of Himmler's rather eloquent correspondence: *Reichsführer! Brief an und von Himmler* (Stuttgart: Deutsche Verlags-Anstalt, 1968).
125. Pytheas of Marseille, *Peri tou okeanou*, written around 320 BC. On Pytheas, see Barry Cunliffe, *The Extraordinary Voyage of Pytheas the Greek: The Man Who Discovered Britain* (London: Allen Lane, 2001).
126. See chap. 1, esp. pp. 35–37.
127. A view shared by Rosenberg, who denounced "Roman race-chaos." See Rosenberg, *Myth of the Twentieth Century*, 44.
128. Such was the motto of the *SS-Leitheft*, a "leadership magazine" designed for the education of SS members and party cadres, quoted in Josef Ackermann, *Heinrich Himmler als Ideologe* (Göttingen: Musterschmidt, 1970), 56.
129. "Plan des Persönlichen Stabs Reichsführer-SS" (1937), quoted in Ackermann, *Heinrich Himmler als Ideologe*, 42.
130. The welcoming of the winter solstice and that of the summer solstice (Sonnenwendfeier) were the two primary German holidays—*Bräuche* or *Sitten*—that the SS tried to resuscitate, imposing celebrations where lighted torches and solemn vows created a cultlike atmosphere of communion with the blood and the ancestral dead.
131. Heinrich Himmler, "Julspruch 1935," quoted in Ackermann, *Heinrich Himmler als Ideologe*, 53.
132. See BABL/N 21—Deutsches Ahnenerbe.

133. Also, notably, in German historiography on antiquity. See Christhard Hoffmann, *Juden und Judentum im Werk deutscher Althistoriker des 19. und 20. Jahrhunderts* (New York: E. J. Brill, 1988).

134. See Klaus von See, *Deutsche Germanenideologie vom Humanismus bis zur Gegenwart* (Frankfurt am Main: Athenäum, 1970), 13 and 100.

135. See Volker Losemann, *Nationalsozialismus und Antike: Studien zur Entwicklung des Faches Alte Geschichte 1933–1945* (Hamburg: Hoffman und Campe, 1977), 118.

136. A précis of the letter was published in *Das Schwarze Korps*, 29 October 1936, 3.

137. Heinrich Himmler, letter to Walter Wüst, 10 December 1937, quoted in Michael Kater, *Das "Ahnenerbe" der SS, 1933–1945: Ein Beitrag zur Kulturpolitik des Dritten Reiches* (Munich: Oldenbourg, 2001), 71; and in Losemann, *Nationalsozialismus und Antike*, 119.

138. Heinrich Himmler, "Rede des Reichsführers-SS auf der SS-Gruppenführertagung in Posen am 4.10.1943," BABL/NS 19/4010, ff. 94–95.

139. Himmler, letter to Wüst, 10 December 1937.

140. Ibid.

141. Heinrich Himmler, letter to Bernhard Rust, 8 March 1938, quoted in Losemann, *Nationalsozialismus und Antike*, 25.

142. Himmler, letter to Wüst, 10 December 1937.

143. On Franz Altheim and his campaign in Italy, see Losemann, *Nationalsozialismus und Antike*, 123–25.

144. Franz Altheim, *Vom Ursprung der Runen* (Frankfurt am Main: Klostermann, 1939).

145. Franz Altheim, *Italien und die dorische Wanderung* (Amsterdam: Pantheon, 1940).

146. Franz Altheim, "Indogermanisches Erbe im Rom," *Die Antike: Zeitschrift für Kunst und Kultur des klassischen Altertums* 17 (1941): 49–59.

147. The Swedish and Italian drawings were reproduced side by side on ibid., 51. After having left their caves in southern Sweden, the Indo-Germans had apparently brightened up their tasteful little grottoes in northern Italy with the same type of wall art.

148. Ibid., 56.

149. Ibid., 55.

150. See Bernard Sergent, *Les Indo-Européens: Histoire, langues, mythes* (Paris: Payot, 1995).

151. Franz Altheim and Erika Trautmann, "Die Elchrune," *Germanien* 13 (1941): 24–25. See also chap. 1, esp. pp. 27–28.

152. Friedrich Matz, "Die Indogermanisierung Italiens," *Neue Jahrbücher für antike und deutsche Bildung*, 1938, Heft 8: 367–400; 1939, Heft 9: 32–47.

153. See chap. 1.

154. Walter Brewitz, "Das Löwentor von Mykenä, ein Nordisches Kultsymbol," *Germanien* 9 (1937): 41–49.

155. See chap. 4.

156. Werner Müller, *Kreis und Kreuz: Untersuchungen zur sakralen Siedlung bei Italikern und Germanien* (Berlin: Deutsches Ahnenerbe Stiftung Verlag, 1938).

157. *Reichsführer!*, 120, letters 111a–b.
158. See Kater, *Das "Ahnenerbe" der SS*, 205.
159. *Deutsche Geschichte, Lichtbildvortrag, Erster Teil: Germanische Frühkeit, "Das Licht aus dem Norden,"* ed. Reichsführer-SS, Chef des Rasse- und Siedlungshauptamtes (Berlin, n.d.), BABL/RD/NSD 41/87, 16–17.
160. *Das Blut, seine Bedeutung, Reinerhaltung und Verbesserung*, ed. vol. 1, *Blut und Boden: Lichtsbildvortrag*, ed Reichsführer-SS, Chef des Rasse- und Siedlungshauptamtes (Berlin, n.d.), BABL/RD/NSD 41/87.
161. Ibid., 25. The men the book was about to show were Reichsgraf Maximilian von Spee and Horst Wessel, both of whom "incarnated the German essence" and were "combatants for the Nordic blood and carriers of its spirit, linked by blood to the modern German man."
162. *Rasse und Volk: Stoffsammlung für die weltanschauliche Schulung*, ed. Beauftragten für die weltanschauliche Schulung der deutschen Volksgruppe in Rumänien, November 1941, Heft 2: 88, Tafel VI.
163. Dietrich Klagges, *Geschichtsunterricht als nationalpolitische Erziehung* (Frankfurt am Main: Moritz Diesterweg Verlag, 1937).
164. Ibid., 207–60.
165. Ibid., 261–88.
166. Karl Schmelze, *Rassengeschichte und Vorgeschichte im Dienste nationaler Erziehung: Eine Ergänzung zu jedem Lehrbuch der Geschichte für höhere Unterrichtsanstalten auf Grund der Entschliessung des Reichsministers des Innern Nr. III 3120/21.6 vom 26. Juni 1933 betr. Richtlinien für die Geschichtslehrbücher* (Bamberg: Buchners Verlag, 1936).
167. *Ergänzungheft*, according to the title and preface, ibid.
168. Ibid., 16.
169. Regarding the notion of overpopulation, see chap. 6 and the ideas of Richard Walther Darré.
170. Schmelze, *Rassengeschichte und Vorgeschichte*, 16.
171. Ibid., 17.
172. Ibid., 18.
173. Ibid.
174. Otto Regenbogen, "Das Altertum und die politische Erziehung," *Neue Jahrbücher für Wissenschaft und Jugendbildung*, 1934, Heft 10: 211–25. See also chap. 3.
175. Walther Gehl, *Geschichte: 6. Klasse Oberschulen, Gymnasien und Oberschulen in Aufbauform; von der Urzeit bis zum Ende der Hohenstaufen* (Breslau: Ferdinand Hirt, 1940).
176. "Non semper in Graecia idem incolae habitaverunt. Antiquissimis temporibus Graeci, qui Germanis et Romanis consanguineri erant, in patriam novam migraverunt." Wilhelm Schaeffer, *Lateinisches Lese- und Übungsbuch*, pt. 2, *Für die vierte und fünfte Klasse der deutschen Oberschule* (Bielefeld: Verlag von Velhagen und Klasing, 1942).
177. See *Personalverzeichnis für das Winterhalbjahr 1933–1934 und Vorlesungsverzeichnis für das Sommerhalbjahr 1934, Ruprecht-Karl-Universität Heidelberg* (Heidelberg, 1934).

178. See *Personal- und Vorlesungszeichnis, Sommersemester 1935, Friedrich-Schiller Universität Jena* (Jena: Universitäts-Buchdruckerei, 1935).

179. See *Universität Wien: Personal- und Vorlesungsverzeichnis für das Wintersemester 1941–1942* (Vienna: Verlag Adolf Holzhausen, Universitätsbuchdrucker, 1941).

180. See *Personal- und Vorlesungsverzeichnis, deutsche Karls-Universität Prag, Zweites Trimester 1940* (Prague, 1940).

181. See *Julius-Maximilians-Universität Würzburg: Personal- und Vorlesungsverzeichnis für das Sommerhalbjahr 1942* (Würzburg, 1942).

182. See *Christian-Albrechts-Universität Kiel: Personal- und Vorlesungsverzeichnis für das Sommerhalbjahr 1935* (Kiel: Walther G. Mühlau Verlag, 1935).

183. "Griechenland," in *Der neue Brockhaus: Allbuch in vier Bänden und einem Atlas* (Leipzig: F. A. Brockhaus, 1938–39), vol. 2, 280.

184. See chap. 4.

185. David Clay Large, *Where Ghosts Walked: Munich's Road to the Third Reich* (New York: Norton, 1997), esp. 336–47, regarding the Tages der deutschen Kunst.

186. See Reinhold Baumstark, ed., *Das neue Hellas: Griechen und Bayern zur Zeit Ludwigs I.*, exhibition catalog of the Bayerischen Nationalmuseum (Munich: München Hirmer, 1999).

187. "Hitlers Rede zur Eröffnung der 'Großen deutschen Kunstausstellung,'" Munich, 1937, in Peter-Klaus Schuster, ed., *Die "Kunststadt" München 1937: Nationalsozialismus und "Entartete Kunst"* (Munich: Prestel, 1987), 248.

188. See Wolfgang Hermann, *Der historische Festzug: Seine Entstehung und Entwicklung im 19. und 20. Jahrhundert* (Munich: Prestel, 1976).

189. See Schuster, *Die "Kunststadt" München 1937*, 84.

190. *Tag der deutschen Kunst—14.-15. Oktober 1933, Fest-Folge*, Munich, Gauleitung NSDAP.

191. See the photographs reproduced in the *Völkischer Beobachter, Norddeutsche Ausgabe*, 17 October 1933, 1 and 5.

192. See *Zweitausend Jahre deutsche Kultur: Festzug am Tag der deutschen Kunst zu München 1938* (Munich: Vertrieb Knorr und Hirth, 1938). For a description of the event, see Egon Kerkschmidt, "Münchner Festzug zum Tag der deutschen Kunst," *Velhagen und Klasings Monatshefte*, 1938–39, 1 Bd., 53 Jg.

193. See Bernd Ogan and Wolfgang W. Weiss, eds., *Faszination und Gewalt: Zur politischen Ästhetik des Nationalsozialismus* (Nuremberg: W. Tümmels Verlag, 1992).

194. See chap. 3.

195. See Jörg Schöning, ed., *Reinhold Schünzel: Schauspieler und Regisseur* (Munich: Edition Text und Kritik, 1989).

196. Schünzel's film was also turned into a French version in the studios of Berlin's UFA, called *Les dieux s'amusent*.

197. See Sabine Hake, *Popular Cinema of the Third Reich* (Austin: University of Texas Press, 2001); Robert C. Reimer, ed., *Cultural History through a*

National Socialist Lens: Essays on the Cinema of the Third Reich (Rochester, NY: Camden House, 2000); and Lutz Koepnick, *The Dark Mirror: German Cinema between Hitler and Hollywood* (Berkeley: University of California Press, 2002).

198. Reinhold Schünzel (1888–1954) had appeared in films by Ernst Lubitsch (he played the role of Choiseul in 1919's *Madame Dubarry*) and later starred in Georg Wilhelm Pabst's *Die Dreigroschenoper* (1931) before appearing in Fritz Lang's *Hangmen Also Die!* (1942).

199. On the conquest and occupation of Greece by the Germans, see Mark Mazower, *Inside Hitler's Greece: The Experience of Occupation, 1941–1944* (New Haven: Yale University Press, 1993).

200. "Der Siegeslauf nach Athen: Der deutsche Sturm über die Thermopylen," *Völkischer Beobachter*, 28 April 1941, 2.

201. See chap. 4.

202. Mazower, *Inside Hitler's Greece*, 223.

203. "Athen ist gefallen," *Völkischer Beobachter*, 28 April 1941, 1.

204. *The Goebbels Diaries, 1939-1941*, trans. and ed. Fred Taylor (London: Hamish Hamilton, 1982), 8 April 1941, 304.

205. See chap. 8.

206. K. Hesse, "Die Erstürmung der Thermopylen," *SS-Leithefte*, 1942, Heft 1: 17–19; and Heinrich Gaese, "Die Lorbeer," *SS-Leithefte*, 1942, Heft 6: 3–4.

207. Gaese, "Die Lorbeer," 3.

208. Ibid., 4.

209. Theotakas's quotation of Cavafy's verse (from "Waiting for the Barbarians") is in Mazower, *Inside Hitler's Greece*, 1.

210. "Griechenland," *Der Angriff: Tageszeitung der deutschen Arbeitsfront*, no. 94 (19 April 1941), 3.

211. "Griechenland," in *Der neue Brockhaus*.

212. See chap. 8.

213. Tito Körner, "Rassenköpfe aus Griechenland," *Volk und Rasse*, 1939, Heft 11–12: 239–41.

214. Ibid., 239.

215. Ibid., 241.

216. Roland Hampe, "Griechenland, das Land der Gegensätze," *Volk und Rasse*, 1941, Heft 7–8: 117–21.

217. Ibid., 119.

218. Ibid., 121.

219. Ibid. The author used the German expression "europäischer Blutkreislauf"; the metaphor was unmistakable.

CHAPTER 3. MENS SANA

Epigraphs. Martin Heidegger, "'The Self-Assertion of the German University' and 'The Rectorate 1933/1934,'" trans. Karsten Harries, *Review of Metaphysics* 38, no. 3 (March 1985): 473, revised version in Günther Neske and Emil Kettering, eds., *Martin Heidegger and National Socialism: Questions and*

Answers (New York: Paragon, 1990), 5–14; and Heinrich Böll, "Stranger, Bear Word to the Spartans We . . . ," in *The Collected Stories of Heinrich Böll*, trans. Leila Vennevitz (New York: Melville House, 2011), 31–39.

1. Hitler, *Mein Kampf*, trans. Ralph Manheim (Boston: Houghton Mifflin, 1943), 15.
2. Eberhardt Jäckel, *Hitler's World View: A Blueprint for Power*, trans. Herbert Arnold (Cambridge, MA: Harvard University Press, 1981), 87.
3. See Albert Speer, *Spandau: The Secret Diaries*, trans. Richard Winston and Clara Winston (New York: Macmillan, 1976), 20 April 1947, 59.
4. *Hitler's Table Talk, 1941–1944: His Private Conversations*, trans. Norman Cameron and R. H. Stevens (New York: Enigma, 2000), night of 21–22 July 1941, 10.
5. Cicero, *De oratore* 2.36.
6. Roman historians were almost unanimous in stating some version of Sallust's "the recording of the events of the past is particularly serviceable" ("magno usui est memoria rerum gestarum"); see Sallust, *The War with Jugurtha*, trans. J. C. Rolfe (Cambridge, MA: Harvard University Press, 1931), 4. The Roman historian whose rather abundant oeuvre has survived most completely, Livy, wrote: "What chiefly makes the study of history wholesome and profitable is this, that you behold the lessons of every kind of experience set forth as on a conspicuous monument; from these you may choose for yourself and for your own state what to imitate, from these mark for avoidance what is shameful in the conception and shameful in the result." Livy, *The History of Rome*, trans. B. O. Foster (Cambridge, MA: Harvard University Press, 1919), 7 (1.10).
7. Thucydides, *History of the Peloponnesian War, Books 1–2*, trans. C. F. Smith (Cambridge, MA: Harvard University Press, 1919), 41 (1.22.4).
8. Polybius, *The Histories*, trans. W. R. Paton., rev. F. W. Walbank and Christian Habicht (Cambridge, MA: Harvard University Press, 2010), 7 (1.1).
9. The expression itself comes from Polybius, who wrote of πραγματικῆς ἱστορίας.
10. The realschule, in Austria as in Germany, was (unlike the more classical gymnasium) oriented toward more so-called "modern" subjects, like languages. The realschule prepared students for neither the Abitur (the German qualification exam) nor a university education but rather for a career in a variety of white-collar occupations, including (in Austria) lower-level positions in the civil service. See Ian Kershaw, *Hitler, 1889–1936: Hubris* (New York: W. W. Norton, 1998), 16.
11. Hitler, *Mein Kampf*, 14. Italics in the original.
12. Ibid.
13. Fritz Stern, *The Politics of Cultural Despair: A Study in the Rise of the Germanic Ideology* (Berkeley: University of California Press, 1961).
14. Paul de Lagarde, Julius Langbehn, and Arthur Moeller van den Bruck.
15. Stern, *Politics of Cultural Despair*, 271.
16. Ibid., xvii.
17. Ibid., xiv.
18. Hitler, *Mein Kampf*, 14.

19. Ibid.

20. Bernhard Rust, ed., *Erziehung und Unterricht in der höheren Schule: Amtliche Ausgabe des Reichs- und Preußischen Ministeriums für Wissenschaft, Erziehung und Volksbildung* (Berlin: Weidmann, 1938), 70.

21. Hitler, *Mein Kampf*, 16.

22. Ibid., 420.

23. Ibid., 129.

24. Ibid., 421.

25. Ibid., 420.

26. Ibid., 421.

27. Ibid. Italics in the original.

28. Ibid., 422.

29. Ibid., 409.

30. Kurt Krippendorf, "Grundsätzliche Erwägungen zur Neugestaltung des Geschichtsunterrichts," *Vergangenheit und Gegenwart: Zeitschrift für den Geschichtsunterricht und staatsbürgerliche Erziehung in allen Schulgattungen* 1933, Heft 9: 483.

31. Ibid., 485.

32. Ibid., 488.

33. A professor of Greek history at the University of Vienna, Fritz Schachermeyr (1895–1987) made a name for himself by publishing two books—*Lebensgesetzlichkeit in der Geschichte* (Biological laws in history) in 1940 and *Indogermanen und Orient* (Indo-Germans and the Orient) in 1944—that opportunistically captured the predominant spirit of racist historiography, of which he was an otherwise fervent advocate (as many of his numerous journal articles demonstrate). After 1945, he continued his brilliant career at Vienna and was recognized as an eminent specialist in Greek prehistory, writing several books and compiling the third volume (on Greece) of the *Propyläen Weltgeschichte* in 1962. For more on Schachermeyr, see the hagiographic but still instructive collection of essays "In Memoriam Fritz Schachermeyr, 1895–1986 [sic]," special issue, *American Journal of Ancient History* 13, no. 1 (1996).

34. On Hans Oppermann, see Jürgen Malitz, "Römertum im 'Dritten Reich': Hans Oppermann," in *Imperium romanum: Studien zu Geschichte und Rezeption, Festschrift für Karl Christ zum 75. Geburtstag*, ed. Peter Kneissl and Volker Losemann (Stuttgart: Franz Steiner Verlag, 1998), 519–44.

35. "Humanistische Bildung im nationalsozialistischen Staate," special issue, *Neue Wege zur Antike*, Erste Reihe, 1933, Heft 9.

36. Hermann Gieselbusch, "Gymnasium in dieser Zeit," in ibid., 1–9.

37. Gerhart Salomon, "Humanismuswende," in "Humanistische Bildung im nationalsozialistischen Staate," 9–16.

38. Benno von Hagen, "Wege zu einem Humanismus im Dritten Reich," in "Humanistische Bildung im nationalsozialistischen Staate," 17–22.

39. Gustav Klingenstein, "Humanistische Bildung als deutsche Waffe," in "Humanistische Bildung im nationalsozialistischen Staate," 23–35.

40. Deutscher Philologenverband, "Die Gegenwartsbedeutung des deutschen Gymnasiums," *Das humanistische Gymnasium*, 1933: 209.

41. Ibid., 210.
42. Fritz Bucherer, "Humanistische Bildung im nationalsozialistischen Staate," *Das humanistische Gymnasium*, 1934: 7.
43. Werner Jaeger, "Die Erziehung des politischen Menschen und die Antike," *Volk im Werden* 1, no. 3 (1933): 43.
44. Ibid., 44.
45. Wilhelm Brachmann, "Der 'humanistische' Gedanke," *Nationalsozialistische Monatshefte: Wissenschaftliche Zeitschrift der NSDAP*, 1937: 496. The Erasmus quote is from *The Apophthegmes of Erasmus*, trans. Nicolas Udall (Boston: Robert Roberts, 1877), 12.
46. Jaeger, "Die Erziehung des politischen Menschen und die Antike," 48.
47. Nazi propaganda celebrated the famous "spirit of Potsdam," referring to a day of unity and national rebirth organized on 21 March 1933 by the new chancellor—who convened the Reichstag in the city's Garrison Church (Garnisonkirche], the site of the tomb of Frederick II, to vote him the exceptional powers outlined in what would become known as the Enabling Act. Including a coterie of brownshirts, the SA, many of Prussia's old landed aristocracy, the Junkers, and Marshall Hindenburg, the Day of Potsdam celebration represented the fusion of the two Germanies, a fusion that might be thought of in various ways: the Prussian and the Nazi; the imperial and the racist; the Germany of the great Frederick and that of the little corporal, Hitler; the army of the great field marshall and that of the common soldier; the president and the chancellor; the Germany of tradition and that of the National Socialist revolution; the Germany of heritage and that of the new man.
48. Jaeger, "Die Erziehung des politischen Menschen und die Antike," 43.
49. Ibid., 44.
50. Ibid., 47.
51. Ibid.
52. Ibid., 48.
53. Ibid.
54. Werner Jaeger, "Humanismus und Jugendbildung," in Jaeger, *Humanistische Reden und Vorträge* (Berlin: De Gruyter, 1937), 71.
55. Wilhelm Brachmann, "Antike und Gegenwart: Ein Beitrag zum Problem des gegenwärten Humanismus in Deutschland und Italien," *Nationalsozialistische Monatshefte: Wissenschaftliche Zeitschrift der NSDAP*, 1941: 932.
56. Ibid.
57. Alfred Bäumler, "Der Kampf um den Humanismus," in Bäumler, *Politik und Erziehung* (Dresden: Junker und Dünnhaupt, 1937), 57.
58. Ibid., 58–59.
59. Ibid., 59.
60. Ibid., 65.
61. Ibid., 63.
62. See chap. 6, esp. pp. 223–24 and Hitler's comparisons between Nazi eugenics and the Spartans' exposure of newborn infants.
63. The expression was coined by Nietzsche in his essay *On the Genealogy of Morals*.
64. See p. 223.

65. See Leo Strauss, "German Nihilism," ed. David Janssens and Daniel Tanguay, *Interpretation: A Journal of Political Philosophy* 26, no. 3 (Spring 1999): 353–78.
66. Alfred Bäumler, "Das Volk und die Gebildeten," broadcast speech, 3 April 1933, in Bäumler, *Männerbund und Wissenschaft* (Berlin: Junker und Dünnhaupt, 1943), 114.
67. Ibid., 115.
68. Alfred Bäumler, "Antrittsvorlesung in Berlin," 10 May 1933 speech, in ibid., 128.
69. Alfred Bäumler, "Der theoretische und der politisch Mensch," in ibid., 94.
70. Wilhelm Frick, "Kampfziel der Deutschen Schule: Ansprache des Reichsministers des Innern Dr. Frick auf der Ministerkonferenz am 9. Mai 1933," special issue, *Friedrich Manns Pädagogisches Magazin*, Heft 1376: 6–7.
71. Rust, *Erziehung und Unterricht in der höheren Schule*, 238.
72. See chap. 4.
73. Alfred Rosenberg, "Von der Auffassung über nationalsozialistische Erziehung," speech of 15 March 1934, in Rosenberg, *Reden und Aufsätze von 1933–1935*, vol. 2 of *Gestaltung der Idee: Blut und Ehre* (Munich: Zentralverlag der NSDAP, Franz Eher Verlag, 1936), 47–58.
74. Ibid., 47.
75. Ibid., 51.
76. Ibid., 54.
77. Ernst Krieck, *Musische Erziehung* (Leipzig: Armanen-Verlag, 1933), esp. the *vorwort* (unnumbered).
78. Ibid., 45.
79. Ernst Krieck, *Menschenformung: Grundzüge der vergleichenden Erziehungswissenschaft* (Leipzig: Verlag Quelle und Mayer, 1925), 205.
80. See chap. 5.
81. Fritz Schachermeyr, "Die Aufgaben der Alten Geschichte im Rahmen der nordischen Weltgeschichte," *Vergangenheit und Gegenwart* 23 (1933): 599.
82. Hans Bogner, "Die Judenfrage in der griechisch-römischen Welt," in *Forschungen zur Judenfrage*, vol. 1, Schriften des Reichsinstitut für Geschichte des neuen Deutschlands (Hamburg: Hanseatische Verlagsanstalt, 1937), 82–83.
83. See chap. 7.
84. Bogner, "Die Judenfrage in der griechisch-römischen Welt," 84.
85. Karl Georg Kuhn, "Weltjudentum in der Antike," in *Forschungen zur Judenfrage*, vol. 2, Schriften des Reichsinstitut für Geschichte des neuen Deutschlands (Hamburg: Hanseatische Verlagsanstalt, 1937), 20.
86. Ernst Krieck, *Nationalpolitische Erziehung* (Leipzig: Armanen-Verlag, 1932), 7.
87. Krieck, *Musische Erziehung*, 36.
88. Ibid., 38.
89. Ibid., 23 (and again in nearly identical form on 32).
90. Hans Bogner, *Die Bildung der politischen Elite* (Oldenburg: Stalling Verlag, 1932), 7.
91. Ibid., 32.
92. Ibid., 35.

93. Ibid., 26.
94. Ibid., 11.
95. Ibid., 46–47.
96. Ibid., 52–53.
97. Martin Heidegger, "'The Self-Assertion of the German University' and 'The Rectorate 1933/34,'" trans. Karsten Harries, *Review of Metaphysics* 38, no. 3 (March 1985): 472.
98. Ibid., 473.
99. See Rüdiger Safranski, *Martin Heidegger: Between Good and Evil*, trans. Ewald Osers (Cambridge, MA: Harvard University Press, 1999), 261–62.
100. August Heissmeyer, SS-Obergruppenführer, Inspekteur der Napolas, "Bericht über die Arbeit der Nationalpolitischen Erziehungsanstalten," BABL/R 43 II/956 b, microfiche 2, f. 54.
101. "Richtlinien für den Geschichtsunterricht" (Zentralblatt Preußen, 1933), 197, quoted in Helmut Genschel, *Politische Erziehung durch Geschichtsunterricht: Der Beitrag der Geschichtsdidaktik und des Geschichtsunterrichts zur politischen Erziehung im Nationalsozialismus* (Frankfurt am Main: Haag und Herchen Verlag, 1980), 19–20.
102. "Ein Streit für und wider die Antike." Schachermeyr, "Die Aufgaben der Alten Geschichte," 589.
103. See chap. 1.
104. Schachermeyr, "Die Aufgaben der Alten Geschichte," 589.
105. Ibid., 592.
106. Ibid., 594.
107. Ibid., 593.
108. Ibid., 596.
109. Ibid., 593.
110. Ibid., 597.
111. Ibid., 594.
112. Ibid., 600.
113. Bogner, "Die Judenfrage in der griechisch-römischen Welt," 81.
114. Hans F. K. Günther, *Die nordische Rasse bei den Indogermanen Asiens: Zugleich ein Beitrag zur Frage nach der Urheimat und Rassenherkunft der Indogermanen* (Munich: Lehmanns Verlag, 1934), 241.
115. Hans F. K. Günther, "Humanitas," in *Altsprachliche Bildung im Neuaufbau der deutschen Schule* (Leipzig: Teubner Verlag, 1937), quoted in Brachmann, "Der 'humanistische' Gedanke," 493.
116. Ibid., 502.
117. Ibid., 491.
118. Ibid., 490.
119. Ibid., 491.
120. Ibid.
121. Ibid., 493.
122. Ibid., 494.
123. Frick, *Kampfziel der deutschen Schule*, 6.
124. Friedrich Klose, "Altrömische Wertbegriffe (*honos* und *dignitas*)," *Neue Jahrbücher für die Antike und deutsche Bildung*, 1938, Heft 6: 268–78.

125. See Claude Digeon, *La crise allemande de la pensée française, 1870–1914* (Paris: Presses Universitaires de France, 1959).
126. Jacques Le Rider, *Freud, de l'Acropole au Sinaï: Le retour à l'Antique des Modernes viennois* (Paris: Presses Universitaires de France, 2002), 22.
127. On these questions and for more general context surrounding these issues, see Françoise Waquet, *Latin, or the Empire of a Sign: From the Sixteenth to the Twentieth Century*, trans. John Howe (New York: Verso, 2001).
128. See Helmut Heiber, *Der Professor im Dritten Reich: Bilder aus der akademischen Provinz*, vol. 1 of *Universität unterm Hakenkreuz* (Munich: K. G. Saur, 1991), 400.
129. Walter Eberhardt, "Die Antike und wir," *Nationalsozialistische Wissenschaft: Schriftenreihe der Nationalsozialistischen Monatshefte*, 1935, Heft 2: 3–15.
130. Ibid., 4.
131. Ibid., 10.
132. Ibid., 11.
133. Ibid.
134. Ibid., 10.
135. A dissenting opinion may be found in Franz Miltner, "Die Antike als Einheit in der Geschichte," in *Rom*, vol. 2 of *Das neue Bild der Antike*, ed. Helmut Berve (Leipzig: Koehler und Amelang, 1942), 433–53.
136. Eberhardt, "Die Antike und wir," 9.
137. Bäumler, "Der Kampf um den Humanismus," 64.
138. Eberhardt, "Die Antike und wir," 11.
139. On the history of international relations in this period, see Robert Frank and René Girault, *Turbulente Europe et nouveaux mondes, 1914–1941*, vol. 2 of *Histoire des relations internationales contemporaines* (Paris: Masson, 1988).
140. See Mussolini's speech of 6 September 1934, quoted on p. 75.
141. On Oppermann, see Malitz, "Römertum um 'Dritten Reich.'"
142. E.g., Hans Oppermann, "Der erzieherische Wert des lateinischen Unterrichts," in "Humanistische Bildung im Nationalsozialistischen Staate," special issue, *Neue Wege zur Antike*, Erste Reihe, 1933, Heft 9: 50–59.
143. Hans Oppermann, "Altertumswissenschaft und politische Erziehung" *Neue Jahrbücher für Wissenschaft und Jugendbildung*, 1935, Heft 11: 368.
144. Bernhard Rust, "Die Grundlagen der nationalsozialistischen Erziehung," *Hochschule und Ausland*, 1935, Heft 1: 1–18. A brief note from the education minister regarding the reform of teaching of ancient languages repeated the general outline of this comparison of Latin and sport: see "Richtlinien für die alten Sprachen," 21 July 1937, 7, BABL/R/4901/4614, f. 403.
145. On Bernhard Rust, see Ulf Pedersen, *Bernhard Rust: Ein nationalsozialistischer Bildungspolitiker vor dem Hintergrund seiner Zeit* (Braunschweig: Forschungsstelle für Schulgeschichte und Schulentwicklung, TU Braunschweig, 1994).
146. See pp. 132–35.

147. Decree of 29 January 1938, "Neuordnung des höheren Schulwesens." A detailed description of curricula in history and classical literature can be found in Rust, *Erziehung und Unterricht in der höheren Schule.*

148. Hans Oppermann, "Die alten Sprachen in der Neuordnung des höheren Schulwesens," *Neue Jahrbücher für antike und deutsche Bildung,* 1938, Heft 3: 127–36.

149. Helmut Berve, "An unsere Leser," *Neue Jahrbücher für antike und deutsche Bildung,* 1938, Heft 1: 2–13.

150. Ludwig Mader and Walter Breywisch, *Zur Eingliederung des altsprachlichen Unterrichts in die nationale Schule* (Frankfurt: Verlag Moritz Diesterweg, 1934), 18–24.

151. Jaeger, "Die Erziehung des politischen Menschen und die Antike," 47.

152. "Richtlinien für die alten Sprachen," f. 405.

153. *Auf dem Wege zum nationalpolitischen Gymnasium: Beiträge zur nationalsozialistischen Ausrichtung des altsprachlichen Unterrichts,* published for the Reichssachsbearbeiters für alte Sprache im NSLB (Frankfurt: Moritz Diesterweg Verlag).

154. On Augustus and the figure of the leader in antiquity, see **chap. 6, esp. pp. 262–64.**

155. Hans Oppermann, "Horaz, Dichtung und Staat," in *Rom,* vol. 2 of *Das neue Bild der Antike,* ed. Helmut Berve (Leipzig: Koehler und Amelang, 1942), 265–95.

156. Hans Oppermann, "Horaz als Dichter der Gemeinschaft," *Auf dem Wege zum nationalpolitischen Gymnasium,* 1938, Heft 6: 61.

157. Ibid., 67.

158. Hans Oppermann et al., *Probleme der augusteischen Erneuerung, Auf dem Wege zum nationalpolitischen Gymnasium—Beiträge zur nationalsozialistischen Ausrightung des altsprachlichen Unterrichts,* published for the Reichsfachbeartbeiters für alte Sprachen im NSLB, Heft 6 (Frankfurt: Verlag Moritz Diesterweg, 1938).

159. Hans Oppermann, "Horaz als Dichter der Gemeinschaft," 71.

160. Ibid., 72.

161. Josef Derbolav, "Weltanschauliche Fragen im Dichtwerk des Horaz," *Neue Jahrbücher für antike und deutsche Bildung,* 1942, Heft 5: 101.

162. Ibid.

163. Ibid., 102.

164. Ibid., 103.

165. Rust, *Erziehung und Unterricht in der höheren Schule,* 243.

166. See (as early as 1933) Kurt Sachse, "Vorschläge zum altsprachlichen Lehrplan eines deutschen Gymnasiums," in "Humanistische Bildung im Nationalsozialistischen Staate," special issue, *Neue Wege zur Antike,* Erste Reihe, 1933, Heft 9: 59–80.

167. Bayerisches Staatsministerium für Unterricht und Kultur ministerialrat Dr. Bauernschmidt, "Richtlinien für den altsprachlichen Unterricht," 29 December 1933, BABL/R/4901/4614, ff. 47–48.

168. Oberstudiendirektor Billen, "Vorschläge für die Gestaltung des Unterrichts in den alten Sprachen," 1936, BABL/R/4901/4614, ff. 245–46.

169. Kollegium des Gymnasiums in Rostock, "Grundsätzliches zum Lehrplan des deutschen Gymnasiums, zugleich als Begründung für eine Stundentafel," 7 July 1946, BABL/R/4901/4614, f. 32.

170. Ibid.
171. Ibid.
172. Ibid.
173. "Richtlinien für Lateinisch," Mecklenburgisches Staatsministerium, Abt. Unterricht, BABL/R/4901/4614, ff. 271–73.
174. "Richtlinien für Griechisch," Mecklenburgisches Staatsministerium, Abt. Unterricht, BABL/R/4901/4614, ff. 279–85.
175. "Richtlinien für Lateinisch," ff. 271–73.
176. Ibid.
177. Bauernschmidt, "Richtlinien für den altsprachlichen Unterricht," ff. 47–48.
178. Ibid.
179. Rust, *Erziehung und Unterricht in der höheren Schule*, 231.
180. Ibid., 241.
181. Ibid., 242.
182. Ibid., 242–43.
183. Ibid., 243.
184. Ibid.
185. Ibid.
186. Ibid., 250. See also chap. 5.
187. Élisabeth Ducultot, *Johann Joachim Winckelmann: Enquête sur la genèse de l'histoire de l'art* (Paris: Presses Universitaires de France, 2000), 123.
188. Ibid., 125.
189. Quoted in Walther Rehm, *Griechentum und Goethezeit: Geschichte eines Glaubens* (Leipzig: Diederich Verlag, 1936), 230.
190. Giovanni Pico della Mirandola, *Oratio de dignitate hominis*, preface to the DCCCC *Conclusiones* (*Nine Hundred Theses*). The phrase was translated by Ernst Cassirer as "the 'sculptor' who must bring forth and in a sense chisel out his own form from the material with which nature has endowed him." Cassirer, "Giovanni Pico della Mirandola: A Study in the History of Ideas," *Journal of the History of Ideas* 3 (1943): 333.
191. Johann Wolfgang Goethe, "Prometheus" (1774).
192. Rehm, *Griechentum und Goethezeit*, 18.
193. Friedrich Hölderlin, "Gesang des deutschen," in Hölderlin, *Sämtliche Werke*, ed. Friedrich Beissner, vol. 2, *Gedichte nach 1800* (Stuttgart: J. G. Cottasche Buchhandlung Nachfolger, 1953), 4.
194. Rehm, *Griechentum und Goethezeit*, 17.
195. Johann Joachim Winckelmann, *Reflections on the Imitation of Greek Works in Painting and Sculpture*, trans. Henry Fusseli (London: A. Millar, 1765), 2.
196. Rehm, *Griechentum und Goethezeit*, 17.
197. Ibid., 20–21.
198. Eliza Marian Butler, *The Tyranny of Greece over Germany: A Study of the Influence Exercised by Greek Art and Poetry over the Great German Writ-*

ers of the Eighteenth, Nineteenth, and Twentieth Centuries (Cambridge: Cambridge University Press, 1935), 6.
199. Ibid., 2.
200. Ibid., 4.
201. Ibid., 80.
202. Friedrich Hölderlin, "The Only One (First Version)," in *Friedrich Hölderlin: Selected Poems and Fragments,* trans. Michael Hamburger (New York: Penguin, 1998), 219.
203. Rehm, *Griechentum und Goethezeit,* 6.
204. For an examination of this phenomenon, see the interesting article on the case of Hölderlin published in 1943: Karl Weibel, "Hölderlins Hellastraum," *Neue Jahrbücher für antike und deutsche Bildung,* 1943, Heft 2.
205. Ducultot, *Johann Joachim Winckelmann,* 147.
206. Ibid., 148.
207. It is also well known that Martin Heidegger did not visit Greece until much later in his life, in 1962. He hesitated even then to make the trip, which his wife Elfriede gave him as an anniversary gift: "That proposal was followed, of course, by a long hesitation due to the fear of disappointment." See Heidegger, *Sojourns: The Journey to Greece,* trans. John-Panteleimon Manoussakis (Albany: SUNY Press, 2005), 4.
208. On the *George-Kreis,* see Karlhans Kluncker, *"Das geheime Deutschland": Über Stefan George und seinen Kreis* (Bonn: Bouvier Verlag, 1985); and Ulrich Raulff, "Der Dichter als Führer: Stefan George," in *Vom Künstlerstaat: Ästhetische und politische Utopien,* ed. Raulff (Munich: Hanser, 2006), 127–43.
209. See esp. Suzanne L. Marchand, *Down from Olympus: Archaeology and Philhellenism in Germany, 1750–1970* (Princeton: Princeton University Press, 1996); and Karl Christ and Arnoldo Momigliano, eds., *L'antichità nell'Ottocento in Italia e Germania/Die Antike im 19. Jahrhundert in Italien und in Deutschland* (Bologna: Il Mulino; Berlin: Duncker und Humblot, 1988). See also Michel Espagne and Gilles Pécout, eds., "Philhellénisme et transferts culturels dans l'Europe du XIXe siècle," special issue, *Revue germanique internationelle* 2005, nos. 1–2.
210. The Hellenophile Charles Maurras, the Athens correspondent for *La gazette de France* at the first Olympic Games, in 1896, described with just a touch of resentment and disdain the rather diaphanous complexion of the royal family, barbarians who had come from the North and found themselves under the hot Greek sun: "Their transparent skin tone [and] pale blue eyes . . . both recall . . . the hyperborean climate. I don't believe it will take long for that whole world to become Hellenized. The Hellenic people can absorb and assimilate all the barbarians they please." Maurras, *Lettres des jeux Olympiques* (Paris: Flammarion, 2004), 48.
211. See Kurt Bittel, *Beiträge zur Geschichte des Deutschen Archäologischen Instituts 1929 bis 1979* (Mainz: Verlag Philipp von Zabern, 1979); and Lothar Wickert, *Beiträge zur Geschichte des Deutschen Archäologischen Instituts 1879 bis 1929* (Mainz: Verlag Philipp von Zabern, 1979).
212. Hans Bogner, *Der Seelenbegriff der griechischen Frühzeit,* Schriften des Reichsinstituts für Geschichte des neuen Deutschlands (Hamburg: Hanseatische Verlagsanstalt, 1939), 14.

213. Ludwig Schemann, *Hauptepochen und Hauptvölker der Geschichte in ihrer Stellung zur Rasse*, vol. 2 of *Die Rasse in den Geisteswissenschaften* (Munich: Lehmanns Verlag, 1930), 104.
214. Martin Heidegger, *Introduction to Metaphysics*, trans. Gregory Fried and Richard Polt (New Haven: Yale University Press, 2000), 40.
215. See Werner Beumelburg, *Sperrfeuer um Deutschland* (Oldenburg: Stalling, 1929).
216. Heidegger, *Introduction to Metaphysics*, 40.
217. Ibid.
218. Ibid., 41.
219. Ibid. Italics in the original.
220. Ibid. Italics in the original.
221. Heidegger, "'Self-Assertion of the German University,'" 473.
222. Heidegger was actually rather critical of Plato, whom he saw as metaphysics' first gravedigger; his distinction between the Ideal and the Real opened the way for the technocratic reification of the world. Aristotle administered the coup de grâce to a pre-Socratic thought attentive to existential questions: by creating an epistemological and axiological caesura between the supralunary and sublunary worlds, Aristotle condemned the sublunar, which he identified with scientific reification and technological exploitation.
223. Safranski, *Martin Heidegger*, 261.
224. Martin Heidegger, "Die Bedrohung der Wissenschaft," in Dietrich Papenfuss and Otto Pöggeler, eds., *Zur philosophischen Aktualität Heideggers*, vol. 1, *Philosophie und Politik* (Frankfurt: Klostermann, 1991), 9.
225. Ibid., 17.
226. Ibid., 19.
227. Ibid., 21.
228. Ibid., 25.
229. Ibid., 18. The teaching of philosophy faced competition from other subjects more obviously useful for the rearmament effort. What increasingly took the place of philosophy was the teaching of "world view," or weltanschaaung. In this regard, it is revealing that the old academic and pedagogue Ernst Krieck (1882–1947), a professor at the Pädagogische Hochschule, was made a professor of philosophy and the rector of the University of Frankfurt am Main in 1933 and the following year named a professor of philosophy at Heidelberg, the university where he would become rector in 1937. Heidegger, who was violently attacked by Krieck in the review *Volk im Werden*, criticized the ideologue by name in the text of his remarks.
230. Ibid., 27.
231. Martin Heidegger, *Nietzsche: Der europäische Nihilismus*, vol. 48 of *Gesamtausgabe*, pt. 2, *Vorlesungen 1923–1944* (Frankfurt: Klostermann, 1986), 205.
232. A possibility opened, in the modern era, through the disenchantment of the world and the thought of Descartes.
233. Martin Heidegger, *Basic Concepts*, trans. Gary E. Aylesworth (Bloomington: University of Indiana Press, 1993), 7.
234. Ibid.

235. Ibid., 8.

236. Martin Heidegger, "Lectures on Hölderlin" (1942), in *Hölderlins Hymne "Der Ister,"* vol. 53 of *Gesamtausgabe* (Frankfurt: Klostermann, 1993), 106, quoted in Luc Ferry and Alain Renaut, *Heidegger and Modernity*, trans. Franklin Philip (Chicago: University of Chicago Press, 1990), 124n50.

237. As does Emmanuel Faye, for example: see his *Heidegger: The Introduction of Nazism into Philosophy in Light of the Unpublished Seminars of 1933–1935*, trans. Michael B. Smith (New Haven: Yale University Press, 2009).

238. Martin Heidegger, lecture of 1 December 1949, quoted in Ferry and Renaut, *Heidegger and Modernity*, 71.

239. "On page 152 Heidegger concerns himself with National Socialism, 'with the inner truth and greatness of this movement (namely with the encounter of planetarally determined technology and modern man) . . .' Since these sentences were published for the first time without any remarks, one may assume that they represent, without alteration, Heidegger's position today." Jürgen Habermas, "Martin Heidegger, on the Publication of Lectures from the Year 1935," trans. Dale Ponikvar, *Graduate Faculty Philosophy Journal* 6, no. 2 (Fall 1977): 157.

240. See François Fédier, introduction to Martin Heidegger, *Écrits politiques, 1933–1966* (Paris: Gallimard, 1995).

241. "'Only God Can Save Us': The *Spiegel* Interview," trans. William J. Richardson, in *Heidegger: The Man and the Thinker*, ed. Thomas Sheehan (New Brunswick, NJ: Transaction Publishers, 2009), 61.

PART 2. IMITATING ANTIQUITY

Epigraphs. Karl Marx, *The Eighteenth Brumaire of Louis Bonaparte*, in Robert C. Tucker, ed., *The Marx-Engels Reader*, 2nd ed. (New York: W. W. Norton, 1978), 595; Alfred Rosenberg, *The Myth of the Twentieth Century: An Evaluation of the Spiritual-Intellectual Confrontations of Our Age*, trans. Vivian Bird (Newport Beach, CA: Noontide, 1982), 12; and Adolf Hitler, "Rede des Führers auf der Kulturtagung des Reichsparteitages zu Nürnberg," 1 September 1933, in Werner Siebarth, ed., *Hitlers Wollen: Nach Kernsätzen aus seinen Schriften und Reden* (Munich: Zentralverlag der NSDAP, 1935), 140 ("Es ist . . . kein wunder dass jedes politisch heroische Zeitalter in seiner Kunst sofort die Brücke schlägt zu einer nicht minder heroischen Vergangenheit. Griechen und Römer werden dann plötzlich den Germanen so nahe, weil alle ihre Wurzeln in einer Grundrasse zu suchen haben, und daher üben auch die unsterblichen Leistungen der alten Völker immer wieder ihre anziehende Wirkung aus auf die ihnen rassisch verwandten Nachkommen").

CHAPTER 4. FROM STONE TO FLESH

Epigraphs. Charlotte Beradt, *The Third Reich of Dreams: The Nightmares of a Nation, 1933–1939*, trans. Adrienne Gottwald (Chicago: Quadrangle Press, 1968), 79–80; and Hermann Jekeli, "Rasse ist Verpflichtung," *Rasse und Volk: Stoffsammlung für die weltanschauliche Schulung*, ed. Beauftragten für die weltanschauliche Schulung der deutschen Volksgruppe in Rumänien, NSDAP, November 1941, Heft 2: 15.

1. Johann Joachim Winckelmann, *History of the Art of Antiquity*, trans. Harry Mallgrave (Los Angeles: Getty Publications, 2006).
2. George Mosse, *The Image of Man: The Creation of Modern Masculinity* (New York: Oxford, 1998).
3. The phrase comes from Juvenal, *Satires* 10.356.
4. Johann Kaspar Lavater, *Essays on Physiognomy*, trans. Thomas Holcroft (London: C. Whittingham, 1804).
5. Johann Kaspar Lavater, *Ausgewählte Schriften*, ed. Johann Kaspar Orelli (Zürich: F. Schulthess, 1859), 21, quoted in Mosse, *Image of Man*, 25. On the science of physiognomy and its reception under National Socialism, see the work of Claudia Schmölders: *Das Vorurteil im Leibe: Einführung in die Physiognomik* (Berlin: Akademie Verlag, 1995) and *Hitlers Gesicht: Eine physiognomische Biographie* (Munich: Beck, 2000).
6. See George Mosse, *Fallen Soldiers: Reshaping the Memory of the World Wars* (New York: Oxford, 1990), 29-32, 72, and 74. Mock-ups of several of these German monuments to the dead are on display at the *Historial de la Grande Guerre* in Péronne. On this theme, see also Michael Jeismann and Reinhardt Koselleck, *Der politische Totenkult: Kriegerdenkmäler in der Moderne* (Munich: Fink, 1994).
7. Mosse, *Image of Man*, 32.
8. Hermann Jekeli, "Rasse ist Verpflichtung," *Rasse und Volk: Stoffsammlung für die weltanschauliche Schulung*, ed. Beauftragten für die weltanschauliche Schulung der deutschen Volksgruppe in Rumänien, NSDAP, November 1941, Heft 2: 15.
9. Ludwig Schemann, *Hauptepochen und Hauptvölker der Geschichte in ihrer Stellung zur Rasse*, vol. 2 of *Die Rasse in den Geisteswissenschaften* (Munich: Lehmanns Verlag, 1930), 105.
10. See chap. 1, as well as the first part of Ingomar Weiler, "Zur Rezeption des griechischen Sports im Nationalsozialismus: Kontinuität oder Diskontinuität in der deutschen Ideengeschichte?," in *Antike und Altertumwissenschaft in der Zeit von Faschismus und Nationalsozialismus: Kolloquium Universität Zürich, 14.-17. Oktober 1998*, ed. Beat Näf (Mandelbachtal: Edition Cicero, 2001), 267-84.
11. See especially J. H. Krause, *Die Gymnastik und Agonistik der Hellenen* (Leipzig: J. A. Barth, 1841).
12. Gerhard Krause and Erich Mindt, *Olympia 1936: Eine nationale Aufgabe* (Berlin: Reichstportverlag, 1935), 83-84.
13. *Völkischer Beobachter*, 2 August 1936, 7.
14. Dr. Hans Kern, "Olympia, das Erbe der Hellenen: Blüte und Verfall der olympischen Spiele der Griechen," *Völkischer Beobachter*, 2 August 1936, 8.
15. By resuscitating the games, Coubertin had performed "a sublime act, for which the peoples of the earth can only thank him." In Berlin's Olympic park, the Olympia Gelände, the plaza leading to the stadium was named in his honor. See Manfred Hausmann, "Der Gedanke von Olympia," *Olympia-Zeitung*, no. 1 (21 July 1936), 2.

16. "Wegbereiter der Wiedergeburt: Winckelmann, Curtius, und Dörpfeld, Pioniere des olympischen Gedankens," *Völkischer Beobachter,* 2 August 1936, 7–8.

17. Hausmann, "Der Gedanke von Olympia," 2.

18. "Olympias klassische Kampfspiele," *Das Schwarze Korps,* 22 May 1935, 8.

19. Alfred Rosenberg, "Die olympischen Spiele im Dienste der ewigen Werte," *Völkischer Beobachter, "Olympia-Sonderausgabe,"* 17 July 1936, section 1, 2.

20. Carl Diem, "Die Geschichte der olympischen Spiele," in *Olympia 1936 und die Leibesübungen im nationalsozialistischen Staat,* ed. Friedrich Mildner, vol. 1 (Berlin: Buchvertrieb Olympiade 1936, 1934), 35.

21. Gerhart Rodenwaldt and Walter Hege, *Olympia* (Berlin: Deutscher Kunstverlag, 1936).

22. On Hans Schlief, see Veit Stürmer, "Hans Schlief: Eine Karriere zwischen Archäologischem Institut und Ahnenerbe e.V.," in *Prähistorie und Nationalsozialismus: Die mittel- und osteuropäische Ur- und Frühgeschichtsforschung in den Jahren 1933–1945,* ed. Achim Leute (Heidelberg: Synchron, 2002), 429–50.

23. "Die Ursprungstätte der olympischen Spiele," *Das Schwarze Korps,* no. 29 (1936), 3.

24. "Olympia: Die Ausgrabung des Führers," *Das Schwarze Korps,* no. 33 (1938), 10–11.

25. *Olympia-Zeitung: Offizielles Organ der XI. Olympischen Spiele 1936 in Berlin,* no. 3 (23 July 1936), 47.

26. Theobald Bieder, *Das Hakenkreuz* (Leipzig: Verlag Theodor Weicher, 1934).

27. See Jean-Marie Brohm, *Jeux olympiques à Berlin* (Brussels: Éditions Complexe, 1983), esp. ch. 1.

28. Hajo Bernett, *Sportpolitik im Dritten Reich: Aus den Akten der Reichskanzlei,* Beiträge zur Lehre und Forschung der Leibeserziehung 39 (Schorndorf bei Stuttgart: Verlag Karl Hofmann, 1971), 51–52.

29. Wilhelm Frick to the Reich Chancellery, 22 January 1936, BABL/R 43 II/731, microfiche 2, f. 51.

30. Hans Lammers to Wilhelm Frick, 24 January 1936, BABL/R 43 II/731, microfiche 2, f. 52.

31. "Deutsch am Wege der Olympiafackel," *Das Schwarze Korps,* 23 July 1936, 8.

32. "Auferstehung des antiken Theaters," *Völkischer Beobachter,* 17 July 1936, section 2, 28.

33. See chap. 5, esp. pp. 204–6.

34. Krause and Mindt, *Olympia 1936,* 19.

35. See Tacitus, *Germania* 3. In describing Hercules's voyages to those lands, Tacitus explained how the Greek demigod had become a German national hero: "Fuisse apud eos et Hercules memorant" ("They further record how Hercules appeared among the Germans" [Tacitus, *Germania,* trans. M. Hutton, rev. E. H. Warmington, in *Tacitus: Agricola, Germania, Dialogus* (Cambridge, MA:

Harvard University Press, 1970), 133]). Hercules was not the only prestigious visitor to those far northern territories; Tacitus would have it that Ulysses made the same voyage, leaving behind an altar, where his cult was long celebrated.

36. Krause and Mindt, *Olympia 1936*, 19.

37. Felicias von Reznicek, "Händel's 'Herakles' auf der Dietrich-Eckart-Bühne," *Olympia-Zeitung*, no. 20 (9 August 1936), 384.

38. *Völkischer Beobachter*, 4 August 1936.

39. See Lothar Schirmer, "Theater und Antike: Probleme der Antikenrezeption auf Berliner Bühnen vom Ende des 18. Jahrhunderts bis zur Gegenwart," in *Berlin und die Antike: Architektur, Kunstgewerbe, Malerei, Skulptur, Theater und Wissenschaft vom 16. Jahrhundert bis heute*, ed. Willmuth Arenhövel and Christa Schreiber (Berlin: Deutsche Archäologisches Institut, 1979), 303–51.

40. *Völkischer Beobachter*, 31 July 1936, 3.

41. "Wir tragen das Feuer," *Olympia-Zeitung*, no. 2 (22 July 1936), 1 and 27.

42. Bernhard Rust, "Rede anlässlich des Empfangs der nationalen Delegationen am Pergamon-Altar," *Völkischer Beobachter*, 31 July 1936, 3.

43. *Völkischer Beobachter*, 29 July 1936, 5.

44. These were, of course, *Der Sieg des Glaubens* (*Victory of Faith*, 1933), *Triumph des Willens* (*The Triumph of the Will*, 1934), and *Tag der Freiheit: Unsere Wehrmacht* (*Day of Freedom: Our Armed Forces*, 1935).

45. Leni Riefenstahl, interviewed by *Lichtbild-Bühne*, 13 April 1938, quoted in Daniel Wildmann, *Begehrte Körper: Konstruktion und Inszenierung der "arischen" Männerkörpers im "Dritten Reich"* (Würzburg: Königshausen und Neumann, 1998), 41.

46. Carl Diem, *Olympische Reise: Unter der Sonne Homers, dazu ein Körnlein attischen Salzes* (Berlin: Deutscher Schriftenverlag, 1937).

47. These details are drawn from Walter Borgers, "Fackelläufe bei olympischen Spielen: Vorgeschichte und Bedeutung," in Borgers, *Olympische Lauffeuer* (Kassel: Agon Verlag, 1994), 6–25.

48. Werner Klingeberg, "Der Weg der Fackel," *Olympia-Zeitung*, no. 1 (21 July 1936), 6.

49. "Griechische Feiertage: Die Entzündung der heiligen Flamme," *Völkischer Beobachter*, 22 July 1936, 12; "Griechenland umjubelt die Fackelläufer," *Völkischer Beobachter*, 23 July 1936, 3; and "Der Weg des olympischen Feuers," *Völkischer Beobachter*, 24 July 1936, 4.

50. Krause and Mindt, *Olympia 1936*, 65.

51. "Appel des Reichsministers Dr. Goebbels, des Reichsministers Frick und des Reichssportführers von Tschammer und Osten," January 1935, quoted in ibid., 76.

52. Krause and Mindt, *Olympia 1936*, 126.

53. Ibid., 13.

54. Ibid., 14.

55. Ibid., 13.

56. Rosenberg, "Die olympischen Spiele im Dienste der ewigen Werte," 2.

57. Adolf Hitler, *Mein Kampf*, trans. Ralph Manheim (Boston: Houghton Mifflin, 1943), 408.

58. Friedrich Richter, "Der olympische Gedanke als Kulturträger," *Völkischer Beobachter,* "*Olympia-Sonderausgabe,*" 17 July 1936, section 1, 5.
59. "Reichsminister Rust eröffnet das internationale Sport-Studentenlager," *Völkischer Beobachter,* 25 July 1936, 6.
60. See chap. 3.
61. "Olympias klassische Kampfspiele," *Das Schwarze Korps,* 22 May 1935, 8.
62. Solon, in dialogue with Lucian, quoted in Krause and Mindt, *Olympia 1936,* 38.
63. See Michèle C. Cone, *Artists under Vichy* (Princeton: Princeton University Press, 1992), 155.
64. The study of genetics was certainly born with the laws of Mendel, but DNA, as the definitive physical identification of the individual, was not discovered until 1944 by Oswald Avery, who demonstrated that deoxyribonucleic acid was responsible for the transmission of hereditary characteristics. The structure of DNA was subsequently discovered by Watson and Crick in 1953. See François Jacob, *The Logic of Life: A History of Heredity,* trans. Betty Spillman (Princeton: Princeton University Press, 1993); and Michel Morange, *A History of Molecular Biology,* trans. Matthew Cobb (Cambridge, MA: Harvard University Press, 2000).
65. This was Hitler's assertion in *Mein Kampf*: "[France] is making such great progress in negrification that we can actually speak of an African state arising on European soil" (644).
66. Mosse, *Image of Man,* 63–64.
67. Anthropologists from the prestigious Kaiser-Wilhelm-Gesellschaft (1911–48) trained the SS's own racial experts. The professor of anthropology Eugen Fischer, the rector of the University of Berlin, himself donated his racial expertise to the doctors of the SS from October 1934 until August 1935. The goal was to train them to recognize a superior or inferior racial type by simple visual observation. See Benno Müller-Hill, *Murderous Science: Elimination by Scientific Selection of Jews, Gypsies, and Others, Germany, 1933–1945,* trans. George R. Fraser (New York: Oxford University Press, 1988); and Robert N. Proctor, *Racial Hygiene: Medicine under the Nazis* (Cambridge, MA: Harvard University Press, 1998).
68. Established on 31 December 1941, the RUSHA was headed by Richard Walther Darré, assigned the rank of *SS-Standartenführer.*
69. Schemann, *Hauptepochen und Hauptvölker der Geschichte in ihrer Stellung zur Rasse,* 78.
70. *Entartete Kunst: Ausstellungsführer,* Reichspropagandaleitung, Amtsleitung Kultur (Berlin, 1937), esp. 27, 29, and 31. A complete reproduction can be found in Peter-Klaus Schuster, ed., *Die Kunststadt München 1937: Nationalsozialismus und 'Entartete Kunst'* (Munich: Prestel Verlag, 1988).
71. *Entartete Kunst,* 31.
72. Adolf Hitler, "Speech at the Opening of the Great German Art Exhibition of 1937," Munich, 18 July 1937, in Anson Rabinach and Sander Gilman, eds., *The Third Reich Sourcebook* (Berkeley: University of California Press, 2013), 497.

73. The *Lancellotti Discobolus,* or *Discobolus Palombara,* was a Roman copy in marble of the famous statue by Myron, dating back to the Antonine period of the imperial era; Myron's original *Discobolus,* cast in bronze, has been lost.

74. Adolf Hitler, "Speech at the Opening of the Greater German Art Exhibition of 1938," in Max Domarus, ed., *Hitler: Speeches and Proclamations, 1932–1945,* trans. Mary Fran Gilbert (Wauconda, IL: Bolchazy-Carducci, 1990–2004), vol. 2, *The Years 1935 to 1938,* 1127.

75. See Deulig Tonwochen Nr. 342/1938, 20 July 1938, and Fox Tönende Wochenschauen Nr. 411/1938, 20 July 1938, Bundesarchiv, Abteilung Filmarchiv.

76. Hitler, "Speech at the Opening of the Great German Art Exhibition of 1938," 1127.

77. *Inside the Third Reich: Memoirs by Albert Speer,* trans. Richard Winston and Clara Winston (New York: Macmillan, 1970), 96–97. Speer subsequently commented: "By the Greeks he meant the Dorians. Naturally his view was affected by the theory, fostered by the scientists of his period, that the Dorian tribe which migrated into Greece from the north had been of Germanic origin and that, therefore, its culture had not belonged to the Mediterranean world."

78. Mosse, *Image of Man,* 170.

79. Through children born, through the example set, and through the service that a healthy body could perform in the name of the people's community, in times of war and in times of peace (through work).

80. See Frederic Spotts, *Hitler and the Power of Aesthetics* (New York: Overlook, 2003), ch. 6.

81. Joseph Goebbels, *Combat pour Berlin* (Paris: Socìete de Presse et d'Éditions, 1966), 38, quoted in Éric Michaud, *The Cult of Art in Nazi Germany,* trans. Janet Lloyd (Stanford: Stanford University Press, 2004), 1.

82. Joseph Goebbels, letter to Wilhelm Furtwängler, 11 April 1933, quoted in Michaud, *Cult of Art in Nazi Germany,* 5.

83. See p. 83.

84. *Das Blut, seine Bedeutung, Reinerhaltung und Verbesserung,* vol. 1 of *Blut und Boden: Lichtbildvortrag,* ed. Reichsführer-SS, Chef des Rasse- und Siedlungshauptamts (Berlin, n.d.), BABL/RD/NSD 41/87, 18, image 41.

85. Ibid., images 27–28.

86. Ibid., 18.

87. Hitler, "Speech at the Opening of the Great German Art Exhibition of 1937," 498.

88. Hitler, *Mein Kampf,* 253.

89. Ibid., 407–8.

90. Ibid., 408.

91. Ibid., 409–10.

92. See *Die Lebensreform: Entwürfe zur Neugestraltung von Leben und Kunst um 1900,* 2 vols. (Darmstadt: Institut Mathildenhöhe, 2001).

93. Hans Surén, *Mensch und Sonne: Arisch-olympischer Geist* (Berlin: Scherl Verlag, 1924; reprinted in 1936 and 1940). An English translation, now out of print, appeared in 1927: *Man and Sunlight,* trans. David Arthur Jones (Slough:

Sollux, 1927). Excerpts can be found in Anton Kaes, Martin Jay, and Edward Dimendberg, eds., *The Weimar Republic Sourcebook* (Berkeley: University of California Press, 1995), 678–79. All translations here by Richard Nybakken.

94. Surén, *Mensch und Sonne*, 190.
95. Ibid., 89 and 91.
96. Ibid., 16.
97. Ibid., 16–17.
98. Ibid., 18.
99. Ibid., 87.
100. Ibid., 88.
101. Ibid., 15.
102. Richard Walther Darré, *Das Bauerntum als Lebensquell der nordischen Rasse* (Munich: Lehmanns Verlag, 1929), 444.
103. "Was ist schamlos?," *Das Schwarze Korps*, 20 January 1938, 8; and "Anstossig?," *Das Schwarze Korps*, 16 April 1936, 13.
104. "Anstossig?," 13.
105. See Klaus Theweleit, *Male Fantasies*, 2 vols., trans. Stephen Conway in collaboration with Erica Carter and Chris Turner (Minneapolis: University of Minnesota Press, 1987–89).
106. Hans Surén, *Mensch und Sonne*, 158.
107. Ibid., 160.
108. Ibid., 163.
109. Ibid., 164.
110. Ibid., 178.
111. Ibid., 179.
112. Ibid., 172.
113. Ibid., 213.
114. Ibid., 171.
115. Ibid., 172.
116. Hermann Goering, preface to Krause and Mindt, *Olympia 1936*.
117. Hitler, *Mein Kampf*, 254.
118. Ibid., 408–9.
119. Victorian puritanism undoubtedly formed part of an economy of urges that aimed to contain and constrain an energy that was better channeled and unleashed in the desired direction. The political management of the passions by contemporary totalitarianisms was brilliantly described by George Orwell in his novel *1984*.
120. Quoted in Henry Jouin, *David d'Angers, sa vie, son œuvre, ses écrits et ses contemporains*, vol. 2 (Paris: E. Plon, 1878), 96.
121. Birgit Bressa, "Nachleber der Antike: Klassische Bilder des Körpers in der NS-Skulptur Arno Brekers" (thesis, Universität Tübingen, 2001), 283.
122. Ibid., 288.
123. "Ihr Körper wird als 'ganzer' präsentiert, geöffnet, mit markiertem Schamdreieck und vor allem immer wieder betonten, geradezu erigierten Brüsten." Silke Wenk, "Aufgerichtete weibliche Körper: Zur allegorischen Skulptur im deutschen Faschismus," in *Inszenierung der Macht: Ästhetische Faszination im Faschismus*, ed. Klaus Behnken and Frank Wagner (Berlin: Nishen, 1987), 116.

124. See Peter Reichel, *Der schöne Schein des Dritten Reiches: Faszination und Gewalt des Faschismus* (Munich: Carl Hanser Verlag, 1991); see also Bernd Ogan and Wolfgang W. Weiss, *Faszination und Gewalt: Zur politischen Ästhetik des Nationalsozialismus* (Nuremberg: W. Tümmels Verlag, 1992).

125. Hans Surén, *Gymnastik der Deutschen*, vol. 2, *Lehren für Berufstätige und Gesetze für Sport und Arbeit, Männer und Frauen* (Stuttgart: Franck'sche Verlagshandlung, 1937), 37.

126. Surén, *Mensch und Sonne*, 191.

127. Ibid., 192.

128. See Michaud, *Cult of Art in Nazi Germany*, 134–40.

129. Charles Baudelaire, "The Painter of Modern Life," in Baudelaire, *"The Painter of Modern Life" and Other Essays*, ed. and trans. Jonathan Mayne (London: Phaidon, 1995), 2.

130. Adolf Hitler, "Address on Art and Politics," given at the Kulturtagung (Culture conference) of the Nuremberg Party Congress, 1935, in *The Speeches of Adolf Hitler*, ed. Norman Baynes, vol. 1 (New York: Howard Fertig, 1969), 574.

131. Paul Schultze-Naumburg, *Kunst und Rasse* (Munich: Lehmann Verlag, 1928), 9.

132. Paul Schultze-Naumburg, *Rassengebundene Kunst*, Volk und Wissen 13 (Berlin: Brehm Verlag, 1935), 11.

133. Ibid., 10.

134. Paul Schultze-Naumburg, *Nordische Schönheit: Ihr Wunschbild im Leben und in der Kunst* (Munich: Lehmann Verlag, 1937), 9.

135. Ibid., 151. See also Schultze-Naumburg, *Kunst und Rasse*, 79.

136. Schultze-Naumburg, *Nordische Schönheit*, 148.

137. Schultze-Naumburg, *Kunst und Rasse*, 68–69.

138. Ibid., 71.

139. Schultze-Naumburg, *Nordische Schönheit*, ch. 10, "Beispiele der Kunstgeschichte," 166–226.

140. Ibid., 111.

141. Ibid., 112.

142. Ibid., 113.

143. Ibid.

144. See Michaud, *Cult of Art in Nazi Germany*, 134–40.

145. Bressa, "Nachleber der Antike," 300.

146. Ibid., 301.

147. Walter Benjamin, "The Work of Art in the Age of Mechanical Reproduction," in Benjamin, *Illuminations*, ed. Hannah Arendt, trans. Harry Zohn (New York: Schocken Books, 1968), 241.

148. Ibid., 241n21.

CHAPTER 5. THE RACIAL STATE AND TOTALITARIAN SOCIETY

Epigraphs. Constantin-François Volney, *Lectures on History, Delivered in the Normal School of Paris* (London: Wilson, 1800), 169, 172 (see also Camille Desmoulins: "Our heads stuffed full of Greek and Latin, we were all college republicans"—quoted in Claude Nicolet, *Histoire, nation, république* [Paris: Odile Jacob, 2000], 50 and 263); and Karl Jaspers, letter to Hannah Arendt, 7 January 1951, in *Hannah Arendt, Karl Jaspers: Correspondence, 1926–1969,* ed. Lotte Kohler and Hans Saner, trans. Robert Kimber and Rita Kimber (New York: Harcourt, Brace, 1992), 163.

1. Karl Popper, *The Spell of Plato,* vol. 1 of *The Open Society and Its Enemies* (Princeton: Princeton University Press, 2013), 161.
2. Ibid., xxxix.
3. Hans Bogner, *Platon im Unterricht,* Auf dem Wege zum nationalpolitischen Gymnasium, Beiträge zur nationalsozialistischen Ausrichtung des altsprachlichen Unterrichts 1 (Frankfurt am Main: Verlag Moritz Diesterweg, 1937), 3. See also Bogner, *Die verwirklichte Demokratie: Die Lehren der Antike* (Hamburg: Hanseatische Verlagsanstalt, 1930), esp. ch. 6, "Platon," 197–217.
4. Martha Zapata, "Die Rezeption der Philosophie Friedrich Nietzsches im deutschen Faschismus," in *"Die besten Geister der Nation": Philosophie und Nationalsozialismus,* ed. Ilse Korotin (Vienna: Picus Verlag, 1994), 186–220.
5. Alfred Bäumler, *Nietzsche, der Philosoph und Politiker* (Leipzig: Reclam, 1931).
6. Alfred Bäumler, "Nietzsche und der Nationalsozialismus," *Nationalsozialistische Monatshefte* 5 (1934): 289–98, reprinted in *Studien zur deutschen Geistesgeschichte* (Dresden: Junker und Dünnhaupt, 1937), 281.
7. Ernst Nolte, *Nietzsche und der Nationalsozialismus* (Munich: Herbig, 2000), 307.
8. Ernst Nolte, "Nietzsche im Nationalsozialismus," in *Neue Wege der Ideengeschichte: Festschrift für Kurt Kluxen zum 85. Geburtstag,* ed. Frank-Lothar Kroll (Paderborn: Schöningh, 1996), 379–89, esp. 380.
9. Kurt Hildebrandt, *Platon: Der Kampf des Geistes um die Macht* (Berlin: Georg Bondi, 1933), 7.
10. See Werner Jaeger, "Die griechische Staatsethik im Zeitalter des Platon: Rede zur Reichsgründungsfeier der Berliner Universität am 18. Januar 1924," in *Die Antike: Zeitschrift für Kunst und Kultur des klassischen Altertums,* ed. Jaeger (Berlin: De Gruyter, 1934), 1–16. This inflection in Platonic exegesis is examined in Theresa Orozco, "Die Platon-Rezeption in Deutschland um 1933," in Korotin, *"Die besten Geister der Nation,"* 141–85.
11. Bogner, *Platon im Unterricht,* 8.
12. Hans F. K. Günther, *Platon als Hüter des Lebens: Platons Zucht- und Erziehungsgedanken und deren Bedeutung für die Gegenwart* (Munich: Lehmann Verlag, 1928), preface.
13. Ibid., 16.
14. Werner Jaeger, "Die Erziehung des politischen Menschen und die Antike," *Volk im Werden* 1, no. 3 (1933): 46.
15. Hildebrandt, *Platon,* 265.
16. See chap. 3.
17. Günther, *Platon als Hüter des Lebens,* 9.
18. Ibid., 11. Throughout the book, Günther ceaselessly chastised the *Philosophieprofessoren* in question, whom he contrasted with the figure of the Greek philosopher.

19. Adolf Rusch, "Platon als Erzieher zum deutschen Menschen," in *Humanistische Bildung im Nationalsozialistischen Staate*, Neue Wege zur Antike, Erste Reihe, Heft 9 (Leipzig: Teubner Verlag, 1933), 44–49.
20. Ibid., 45.
21. Oberstudiendirektor Billen, "Vorschläge für die Gestaltung des Unterrichts in den alten Sprachen," 1936, BABL/R/4901/4614, ff. 245–46.
22. *Richtlinien für Griechisch*, Mecklemburgische Staatsministerium, Abt. Unterricht, BABL/R/4901/4614, ff. 281–82.
23. See Ludwig Ferdinand Clauss, *Rasse und Seele: Eine Einführung in den Sinn der leiblichen Gestalt* (Munich: Lehmanns Verlag, 1926).
24. *Richtlinien für Griechisch*, ff. 281–82.
25. See Bernhard Rust, ed., *Erziehung und Unterricht in der höheren Schule: Amtliche Ausgabe des Reichs- und Preußischen Ministeriums für Wissenschaft, Erziehung und Volksbildung* (Berlin: Weidmann, 1938), 250.
26. Günther, *Platon als Hüter des Lebens*, 19.
27. Ibid., 19 and 62.
28. Hildebrandt (1881–1966), a member of Stefan George's circle, wrote several books on Plato, Nietzsche, and Wagner. He also published essays on the state and racial policy (e.g., *Staat und Rasse: Drei Vorträge* [Breslau: Ferdinand Hirt, 1928]).
29. Hildebrandt, *Platon*, 226.
30. Ibid., 247.
31. Ibid., 229.
32. See pp. 211–14.
33. Hildebrandt, *Platon*, 226.
34. Ibid., 234.
35. Ibid., 238.
36. Ibid., 240.
37. Ibid., 241.
38. Joachim Bannes, *Hitlers Kampf und Platons Staat: Eine Studie über den ideologischen Aufbau der Nationalsozialistischen Freiheitsbewegung* (Berlin: De Gruyter, 1933).
39. Bogner, *Platon im Unterricht*, 15.
40. Hildebrandt, *Platon*, 395.
41. Plato, *Auslese und Bildung der Führer und Wehrmänner: Eine Auslese aus dem "Staat,"* trans. Hans Holtorf (Berlin: Teubner Verlag, 1936), 1–2.
42. Hans Heyse, *Die Idee der Wissenschaft und die deutsche Universität: Rede, gehalten bei der feierlichen Übernahme des Rektorates der Albertus-Universität zu Königsberg am 4. Dezember 1933* (Königsberg: Gräfe und Unzer Verlag, 1933), 12.
43. Günther, *Platon als Hüter des Lebens*, 22.
44. Ibid., 29.
45. Ibid., 28.
46. Hildebrandt, *Platon*, 260.
47. Bogner, *Platon im Unterricht*, 13.
48. Hans Bogner, *Die Bildung der politischen Elite* (Oldenburg: Stalling Verlag, 1932), 36.

49. On these aspects, see Luc Brisson, *Lectures de Platon* (Paris: Vrin, 2000); and Monique Canto-Sperber, ed., *Philosophie grecque* (Paris: Presses Universitaires de France, 1998).
50. Hildebrandt, *Platon*, 396.
51. Fritz Lenz, *Menschliche Auslese und Rassenhygiene (Eugenik)*, vol. 2 of *Menschliche Erblichkeitslehre und Rassenhygiene* (Munich: Lehmann Verlag, 1932), 413.
52. Richard Walther Darré, *Neuadel aus Blut und Boden* (Munich: Lehmann Verlag, 1930).
53. Günther, *Platon als Hüter des Lebens*, 24.
54. Ibid., 14.
55. Ibid., 20.
56. Ibid., 30.
57. Ibid., 34.
58. Ibid., 33.
59. Hildebrandt, *Staat und Rasse*, 37.
60. Ibid., 35.
61. Ibid., 36.
62. Ibid., 41.
63. Ibid.
64. Ibid., 42.
65. Günther, *Platon als Hüter des Lebens*, 66.
66. Ibid., 29.
67. Walter Hohmann and Wilhelm Schiefer, *Lehrbuch der Geschichte für höhere Schulen: Oberstufe* (Frankfurt am Main: Verlag Moritz Diesterweg, [1940]), 64.
68. "The race of Asia Minor habitually plays concepts off one another, criticizes old arguments, questions and destroys inherited wisdom." Hans Günther, *Rassengeschichte des Hellenischen und des Römischen Volkes* (Munich: Lehmann Verlag, 1929), 60.
69. Ibid. On the racial scientific interpretation of the sophistic, see also Alfred Rosenberg, *The Myth of the Twentieth Century: An Evaluation of the Spiritual-Intellectual Confrontations of Our Age*, trans. Vivian Bird (Newport Beach, CA: Noontide, 1982).
70. Günther, *Rassengeschichte des Hellenischen und des Römischen Volkes*, 70.
71. The *école unique* was a proposal to create free public education for all French youth, regardless of class or confession, eliminating the existing distinctions in the secondary-school system.
72. Günther, *Rassengeschichte des Hellenischen und des Römischen Volkes*, 71.
73. Hildebrandt, *Platon*, 243.
74. Ibid., 246.
75. Ibid., 246–47.
76. Hans Bogner, *Platon im Unterricht*, 9.
77. Ibid., 10.
78. Ibid., 9.

79. See Tacitus, *Germania* 11.
80. See Claude Nicolet, *La fabrique d'une nation: La France entre Rome et les Germains* (Paris: Perrin, 2003), esp. ch. 3.
81. "Die Thingstätten," *Der Deutsche*, no. 152 (4 July 1934).
82. See Lenz Meinhold, *Die Heidelberger Thingstätte: Die Thingbewegung im Dritten Reich, Kunst als Mittel politischer Propaganda* (Heidelberg: Schutzgemeinschaft Heiligenberg e.V., 1975).
83. See BABL/R 55/264. On the architecture and significance of the *Thingstätten*, see Anna Teut, *Architektur im Dritten Reich 1933–1945* (Berlin: Ullstein, 1967), esp. ch. 5, "Die dritte Bühne," 227–34.
84. See Hanns Johst, *Schlageter* (1932). Johst was later named the director of the Berlin State Theater, the president of the Reichsschriftungskummer (Reich writers' union), and an SS-Brigadeführer.
85. See Richard Euringer, *Deutsche Passion* (1933), and Jurt Heynicke, *Der Weg ins Reich* (1935).
86. See chap. 3, esp. pp. 110–13.
87. Alfred Bäumler, "Sinn und Aufbau der deutschen Leibesübungen," in Bäumler, *Männerbund und Wissenschaft* (Berlin: Junker und Dünnhaupt, 1943), 70.
88. Ibid., 58.
89. Rosenberg, *Myth of the Twentieth Century*, 181.
90. Ernst Krieck, *Musische Erziehung* (Leipzig, Armanen-Verlag, 1933), 20.
91. Ludwig Schemann, *Hauptepochen und Hauptvölker der Geschichte in ihrer Stellung zur Rasse*, vol. 2 of *Die Rasse in den Geisteswissenschaften* (Munich: Lehmanns Verlag, 1930), 132.
92. Hohmann and Schiefer, *Lehrbuch der Geschichte für höhere Schulen*, 69.
93. See Jean-Pierre Vernant, *Les origines de la pensée grecque* (Paris: Presses Universitaires de France, 1962); and Michel Villey, *La formation de la pensée juridique moderne* (Paris: Montchrétien, 1975).
94. Schemann, *Hauptepochen und Hauptvölker der Geschichte*, 145–46.
95. Fritz Schachermeyr, "Die Aufgaben der alten Geschichte im Rahmen der Nordischen Weltgeschichte," *Vergangenheit und Gegenwart* 23 (1933): 599.
96. Ibid., 599n15.
97. Fritz Schachermeyr, *Indogermanen und Orient: Ihre kulturelle und machtpolitische Auseinandersetzung im Altertum* (Stuttgart: W. Kohlhammer Verlag, 1944), 305.
98. Max Pohlenz, "Die Stoa: Geschichte einer geistigen Bewegung," in *Hellas*, vol. 1 of *Das Neue Bild der Antike*, ed. Helmut Berve (Leipzig: Koehler und Amelang, 1942), 356.
99. Ibid., 360.
100. Cicero, *De officiis* 1.16.
101. See chap. 8 on democracy as a symptom and catalyst of racial decadence.
102. Schemann, *Hauptepochen und Hauptvölker der Geschichte*, 145.
103. On these concepts, see Carlos Levy, *Les philosophes hellénistiques* (Paris: Livre de Poche, 1997); and Lucien Jerphagnon, *Histoire de la pensée: Antiquité et Moyen Age* (Paris: Tallandier, 1989).

104. See Paul Petit, *La crise de l'empire (161–284)* (Paris: Le Seuil, 1978); and Lucien Jarphagnon, *Histoire de la Rome antique: Les armes et les mots* (Paris: Tallandier, 1987).
105. Rosenberg, *Myth of the Twentieth Century*, 41–42.
106. Günther, *Rassengeschichte des Hellenischen und des Römischen Volkes*, 106.
107. Ibid.
108. Schachermeyr, *Indogermanen und Orient*, 307.
109. Pohlenz, "Die Stoa," 354–55.
110. Fritz Geyer, *Rasse, Volk und Staat im Altertum* (Leipzig: Teubner Verlag, 1936), 78.
111. Ibid., 79.
112. Hohmann and Schiefer, *Lehrbuch der Geschichte für höhere Schulen*, 67.
113. Walther Gehl, *Geschichte, 6. Klasse, Oberschulen, Gymnasien und Oberschulen in Aufbauform: Von der Urzeit bis zum Ende der Hohenstaufen* (Breslau: Fredinand Hirt, 1940), 58–60.
114. Adolf Hitler, *Mein Kampf*, trans. Ralph Manheim (Boston: Houghton Mifflin, 1943), 290.
115. Günther, *Kleine Rassenkunde Europas* (Munich: Lehmann Verlag, 1925), 146–47; Schemann, *Hauptepochen und Hauptvölker der Geschichte*, 146.
116. According to Hans Günther, "Plato came from the original Hellenic nobility and thus was part of its Nordic essence, even if one can detect the Dinaric influence in him." Günther, *Rassengeschichte des Hellenischen und des Römischen Volkes*, 59.
117. Bogner, *Platon im Unterricht*, 35.
118. Ibid., 17.
119. Günther, *Platon als Hüter des Lebens*.
120. Ibid., 29. In *The Myth of the Twentieth Century*, Rosenberg repeatedly described Socrates' hideousness: "elephantine" ("elefantenstark," 180), "a slovenly satyr" ("ein struppiger Satyrtyp," 182), "the hideous Socrates" ("der hässliche Sokrates," ibid.).
121. Günther, *Rassengeschichte des Hellenischen und des Römischen Volkes*, 29.
122. See Rosenberg, *Myth of the Twentieth Century*, 182.
123. Paul Schultze-Naumburg, *Kunst und Rasse* (Munich: Lehmann, 1928), 75.
124. Rosenberg, *Myth of the Twentieth Century*, 180–82.
125. Ibid., 181.
126. Ibid.
127. Antisthenes (445–360) was one of the first of the Cynics in Athens.
128. Rosenberg, *Myth of the Twentieth Century*, 181.
129. Ibid., 182.
130. Ibid., 181.
131. Ibid., 182.
132. Schachermeyr, "Die Aufgaben der alten Geschichte im Rahmen der Nordischen Weltgeschichte," *Vergangenheit und Gegenwart* 23 (1933): 599.

133. Joachim Bannes, *Hitlers Kampf und Platons Staat*, 8.

134. Helmut Berve, *Sparta* (Leipzig: Bibliographisches Institut AG, 1937), 7.

135. See Thucydides, *The Peloponnesian War* 1.10.1–4. Thucydides allowed himself a few methodological reflections on the weight that the historian may give to evidence from ruins in his inquiry into the past.

136. See François Ollier, *Le mirage spartiate: Étude sur l'idéalisation de Sparte dans l'antiquité grecque de l'origine jusqu'aux Cyniques* (Paris: De Boccard, 1933); and Ollier, *Le mirage spartiate II: Étude sur l'idéalisation de Sparte dans l'antiquité grecque du début de l'école cynique jusqu'à la fin de la cité* (Paris: Les Belles Lettres, 1943).

137. Elizabeth Rawson, *The Spartan Tradition in European Thought* (Oxford: Oxford University Press, 1969).

138. Carl Ottfried Müller, *Die Dorier* (Breslau: Josef Max Verlag, 1824).

139. See chap. 9, esp. pp. 373–76.

140. Karl Christ, "Spartagorschung und Spartabild: Eine Einleitung," in *Sparta*, ed. Christ (Darmstadt: Wissenschaftliche Buchsgesellschaft, 1986), 59.

141. Helmut Berve, "Was is von der griechischen Geschichte lebendig?," *Süddeutsche Monatshefte* 33 (1935–36): 50.

142. Viktor Ehrenberg, "Ein totalitärer Staat," radio address from Prague, in Christ, *Sparta*, 219.

143. Ibid., 224.

144. Ibid., 228.

145. Henri Lichtenberger, *L'Allemagne nouvelle* (Paris: Flammarion, 1937), ch. 5, 153.

146. Ibid.

147. Gottfried Benn, "Dorische Welt: Eine Untersuchung über die Beziehung von Kunst und Macht," in Benn, *Kunst und Macht* (Stuttgart: Deutsche Verlagsanhalt, 1934), 45.

148. Ibid., 14.

149. Ibid. 26.

150. Ibid., 33.

151. Ibid., 29.

152. After the war, Otto Wilhelm von Vacano (1910–97) would become a renowned expert on Etruria. Until the 1990s, he held the chair in classical archaeology at the University of Tübingen.

153. Otto Wilhelm von Vacano, *Sparta: Der Lebenskampf einer nordischen Herrenschicht* (Kempten: Bücherei der Adolf-Hitler-Schulen, 1940), 7.

154. Ibid., 8.

155. Ibid., 24.

156. Ibid., 23.

157. Ibid., 26.

158. Kurt Petter, "Meine Kamaraden," preface (unnumbered) to ibid.

159. Gehl, *Geschichte*, 35.

160. Ibid., 37.

161. Hitler, *Mein Kampf*, 416. Italics in the original.
162. Berve, *Sparta*, 45.
163. Bernhard Rust, "Ansprache bei der Eröffnung der Hochschule für Lehrerbildung in Lauenburg/Pommern am 24.6.1933," quoted in Christ, *Sparta*, 53.
164. Bernhard Rust, "Nationalsozialismus und Wissenschaft," quoted in Christ, *Sparta*, 53; Ernst Krieck, *Das nationalsozialistische Deutschland und die Wissenschaft: Heidelberger Reden* (Hamburg: Hanseatische Verlagsanstalt, 1936), 17.
165. ". . . dass sie den Beweis dafür erbringen soll, dass Hellas nicht erst seit dem Humanismus bei uns ist, dass vielmehr Doris immer schon in Deutschland liege." Bernhard Rust, quoted in *Völkischer Beobachter*, 17 July 1936, 1.
166. Fritz Todt, ed., *Deutschlands Autobahnen: Adolf Hitlers Strassen* (Bayreuth: Gauverlag Bayerische Ostmark, 1937), 114.
167. Joseph Goebbels, speech of 18 February 1943, in *Goebbels-Reden*, vol. 2, *1939–1945* (Düsseldorf: Droste Verlag, 1971), 195.
168. Berve, *Sparta*, 147.
169. Ibid., 39.
170. Lenz, *Menschliche Auslese und Rassenhygiene (Eugenik)*, 16.
171. Ibid.
172. Ibid., 236.
173. Ibid., 17.
174. Günther, *Platon als Hüter des Lebens*.
175. Günther, *Rassengeschichte des Hellenischen und des Römischen Volkes*, 60.
176. Ludwig Schemann, *Hauptepochen und Hauptvölker der Geschichte*, 81. On Greek, and particularly Spartan, eugenics, see 79–82.
177. *Hitler's Second Book: The Unpublished Sequel to Mein Kampf*, ed. Gerhard Weinberg, trans. Krista Smith (New York: Enigma, 2006), 19–20.
178. Adolf Hitler, speech of 4 August 1929, in Hitler, *Reden, Schriften, Anordnungen*, ed. Institut für Zeitgeschichte München (Munich: Saur, 1992–2003), vol. 3, pt. 2, 348.
179. Adolf Hitler, speech of 18 October 1928, in ibid., vol. 2, pt. 2, 164.
180. Eugen Kogon, *The Theory and Practice of Hell: The German Concentration Camps and the System behind Them*, trans. Heinz Norden (New York: Farrar, Straus and Giroux, 2006), 3–4.
181. *Hitler's Table Talk, 1941–1944: His Private Conversations*, trans. Norman Cameron and R.H. Stevens (New York: Enigma, 2000), conversation of 17 February 1942, 313.
182. See chap. 6, esp. pp. 279–82, regarding Nazi colonization.
183. Richard Walther Darré, *Das Bauerntum als Lebensquell der nordischen Rasse* (Munich: Lehmann Verlag, 1929), 169.
184. Ibid., 166.
185. Ibid., 167.
186. Ibid., 169.
187. Ibid., 182.

CHAPTER 6. FROM EMPIRE TO REICH

Epigraphs. Charlie Chaplin as Adenoïd Hynkel in *The Great Dictator* (1940); Thucydides, *History of the Peloponnesian War, Books 1-2,* trans. Charles Forster Smith (Cambridge, MA: Harvard University Press, 1919), 19 (1.10.1–4); and Charles Baudelaire, "Spleen (II)," in Baudelaire, *The Flowers of Evil,* trans. James McGowan (Oxford: Oxford University Press, 2008), 147.

1. Adolf Hitler, *Mein Kampf,* trans. Ralph Manheim (Boston: Houghton Mifflin, 1943), 423.
2. *Hitler's Table Talk, 1941–1944: His Private Conversations,* trans. Norman Cameron and R. H. Stevens (New York: Enigma, 2000), night of 21–22 July 1941, 10.
3. Ibid., night of 31 March 1942, 381.
4. See Hitler, *Mein Kampf,* 300–308.
5. Ibid., 612.
6. Adolf Hitler, "Rede auf einer NSDAP-Versammlung in München," 2 May 1928, in Hitler, *Reden, Schriften, Anordnungen,* ed. Institut für Zeitgeschichte München (Munich: K. G. Saur, 1992–2003), vol. 2, pt. 2, 801–30.
7. See Claude Nicolet, *The World of the Citizen in Republican Rome,* trans. P. S. Falla (Berkeley: University of California Press, 1980), 1.
8. *Hitler's Table Talk,* night of 3 May 1942, 455.
9. See the section "on democracy as racial bastardization" in chap. 8, pp. 341–47.
10. This was the nickname—a sarcastic abbreviation of *Größter Feldherr Aller Zeiten* (Greatest field commander of all time)—given to Hitler by his generals, who were staggered to see him take operational command.
11. Alfred Rosenberg, *The Myth of the Twentieth Century: An Evaluation of the Spiritual-Intellectual Confrontations of Our Age,* trans. Vivian Bird (Newport Beach, CA: Noontide, 1982), 65.
12. *Hitler's Table Talk,* midday, 25 April 1942, 442.
13. Ibid., dinner, 3 June 1942, 511.
14. This entry does not appear in the English-language translation *Hitler's Table Talk,* but only in the German version compiled by Henry Picker: *Hitlers Tischgespräche im Führerhauptquartier 1941–1942* (Stuttgart: Sewald, 1976), lunch, 2 July 1942, 402.
15. German tanks in the Second World War were all named after animals: Tiger, King Tiger, Panther, Elephant . . . and Mouse, a prototype (only two were built) that weighed 188 metric tons (207 short tons) and consumed 1,500 liters (396 gallons) of gas for every 100 kilometers (62 miles)—the largest tank ever built, whose sole defect was that it could barely move.
16. *Hitler's Table Talk,* midday, 6 September 1942, 695.
17. Simone Weil, "The Great Beast: Reflections on the Origins of Hitlerism," in *Simone Weil: Selected Essays, 1934–1943,* trans. Richard Rees (Oxford: Oxford University Press, 1962), 96.
18. Tacitus, *Agricola* 30.6 ("Auferre trucidare rapere falsis nominibus imperium, atque ubi solitudinem faciunt, pacem appellant"), trans. M. Hutton, rev. R. M. Ogilvie, in *Tacitus: Agricola, Germania, Dialogus* (Cambridge, MA: Harvard University Press, 1970), 81.

19. Weil, "Great Beast," 101.
20. Ibid., 102.
21. Weil suggested that if Hitler were to be as successful as the Romans, "our country would be crushed, along with others, under a *pax Germanica* whose benefits would be fulsomely extolled in two thousand years' time by our descendants" (ibid., 119). France would indeed be effectively crushed, but its descendants would not have to wait nearly so long.
22. Ibid.
23. *Hitler's Table Talk,* midday, 23 April 1942, 435.
24. Ibid., midday, 27 January 1942, 253.
25. *Hitlers zweites Buch: Ein Dokument aus dem Jahre 1928,* ed. Gerhard Weinberg (Stuttgart: Deutsche Verlags Anstalt, 1961), translated by Krista Smith as *Hitler's Second Book: The Unpublished Sequel to Mein Kampf* (New York: Enigma, 2006).
26. *Hitler's Second Book,* 115.
27. See chap. 7, esp. pp. 287–90.
28. *Hitler's Table Talk,* evening of 2 November 1941, p 111.
29. Ibid., dinner, 27 June 1942, 537–38.
30. Fritz Todt, ed., *Deutschlands Autobahnen: Adolf Hitlers Strassen* (Bayreuth: Gauverlag Bayerische Ostmark, 1937).
31. Ibid., 22.
32. Ibid., 3.
33. Ibid.
34. Ibid., 22.
35. Ibid., 9.
36. Fritz Todt, *Die Strassen Adolf Hitlers,* ed. Otto Reismann (Berlin: Hermann Hillger, [1937]), 10.
37. Ibid., 8.
38. Ibid., 6.
39. *Hitler's Table Talk,* evening of 26 February 1942, 338.
40. Ibid., evening of 2 November 1941, 111.
41. Todt, *Die Strassen Adolf Hitlers,* 3.
42. Ibid.
43. Emil Maier-Dorn, "Die kulturelle Bedeutung der Reichsautobahnen," *Die Strasse* 5, no. 23 (1938): 736, quoted in Erhard Schütz and Eckhard Gruber, *Mythos Reichsautobahn: Bau und Inszenierung der "Strasse des Führers" 1933–1941* (Berlin: Ch. Links Verlag, 1996), 94.
44. Josef Weinheber, "Ode an die Strassen Adolf Hitlers," in Weinheber, *Blut und Stahl: 3 Oden* (Potsdam: Stichnote, 1941), quoted in Schütz and Gruber, *Mythos Reichsautobahn,* 141.
45. Ernst Bloch, "Deutschfrommes Verbot der Kunstkritik," in Bloch, *Literarische Aufsätze* (Frankfurt am Main: Suhrkamp, 1965), 46, quoted in Schütz and Gruber, *Mythos Reichsautobahn,* 94.
46. A classmate of Speer's in Munich and later at the Technische Hochschule in Berlin-Charlottenburg, Friedrich Tamms (1904–80) was named the *Beratender Architekt für die Reichsautobahnen* in 1935 before rejoining Speer at the Generalbauinspektion in Berlin in 1939. See Werner Durth, *Deutsche*

Architekten: Biographische Verflechtungen 1900–1970 (Munich: Deutscher Taschenbuch Verlag, 1986).

47. Regarding the notebook containing Hitler's sketches, see Frederic Spotts, *Hitler and the Power of Aesthetics* (New York: Overlook, 2003); and George Mosse, *The Nationalization of the Masses: Political Symbolism and Mass Movements in Germany from the Napoleonic Wars through the Third Reich* (New York: Howard Fertig, 1975), 185.

48. Albert Speer, *Spandau: The Secret Diaries,* trans. Richard Winston and Clara Winston (New York: Macmillan, 1976), 20 November 1952, 213.

49. On this view of the psychological foundations of power, see Hitler, *Mein Kampf,* 107.

50. Ibid., 264.

51. Ibid.

52. Ibid., 265.

53. Ibid.

54. *Inside the Third Reich: Memoirs by Albert Speer,* trans. Richard Winston and Clara Winston (New York: Macmillan, 1970), 102.

55. Ibid., 68.

56. See p. 369 regarding the commentary on one passage from *Mein Kampf.*

57. Adolf Hitler, speech at the Kulturtagung (Culture conference) at the Nuremberg Party Congress, 1937, in *The Speeches of Adolf Hitler,* ed. Norman Baynes, vol. 1 (New York: Howard Fertig, 1969), 593.

58. Joseph Vogt, "Unsere Stellung zur Antike," *Jahresbericht der Schlesischen Gesellschaft für vaterländische Kultur,* 1937, Geisteswissenschaftliche Reihe 3–4: 13.

59. Ibid., 13–14.

60. Gerhart Rodenwaldt, "Römische Staatsarchitektur," in *Rom,* vol. 2 of *Das neue Bild der Antike,* ed. Helmut Berve (Leipzig: Koehler und Amelang, 1942), 358. *Maiestas imperii* (majesty of the empire) comes from Vitruvius, *De architectura* 1.2.

61. Ibid., 359 and 376. *Pro maiestate imperii* (for the dignity of the empire) is from Suetonius, *Divus Augustus* 2.28.

62. Ibid., 373.

63. Speer, *Inside the Third Reich,* 42.

64. Ibid., 50.

65. Speer, *Spandau,* 7 May 1955, 273.

66. Ibid., 2 October 1946, 5.

67. Ibid., 12 March 1949, 126.

68. Speer, *Inside the Third Reich,* 62.

69. Ibid., 63.

70. Ibid., 146–47.

71. Ibid., 42.

72. Longevity in the collective memory does not necessarily require leaving behind durable physical traces for posterity. Leaving ruins and a funereal myth could be an even more effective means of bequeathing a lasting impression in the mind.

73. Speer, *Inside the Third Reich*, 42.
74. Ibid., 96.
75. Ibid., 42.
76. Ibid., 159.
77. Ibid., 159–60.
78. Speer, *Spandau*, 16 July 1959, 338.
79. Speer, *Inside the Third Reich*, 160. Speer described how his theory developed around a table at Maxim's in 1941, while he was in the company of several distinguished French dining companions, including Charles Despiau and Jean Cocteau. No doubt this was on the occasion of the Breker exhibition, which had attracted the interest of a large part of the Parisian intelligentsia of the era.
80. Ibid., 78.
81. The title of ch. 5 of Speer's memoirs; see ibid., 50.
82. Ibid., 133.
83. Speer, *Spandau*, 24 October 1948, 112.
84. Jochen Thies, *Architekt der Weltherrschaft: Die Endziele Hitlers* (Düsseldorf: Droste Verlag, 1976).
85. This was Speer's sentiment as well: "These monuments were an assertion of [Hitler's] claim to world dominion long before he dared to voice any such intention even to his closest associates." Speer, *Inside the Third Reich*, 69.
86. Thies, *Architekt der Weltherrschaft*, 72–73.
87. Adolf Hitler, speech to officers of the Wehrmacht, 10 February 1939, quoted in ibid., 79–80.
88. Adolf Hitler, speech at the inauguration of the new Reichs Chancellery, quoted in *Völkischer Beobachter*, 10 January 1939.
89. Quoted in Thies, *Architekt der Weltherrschaft*, 79–80.
90. At Herzberg, in the Niederlausitz.
91. Thies, *Architekt der Weltherrschaft*, 80–81.
92. Speer, *Inside the Third Reich*, 69.
93. *Hitler's Table Talk*, night of 21 October 1941, 81. See also Thies, *Architekt der Weltherrschaft*, 81.
94. Speer, *Spandau*, 26 March 1947, 49.
95. *Hitler's Table Talk*, night of 3–4 January 1942, 174.
96. See the sophisticated reflections on the notion of such monuments by the Latinist Jacques Gaillard in *Rome, le temps, le choses* (Arles: Actes Sud, 1995).
97. *Hitler's Table Talk*, evening of 3 January 1942, 111.
98. Friedrich Nietzsche "On the Uses and Disadvantages of History for Life," in Nietzsche, *Untimely Meditations*, trans. R.J. Hollingdale, ed. Daniel Brezeale (Cambridge: Cambridge University Press, 1997), 67.
99. Ibid., 69.
100. "I have often heard that Quintus Maximus, Publius Scipio, and other eminent men of our country were in the habit of declaring that their hearts were set mightily aflame for the pursuit of virtue whenever they gazed upon the masks of their ancestors. Of course they did not mean to imply that the wax or the effigy had any such power over them, but rather that it is the memory of great deeds that kindles in the breasts of noble men this flame that cannot be

quelled until they by their own prowess have equalled the fame and glory of their forefathers." Sallust, *The War with Jugurtha*, trans. J.C. Rolfe (Cambridge, MA: Harvard University Press, 1921), 136, 138 (4.5–6).

101. *Hitler's Table Talk*, evening of 21 October 1941, 81.
102. Speer, *Inside the Third Reich*, 69.
103. Ibid., 55.
104. Ibid., 67. Speer was describing the *Colossus Neronis*, the emperor's grand statue in the Domus Aurea.
105. Ibid., 68. Speer added, in a detailed volumetric comparison, that the stadium would enclose more than eleven million cubic yards, "some three times more than the pyramid of Cheops."
106. Ibid., 156.
107. Speer, *Spandau*, 21 July 1950, 156.
108. Suetonius, *Vita Neronis* 6.55.
109. See Paul Veyne, *Bread and Circuses: Historical Sociology and Political Pluralism*, trans. Brian Pearce (London: Penguin, 1990); and Lucien Jerphagnon, *Le divins Césars: Idéologie et pouvoir dans la Rome impériale* (Paris: Tallandier, 2004).
110. See Tacitus, *Germania* 2.
111. See Speer, *Inside the Third Reich*, 157.
112. Ibid., 135. The sketchbook is now preserved at the University of Göttingen. See Mosse, *Nationalization of the Masses*, 185.
113. Speer, *Inside the Third Reich*, 153.
114. See Scobie, *Hitler's State Architecture*, 30–35.
115. Speer, *Inside the Third Reich*, 154.
116. See chap. 4.
117. Speer, *Inside the Third Reich*, 134.
118. *Hitler's Table Talk*, night of 21–22 July 1941, 10.
119. See Spotts, *Hitler and the Power of Aesthetics*, 50.
120. On these aspects of Nazism, see Angela Schönberger, *Die neue Reichskanzlei von Albert Speer: Zum Zusammenhang von nationalsozialistischer Ideologie und Architektur* (Berlin: Mann, 1981), 88–148.
121. The vessel that was sunk by the Soviet navy on 30 January 1945, later immortalized by Günther Grass in his novel *Crabwalk* (2002), the first to take as its subject the tragedy of the *Kriegsvertriebene* (those Germans displaced as a result of the war) in the winter of 1945.
122. On the führer's total responsibility, including that of making the supreme sacrifice, see Hitler, *Mein Kampf*, 91.
123. Hitler's table talks concerning every true leader's responsibility to remain celibate were legion. Hitler married his companion Eva Braun only on the day of their double suicide, 30 April 1945.
124. This minor detail of Machiavellian logic was lampooned by Chaplin in a famous scene from *The Dictator*, in which Benzino Napaloni faces Hynkel's desk upon a prie-dieu.
125. Speer, *Inside the Third Reich*, 55.
126. Ibid., 67. The *allgemeine Wehrpflicht* was reestablished on 16 March 1935.

127. Ibid., 63.

128. Robert Brasillach, *Notre avant-guerre* (Paris: Livre de Poche, 1992), 343. See also Brasillach, "La poésie du national-socialisme," *Notre Combat* 42 (April 1943): 6–7.

129. Quoted in Dominique Desanti, *Drieu La Rochelle: Le séducteur mystifié* (Paris: Flammarion, 1978), 315; and in Michel Winock, *Le siècle des intellectuels* (Paris: Le Seuil, 1997), 292.

130. André François-Poncet, *Souvenirs d'une ambassade à Berlin, septembre 1931–octobre 1938* (Paris: Flammarion, 1946), 263.

131. Speer, *Inside the Third Reich*, 142–43.

132. Ibid. More sarcastically, he remarked: "Had Hitler been interested in breeding horses, a passion for horse breeding would undoubtedly have sprung up among the leading men in the Reich."

133. See pp. 279–82 regarding the Nazi colonization of the East.

134. Speer later described it as a "a cubic mass . . . elevated on stout pillars, which seemed to be checking this onslaught." Speer, *Inside the Third Reich*, 81.

135. Ibid.

136. Miguel Abensour, *De la compacité: Architecture et régimes totalitaires* (Paris: Sens et Tonka, 1997), 15.

137. Speer, *Inside the Third Reich*, 134.

138. Abensour, *De la compacité*, 30.

139. Ibid., 39 and 51–53.

140. There was also a diversity of styles in Nazi Germany, which aligned with the type of architecture: communal buildings were often in a folkloric style, industrial edifices in a functionalist style. But the symbolic architecture of the state was uniformly neoclassical. On this functional diversity of styles, see Anna Teut, *Architektur im Dritten Reich 1933–1945*.

141. Fritz Schachermeyr, "Die nordischen Führerpersönlichkeit im Altertum," in *Humanistische Bildung im nationalsozialistischen Staate*, Neue Wege zur Antike, Erste Reihe, Heft 9 (Berlin: Teubner Verlag, 1933), 37.

142. Ibid., 39.

143. Ibid., 41.

144. Ibid., 43.

145. Helmut Berve, *Perikles*, Leipziger Universitätsreden 2 (Leipzig: Barth Verlag, 1940), 3.

146. Ibid., 7.

147. For more on this potential interpretation of the Third Reich, see Götz Aly, *Hitler's Beneficiaries: Plunder, Racial War, and the Nazi Welfare State*, trans. Jefferson Chase (New York: Metropolitan, 2007).

148. Berve, *Perikles*, 8.

149. Ibid., 21.

150. Ibid.

151. Ibid., 23.

152. Ibid., 15.

153. See Vincent Azoulay, *Xénophon et les grâces du pouvoir: De la charis au charisme* (Paris: Presses de la Sorbonne, 2004).

154. Berve, *Perikles*, 28.

155. See chap. 7, esp. pp. 301–3.

156. See the passages on Caesar in Jules Isaac, *Genèse de l'antisémitisme: Essai historique* (Paris: Calmann-Lévy, 1956).

157. See especially Hans Oppermann et al., *Probleme der augusteischen Erneuerung*, Auf dem Wege zum nationalpolitischen Gymnasium 6 (Frankfurt: Diesterweg, 1938); and Hans Volkmann, "Mos maiorum als Grundzug des augusteischen Prinzipats," in Berve, *Rom*, 246–64.

158. Heinrich von Treitschke, *Deutsche Geschichte*, vol. 1 (1879), 28; regarding the phrase in its original context, see Christian Meier, *From Athens to Auschwitz: The Uses of History*, trans. Deborah Lucas Schneider (Cambridge, MA: Harvard University Press, 2005), 109.

159. Hitler, speech of 16 September 1935, in Max Domarus, ed., *Hitler: Speeches and Proclamations, 1932–1945*, trans. Mary Fran Gilbert (Wauconda, IL: Bolchazy-Carducci, 1990–2004), vol. 2, *The Years 1935 to 1938*, 711; also quoted in Meier, *From Athens to Auschwitz*, 108n12.

160. *Die Tagebücher von Joseph Goebbels, Teil 1: Aufzeichnungen 1923–1941*, vol. 1, *Oktober 1923–November 1925*, ed. Elke Frölich (Munich: K. G. Saur Verlag, 2004), 19 July 1924, 173.

161. A famous Nazi poster, which appeared on the Day of Potsdam (21 March 1933), carried the proclamation "What the king conquered, the prince gave shape, the field marshal defended, and the solder has saved and unified."

162. Adolf Hitler, speech of 23 March 1926 in Munich, in Hitler, *Reden, Schriften, Anordnungen*, vol. 1, 357.

163. Speer, *Spandau*, 20 April 1947, 58–59.

164. Tacitus, *Historiae* 1.3.

165. Hitler, *Mein Kampf*, 426.

166. Hitler, speech before the Reichstag on 23 March 1933, in Baynes, *Speeches of Adolf Hitler*, 568.

167. Wilhelm Frick, "Richtlinien für die Geschistslehrbücher" *Zentralblatt für die gesamte Unterrichtsverwaltung in Preußen*, 1933, Heft 15: 197–99.

168. Vappu Tallgren, *Hitler und die Helden: Heroismus und Weltanschauung*, Annales Academiae Scientiarum Fennicae: Dissertationes humanarum litterarum 29 (Helsinki: Suomalainen tiedeakatemia, 1981).

169. Franz Martin Mayer, *Das Altertum*, vol. 1 of *Lehrbuch der Geschichte für die unteren Klassen der Mittelschulen* (Vienna: Tempsky, 1902).

170. Tallgren, *Hitler und die Helden*, 99–100.

171. Ibid. On the figure of Pericles in the Third Reich, see pp. 262–64.

172. See Ernst Hanfstaengl, *Zwischen Weißem und Braunem Haus: Memoiren eines politischen Aussenseiters* (Munich: Piper, 1970), quoted in Tallgren, *Hitler und die Helden*, 140.

173. Joachim Fest, *Hitler*, trans. Richard Winston and Clara Winston (New York: Harcourt Brace Jovanovich, 1974), 382.

174. See Ian Kershaw, *Hitler, 1889–1936: Hubris* (London: Penguin, 1998).

175. Josef Greiner, *Das Ende des Hitler-Mythos* (Vienna: Amalthea Verlag, 1947), 83.

176. Ibid., 84.

177. Hitler allegedly told Greiner that he had read somewhere that in the catacombs, the tombs of converted Jews were marked with the Star of David, while those of the ancient Roman pagans were decorated with the swastika. This fact "gave Hitler endless pleasure. He thought this meant he had proof that the converted Romans, in spite of the community of Christian faith, wanted nothing to do with the Jews, not even in death." Ibid.

178. See August Kubizek, *Adolf Hitler: Mein Jugendfreund* (Graz: Leopold Stocker Verlag, 1953).

179. Hanfstaengl, *Zwischen Weißem und Braunem Haus*, 45.

180. Gustav Schwab, *Die schönsten Sagen des klassischen Altertums*. A classic, compiled between 1838 and 1840, frequently translated and republished in multiple editions (five by 1862), for example in 2001 by Insel Verlag and in 2002 in Reclam's Orange series. English translation: *Gods and Heroes of Ancient Greece*, trans. Olga Marx and Ernst Morwitz (New York: Pantheon, 1946).

181. Adolf Hitler, "Politik der Woche," *Völkischer Beobachter*, 13 April 1929. On the ancient figure of Ephialtes, see Herodotus, *Histories* 7.213.

182. Adolf Hitler, "Sage mir, wer Dich lobt . . . ," *Völkischer Beobachter*, 8 April 1931.

183. Alexander Demandt, "Klassik als Klischee: Hitler und die Antike," *Historische Zeitschrift* 274 (2002): 281–313.

184. Jacques Le Rider, *Freud, de l'Acropole au Sinaï: Le rètour à l'Antique des Modernes viennois* (Paris: Presses Universitaires de France, 2002), esp. the introduction, "Les Anciens et les Modernes, de 1800 à 1900."

185. It should come as no surprise that Hitler, who had his documents compiled on a special typewriter, the *Führerschreibmachine*, with outsize characters and spacing so that he could read them without glasses and thus mask his farsightedness in public, took an interest in such matters.

186. An outrage that equaled the hope of these same Germanophiles upon the Nazis' rise to power. The journal *Die deutsche Schrift*, in its edition of September 1934, even called for a "Night of the Long Knives" against the *Lateinschriftler* (Latin writers). See BABL/R 43/II/953, microfiche 2, f. 71.

187. Martin Bormann, letter to Hans Lammers, 7 November 1941, BABL/R 43/II/953, microfiche 1, f. 23. *Deutsche Schrift* is the same as *gothische Schrift*, or Gothic script.

188. It is remarkable that, in the publications of the period, all the classes of documents that came from the party or the state—every kind of legal document down to the slightest propaganda leaflet—saw their font changed in the course of 1941.

189. *The Goebbels Diaries, 1939–1941*, ed. and trans. Fred Taylor (London: Hamish Hamilton, 1981), 8 April 1941, 304. A few weeks later, on 30 April, he wrote: "[Hitler] is sad to have had to attack Greece in the first place. The Greeks have done nothing to deserve it. He intends to treat them as humanely as possible. . . . We watch our entry into Athens on the newsreel. The Führer finds it hard to enjoy it, so moved is he by Greece's fate." Ibid., 341–42.

190. Ibid., 8 April 1941, 304.

191. Speer, *Spandau*, 24 October 1948, 112.

192. Speer, *Spandau*, 20 April 1947, 58. The conversation in question occurred on 20 April 1943. Charlemagne was a problematic figure for the Nazis and had been vilified by the SS; as the enemy of Widukind and "butcher of the Saxons" (*Sachsenschlächter*), he had used force to convert the proud Germanic peoples to Oriental, Semitic Christianity.

193. Ibid.

194. See the quote on p. 321.

195. Nicole Loraux, *The Invention of Athens: The Funeral Oration in the Classical City*, trans. Alan Sheridan (Cambridge, MA: Harvard University Press, 1986).

196. Greiner, *Das Ende des Hitler-Mythos*, 85 and 86.

197. Ibid., 85.

198. Speer, *Inside the Third Reich*, 42–43.

199. Ibid., 106.

200. *Hitler's Table Talk*, night of 21–22 July 1941, 10–11.

201. See Hannah Arendt, *Between Past and Future* (New York: Meridian, 1954), esp. the introduction and chs. 1 and 2; and Gaillard, *Rome, le temps, les choses*.

202. See Fabrice d'Almeida, *High Society in the Third Reich*, trans. Steven Rendall (Cambridge: Polity, 2008).

203. An anecdote in the original, German version of the table talks; see *Hitlers Tischgespräche im Führerhauptquartier*, 334n309.

204. Josef Wackerle, "Relief im Teehaus des Führers im Obersalzberg," depicted in *Die Kunst im deutschen Reich*, 1939.

205. A conversation not found in the English-language edition of the table talks. See *Hitlers Tischgespräche im Führerhauptquartier*, 2 July 1942, 402.

206. On this point, see Joachim Fest, *Inside Hitler's Bunker: The Last Days of the Third Reich*, trans. Margot Bettauer Dembo (New York: Farrar, Straus and Giroux, 2004), 127.

207. Bogner, *Der Seelenbegriff der griechischen Frühzeit* (Hamburg: Hanseatische Verlagsanstalt, 1939), 19.

208. On Darré and the ideological underpinnings of *Blut und Boden*, see Gustavo Corni and Horst Gies, *Blut und Boden: Rassenideologie und Agrarpolitik im Staat Hitlers* (Idstein: Schulz-Kirchner, 1994); and Matthias Eidenbenz, *"Blut und Boden": Zu Funktion und Genese der Metaphern des Agrarismus und Biologismus in der nationalsozialistischen Bauernpropaganda R. W. Darrés* (Bern: Peter Lang, 1993).

209. The RUSHA was created in 1931 by Himmler, who placed Darré in charge.

210. Richard Walther Darré, *Das Bauerntum als Lebensquell der nordischen Rasse* (Munich: Lehmann Verlag, 1929).

211. Ibid., 11.

212. Hitler, *Mein Kampf*, 290, quoted in ibid., 59.

213. Darré, *Das Bauerntum als Lebensquell der nordischen Rasse*, 190.

214. Ibid., 196.

215. Ibid., 58–59.

216. Ibid., 196. The term used by Darré was *Bauerntreck*.
217. Ibid, 191.
218. On the *ver sacrum*, see Jacques Heurgon, *Trois études sur le "ver sacrum"* (Brussels: Latomus, 1957). It should be noted that the idea of the *ver sacrum*, so poetically resuscitated by Nietzsche, was also a leitmotif of the Viennese Sezession; its journal was named *Ver sacrum* by Klimt in 1898 and its office facing the Karlskirche bore that inscription, the proclamation of a renaissance of the arts and a renewed fertility of creation.
219. Darré, *Das Bauerntum als Lebensquell der nordischen Rasse*, 195.
220. Ibid., 198–99.
221. Ibid., 201.
222. Ibid., 200.
223. Ibid., 154.
224. Ibid., 157.
225. "During the process of publishing this book, the author's attention was drawn to a new work by Günther, *Rassengeschichte des hellenischen und [des] römischen Volkes*, which presents additional proof of the Nordic origins of the Greeks and Romans." Ibid., 150n1.
226. Ibid., 160.
227. Ibid., 159.
228. Ibid., 161.
229. Christian Ingrao, *Les intellectuels SS du SD, 1900–1945* (doctoral thesis, Université de Picardie Jules-Verne, Amiens, 2001), 393.
230. Ibid., 390.
231. Ibid., 387–88.
232. Wolfgang Wippermann, *Der "Deutsche Drang nach Osten": Ideologie und Wirklichkeit eines politischen Schlagwortes* (Darmstadt: Wissenschaftliche Buchgesellschaft, 1981).
233. The fate of Eisenstein's film was inextricably linked to the oscillations of official Soviet policy. Celebrated as a masterpiece in 1938, the film was retired from the big screen after the signing of the German-Soviet pact of 23 August 1939, before being converted into a symbol of the Great Patriotic War following the German invasion of 22 June 1941. *Habent sua fata libelli*.
234. This hypocoristic, an abridgement of "Reichsführer Heinrich," was Himmler's nickname among the ranks of the SS.
235. Otto Wilhelm von Vacano, *Sparta: Der Lebenskampf einer nordischen Herrenschicht* (Kempten: Bücherei der Adolf-Hitler-Schulen, 1940), 8.
236. Heinrich Himmler, "Rede das Reichsführers-SS am 19.6.1942 vor dem Führerkorps der Division Das Reich," BABL/NS 19/4009, f. 127, 50.
237. See esp. *Das Reich und Europa*, Reichsführer-SS, SS-Hauptamt (Berlin, n.d.), BABL/RD/NSD 41/115, 2.
238. Heinrich Himmler, "Das Reichsführer-SS vor den Oberabschnittführern und Hauptamtchefs im Haus der Flieger in Berlin am 9. Juni 1942," BABL/NS 19/4009, f. 5, 18.
239. Reinhard Heydrich, speech of 2 October 1941, in Czesław Madajczyk, ed., *Vom Generalplan Ost zum Generalsiedlungsplan* (Munich: K.G. Saur, 1994), 21.

240. Eugen Kogon, *The Theory and Practice of Hell: The German Concentration Camps and the System behind Them*, trans. Heinz Norden (New York: Farrar, Straus and Giroux, 2006), 3.

241. See chap. 5, esp. pp. 221–26.

242. See Mechtild Rössler and Sabine Schleiermacher, eds., *Der "Generalplan Ost": Hauptlinien der nationalsozialistischen Planungs- und Vernichtungspolitik* (Berlin: Akademie Verlag, 1993).

243. Speer, *Spandau*, 26 March 1947, 48.

244. See the quote on p. 223.

245. Speer, *Spandau*, 21 July 1950, 156.

246. Heydrich, speech of 2 October 1941, in Madajczyk, *Vom Generalplan Ost zum Generalsiedlungsplan*, 21.

247. *Die Sicherung Europas*, ed. Reichsführer-SS, SS-Hauptamt (n.p., n.d.).

248. *Dich ruft die SS*, SS-Hauptamt (Berlin: Verlag Hermann Hillger, n.d), BABL/RD/NSD 41/127, 68.

249. Speech by SS-Reichsführer Heinrich Himmler in Charkow (Kharkiv), April 1943, BABL/NS 19/4010, f. 142.

PART 3. RELIVING ANTIQUITY

Epigraph. Adolf Hitler, *Mein Kampf*, trans. Ralph Manheim (Boston: Houghton Mifflin, 1943), 291–92.

CHAPTER 7. HISTORY AS RACIAL STRUGGLE

Epigraphs. Christopher Isherwood, *Goodbye to Berlin* (New York: New Directions, 2012), 96; and Alfred Rosenberg, "Innere und äussere Freiheit des Deutschen," in *Ich kämpfe! Sonderdruck zum 10. Jahrestag der Machtergreifung, 30. Januar 1943*, ed. Hauptkulturamt in der Reichspropagandaleitung der NSDAP (Munich: Zentralverlag der NSDAP, 1943), 35.

1. Adolf Hitler, *Mein Kampf*, trans. Ralph Manheim (Boston: Houghton Mifflin, 1943), 421.

2. See Pierre-André Taguieff, *La couleur et le sang: Doctrines racistes à la française* (Paris: Mille et une nuits, 1998); and Taguieff, "Racisme aryaniste, socialisme et eugénisme chez Georges Vacher de Lapouge (1854–1936)," in "Classer/Penser/Exclure: De l'eugénisme à l'hygiène raciale," ed. Yves Ternon and Rita Thalmann, special issue, *Revue d'histoire de la Shoah* 183 (July–December 2005): 69–134.

3. Hitler, *Mein Kampf*, 296.

4. Adolf Hitler, speech of 15 March 1942, in *"Es spricht der Führer": 7 exemplarische Hitler-Reden*, ed. Hildegard von Kotze and Helmuth Krasnick (Gütersloh: Sigbert Mohn Verlag, 1966), 307.

5. Ibid.

6. See, for instance, *Hitler's Table Talk, 1941–1944: His Private Conversations*, trans. Norman Cameron and R.H. Stevens (New York: Enigma, 2000), 28 January 1942, 261–62.

7. Hitler, *Mein Kampf*, 289.

8. Ibid., 423.
9. Ibid., 420.
10. This portion of Goebbels's diaries has not been translated into English. See *Die Tagebücher von Joseph Goebbels, Teil 1: Aufzeichnungen 1923–1941*, vol. 8, *April–November 1940*, ed. Jana Richter (Munich: K.G. Saur Verlag, 1998), 23 April 1940, 68.
11. *Hitlers Briefe und Notizen: Sein Weltbild in handschriftlichen Dokumenten*, ed. Werner Maser (Düsseldorf: Droste, 1988), 289–97.
12. E.g., Rudolf Benze, *Geschichte im Rassenkampf* (Berlin: Brehm, 1934).
13. Walter Groß, *Der Rassengedanke im neuen Geschichtsbild* (Berlin: Junker und Dünnhaupt, 1936).
14. Dietrich Klagges, "Die Rassenfrage ist der Schlüssel zur Weltgeschichte," in Klagges, *Geschichtsunterricht als nationalpolitische Erziehung* (Frankfurt: Moritz Diesterweg Verlag, 1937), 87–101.
15. "The racial question gives the key not only to world history but to all human culture" ("Die Rassenfrage ist der Schlüssel zur Weltgeschichte und zur menschlichen Kultur"). Hitler, *Mein Kampf*, 339.
16. Fritz Schachermeyr, *Lebensgesetzlichkeit in der Geschichte: Versuch einer Einführung in das geschichtsbiologische Denken* (Frankfurt: Klostermann, 1940).
17. Fritz Schachermeyr, "Die Aufgaben der alten Geschichte im Rahmen der nordischen Weltgeschichte," *Vergangenheit und Gegenwart* 23 (1933): 594.
18. Fritz Geyer, *Rasse, Volk und Staat im Altertum* (Leipzig: B.G. Teubner, 1936), foreword (unnumbered).
19. Walther Gehl, *Geschichte, 6. Klasse, Oberschulen, Gymnasien und Oberschulen in Aufbauform: Von der Urzeit bis zum Ende der Hohenstaufen* (Breslau: Fredinand Hirt, 1940).
20. *Das Reich und Europa*, ed. Reichsführer SS, SS-Hauptamt, Berlin, BABL, RD/NSD 41/115, 4.
21. *Deutschland ordnet Europa neu!*, ed. Chef der Ordnungspolizei—SS-Hauptamt, Schriftenreihe für die weltanschauliche Schulung der Ordnungspolizei, 1942, Heft 4, BABL, RD 18/16, 19.
22. Adolf Hitler, speech before the Reichstag, 11 December 1941, in Max Domarus, ed., *Hitler: Speeches and Proclamations, 1932–1945*, trans. Mary Fran Gilbert (Wauconda, IL: Bolchazy-Carducci, 1990–2004), vol. 4, *The Years 1941 to 1945*, 2534–35.
23. An entry not recorded in the English-language version of Hitler's table talks by Norman Cameron and R.H. Stevens; see instead *Hitlers Tischgespräche im Führerhauptquartier 1941–1942*, ed. Henry Picker (Bonn: Athenäum, 1951), 9 April 1942, 209.
24. *Hitler's Table Talk, 1941–1944: His Private Conversations*, trans. Norman Cameron and R.H. Stevens (New York: Enigma, 2000), 12 November 1941, 125.
25. "In the Catalaunian Fields," the Huns' assault "from Asia was repelled after a bloody battle." Heinrich Himmler, "Rede des Reichsführers-SS am 23.11.1942—SS Junkerschule Tölz," BABL/NS/19/4009, f. 188, 9.

26. Heinrich Himmler, "Der Reichsführer-SS zu den Ersatzmannschaften für di Kampfgruppe Nord am Sonntag, dem 13. Juli 1941, in Stettin," BABL/NS/19/4008, f. 35.

27. *Der Untermensch,* ed. SS-Hauptamt—Schulungsamt, Nordland-Verlag (n.p., n.d.), BABL/RD/NSD 41/141, 3.

28. "Die wichtigsten Völkerwanderungszüge," in *Sicherung Europas,* ed. Reichsführer-SS, SS-Hauptamt (n.p., n.d.).

29. Fritz Taeger, *Orient und Occident in der Antike* (Tübingen: J.C.B. Mohr, 1936), 5; Fritz Schachermeyr, *Indogermanen und Orient: Ihre kulturelle und machtpolitische Auseinandersetzung im Altertum* (Stuttgart: W. Kohlhammer Verlag, 1944).

30. Taeger, *Orient und Occident in der Antike,* 27.

31. "Kriegseinsatz der deutschen Geisteswissenschaften": see Frank-Rutger Hausmann, *"Deutsche Geisteswissenschaft" im Zweiten Weltkrieg: Die "Aktion Ritterbusch" (1940–1945)* (Dresden: Dresden University Press, 1998).

32. Joseph Vogt, "Unsere Fragestellung," in *Rom und Karthago: Ein Gemeinschaftswerk,* ed. Vogt (Leipzig: Koehler und Amelang, 1943), 5.

33. Ibid., 6.

34. Ibid., 7.

35. Ibid., 8. This question was addressed explicitly by Fritz Schachermeyr in his contribution to the volume; see following note.

36. Fritz Schachermeyr, "Karthago in rassengeschichtlicher Betrachtung," in Vogt, *Rom und Karthago,* 9–43.

37. Matthias Gelzer, "Der Rassengegensatz als geschichtlicher Faktor beim Ausbruch der römisch-karthagischen Kriege," in Vogt, *Rom und Karthago,* 178–202.

38. Fritz Taeger, "Völker- und Rassenkämpfe im westlichen Mittelmeer," in Vogt, *Rom und Karthago,* 44–82.

39. Joseph Vogt, "Das Puniertum und die Dynastie des Septimius Severus," in Vogt, *Rom und Karthago,* 346–66.

40. Alfred Rosenberg, *The Myth of the Twentieth Century: An Evaluation of the Spiritual-Intellectual Confrontations of Our Age,* trans. Vivian Bird (Newport Beach, CA: Noontide, 1982), 25.

41. Ibid.

42. Houston Stewart Chamberlain, *The Foundations of the Nineteenth Century,* trans. John Lees, vol. 1 (London: John Lane, 1912), 115 and 117–18.

43. *The Goebbels Diaries: The Last Days,* trans. Richard Barry (London: Martin Secker and Warburg, 1978), 12.

44. See chap. 9, esp. pp. 376–83. German newspapers developed a comparison between the Second Punic War and the threat that the Red Army posed for Berlin.

45. Rosenberg, *Myth of the Twentieth Century,* 25.

46. Ferdinand Fried attributed the alleged hate that the Jews felt for Rome to a spirit of revanche and thirst for vengeance, a spirit of Semitic solidarity with the civilization destroyed by Scipio Africanus. See Fried, *Der Aufstieg der Juden* (Reichsbauernstadt Goslar: Verlag Blut und Boden, 1937), 99.

47. See chap. 8, esp. pp. 305–10.

48. *Dieser Krieg ist ein weltanschaulicher Krieg,* Schulungsgrundlagen für die Reichsthemen der NSDAP für das Jahr 1941/1942, Der Beauftragte des Führers fur die Überwachung der gesamten geistigen und weltanschaulichen Schulung und Erziehung der NSDAP (Berlin, 1942), BABL/RD/NSD 16/29.

49. Dr. Stellrecht, "Sechstausend Jahre Rassenkampf," in ibid., 39–46.

50. Ibid., 43.

51. "Roms Aufstieg zur Weltmacht im Rassenkampf gegen das Semitentum," in Gehl, *Geschichte,* 80–87.

52. Walter Hohmann and Wilhelm Schiefer, *Lehrbuch der Geschichte: Oberstufe,* vol. 1 (Frankfurt: Diesterweg, 1940), 91.

53. Ibid., 95.

54. Bernhard Rust, ed., *Erziehung und Unterricht in der höheren Schule: Amtliche Ausgabe des Reichs- und Preußischen Ministeriums für Wissenschaft, Erziehung und Volksbildung* (Berlin: Weidmann, 1938), 74.

55. Fritz Schachermeyr, "Die nordische Führerpersönlichkeit im Altertum," in *Humanistische Bildung im nationalsozialistischen Staate,* Neue Wege zur Antike, Erste Reihe, Heft 9 (Leipzig and Berlin: Teubner Verlag, 1933), 42.

56. Ibid.

57. Hohmann and Schiefer, *Lehrbuch der Geschichte,* 95.

58. H. Rübel, "Römische Geschichte in rassischer Beleuchtung," *Volk und Rasse* 1 (1943): 11.

59. Hans Oppermann, *Der Jude im griechisch-römischen Altertum,* ed. Beauftragen des Führers für die Überwachung der gesamten geistigen und weltanschaulichen Schulung und Erziehung der NSDAP (Munich: Franz Eher Verlag, Zentralverlag der NSDAP, 1943), 6.

60. Ibid., 8.

61. Fried, *Der Aufstieg der Juden,* 101.

62. Schachermeyr, *Indogermanen und Orient,* 447.

63. See notably the title, edited by the SA, E. V. von Rudolf, *Der Judenspiegel: Judentum und Antisemitismus in der Weltgeschichte,* Kampfschriften der Obersten SA-Führung 1 (Munich: Fritz Ehler Verlag, Zentralverlag der NSDAP, 1937), BABL/RD/NSD 40/25-1.

64. *3000 Jahre jüdischer Hass,* Schulungs-Unterlage no. 13, Der Reichsorganisationsleiter der NSDAP, Hauptschulungsamt (n.p., n.d.), BABL/RD/NSD 9/34-13, 2.

65. Hans Bogner, "Die Judenfrage in der griechisch-römischen Welt," in *Forschungen zur Judenfrage,* vol. 1, Schriften des Reichsinstitut für Geschichte des neuen Deutschlands (Hamburg: Hanseatische Verlagsanstalt, 1937), 82.

66. Oppermann, *Der Jude im griechisch-römischen Altertum,* 14.

67. Fried, *Der Aufstieg der Juden,* 100.

68. Ibid., 101.

69. *3000 Jahre jüdischer Hass,* 4.

70. Ibid., 5.

71. Fried, *Der Aufstieg der Juden,* 125.

72. Ibid., 124.

73. *3000 Jahre jüdische Hass,* 5–6.

74. Fried, *Der Aufstieg der Juden*, 99.
75. *3000 Jahre jüdischer Hass*, 7.
76. Ibid., 8. The booklet repeated a phrase from *Mein Kampf*: "Mit dem Juden gibt es kein Paktieren, sondern nur das harte Entweder-Oder" ("There is no making pacts with Jews; there can only be the hard: either—or" [206]).
77. Oppermann, *Der Jude im griechisch-römischen Altertum*, 8.
78. Karl Georg Kuhn, "Weltjudentum in der Antike," in *Forschungen zur Judenfrage*, vol. 2, Schriften des Reichsinstitut für Geschichte des neuen Deutschlands (Hamburg: Hanseatische Verlagsanstalt, 1937), 15.
79. See Pierre Vidal-Naquet, *Flavius Josèphe ou Du bon usage de la trahison: Préface à "La guerre des Juifs"* (Paris: Minuit, 1976); and Vidal-Naquet, *Flavius Josèphe et "La guerre des Juifs"* (Paris: Bayard–Bibliothèque nationale de France, 2005). See also Mireille Hadas-Lebel, *Flavius Josèphe* (Paris: Fayard, 1989).
80. Oppermann, *Der Jude im griechisch-römischen Altertum*, 12.
81. Kuhn, "Weltjudentum in der Antike," 19.
82. Oppermann, *Der Jude im griechisch-römischen Altertum*, 10.
83. Kuhn, "Weltjudentum in der Antike," 19.
84. Oppermann, *Der Jude im griechisch-römischen Altertum*, 11.
85. Ibid. See also Kuhn, "Weltjudentum in der Antike," 19.
86. Gerhard Kittel, *Die historischen Voraussetzungen der jüdischen Rassenmischung* (Hamburg: Hanseatische Verlagsanstalt, 1939), 22. See also Oppermann, *Der Jude im griechisch-römischen Altertum*, 5.
87. Oppermann, *Der Jude im griechisch-römischen Altertum*, 13.
88. Eugen Fischer and Gerhard Kittel, *Das antike Weltjudentum: Tatsachen, Texte, Bilder*, vol. 7 of *Forschungen zur Judenfrage* (Hamburg, Hanseatische Verlagsanstalt, 1943), 5.
89. Ibid., 9.
90. Ibid. Their use of the German term *Lehrmeisterin* was an explicit nod to *Mein Kampf*. See chap. 3, esp. pp. 99–105.
91. Fischer and Kittel, *Das antike Weltjudentum*, 10.
92. See "Der Assimilationsjude," in ibid., 49–53.
93. Fischer and Kittel, *Das antike Weltjudentum*, 10.
94. Fried, *Der Aufstieg der Juden*, 114.
95. See Kuhn, "Weltjudentum in der Antike," 18.
96. Bogner, "Die Judenfrage in der griechisch-römischen Welt," 87.
97. *Der Kampf um unsere Weltanschauung: Gedankenführungen zu Weltanschaulichpolitischen Vorträgen zur Partei- und Wehrmachtschulung*, Amt Wehrmachtschulung der Dienststelle des Reichsleiters Rosenberg (Stein: Slatner, n.d.), BABL/RD/BDC 4.1, 138–41.
98. Ibid., 139–40.
99. Theodor Mommsen, *The History of Rome*, trans. William P. Dickson, vol. 4, pt. 2 (London: Richard Bentley, 1866), 539.
100. Eugen Täubler, "Nachwort," in Theodor Mommsen, *Judaea und die Juden* (Berlin: Schocken Verlag, 1936).
101. Richard Fester, *Das Judentum als Zersetzungselement der Völker: Weltgeschichtliche Betrachtungen* (Hamburg: Hanseatische Verlagsanstalt, 1941).

102. See ibid., 5.
103. Joseph Goebbels, speech of 18 February 1943, in *Goebbels-Reden*, vol. 2, *1939–1945*, ed. Helmut Heiber (Dusseldorf: Droste Verlag, 1971), 178. An English-language translation of the quote can be found in *Landmark Speeches of National Socialism*, ed. and trans. Randall Bytwerk (College Station: Texas A&M University Press, 2008), 118.
104. For more on the film, see Stefan Mannes, *Antisemitismus im nationalsozialistischen Propagandafilm: "Jud Süss" und "Der ewige Jude"* (Cologne: Teiresias, 1999).
105. *Der ewige Jude* (1940), directed by Fritz Hippler. The other major cinematographic monument to Nazi anti-Semitism was of course the seventeenth-century period piece *Jud Süss* (1940), directed by Veit Harlan.
106. Fried, *Der Aufstieg der Juden*, 99.
107. See Stig Hornshøj-Møller, *"Der ewige Jude": Quellenkritische Analyse eines antisemitischen Propagandafilms* (Göttingen: Institut für den Wissenschaftlichen Film, 1995). The author suggests that Hitler's approval of the film on 20 May 1940 was his initial signal of assent to the extermination of the Jews in Europe.
108. Schachermeyr, *Indogermanen und Orient*, 481.
109. Ibid., 482.
110. Ibid., 486.
111. For more on Berenice, see Juhn, "Weltjudentum in der Antike," 28.
112. Joseph Vogt, *Kaiser Julian und das Judentum: Studien zum Weltanschauungskampf der Spätantike*, Morgenland, Darstellungen aus Geschichte und Kultur des Ostens 30 (Leipzig: Hinrichs Verlag, 1939).
113. *Hitler's Table Talk*, midday, 27 February 1942, 343.
114. "I know nothing of the Other World, and I have the honesty to admit it." Ibid., evening of 11 November 1941, 124.
115. Ibid., midday, 13 December 1941, 145.
116. Ibid., 143.
117. Ibid., midday, 21 October 1941, 76.
118. Ibid., night of 29–30 November 1944, 721.
119. Ibid., midday 21 October 1941, 76.
120. Rosenberg, *Myth of the Twentieth Century*, 38.
121. Ibid., midday, 21 October 1941, 76–77.
122. Ibid., 77.
123. A similar analysis of the move from Christlike to Christian and the effects of Pauline theology can be found in Nietzsche's *The Antichrist* and *The Genealogy of Morals*. Nietzsche's categories drew upon the psychological and the ethical, however, and not the racial.
124. *Hitler's Table Talk*, midday, 21 October 1941, 78.
125. Ibid., midday, 13 December 1941, 143.
126. See Christian Gerlach, *Krieg, Ernährung, Völkermord: Forschungen zur deutschen Vernichtungspolitik im Zweiten Weltkrieg* (Hamburg: Hamburger Edition, 1998).
127. *Hitler's Table Talk*, night of 27–28 January 1942, 261.
128. Rosenberg, *Myth of the Twentieth Century*, 38.

129. *Hitler's Table Talk,* midday, 17 February 1942, 313.
130. Rosenberg, *Myth of the Twentieth Century,* 38.
131. *Hitler's Table Talk,* midday, 27 January 1942, 253.
132. Ludwig Schemann, *Hauptepochen und Hauptvölker der Geschichte in ihrer Stellung zur Rasse,* vol. 2 of *Die Rasse in den Geisteswissenschaften* (Munich: Lehmanns Verlag, 1930), 167.
133. Ibid., 168–71.
134. Fried, *Der Aufstieg der Juden,* 122.
135. See pp. 275–78.
136. *Das Reich und Europa,* 2.
137. *Hitler's Table Talk,* midday, 17 February 1942, 313.
138. Ibid., evening of 11 November 1941, 123–24.
139. Ibid., evening of 25 October 1941, 88.
140. Ibid., 88–89.
141. Ibid., evening of 5 July 1942, 563.
142. Ibid., midday, 13 December 1941, 144.
143. Ibid., midday, 14 October 1941, 60.
144. See Hermann Rauschning, *The Voice of Destruction* (New York: G. P. Putnam's Sons, 1940), esp. ch. 4 ("Antichrist").
145. Hitler, quoted in ibid., 50.
146. Hitler, *Mein Kampf,* 454.
147. Ibid.
148. *The Goebbels Diaries, 1939–1941,* ed. and trans. Fred Taylor (London: Hamish Hamilton, 1982), 8 April 1941, 304–5.
149. Rosenberg, *Myth of the Twentieth Century,* 35.
150. Richard Walther Darré, *Das Bauerntum als Lebensquell der nordischen Rasse,* 445.
151. *Hitler's Table Talk,* midday, 14 December 1941, 146.
152. Ibid., midday, 28 August 1942, 667.
153. Ibid., midday, 17 February 1942, 314.
154. Rauschning, *Voice of Destruction,* 50.
155. *Hitler's Table Talk,* night of 11–12 July 1941, 7.
156. Ibid., night of 3–4 February 1942, 288.
157. Hitler, *Mein Kampf,* 454–55.
158. *Hitler's Table Talk,* midday, 21 October 1941, 77.
159. Ibid., midday, 27 February 1942, 342.
160. A popular *Flüsterwitz* (whispered joke) in 1930s Germany described Hitler and Frederick together in heaven, with Old Fritz trying desperately to explain to the führer that *façon* was spelled with a *ç* and not an *SS*.
161. *Hitler's Table Talk,* midday, 21 October 1941, 77.
162. Ibid., midday, 27 January 1942, 253–54.
163. Ibid., midday, 21 October 1941, 76.
164. Ibid., midday, 25 October 1941, 87.
165. *Hitlers Tischgespräche im Führerhauptquartier,* midday 21 October 1941, 77. (The reference to Saul as a *Kommissar* does not appear in the entry as translated in *Hitler's Table Talk.*)

166. *Hitler's Table Talk,* night of 19 October 1941, 75–76.
167. This entry appears only in the Picker version: see *Hitlers Tischgespräche im Führerhauptquartier,* 27 January 1942, 95.
168. *Hitler's Table Talk,* night of 11–12 July 1941, 7.
169. Ibid., midday, 21 October 1941, 78.
170. Ibid., 79.
171. *Deutschland ordnet Europa neu!,* 19.
172. Fried, *Der Aufstieg der Juden,* 113.
173. *Hitler's Table Talk,* midday, 17 February 1942, 314.
174. Ibid., midday, 21 October 1941, 78.
175. Hitler, *Mein Kampf,* 423.
176. Rosenberg, *Myth of the Twentieth Century,* 94.
177. Ibid.
178. Ibid., 4.
179. *Hitler's Table Talk,* midday, 13 December 1941, 143.
180. Ibid., midday, 21 October 1941, 76.
181. Ibid., 79.
182. Adolf Hitler, interview of 21 February 1936 with Bertrand de Jouvenel, quoted in J. P. Stern, *Hitler: The Führer and the People* (Berkeley: University of California Press, 1975), 40.
183. Hitler, *Mein Kampf,* 118.

CHAPTER 8. *VOLKSTOD* OR *RASSENSELBSTMORD*

Epigraph. Paul Valéry, "The Crisis of the Mind," in *History and Politics: The Collected Works of Paul Valéry,* vol. 10, ed. Jackson Mathews (New York: Bollingen Foundation, 1962), 23.

1. *Hitler's Table Talk, 1941–1944: His Private Conversations,* trans. Norman Cameron and R. H. Stevens (New York: Enigma, 2000), night of 28–29 January 1942, 261.
2. Richard Korherr, *Geburtenrückgang: Mahnruf an das deutsche Volk* (Munich: Süddeutsche Monatshefte, 1935), BABL/RD/NSD 70/185.
3. Richard Korherr, "Die Bevölkerungspolitik der alten Kulturvölker," in *Congrès international de la population, Paris 1937,* vol. 2, Actualités scientifiques et industrielles 711 (Paris: Hermann, 1937), 1.
4. The first article in the series was Richard Korherr, "Der Untergang der alten Kulturvölker: Eine Statistik in Worten I," *Allgemeines statistisches Archiv* 27 (1938): 29–50; the second appeared in 28 (1938): 72–89, 299–321, and 447–61.
5. Heinrich Himmler, "Geleitwort von Reichsführer-SS Heinrich Himmler," in Korherr, *Geburtenrückgang,* 3.
6. Heinrich Himmler, "Rede des Reichsführers-SS am 16. September 1942 in der Felkommandostelle vor den Teilnehmern an der SS- und Polizeiführertagung, einberufen von SS-Obergruppenführer Prütsmann, Höhere SS- und Polizeiführer Russland-Süd," BABL/NS 19/4009, f. 120. A little later on, Himmler added that the only Nordics to save themselves from death by declining birthrate were Con-

fucians, who, in worshiping their ancestors, emphasized the need to produce children to continue the circle of life and educate and reinforce the *Sippe,* or clan (ff. 120–21).

7. *Rassenpolitik,* ed. Chef der Ordnungspolizei—SS-Hauptamt, Schriftenreihe für die weltanschauliche Schulung der Ordnungspolizei, Heft 4 bis 6, (Berlin, 1943), BABL/RD 18/4, 28–29.

8. *Hitler's Table Talk,* night of 28–29 January 1942, 261.

9. Erwin Baur, "Der Untergang der Kulturvölker im Lichte der Biologie," *Volk und Rasse* 2 (1932): 65–79.

10. Ibid., 65.

11. Ibid., 66.

12. Fritz Lenz, *Menschliche Auslese und Rassenhygiene (Eugenik),* vol. 2 of *Menschliche Erblichkeitslehre und Rassenhygiene* (Munich: Lehmanns Verlag, 1932), 88.

13. Ibid., 78.

14. Lenz explored them in greater detail in ibid., 235.

15. Ibid., 89.

16. Fritz Geyer, *Rasse, Volk und Staat im Altertum* (Leipzig: B. G. Teubner Verlag, 1936), 48–49.

17. See Hans Gunther, *Rassengeschichte des Hellenischen und des Römischen Volkes* (Munich: Lehmann Verlag, 1929), 39–40 (on Sparta) and 52–53 (on Athens).

18. Walther Gehl, *Geschichte: 6. Klasse Oberschulen, Gymnasien und Oberschulen in Aufbauform; von der Urzeit bis zum Ende der Hohenstaufen* (Breslau: Ferdinand Hirt, 1940), 55.

19. Ludwig Schemann, *Hauptepochen und Hauptvölker der Geschichte in ihrer Stellung zur Rasse,* vol. 2 of *Die Rasse in den Geisteswissenschaften* (Munich: Lehmanns Verlag, 1930), 164.

20. See Richard Walther Darré, *Das Bauerntum als Lebensquell der nordischen Rasse* (Munich: Lehmanns Verlag, 1929), 168–69.

21. Schemann, *Hauptepochen und Hauptvölker der Geschichte,* 164.

22. Lenz, *Menschliche Auslese und Rassenhygiene (Eugenik),* 78.

23. *Inside the Third Reich: Memoirs by Albert Speer,* trans. Richard Winston and Clara Winston (New York: Macmillan, 1970), 440.

24. Lenz, *Menschliche Auslese und Rassenhygiene (Eugenik),* 235.

25. Which Lenz described in ibid., 368.

26. Ibid., 235.

27. Ibid., 236.

28. H. Rübel, "Römische Geschichte in rassischer Beleuchtung," *Volk und Rasse* 1 (1943): 10.

29. Geyer, *Rasse, Volk und Staat im Altertum,* 137.

30. Schemann, *Die Rasse in den Geisteswissenschaft,* 77.

31. Rübel, "Römische Geschichte in rassischer Beleuchtung," 5.

32. Schemann, *Die Rasse in den Geisteswissenschaft,* 77.

33. Fritz Lenz, *Menschliche Auslese und Rassenhygiene (Eugenik),* 88. See also Karl Kynast, *Apollon und Dionysos: Nordisches und Unnordisches inner-*

halb der Religion der Griechen, eine rassenkundliche Untersuchung (Munich: Lehmanns Verlag, 1927), 77.

34. Ferdinand Fried, *Latifundien vernichteten Rom! Eine Studie der römischen Agrarverhältnisse und ihrer Auswirkungen auf Volk und Staat* (Reichsbauernstadt Goslar: Verlag Blut und Boden, 1938).

35. Darré, *Das Bauerntum als Lebensquell der nordischen Rasse,* 168–83 (on the example of Sparta).

36. Fried, *Latifundien vernichteten Rom!,* 115.

37. Paul Hanschke, "Der Einbruch des Orientalischen in das klassische römische Schrifttum als Vorbereitung des Christentums," *Neue Jahrbücher für antike und deutsche Bildung,* 1938, Heft 3: 116–26.

38. Ulrich Knoche, "Der Beginn des römischen Sittenverfalls," *Neue Jahrbüher für Antike und deutsche Bildung,* 1939, Heft 10: 99–123.

39. Ennius, *Annales,* quoted in Cicero, *On the Republic,* in *On the Republic; On the Laws,* trans. Clinton W. Keyes (Cambridge, MA: Harvard University Press, 1928), 245 (5.1).

40. Viktor Pöschl, "Cato als Vorbild römischer Lebenshaltung," *Neue Jahrbücher für die Antike und deutsche Bildung,* 1939, Heft 10: 411–21.

41. Geyer, *Rasse, Volk und Staat im Altertum,* 119.

42. Fried, *Latifundien vernichteten Rom!,* 120.

43. Ibid., 121.

44. Walter Hohmann and Wilhelm Schiefer, *Lehrbuch der Geschichte: Oberstufe,* vol. 1 (Frankfurt: Diesterweg, 1940), 102.

45. *Rassenpolitik,* 46–47.

46. Adolf Hitler, *Mein Kampf,* trans. Ralph Manheim (Boston: Houghton Mifflin, 1943), 289.

47. Walter Brewitz, "Die Entnordung der Römer," *Volk und Rasse* 9 (1936):369.

48. Ibid., 370.

49. Ibid., 369.

50. Ibid., 372.

51. Ibid., 373.

52. Ibid., 369.

53. Alfred Rosenberg, *The Myth of the Twentieth Century: An Evaluation of the Spiritual-Intellectual Confrontations of Our Age,* trans. Vivian Bird (Newport Beach, CA: Noontide, 1982), 26.

54. Ibid., 27.

55. On Roman bastardization, see Fritz Schachermeyr, *Indogermanen und Orient: Ihre kulturelle und machtpolitische Auseinandersetzung im Altertum* (Stuttgart: W. Kohlhammer Verlag, 1944), 459.

56. *Deutschland ordnet Europa neu!,* ed. Chef der Ordnungspolizei—SS Hauptamt, Schriftenreihe für die weltanschauliche Schulung der Ordnungspolizei, 1942, Heft 4, BABL, RD 18/16, 16.

57. Ibid.

58. Fritz Taeger, *Orient und Occident in der Antike* (Tübingen: J. C. B. Mohr, 1936), 25–26.

59. Schachermeyr, *Indogermanen und Orient*, 493.
60. Ibid.
61. *Deutschland ordnet Europa neu!*, 17.
62. Domitius Ulpianus, known as Ulpian, was a Roman jurist who died in 228. His place and date of birth remain unknown, as are those of Papinian.
63. Aemilius Papinianus, or Papinian, was a Roman jurist who died in 212, on the orders of Emperor Caracalla. He had previously been a praetorian prefect under Septimius Severus.
64. Ferdinand Fried, *Der Aufstieg der Juden* (Reichsbauernstadt Goslar: Verlag Blut und Boden, 1937), 125.
65. Walter Brewitz, "Die Entnordung der Römer," 370.
66. Fried, *Der Aufstieg der Juden*, 125.
67. Schachermeyr, *Indogermanen und Orient*, 492.
68. Joseph Vogt, "Das Puniertum und die Dynastie des Septimius Severus," in *Rom und Karthago: Ein Gemeinschaftswerk*, ed. Vogt (Leipzig: Koehler und Amelang, 1943), 346–66.
69. Fried, *Der Aufstieg der Juden*, 123–30.
70. Ibid., 123.
71. Ibid., 122.
72. Ibid., 124.
73. See most notably Alexander Demandt, *Der Fall Roms: Die Auflösung des römischen Reiches im Urteil der Nachwelt* (Munich: C.H. Beck Verlag, 1984).
74. Geyer, *Rasse, Volk und Staat im Altertum*, 172.
75. Fritz Schachermeyr, "Die Aufgaben der alten Geschichte im Rahmen der nordischen Weltgeschichte," *Vergangenheit und Gegenwart* 23 (1933): 596–97.
76. Ibid., 597.
77. Ernst Kornemann, *Das Imperium Romanum, sein Aufstieg und Niedergang: Ein Beitrag zur ersten europäischen Großraumgestaltung*, Vorträge der Friedrich-Wilhelms-Universität zu Breslau im Kriegswinter 1940/41 (Breslau: Korn, 1941), 28.
78. Wilhelm Frick, "Richtlinien für die Geschichtslehrbücher—20. Juli 1933," *Zentralblatt für die gesamte Unterrichtsverwaltung in Preußen*, ed. Ministerium für Wissenschaft, Kunst und Volksbildung, 5 August 1933, Heft 15: 198.
79. Bernhard Rust, ed., *Erziehung und Unterricht in der höheren Schule: Amtliche Ausgabe des Reichs- und Preußischen Ministeriums für Wissenschaft, Erziehung und Volksbildung* (Berlin: Weidmann, 1938), 74.
80. Ibid., 92.
81. See pp. 220–21, 290, and 342.
82. Walter Groß, *Deine Ehre ist die Treue zum Blute deines Volkes*, Schriftenreihe für die Wochenendschulungen der Hitlerjugend 3, Reichsjugendführung, (Berlin, 1943), BABL/NSD 43/155-3, 7–8.
83. The SS motto, of course, was *Meine Ehre heisst Treue* (My honor is called loyalty).
84. Walter Groß, *Deine Ehre ist die Treue zum Blute deines Volkes*, 13.
85. "Jason und Medea: Die Tragödie der rassischen Mischehe," *SS-Leitheft* 7, no. 6a (1941): 18.

86. Ibid., 19.
87. Ibid., 18.
88. Ibid., 19.
89. Ibid., 20.
90. Ibid., 19.
91. *Der Boden: Blutliche Bedeutung der Bodenständigkeit, Bauernfeindlichkeit der Internationalen Raumfrage*, vol. 2 of *Blut und Boden: Lichtbildvortrag*, ed. Reichsführer-SS Chef des Rasse- und Siedlungshauptamtes, Berlin, BABL/NSD 41/87, image 32.
92. Hermann Jekeli, "Rasse ist verpflichtung," *Rasse und Volk: Stoffsammlung für die weltanschauliche Schulung*, ed. Beauftragten für die weltanschauliche Schulung der deutschen Volksgruppe in Rumänien, NSDAP, November 1941, Heft 2: 16.
93. Ibid., 17.
94. Hitler, *Mein Kampf*, 91.
95. Joseph Goebbels, article in *Völkischer Beobachter*, "Olympia-Sonderausgabe," 17 July 1936, section 1, 6.
96. Hans Bogner, *Die verwirklichte Demokratie: Die Lehren der Antike* (Hamburg: Hanseatische Verlagsanstalt, 1930).
97. Ibid., 126–42.
98. Hohmann and Schiefer, *Lehrbuch der Geschichte*, 61.
99. Gehl, *Geschichte*, 53–54 and 57–60.
100. See p. 118.
101. Hans Bogner, *Die Bildung der politischen Elite* (Oldenburg: Stalling Verlag, 1932), 52.
102. Ibid.
103. Ibid., 53.
104. Geyer, *Rasse, Volk und Staat im Altertum*, 44.
105. Ibid., 51.
106. Ludwig Schemann delved into the Aristotelian critique of democracy in *Die Rassen in den Geisteswissenschaften*, 134–35.
107. For an interpretation of German historiography on Athenian democracy, see Beat Näf, *Von Perikles zu Hitler? Die athenische Demokratie und die deutsche Althistorie bis 1945* (New York: Peter Lang, 1986).
108. Rosenberg, *Myth of the Twentieth Century*, 23.
109. Alfred Rosenberg, speech at the Palais Bourbon, 28 November 1940, in *Völkischer Beobachter*, 29 November 1940, 1 and 4.
110. Joseph Arthur de Gobineau, *The Inequality of Human Races*, trans. Adrian Collins (London: William Heinemann, 1915), 210.
111. Ibid., 36.
112. Collins's translation: ibid., xiii.
113. Georges Vacher de Lapouge, "Les sélections sociales," *Revue d'anthropologie*, 15 September 1887, quoted in Pierre-André Taguieff, *La couleur et le sang: Doctrines racistes à la française* (Paris: Mille et une nuits, 1998), 36.
114. Georges Vacher de Lapouge, letter to Julius Langbehn, 3 September 1890, quoted in Taguieff, *La couleur et le sang*, 116.

115. Kynast, *Apollon und Dionysos*, 72.
116. Rosenberg, *Myth of the Twentieth Century*, 23.
117. Ibid., 4.
118. Ibid., 89.
119. Ibid., 24.
120. Fritz Schachermeyr, "Die nordische Führerpersönlichkeit im Altertum," in *Humanistische Bildung im nationalsozialistischen Staate*, Neue Wege zur Antike, Erste Reihe, Heft 9 (Leipzig and Berlin: Teubner Verlag, 1933), 42.
121. Schachermeyr, *Indogermanen und Orient*, 240.
122. Taeger, *Orient und Occident in der Antike*, 16.
123. Ibid., 17.
124. Schachermeyr, *Indogermanen und Orient*, 240.
125. Ibid., 241.
126. Ibid., 242.
127. Taeger, *Orient und Occident in der Antike*, 17.
128. Schachermeyr, *Indogermanen und Orient*, 392–93.
129. Ibid., 393.
130. "Griechenland," in *Der neue Brockhaus: Allbuch in vier Bänden und einem Atlas* (Leipzig: F. A. Brockhaus, 1938–39), vol. 2, 280.
131. For another example of the contrasts between Philip and Alexander and between Augustus and Caesar, see Ernst Kornemann, "Gli studi germanici sulla figura e l'opera di Augusto e sulla fondazione dell'impero romano," *Quaderni Augustei: Studi stranieri* 4 (1937).
132. Schachermeyr, "Die nordische Führerpersönlichkeit im Altertum," 42.
133. Ibid.
134. Hohmann and Schiefer, *Lehrbuch der Geschichte*, 74.
135. Rosenberg, *Myth of the Twentieth Century*, 90.
136. Ibid., 112.
137. Ibid., 90.
138. Schemann, *Die Rasse in der Geisteswissenschaften*, 139.
139. Ibid., 147.
140. Schachermeyr, *Indogermanen und Orient*, 254.
141. Ibid., 256.
142. Taeger, *Orient und Occident in der Antike*, 20.
143. Ibid., 22.
144. Schachermeyr, *Indogermanen und Orient*, 296.
145. Ibid., 297.
146. Ibid., 258.
147. See chap. 3, esp. pp. 142–49, regarding the thought of Martin Heidegger.
148. Schachermeyr, *Indogermanen und Orient*, 259.
149. Günther, *Rassengeschichte des hellenischen und des römischen Volkes*, 61.
150. Ibid., 65–66.
151. Ibid., 60.
152. Ibid., 67–68.
153. Rosenberg, *Myth of the Twentieth Century*, 65–66.
154. Ibid., 94.
155. *Hitler's Table Talk*, midday, 12 November 1941, 125.

156. See Philippe Burrin, *Ressentiment et apocalypse: Essai sur l'antisémitisme nazi* (Paris: Seuil, 2004).

157. Rosenberg, *Myth of the Twentieth Century,* 42.

158. Alfred Rosenberg, "Nordische Wiedergeburt: Rede in Lübeck anlässlich der zweiten Reichstagung der Nordischen Gesellschaft," 26 June 1935, in Rosenberg, *Reden und Aufsätze von 1933–1935,* vol. 2 of *Gestaltung der Idee: Blut und Ehre* (Munich: Zentralverlag der NSDAP, Franz Eher Verlag, 1936), 342–43.

159. Ibid., 343.

160. Joseph Goebbels, speech of 18 February 1943, in *Landmark Speeches of National Socialism,* ed. and trans. Randall Bytwerk (College Station: Texas A&M University Press, 2008), 122.

161. Ibid., 114.

162. Ibid., 135.

163. Ibid., 123.

164. Hitler, *Mein Kampf,* 288.

165. J.P. Stern, *Hitler: The Führer and the People* (Berkeley: University of California Press, 1975), 65.

166. Adolf Hitler, speech before the Reichstag at the Opera Kroll in Berlin, 30 January 1939, in Max Domarus, ed., *Hitler: Speeches and Proclamations, 1932–1945,* trans. Mary Fran Gilbert (Wauconda, IL: Bolchazy-Carducci, 1990–2004), vol. 3, *The Chronicle of a Dictatorship,* 1449.

167. Adolf Hitler, speech of 30 May 1942, in ibid., vol. 4, *The Years 1941 to 1945,* 2641.

168. *Hitler's Table Talk,* night of 11–12 July 1941, 7.

169. Ibid., night of 20–21 February 1942, 322.

170. See Christian Ingrao, "Le suicide comme sortie de guerre: Allemagne-Japon, 1945," in *Sorties de guerre,* ed. Stéphane Audoin-Rouzeau and Roland Beller (Paris: Le Découverte, 2003); and Frank-Lothar Kroll, "Der Faktor 'Zukunft' in Hitlers Geschichtsbild," in *Neue Wege der Ideengeschichte: Festschrift für Kurt Kluxen zum 85. Geburtstag,* ed. Kroll (Paderborn: Schöningh, 1986), 391–409.

171. *Hitler's Table Talk,* night of 2–3 November 1941, 110.

172. Ibid., evening of 17 February 1942, 316.

CHAPTER 9. THE CHOREOGRAPHY OF THE END

Epigraphs. Ernst Jünger, *On the Marble Cliffs,* trans. Stuart Hood (New York: Penguin, 1970), 107; and Jean-Paul Sartre, "Erostratus," in *"The Wall (Intimacy)" and Other Stories,* trans. Lloyd Alexander (New York: New Directions, 1948), 46–47.

1. Joseph Goebbels, press conference of 21 April 1945, quoted in Joachim Fest, *Inside Hitler's Bunker: The Last Days of the Third Reich,* trans. Margot Bettauer Dembo (New York: Farrar, Straus and Giroux, 2004), 56.

2. *Die Tagebücher von Joseph Goebbels, Teil II: Diktate 1941–1945,* ed. Elke Fröhlich, vol. 7, *Januar–März 1943* (Munich: K.G. Saur Verlag, 1993), 23 January 1943, 175.

3. Ibid., 28 January 1943, 211.
4. Adolf Hitler to Martin Bormann, quoted in Joachim Fest, *Hitler*, trans. Richard Winston and Clara Winston (New York: Harcourt, 1974), 725.
5. *The Goebbels Diaries: The Last Days*, trans. Richard Barry (London: Martin Secker and Warburg, 1978), 11 March 1945, 102.
6. Adolf Hitler, "My Political Testament," in Max Domarus, ed., *Hitler: Speeches and Proclamations, 1932–1945*, trans. Mary Fran Gilbert (Wauconda, IL: Bolchazy-Carducci, 1990–2004), vol. 4, *The Years 1941 to 1945*, 3055–57.
7. Hannah Arendt, "On the Nature of Totalitarianism," in Arendt, *Essays in Understanding, 1930–1954*, ed. Jerome Kohn (New York: Schocken Books, 1994), 340.
8. Immanuel Kant, "Der Streit der Fakultäten," in *Kants Werke: Akademie Textausgabe*, vol. 7 (Berlin: W. de Gruyter, 1968), 79–80, quoted in Reinhard Koselleck, *Futures Past: On the Semantics of Historical Time*, trans. Keith Tribe (New York: Columbia University Press, 2004), 39.
9. Richard Wagner, *Rienzi, der Letzte der Tribunen*, act 1, scene 1. All English-language quotations from Richard Wagner, *Rienzi: The Last of the Tribunes*, trans. John Jackson (New York: New York Metropolitan Opera House, 1885–86).
10. Ibid., act 1, scene 2.
11. As demonstrated by Rienzi's famous prayer in ibid., act 5, scene 1.
12. Ibid., act 5, scene 4.
13. August Kubizek, *The Young Hitler I Knew: The Memoirs of Hitler's Childhood Friend*, trans. Geoffrey Brooks (Barnsley: Frontline, 2006), 116.
14. Ibid., 117.
15. Ibid., 118.
16. Ibid.
17. Ibid., 119.
18. Albert Speer, *Spandau: The Secret Diaries*, trans. Richard Winston and Clara Winston (New York: Macmillan, 1976), 15 January 1951, 173.
19. *Inside the Third Reich: Memoirs by Albert Speer*, trans. Richard Winston and Clara Winston (New York: Macmillan, 1970), 68.
20. Ibid., 55–56.
21. Adolf Hitler, speech at the Kulturtagung (Culture conference) of the Nuremberg Party Congress, 6 September 1938, in *The Speeches of Adolf Hitler*, ed. Norman Baynes, vol. 1 (New York: Howard Fertig, 1969), 597.
22. Speer, *Inside the Third Reich*, 103–4.
23. Speer, *Spandau*, 24 April 1952, 195.
24. E.g., Hermann Rauschning, *The Voice of Destruction* (New York: G. P. Putnam and Sons, 1940), 121.
25. Domarus, *Hitler*, vol. 1, *The Years 1932 to 1934*, 486.
26. Speer, *Inside the Third Reich*, 56.
27. Ibid.
28. Adolf Hitler, speech at the Kulturtagung of the Nuremberg Party Congress, 1935, in Baynes, *Speeches of Adolf Hitler*, 573.
29. Adolf Hitler, speech at the opening of the House of German Art in Munich, 1937, in Baynes, *Speeches of Adolf Hitler*, 586.

30. Hitler, speech at the Kulturtagung of the Nuremberg Party Congress, 1935, 573.
31. Hitler, speech at the Kulturtagung of the Nuremberg Party Congress, 1937, in Baynes, *Speeches of Adolf Hitler*, 593.
32. Hitler, speech at the Kulturtagung of the Nuremberg Party Congress, 1935, 573.
33. Ibid., 583.
34. Ibid., 573.
35. Adolf Hitler, *Mein Kampf*, trans. Ralph Manheim (Boston: Houghton Mifflin, 1943), 265.
36. See, for instance, "Warum tragen die SS-Männer den Totenkopf an der Mütze?," *Das Schwarze Korps*, 2 December 1937, 2; "SS-Mann, dein Symbol," *Das Schwarze Korps*, 25 January 1940, 8; and "Der Totenkopf, Zeichen unseres Lebenswillens," *Die Deutsche Polizei*.
37. See chap 7, esp. pp. 290–93, and chap. 8, esp. pp. 351–54.
38. See pp. 351–54.
39. On eschatology and belief in the end of days, see Norman Cohn, *The Pursuit of the Millennium: Revolutionary Millenarians and Mystical Anarchists of the Middle Ages* (Oxford: Oxford University Press, 1957); and Alexander Demandt, *Endzeit? Die Zukunft der Geschichte* (Berlin: Siedler, 1993).
40. Alfred Rosenberg, *The Myth of the Twentieth Century: An Evaluation of the Spiritual-Intellectual Confrontations of Our Age*, trans. Vivian Bird (Newport Beach, CA: Noontide, 1982), 66.
41. See Hitler, *Mein Kampf*, 206: "There is no making pacts with Jews; there can only be the hard: either-or."
42. *Die Tagebücher von Joseph Goebbels*, 2 March 1943, 454, quoted in Bernd Wegner, "The Ideology of Self-Destruction: Hitler and the Choreography of Defeat," *German Historical Institute London Bulletin* 26 (2004): 27.
43. Bernd Wegner, "Hitler, der Zweite Weltkrieg und die Choreographie des Untergangs," *Geschichte und Gesellschaft* 26 (2000): 507.
44. Adolf Hitler, speech before the Reichstag, 1 September 1939, in Domarus, *Hitler*, vol. 3, *The Years 1939 to 1940*, 1755.
45. Wegner, "Hitler, der Zweite Weltkrieg und die Choreographie des Untergangs," 508.
46. Ibid., 500.
47. Private remark by Hitler from 1944, quoted in ibid., 509.
48. Ibid., 501.
49. Ibid., 509.
50. See chap. 5, esp. pp. 221–26.
51. See chap. 2, pp. 91–96 regarding the transition from symbolic to territorial annexation.
52. See *Landmark Speeches of National Socialism*, ed. Randall Bytwerk (College Station: Texas A&M University Press, 2008), 112–39.
53. See pp. 221–26.
54. "Appell des Reichsmarschalls Goering an die Wehrmacht am 30. Januar 1943." Göring's radio address was published in the *Völkischer Beobachter*, 3 January 1943, 3–4, and subsequently reproduced in Otto Wilhelm von Vacano,

Sparta: Der Lebenskampf einer nordischen Herrenschicht (Kempten: Bücherei der Adolf-Hitler-Schulen, 1940), 120.

55. Ibid.

56. *Völkischer Beobachter*, 7 February 1943, 3.

57. See Ulrich Albrecht, "Hitlers 11. September?," lecture, Freie Universität Berlin, 8 October 2002.

58. For more on *Der alte Fritz*, see Johannes Kunisch, *Friedrich der Grosse: Der König und seine Zeit* (Munich: C.H. Beck, 2005). The anecdote about Hitler's and Goebbels's excitement at the news of Roosevelt's death is also noted in Fest, *Inside Hitler's Bunker*, 13–14. See also Hugh Trevor-Roper, *The Last Days of Hitler* (Chicago: University of Chicago Press, 1987), 140:

> Goebbels told [Count] Schwerin von Krosigk how he had recently been reading aloud to the Fuehrer, to solace him in his universal discomfiture. He was reading from his favourite book, Carlyle's *History of Frederick the Great*; and the chapter he was reading described 'how the great king himself no longer saw any way out of his difficulties, no longer had any plan; how all his generals and ministers were convinced that his downfall was at hand; how the enemy was already counting Prussia as destroyed; how the future hung dark before him, and in his last letter to his minister, Count Finckenstein, he gave himself one last respite: if there was no change by February 15th, he would give it up and take poison. "Brave king!" says Carlyle, "wait yet a little while, and the days of your suffering will be over. Already the sun of your good fortune stands behind the clouds, and soon will rise upon you." On February 12th the Czarina died; the Miracle of the House of Brandenburg had come to pass.' At this touching tale, said Goebbels, 'tears stood in the Fuehrer's eyes.'

59. Goebbels, *Final Entries*, 28 February 1945, 11–12.

60. Joseph Goebbels, "Die Geschichte als Lehrmeisterin," *Das Reich: Deutsche Wochenzeitung*, 1 April 1945, 1.

61. Ibid.

62. Ibid., 2.

63. Ibid.

64. Ibid.

65. Walter Frank, "Hannibal von den Toren: Senat und Volk von Rom in den Punierkriegen," *Das Reich*, 8 April 1945, 3, and 15 April 1945, 3–4.

66. Ibid., 8 April, 3.

67. Ibid., 15 April, 3.

68. Ibid., 8 April, 3. The quote is from Leopold von Ranke, *Weltgeschichte*, vol. 2, *Die Römische Republik und ihre Weltherrschaft* (Leipzig: Duncker und Humblot, 1882), 225.

69. Frank, "Hannibal von den Toren," 15 April, 4.

70. Ibid., 3.

71. Ibid., 4.

72. Hugo Landgraf, "Roms Triumph über Hannibal: Die Widerstandskraft einer Soldatennation entschied den Zweiten Punischen Krieg," *Völkischer Beobachter*, 15 April 1945, 4.

73. "Volk in der Entscheidung: Ungebrochener Kampfgeist in Schicksalsstunden der Jahrhundert bewährt," *Völkischer Beobachter*, 15 April 1945, 4.

74. Landgraf, "Roms Triumph über Hannibal."
75. "Cannae," *SS-Leitheft,* 1944, Heft 10: 15-18.
76. Ibid, 16.
77. Ibid., 18.
78.
>Feiger Gedanken
>bängliches Schwanken,
>weibisches Zagen,
>ängstliches Klagen
>wendet kein Elend,
>macht dich nicht frei.
>Allen Gewalten
>zum Trutz sich erhalten,
>nimmer sich beugen,
>kräftig sich zeigen,
>rufet die Arme
>der Götter herbei!
>
>Cowardly thoughts'
>fearful wavering,
>womanish hesitancy,
>anxious complaining
>wards off no misery,
>won't make you free.
>In face of all forces
>maintaining defiance,
>yielding never,
>showing oneself strong—
>summons the arms
>of the gods to one's side.

Johan Wolfgang Goethe, "Beherzigung," from *Lila* (set to music by Johann Friedrich Reichardt and Hugo Wolf, 1887), in Dietrich Fischer-Dieskau, ed., *The Fischer-Dieskau Book of Lieder,* trans. George Bird and Richard Stokes (New York: Limelight, 1995), 71.
79. Landgraf, "Roms Triumph über Hannibal."
80. Ibid.
81. Frank, "Hannibal von den Toren," 15 April 1945, 3.
82. Ibid.
83. Ibid., 4.
84. Kurt Pastenacci, "Sind Kriege Rechenexempel? Eine historische Untersuchung," *Die Deutsche Polizei,* March 1945, 35-37, BABL/RD 19/1-13.
85. Ibid, 36.
86. Ibid., 37.
87. Landgraf, "Roms Triumph über Hannibal."
88. Adolf Hitler, "Sage mir, wer Dich lobt . . . ," *Völkischer Beobachter,* 8 April 1931.
89. Hitler, speech at the Kulturtagung of the Nuremberg Party Congress, 1935, 570.
90. See Trevor-Roper, *Last Days of Hitler,* 226.

91. Fest, *Inside Hitler's Bunker*, esp. ch. 6.
92. Ibid., 125.
93. Ibid., 128.
94. Ibid., 127.
95. Hermann Rauschning, *The Revolution of Nihilism: Warning to the West* (New York: Longmans, 1939).
96. This sense of indifference in the face of the absurdity of life can be heard in the "Teufelslied" (Devil's song), a marching tune preferred by the Waffen-SS. As one verse proclaims:

> Wir pfeifen auf Unten und Oben,
> Und uns kann die ganze Welt
> Verfluchen oder auch loben,
> Grad wie es ihnen gefällt.
>
> We care about nothing around us,
> And the whole world can
> Curse or praise us,
> Just as it pleases.

97. Sebastian Haffner, *The Meaning of Hitler*, trans. Ewald Osers (London: Phoenix, 2000), 112.
98. J.P. Stern, *Hitler: The Führer and the People* (Berkeley: University of California Press, 1975), 28.
99. Ibid., 29.
100. Hitler, *Mein Kampf*, 206.
101. Goebbels, quoted in Fest, *Inside Hitler's Bunker*, 127.
102. Fest, *Hitler*, 725.
103. "Hitlers Lagesbesprechungen," *Der Spiegel*, no. 3 (10 January 1966), 37, quoted in translation in Ian Kershaw, *Hitler: Nemesis* (New York: W.W. Norton, 2001), 811.
104. Speer, *Inside the Third Reich*, 440.
105. *Hitler's Table Talk, 1941–1944: His Private Conversations*, trans. Norman Cameron and R.H. Stevens (New York: Enigma, 2000), evening of 25 October 1941, 89.
106. Suetonius, *Vita Neronis* 49.1.
107. Fest, *Hitler*, 726.
108. See Fest, *Inside Hitler's Bunker*, 169; see also Robert Sherwood, *Roosevelt and Hopkins: An Intimate History*, rev. ed. (New York: Universal, 1950), 887.

CONCLUSION

1. Mircea Eliade, *The Myth of Eternal Return: Or, Cosmos and History*, trans. Willard Trask (New York: Bollingen Foundation, 1954).
2. Ecclesiastes 1:9.
3. Alfred Rosenberg, *The Myth of the Twentieth Century: An Evaluation of the Spiritual-Intellectual Confrontations of Our Age*, trans. Vivian Bird (New-

port Beach, CA: Noontide, 1982), 181; *Hitlers Tischgespräche im Führerhauptquartier 1941–1942,* ed. Henry Picker (Bonn: Athenäum, 1951), midday, 21 October 1941, 77; *Hitler's Table Talk, 1941–1944: His Private Conversations,* trans. Norman Cameron and R.H. Stevens (New York: Enigma, 2000), midday, 14 December 1941, 146.

4. In addition to these diametrically opposed practices there was the burlesque mocking of Claudius in Seneca's *Apocolocyntosis,* the parodying and satirizing of memory that provided a novel form of catharsis.

5. Lucien Jerphagnon, "*Damnatio memoriae:* Essai sur le traitement des nuisances en histoire," in Jerphagnon, *Au bonheur des sages* (Paris: Desclée de Brouwer, 2004), 233–50.

6. Goebbels quoted in Joachim Fest, *The Face of the Third Reich: Portraits of the Nazi Leadership,* trans. Michael Bullock (New York: Da Capo, 1999), 97.

7. Suetonius, *Vita Neronis* 6.49.1.

8. Robert Antelme, *The Human Race,* trans. Jeffrey Haight and Anne Mahler (Evanston, IL: Marlboro, 1992), 79.

Index

Abensour, Miguel, 261
academics, dissident, 101
academics, Third Reich, 7, 11; after 1945, 47; on antiquity, 6; Aryanization of, 86; compromises of, 46; ideological works of, 2–3; Nordicist, 27, 29; in NSLB, 130–31; service to Nazism, 46–47; support for Nordic unity, 50. *See also* classicists; historians
Academie française, linguistic standards of, 19
academies, Nazi: on Prometheus, 31. *See also* curricula; education, Nazi; Gymnasien; pedagogy
Achaeans, Nordic character of, 60, 65, 85
Acropolis (Athens): construction of, 263–64; swastika over, 92
Actium, Battle of, 131
Adamic myth, alternatives to, 21–22
Adolf-Hitler-Schulen, textbooks on Lacedaemonians, 219. *See also* education, Nazi; pedagogy
Adonis, Nazi ideal of, 13
Aeneas: in Nazi decorative art, 257; torch of, 169
agōgē, Spartan: for Nazi new man, 219–21
agon, Hellenic, 159; and German sport, 178–82
agrarianism: of Indo-Germanic people, 274–75, 276–77, 284; of NSDAP, 274

Ahnenerbe (German Ancestral Heritage Society), 27; archaeological research of, 79–80; and Atlantean hypothesis, 36; charter of, 78, 79; classical philology of, 80; Department of Classical Antiquity, 75–82; edition of *Codex Aesinas*, 80; excavations of, 80–81; *Germanenkunde* of, 77–78; Lehr- und Forschungseinrichtung für indogermanisch-arische Philologie under Kulturwissenschaft, 81; publications of, 9; on Roman Nordicism, 79
Albani, Cardinal Alessandro, 156
Alcibiades, 343
Alexander the Great: as Asiatic king, 348; conquest of East, 397, 399; contrast with Philip, 348; de-Nordification under, 304, 305, 347, 348, 349; Greco-Oriental empire of, 290; Greek-Persians under, 349; imperialism of, 264; in Nazi decorative art, 257; Nordic appearance of, 347, 348; *proskynesis* before, 348; as race traitor, 349; world empire of, 347–48, 349
Alexander Nevsky, 279
Alexandrine Empire: cultural globalization of, 347; de-Nordification of, 350; miscegenation in, 356
allegory, ancient: Nazi use of, 257
Allies: bombardment of Germany, 388, 389; dynamiting of Nazi architecture,

Allies *(continued)*
   397; unconditional surrender demands, 370–71
Alpines, among German people, 224, 281
Altes Museum (Berlin): Pergamon Altar, 165, 192; warriors' helmets in, 56
Altheim, Franz: on *Elchrune,* 81; "Germans and Iranians," 27; publications of, 80–81
Amazons, as Nordic, 59
ancestry, Nordic: among ancient peoples, 32–33, 38, 39. *See also* Greeks, Nordic; Nordic people; Romans, Nordic
Ancients and Moderns, French quarrel of, 163–64
Der Angriff, on modern Greeks, 94
annexations, Nazi: Hitler's justification of, 92–93
Antelme, Robert: *The Human Race,* 399
anthropology, German nineteenth-century, 19
anthropology, racial, 56–60; and ancient history, 120–21. *See also* racial science
anthropometry, nineteenth-century, 173
anti-intellectualism, Nazi, 99, 196, 226
Die Antike (journal), Indo-Germanic heritage in, 80
antiquity, Germanic: and *Germanentum,* 76; proponents of, 4. *See also* prehistory, German
antiquity, Greco-Roman: anti-Semitism in, 121; *Assimilationsjude* in, 116; blonds in, 56–58, 97, 201–2; Christian destruction of, 310–13, 320, 388; civic culture of, 134, 150; concept of history in, 99, 100; creative forces of, 134; defense against Bolshevism, 123; denatalism in, 326; eighteenth-century revival of, 156–58; end of, 336–37, 359; exemplars of, 284; foreign peoples of, 116–17; *Führerpersönlichkeit* in, 262–64; *Germanentum* and, 76, 122, 123; Germanists' use of, 124; Germanophile rejection of, 149–50; German values in, 108–9; Great Man theory in, 266, 267, 268, 271; Günther on, 25, 52–55; Himmler and, 78–79; Hitler's admiration for, 70, 71, 73–74, 77, 96, 230, 268–73; human-divine relationships in, 314; Indo-Germanic appropriation of, 75, 111, 162; Jewish destruction of, 289, 353–54; Jewish question in, 298–301; Latin versus Greek quarrel on, 125–28; leadership in, 262–68; lebensraum in, 273–78; Malthusianism in, 325–27; Nazi inauthenticity concerning, 147–49, 152; Nazi interpreters of, 2–3, 6, 10–11; in Nazi symbolism, 40; Nazi use of, 1–8, 147, 393, 396; as political weapon, 147; prophetic warning from, 395; public monuments of, 242, 251, 252; racialized vision of, 4–5, 122, 214; reassurance of German pride, 5, 97; relationship with natural world, 314; role in European power, 1; SS study of, 78; toleration in, 315; totalitarian use of, 2. *See also* civilization, Greco-Roman
antiquity, Greek: German scholarship on, 126; versus Roman antiquity, 125–28
antiquity, Indo-Germanic: depopulation in, 327
antiquity, Roman: clichés of, 151; versus Greek antiquity, 125–28; Renaissance study of, 126
anti-Semitism: in Greco-Roman antiquity, 121; inversion of reality in, 300; in Latin literature, 303; Orientalism in, 298; resentment in, 299; in SS manual, 300; in Wehrmacht propaganda, 303–4. *See also* miscegenation, racial; racial conflict
Antisthenes, continuation of Socrates, 213
apocalypse, Horsemen of, 292
apocalypse, Nazi, 351–54, 356, 370; Hitler's discourse on, 353–54; mobilization for, 352; racial discourse of, 351–53
Apollo: cult of light, 61, 62; versus Dionysus, 60–62, 115, 117; Nordic characteristics of, 61
apotheosis, Nazi, 365, 397
apotheosis, Roman: versus *damnatio memoriae,* 398
Arbeit und Brot campaign, 263
archaeology, Nazi, 3, 9, 96; Ahnenerbe's, 79–80; Himmler's projects in, 70, 74, 78; Hitler on, 70; on Indo-German migration, 80–81; in Olympic propaganda, 162, 164; public consumption of, 81
archaeology, Nordicist, 81
archetypes, German search for, 138
archetypes, Greek: German idealization of, 140
archetypes, Nordic: beauty of, 172, 191; and Jewish countertypes, 173–75, 177, 178; preservation for posterity, 176, 191

architecture: as expression of community, 243; French Empire, 246; German neoclassical, 140; global neoclassicism in, 260; hieratic tradition of, 260; role in colonization, 281; role in totalitarianism, 261; Stalinist, 261

architecture, Greco-Roman: in city of Rome, 254; immortality of, 368; imperialism of, 244; as Indo-Germanic, 60; influence on Nazi architecture, 2, 6, 241–44, 250–52, 283; monumentality of, 253

architecture, Nazi, 10; as allegory of *Führerprinzip*, 262; Allies' dynamiting of, 397; appeal to passions, 241; of Berlin, 246, 248, 251, 252–56; of Berlin *Olympiastadium*, 163–64, 165, 167, 251; Chaplin's parody of, 255–56; classical revival in, 243–44; for colonization, 281–82; cost of, 243, 255, 364; as cultural monument, 241–46; diachronic view of, 365; Doric style of, 88, 90, 245, 260, 284; effect of German power on, 246; exceptionalism in, 252; and Fascist EUR, 75; in German cities, 258–61; gigantism in, 246, 247, 252, 258–61; Greco-Roman influence on, 2, 6, 241–44, 250–52, 283–84; hieratism in, 258–61; Hitler's justification for, 368; Hitler's taste in, 241, 246, 252, 254, 268, 271–72; hybris in, 246–48; immortality in, 245; imperialism in, 241–46, 260; infrastructural, 240–41; links to past, 261; militarism and, 247; monumentality of, 246, 247–48, 250–52, 254, 261, 393; in Munich, 88–89; neoclassical, 165, 167; neo-empire style, 245–46; of Nuremberg, 230; of Olympic complex, 243; for posterity, 364; purpose of, 364–65; racial history in, 284; reflection of racial purity, 261; rivalry with American architecture, 248; stagecraft of, 261; stylistic changes in, 245–46; symbolism of, 241–48, 254, 283; testament to ancestors, 365; of Thingstätten, 205; Versailles treaty and, 247–28. *See also* ruins, Nazi

Ardennes, Battle of, 376
Arendt, Hannah: on totalitarianism, 6–7
Arent, Benno von, 255
Argonauts, as *Drang nach Osten*, 340
aristocracy, Germanic: sovereignty of, 230–33

Aristophanes, satirization of Cleon, 342
Aristotle: environmental determinism of, 67; Nazi neglect of, 206–7; political man of, 112, 206; rationalism of, 115, 207; on *zoon politikon*, 112. Works: *Metaphysics*, 195; *Politics*, 206
Armageddon, Nazi defeat as, 370
Arminius (Herman): classical civilization of, 71–72; defeat of Varus, 71, 78; Hitler and, 393; in Nazi ethos, 4
Arno Breker Steinbildhauerwerkstätten GmbH, 190
art: dialectic with body, 187; eternal language of, 390; Weimar, 189. *See also* sculpture
art, classical: rediscovery of, 156
art, degenerate, 174–75, 260; contamination from, 189; as cultural Bolshevism, 175; as mental illness, 175; subhumanity of, 189
art, European: Nazi plundering of, 41
art, German: Athena in, 10, 89, 96, 169; classicist, 88–91; kitsch in, 90, 151; state protection of, 89; in wood, 69
art, Greek: Hyperborean race in, 60; Nordic creativity in, 85; Weimar appreciation of, 138
art, Nazi, 7, 9; biological determinism in, 187; as challenge, 186; distribution of, 190; Nordic ideal of, 156, 176–77; performative function of, 186, 191; physical standards of, 172; for posterity, 368; public consumption of, 191; racial cultivation in, 186–87; racial ideal of, 173–75, 185; type and countertype in, 174–75. *See also* sculpture, Nazi
art, Nordic: creativity of, 85; expression of Indo-Germanic race, 188; Nazi, 156, 176–77
Artemis, Temple of (Ephesus), destruction of, 384
art history, Nordicist, 58–59, 60
artists, physical being of, 187–88
Aryanism: enduring culture of, 274; Nazi use of, 5; proof of, 3; of SS members, 3
Aryan migration: myth of, 20–24, 29–30, 33–35; teaching of, 37, 39
Aryan myth: in German identity, 136, 395; Hitler's support for, 77; Nazi use of, 5, 66. *See also* mythmaking
Aryan race: chaos following defeat of, 370; destruction through miscegenation, 127, 151, 395; enmity with Jews, 30, 352; Hitler's prophecy concerning, 360;

Aryan race *(continued)*
immortality of, 48; Northern origins of, 30; as Prometheus, 30–31, 49; at Thermopylae, 375. *See also* Indo-Germanic people
asceticism: eastern, 313; Oriental-Semitic, 181
Asia, Indo-Germanic homeland in, 26–27. *See also* East
Asiatic races: assault on ancient civilization, 351; as Horsemen of the Apocalypse, 292; nomadism of, 275
Athena: at Berlin Olympics, 165; in German art, 10, 89, 96, 170; as goddess of light, 62
Athens, classical: class-based politics of, 342; defeat by Sparta, 215; democracy of, 118, 215, 263, 270; de-Nordification of, 338; eupatridae of, 201; foreigners in, 341; imperialism of, 263; Nordic leadership of, 85, 201–2, 262; ostracism in, 343; racial miscegenation in, 208, 341; as symbol for philosophy, 249
Athens, modern: non-bombardment of, 270
athletes, Greek: sculpture of, 156
athleticism, German national, 170
Atlantis: Indo-Germanic myth of, 34–37; northern site for, 36; Plato's account of, 35; as Ultima Thule, 35
Augustus (emperor of Rome): civic crown of, 256; Hitler and, 244, 264, 283; Horace's celebration of, 131–32; in Nazi curriculum, 136; Nazi glorification of, 283; Nordic blood of, 333, 334, 341, 348, 355; as Nordic *führer*, 264; protonatalism of, 326, 329
Aurelius, Marcus: Stoicism of, 211
Austria, invasion of, 193–94
autobahn, Nazi, 240, 268
autochthony, Athenian, 20
autochthony, German: myth of, 48; and national identity, 18–20; Tacitus on, 19–20

backwardness, German, 96; archaeological evidence of, 70–71; versus Greco-Roman civilization, 66–69
Bannes, Joachim: *Hitlers Kampf und Platos Staat*, 199
Barcelona Expo (1929), functionalism of, 260
Baths of Diocletian, 254
Baudelaire, Charles, 187
Bäumler, Alfred: on German humanism, 110–11; "Nietzsche and National Socialism," 194; on Nordic purity, 127; on political man, 112–13, 206; use of Aristotle, 206
Baur, Erwin: eugenics work of, 327; Nordicism of, 27
Beauftragter des Führers für die Überwachung der... NSDAP (1934), 29
Beaune, Colette, 5
beauty, Greek ideal of, 158, 167, 188
beauty, racial: archetypes of, 172, 191; expression in art, 188; and Nazi eugenics, 189
Beer Hall Putsch (Munich, 1931), 88
"The Beginning of Roman Moral Decadence" (*Neue Jahrbücher*), 331–32
Being: Heidegger's philosophy of, 142, 143, 152; Nazi mechanization of, 145; ontological, 142
Beloch, Karl Julius: *Griechische Geschichte*, 52–53
Benda, Julian, 47
Benjamin, Walter: "The Work of Art in the Age of Mechanical Reproduction," 190
Benn, Gottfried: *Kunst und Macht*, 218–19
Benze, Rudolf, 289
Berenice (Herodian dynasty), 305
Berillon, Alphonse, 58
Berlin: arc de triomphe of, 253; as Athens of the North, 88; battle for (1945), 358, 360; city plan of, 248, 254–55; Doric capitals of, 255; east-west axis of, 255; gauleiters' imitation of, 259–60; Grosse Halle, 253–54, 384; Nazi imperialism in, 253; as new Rome, 397; north-south axis of, 255; Olympic bond with, 169; Pergamonmuseum, 258; Prussian royal axis of, 254–55; rebuilding as "Germania," 246, 251, 252–56, 259, 384; renaming as Germania, 252–56, 259, 689; Repräsentationsbauten of, 260; Roman baths of, 254; *Romanitas* of, 253; Roman plan of, 255; Unter den Linden, 255
Berve, Helmut, 47, 130; on Pericles, 263–64; on Sparta, 214, 216–17, 221, 222
Bewegung, Nazi: architectural inspiration for, 366
"Die Beweiskraft des Virbildes" (*Das Reich*), 377
Bilabel, Friedrich, 86
biological determinism, Nordicist, 59–60, 76; in art, 187; egalitarianism and, 209; view of history, 323
bios theoretikos, Western tradition of, 99

birthrate, ancient, 325
birthrate, Nordic: decline in, 325–27
Bismarck, Otto von, 215, 216
Black Order, Himmler's, 9, 162, 279, 292
blacks, in Nazi discourse, 173
blitzkrieg, German: into Greece (1941), 91–96, 97; mechanization of, 146
Bloch, Ernst, 240
Bloch, Marc, 48
blonds, Nordic: in antiquity, 56–58, 97, 201–2; decimation of, 201–2; in North Africa, 38; Roman, 58
blood: community of, 134, 191; in educational models, 133–34; Germanic, 76; Nordicist theory of, 59, 123. *See also* racial purity
bodily perfection: and interior virtue, 157–58; in Nazi utopia, 190
body: dialectic with art, 187; Germanic-Hellenic ennobling of, 182, 226; identification with spirit, 59, 171; Semitic stigmatization of, 180–81. *See also* nude sculpture, Nazi
body, Aryan: emulation of, 186, 191; versus Jewish body, 172–73; staging of, 185
body, German: individual responsibility for, 177; masculine ideal of, 158; Nazi cult of, 150; as possession of state, 177; racial, 172–75; rejuvenation of, 178
body, Greek: German fascination with, 156–59
Bogner, Hans: on Athenian democracy, 342; on Greek colonization, 274; on Jewish-Roman conflict, 299; on Olympic idea, 204; on Plato, 194, 195, 199; on racial miscegenation, 116; on Socrates, 212; on teaching of antiquity, 121. Works: *Der Seelenbegriff der griechischen Frühzeit*, 55–56, 141; *The Training of a Political Elite*, 118
Bolshevism: antiquity as weapon against, 123; as Asiatic attack, 351; Christianity as, 313–22, 396; Hitler on, 353–54; Jewish hatred in, 317; mobilization of oppressed, 316–17; Nazi fight against, 316, 319; Paul as precursor of, 308; in propaganda of defeat, 373; racial conflict in, 292. *See also* Judeo-Bolshevism
bonfires, solstice, 28
book burning, 174, 311; at University of Berlin, 113
Bormann, Martin: on Gothic script, 270; on Leonidas, 386
Boudicca, fate of, 384
Boulainvilliers, Henri de, 205
Bourdieu, Pierre, 8
boxing, Hitler on, 183
Brachmann, Wilhelm, 107; on Greek heritage, 123–24
Brasillach, Robert, 259
Braun, Eva, 365
Braunes Haus (Munich), 88
Breker, Arno: athlete sculptures of, 172; nudes of, 2, 9, 183–84; Prometheus figures of, 30; reproduction of works, 189–90; syncretic images of, 184. Works: *Auszug zum Kampf*, 184; *Die Partei*, 30, 183; *Der Wächter*, 184; *Die Wehrmacht*, 183–84
Brenner Pass incident (1934), 127–28
Bressa, Birgit, 185; on Beker, 190
Breywisch, Walter, 130
bridges, Roman: Nazi imitation of, 240–41
British Empire, Hitler's obsession with, 247
Brockhaus encyclopedia: on Alexander the Great, 348; on modern Greeks, 94; Nordicism in, 87
Die Brücke (artists' group), 89
Brutus, Lucius Junius, 271
Bucherer, Fritz, 106
Burckhardt, Jacob, 141; *Griechische Kulturgeschichte*, 159–60; on Sparta, 216
Butler, Eliza: *The tyranny of Greece over Germany*, 139–40

Caesar, Julius, 218; *The Gallic Wars*, 19, 135, 283; on Germania, 136; Hitler's emulation of, 234, 249, 283; imperialism of, 264; Jewish policy of, 264; *phronesis* of, 234; racial characteristics of, 63, 348; strategies of, 271
"Caesar," symbolism of, 249
Calgacus, Tacitus on, 235
Campanella, Tommaso: *The City of the Sun*, 187
Cannae, Battle of: Roman defeat at, 379, 380
capitalism: Jewish, 306; of Roman latifundia, 330
Caracalla (emperor of Rome): as "Negroid," 45; Oriental-Asiatic blood of, 336, 355; racial chaos under, 333, 335; Stoicism of, 209
Carthage: as mercantile state, 297; racial-political allegory of, 293–96; Roman destruction of, 235, 383, 389; as Semitic nemesis, 322. *See also* Punic Wars

cartography: of Indo-Germanic migration, 34–35; Nordicist, 39–40, 43
Cassirer, Ernst: *Essay on Man*, 10
Catalaunian Field, Battle of, 291–92
Catholic Church, Hitler on, 312
Cato the Elder, 271; on decadence, 332; *Delenda est Carthago* speech, 295; Nordic appearance of, 63
Cavafy, Constantine, 94
Céline, Louis-Ferdinand, 218
Chamberlain, Houston Stewart, 24, 195, 294; on emperors' racial characteristics, 334; *The Foundations of the Nineteenth Century*, 295; Social Darwinism of, 321
Chaplin, Charlie: *The Great Dictator*, 230, 255–56
Charlemagne: Hitler's admiration for, 270–71, 272; *renovatio imperii* by, 271, 283
Charles V (Holy Roman emperor), imperial ambitions of, 283
Chinese, as corrupted Aryans, 32–33
Christ, Karl, 216
Christian-Albrechts-Universität (Kiel), racial sciences at, 87
Christianity, Judaized: apodictic creed of, 312; as Bolshevism, 313–22, 396; as conspiracy, 309, 317, 318; cultural vandalism of, 320; destruction of ancient culture, 310–13, 320, 353–54; egalitarian, 308; Hitler's opposition to, 305–6, 311, 314–16; immobilization of German people, 314; incoherence of, 311; intolerance of, 314; mobilization of oppressed, 307, 316–17; Nazi condemnation of, 180–81, 191; obscurantism of, 310–13; Pauline, 296; repudiation of body, 313; role in racial degeneration, 313; self-hatred in, 313; SS confrontation with, 77; subversion of Roman Empire, 305–10, 315, 317–21, 322–23, 331; supranational ideology of, 318; universality of, 318, 319; as victory of darkness, 310, 312–13, 314
Cicero: anti-Semitism of, 303; on history, 99; Stoicism of, 209. Works: *Catiline Orations*, 135–36; *Republic*, 136
Cincinnatus, 271
cinema, Hitler's love of, 273
cities, ancient: public monuments of, 242, 251, 252
cities, German: Berlin model for, 259–60; Nazi architecture of, 258–61
cities, public/private space in, 241–42

city-states, Greek: fatalities in warfare, 327–28; natural law in, 202; as Nazi model, 225; Plato's ideal of, 195, 197, 198, 202, 210; racial aristocracy of, 281; war among, 199, 327–29
civilization: Apollonian-Dionysian dichotomies of, 60–62, 117; demise of, 327, 333, 351–54, 355; Indo-German creation of, 15, 34, 325; Nazi *Endkampf* for, 370; Nordic origin of, 18, 32; rise and fall of, 286; SA's, 72
civilization, Greco-Roman: Asiatic assaults on, 351; Christian destruction of, 310–13, 320, 353–54; de-Nordification of, 346; fall of, 288, 324, 333, 355; versus German backwardness, 66–69; Hitler's love of, 70, 71; Latin querelle concerning, 125–28; mortality of, 327–29; Nazi annexation of, 85; in Nazi education, 128–31; Nordic origins of, 82–83, 136. *See also* antiquity
civilization, Indo-European: myths of, 22
civilization, Indo-Germanic: claims for, 18, 32; fall of, 324–25, 327
civilization, Nordic: Hitler on, 49; Jewish war against, 298, 301; in Mediterranean, 85; as origin of all civilization, 18, 32; origins of, 50; teaching of, 40
civil wars, Roman: depopulation in, 328, 329, 330; and racial identity, 329
classical literature: body and mind in, 150; and curriculum of 1938, 135–36, 197; as expression of racial identity, 133; German values in, 130; Indo-Germanic-ness of, 134; instruction time for, 129; mixed-blood authors of, 133–34; in Nazi education, 128–31; Nazification of, 108–10, 132; in nineteenth-century Germany, 125; Nordic authors of, 134; political virtue in, 128–31, 133, 134; racist discourse concerning, 132. *See also* Latin literature
classicism: eighteenth-century, 156–58; French, 126–27, 137, 152; versus Germanophilia, 69–73, 119–22; Soviet, 261. *See also* Weimar classicism
classicism, Nazi: in educational reforms, 105–6; versus Germanophilia, 69–73; Hitler's, 70, 71, 73–74, 78, 150–51, 235, 245, 246, 268, 270, 289; in Munich, 88–81; place in Nazi state, 213–14
classicists, Third Reich: accommodations made by, 132–33; defense against Germanophiles, 124–25; devotion to

state, 108; and Nazi humanism, 106–10; Nordicism of, 29; reaction to educational reforms, 105–6; sincerity of, 7; on total man, 114. *See also* academics, Third Reich
Clauss, Ludwig Ferdinand, 55, 179; psychoracial typology of, 197
Cleon, class-based politics of, 342
Codex Aesinas, Ahnenerbe edition of, 80
coloniae: Greek, 274; Nordic, 277; Spartan, 279–82
coloniae, Roman: city plans of, 255; Nazi emulation of, 233, 260; Roman legionnaires in, 282
colonization: German frustration with, 276; role of architecture in, 281; victors' viewpoint on, 235
colonization, German: expansion of Occident, 291; medieval, 279
colonization, Nazi, 273–78; architecture of, 281–82; in the East, 278–79, 280–82; enslavement in, 281; Greek model of, 281; methods of, 280; in Nazi imaginary, 278–79; as new Roman Empire, 354; *Ostwall* for, 282; peasant warriors in, 281–82; permanence for, 281; racial hierarchy in, 281; slavery discourse in, 280; space for, 250; SS plan for, 278, 280; Wehrmacht in, 280
Colosseum, Hitler's admiration for, 272
Communist Party of the Soviet Union (CPSU), commissars of, 316
community: architectural expression of, 243; Aryan, 231; of blood, 134, 191; unitarian conception of, 213
community, Nazi: holistic, 204, 211; lack of class conflict, 222; political, 113, 125; sports in, 192
Confederation of the Rhine (1806–13), 137
Confucius, racial purity of, 32
Congrès international de la population (1937), 325
conspiracies, imagined, 7
Constantine (emperor of Rome), 315
Constitutio Antoniniana, Roman citizenship under, 209
Conte, Édouard, 28
contemplation, Western tradition of, 99
contraception, ancient use of, 328–39, 355
Conze, Alexander, 42
cosmology, Stoic, 207–8
Coubertin, Pierre de, 160–61, 162; internationalism of, 182; and Olympic flame, 167

creativity, cultural and natural, 188
creativity, Nordic, 32; in ancient texts, 134; classical nourishing of, 71; evidence for, 40; Greek art under, 85; in Hellenism, 350; teaching of, 84
Critias, collaboration with Lacedaemonians, 227
Crouzet, Denis, 10
cultural production, state-based, 231
culture, European: militarism and, 232; Nazi annexation of, 41–42
culture, Greek: at Berlin Olympics, 159–64; versus *Germanentum,* 122; and German medieval practices, 163; in Olympic propaganda, 160–63; as racial culture, 116–17; Roman corruption of, 111
culture, Indo-Germanic: creation of Greco-Roman culture, 79–80; fight for existence, 288; invention of, 40–43; Jewish subversion of, 123, 322; Nazi reassertion of, 5; spiritual values of, 122
culture, Latinate: German solidarity against, 126–27
culture, Nordic: and Greek art, 174; and medieval German art, 174; as original culture, 274; and Renaissance art, 174; SS propaganda on, 75–76
curricula, Nazi: discourse of antiquity in, 11; Plato in, 136, 196–97, 200. *See also* education, Nazi; pedagogy
Curtius, Ernst: excavation of Olympia, 161; *Der Wettkampf,* 159
Cynoscephalae, Battle of: Stoicism following, 209

damnatio memoriae: Allied practice of, 398; Nero's, 388; Roman, 397–98
d'Angers, David, 185
Darré, Richard Walther: agrarianism of, 274, 278, 284, 328; antimodernism of, 274, 278; *Das Bauerntum als Lebensquell der nordischen Rasse,* 274, 330; on Chinese people, 32; on Christianity, 313; on depopulation, 328; development of racial policies, 274–75; on lebensraum, 275; marginalization of, 278, 279; Nordicism of, 28, 32–33, 54; on Plato, 201; RUSHA leadership, 274, 277; on Spartans, 181, 225–26, 228
David, Jacques-Louis: classicism of, 157
Day of Potsdam (1933), 108
death: Hitler's obsession with, 365; immortality in, 369–73; Nazi ideology of, 364, 369, 395

Decius Mus (consul), in Nazi decorative art, 257
decorative arts, Nazi: classical mythology in, 256–58; of Reich Chancellery, 257
defeat, Nazi: as Armageddon, 370; cataclysmic, 394, 395; and fall of Rome, 387; as *finis Germaniae*, 390, 391; heroic myth of, 359; Hitler's choreography of, 372–73, 383; intransigence toward, 357–58, 360, 369–71, 385–86; Jewish question and, 371; meaning of, 359; morale-building before, 376–83; as *Niebelungenlied*, 358; nothingness in, 385; perseverance in face of, 373–76, 383; propaganda on, 373, 376; sacrifice in, 395; self-destruction in, 384–85; as spectacle, 358; suicide in, 376, 390, 391
defeatism, Nazi propaganda on, 381
defeats, Roman, 379, 380
deforestation, medieval, 68
degeneracy, racial, 172; in Hellenism, 213, 290, 338, 347–51; of Nordic Greeks, 94–95, 133–34, 201–2, 337, 344; of Romans, 133–34, 211
De Maistre, Joseph, 213
Demandt, Alexander, 269
democracy: egalitarian, 344–45; miscegenation in, 341–47, 356; Nordic, 341; Roman, 232; Spartan dislike for, 219
democracy, Athenian, 118, 215, 263, 270; *Adelsherrschaft* in, 342, 343; class struggle in, 343; demagogues in, 342; egalitarianism in, 342–43; as *Massherenschaft*, 343, 344; mesocracy in, 342; murder of Socrates, 345; racial bastardization of, 341–42
democracy, Germanic, 341–42; exclusivist model of, 342
denatalism, 325–27
de-Nordification (*Entnordnung*), 28; under Alexander the Great, 304, 305, 347, 348, 349; of Athens, 338; of Greco-Roman civilization, 214, 346; of Greece, 201, 207, 226, 346; of Hellenistic culture, 350; of Romans, 333–37, 355; of southern Europe, 338; of Sparta, 226. *See also* miscegenation, racial
"The De-Nordification of the Roman People" (*Volk und Rasse*), 333
depopulation, 325–27; in ancient warfare, 327–28, 329, 330; Nazi concern over, 327–30; through contraception, 328–39
Déroulède, Paul: celebration of Rome, 151
destruction, Nazi will to, 235, 384–85

"Destruction Measures within Reich Territory." *See* Nero Decree
Deutsche Arbeitsfront (DAF), 221–22
Deutsche Autobahnen: Adolf Hitlers Strassen, 237–38
Die deutschen Leibesübungen des Mittelalters in Buch und Bild (exhibit), 163
Die deutsche Polizei (journal): ideological pamphlets of, 39; Nordic migration in, 44
Deutscher Philologenverband (Association of German Philologists), manifesto of 1933, 106
Deutsches Ahnenerbe e. V., 27; archaeological research of, 79–80; and Atlantean hypothesis, 36; charter of, 78, 79; classical philology of, 80; Department of Classical Antiquity, 75–82; edition of *Codex Aesinas*, 80; excavations of, 80–81; *Germanenkunde* of, 77–78; Lehr- und Forschungseinrichtung für indogermanisch-arische Philologie under Kulturwissenschaft, 81; proof of Roman Nordicism, 79; publications of, 9
Deutsche Stadion (Nuremberg): cost of, 243; size of, 251
Deutschland Erwache! (NSDAP motto), 31, 256
Deutschland ordnet Europe neu! (1942), racialized Europe in, 44–45
"Deutschland über Alles in der Welt," 248
Deutschtum (Germanness), Nazi, 2; defect in, 4
Diadochi, rule of Alexandrine empire, 347, 350
diaspora, Jewish: into Nordic West, 321
Diem, Carl, 161, 168
Dieser Krieg ist ein weltanschaulicher Krieg (pamphlet), 296
Dietrich-Eckart Bühne, Handel's *Herakles* at, 165
Dinarics, among German people, 224, 281
Diodorus of Sicily, Günther's use of, 53
Dionysus: versus Apollo, 60–62; bacchanalian cult of, 61, 62; chthonic characteristics of, 61; Nietzschean ideal of, 60, 115
Discobolus, Lancelloti: state reception for, 176, 191
Discobolus, Myron's, 167, 176, 186
Dorians, 216; German historians on, 53; open villages of, 277; territoriality of, 279. *See also* Spartans

Drang nach Osten (Drive to the East), 4, 238, 279, 399; Argonauts as, 340
Drieu La Rochelle, Pierre, 259
Droysen, Johann Gustav, 141; on Alexander the Great, 216
Durchhalten (perseverance), 373–76; in Nazi intransigence, 369, 383

East: Alexander the Great's conquest of, 397, 399; asceticism from, 313; as instrument of Jews, 388; medieval German colonization of, 279; Nazi blitzkrieg in, 251, 280; Nazi colonization of, 278–79, 280–82; Nazi *Endkampf* with, 370; racial determinism of, 68; Wehrmacht colonization of, 280, 281–82
eastern front, stalemate on, 233
Easternization: in fall of Rome, 330–33; of Greece, 332
East-West struggle: Jews in, 299; millenary, 292; in Nazi education, 296–98; as preventive war, 299; as *Weltanschauungskampf*, 305
Eberhardt, Walter, 128; on Fascist Italy, 127; on Greek versus Latin education, 125–26
economy, German: state intervention in, 263
education, German nineteenth-century: Latin versus Greek in, 125–28. *See also* Gymnasien, German
education, Nazi: ancient history in, 119–22; body/soul unity in, 171, 181; classical literature in, 128–31; for community, 119, 125; conference on (May, 1933), 134–35; East-West struggle in, 296–98; German prehistory in, 119; Greek *paideia* and, 109; Hitler on, 99; Horace in, 131–32; physical education in, 104–5, 150, 178–79, 183; Plato in, 196; racial miscegenation in, 338–39; for racial state, 178–79; secondary, 122–24; Spartan model of, 118–19, 219–21; SS propaganda in, 82–86; state-oriented, 106; for survival of Reich, 125; in *Völkisch* state, 104–5; *Wehrsport* in, 119. *See also* curricula, Nazi; Greek language teaching; Latin language teaching; *paideia*; pedagogy
educational reform, Nazi, 99; of 1938, 39, 49–50, 83, 84, 102–3, 129, 135–36, 197, 297, 338; classicists' reaction to, 105–6; decree of 1935, 38–39, 83; of humanities, 105–10

egalitarianism: in democracy, 342–45; in fall of Rome, 308; Greek, 338; of Judaized Christianity, 308; and racial miscegenation, 209, 227; threat to Nordic elite, 323
Egyptians, Nordic origins of, 32
Ehrenberg, Viktor, 217
Ehrentempel (Munich), 88, 244
Eiselen, Ernst, 157
Eisenstein, Sergey: *Alexander Nevsky*, 279; Stalin's commissions for, 2
Elagabalus (emperor of Rome), Syrian blood of, 335
Elchrune (life rune), 27, 50, 81
Eleans, open villages of, 277
Eliade, Mircea, 396
elites, German: training of, 117–19
Elizabeth (empress of Russia), death of, 376
emperors, Roman: racial characteristics of, 333–34, 335, 336
empires, Western: Roman model for, 282–83
Encke, Erberhard, 166
Enlightenment: *Bildung* of, 76; concept of origins, 20–21; decadence of, 290; humanism of, 107, 203; rationality of, 102, 150; spiritual contamination from, 339
Ennius, on *mos maiorum*, 332
Entartete Kunst (Degenerate art) exhibit, 174–75
environmental determinism: in classical ethology, 67; of German backwardness, 66–69; of Italo-Alpine forests, 69
Ephialtes, 269
epics, Teutonic: in Nazi ethos, 4
Erasmus, humanism of, 107
eschatology, Nazi, 351, 354, 370, 390; nihilism of, 385
ethnotypes, Teutonic, 20
Etruscans, Nordic victory over, 85
euergetism, Roman, 252, 254
eugenics: idealized Greek figure in, 8; as natural law, 223; Seneca on, 223; Spartan practice of, 222–25, 228
eugenics, Nazi: artistic, 187; euthanasia in, 224; founders of, 327; and Nazi art, 156; and Nordic beauty, 189; Plato and, 200–204; racial canon of, 176; Spartan model for, 222–25, 228; training programs of, 176; for völkisch state, 175–76, 204
EUR (Esposizione Universale Roma), Nazi architecture and, 75

Euripides, *Medea*, 340
Europe: Nazi vision of, 1, 43–45; as Nordic empire, 43; Roman unification of, 44–45
Europe, southern: de-Nordification of, 338
euthanasia, Nazi: T4 program, 224
Der ewige Jude (film, 1941), 304–5
expansionism, Nazi: anxieties over, 230; global, 247; Indo-Germanicization in, 260
ex septentrione lux: versus *ex oriente lux,* 33, 34, 38, 49; propaganda of, 44
extermination: Jewish, 148, 224, 250; of Gypsies, 148; as racial self-defense, 299

Fabius Maximus Cunctator: delaying tactics of, 381–82; dictatorships of, 379–80; Hitler as, 382; resistance to popular will, 382, 383; victory of, 388
Febvre, Lucien: *Rabelais,* 10
Fest, Joachim, 268; on will to destroy, 384
Fester, Richard, 304
Festung Europa, 291; in Nazi discourse, 290
film, German, 11; classically themed, 90–91
film, Nazi, 166–67; propaganda, 173. See also Riefenstahl, Leni
Final Solution, 308, 314, 354; statistics for, 325
Fischer, Eugen: on Jewish question, 327; Nordicism of, 27. Works: *Das antike Weltjudentum,* 302–3; *Deutsche Köpfe nordischer Rasse,* 58
flames, sacred, 28, 167; Aeneas's, 169; in topography of ancient houses, 277
Flavian dynasty, Phalian/Dalic blood of, 333
Förster, Elizabeth, 194
France: contrast with Germany, 18; Empire style, 246; racial miscegenation in, 173, 344; relationship with ancient Rome, 137; unity of, 18. See also French Revolution
Frank, Walter: "Hannibal von den Toren," 379–80, 382; suicide of, 380
Frankfurt School, 46
Franz Josef (emperor of Austria), on Philhellenism, 269
Frederick Barbarossa, 279
Frederick II, the Great (king of Prussia), 372; comparison with Philip of Macedon, 216; Nazi invocation of, 371; Philhellenism of, 2; on salvation, 315; Seven Years' War of, 264, 373, 376, 377, 391

Freikörperkultur, 179. See also nudity
Freikorps, Günther in, 24
French Empire style, Speer on, 246
French Revolution, 126; Roman tropes of, 147, 157; Stoicism and, 210
Frick, Wilhelm: "Directives for History Textbooks," 267, 337; and *Olympiastadium,* 164; on political community, 113, 125; on political education, 134–35; racial science of, 25; on teaching of history, 119
Fried, Ferdinand: on Jewish impurity, 298–99; on Jewish revolt against Rome, 318; on re-Nordification of Rome, 309; on Roman jurists, 335–36; on Roman peasant-soldiers, 332. Works: *Latifundien vernichteten Rom!,* 330–31; *The Rise of the Jews,* 300, 336
Frobenius, Leo, 62
Führeraristokratie, Hitler's, 232
führer-as-sculptor metaphor, 177
Führergedanke, Plato's role in, 200
Führerpersönlichket, in antiquity, 262–64
Führerprinzip: Alexander the Great's betrayal of, 349; centralized state of, 232–33

Galton, Francis, 200; racism of, 321
Gauls, Roman, 72–73
Geary, Patrick, 48
Gehl, Walther, 220; on Attic democracy, 342; on racial war, 297
Gelzer, Matthias, 294
genealogy: German study of, 3; medieval, 5; of Nordic origins, 45–48; racist, 3
Generalplan Ost, enslavement in, 281
geopolitics, Nordic, 276
George, Stefan: revival of antiquity, 140
Germanentum (Germanicness), 66; Greco-Roman antiquity and, 76, 122, 123; Hellas and, 167–70, 182, 192; Hellenism as metaphor for, 139–40; Himmler's, 72; Hitler on, 70–71, 73–74; Nazism and, 149; racial relationship with Greece, 127; renaissance of, 182; and *Romanitas,* 125–28; in teaching of history, 121
German History (1937–1940), Nordicist history in, 39
"Germania": as new Rome, 397; rebuilding of Berlin as, 246, 251, 252–56, 259, 384
Germanien (SS journal), 253; Indo-Germanic studies in, 81

German language: dialects of, 18–19; primitivity of, 48; relationship to Greek, 54–55; relationship to Italian, 62–63
German Newsreel Archives, 11
Germanophilia: versus classicism, 69–73, 119–22; classicists' defense against, 124–25; Nazi hope for, 149; rejection of antiquity, 149–50; role of humanities in, 122–23; Saxon prehistory in, 97; SS, 69–71, 73, 74, 76
Germans, ancient: immobilization by Christianity, 314; legislative assemblies of, 205; Roman perspective on, 73; Teutonic clichés on, 72. *See also* prehistory, German
Germans, modern: betrayal of Hitler, 387; biological solidarity of, 108; continuity with ancient peoples, 394–95; as *Dichter und Denker*, 170; emulation of ancients, 271; Helotry among, 281; historicizing duty of, 146; kinship with Greeks and Romans, 64–65; mobilization for apocalypse, 352; preservation of Nordic blood, 337, 356; race potential of, 394; siege mentality of, 143; solidarity with ancient Nordic peoples, 123; special relationship with Greece, 136–42
Germany: contrast with France, 18; Great Men of, 266; interwar international relations of, 127–28; mythological vacuum of, 140; as Nordic *Urheimat*, 29; political access in Greece, 141; religious divisions of, 19; self-creation of, 48; sovereign states of, 18; unification of, 236. *See also* Third Reich; Weimar Republic
Germany, ancient: Roman aversion to, 67, 68–69; as womb of civilizations, 34. *See also* prehistory, German
Germany, medieval: colonization of East, 279; *Drang nach Osten* of, 238; Gothic cathedrals of, 242; Greek culture and, 163; Himmler's love of, 279; Nordic culture of, 174; politics of empire, 45
Germany, Nazi: Allied bombardment of, 388, 389; eastern frontier of, 279–82; physical renewal of, 218; political community of, 113; racial unification of, 237; rearmament of, 152; road construction in, 237–41. *See also* Third Reich
Germany, nineteenth-century: education in, 125; French threats to, 137, 139;

Helleno-German kinship in, 139–41; Victorian morality of, 184
Geschichte, versus *Historie*, 46, 99
Gewalt (violence), in Hitler's aesthetics, 247
Geyer, Fritz: on democracy, 343; on Easternization of Rome, 329, 332; on end of antiquity, 336–37; on Peloponnesian Wars, 328; *Rasse, Volk und Staat im Altertum*, 290
Gobineau, Arthur de, 24, 286; on miscegenation, 209, 344; Nordicism of, 53; view of democracy, 343–44
God, death of, 385
Goebbels, Joseph, 91; and Berlin Olympics, 168; brown-red Nazism of, 222, 374; on Christianity, 312; on defeat, 359, 386–87; discourse of spectacle, 358; on German democracy, 341–42; "Die Geschichte als Lehrmeisterin," 377; on Great Men, 265–66; on Hitler's classicism, 270, 289; on international Jewry, 304; intransigence in defeat, 358, 383, 386; on Jewish question, 371; morale-building propaganda of, 377–78; on Nazi remembrance, 398; and *Olympiastadium*, 164; on Punic War, 295, 379; remembrance of, 398; on shaping of masses, 177; Spartan tropes of, 222; total war proclamation, 352, 373–74; on victory, 378–79
Goethe, Johann Wolfgang von: avoidance of Greece, 140; martial verses of, 381; Napoleon's request to, 139; "Prometheus," 31
"The Golden Centuries of German Culture" (parade, 1933), 89
Gorgon, in Nazi decorative arts, 258
Göring, Hermann: at Berlin Olympics, 165; on physical training, 183; Spartan imagery of, 374–75; on Stalingrad defeat, 374
Gothic cathedrals, 242
Gothic script, Hitler's rejection of, 270
Great Flood myth, Indian subcontinent in, 21
Great Man theory (history): in antiquity, 266, 267, 268, 271; Goebbels on, 265–66; Hitler and, 265–68, 269, 270–71; in Nazi defeat, 359
Greco-Persian Wars, 91, 346; defense against Asian race in, 85, 92, 93; as racial conflict, 297
Greece: de-Nordification of, 207, 226, 346; depopulation of, 355; egalitarianism in,

486 | Index

Greece *(continued)*
338; fall to East, 297; German blitzkrieg into (1941), 91–96, 97; as German model, 138; German royal family of, 141; inclusion in Nordicism, 29, 30; Indo-Germanic aspects of, 26, 79, 97; Indo-Germanic migrations to, 60; Mussolini's armies in, 270; Nordicist history of, 85; in Nordic pedagogy, 38; oligarchy versus democracy in, 118; Orientalization of, 297, 332; Philhellenist avoidance of, 140; racial laws of, 341; racial suicide of, 338; racist reinterpretations of, 227; special relationship with Germany, 136–42; *translatio studii et imperii* from, 346; in Weimar classicism, 138–39

Greek language, relationship to German, 54–55

Greek language teaching: German values in, 108–9; guidelines for, 136; versus Latin, 125–26; Nazi reforms affecting, 106; Plato in, 197; in secondary schools, 122, 123, 124

Greeks, ancient: Apollonian-Dionysian dichotomy among, 61–62; Hellenistic, 116–17; Homeric, 55; Jewish imitation of, 302; Levantine, 345; physical deformity of, 350–51; racial types of, 60

Greeks, modern: at Berlin Olympics, 92; Nazi terrorization of, 92; phenomenological evident for, 95; racial composition of, 93, 94–96; resistance to Nazis, 93

Greeks, Nordic, 5, 6, 7–8, 38, 39; academic validation of, 96–97; active ideal of, 160; Asiatics and, 294, 337, 346; body and spirit in, 171; ethology of, 52–55; Germanists' depictions of, 124; Hellenistic corruption of, 115–17, 208; heroic mythology of, 369; Hitler on, 93; holistic body politic of, 210; Jewish persecution of, 300; miscegenation among, 285–86, 337–38, 339, 346, 356; purity of, 127; racial degeneration of, 94–95, 133–34, 201–2, 337, 344; racial heritage from, 160–61; scholarly validation of, 51; sculptural proof of, 158–59; in teaching of history, 120; total man of, 114; use of conraception, 328–39; use of swastika, 163

Grégoire, Abbé, 21

Greiner, Josef, 268

"Greuelpropaganda im Altertum-Fortsetzung" (*Das Schwarze Korps*, 1935), 73

Grimm, Jacob: *Geschichte der Deutschen Sprache*, 23

Grösfaz, Hitler as, 233, 283

Gross, Walter, 289; *Deine Ehre ist die Treue zum Blute deines Volkes*, 339–40

Grosse deutsche Kunstausstellung (exhibition), 174

Günther, Hans, 49; academic career of, 25; accolades of, 25; on ancient racial history, 338; on Apollonian-Dionysian dichotomy, 61; art historical descriptions of, 59; on Attic noblesse, 201; citation of Jordanes, 28; classicism of, 122–23; on eugenics, 203; in Freikorps, 24; on Germanomania, 121–22; Greek ethology of, 52–55; on Helen of Troy, 56–57; on Hellenism, 350; at Jena, 86; linguistics of, 53; mentoring of SS, 28, 29; mythography of, 53; Nordicism of, 24–28; on Nordic Romans, 62–64; pedagogical use of, 38; on Plato, 195, 196, 200, 223; Platonic racism of, 212; racial symptomatology of, 203; on Socrates, 212–13; on Stoicism, 209, 211; use of paleontology, 56. Works: *Deutsche Köpfe nordischer Rasse*, 58; *Die nordische Rasse bei den Indogermanen Asiens*, 26–27; *Rassenkunde des Deutschen Volkes*, 24, 26, 28, 52–55

Gustloff, Wilhelm, 265

Guts Muth, J.F.C., 157, 160

Gymnasien, German: defense of, 107; Greek paradigm for, 151; motto of, 157; and Nazi education, 109; and physical training, 178; production of leaders, 109. *See also* education, German nineteenth-century

Gymnasien, Greek: pedagogical method of, 100

Gypsies, extermination of, 148

Hadrian (emperor of Rome): and Antinous, 140; defeat of Jews, 300, 301; non-Nordic blood of, 333

hakenkreuz: Nordic Greek use of, 163; as Nordic symbol, 42–43; settings of, 256–57. *See also* swastika

Hanfstaengl, Ernst, 268, 269

Hannibal: elephants of, 379; in Nazi propaganda, 379–83, 389; Stalin as, 391; technology of, 234

Harlan, Veit: *Der ewige Jude*, 173

Haus der deutsche Kunst (Munich), 88–91;
  Great German Art exhibition at, 174;
  opening of, 174, 175, 368
Hegel, Georg Wilhelm Friedrich: on
  Athenian democracy, 215; on East-West
  migration, 33; *Lectures on the
  Philosophy of World History*, 23;
  Rosenberg's attack on, 33–34
Heidegger, Martin, 90, 127; on armed
  services, 198; break with Nazism,
  144–47, 148; concept of *Verfallen*, 142;
  on death of God, 385; engagement with
  NSDAP, 142, 148–49; on German
  universities' mission, 143–44; and Greek
  metaphysics, 142–47; hosting of Nazi
  youth, 119; on Indo-Germanic people,
  147; ontology of, 218; rectoral address
  (1933), 142, 144; rectorate at
  Heidelberg, 119, 148–49; rehabilitation
  of pre-Socratics, 142; on service to state,
  144; on technological modernity, 143;
  on use of antiquity, 147–48, 152; on
  Wehrsport, 119, 144; on Western
  destiny, 142. Works: *Basic Concepts*,
  147–48; *Introduction to Metaphysics*,
  148; "The Threat to Science", 144
Heidelberg, Indo-Germanic studies at, 86
Heidemann, Hans, 166
Heiligenberg, *Thingplatz* of, 205
Heissmeyer, August, 119
Helen of Troy, Nordic characteristics of,
  56–57
Hellenism: Alexandrine, 302, 347, 350;
  corruption of Nordic Greece, 115–17,
  208; cosmopolitanism of, 210; fight for
  existence, 319; individualism of, 115;
  Nordic creativity in, 350; Orientalized,
  115–16; racial degeneration of, 213,
  290, 338, 347–51; and *Romanitas*, 133;
  Semitic subversion in, 350; "Westic-
  Mediterranean" blood in, 350
Helots, Spartan: in Nazi colonization
  discourse, 280, 281; Nordic domination
  of, 226, 228; in SS culture, 280–81
Henry the Fowler (king of Germany), 279
Henry the Lion, in Nazi ethos, 4, 279
Henry II the Pious, defeat of Mongols, 93
Heraclitus, 368; concept of time, 396; on
  war, 198
Hercules: labors of, 53; as Nordic hero,
  165
Hermannsdenkmal monument (Detmold),
  72
Herodes Atticus, Athenian stadium of, 259

Herodotus, 375; Günther's use of, 53; on
  roads, 238, 239
heroes, funeral orations of, 271
heroes, Nazi, 265, 266; apotheosis of, 365;
  farmers, 274; tragic sacrifice of, 364. *See
  also* Great Man theory
Herostratus, 383; destruction of Temple of
  Artemis, 384
Herrenmenschen, Homeric Greeks as, 55
Herriot, Édouard: école unique of, 204
Herrmann, Albert: *Unsere Ahnen und
  Atlantis*, 36
Hesiod, on nobility of labor, 109
Heydrich, Reinhard: on frontier security,
  282; on Helotization, 280
Heyse, Hans, 200
Hildebrandt, Kurt: on eugenics, 202–4; on
  Plato, 195, 198, 199, 202–3; *Staat und
  Rasse*, 202–3
Himmler, Heinrich: archaeological projects
  of, 70, 74, 78; and Atlantean hypothesis, 36; Black Order of, 9, 162, 279,
  292; claims of racial morality, 112; on
  German birthrates, 326; Germanophilia
  of, 69–70, 72, 73, 76–77; on Greek
  racial greatness, 82; and Hitler's
  classicism, 78; love of esoterica, 36, 82;
  love of German Middle Ages, 279;
  mysticism of, 76; Nordicism of, 28; on
  past, present, and future, 9; on
  peasant-solder colonizers, 282;
  protonatalism of, 326; racial-anthropological projects of, 82; on Roman
  antiquity, 78–79; on separate peace,
  370; on *ver sacrum*, 280
historians, Third Reich: devotion to state,
  108; obedience to educational reforms,
  105; service to Nazism, 46–47. *See also*
  academics
historical reenactments, German, 89–90
Historie, versus *Geschichte*, 46, 99
historiography, German nineteenth-century,
  8; on antiquity, 52–53, 140–41; on
  image of Germans, 28; inertia in, 120;
  on invasion of Rome, 65–66; Nazi use
  of, 47
historiography, nationalistic: European
  nationalism and, 48
history: ancient concept of, 99, 100; Cicero
  on, 99; cyclical, 321, 323; function of,
  250; Great Man theory of, 265–68;
  Hegelian reading of, 10; Hitler's view of,
  99–105; humanist versus racist, 110;
  lessons of, 102; minimalist, 103;

history *(continued)*
  monocausal explanations of, 7;
  monumental, 250; Nazi appropriation
  of, 7, 15, 45–46, 394; Nazi distrust of,
  396; Nazi ideology of, 12, 46; Nazi
  mythmaking in, 45–46; Nazi philosophy
  of, 320, 321, 323; in Nazi *Völkisch*
  state, 104; political uses of, 83, 103–4;
  proofs from, 104; as racial conflict,
  287–90, 320; racial past in, 46; racial
  reading of, 336; systematic, 99
history, ancient: Asiatic assaults in, 351;
  body and mind in, 150; glorification of,
  13; imitation of, 13; mythologized, 387;
  in Nazi education, 119–22; Nazi
  reforms affecting, 106, 109; Nazi
  relationship with, 167; Nordic
  perspective on, 120–21, 324; as
  premonition, 13; projection of Nazi
  ideology onto, 13; and racial anthropology, 120–21; rewriting of, 12, 323; in
  secondary schools, 122, 123, 124; teaching of, 37
history, German: as European history, 43;
  Nazi invention of, 48; Nordicist
  teaching of, 39; popular works on, 40;
  reversals of fortune in, 381. *See also*
  prehistory, German
history, Indo-Germanic: Roman history as,
  12; swastika in, 42–43
history, Roman: ancient historiographers
  on, 99; Hitler on, 12, 128, 230, 268–71,
  397; Hitler's use of, 233–37; Indo-Germanic history as, 12; lessons from, 230;
  racial conflict in, 294; racial reading of,
  336
Hitler, Adolf, 99; admiration for antiquity,
  70, 71, 73–74, 77, 96, 230, 268–73;
  admiration for Mussolini, 269; aesthetic
  sense of, 245–46, 247, 367, 384;
  agnosticism of, 306, 315; anti-Christianity of, 305–6, 311, 314–16; apocalyptic
  discourse of, 353–54; appearance of
  optimism, 372; architectural taste of,
  241, 246, 252, 254, 268, 271–72; on
  Arminius, 72; art of, 385; on Asiatic
  assaults, 351; attention to decorative
  arts, 256–58; and Augustus, 244, 264,
  283; Austrian nationality of, 269; as
  autodidact, 268–73, 284; on betrayal,
  387; on blonds, 58; on boxing, 183;
  choreographing of defeat, 372–73, 383,
  395, 398; classicism of, 70, 71, 73–74,
  78, 150–51, 235, 245, 246, 268, 270;
  289; on crisis of culture, 218; on death
  of Rome, 354; declaration of war
  (1939), 371; on demise of antiquity,
  354; on denatalism, 326; desire for
  immortality, 243; on *Discobolus*, 176,
  186, 191; education of, 99, 102, 267;
  emulation of Caesar, 234, 249, 283;
  environmental determinism of, 67–69;
  fascination with *Rienzi*, 11, 262–64,
  360–61; on German backwardness,
  66–67; on *Germanentum*, 70–71; and
  Great Man theory, 265–68, 269,
  270–71; on Greek ancestors, 66; on
  Greek beauty, 158; as Herostratus, 383;
  hypochondria of, 365; imprisonment of,
  369; indulgence in fantasy, 273, 311;
  intransigence in defeat, 358, 372–73,
  384, 386–87; justification of annexations, 92–93; as Leonidas, 386; at Linz
  realschule, 99, 102; on local government, 232–33; on loss of war, 366; love
  of cinema, 273; on materialism, 262; on
  meaning of defeat, 359; megalomania
  of, 246, 248, 250, 252, 254; mythbuilding by, 320, 384, 386–87, 397; on
  new man, 175; and Nietzsche, 194–95;
  on Nordic civilization, 49; Nordicism
  of, 29; obsession with death, 365; on
  Olympiastadium, 164; as *pater patriae*,
  256; Pericles and, 262–64, 268; plunder
  of museums, 15; on preservation of
  species, 306; on Prometheus myth, 49;
  as prophet, 352–53, 359–60; on purpose
  of architecture, 364–65; racial
  Darwinianism of, 288; reading of
  Tacitus, 68; reading tastes, 268–69;
  relationship with Mussolini, 74, 127;
  remembrance of, 398; on road
  construction, 237; on Roman diet, 233;
  on Roman genealogy, 7; on Roman
  history, 12, 128, 230, 268–71, 397; as
  sculptor, 177; self-representations of,
  361, 366; silverware of, 273; on Sparta,
  223–24, 225, 228, 236; on sports, 176;
  on St. Paul, 306, 307–9; suicide of, 384;
  support for Aryan myth, 77; table talks
  of, 67–69; on teaching of history,
  266–67; on unconditional resistance,
  371; use of Mommsen, 304; vegetarianism, 233; on Versailles Treaty, 371–72;
  Viennese manners of, 273; visit to
  Rome, 254, 272
  —*Mein Kampf*, 66–67; antiquity in, 271,
  288; Aryan-Jewish enmity in, 30; binary

Index | 489

logic of, 385; Christianity in, 305, 312, 314; composition of, 369; demise of civilizations in, 333; educational ideas in, 99, 129, 287, 288; *führer* figure in, 262; Great Man theory in, 266–67, 268, 271; Greco-Roman antiquity in, 150–51; laws of nature in, 352; Pericles in, 263; physical training, 178–79; Pötsch in, 267–68; Prometheus in, 169; on public architecture, 242; racial conflict in, 287; on racial unity, 1, 319; Roman history in, 230; single adversary theory of, 321; sovereignty in, 231; Spartan education in, 221; teaching of history in, 287, 288; typology of race in, 211; view of history, 99, 101, 102–5
—*Skizzenbuch*, 253
—"Why Are We Anti-Semites?," 23–24
—*Zweites Buch*, 223–24, 236
Hitlerjugend, racial propaganda for, 339–40
Hoheitsadler (Romanesque eagle), 89
Hohmann, Walter, 297, 298, 332, 342
Hölderlin, Friedrich: "Gesang der Deutschen," 160; love of Greece, 138, 139, 140
Holocaust, technological modernity of, 148
Holtorf, Hans, 200
Holy Roman Empire: French victory over, 18; Hitler on, 69–70; Nazi use of, 4
Homer: blonds in, 56–57; Greek soul in, 55; Nordic figures of, 59
homoioi: national unity of, 374; Spartan, 222
Hopkins, Harry L., 389
hoplites, Greek: German statues of, 184
Horace: aestheticism of, 131; association with *Volksgemeinschaft*, 132; celebration of Augustus, 131–32; in Nazi education, 131–32, 151
"Horst-Wessel-Lied," 248
Hosaeus, Hermann: bas-relief nude of, 375
houses, ancient: semiotics of, 277
houses, Germanic: and Greco-Roman houses, 277
Huber, Erwin, 167
humanism: apolitical, 107; body and soul in, 150; conflict with Nazism, 110; equality in, 76; European, 110; individualistic, 213; Nazi attacks on, 195–96; Nordicist, 110; Plato's, 195; racial perspective on, 108; Renaissance, 110; Schiller's, 114
humanism, Enlightenment, 107, 203; Nazi opposition to, 210–11

humanism, Nazi, 106–13; Indo-Germanic elements of, 115; legitimization of, 111–12; manifestos for, 106–10; for political man, 106–10; racial morality of, 112; racial selection in, 116; "third," 106–10
humanities: in German culture, 107–8; Nazi reform of, 105–10; in understanding of Indo-German heritage, 122–23
humanities, Indo-Germanic, 122–25; role in racial identity, 123
humanities, Nazi: service to community, 113
humanity, Socrates' conception of, 212
humanity, Germanic: relationship with technology, 149; universal domination of, 79
Humboldt, Wilhelm von: *Geschichte des Verfalls und Untergangs der griechischen Freistaaten*, 140–41; on Greek-German relationship, 138; on Sparta, 215
Hyperborean peoples: in Greek art, 60; Nordicist theory of, 53

iconoclasm, Christian, 272
iconography, Nazi: classical influences in, 11; Prometheus in, 31
idealism, Platonic, 196
idealism, Aryan: versus Jewish materialism, 231
identity: origin and, 17; psychological, 55. *See also* national identity, German
identity, Greek: Nazi seizure of, 10
identity, racial: Indo-Germanic humanities in, 123; maps of, 43
identity, Roman: civil wars and, 329; Nazi seizure of, 10
ideology, Nazi: of death, 364, 369; exclusionary, 149, 393; of historical mythology, 12, 46; indoctrination into, 9; the past in, 393; projection onto ancient history, 13; revision of antiquity, 397
imperialism, German: French opposition to, 126–27; Indo-Germanic people under, 124; oppressiveness of, 114; road construction in, 237–38; Russian resistance to, 2
imperialism, Nazi: in architecture, 241–46, 260; in Berlin, 253; in infrastructure, 237–41
imperialism, Roman: architecture of, 244; and French aggression, 137; monumentality of, 240

imperium romanum, European pretenders to, 1
India: in Great Flood myth, 21; origin myths of, 20–23, 395; travel narratives of, 21. *See also* Out-of-India (*Urheimat*) theory
indigenae, Roman idea of, 19–20
individualism, Western: versus group membership, 99; private space in, 242; "Spartanism" and, 217; Stoic, 211
Indo-Europeans: Asian homeland of, 81; origin myths of, 20–23
Indo-Germanic migration, 45; belief in, 91; to Greece, 60; linguistic arguments for, 55; maps of, 34–35, 39–40; Nazi archaeological study of, 80–81; overpopulation and, 84
Indo-Germanic past: invention of, 40–43; setback to, 9
Indo-Germanic people: active ideal of, 159–60; agrarian, 274–75, 276–77, 284; appropriation of Greco-Roman antiquity, 75, 111, 162; of Asia, 25–27; assimilation of Jews into, 302; civilizational claims of, 15, 18, 32, 325; cultural creativity of, 15, 79–80, 285; decisiveness of, 111; effect of liberalism on, 124; environmental determinism of, 69; under German imperialism, 124; Heidegger on, 147; heroic ethos of, 84; imaginary of, 82; Jewish hatred for, 321; lebensraum for, 273–78; miscegenation among, 333; neglect of Nordic blood, 356; new humanism of, 108; Nordicist teaching on, 39; Nordic tongue of, 27; psychological identity of, 55; in racial past, 40; racial scientists on, 55–56; versus Semitic people, 78; showdown with East, 293; sun worship of, 82; textbook accounts of, 83–85; as true humans, 112; *ver sacrum* ritual for, 280; as warrior-peasants, 277–78. *See also* Aryan race; Nordic peoples
Indomania, German, 22–23
Ingrao, Christian, 278
insignia, Nazi: Hitler's attention to, 256
Italian language, relationship to German, 62–63
Italy: deforestation of, 69; Indo-German aspects of, 79; relationship with ancient Rome, 137; Roman unification of, 85
Italy, Fascist: abandonment of Axis, 79; anti-German contempt in, 127; cultural politics of, 2; invasion of Ethiopia, 127; and Nazi Germany, 12; in Pact of Steel, 78, 97, 127; relations with Germany, 127–28; use of antiquity, 2

Jäckel, Eberhardt, 99
Jaeger, Werner: on grammatical formalism, 130; on Plato, 195–96; third humanism of, 106–10
Jahn, Friedrich Ludwig, 160; *Die deutsche Turnkunst*, 157
Jason and Medea, racialized myth of, 340–41
Jena, University of: Indo-Germanic studies at, 86
Jerphagnon, Lucien, 10
Jerusalem, Roman conquest of, 296, 322
Jesus, Paul's subversion of, 306, 307
Jewish conspiracy, 309, 317, 318, 396; genealogy of, 322; protean character of, 322; against Rome, 321–22; universal, 320
Jewish question, 327; in antiquity, 298–301; Nazi defeat and, 371
Jewry, international: and global empire, 305; Hitler's prophecy on, 353; in Pax Romana, 303; in propaganda films, 304–5
Jews: anthropometric characteristics of, 173; as cause of decadence, 289; East as instrument of, 388; intermarriage with Germans, 334; materialism of, 262; millennial war with Aryans, 352; Nordicist theories on, 58; Orientalism and, 298; as parasites, 300, 303; rise to power, 303; trickery of, 303
Jews, ancient: abandonment of Hebrew, 302; adoption of host names, 302; assimilation of, 116, 173, 301–5, 304; conflict with Rome, 296, 299, 300–301; corruption of host race, 301–2; destruction of Greco-Roman antiquity, 289, 353–54; in East-West struggle, 299; linguistic assimilation of, 302; merchants, 301; nomadism of, 301; pogrom against Persians, 300; racial makeup of, 299; war against Nordic civilization, 296, 298, 301
J. F. Lehmanns Verlag: Nazi publications of, 24, 57, 60, 64; racial anthropology contributors, 95
Jones, William, 22
Jordanes (historian), 50; Günther's citation of, 28
Josephus, Flavius: perjury of, 301

Jouvenel, Bertrand de, 321
Judeo-Bolshevism: final phase of, 356; plot against Nazi Germany, 323; *Schicksalkampf* with Nordic peoples, 352; weakness in face of, 385. See also Bolshevism
Le Juif éternel (exhibition), 172
Julia Mamaea, Empress: non-Nordic blood of, 333–34
Julian the Apostate (emperor of Rome), Hitler's admiration for, 315–16
Julius Paulus (jurist), 336
Juvenal: anti-Semitism of, 303; on Easternization, 331, 355–56; *Satires*, 331

Der kampf um unsere Weltanshauung (training pamphlet), 303
Kant, Immanuel: Nazi view of, 196; on prophecy, 360
KdF-Schiff Wilhelm Gustloff, Roman mosaics of, 257
kinship, Helleno-German, 1, 64–65, 204; at Berlin Olympics, 136, 159–70, 192; physical training in, 179; pre-Nazi idea of, 47; racial, 136–42
kitsch, antique: Hitler's taste for, 272
kitsch, German: 90, 151; *Völkisch*, 72
Kittel, Gerhard: *Das antike Weltjudentum*, 302–3
Kladderadatsch (satirical weekly), führer-as-sculptor metaphor, 177
Klagges, Dietrich: *Geschichtsunterricht als nationalpolitische Erziehung*, 83; "The Racial Question is the Key to World History," 289
Klein, Richard, 89
Klingeberg, Werner, 168
Kogon, Eugen, 225, 281
Kokoschka, Oscar, 175
Königsplatz (Munich), 243; Nazi architecture of, 88
Korherr, Richard: "The Death of Ancient Civilizations," 326; *Geburtenrückgang*, 325–26
Kornemann, Ernst, 337
Körperkultur, Nordic, 192
Kossina, Gustaf, 37, 38, 150; prehistorical studies of, 70
Krause, Hans-Konrad, 54
Kreis, Wilhelm, 252
Krieck, Ernst, 198; on Aristotle, 207; on Greek man, 117; on Greek paideia, 114–15

Kriegseinsatz der deutschen Geisteswissenshchaften, 294
Kubizek, August, 269; credibility of, 363; on *Rienzi*, 362–63
Kuhn, Georg, 302
Kulturbolschewismus (cultural Bolshevism), 175, 189
Kulturkampf, against French classicism, 126–27, 137
Die Kunst im Deutschen Reich (revue), on bridges, 240
Die Kunst im Dritten Reich (art review), 89; antiquity in, 11
Kunst- und Kulturgutraub, Nazi: objectives of, 41
Kynast, Karl, 60, 115; *Apollon und Dionysos*, 345

Lacedaemonians: in Adolf-Hitler-Schulen textbooks, 219; Critias's collaboration with, 227; discretion of, 214; kinship with Chinese, 32–33. See also Spartans
Lake Trasimene, Roman defeat at, 379
Lammers, Hans, 164; on Gothic script, 270
Landsberg Prison, Hitler in, 369
Lange, Heinrich, 376
Laocoön (sculpture), 156, 158
Lapis Niger (Roman Forum), 78
latifundia, Roman: capitalistic, 330; Eastern slaves on, 331, 355
Latin language: as mental gymnastics, 128, 129; Roman character in, 130
Latin language teaching: defenders of, 151; German values in, 108–9; "grammaticism" in, 130; versus Greek, 125–26; guidelines for, 135–36; Hitler on, 288–89; Nazi reforms affecting, 106; in Philhellenic Germany, 151; Roman virtue in, 128–31; in secondary schools, 122, 123, 124
Latin literature: anti-Semitism in, 303; Easternization of, 331
Latium, racial republic of, 296, 297
Lavater, Johann Kaspar: *Essays on Physiognomy*, 157
law, natural: eugenics as, 223; in Greek city-states, 202; *Kampf* as, 358–59
law, Roman: degeneration of, 45; Judaization of, 335–36; Western law from, 230
leadership: in antiquity, 262–68; cult of, 265–68; Nordic, 85, 201–2, 262–64
leadership, Nazi: belief in Nazi myth, 398; democratic, 342; and Greek leaders, 262–63

Lebensbejahung (affirmation of life), 331
lebensraum: in antiquity, 273–78;
  Indo-Germanic, 273–78; Nazi, 67, 276;
  and Treaty of Versailles, 276
Lebensreform (back-to-nature movement),
  115; physical exercise in, 179
legionnaires, Roman: diet for, 233;
  Easternization of, 331; German, 71–72,
  309; mercenaries, 236; settlement of
  colonies, 282; supplying of, 233; and
  Teutonic Knights, 290–91; *Wehrmacht*
  and, 233–37
Lehmann, Julius Friedrich, 24
Leistungsmenchen (men of achievement), 55
Lemcke, Walter, 168
Lenz, Fritz: on class struggle, 330; eugenics
  work of, 222–23, 327–28; Nordicism
  of, 27
Leonidas (king of Sparta): as allegory of
  sacrifice, 375–76; farewell to wife, 223;
  and Persian effeminacy, 180; at
  Thermopylae, 91, 92, 93, 373, 388, 391
Leonidas-Staffel (suicide squadron), 376
Le Rider, Jacques, 269
Lessing, Gotthold Ephraim, 126
Lewald, Theodor, 168
Library of Alexandria, destruction of, 311
Lichtenberger, Henri: *L'Allemagne nouvelle*,
  217–18
Liebelfels, Jörg von, 23
light, Apollonian cult of, 61, 62
linguistics, Nordicist, 53–55, 86
Linz realschule, Hitler at, 99, 102
List, Guido von, 23
Livia (wife of Augustus), Nordic blood of,
  333
Livy, *The History of Rome*, 135
Loraux, Nicole, 271
Losemann, Völker, 80
Louis, Spiridon, 92
Ludwig I (king of Bavaria), Philhellenism of,
  2, 88, 90
Luftwaffe KG 200, suicide missions of, 376
Luther, Martin: Bible translation of, 18;
  defiance of Rome, 137; intellectualiza-
  tion of faith, 139–40
Lycurgus, eugenics of, 222–23
Lysander, 345

Mader, Ludwig, 130
magna mater alma (Great Mother), Nordic
  closeness to, 179
Mahnkopf, Johannes: *On the Prehistory of
  the Greater German Reich*, 41

Malthusianism, 276; in Greco-Roman
  antiquity, 325–27
Männerbund: Nazi celebration of, 131;
  training of, 117. *See also* soldiers,
  German
Marathon, Battle of, 290, 291
March, Werner, 251
marriage, interracial: Greek-Persian, 349;
  Jason and Medea, 340–41; Jews with
  Germans, 334; patricians with
  plebeians, 334. *See also* miscegenation,
  racial
Mars, in Nazi decorative arts, 258
Martial, anti-Semitism of, 303
Marx, Karl: on French classicism, 152; as
  Indo-Germanic foe, 396; name change
  of, 317–18, 323; and Paul the apostle,
  318
Marxism: dialectical materialistic of, 262,
  266; universal method of, 318
Maximinus Thrax (emperor of Rome),
  racial degeneracy of, 333
May, Karl: novels of, 273, 397
Mazower, Mark, 92
media, Nazi: coverage of Greek invasion,
  94–95; dissemination of Nordicism, 87
*Medieval German Physical Education in
  Words and Images* (exhibition), 221
Meller, Willy, 31, 184
Menschenbild, Nazi, 129
metaphysics, Greek: Heidegger and, 142–47
Michaud, Éric, 187
Middle Ages, genealogies from, 5. *See also*
  Germany, medieval
Minerva, in Nazi decorative arts, 258. *See
  also* Athena
Ministry of Public Enlightenment and
  Propaganda, files of, 166
Minorca, Jewish infiltration of, 302
miscegenation, racial: under Alexander the
  Great, 304, 305, 356; among Indo-
  Germanic peoples, 333; among Nordic
  Greeks, 285–86, 337–38, 339, 346, 356;
  among Romans, 127, 151, 285–86, 297,
  298, 309, 329–37, 341; as blood
  poisoning, 333, 338, 394; decline
  through, 337; in democracy, 341–47,
  356; egalitarianism and, 209, 227; in
  France, 344; in Hellenistic world, 290;
  Indo-Germanic destruction through,
  285, 339; in myth of Jason and Medea,
  340–41; in Nazi education, 338–39;
  Nazi humanism on, 116; perversion of
  spirit in, 313; in racial conflict, 288;

unlawful, 178; violation of laws of
nature, 334; warning to Germany about,
337–41. *See also* de-Nordification;
marriage, interracial; racial purity
Mischlinge (half-breeds), 172
modernity: versus agrarian utopias, 274,
278; egalitarianism of, 204; feminine,
219; mind/body perfection in, 158
modernity, Nazi: technological, 146–47,
148, 152, 278, 378
Mommsen, Theodor: *Römische Geschichte*,
304, 378
Montesquieu, Charles-Louis de Secondat,
205; environmental determinism of, 67
Monumentalität, in Hitler's aesthetics, 247
monuments, Nazi: planned obsolescence of,
367. *See also* architecture, Nazi
monuments, Roman: colossal, 251, 252
monuments to dead, German, 158
Mooslahnerkopf Teehaus (Obersalzberg),
neoclassical sculpture of, 273
mosaics, Nazi use of, 257
mos maiorum, Roman, 332, 355, 382
Mosse, George, 10, 157
Mostra Augustea della Romanità, Hitler's
visit to, 254
Mount Olympus, Nazi archaeologists at, 3
Mount Taygetus, exposure of children on,
224, 228
Müller, Hermann: *Das nordische Griechenthum*, 52
Müller, Karl Ottfried: *Die Dorier*, 53, 216
Müller, Werner, 81
Munich: architecture of, 88–89, 258;
German classic art in, 2, 88–91;
historische Festzuge of, 88–90;
Königsplatz, 88, 243
Museeninsel (Berlin), classical holdings of, 31
Mussolini, Benito: in Brenner Pass incident,
127–28; death of, 384; Hitler's
admiration for, 269; imperial designs of,
2; as mentor, 75; relationship with
Hitler, 74, 127; as true Roman, 79
Mycenae: Nordic character of, 65;
raciological exegesis of, 58
mythmaking, Nazi, 4–5, 9, 45–46, 366,
397; Aryans in, 5, 66; death in, 369;
heroic defeat in, 359; leaders', 398;
Nordic people in, 15, 23, 394, 399; of
origins, 4–5, 17–18; racial, 9, 340–41;
ruins in, 387. *See also* origin myths
mythography, Günther's use of, 53
mythology, historical: in Nazi ideology, 12,
46

Napola (National political institutes of
education), Greek model for, 150
Napoleon (emperor of France): humiliation
of Germany, 139; imperial ambitions of,
283; neoclassicism of, 137; road
construction of, 238–39
national identity, German: academic
reinforcement of, 47; Aryan myth of,
136; autochthony and, 18–20; crisis of
nineteenth century, 23; cultural, 18–19;
role of Greece in, 139, 140, 163–64;
role of history in, 104; role of
humanities in, 123; self-esteem in, 49;
Tacitus's influence on, 20. *See also*
identity
nationalism, European: and nationalist
historiography, 48
nationalism, Greek nineteenth-century, 2
Nationalpolitische Erziehungsanstalten
(National political institutes of
education), 119
Nationalsozialistische Führungsoffiziere
(NSFO), 42
Nationalsozialistische Lehrerbund (NSLB),
journal of, 130–31
nature, laws of: historians' understanding
of, 289; Hitler on, 306, 352; miscegenation as, 334; Nazism and, 202; racial
conflict as, 319–20; totalitarianism as,
360
Nazism: absolute evil of, 398; academic
organizations of, 7; academics' service
to, 46–47; anxiety over history, 48;
artistic organizations of, 7; canonical
texts of, 11; Cartesianism of, 148;
Chaplin's parody of, 230, 255–56;
conflict with humanism, 110; creative
will of, 68; cult of body, 150; cultural
inferiority complex of, 73–76; desire for
ideal, 396–97; exclusionary ideology of,
149, 393; as form of seduction, 186;
geostrategic euphoria of, 251; and
Germanentum, 149; hope for Germanophiles, 149; ideological training for, 9,
11–12; intellectual censorship by, 27;
laws of nature and, 202; mythical
origins of, 4–5, 7, 17–18; as *Mythos*,
387; nihilism of, 369, 385; Nordic
origin myth and, 23, 394; official
Nordicism of, 28–30; "pastification" of,
367; prudery in, 184–85; racial myths
of, 9, 340–41; relationship with
antiquity, 2; relationship with

Nazism *(continued)*
    modernity, 148; rise to power, 99; self-mythologization of, 366; *Stehen und Kämpfen* mentality of, 369–73; on Stoicism, 207–11; suppression of philosophy, 146; symbolic universe of, 10–11; technological modernity of, 146–47, 148, 152, 378; Teutonic archetypes to, 4; *translatio studii et imperii* to, 64–66, 170; use of Aryan myth, 5, 66; validation *ab historia*, 46
Naztionalsozialistische Wissenschaft (journal), on Latin education, 125–26
negrification, 173
Nero (emperor of Rome): building program of, 388; burning of Rome, 388–89; colossal monuments of, 251; *damnatio memoriae* of, 388; Golden House of, 252; Nova Roma of, 389; renaming of Rome, 252
Nero Decree (*Nero-Befehl*), 387, 399; partial application of, 388
Netzer, Hubert, 184
Das neue Bild der Antike, 244
Neue Jahrbücher für antike und deutsche Bildung (review), 129–30; on Horace, 131, 132
Neue Sachlichkeit, degenerate art of, 260
Neue Wege zur Antike (journal), humanist education in, 105–6
new man, Nazi, 13; at Berlin Olympics, 175; as body, 190–91; classical ideal of, 8–9, 149; Hitler on, 175; in Nazi propaganda, 393, 394; physical training of, 8; Plato and, 196; psychological molding of, 8; Spartan education for, 219–21; ties to Rome, 151; Winckelmann's influence on, 158
Niebelungenlied, Amazon figures in, 59
Nietzsche, Friedrich: on death of God, 385; Dionysian ideal of, 60, 115; on function of history, 250; in genesis of Nazism, 194–95; *Lebensphilosophie* of, 194; Philhellenism of, 141; on Sparta, 216; *Übermensch* of, 194; and Wagner, 195. Works: "Homers Wettkampf," 159–60; *Untimely Mediations*, 250
Night of the Long Knives (1934), 28
Nizan, Paul, 46
NKVD, scorched-earth tactics of, 317
Nolte, Ernst, 194
nomadism, of non-Aryan races, 275
Nordicism: academics on, 27; of ancient languages, 123; on archaeological research, 81; body and soul in, 123; corruption of, 32; of Greco-Roman portraits, 58–59, 83; Günther's, 24–28; linguistic evidence for, 53–55; of Nazi leaders, 64, 262–64; Nazi radicalization of, 47; in Nazi textbooks, 85–86; NSDAP's, 28–30; Plato's, 194–98; in SS propaganda, 82–83; symbols of, 27–28; teaching of, 37–40, 82–86
Nordicism, Greek: at Berlin Olympics, 88; of the soul, 55–56; Spartan, 53, 95, 216, 219; of temples, 82–83. *See also* Greeks, Nordic
Nordic peoples: agrarianism of, 284; anthropometric characteristics of, 56–58; Apollonian liberty of, 313; body/soul unity of, 114–15, 171, 181; cataclysm destroying, 386; closeness to nature, 179; cultural claims for, 52, 274; declining birthrates of, 325–27; defeat of racial inferiors, 373; demographic fertility of, 276; deterioration of, 40; disappearance of, 387; Doric spirit of, 284; egalitarian threat to, 323; elimination from antiquity, 214; historical responsibility toward, 124; Jewish assault on, 322; lebensraum for, 273–78; limiting of humanity to, 150; maps of, 43; Mediterranean colonies of, 277; Nazi myths of, 15, 399; as peasant-warriors, 275; racial soul of, 122; *Schicksalkampf* with Judeo-Bolsheviks, 352; in Second Punic War, 329; self-possession of, 61; sins against race, 394; sociobiological refoundation of, 278; solidarity with modern Germans, 123; southern migration of, 29–30, 33–35, 285, 394–95; tragic history of, 391. *See also* Aryan race; Greeks, Nordic; Indo-Germanic people; Romans, Nordic
Nordische Gesellschaft (Nordic Society), 352
NSDAP (Nationalsozialistische Deutsche Arbeiterpartei): agrarian utopia concept, 274; civic crown of, 256; Heidegger's engagement with, 142, 148–49; Indo-Germanic Reich of, 28; Nordicism of, 28–30; power structure of, 232; racial-genetic platform of, 23–24
nude sculpture, Nazi, 375, 393–94; eroticism of, 184–86; feminine, 185–86; sexual distancing of, 185; warriors, 183–84, 375. *See also* sculpture, Nazi

nudity: in art, 181; Greco-Roman, 179, 180–82, 191; in Olympic sport, 181–82
Nuremberg: Deutsche Stadion, 243, 251, 258–59; Kongresshalle, 366; Nazi architecture of, 230, 258–59; Reichsparteitagsgelände, 258–59; ruins of, 367, 390; Zeppelinfeld, 258, 259, 367
Nuremberg Congress, *chorégies* (1935), 259
Nuremberg Laws (1935), 43
Nuremberg rallies, 90; Hitler's choreographing of, 366

obscurantism, Christian: versus ancient purity, 310–13
Oexle, Otto Gerhard, 6
Olympia: bond with Berlin, 169; excavation of, 159, 161, 162; sacred flame at, 168
Olympia (art photography, 1936), 162
Olympia 1936: Eine nationale Aufgabe, 160
"Olympia: The Führer's Excavations" (*Das Schwarze Korps*), 162
Olympia-Zeitung (newspaper), 161, 162–63, 165–66; on Hercules, 165; torch relay in, 168; "Yesterday: 600 and 2,000 Years Ago," 163
Olympic Games: Aryan spirit of, 182; of 1896, 92; flame at, 167; as German creation, 161–62; nude sports in, 181–82
Olympic Games (Berlin, 1936), 11; ancient kitsch in, 151; ceremonies at, 165–66; exhibitions at, 162, 163, 166; Greek athletes at, 92; Greek culture at, 159–64; Greek Nordicism of, 88; Helleno-German kinship at, 136, 159–70, 192; as national duty, 170; new man at, 175; Nordic athletes at, 167, 175, 192; *Olympiastadium*, 163–64, 167, 192, 251; Olympic cauldron, 169; propaganda for, 160–63; racial identity at, 160; theater at, 165; torch relay, 167–70; total man at, 114; *Wettkampf* at, 192
Olympic torch relay, 167–70, 192; route for, 168, 169; *translatio igni* in, 170; travel time, 169
Olympus, German excavation of, 141
onomastics, Nordicist, 54–55
ontology, Greek: Heidegger on, 142
Operation Barbarossa, 280; destruction of Judeo-Asiatics, 370
Oppermann, Hans: on Horace, 131; on Jewish-Roman conflict, 299–300; on Jews in antiquity, 298; on Latin teaching, 128; on Nazi humanism, 105–6
Ordensburgen (Nazi academies), on Prometheus, 31
Ordnungspolizei: ideological pamphlets of, 39; Nordicism of, 29
Organisation Todt, bridge construction under, 240–41
Orientalism: Caracalla's, 336, 355; of Greece, 332; Hellenistic, 115–16; Jewishness and, 298
origin: Enlightenment ideas of, 20–21; identity and, 17
origin myths: Adamic, 21; Atlantean, 35–37; cartography of, 34–35; Günther's contribution to, 24–28; India in, 20–23, 395; Indo-Germanic, 22, 23, 24–28, 34–37. *See also* mythmaking
origin myths, Nordic, 23, 394; Eastern civilizations in, 32–33; genealogy in, 45–48; homeland in, 29; nationalism in, 23; racialist movements and, 23
origins, German, 18–20; Nazi discourse on, 40
origins, Nordic: in Nazi propaganda, 49; role in German expansion, 50; transmission of theories, 37–40, 49
Orsippus of Megara, 182
Orwell, George: *1984*, 7
ostracism, Athenian, 343
Ostsiedlung, for SS veterans, 282
Otto I (Holy Roman emperor), imperial ambitions of, 283
Otto I (king of Greece), 95, 141
Out-of-India (*Urheimat*) theory, 22; Günther on, 25–26, 52; maps of, 34–35; Nazi rejection of, 42, 49. *See also* India
overpopulation, Indo-Germanic, 84

Pact of Steel (Berlin-Rome), 78, 97, 127
paideia, German: Nazi celebration of, 170–72; *volle Mensch* in, 170–72
paideia, Greek: body/soul unity in, 115, 117; Hellenistic, 116–17; musical training in, 115; and Nazi education, 109; Nazi paradigm for, 113–17; physical training in, 115; training of political soldiers, 118
Palais Garnier (Paris), neobaroque of, 245
Palatinate, devastation (1689), 137
paleontology, Nordicist use of, 56
Palestine, Roman war in, 296

496 | Index

Panhellenic games, Greek: sacred flame at, 167
Panofsky, Erwin, 10
Pantheon, Roman: Hitler's admiration for, 272; Nazi copy of, 254
Panzer tanks, "Elephant," 234
Papinian (jurist), Judaized law of, 335–36
parades, classically themed, 89–90, 97, 169
Paris: Arc de Triomphe, 272; Hitler's visit to, 272
Paris International Exposition (1937), German pavilion at, 260
parvenus, Nazi, 272–73
patricians, Roman: intermarriage with plebeians, 334
Paul, Saint: conspiracy tactics of, 322; conversion of, 307; as Indo-Germanic foe, 396; and Marx, 318; mobilization of masses, 322; name change of, 317–18, 323; as political commissar, 316, 396; as precursor of Bolshevism, 308; rallying of proletariat, 315; subversion of Jesus, 306, 307; universal message of, 318
Paulus, General Friedrich: surrender of, 352, 358, 374
Pax Romana: international Jewry in, 303; and Pax Franco-Gallica, 127
Peace of Westphalia (1648), 18
pedagogy, German: harmful, 104; Hitler's criticism of, 101. *See also* education; Gymnasien; paideia
pedagogy, Nazi, 9; anti-intellectualism of, 196; political opportunism in, 99; on re-Nordification of Rome, 309; textbooks, 83–86
pedagogy, Nordicist, 37–40, 49–50; decrees concerning, 38–39; Greco-Roman antiquity in, 38; SS, 82–86; transmission of, 40
Pelasgians, Greek, 60
Peloponnesian League, defeat of Athens, 215
Peloponnesian War, 263, 264; depopulation in, 328, 339; racial decline following, 339
Pericles: building program of, 263, 264; democratic politics of, 263; as *führer*, 263–64; Great Man theory of, 267; Hitler and, 262–64, 268
Perioeci, Spartan: Nordic domination of, 226, 228
Persians: effeminacy of, 180; Jewish pogrom against, 300; Nordic elites, 349

Persius, anti-Semitism of, 303
personality, Nazi cult of, 265, 266
Petacci, Clara, 384
Petter, Kurt, 219–20
phenotypes, Nordic, 58–59, 173, 179; mutation of, 351
Philhellenism, German, 95, 195; Frederick the Great's, 2; glorification of Athens, 215; and Greco-German racial kinship, 136–42; historiography of, 140; Ludwig I's, 2, 88, 90; racial, 82; Sparta in, 216; and travel to Greece, 140; in Weimar classicism, 269
Philip the Arab (emperor of Rome), racial degeneracy of, 333
Philip of Macedon: contrast with Alexander, 348; defeat of Sparta, 216; as Indo-Germanic king, 348
philosopher kings, Platonic, 198; racial purity of, 201
philosophers, racial qualifications for, 200–201
philosophy, ancient: Nazi concepts in, 227; Nazi reforms affecting, 109
philosophy, European: Nazi suppression of, 146; replacement with ideology, 146; and Western politics, 143
philosophy departments, university: Indo-Germanic studies in, 86–87
physical training: in Greek paideia, 115; in Helleno-German kinship, 179; in *Mein Kampf*, 178–79; in Nazi education, 104–5, 150, 178–79; for new man, 8. *See also* sports
physiognomy, Nazi, 59
Plato: Academy of, 144; account of Atlantis, 35; aporetic dialogues of, 199–200; as defender of race, 213; on democracy, 356; de-Nordification in time of, 201, 338; Dinaric blood of, 212; eugenicist reading of, 200–204; as forerunner of Führer, 199–204; holistic state of, 210, 211; influence on Xenophon, 197–98; in Nazi curriculum, 136, 196–97, 200; Nazi interpretation of, 194–98; and Nazi racism, 200–204; new man of, 109; Nordicism of, 194–98, 227, 345; as Nordic warrior, 199; philosopher kings of, 198, 201; philo-Spartanism of, 227, 345; political writings, 195, 196; politicized reading of, 131; role *in Volksgemeinschaft*, 196; on the soul, 115; struggle against racial decadence, 290; totalitarianism of, 193–94;

tripartite state of, 200; as *volle Mensch*, 196, 198; warriors of, 198
—*Apology*, 212
—*Gorgias*, 345
—*Laws*, 195
—*Republic*, 144, 195, 199; eugenicist interpretation of, 200–201; racial policy of, 202; tripartite state of, 200
—*The Statesman*, 195
Plutarch: *Bioi paralleloi*, 266; on Olympic flame, 168
Pohlenz, Max, 208
Poland, Wehrmacht invasion of, 390
political man: Aristotle's, 112, 206; versus humanist man, 113
political man, Nazi: humanism for, 106–10; as rediscovery of Greek man, 112–13; soldiers, 109, 112, 117–18, 134; and teaching of classics, 134; training for, 125
politics, as *werdende Geschichte*, 103
Polybius, on systematic history, 99
Pompeii, excavation of, 157
Popper, Karl, 6; *The Open Society and Its Enemies*, 194; on Plato, 193–94
pornography, anti-Semitic, 185
portraits, Greco-Roman: Nordic traits of, 58–59, 83, 177
Pötsch, Leopold, 99, 102, 267–68
Potsdam Conference (1945), 389
power, Roman: centralized, 232; Renaissance monuments to, 1; symbolism of, 249
power: Nazi will to, 235, 239, 297, 366–67
Prague, University of: National Socialist ideology at, 86
prehistorians, German, 24; conflict with classicists, 119
prehistory, German: Himmler's interest in, 70; Hitler's dislike of, 69–71; Nazi teaching of, 119, 267; promotion of scholarship on, 124; teaching of, 39; Teutonic clichés in, 72–73; in textbooks, 37. *See also* antiquity, Germanic; Germany, ancient
procreation, interracial: prohibition of, 84. *See also* miscegenation
Prometheus: as Aryan metaphor, 169; Aryans as, 30–31, 49; in Nazi sculpture, 30–31; as sculptor, 138; in Weimar classicism, 31
propaganda, Nazi: after Stalingrad, 381; ancient history in, 12; for Berlin Olympics, 160–63; creation of ideal subject, 8; defeat in, 373, 376; Europe in, 43; Frederick the Great in, 376, 377–78; intransigence of, 371, 372; leitmotivs of, 393; morale-building, 376–83; new man in, 393, 394; Nordic origins in, 49; Punic Wars in, 376–83; racial, 339–40, 393; on re-Nordification of Rome, 309; roads in, 240; Romans in, 378; sacrifice in, 373; world domination in, 378
propaganda, SS, 43–44; on Nordic culture, 75–76; in schools, 82–86. *See also* SS
Propaganda Ministry, archives of, 11
prosopography, Nordicist, 57
The Protocols of the Elders of Zion, 317
protonatalism, Roman, 326, 329
Prussia: as symbol for discipline, 249; unification of Germany, 236
pseudomedievalism, Nazi, 279
psychology, racial, 55
Punic Wars: Hitler on, 273; as Nazi exemplar, 376–83, 391; Nordic race in, 329; as racial conflict, 293–96, 297–98; Roman defeats in, 379, 380; Roman perseverance in, 378, 379–83; Second, 3, 329, 377, 378, 380, 389, 391. *See also* Carthage
Purim (Jewish holiday), commemoration of Persian pogrom, 300
puritanism, Victorian, 184
putsch, failed (Nov. 1923), 265
Pyramid of Cheops, construction of, 238
Pytheas of Marseilles, on Ultima Thule, 35, 77

"le querelle du latin," in German education, 125–28
Quintilian, anti-Semitism of, 303

race: in artistic creation, 187–88; in explanation of history, 294, 394; state policy on, 25
racial conflict: in Battle of Catalaunian Field, 291–92; betrayal of Hitler, 387; in Bolshevism, 292; and class conflict, 321, 330; classical examples of, 13; continuity in, 291; extermination in, 386; and fall of Rome, 334; Greco-Persian Wars as, 297; historians of antiquity on, 293; history as, 287–90, 320; with Jews, 296; as law of nature, 319–20; miscegenation in, 288; in Nazi defeat, 385; Nazi discourse of, 6, 356, 393, 396; Nordic-Semitic, 296–98;

racial conflict *(continued)*
  Punic Wars as, 293–96, 297–98;
  territorial domination in, 287; timeless,
  396; as total war, 358. *See also*
  anti-Semitism
racial hierarchy: in Nazi colonization, 281;
  Roman, 335; Spartan, 220, 228
racial history, Nazi writers on, 289–90,
  292–93
racial hygiene, Nazi, 176
racialist movements, and Nordic origin
  movements, 23
racial purity: architectural reflection of,
  261; Aryan loss of, 285; versus
  Christian obscurantism, 310–13;
  corruption of, 32; disruption of, 333; in
  Greece, 127; Günther on, 2; historical
  verification of, 3; observable traits of,
  172–73; of philosopher kings, 201; in
  teaching of classics, 133–34. *See also*
  blood; miscegenation, racial
racial science (*Rassenkunde*), Nazi, 10; at
  Christian-Albrechts-Universität, 87;
  culturally based arguments of, 55–56;
  on end of antiquity, 337; Günther's, 24;
  historians' understanding of, 289, 290;
  scholarship of, 18
racial unity: European, 44–45; Greco-
  Roman and German, 1; in *Mein Kampf*,
  1, 319
racism: biological determinism of, 3;
  Darwinian, 288; Platonic interpretation
  of, 200–204
racism, Nazi: biological determinism in,
  323; symptomatology of, 203; view of
  history in, 360
Ranke, Leopold von: on Punic Wars, 380
Rassenpolitik (pamphlet), 326
Rassenschande (crimes against race), 178
Rassenselbstmord (racial suicide), 326, 338
Rassenverbundenheit, in teaching of
  classics, 133
rationalism: Aristotle's, 115, 207; German
  hostility to, 102
Rauschning, Hermann, 74
Rawson, Elizabeth: *The Spartan Tradition
  in European Thought*, 215
reality, Nazi concept of, 396
Reche, Otto: *Europas Geschichte als
  Rassenschicksal*, 64; *Rasse und Heimat
  der Indogermanen*, 63–64; *Reallexikon
  der Vorgeschichte*, 53
Red Army, reprisals of, 370
Reformation, German, 18, 19

Regenbogen, Otto, 84
Rehm, Walther, 129, 140
Das Reich (newspaper), 11; morale-building
  in, 379; on Roman history, 3
Reich Chancellery, 247, 252; archives of,
  11; eradication of, 397; Hitler on,
  242–43; Hitler's office in, 257–58;
  mosaics of, 257, 284; Roman iconogra-
  phy of, 257–58; Speer's design for, 30,
  243, 365
Reich Education Ministry, archives of, 11
Reichel, Peter, 186
Reich Ministry for Public Enlightenment
  and Propaganda, 205
Reich Ministry for Science and Education:
  on Plato, 197; professional development
  courses of, 39; teachers' memoranda to,
  132–35
Reichsautobahn (neologism), 240
Reichsbund für deutsche Freilicht- und
  Volksschauspiele e. V., 204–5
Reichsinstitut für Geschichte des neuen
  Deutschlands, 380
Reichspost, Prometheus image of, 31
Reinerth, Hans, 77
Reitsch, Hanna, 376
remembrance: natural selection of, 368;
  Nazi, 398, 399
Renaissance: as Germanic, 188; monuments
  to Rome, 1; Nordic art of, 188; Roman
  antiquity in, 126
Renan, Ernest: "What Is a Nation?," 18
renovatio imperii, 394; Charlemagne's, 271,
  283
repetition, in discourse of antiquity, 6
res cogitans, and *res extensa*, 152
Res gestae divi Augusti, 244
restauratio imperii, European dream of, 1
Rheinlandbastarde (illegitimate black
  children), 173
Ribbentrop, Joachim von, 272
"Richtlinien für die Geschichtslehrbücher,"
  37
Riefenstahl, Leni, 169–70; *Das blaue Licht*,
  166; Nationaler Filmpreis of, 166;
  Olympia, 11, 92, 166–67, 192
Riesenhaftigkeit (hugeness), in Hitler's
  aesthetics, 247
Ringstrasse, Viennese: neobaroque of, 245
road construction, Napoleonic, 238–39
road construction, Nazi, 237–41; Speer's,
  241
roads, Nazi: cultural significance of,
  237–38, 268; glorification of, 239–40;

monumentality of, 240; troop movement on, 238–39; will to power in, 239
roads, Roman, 237, 238; construction techniques of, 239
Robert, Hubert, 367
Rodenwaldt, Gerhart, 244
Roman Empire: Attila's invasions of, 322; centralized power of, 232; conflict with Jews, 296, 299, 300–301; decadence of, 294; easternization of, 329; euergetism of, 252, 254; foreshadowing of Third Reich, 379; Germanic immigration into, 65–66; German soldiers of, 71–72, 309; German *ver sacrum* for, 310; German vitality in, 309; hegemony under, 235–36, 247, 249; Hitler on, 230–31, 249; Jewish conspiracy against, 321–22; Jewish merchants of, 301; Jewish revolt against, 318; as model for Western empires, 282–83; moral degeneration of, 332; as Nazi model, 248–50; as Nazi predecessor, 230, 337; in Nazi symbolism, 230; as Nordic creation, 85; racially related people of, 236; racial miscegenation in, 127, 151, 285–86, 297, 298, 309, 329–37, 341; re-Nordification of, 309; resurrection of, 283; road system of, 237, 238; as savior of Nordic race, 295; subversion by Judaized Christianity, 305–10, 315, 317–21, 322–23, 331; as symbol of power, 249; unification of Europe, 44–45; United States as, 389; victory over Huns, 291–92
—fall of, 305–10; Christianity and, 331; Easternization in, 297, 330–33; egalitarianism in, 308; Hitler on, 354; and Nazi defeat, 387; Nazi theory of, 324; racial conflict and, 334; *Völkerwanderungen* in, 309
Romanitas: Berlin's, 253; French celebration of, 269; in German culture, 269; *Germanentum* and, 125–28; Hellenism and, 133; in Nazi architecture, 283–84
Roman Republic: Fabius's defense of, 380; German democracy and, 233; Hitler on, 232; perseverance in Punic Wars, 378, 379–83. *See also* Punic Wars
Romans, ancient: blond slaves of, 65; mixed blood of, 127, 151; in Nazi propaganda, 378; racial aristocracy of, 307; racially degenerate, 133–34, 211; superstition of, 234

Romans, Nordic, 6, 7–8, 38, 39; academic validation of, 96–97; Ahnenerbe's proof of, 79; battle with Semitic Carthage, 293; blond, 58; de-Nordification of, 333–37, 355; ethology of, 52–55; Germanists' depictions of, 124; Günther on, 62–64; hostility toward Judaism, 268; Jewish persecution of, 300; parasitism affecting, 332; racial scientists on, 63; scholarly validation of, 51; spring migrations of, 275–76; in teaching of history, 120; use of contraception, 328–39; *ver sacrum* ritual of, 275–76, 279, 399
romanticism, German: holistic community of, 211
Rome: bastardized heritage of, 110; civil wars of, 328, 329, 330; as *colluvium*, 62–64; corruption of Greek culture, 111; denatalism in, 326; Fascist images of, 12; German antipathy toward, 137; Great Men of, 271; Hippodamian city plan of, 255; Hitler's idea of, 248; Hitler's visit to, 254, 272; inclusion in Nordicism, 29, 30; Latinate union of, 236; *mos maiorum* of, 332, 355, 382; Nordicist history of, 85; in Nordic pedagogy, 38; peasant soldiers of, 330–31, 332, 355; in propaganda of defeat, 373; racial castes of, 329–30; racial hierarchy of, 335; racial history of, 294, 341; racial oligarchy of, 283; Teutonic invaders of, 65; tolerance in, 65, 315; urban planning of, 255; urban synoecism of, 255
Rom und Karthago (1943), 12, 382–83; racial conflict in, 293
Roosevelt, Franklin Delano: death of, 376–77
Rosenberg, Alfred, 5, 49; on Alexander the Great, 349; anti-Pauline discourse of, 308; on Apollonian-Dionysian dichotomy, 61–62; on Aristotle, 207; on Aryan defeat, 351; on Atlantean hypothesis, 35–36; attack on Hegel, 33–34; biological determinism of, 313; on Caesar, 264; on democracy, 344; on emperors' racial characteristics, 334; Germanophilia of, 76; on Judaized Christianity, 306–7; on miscegenation, 319, 334–35; *The Myth of the Twentieth Century,* 33, 35, 61–62, 163, 207, 264, 294, 313, 349, 351–52; on Nietzsche, 195; on Nordic apocalypse,

Rosenberg *(continued)*
  352; on Nordic Greeks, 65; Nordicism of, 28, 29, 128; Olympic propaganda of, 161; on Plato, 345; on Punic War, 295–96; on Roman warfare, 233; on Socrates, 212, 213; Sonderstab Vor- und Frühgeschichte of, 77; speeches of, 1; on swastika, 42; view of humanism, 114
Rousseau, Jean-Jacques, 203
Ruinenwerte, theory of, 366–69
ruins, ancient: inspiration from, 366, 390, 395; nihilistic vitalism of, 369; paintings of, 261
ruins, Nazi, 366, 397; Hitler's investment in, 368–69; mythical status of, 387; of Nuremberg, 367, 390; and ruins of antiquity, 390, 395; as sacred space, 398–99; stagecraft in, 367
Rusch, Adolf, 196
RUSHA (SS Office for Race and Settlement), 173; Darré's leadership of, 274, 277
Rust, Bernhard, 38, 79, 83, 119; on Berlin Olympiad, 166; defense of Latin, 128–29; "Die Grundlagen der nationalsozialistischen Erziehung," 128; on Sparta, 221; teachers' memoranda to, 132–35; on *volle Mensch*, 171

SA: civilization of, 72; opposition to Nordicism, 28; political soldiers of, 113; *Reichswettkämpfe* (fitness contests) of, 176
Sabines, *ver sacrum* ritual of, 275
Sallust, *The War with Jugurtha*, 135
Sanskrit, as mother tongue, 22
Sartre, Jean-Paul: on Herostratus, 384
Schachermeyr, Fritz, 7; on Alexander the Great, 347, 348; on Caesar, 348; on Carthage, 294; on de-Nordification, 346; on Elagabalus, 335; on Hellenism, 116, 208, 209; on individualism, 210; on international Jewry, 305; on Jewish hate, 299; on Nazi humanism, 105–6; on Nordic leader, 262; on racial science, 337; on Roman jurists, 335–36; on vigilance in classical studies, 213–14. Works: "Die Aufgaben der Alten Geschichte . . . ," 119–21; *Indogermanen und Orient*, 292, 350; *Lebensgesetzlichkeit in der Geschichte*, 289
Schemann, Ludwig, 61; on Alexandrine era, 349–50; on Aristotle, 207; on depopulation, 328; on fall of Rome, 309; on Hellenic ancestry, 142; on Nordic phenotypes, 173; on Roman colluvium, 63; on Sparta, 223; on Stoicism, 209, 211
Schicksalkampf (battle for destiny), Nazi, 370
Schiefer, Wilhelm, 297, 298, 332, 342
Schiff, Alfred, 168
Schiller, Friedrich: humanism of, 114
Schlageter, Albert Leo, 93, 205; death of, 265
Schlegel, Friedrich: "On the Language and Wisdom of the Indians," 22
Schlief, Hans: Olympia excavations of, 162
Schliemann, Heinrich, 42
Schmelze, Karl: *Rassengeschichte und Vorgeschichte im Dienste nationaler Erziehung*, 84
Schöttler, Peter, 6
Schrötter, Kurt: *Tod under Unsterblichkeit*, 41
Schuchhardt, Carl, 26; "Die Indogermanisierung Griechenlands," 60
Schultze-Naumburg, Paul, 69, 159; on Socrates, 212. Works: *Kunst und Rasse*, 187, 189; *Nordische Schönheit*, 189
Schünzel, Reinhold: *Amphitryon*, 11, 90–91; *Halbjude* status of, 91
Schwab, Gustav: *Die schönsten Sagen des klassischen Altertums*, 269
Das Schwarze Korps (SS weekly): on ancient Olympics, 171–72; on Atlantean hypothesis, 36; on blond hair, 57–58; on Curtius, 161; on Nordic homeland, 36; on nudity in art, 181; on *Olympiastadium*, 164; on Teutonic clichés, 72; vilification of Rome, 77
sciences, complicity with Nazism, 145, 146. *See also* racial science
Scipio Africanus, Publius Cornelius, 322, 382; victory at Zama, 381
Scobie, Alexander, 6
scorched-earth policy, Nazi, 328, 387, 388
sculpture, ancient: Nordic traits of, 156, 158–59, 177; Winckelmann on, 156, 158
sculpture, Greek: aesthetic ideal of, 156–58; of athletes, 156; Jewish countertypes to, 174; Nazi appropriation of, 172
sculpture, Nazi: of athletes, 172; of Greek hoplites, 184; neoclassical, 273; Prometheus in, 30–31; syncretism in, 184. *See also* nude sculpture, Nazi
See, Klaus von, 78
self, renunciation of, 113

Semitic races: migratory routes of, 305; nomadism of, 275; Roman defeat of, 293
Seneca: anti-Semitism of, 303; on eugenics, 223; Nazi use of, 111; Stoicism of, 211
Septimius Severus (emperor of Rome): African blood of, 333; and Punic people, 294; racial revanchism of, 336
Siegelin, Wilhem, 36; *Die blonden Haare der indogermanischen Völker,* 57
sin, original: Nazi condemnation of, 180, 181
"Sind Kriege Rechenexempel?" (*Die Deutsche Polizei*), 388
Skorzeny, Otto, 376
skulls, Nordic, 56; in Egyptian tombs, 37–38; in Greek sculpture, 159
slaves, Eastern: effect on racial identity, 329; on latifundia, 331; Nordic Greeks', 337; procreative abilities of, 329
Slavs, war of extermination against, 249
Social Darwinism, 321; Nazi adherence to, 325
social sciences, Nazi, 120
Socrates: anti-Nordic appearance of, 212, 227; conception of humanity, 212; maieutics of, 212; Nazi repudiation of, 198, 211–14; and Sophists, 212
soldiers, citizen: classical model for, 109, 117
soldiers, German: cardinal virtues of, 374; ideological indoctrination of, 44, 91; intransigence in defeat, 357–58; as Nordic heroes, 92; political, 112, 117–18, 134, 198; training of, 117–18; of World War I, 390
soldiers, SS: Nordic blood of, 83
Solon, on gymnastic training, 183
solstice celebrations, 28
Sonnenwendplatz (Solstice Plaza), Prometheus statue of, 31
Sophists: as Asiatic, 203; individualism of, 203; Socrates and, 212
soul, Greek: in the *Iliad,* 55; kinship with German soul, 55–56, 142
soul, Nordic: and Nordic body, 123; racial, 122
sovereignty: architectural expression of, 241; of Germanic aristocracy, 230–33; Roman principle of, 230–33
Soviet Union: architecture of, 261; classicism in, 261; German invasion of, 68, 354; multiethnicity of, 261; Nazi retreat from, 387; Nazi war against, 249. *See also* Stalingrad

Sparta: abandonment of peasant base, 226; Apollonian principle of, 218; breeding policy of, 218; communitarianism of, 214, 217; defeat by Philip, 216; denatalism of, 326; de-Nordification of, 226; education in, 118, 219–21; German interest in, 215; glorification of the fallen, 373–74; land division in, 226; militarism of, 217; myth of, 13, 214–16, 373; as Nazi model, 111, 214–16, 223, 225, 228, 279; Nordicism of, 53, 95, 216, 219, 221, 222; nude sports in, 180, 181; *oliganthropia* of, 226; oligarchy of, 118; physical training in, 220; Plato's links to, 227; proletarianism of, 216; in propaganda of defeat, 373, 383; protototalitarianism of, 216, 220; racial hierarchy of, 220, 228; racialized military state of, 236; SS use of, 224; in Weimar classicism, 215. *See also* Thermopylae
"Spartanism," Nazi: totalitarianism and, 216–19; Western individualism and, 217
Spartans: exposure of infants, 224, 228; Helots, 226, 228, 280–81; *homoioi,* 222; in Nazi propaganda, 373, 383; peasant-warriors, 219, 220, 225–26, 279–82; Perioeci, 226, 228; practice of eugenics, 222–25, 228; as Prussians, 216. *See also* Lacedaemonians
speculation, in Roman culture, 331
Speer, Albert, 74, 176; admiration for Troost, 244; arc de triomphe of, 253; classical training of, 284; on colonization, 281; and cost of architecture, 364; on defeat, 365–66, 387; Deutsche Stadion of, 243, 251, 258–59; on economic collapse, 373; on Great Man theory, 266; on Hitler and history, 99; on Hitler's classicism, 270; on Hitler's megalomania, 248; on Hitler's mortality, 365; imitation of Berlin, 259; imprisonment of, 244–45; on Nazi classicism, 260–61; neo-Roman buildings of, 2, 10, 244–45, 283; and Nero Decree, 388; on Nuremberg Reichsparteitagsgelände, 258; on Paris International, 260; Reich Chancellery of, 30, 243, 365; road project of, 241; theory of ruin value, 367
Spengler, Oswald, 286
Sport der Hellenen (exhibition), 162
sports: nudity in, 180, 181–82; shaping of character, 128

sports, Nazi, 191; Aryan-Olympic spirit in, 183; goal of, 172; Greek agon and, 178–82; ideal of, 170–71; political imperative of, 183; role in war, 182–84; in service of community, 192; service to state, 182; steel metaphor for, 183. *See also* physical training
SS (Schutzstaffel): Aryan members of, 3; confrontation with Christianity, 77; educational material for, 60; embodiment of Nordic culture, 44; Germanophilia of, 69–71, 73, 74, 76; Günther's mentoring of, 28, 29; Helots in culture of, 280–81; Nordicism of, 28–29, 224; Office for Race and Settlement, 173; *Ostkolonization* plan, 278, 280; racial elitism of, 224–25, 228; slavery discourse of, 280; study of antiquity, 78; suicide missions of, 376, 388; *Totenkopf* insignia of, 369; and *ver sacrum* ritual, 310; winter solstice celebration, 28. *See also* propaganda, SS; Waffen-SS
SS-Leithefte (magazine): on Battle of Cannae, 381; on interracial marriage, 340–41; on invasion of Greece, 93
Staatliches Schauspielhaus (Berlin), Greek drama at, 165
stagecraft: Hitler's interest in, 367, 368; of Nazi architecture, 261
Stalin, Joseph: Asiatic hordes of, 351; as Hannibal, 295
Stalingrad, Battle of, 216; German prisoners of, 374; glorification of, 374; as heroic drama, 358; and myth of Sparta, 373; Nazi defeat at, 356; Nazi propaganda following, 381; and Punic Wars, 382; and Thermopylae, 374–75
Stamm (German assembly), 341
Stämme (tribes), German, union of, 236
Standarten, Nazi: swastika on, 256
state, modern: Roman concept of, 230–31
Statue of Liberty, height of, 251
Stehen und Kämpfen (edict), 369–73
Stern, Fritz, 10; on German education, 101
Stern, J. P., 352, 385
Stoicism: *chosmopolis* of, 209; cosmology of, 207–8; egalitarianism of, 209–10, 227; and French Revolution, 210; individualism of, 211; Nazi dislike of, 207–11, 213; Roman, 209
Strabo, on Germans, 73
Die Strasse (journal), 239
Stresa Front, 128
Stresemann, Gustav, 232

Sturm und Drang movement, 126
subject and object, Cartesian split between, 152
Suetonius, *Vita Augusti*, 244
Sulla (dictator), Nordic appearance of, 63, 334
sun, healing properties of, 180
Surén, Hans: on state-sponsored physical education, 183. Works: *Gymnastik der Deutschen*, 186; *Mensch und Sonne*, 179–80, 182
Susa, Greek-Persian weddings at, 349
swastika, 42; Nordic Greek use of, 163; as Nordic symbol, 42–43; settings of, 256–57. *See also* hakenkreuz
Sweden, life rune in, 50
symbolism, Nazi, 10–11; allegorical language of, 257; classical antiquity in, 40; eagle, 89, 256; Hitler's attention to, 256; Roman imperial, 230
symbols, Indo-German, 81–82

table talks, Nazi leaders', 11
Tacitus: anti-Semitism of, 303; on desolation of peace, 235; ethnography of, 19–20; on German environment, 68; German translations of, 205; influence on German character, 20; *Das Schwarze Korps* on, 73
—*Agricola*, 80
—*Germania*, 19–20, 136, 252; Germanic democracy in, 341; on Hercules, 165; Hitler's reading of, 68; manuscript of, 80
Taeger, Fritz, 64; on Alexander the Great, 347–48; *East and West in Antiquity*, 292–93; on Elagabalus, 335; on Hellenization, 350
Tages der deutschen Kunst (Days of German Art, Munich), 88–91, 96, 169, 206
Tallgren, Vappu, 267–68
Tamms, Friedrich: bridge project of, 240–41
Täubler, Eugen, 304
teachers: defense of classical literature, 130–31, 133; memoranda to Reich Ministry for Science and Education, 132–35; national-conservative views of, 133; professional development of, 39
technology, human relationship with, 149. *See also* modernity, Nazi: technological
Temple of Jerusalem, destruction of, 300
temples, Greek: Nordicist theory of, 82–83
Ten Commandments, "slave morality" of, 111

Teutoburg, Battle of: Arminius's victory at, 71
Teutonic clichés, *Das Schwarze Korps* on, 72
Teutonic Knights: *Drang nach Osten* of, 279, 399; Nazi use of, 4; Roman legionnaires and, 290–91
textbooks, Nazi, 83–86; Aryanized, 83; directives for, 37, 83, 267, 337, 338; Indo-Germans in, 83–85; migration in, 84; Nordicist dogma in, 85–86; university, 84–85. *See also* curricula; education; pedagogy
textbooks, Weimar, 83
theater, Greek: and Nazi theater, 204–6
Theotokas, Giorgios, 94
Thermopylae, German assault on (1941), 91, 93
Thermopylae, Battle of: Aryans at, 375; Nazi glorification of, 373; Nazi recreation of, 386; and Stalingrad defeat, 374–75
Thies, Jochen: *Architekt der Weltherrschaft*, 247
Thiesse, Anne-Marie, 48
Thingstätten (theaters), choral performance in, 205–6
Third Reich: anti-miscegenation laws, 178; censorship of, 27; continuity with Rome, 235; devolution of scholarship under, 46–48; economic collapse of, 373; and Fascist Italy, 12; final battles of, 11; foreshadowing by Roman Empire, 379; Four-Year Plan, 146, 152, 278; hegemony under, 236; holistic community of, 204, 211; human raw material of, 177; imperial infrastructure of, 237–41; Judeo-Bolshevik plot against, 323; masculine military virtue of, 184; Nietzsche's philosophy under, 194–95; as organizer of Europe, 45; in Pact of Steel, 78, 97, 127; physical renewal of, 218; racial unification of, 237; rearmament of, 152; relations with Fascist Italy, 127–28; reverence for past, 2, 261, 365; road construction in, 237–41; Roman virtue for, 128–31; as *römische Weltreich*, 249; Spartan model for, 111, 214–16, 218, 223, 225, 228, 279; technological mechanization of, 145, 152, 378. *See also* Germany, Nazi
Thirty Tyrants, 345; struggle against racial decadence, 290
Thirty Years' War, 143

Thorak, Josef: athlete sculptures of, 172; *The Judgment of Paris*, 185; "neo-Grec" nudes of, 2, 9, 10
Thousand-Year Reich, chiliasm of, 386
Three Thousand Years of Jewish Hate (NSDAP pamphlet), 299
Thucydides: *The Peloponnesian War*, 99; on Spartans, 214–15
Thule Gesellschaft, Atlantis in, 35
Thuringia, Nazi majority in, 25
Tiberius (emperor of Rome): protonatalism of, 326; racial purity under, 338
Till, Rudolf, 80
time: eternal return of, 396; Nazi relationship to, 390, 395–97; reality unfolding in, 396; sacred, 396
Titus (emperor of Rome): defeat of Jews, 300, 301, 322; Palestine under, 305
Todt, Fritz, 237–39
torch, Olympic: design of, 168
totalitarianism: control of space, 10; diachronical function of, 7; as law of nature, 360; lies of, 6–8; public acceptance of, 6; role of architecture in, 261; "Spartanism" and, 216–19; use of antiquity, 2, 6
total man. *See volle Mensch*
Totenburgen (funerary complexes), 252
Toward the National Political School (journal), 130–31
Trautmann, E.: on *Elchrune*, 81
Treitschke, Heinrich von: Great Man theory of, 265
Troost, Gerdy, 273
Troost, Paul Ludwig, 273; Braunes Haus of, 244; classical training of, 284; Ehrentempel of, 244; neo-Doric architecture of, 88, 90; Spartan traditionalism of, 244
Truman, Harry, 377
Tschammer und Osten, Hans, 170
Turnbewegung (gymnastics movement), 160
Two Thousand Years of German culture (parade, 1933), 90
typography, Roman: Nazi use of, 270
typology, racial, 197, 211
Tyrtaeus, 151, 215; martial verse of, 109

Ulpian (jurist), Judaized law of, 335–36
Ultima Thule: Atlantis as, 35; Hitler on, 77
Umwelt, Nazi antiquity in, 10
uniforms, Nazi: design of, 256
unity, European: racial concept of, 44–45
universalism, Nazi dislike of, 210

universities, English: sports-rhetoric link in, 109
universities, German: abdication of ethics, 45–46; *Führerprinzip* in, 144; Heidegger on, 145–46; Indo-Germanic studies in, 86–87; mission of, 143–44; *Wehrsport* in, 86, 144
University of Berlin, book burning at, 113
University of Jena, racial science at, 25
Der Untermensch (SS pamphlet), 292

Vacano, Otto Wilhelm von, 279, 309; on Sparta, 219
Vacher de Lapouge, Georges, 24, 321; *L'Aryen*, 38; on class struggle, 330; Nordicism of, 53; selectionism of, 25; view of democracy, 343–44
Val Camonica (Italy), Ahnenerbe excavation of, 80–81
Valéry, Paul: "On Myths and Mythology," 15
Valhalla, for suicide missions, 376
Valkyries, 59
van der Rohe, Mies, 260
Varus, Publius Quinctilius, 126; Arminius's defeat of, 71, 78
Vercingetorix, 384
Verlag Blut und Boden (publisher), 330
Vernant, Jean-Pierre: *Pensée greque*, 10
ver sacrum ritual, 275–76, 279, 399; for Indo-Germanic people, 280; SS and, 310
Versailles treaty: effect on Nazi architecture, 247–28; German humiliation in, 5, 17, 49, 231, 389–90; lebensraum and, 276; Nazi violation of, 258
Vespasian (emperor of Rome), Westphalian appearance of, 333
Via dei Fori Imperiali (Rome), 2
viaducts, Roman: Nazi imitation of, 240
Vienna, Jewish infiltration of, 302
Vienna, University of: National Socialist ideology at, 86
virtue, Greco-Roman, 84; in Latin language teaching, 128–31; political, 128–31, 133, 134
vita activa, as Platonic, 197
vita contemplativa, medieval, 99
vitalism: Nazi, 369; Nietzsche's, 194
Vogt, Joseph, 47; on East-West conflict, 305; on Nazi architecture, 243–44; on Punic Wars, 293–96; on Severan dynasty, 336
Volk: decay through miscegenation, 334; unconditional resistance by, 371

Völkerwanderungen (migration of peoples): in fall of Rome, 309; to Rome, 65–66. See also Indo-Germanic migration
Volk im Werden (journal), Nazi humanism in, 106
"Volk in der Entscheidung" (*Völkischer Beobachter*), 380–81
Völkischer Beobachter (journal), 11; Berlin Olympics in, 160, 161, 162–63, 166, 169, 341–42; on Fabius Maximus, 383; on Greek ideal, 171; heroic nudes in, 375; morale-building in, 379, 380; on *Olympiastadium*, 165; on Roman history, 3; on Thermopylae assault (1941), 91; on unconditional resistance, 371
Volksgemeinschaft: association of Horace with, 132; classicist defense of, 150; cultural demonstrations for, 205; eugenics for, 204; Greek loss of, 202; holistic, 204; knowledge in service of, 145; Plato's role in, 196; relationship of Nazi architecture to, 262; role of sport in, 172; Spartan, 220–21, 221
Volkssturm, in Nazi defeat, 383
Volkstod (death of a people), 324–25; birthrate and, 326
Volk und Rasse (magazine): on modern Greeks, 94–96; on Roman racial conflict, 298; Roman slavery in, 329
volle Mensch, 191; at Berlin Olympics, 114; classicists on, 114; versus divided man, 113–17, 170; in German paideia, 170–72; glorification of, 226
Voltaire, on Sparta, 217
voluntarism, Nazi, 369
vultus animi speculum (adage), 157

Wackerle, Josef, 89; bas-reliefs of, 273
Waffen-SS, 292; assault on Thermopylae, 91, 93; promises of land, 282
Wagner, Richard: on German radio, 381; Hitler's love of, 369, 397; nationalist followers of, 362; and Nietzsche, 195; revolutionary liberalism of, 362
—*Rienzi*: Hitler's fascination with, 11, 360–61, 362–64; restoration of Rome in, 361; romantic hero of, 361–62; self-sacrifice in, 362; sentimentalism of, 360; Wagner's repudiation of, 364
—*The Ring of the Nibelung*, 346
Wagner, Winifred, 363
Walhalla (temple), 88, 97
wall drawings, Indo-Germanic, 80, 81

Wannsee Conference, 308, 324
warfare: eschatological, 390; imaginary thinking about, 358; as natural law, 358–59; Nordic allegory for, 184; resolution in, 378; role of sports in, 182–84
warfare, ancient: depopulation through, 327–28, 329, 330, 339; slavery and, 328
warfare, Roman: emulation of, 283; Hitler on, 233–35; Nazi imitation of, 233–37; technology in, 234; weaponry of, 233–34. *See also* civil wars, Roman; Punic Wars
War of the League of Augsburg (1688–97), 137
warriors' helmets, Greek: anthropological evidence from, 56
Warsaw Ghetto, Jews of, 173
weaponry, Nazi: illusions concerning, 371
weaponry, Roman, 233–34
Wegner, Bernd, 371, 372
Wehrmacht: advance on Moscow, 354; anti-Semitism propaganda for, 303–4; armored vehicles of, 234; assault on Thermopylae, 91, 93; colonization of East, 280, 281–82; High Command of, 92; invasion of Poland, 390; as peasant-soldier colonizers, 281–82; rations for, 233; reorganization of, 258; and Roman legions, 233–37; sacrifice of, 374; Supreme Command of, 371; unconditional resistance by, 371. *See also* soldiers, German
Wehrsport: in Nazi education, 119; in universities, 86
Weil, Simone, 235
Weimar classicism, 2; apolitical nature of, 107–8; German culture under, 107; Philhellenism of, 269; Plato studies of, 195; Prometheus in, 31; Sparta in, 215; universality of reason in, 150; worship of Greece, 138–39. *See also* classicism
Weimar Republic: allegories from antiquity, 264; constitution of, 118; contemporary art of, 189; educational system of, 101; political life under, 108; sovereignty of, 231; textbooks of, 83; Young Plan of, 269

Weinheber, Josef: "Ode an die Strassen Adolf Hitlers," 239–40
Weizsäcker, Ernst von, 372
Weltgeist (world spirit), Hegelian, 23; East-West migration of, 33
Wenk, Silke, 185
Wessel, Horst, 265
Westic peoples, among German people, 281
Wettkampf (agon): at Berlin Olympics, 192; in Greek/German culture, 159
Wilamowitz-Moellendorff, Ulrich von, 125
Wilde, Oscar: *The Portrait of Dorian Gray*, 158
Wilhelm II, Kaiser: educational modernism of, 125
Wille und Macht (youth magazine), 40
Winckelmann, Johann Joachim, 58, 94, 127, 195; avoidance of Greece, 140; German intellectuals after, 245; and Nazi new man, 158; Nazi use of, 156, 158; in Olympic propaganda, 161; on primordial Greeks, 138; search for Greek models, 111; on Sparta, 215. Works: *Gedanken über die Nachahmung der griechischen Werke*, 139; *Geschichte der Kunst des Altertums*, 137–38, 156–57
Woltmann, Ludwig: *Politische Anthropologie*, 216
women, Germanic: phenotypes of, 59
Wucht (force), in Hitler's aesthetics, 247
Wüst, Walther, 78, 79, 80; "India and Germany," 27; *Tod und Unsterblichkeit*, 41

Xenophon, 345; *Anabasis*, 136; Plato's influence on, 197–98; on Socrates, 212

youth, German: masculine ideal of, 158; Nordic character of, 135; political training of, 113; racial consciousness of, 134
The Youth of the World (film), 166

Zeno, Semitic roots of, 208, 210
Zschaetzsch, Karl Georg: *Atlantis*, 35, 36
Zwangsarbeiter (compulsory worker), 280

www.ingramcontent.com/pod-product-compliance
Lightning Source LLC
Chambersburg PA
CBHW021332230426
43666CB00006B/274